MW00396695

Implementing Cisco Unified Communications Voice over IP and QoS (CVOICE) Foundation Learning Guide

Fourth Edition

Kevin Wallace, CCIE No. 7945

Cisco Press

800 East 96th Street

Indianapolis, IN 46240

Implementing Cisco Unified Communications Voice over IP and QoS (CVOICE) Foundation Learning Guide Fourth Edition

Kevin Wallace, CCIE No. 7945

Copyright© 2011 Cisco Systems, Inc.

Published by:
Cisco Press
800 East 96th Street
Indianapolis, IN 46240 USA

Printed in the United States of America

Second Printing December 2011

Library of Congress Cataloging-in-Publication data is on file.

ISBN-13: 978-1-58720-419-7

ISBN-10: 1-58720-419-3

Warning and Disclaimer

This book is designed to provide information about Cisco Voice over IP (CVOICE) certification. Every effort has been made to make this book as complete and as accurate as possible, but no warranty or fitness is implied.

The information is provided on an "as is" basis. The authors, Cisco Press, and Cisco Systems, Inc. shall have neither liability nor responsibility to any person or entity with respect to any loss or damages arising from the information contained in this book or from the use of the discs or programs that may accompany it.

The opinions expressed in this book belong to the author and are not necessarily those of Cisco Systems, Inc.

Trademark Acknowledgments

All terms mentioned in this book that are known to be trademarks or service marks have been appropriately capitalized. Cisco Press or Cisco Systems, Inc. cannot attest to the accuracy of this information. Use of a term in this book should not be regarded as affecting the validity of any trademark or service mark.

Corporate and Government Sales

The publisher offers excellent discounts on this book when ordered in quantity for bulk purchases or special sales, which may include electronic versions and/or custom covers and content particular to your business, training goals, marketing focus, and branding interests. For more information, please contact: U.S. Corporate and Government Sales   1-800-382-3419   corpsales@pearsontechgroup.com

For sales outside the United States, please contact: International Sales   international@pearsoned.com

Feedback Information

At Cisco Press, our goal is to create in-depth technical books of the highest quality and value. Each book is crafted with care and precision, undergoing rigorous development that involves the unique expertise of members from the professional technical community.

Readers' feedback is a natural continuation of this process. If you have any comments regarding how we could improve the quality of this book, or otherwise alter it to better suit your needs, you can contact us through email at feedback@ciscopress.com. Please make sure to include the book title and ISBN in your message.

We greatly appreciate your assistance.

Publisher: Paul Boger

Associate Publisher: Dave Dusthimer

Executive Editor: Brett Bartow

Managing Editor: Sandra Schroeder

Development Editor: Dayna Isley

Senior Project Editor: Tonya Simpson

Book Designer: Louisa Adair

Cover Designer: Sandra Schroeder

Manager, Global Certification: Erik Ullanderson

Business Operation Manager, Cisco Press: Anand Sundaram

Technical Editors: Michael J. Cavanaugh, Jacob Uecker

Copy Editor: Bill McManus

Proofreader: Sheri Cain

Editorial Assistant: Vanessa Evans

Composition: Mark Shirar

Indexer: Tim Wright

Americas Headquarters
Cisco Systems, Inc.
San Jose, CA

Asia Pacific Headquarters
Cisco Systems (USA) Pte. Ltd.
Singapore

Europe Headquarters
Cisco Systems International BV
Amsterdam, The Netherlands

Cisco has more than 200 offices worldwide. Addresses, phone numbers, and fax numbers are listed on the Cisco Website at **www.cisco.com/go/offices.**

About the Author

Kevin Wallace, CCIE No. 7945, is a certified Cisco instructor and holds multiple Cisco certifications, including the CCSP, CCVP, CCNP, and CCDP, in addition to multiple security and voice specializations. With Cisco experience dating back to 1989 (beginning with a Cisco AGS+ running Cisco IOS 7.x), Kevin has been a network design specialist for the Walt Disney World Resort, a senior technical instructor for SkillSoft/Thomson NETg/KnowledgeNet, and a network manager for Eastern Kentucky University. Kevin holds a bachelor's of science degree in electrical engineering from the University of Kentucky. Also, Kevin has authored multiple books for Cisco Press, including *CCNP TSHOOT 642-832 Official Certification Guide*, *Routing Video Mentor*, and the Video Mentor component of the *TSHOOT 642-832 Cert Kit*, all of which target the current CCNP certification. Kevin lives in central Kentucky with his wife, Vivian, and two daughters, Stacie and Sabrina. You can follow Kevin online through the following social media outlets:

- Web page: http://1ExamAMonth.com

- Facebook Fan Page: Kevin Wallace Networking

- Twitter: http://twitter.com/kwallaceccie

- YouTube: http://youtube.com/kwallaceccie

- Network World blog: http://nww.com/community/wallace

- iTunes: 1ExamAMonth.com Podcast

About the Technical Reviewers

Michael J. Cavanaugh, CCIE No. 4516 (Routing & Switching, Voice) and MCSE +Messaging, has been in the networking industry for more than 24 years. His employment with companies such as Wachovia, General Electric, Cisco Systems, Bellsouth Communications Systems, AT&T Communications Systems, and Adcap Network Systems has allowed him to stay at the forefront of technology and hold leading-edge certifications. He spent the last ten years focused on Cisco Unified Communications design, professional services, consulting, and support. As an author, Michael has written multiple books for Cisco Press, and as an instructor, he holds technical deep-dive sessions (Geeknick.com) for customers in Georgia and Florida. Michael maintains a YouTube channel (Networking Technologies Explained), where he indulges in his true passion, learning the practical applications of new technologies and sharing his real-world experience and knowledge with end customers and fellow engineers.

Jacob Uecker, CCIE No. 24481, is currently a network engineer for Torrey Point Group. He also teaches CCNA classes through the Cisco Networking Academy at the College of Southern Nevada. Previously, Jacob helped design, build, and maintain in-room data networks for some of the largest hotels in the world and served as a network weasel for a U.S. government contractor. He graduated from UNLV with a master's degree in computer science in 2005 and lives in Las Vegas, Nevada, with his wife and son.

Dedications

As a young boy, my curiosity drove me to learn, experiment, and build things. Also, I promised myself at a young age that I would never forget what it was like to be a kid. My daughters (Stacie and Sabrina) and my wife (Vivian), who I embarrass on a regular basis, would tell you I've kept that promise.

But it was that hunger to learn more…to play…that led me on my journey of discovery in the networking world. So, I dedicate this book to the child in all of us. May we always be curious.

Acknowledgments

Thanks to all the great folks at Cisco Press, especially Brett Bartow, for their commitment to make this the best book it can be. You guys are totally professional and are a huge asset to Cisco learners everywhere.

My family deserves tremendous credit and acknowledgment for this book. It's a tough balancing act…to be a husband, a father, and an author. Family is definitely number one for me, and if I thought my hours of writing would hurt my family, then I would walk away from the keyboard. Fortunately, though, I am blessed with inexplicable support from my beautiful wife, Vivian, and two amazing daughters, Sabrina and Stacie. And speaking of being blessed, I thank God and His Son Jesus Christ for having a personal relationship with me. I fully realize that readers of this book come from a variety of faiths and traditions. So, I don't make such statements to be "preachy," I simply want you to know from where my strength comes.

Contents at a Glance

Contents

Icons Used in This Book

 Router

 Switch

 PC

 Server

 Analog Phone

 IP Phone

 Voice-Enabled Router

 Cisco Unified Communications Manager

 Voice Gateway

 Cisco Unified Communications Manager Express Router

 SIP Server

 Modem or CSU/DSU

 PBX

 Multilayer Switch

 Access Server

 Unified Communications Gateway

 Communications Server

Command Syntax Conventions

The conventions used to present command syntax in this book are the same conventions used in the Cisco IOS Command Reference. The Command Reference describes these conventions as follows:

- **Boldface** indicates commands and keywords that are entered literally as shown. In actual configuration examples and output (not general command syntax), boldface indicates commands that are manually input by the user (such as a show command).

- *Italic* indicates arguments for which you supply actual values.

- Vertical bars (|) separate alternative, mutually exclusive elements.

- Square brackets ([ ]) indicate an optional element.

- Braces ({ }) indicate a required choice.

- Braces within brackets ([{ }]) indicate a required choice within an optional element.

Introduction

With the rapid adoption of Voice over IP (VoIP), many telephony and data network technicians, engineers, and designers are now working to become proficient in VoIP. Professional certifications, such as the CCNP Voice certification, offer validation of an employee's or a consultant's competency in specific technical areas.

This book mirrors the level of detail found in the Cisco CVOICE Version 8.0 course, which many CCNP Voice candidates select as their first course in the CCNP Voice track. Version 8.0 represents a significant update over the previous version, Version 6.0, of the CVOICE course. Specifically, Version 8.0 integrates much of the content previously found in the Implementing Cisco IOS Unified Communications (IIUC) 1.0 and Implementing Cisco QoS (QOS) 2.3 courses. This content includes coverage of Cisco Unified Communications Manager Express (CUCME) and quality of service topics.

A fundamental understanding of traditional telephony, however, would certainly benefit a CVOICE student or a reader of this book. If you think you lack a fundamental understanding of traditional telephony, a recommended companion for this book is the Cisco Press book *Voice over IP First-Step* (ISBN: 978-1-58720-156-1), which is also written by this book's author. *Voice over IP First-Step* is written in a conversational tone and teaches concepts surrounding traditional telephony and how those concepts translate into a VoIP environment.

Additional Study Resources

This book contains a CD with 14 supplemental video lab demonstrations. The video lab titles are as follows:

- Lab 1: DHCP Server Configuration
- Lab 2: CUCME Auto Registration Configuration
- Lab 3: ISDN PRI Configuration for an E1 Circuit
- Lab 4: Configuring a PSTN Dial Plan
- Lab 5: Configuring DID with Basic Digit Manipulation
- Lab 6: H.323 Gateway and VoIP Dial Peer Configuration
- Lab 7: Dial Peer Codec Selection
- Lab 8: Voice Translation Rules and Voice Translation Profiles
- Lab 9: MGCP Gateway Configuration
- Lab 10: Configuring PSTN Failover
- Lab 11: Class of Restriction (COR) Configuration
- Lab 12: Configuring a Gatekeeper
- Lab 13: Configuring a Gateway to Register with a Gatekeeper
- Lab 14: Configuring AutoQoS VoIP

In addition to the 14 video labs, this book periodically identifies bonus videos (a total of 8 bonus videos), which can be viewed on the author's web site (1ExamAMonth.com). These bonus videos review basic telephony theory (not addressed in the course). This telephony review discusses analog and digital port theory and configuration. Other fundamental concepts (that is, dial-peer configuration and digit manipulation) are also addressed. Finally, these bonus videos cover three of the most challenging QoS concepts encountered by students.

With the combination of the 14 video labs on the accompanying CD and the 8 bonus online videos, you have 22 videos to help clarify and expand on the concepts presented in the book.

Goals and Methods

The primary objective of this book is to help the reader pass the 642-437 CVOICE exam, which is a required exam for the CCNP Voice certification.

One key methodology used in this book is to help you discover the exam topics that you need to review in more depth, to help you fully understand and remember those details, and to help you prove to yourself that you have retained your knowledge of those topics. This book does not try to help you pass by memorization, but helps you truly learn and understand the topics by using the following methods:

- Helping you discover which test topics you have not mastered

- Providing explanations and information to fill in your knowledge gaps, including detailed illustrations and topologies as well as sample configurations

- Providing exam practice questions to confirm your understanding of core concepts

Who Should Read This Book?

This book is primarily targeted toward candidates of the CVOICE exam. However, because CVOICE is one of the Cisco foundational VoIP courses, this book also serves as a VoIP primer to noncertification readers.

Many Cisco resellers actively encourage their employees to attain Cisco certifications, and seek new employees who already possess Cisco certifications, to obtain deeper discounts when purchasing Cisco products. Additionally, having attained a certification communicates to your employer or customer that you are serious about your craft and have not simply "hung out a shingle" declaring yourself knowledgeable about VoIP. Rather, you have proven your competency through a rigorous series of exams.

How This Book Is Organized

Although the chapters in this book could be read sequentially, the organization allows you to focus your reading on specific topics of interest. For example, if you already possess a strong VoIP background but want to learn more about Cisco Unified

Communications Manager Express, you can jump right to Chapter 3. Alternately, if you are interested in quality of service (QoS), and not necessarily for VoIP purposes, you can read about basic QoS theory in Chapter 7 and see how to configure various QoS mechanisms in Chapter 8. Specifically, the chapters in this book cover the following topics:

- **Chapter 1, "Introducing Voice Gateways":** This chapter describes the characteristics and historical evolution of unified communications networks, the three operational modes of gateways, their functions, and the related call leg types. Also, this chapter explains how gateways route calls and which configuration elements relate to incoming and outgoing call legs. Additionally, Chapter 1 describes how to connect a gateway to traditional voice circuits using analog and digital interfaces. Finally, DSPs and codecs are addressed.

- **Chapter 2, "Configuring Basic Voice over IP":** This chapter describes how VoIP signaling and media transmission differs from traditional voice circuits, and explains how voice is sent over IP networks, including analog-to-digital conversion, encoding, and packetization. Characteristics of the gateway protocols H.323, SIP, and MGCP are presented, along with special considerations for transmitting DTMF, fax, and modem tones. Finally, this chapter introduces the concept of dial peers.

- **Chapter 3, "Supporting Cisco IP Phones with Cisco Unified Communications Manager Express":** This chapter focuses on Cisco Unified Communications Manager Express (CUCME). After a discussion of CUCME theory and components, this chapter covers CUCME configuration.

- **Chapter 4, "Introducing Dial Plans":** This chapter describes the characteristics and requirements of a numbering plan. Also, the components of a dial plan, and their functions, are explained.

- **Chapter 5, "Implementing Dial Plans":** This chapter describes how to configure a gateway for digit manipulation, how to configure a gateway to perform path selection, and how to configure calling privileges on a voice gateway.

- **Chapter 6, "Using Gatekeepers and Cisco Unified Border Elements":** This chapter describes Cisco gatekeeper functionality, along with configuration instructions. Additionally, this chapter addresses how a gatekeeper can be used to perform call admission control (CAC). Also covered in Chapter 6 is Cisco Unified Border Element (UBE) theory and configuration.

- **Chapter 7, "Introducing Quality of Service":** This chapter explains the functions, goals, and implementation models of QoS, and what specific issues and requirements exist in a converged Cisco Unified Communications network. Also addressed in this chapter are the characteristics and QoS mechanisms of the DiffServ QoS model, as contrasted with other QoS models.

- **Chapter 8, "Configuring QoS Mechanisms":** This chapter explains the operation and configuration of various QoS mechanisms, including classification, marking, queuing, congestion avoidance, policing, shaping, Link Fragmentation and Interleaving (LFI), and header compression. Additionally, all variants of Cisco AutoQoS are described, along with configuration guidance.

Appendix A, "Answers Appendix," lists the answers to the end-of-chapter review questions.

Chapter 1

Introducing Voice Gateways

After reading this chapter, you should be able to perform the following tasks:

- Describe the characteristics and historical evolution of unified communications networks, the three operational modes of gateways, their functions, and the related call leg types.

- Explain how gateways route calls and which configuration elements relate to incoming and outgoing call legs.

- Describe how to connect a gateway to traditional voice circuits using analog and digital interfaces.

- Define DSPs and codecs, and explain different codec complexities and their usage.

Cisco Unified Communications gateways play an important role in the Cisco Unified Communications environment. Their primary function is to convert voice formats, signals, and transmission methods as voice information travels over various network types. This chapter describes the various types of voice gateways and how to deploy them in different Cisco Unified Communications environments. Furthermore, it explains the call-routing process, the direct inward dialing (DID) feature, the various types of voice ports and their characteristics, coder-decoders (codecs), digital signal processors (DSP), and their implementation.

The Role of Gateways

This section describes the operational modes of a voice gateway and how the gateway fits in the Cisco Unified Communications architecture. It explains the voice gateway functions in each Cisco Unified Communications deployment model and the call legs that are associated with each operational mode.

Traditional Telephony Networks

The following components are common elements in such a telephony network, as shown in Figure 1-1.

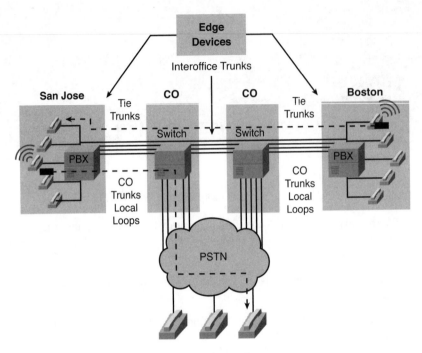

Figure 1-1   *Traditional Telephony Network*

- **Telephones:** Analog telephones are the most common type of phone in a traditional telephony network. Analog phones directly connect to the public switched telephone network (PSTN).

- **Central office (CO) switch:** These switches terminate the local loop and manage signaling, digit collection, call routing, call setup, and call teardown.

- **Private branch exchange (PBX):** A PBX is a privately owned switch that is located on the customer premises. A PBX is a smaller, privately owned version of the CO switches that telephone companies (telcos) use. Many businesses still have a PBX telephone system. Large offices with more than 50 telephones or handsets still use a PBX to connect users, both in-house and to the PSTN.

- **Trunk:** Trunks provide the path between two switches and can be of different types:

    - **CO trunk:** A CO trunk is a direct connection between a local CO and a PBX, which can be analog or digital.

    - **Tie trunk:** A tie trunk is a dedicated circuit that connects PBXs to each other.

- **Interoffice trunk:** An interoffice trunk is typically a digital circuit that connects the COs of two local telcos.

Traditional telephony differs in many aspects from modern unified communications. One important difference is the closed nature of traditional telephony. Integration with modern software applications, databases, and a rapidly evolving computing environment is difficult. Traditional telephony uses circuit-switching technology to establish a voice channel end to end. This approach does not allow sharing of the network infrastructure for emerging applications and services.

A traditional telephony environment addresses these areas:

- **Signaling:** Signaling is the ability to generate and exchange the control information that will be used to establish, monitor, and release connections between two endpoints. Voice signaling requires the ability to provide supervisory, address, and alerting functionality between nodes. The PSTN network uses Signaling System 7 (SS7) to transport control messages. SS7 uses out-of-band signaling, which, in this case, is the exchange of call control information in a separate dedicated channel.

- **Database services:** Database services include access to billing information, caller name (CNAM) delivery, toll-free database services, and calling-card services. An example is providing a call notification service that places outbound calls with prerecorded messages at specific times to notify users of such events as school closures, wakeup calls, or appointments.

- **Bearer control:** Bearer control defines the bearer channels that carry voice calls. Proper supervision of these channels requires that the appropriate call connect and call disconnect signaling is passed between end devices. Correct signaling ensures that the channel is allocated to the current voice call and that the channel is properly deallocated when either side terminates the call. Connect and disconnect messages are carried by SS7 in the PSTN network.

As you will learn in your continued unified communications studies, unified communications solutions exist for signaling, database services, and bearer control.

Cisco Unified Communications Overview

The Cisco Unified Communications system fully integrates communications by enabling data, voice, and video to be transmitted over a single network infrastructure using standards-based IP. The Cisco Unified Communications system incorporates and integrates the following communications technologies:

- IP communications is the technology that transmits voice and video communications over a network using IP standards. Cisco Unified Communications includes hardware and software products, such as call-processing agents, IP phones (both wired and wireless), voice-messaging systems, video devices, and many special applications.

- Mobile applications enhance access to enterprise resources, increase productivity, and increase the satisfaction of mobile users.

■ Customer care enables efficient and effective customer communications across a global network. This strategy allows organizations to draw from a broader range of resources to service customers. They include access to a large pool of agents and multiple channels of communication, as well as customer self-help tools.

■ Telepresence and conferencing enhance the virtual meeting environment with an integrated set of IP-based tools for voice, video, and web conferencing.

■ Messaging provides the functionality for sending and managing of voice and video messages for users.

■ Enterprise social software includes applications that enable communications with the enterprise that are not strictly limited to business-oriented activities.

Cisco Unified Communications Architecture

Leveraging the framework provided by Cisco IP hardware and software products, the Cisco Unified Communications system has the capability to address current and emerging communications needs in the enterprise environment. The Cisco Unified Communications family of products is designed to optimize feature functionality, reduce configuration and maintenance requirements, and provide interoperability with a wide variety of other applications.

The Cisco Unified Communications architecture, as illustrated in Figure 1-2, consists of these logical layers:

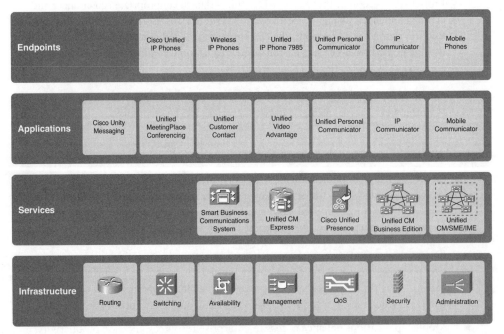

Figure 1-2   *Cisco Unified Communications Architecture*

■ **Infrastructure:** Infrastructure consists of Cisco network components. It provides and maintains a high level of availability, quality of service (QoS), and security for the network.

■ **Services:** Services are responsible for providing the core functionality of Cisco Unified Communications, such as signaling and call routing.

■ **Applications:** Applications include a wide array of software that offers a collection of features to the users.

■ **Endpoints:** Endpoints include end-user hardware and software products that constitute attachment points to the Cisco Unified Communications system.

Cisco Unified Communications Business Benefits

The business advantages that influence the implementation of Cisco Unified Communications have changed over time. Starting with simple media convergence, these advantages have evolved to include call-switching intelligence and the total user experience. Consider the following business drivers for a unified communications solution:

■ **Cost savings:** Traditional time-division multiplexing (TDM), which is used in the PSTN environment, dedicates 64 kbps of bandwidth per voice channel. This approach results in unused bandwidth when there is no voice traffic. VoIP shares bandwidth across multiple logical connections, which makes more efficient use of the bandwidth and therefore reduces bandwidth requirements.

■ **Flexibility:** The sophisticated functionality of IP networks allows organizations to be flexible in the types of applications and services that they provide to their customers and users. Service providers can easily segment customers. This segmentation helps them to provide different applications, custom services, and rates, depending on the traffic volume needs and other customer-specific factors.

■ **Advanced features:** Here are some examples of the advanced features provided by Cisco Unified Communications:

   ■ **Advanced call routing:** When multiple paths exist to connect a call to its destination, some of these paths might be preferred over others based on cost, distance, quality, partner handoffs, traffic load, or various other considerations. Least-cost routing and time-of-day routing are two examples of advanced call routing that can be implemented to determine the best possible route for each call.

   ■ **Unified messaging:** Unified messaging improves communications and productivity. It provides a single user interface for messages that have been delivered over various media. For example, users can read their email, hear their voice mail, and view fax messages by accessing a single inbox.

   ■ **Integrated information systems:** Organizations use Cisco Unified Communications to affect business process transformation. These processes include centralized call control, geographically dispersed virtual contact centers, and access to resources and self-help tools.

- **Long-distance toll bypass:** Long-distance toll bypass is an attractive solution for organizations that place a significant number of calls between sites that are charged traditional long-distance fees. In this case, it might be more cost effective to use VoIP to place those calls across the IP network. If the IP WAN becomes congested, calls can overflow into the PSTN, ensuring that there is no degradation in voice quality.

- **Voice and video security:** There are mechanisms in the IP network that ensure secure IP conversations. Encryption of sensitive signaling header fields and message bodies protects the packets in case of unauthorized packet interception.

- **Customer care:** The ability to provide customer support through multiple media, such as telephone, chat, and email, builds solid customer satisfaction and loyalty. A pervasive IP network allows organizations to provide contact center agents with consolidated and up-to-date customer records along with the related customer communication. Access to this information allows quick problem solving, which, in turn, builds strong customer relationships.

- **Telepresence and conferencing services:** These services save time and resources by providing a media-rich communications platform for users in a distributed enterprise environment.

Originally, return on investment (ROI) calculations centered on toll-bypass and converged network savings. Although these savings are still relevant today, advances in voice technologies allow organizations and service providers to differentiate their product offerings by providing advanced features such as those in the preceding list.

Cisco Unified Communications Gateways

Unified communications gateways are connection points between different communications networks. Depending on the deployment type, a gateway can perform one or several of these functions:

- Act as a voice switch that interconnects multiple traditional telephony circuits. The circuits can be analog or digital. The gateway participates in signaling and might have to convert the media channels. Gateways provide physical access for local analog and digital voice devices such as telephones, fax machines, key sets, and PBXs.

- Act as a PSTN-to-VoIP gateway that provides translation between VoIP and non-VoIP networks, such as the PSTN. In addition to the functionality of traditional voice switches, the PSTN-to-IP gateways enable voice and video communications between traditional PSTN infrastructure and converged IP networks.

- Act as a Cisco Unified Border Element (often written as *Cisco UBE* or *CUBE*) that interconnects two IP networks and allows communications between endpoints distributed among them. The Cisco UBEs might implement filtering, address translation, and security-related functions.

Gateway Operation

Cisco Unified Communications gateways use several control and call-signaling protocols. Among these protocols are

- **H.323:** H.323 is a standard that specifies the components, protocols, and procedures that provide multimedia communication services and real-time audio, video, and data communications over packet networks, including IP networks. H.323 is part of a family of International Telecommunication Union Telecommunication Standardization sector (ITU-T) recommendations called H.32x that provides multimedia communication services over a variety of networks. H.32x is an umbrella of standards that defines all aspects of synchronized voice, video, and data transmission. It also defines end-to-end call signaling.

- **Media Gateway Control Protocol (MGCP):** MGCP is a method for PSTN gateway control or thin device control. Specified in RFC 2705, MGCP defines a protocol that controls VoIP gateways that are connected to external call control devices, referred to as call agents. MGCP provides the signaling capability for edge devices, such as gateways, that might not have implemented a full voice-signaling protocol such as H.323. For example, anytime an event, such as off-hook, occurs on a voice port of a gateway, the voice port reports that event to the call agent. The call agent then signals the voice port to provide a service, such as dial-tone signaling.

- **Session Initiation Protocol (SIP):** SIP is a detailed protocol that specifies the commands and responses to set up and tear down calls. SIP also details features such as security, proxy, and Transmission Control Protocol (TCP) or User Datagram Protocol (UDP) services. SIP and its partner protocols, Session Announcement Protocol (SAP) and Session Description Protocol (SDP), provide announcements and information about multicast sessions to users on a network. SIP defines end-to-end call signaling between devices. SIP is a text-based protocol that borrows many elements of HTTP, using the same transaction request and response model and similar header and response codes. It also adopts a modified form of the URL addressing scheme used within email that is based on Simple Mail Transfer Protocol (SMTP).

- **Skinny Client Control Protocol (SCCP):** SCCP is a Cisco proprietary protocol used between Cisco Unified Communications Manager and Cisco IP Phones. The end stations (IP phones) that use SCCP are called Skinny clients, which consume less processing overhead. The client communicates with the Cisco Unified Communications Manager (often referred to as Call Manager, and abbreviated UCM) using connection-oriented (TCP-based) communication, which is sometimes used to establish a call with another H.323-compliant end station.

The following sections describe each of these protocols in greater detail.

The H.323 Protocol Suite

H.323 is a suite of protocols defined by the ITU for multimedia conferences over LANs. The H.323 protocol was designed by the ITU-T and was initially approved in February 1996. It was developed as a protocol that provides IP networks with traditional telephony functionality. Today, H.323 is the most widely deployed standards-based voice and video-conferencing standard for packet-switched networks.

The protocols specified by H.323 include the following:

- **H.225 Call Signaling:** H.225 call signaling is used to establish a connection between two H.323 endpoints. This is achieved by exchanging H.225 protocol messages on the call-signaling channel. The call-signaling channel is opened between two H.323 endpoints or between an endpoint and an H.323 gatekeeper.

- **H.225 Registration, Admission, and Status:** Registration, admission, and status (RAS) is the protocol between endpoints (terminals and gateways) and gatekeepers. RAS is used to perform registration, admission control, bandwidth changes, status, and disengage procedures between endpoints and gatekeepers. A RAS channel is used to exchange RAS messages. This signaling channel is opened between an endpoint and a gatekeeper prior to the establishment of any other channels.

- **H.245 Control Signaling:** H.245 control signaling is used to exchange end-to-end control messages governing the operation of an H.323 endpoint. These control messages carry information related to the following:

  - Capabilities exchange

  - Opening and closing of logical channels used to carry media streams

  - Flow-control messages

  - General commands and indications

- **Audio codecs:** An audio codec encodes the audio signal from a microphone for transmission by the transmitting H.323 terminal and decodes the received audio code that is sent to the speaker on the receiving H.323 terminal. Because audio is the minimum service provided by the H.323 standard, all H.323 terminals must have at least one audio codec supported, as specified in the ITU-T G.711 recommendation (coding audio at 64 kbps). Additional audio codec recommendations, such as G.722 (64, 56, and 48 kbps), G.723.1 (5.3 and 6.3 kbps), G.728 (16 kbps), and G.729 (8 kbps), might also be supported.

- **Video codecs:** A video codec encodes video from a camera for transmission by the transmitting H.323 terminal and decodes the received video code on a video display of the receiving H.323 terminal. Because H.323 specifies support of video as optional, the support of video codecs is optional as well. However, any H.323 terminal providing video communications must support video encoding and decoding as specified in the ITU-T H.261 recommendation.

In Cisco IP Communications environments, H.323 is widely used with gateways, gate-keepers, and third-party H.323 clients, such as video terminals. Connections can be configured between devices using static destination IP addresses.

Note Because H.323 is a peer-to-peer protocol, H.323 gateways are not registered with Cisco Unified Communications Manager as an endpoint is. An IP address is configured in the Cisco UCM to direct calls to the H.323 device.

MGCP

MGCP is a client/server call control protocol built on a centralized control architecture. MGCP offers the advantage of centralized gateway administration and provides for largely scalable IP telephony solutions. All dial plan information resides on a separate call agent. The call agent, which controls the ports on the gateway, performs call control. An MGCP gateway does media translation between the PSTN and VoIP networks for external calls. In a Cisco-based network, Cisco Unified Communications Managers function as call agents.

MGCP is a plain-text protocol used by call control devices to manage IP telephony gateways. MGCP was defined under RFC 2705, which was updated by RFC 3660, and superseded by RFC 3435, which was updated by RFC 3661.

With MGCP, Cisco UCM knows of and controls individual voice ports on an MGCP gateway. This approach allows complete control of a dial plan from Cisco UCM and gives Communications Manager per-port control of connections to the PSTN, legacy PBX, voice-mail systems, and plain old telephone service (POTS) phones. MGCP is implemented with use of a series of plain-text commands sent via User Datagram Protocol (UDP) port 2427 between the Cisco UCM and a gateway.

Note that for an MGCP interaction to take place with Cisco UCM, an MGCP gateway must have Cisco UCM support. If you are a registered customer of the Software Advisor, you can use this tool to make sure your platform and your Cisco IOS software or Cisco Catalyst operating system version are compatible with Cisco UCM for MGCP. Also, make sure your version of Cisco UCM supports the gateway.

A Primary Rate Interface (PRI) and Basic Rate Interface (BRI) backhaul is an internal interface between the call agent (such as Cisco UCM) and Cisco gateways. It is a separate channel for backhauling signaling information. A backhaul forwards PRI Layer 3 (Q.931) signaling information via a TCP connection.

An MGCP gateway is relatively easy to configure. Because the call agent has all the call-routing intelligence, you do not need to configure the gateway with all the dial peers it would otherwise need. A downside is that a call agent must always be available. Cisco MGCP gateways can use Survivable Remote Site Telephony (SRST) and MGCP fallback to allow the H.323 protocol to take over and provide local call routing in the absence of a Communications Manager (for example, during a WAN outage). In that case, you must configure dial peers on the gateway for use by H.323.

Session Initiation Protocol

SIP is a protocol developed by the Internet Engineering Task Force (IETF) Multiparty Multimedia Session Control (MMUSIC) Working Group as an alternative to H.323. SIP features are compliant with IETF RFC 2543, published in March 1999; RFC 3261, published in June 2002; and RFC 3665, published in December 2003. Because SIP is a common standard based on the logic of the World Wide Web and is very simple to implement, it is widely used with gateways and proxy servers within service provider networks for internal and end-customer signaling.

SIP is a peer-to-peer protocol where user agents (UA) initiate sessions, similar to H.323. However, unlike H.323, SIP uses ASCII-text-based messages to communicate. Therefore, you can implement and troubleshoot SIP very easily.

Because SIP is a peer-to-peer protocol, the Cisco UCM does not control SIP devices, and SIP gateways do not register with Cisco UCM. As with H.323 gateways, only the IP address is available on Cisco UCM to make communication between a Cisco UCM and a SIP voice gateway possible.

Skinny Client Control Protocol

SCCP is a Cisco proprietary protocol that is used for the communication between Cisco UCM and terminal endpoints. SCCP is a client/server protocol, meaning any event (such as on-hook, off-hook, or buttons pressed) causes a message to be sent to a Cisco UCM. Cisco UCM then sends specific instructions back to the device to tell it what to do about the event. Therefore, each press on a phone button causes data traffic between Cisco UCM and the terminal endpoint. SCCP is widely used with Cisco IP Phones. The major advantage of SCCP within Cisco UCM networks is its proprietary nature, which allows you to make quick changes to the protocol and add features and functionality.

SCCP is a simplified protocol used in VoIP networks. Cisco IP Phones that use SCCP can coexist in an H.323 environment. When used with Cisco Communications Manager, an SCCP client can interoperate with H.323-compliant terminals.

Comparing VoIP Signaling Protocols

The primary goal for all four of the previously mentioned VoIP signaling protocols is the same—to create a bidirectional Real-time Transport Protocol (RTP) stream between VoIP endpoints involved in a conversation. However, VoIP signaling protocols use different architectures and procedures to achieve this goal.

H.323

H.323 is considered a peer-to-peer protocol, although H.323 is not a single protocol. Rather, it is a suite of protocols. The necessary gateway configuration is relatively complex, because you need to define the dial plan and route patterns directly on the gateway. Examples of H.323-capable devices are the Cisco VG224 Analog Phone Gateway and the Cisco 2600XM Series, Cisco 2800 Series, 2900 Series, and 3900 Series routers.

The H.323 protocol is responsible for all the signaling between a Cisco UCM cluster and an H.323 gateway. The ISDN protocols, Q.921 and Q.931, are used only on the Integrated Services Digital Network (ISDN) link to the PSTN, as illustrated in Figure 1-3.

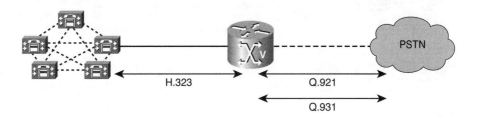

Figure 1-3   *H.323 Signaling*

MGCP

The MGCP protocol is based on a client/server architecture. That simplifies the configuration because the dial plan and route patterns are defined directly on a Cisco UCM server within a cluster. Examples of MGCP-capable devices are the Cisco VG224 Analog Phone Gateway and the Cisco 2600XM Series, 2800 Series, 2900 Series, and 3900 Series routers. Non-IOS MGCP gateways include the Cisco Catalyst 6608-E1 and Catalyst 6608-T1 module.

MGCP is used to manage a gateway. All ISDN Layer 3 information is backhauled to a Cisco UCM server. Only the ISDN Layer 2 information (Q.921) is terminated on the gateway, as depicted in Figure 1-4.

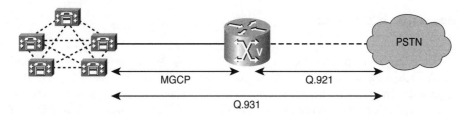

Figure 1-4   *MGCP Signaling*

SIP

Like the H.323 protocol, SIP is a peer-to-peer protocol. The configuration necessary for the gateway is relatively complex because the dial plan and route patterns need to be defined directly on the gateway. Examples of SIP-capable devices are the Cisco 2800 Series, 2900 Series, and 3900 Series routers.

The SIP protocol is responsible for all the signaling between a Cisco UCM cluster and a gateway. The ISDN protocols, Q.921 and Q.931, are used only on an ISDN link to the PSTN, as illustrated in Figure 1-5.

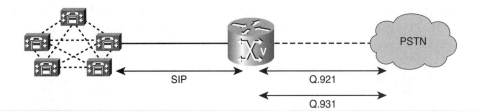

Figure 1-5   *SIP Signaling*

SCCP

SCCP works in a client/server architecture, as shown in Figure 1-6, which simplifies the configuration of SCCP devices such as Cisco IP Phones and Cisco ATA 180 Series and VG200 Series FXS gateways.

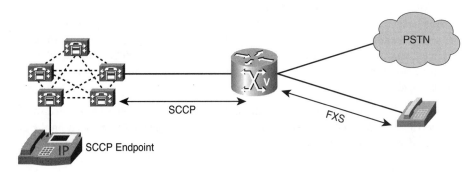

Figure 1-6   *SCCP Signaling*

SCCP is also used on Cisco VG224 and VG248 Analog Phone Gateways, in addition to analog telephone adapters (ATA). ATAs enable communications between Cisco UCM and a gateway. The gateway then uses standard analog signaling to an analog device connected to the ATA's foreign exchange station (FXS) port. Recent versions of Cisco IOS voice gateways—for example, the 2900 series—also support SCCP controlled Foreign Exchange Station (FXS) ports.

Gateway Deployment Example

Gateways are deployed usually as edge devices on a network. Because gateways might interface with both the PSTN and a company WAN, they must have appropriate hardware and utilize an appropriate protocol for that network. Figure 1-7 represents a scenario where three types of gateways are deployed for VoIP and PSTN interconnections.

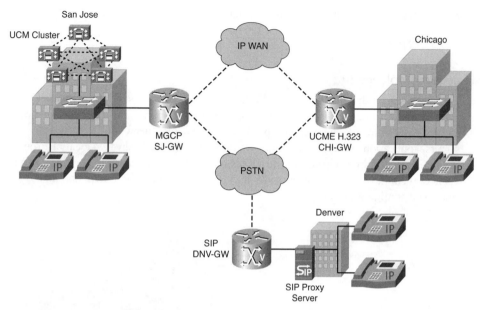

Figure 1-7 *Gateway Deployment Example*

The scenario shown in Figure 1-7 displays the unified communications network of a company that was recently formed as a result of a merger of three individual companies. In the past, each company had its own strategy in terms of how it connected to the PSTN:

■ The San Jose location used a Cisco UCM environment with an MGCP-controlled unified communications gateway to connect to the PSTN.

■ The Chicago location used a Cisco UCM Express environment with an H.323-based unified communications gateway to connect to the PSTN.

■ The Denver location used a Cisco SIP proxy server and SIP IP phones as well as a SIP-based unified communications gateway to connect to the PSTN. Because the Denver location is only a small office, it does not use the WAN for IP telephony traffic to the other locations. Therefore, Denver's local VoIP network is connected only to the PSTN.

IP Telephony Deployment Models

Each IP telephony deployment model differs in the type of traffic that is carried over the WAN, the location of the call-processing agent, and the size of the deployment. Cisco IP telephony supports these deployment models:

■ Single site

■ Multisite with centralized call processing

- Multisite with distributed call processing

- Clustering over the IP WAN

Single-Site Deployment

The single-site model for Cisco Unified Communications consists of a call-processing agent cluster located at a single site, or campus, with no telephony services provided over an IP WAN. Figure 1-8 illustrates a typical single-site deployment. All Cisco UCM servers, applications, and DSP resources are located in the same physical location. You can implement multiple clusters inside a LAN or a metropolitan-area network (MAN) and connect them through intercluster trunks if you need to deploy more IP phones in a single-site configuration.

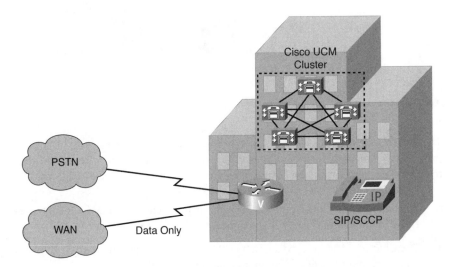

Figure 1-8 *Single-Site Deployment*

An enterprise typically deploys the single-site model over a LAN or MAN, which carries the voice traffic within the site. Gateway trunks that connect directly to the PSTN handle all external calls. If an IP WAN exists between sites, it is used to carry data traffic only; no telephony services are provided over the WAN.

Design Characteristics of Single-Site Deployment

The single-site model has the following design characteristics:

- Single Cisco UCM cluster.

- Maximum of 30,000 SCCP or SIP IP phones or SCCP video endpoints per cluster.

- Maximum of 2100 H.323 devices (gateways, multipoint control units [MCUs], trunks, and clients) or MGCP gateways per UCM cluster.

- PSTN for all calls outside the site.

- DSP resources for conferencing, transcoding, and media termination point (MTP) services.

- Voice-mail, unified messaging, Cisco Unified Presence, audio, and video components.

- Capability to integrate with legacy PBX and voice-mail systems.

- H.323 clients, MCUs, and H.323/H.320 gateways that require a gatekeeper to place calls must register with a Cisco IOS Gatekeeper (Cisco IOS Release 12.3(8)T or greater). UCM then uses an H.323 trunk to integrate with a gatekeeper and provide call-routing and bandwidth-management services for H.323 devices registered to it. Multiple Cisco IOS Gatekeepers might be used to provide redundancy.

- MCU resources are required for multipoint video conferencing. Depending on conferencing requirements, these resources might be either SCCP or H.323, or both.

- H.323/H.320 video gateways are needed to communicate with H.320 videoconferencing devices on a public ISDN network.

- High-bandwidth audio (for example, G.711, G.722, or Cisco Wideband Audio) between devices within the site.

- High-bandwidth video (for example, 384 kbps or greater) between devices within the site. The Cisco Unified Video Advantage Wideband Codec, operating at 7 Mbps, is also supported.

Benefits of Single-Site Deployment

A single infrastructure for a converged network solution provides significant cost benefits and enables Cisco Unified Communications to take advantage of many IP-based applications in an enterprise. Single-site deployment also allows each site to be completely self-contained. There is no dependency for service in the event of an IP WAN failure or insufficient bandwidth, and there is no loss of call-processing service or functionality.

The main benefits of the single-site model are the following:

- Ease of deployment.

- A common infrastructure for a converged solution.

- Simplified dial plan.

- No transcoding resources are required because of the use of a single high-bandwidth codec.

Design Guidelines for Single-Site Deployment

Single-site deployment is a subset of the distributed and centralized call-processing model. Future scalability requires that you adhere to the recommended best practices specific to the distributed and centralized call-processing model. When you develop a stable, single site that is based on a common infrastructure philosophy, you can easily expand the IP telephony system applications, such as video streaming and videoconferencing, to remote sites.

Follow these guidelines and best practices when implementing the single-site model:

■ Provide a highly available, fault-tolerant infrastructure based on a common infrastructure philosophy. A sound infrastructure is essential for easier migration to Cisco Unified Communications, integration with applications such as video streaming and video conferencing, and expansion of your Cisco Unified Communications deployment across the WAN or to multiple UCM clusters.

■ Know the calling patterns for your enterprise. Use the single-site model if most of the calls from your enterprise are within the same site or to PSTN users outside your enterprise.

■ Use G.711 codecs for all endpoints. This practice eliminates the consumption of DSP resources for transcoding, and those resources can be allocated to other functions, such as conferencing and MTPs.

■ Use SIP, SRST, and MGCP gateways for the PSTN. This practice simplifies dial plan configuration. H.323 might be required to support specific functionality, such as support for SS7 or Nonfacility Associated Signaling (NFAS), which allows a single channel on one digital circuit to carry signaling information for multiple digital circuits.

■ Implement the recommended network infrastructure for high availability, connectivity options for phones (in-line power), QoS mechanisms, and security.

Multisite WAN with Centralized Call-Processing Deployment

The model for a multisite WAN deployment with centralized call processing consists of a single call-processing agent cluster that provides services for multiple remote sites and uses the IP WAN to transport Cisco Unified Communications traffic between sites. The IP WAN also carries call control signaling between central and remote sites. Figure 1-9 illustrates a typical centralized call-processing deployment, with a UCM cluster as the call-processing agent at the central site and an IP WAN with QoS enabled to connect all the sites. The remote sites rely on the centralized UCM cluster to handle their call processing. Applications such as voice-mail and interactive voice response (IVR) systems are typically centralized as well to reduce the overall costs of administration and maintenance.

WAN connectivity options include the following:

■ Leased lines

■ Frame Relay

■ ATM

■ ATM and Frame Relay Service Inter-Working (SIW)

■ Multiprotocol Label Switching (MPLS) VPN

■ Voice- and Video-Enabled IP Security Protocol (IPsec) VPN (V3PN)

Routers that reside at WAN edges require QoS mechanisms, such as priority queuing and traffic shaping, to protect voice traffic from data traffic across the WAN, where bandwidth is typically scarce. In addition, a call admission control scheme is needed to avoid over-subscribing the WAN links with voice traffic and deteriorating the quality of established calls. For centralized call-processing deployments, the locations construct within UCM provides call admission control.

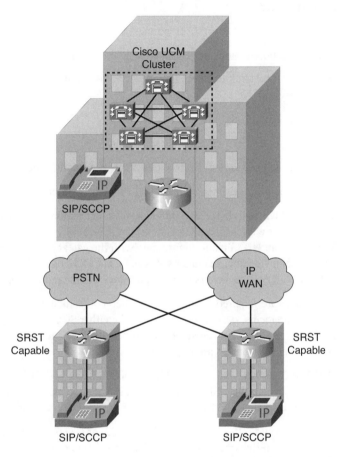

Figure 1-9 *Multisite WAN with Centralized Call Processing*

A variety of Cisco gateways can provide remote sites with PSTN access. When the IP WAN is down, or if all the available bandwidth on the IP WAN has been consumed, users at remote sites can dial a PSTN access code and place their calls through the PSTN. The Cisco Unified SRST feature, available for both SCCP and SIP phones, provides call processing at the branch offices for Cisco IP Phones if they lose their connection to the remote primary, secondary, or tertiary UCM server or if the WAN connection is down. Cisco Unified SRST functionality is available on Cisco IOS gateways running the SRST feature or on Cisco Unified Communications Manager Express (Unified CME) Release 4.0 and later running in SRST mode. Unified CME running in SRST mode provides more features for the phones than SRST on a Cisco IOS gateway.

Design Characteristics of Multisite WAN with Centralized Call-Processing Deployment

The multisite model with centralized call processing has the following design characteristics:

- Single UCM cluster.

- Maximum of 30,000 SCCP or SIP IP phones or SCCP video endpoints per cluster.

- Maximum of 1000 locations per UCM cluster.

- Maximum of 2100 H.323 devices (gateways, MCUs, trunks, and clients) or 1100 MGCP gateways per UCM cluster.

- PSTN for all external calls.

- DSP resources for conferencing, transcoding, and MTP.

- Voice-mail, unified messaging, Cisco Unified Presence, audio, and video components.

- Capability to integrate with legacy PBX and voice-mail systems.

- H.323 clients, MCUs, and H.323/H.320 gateways that require a gatekeeper to place calls must register with a Cisco IOS Gatekeeper (Cisco IOS Release 12.3(8)T or later). UCM then uses an H.323 trunk to integrate with the gatekeeper and provide call-routing and bandwidth-management services for the H.323 devices registered to it. Multiple Cisco IOS Gatekeepers might be used to provide redundancy.

- MCU resources are required for multipoint video conferencing. Depending on conferencing requirements, these resources might be either SCCP or H.323, or both, and might all be located at a central site or might be distributed to the remote sites if local conferencing resources are required.

- H.323/H.320 video gateways are needed to communicate with H.320 videoconferencing devices on a public ISDN network. These gateways might all be located at the central site or distributed to the remote sites if local ISDN access is required.

- High-bandwidth audio (for example, G.711, G.722, or Cisco Wideband Audio) between devices in the same site and low-bandwidth audio (for example, G.729 or G.728) between devices in different sites.

- High-bandwidth video (for example, 384 kbps or greater) between devices in the same site and low-bandwidth video (for example, 128 kbps) between devices at different sites. The Cisco Unified Video Advantage Wideband Codec, operating at 7 Mbps, is recommended only for calls between devices at the same site.

- Minimum of 768 kbps or greater WAN link speeds. Video is not recommended on WAN connections that operate at speeds lower than 768 kbps.

- UCM locations provide call admission control, and automated alternate routing (AAR) is also supported for video calls, which allows calls to flow over the PSTN if a call across the WAN is rejected by the locations feature.

- SRST versions 4.0 and later support video. However, versions of SRST prior to 4.0 do not support video, and SCCP video endpoints located at remote sites become audio-only devices if the WAN connection fails.

- Cisco Unified CME versions 4.0 and later might be used for remote site survivability instead of an SRST router. Unified CME also provides more features than the SRST router during WAN outage.

- Cisco Unified CME can be integrated with Cisco Unity Express (CUE) in the branch office or remote site. The Cisco Unity server is registered to the UCM at the central site in normal mode and can fall back to Unified CME in SRST mode when the centralized UCM server is not reachable, or during a WAN outage, to provide the users at the branch offices with access to their voice mail with message waiting indicators (MWI).

Design Guidelines for Multisite WAN with Centralized Call-Processing Deployment

Follow these guidelines when implementing the multisite WAN model with centralized call processing:

- Minimize delay between Cisco UCM and remote locations to reduce voice cut-through delays (also known as *clipping*). The ITU-T G.114 recommendation specifies a 150 ms maximum one way.

- Use HSRP for network resiliency.

- Use the locations mechanism in Cisco UCM to provide call admission control into and out of remote branches.

- The number of IP phones and line appearances supported in SRST mode at each remote site depends on the branch router platform, the amount of memory installed, and the Cisco IOS release. SRST on a Cisco IOS gateway supports as many as 1500 phones, whereas Unified CME running in SRST mode supports 240 phones. Generally speaking, however, the choice of whether to adopt a centralized call-processing approach or distributed call-processing approach for a given site depends on a number of factors, such as

  - IP WAN bandwidth or delay limitations

  - Criticality of the voice network

  - Feature set needs

  - Scalability

  - Ease of management

  - Cost

Note   If a distributed call-processing model is deemed more suitable for a customer's business needs, the choices include installing a UCM cluster at each site or running Unified CME at the remote sites.

- At the remote sites, use the following features to ensure call-processing survivability in the event of a WAN failure:

  - For SCCP phones, use SRST on a Cisco IOS gateway or Unified CME running in SRST mode.

  - For SIP phones, use SIP SRST.

  - For devices attached to analog or digital voice ports, use MGCP Gateway Fallback.

SRST or Unified CME in SRST mode, SIP SRST, and MGCP Gateway Fallback can reside with each other on the same Cisco IOS gateway.

For specific sizing recommendations, refer to the Cisco Unified Communications System SRND based on Cisco UCM 8.x at the following link: https://www.cisco.com/en/US/docs/voice_ip_comm/cucm/srnd/8x/uc8x.html.

Multisite WAN with Distributed Call-Processing Deployment

The model for a multisite WAN deployment with distributed call processing, as illustrated in Figure 1-10, consists of multiple independent sites, each with its own call-processing agent cluster connected to an IP WAN that carries voice traffic between the distributed sites.

An IP WAN interconnects all the distributed call-processing sites. Typically, the PSTN serves as a backup connection between the sites in case the IP WAN connection fails or does not have any available bandwidth. A site connected only through the PSTN is a standalone site and is not covered by the distributed call-processing model.

WAN connectivity options include the following:

- Leased lines

- Frame Relay

- ATM

- ATM and Frame Relay SIW

- MPLS VPN

- IPsec V3PN

Multisite distributed call processing allows each site to be completely self-contained. In the event of an IP WAN failure or insufficient bandwidth, a site does not lose call-processing service or functionality. Cisco UCM simply sends all calls between the sites across the PSTN.

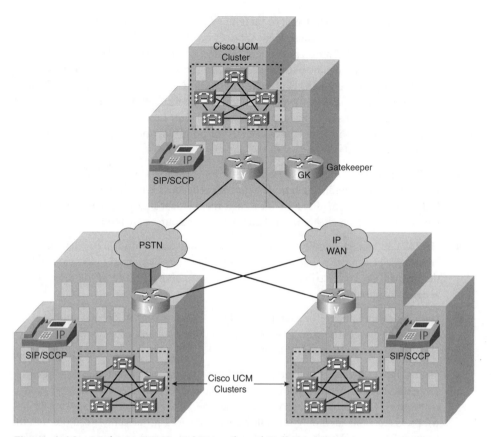

Figure 1-10 *Multisite WAN with Distributed Call Processing*

Design Characteristics of Multisite WAN with Distributed Call-Processing Deployment

The multisite model with distributed call processing has the following design characteristics:

- Maximum of 30,000 SCCP or SIP IP phones or SCCP video endpoints per cluster.

- Maximum of 2100 MGCP gateways or H.323 devices (gateways, MCUs, trunks, and clients) per UCM cluster.

- PSTN for all external calls.

- DSP resources for conferencing, transcoding, and MTP.

- Voice-mail, unified messaging, and Cisco Unified Presence components.

- Capability to integrate with legacy PBX and voice-mail systems.

- H.323 clients, MCUs, and H.323/H.320 gateways that require a gatekeeper to place calls must register with a Cisco IOS Gatekeeper (Cisco IOS Release 12.3(8)T or later).

UCM then uses an H.323 trunk to integrate with the gatekeeper and provide call-routing and bandwidth-management services for the H.323 devices registered to it. Multiple Cisco IOS Gatekeepers might be used to provide redundancy. Cisco IOS Gatekeepers might also be used to provide call routing and bandwidth management between the distributed UCM clusters. In most situations, Cisco recommends that each UCM cluster have its own set of endpoint gatekeepers and that a separate set of gatekeepers be used to manage intercluster calls. It is possible in some circumstances to use the same set of gatekeepers for both functions, depending on the size of the network and complexity of the dial plan.

- MCU resources are required in each cluster for multipoint video conferencing. Depending on conferencing requirements, these resources might be either SCCP or H.323, or both, and might all be located at the regional sites or distributed to the remote sites of each cluster if local conferencing resources are required.

- H.323/H.320 video gateways are needed to communicate with H.320 videoconferencing devices on the public ISDN network. These gateways might all be located at the regional sites or distributed to the remote sites of each cluster if local ISDN access is required.

- High-bandwidth audio (for example, G.711, G.722, or Cisco Wideband Audio) between devices in the same site, but low-bandwidth audio (for example, G.729 or G.728) between devices in different sites.

- High-bandwidth video (for example, 384 kbps or greater) between devices in the same site, but low-bandwidth video (for example, 128 kbps) between devices at different sites. The Cisco Unified Video Advantage Wideband Codec, operating at 7 Mbps, is recommended only for calls between devices at the same site. Note that the Cisco VT Camera Wideband Video Codec is not supported over intercluster trunks.

- Minimum of 768 kbps or greater WAN link speeds. Video is not recommended on WAN connections that operate at speeds lower than 768 kbps.

- Call admission control is provided by UCM locations for calls between sites controlled by the same UCM cluster and by the Cisco IOS Gatekeeper for calls between UCM clusters (that is, intercluster trunks). Automated Alternate Routing (AAR) is also supported for both intracluster and intercluster video calls.

Benefits of Multisite WAN with Distributed Call-Processing Deployment

The main benefits of the multisite WAN with distributed call-processing deployment model are as follows:

- Cost savings when you use the IP WAN for calls between sites

- Use of the IP WAN to bypass toll charges by routing calls through remote site gateways, closer to the PSTN number dialed (that is, tail-end hop-off [TEHO])

- Maximum utilization of available bandwidth by allowing voice traffic to share an IP WAN with other types of traffic

- No loss of functionality during an IP WAN failure

- Scalability to hundreds of sites

Design Guidelines for Multisite WAN with Distributed Call-Processing Deployment

A multisite WAN deployment with distributed call processing has many of the same requirements as a single-site or a multisite WAN deployment with centralized call processing. Follow the best practices from these other models in addition to the ones listed here for the distributed call-processing model.

Gatekeeper or SIP proxy servers are among the key elements in the multisite WAN model with distributed call processing. They each provide dial plan resolution, with the gatekeeper also providing call admission control. A gatekeeper is an H.323 device that provides call admission control and E.164 dial plan resolution.

Best Practices for Multisite WAN with Distributed Call-Processing Deployment

The following best practices apply to the use of a gatekeeper:

- Use a Cisco IOS Gatekeeper to provide call admission control into and out of each site.

- To provide high availability of the gatekeeper, use HSRP gatekeeper pairs, gatekeeper clustering, and/or alternate gatekeeper support. In addition, use multiple gatekeepers to provide redundancy within the network.

- Size the platforms appropriately to ensure that performance and capacity requirements can be met.

- Use only one type of codec on the WAN because the H.323 specification does not allow for Layer 2, IP, UDP, or RTP header overhead in the bandwidth request.

Using one type of codec on the WAN simplifies capacity planning by eliminating the need to over-provision the IP WAN to allow for a worst-case scenario.

Gatekeeper networks can scale to hundreds of sites, and the design is limited only by the WAN topology.

SIP devices provide resolution of E.164 numbers as well as SIP uniform resource identifiers (URI) to enable endpoints to place calls to each other. UCM supports the use of E.164 numbers only.

The following best practices apply to the use of SIP proxies:

- Provide adequate redundancy for the SIP proxies.

- Ensure that SIP proxies have the capacity for the call rate and number of calls required in the network.

Call-Processing Agents for the Distributed Call-Processing Model

Your choice of call-processing agent will vary, based on many factors. The main factors, for the purpose of design, are the size of the site and the functionality required.

For a distributed call-processing deployment, each site has its own call-processing agent. The design of each site varies with the call-processing agent, the functionality required, and the fault tolerance required. For example, in a site with 500 phones, a UCM cluster containing two servers can provide one-to-one redundancy, with the backup server being used as a publisher and Trivial File Transfer Protocol (TFTP) server.

The requirement for IP-based applications also greatly affects the choice of call-processing agent because only UCM provides the required support for many Cisco IP applications.

Table 1-1 lists recommended call-processing agents for distributed call processing.

Table 1-1   *Recommended Call-Processing Agents*

Call-Processing Agent	Recommended Size	Comments
Cisco Unified Communications Manager Express (Unified CME)	Up to 240 phones	For small remote sites. Capacity depends on Cisco IOS platform.
Cisco UCM	50 to 30,000 phones	Small to large sites, depending on the size of the UCM cluster. Supports centralized or distributed call processing.
Legacy PBX with VoIP gateway	Depends on PBX	Number of IP WAN calls and functionality depend on the PBX-to-VoIP gateway protocol and the gateway platform.

Clustering over the IP WAN Deployment

Cisco supports Cisco UCM clusters over a WAN, as illustrated in Figure 1-11. Clustering over the WAN involves having the applications and UCM of the same cluster distributed across the IP WAN.

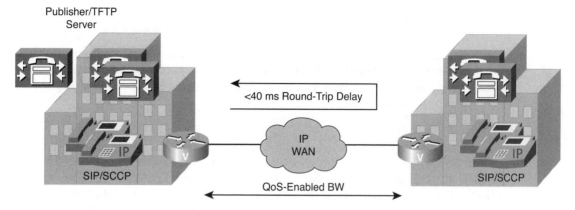

Publisher/TFTP
Server

<40 ms Round-Trip Delay

IP
WAN

QoS-Enabled BW

SIP/SCCP

SIP/SCCP

Figure 1-11   *Clustering over the IP WAN*

Clustering over the WAN can support two types of deployments:

- **Local failover deployment model:** Local failover requires that you place UCM subscriber and backup servers at the same site, with no WAN between them. This deployment model is ideal for two to four sites with UCM.

- **Remote failover deployment model:** Remote failover allows you to deploy the backup servers over the WAN. Using this deployment model, you might have up to eight sites with UCM subscribers being backed up by UCM subscribers at another site.

Note   The remote failover deployment model might need higher bandwidth because a large amount of intracluster traffic flows between the subscriber servers.

You can also use a combination of the two deployment models to satisfy specific site requirements. For example, two main sites might each have primary and backup subscribers, with another two sites containing only a primary server each and utilizing either shared backups or dedicated backups at the two main sites.

Benefits of the Clustering over the IP WAN Deployment

Although stringent requirements exist, the clustering over the IP WAN deployment design offers these advantages:

- Single point of administration for users for all sites within a cluster

- Feature transparency

- Shared line appearances

- Extension mobility within the cluster

- Unified dial plan

These features make this solution ideal as a disaster recovery plan for business continuance sites or as a single solution for as many as eight small or medium-size sites.

The cluster design is also useful for customers who require more functionality than the limited feature set offered by SRST. This network design also allows remote offices to support more Cisco IP Phones than SRST in the event that the connection to the primary Cisco UCM server is lost.

WAN Considerations

For clustering over the WAN to be successful, you must carefully plan, design, and implement various characteristics of the WAN itself. The Intra-Cluster Communication Signaling (ICCS) between UCM servers consists of many traffic types. The ICCS traffic types are classified as either priority or best effort. Priority ICCS traffic is marked with IP Precedence 3 (DSCP 24 or PHB CS3). Best-effort ICCS traffic is marked with IP Precedence 0 (DSCP 0 or PHB BE).

The following design guidelines apply to the indicated WAN characteristics:

- **Delay:** The maximum one-way delay between any UCM servers for all priority ICCS traffic should not exceed 40 ms, or 80 ms round-trip time (RTT). Delay for other ICCS traffic should be kept reasonable to provide timely database access. Propagation delay between two sites introduces 6 microseconds per kilometer without any other network delays being considered. This equates to a theoretical maximum distance of approximately 3000 km for 20 ms delay or approximately 1860 miles. These distances are provided only as relative guidelines and in reality will be shorter because of additional delay incurred within the network.

- **Jitter:** Jitter is the varying delay that packets incur through the network because of processing, queue, buffer, congestion, or path variation delay. Jitter for the IP Precedence 3 ICCS traffic must be minimized using QoS features.

- **Packet loss and errors:** The network should be engineered to provide sufficient prioritized bandwidth for all ICCS traffic, especially the priority ICCS traffic. Standard QoS mechanisms must be implemented to avoid congestion and packet loss. If packets are lost because of line errors or other "real world" conditions, an ICCS packet will be retransmitted because it uses the TCP protocol for reliable transmission. The retransmission might result in a call being delayed during setup, disconnect (teardown), or other supplementary services during the call. Some packet-loss conditions could result in a lost call, but this scenario should be no more likely than errors occurring on a T1 or E1, which affect calls via a trunk to the PSTN/ISDN.

- **Bandwidth:** Provision the correct amount of bandwidth between each server for the expected call volume, type of devices, and number of devices. This bandwidth is in addition to any other bandwidth for other applications sharing the network, including voice and video traffic between the sites. The bandwidth provisioned must have QoS enabled to provide the prioritization and scheduling for the different classes of traffic. The general rule for bandwidth is to overprovision and undersubscribe.

- **QoS:** The network infrastructure relies on QoS engineering to provide consistent and predictable end-to-end levels of service for traffic. Neither QoS nor bandwidth alone is a solution. Rather, QoS-enabled bandwidth must be engineered into the network infrastructure.

Modern Gateway Hardware Platforms

The Cisco 2900 Series and 3900 Series Integrated Services Routers (ISR) are among the more modern gateway hardware platforms.

Cisco 2900 Series Integrated Services Routers

The Cisco 2900 Series Integrated Services Routers, an example of which is shown in Figure 1-12, comprise four models: Cisco 2901 Integrated Services Router, Cisco 2911 Integrated Services Router, Cisco 2921 Integrated Services Router, and Cisco 2951 Integrated Services Router. These Integrated Services Routers Generation 2 platforms are future-enabled with multicore CPUs, support for high-capacity DSPs for future enhanced video capabilities, high-powered service modules with improved availability, and Gigabit Ethernet switching with enhanced Power over Ethernet (PoE). Additionally, a new Cisco IOS Software Universal Image and Services Ready Engine module enables you to decouple the deployment of hardware and software. This decoupling provides a flexible technology foundation that can quickly adapt to evolving network requirements.

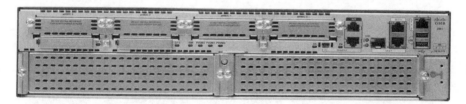

Figure 1-12 *Cisco 2900 Series Router*

Cisco 3900 Series Integrated Services Routers

The Cisco 3900 Series Integrated Services Routers, an example of which is provided in Figure 1-13, comprise two models: Cisco 3925 and Cisco 3945 Integrated Services Routers. In addition to providing the functionality of the Cisco 2900 Series Routers, the Cisco 3900 Series Routers offer superior performance and flexibility for network deployments from small business offices to large enterprise offices, while providing industry-leading investment protection.

Well-Known Older Enterprise Models

The Cisco 2800 and 3800 Series ISRs are modular access routers that have voice gateway capabilities. These models are well known and widely used.

Figure 1-13 *Cisco 3900 Series Router*

Cisco 2800 Series Integrated Services Routers

The Cisco 2800 Series Integrated Services Routers, as pictured in Figure 1-14, comprise four models (listed from top to bottom): Cisco 2801, Cisco 2811, Cisco 2821, and Cisco 2851. The 2800 Series provides increased security, voice, and overall performance, embedded service options, and dramatically increased slot performance and density, as compared to older 2600 Series models. It also maintains support for most of the more-than-90 modules available for the Cisco 1700 Series Modular Access Routers, 2600 Series Multiservice Platforms, and 3700 Series Multiservice Access Routers.

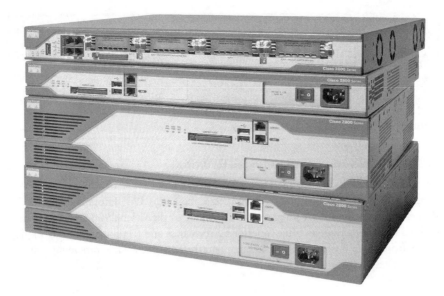

Figure 1-14 *Cisco 2800 Series Routers*

The 2800 Series can deliver simultaneous, high-quality, wire-speed services up to multiple T1/E1/xDSL connections. The routers offer embedded encryption acceleration and, on the motherboard, voice digital signal processor (DSP) slots. They also offer intrusion prevention system (IPS) and firewall functions, optional integrated call-processing and voice-mail support, high-density interfaces for a wide range of wired and wireless connectivity requirements, and sufficient performance and slot density for future network expansion requirements and advanced applications.

Cisco 3800 Series Integrated Services Routers

The Cisco 3800 Series Integrated Services Routers, as shown in Figure 1-15, also feature embedded security processing, significant performance and memory enhancements, and high-density interfaces that deliver the performance, availability, and reliability required to scale mission-critical security, IP telephony, business video, network analysis, and web applications in today's enterprise environments. The 3800 Series routers deliver multiple concurrent services at wire-speed T3/E3 rates.

Figure 1-15   *Cisco 3800 Series Routers*

The integrated services routing architecture of the 3800 Series is based on the 3700 Series. These routers are designed to embed and integrate security and voice processing with advanced wired and wireless services for rapid deployment of new applications, including application layer functions, intelligent network services, and converged communications. The 3800 Series supports the bandwidth requirements for multiple Fast Ethernet interfaces per slot, TDM interconnections, and fully integrated power distribution to modules supporting 802.3af Power over Ethernet (PoE). The Cisco 3800 Series also supports the existing portfolio of Cisco modular interfaces. This accommodates network expansion or changes in technology as new services and applications are deployed. By integrating the functions of multiple separate devices into a single compact unit, the 3800 Series reduces the cost and complexity of managing remote networks.

Specialized Voice Gateways

To fit special needs within the customer unified messaging system, Cisco offers stand-alone voice gateways for specific purposes. Each of these voice gateways fulfills a different need, such as the integration of analog devices into the unified messaging system, enhanced performance, business-class functionality, adaptability, serviceability, and manageability.

Cisco ATA 186

The Cisco Analog Telephone Adaptor 186 (Cisco ATA 186), as illustrated in Figure 1-16, is a handset-to-Ethernet adapter that allows traditional telephone devices to function as VoIP devices. Customers can use IP telephony applications by connecting their analog devices to analog telephone adapters.

Figure 1-16   *Cisco ATA 186*

The Cisco ATA 186 supports two voice ports, each of which has an independent telephone number and a single 10BASE-T Ethernet port. This adapter can make use of existing Ethernet LANs, in addition to broadband pipes such as DSL, fixed wireless, and cable modem deployments.

Cisco VG248 Analog Phone Gateway

The Cisco VG248 Analog Phone Gateway, as depicted in Figure 1-17, provides support for traditional analog devices while taking advantage of the new capabilities that Cisco Unified Communications affords. The Cisco VG248 Analog Phone Gateway offers 48 analog ports for use as extensions to the Cisco Unified Communications Manager system.

Cisco AS5350XM Series Universal Gateway

The Cisco AS5350XM Series Gateway, an example of which is provided in Figure 1-18, is the only one-rack-unit gateway that provides data, voice, and fax services, as well as Session Border Controller (SBC) functionality. The SBC feature is used at provider interconnects and typically provides complete session state, security, and reporting services. The Cisco AS5350XM offers high reliability in a compact, modular design. This cost-effective platform is ideally suited for ISPs and enterprises that require innovative universal or voice services. The Cisco AS5350XM supports PSTN signaling, gateway signaling, voice codecs, fax, VoiceXML, RADIUS, Tool Command Language (TCL), and interactive voice response. The SBC functionality provides additional opportunities for IP-to-IP trunking applications.

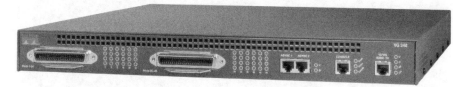

Figure 1-17   *Cisco VG248 Gateway*

Figure 1-18   *Cisco AS5350XM Series Gateway*

Cisco AS5400 Series Universal Gateway Platforms

The Cisco AS5400XM Series Universal Gateway, as shown in Figure 1-19, is 2 rack units (RU) in height and provides data, voice, and fax services, as well as SBC functionality. High density, low power consumption, and a robust feature set make the Cisco AS5400XM Series Universal Gateway ideal for several network deployment architectures, especially for colocation environments and for large points of presence (POP). The Cisco AS5400XM Universal Gateway offers reliable, scalable data and voice gateway functions and SBC services. The Cisco AS5400XM supports PSTN signaling, gateway signaling, voice codecs, fax, VoiceXML, RADIUS, TCL, and IVR.

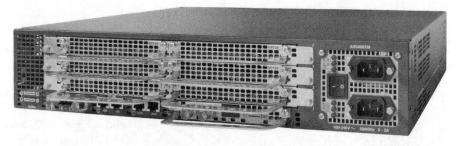

Figure 1-19   *Cisco AS5400XM Series Universal Gateway*

Cisco 7200 Series Routers

Cisco 7200 Series Routers, an example of which is shown in Figure 1-20, are service routers for Enterprise Edge and Service Provider Edge applications. These compact routers provide serviceability and manageability coupled with high-performance modular processors such as the Cisco 7200 Network Processing Engine NPE-G1 (NPE-G1).

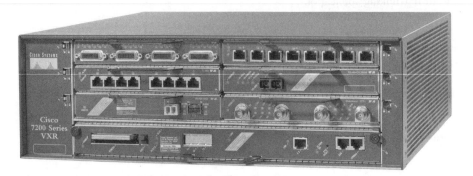

Figure 1-20   *Cisco 7200 Series Router*

Gateway Operational Modes

Voice gateways can be deployed in three modes. A single gateway can operate in one mode or multiple modes at the same time. These modes are as follows:

■   A voice-switching gateway, as shown in Figure 1-21, connects various analog and digital voice circuits. This functionality is equivalent to the operation of central office switches and PBXs in traditional telephony.

Figure 1-21   *Voice-Switching Gateway*

■   A VoIP gateway, as depicted in Figure 1-22, connects the traditional telephony network to the IP network. It converts the signaling and media transmission methods used on one side to the other side. VoIP gateways provide physical access for local analog and digital voice devices such as telephones, fax machines, key sets, and PBXs.

■   Cisco Unified Border Element (Cisco UBE), which is illustrated in Figure 1-23, interconnects two IP networks. It terminates the signaling sessions and either passes through or terminates the media channels.

Figure 1-22 *VoIP Gateway*

Figure 1-23 *Cisco Unified Border Element*

The following sections first introduce voice gateway call legs, both POTS and VoIP call legs, and then describe how these call legs define the mode of operation for a voice gateway.

Voice Gateway Call Legs

A voice call over a packet or traditional telephony network is segmented into discrete call legs. When a gateway receives a call setup, it performs a routing decision and sends the call setup request to the next device. The incoming part of the call is referred to as the incoming call leg and the outgoing part of the call is referred to as the outgoing call leg.

On Cisco IOS routers, the call legs are associated with dial peers. One dial peer corresponds to one call leg. A call leg is a logical connection between two gateways or between a gateway and a telephony device, as shown in Figure 1-24. If the gateway receives or forwards the call over an analog or digital voice circuit, the corresponding call leg is referred to as POTS. If the gateway receives or forwards the call over an IP interface, the corresponding call leg is referred to as VoIP.

The call legs are relevant for call routing. Before a gateway makes the call-routing decision, it must apply the settings defined in the incoming call leg. In the case of POTS incoming call legs, these parameters define how the gateway collects the dialed digits and optional applications. In the case of VoIP incoming call legs, these parameters describe the voice transmission methods, such as codec, voice activity detection (VAD), and dual-tone multifrequency (DTMF)-related features. These parameters must be successfully negotiated between the local and preceding gateway before the call can be forwarded to the next gateway in the path. You learn more about call legs in the upcoming section, "How Voice Gateways Route Calls."

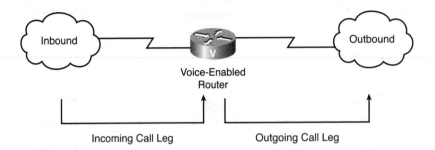

Figure 1-24 *Voice Call Legs*

Voice-Switching Gateway

A voice-switching gateway, as depicted in Figure 1-25, has traditional telephony interfaces. Multiple call-signaling protocols exist, such as SS7, ISDN, Q Signaling (QSIG), and the analog signaling methods, including supervisory signaling (loop-start, ground-start, immediate-start, wink-start, delay-start), address signaling (pulse, DTMF), and informational signaling. The voice-switching gateway receives and forwards the call setup request over analog or digital voice circuits. The gateway might have to convert the call signaling and the voice format when the call traverses the gateway from one port to another. The incoming and the outgoing call legs are the POTS call legs.

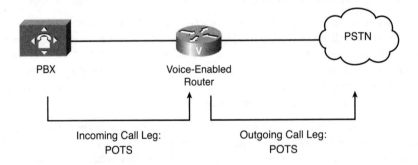

Figure 1-25 *Voice-Switching Gateway*

VoIP Gateway

The gateway provides translation between VoIP and non-VoIP networks, such as the PSTN. It converts the signaling and voice signal between traditional telephony circuits and the VoIP transmission in an IP network. One of the call legs is a POTS call leg, while the other is a VoIP call leg.

In Figure 1-26, the originating gateway has the POTS incoming call leg and the VoIP outgoing call leg. The VoIP terminating gateway has the VoIP incoming call leg and the POTS outgoing call leg. Both gateways must first successfully negotiate the VoIP parameters associated with their respective outgoing and incoming call legs before the VoIP terminating gateway can forward the call to the destination PSTN network.

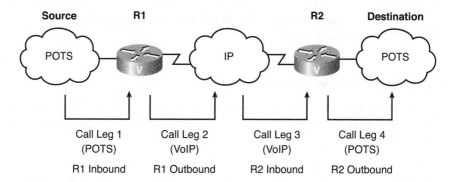

Figure 1-26 *VoIP Gateway*

Cisco Unified Border Element

Cisco Unified Border Element, as illustrated in Figure 1-27, forwards an incoming VoIP call as another, outgoing VoIP call. It receives a call setup request, negotiates parameters, and forwards the call setup request to the next gateway. The incoming signaling protocol might differ from the outgoing signaling protocol. When the call is successfully signaled end to end, Cisco UBE might either proxy the media channel, which is referred to as *flow-through*, or let the media channel pass through the gateway without any modification, which is referred to as *flow-around*. The media proxy function is necessary when the VoIP traffic parameters of the incoming call leg differ from the VoIP parameters of the outgoing call leg. When Cisco UBE proxies the media channel, it changes the IP addresses of the media packets. This feature is very useful for security or connectivity reasons. Both call legs of a Cisco UBE are VoIP call legs.

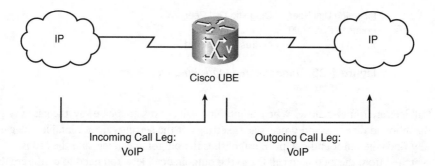

Figure 1-27 *Cisco Unified Border Element*

How Voice Gateways Route Calls

A primary function of the Cisco Unified Communications gateways is to route calls. The process of call routing includes the processing of incoming and outgoing call legs. This section describes how call legs are created when inbound and outbound dial peers are matched. It provides details about the dial-peer matching process and explains the direct inward dialing (DID) feature. Additionally, this section addresses the configuration of POTS dial peers. The configuration of VoIP dial peers is covered in Chapter 2, "Configuring Basic Voice over IP."

Gateway Call-Routing Components

Dial peers are essential to implementing dial plans and providing voice services over an IP packet network. Dial peers are used to identify call source and destination endpoints and to define the characteristics that are applied to each call leg in the call connection.

A traditional voice call over the PSTN uses a dedicated 64-kbps end-to-end circuit. In contrast, a voice call over the packet network is made up of discrete segments or call legs. As previously mentioned, a call leg is a logical connection between two routers or between a router and a telephony device. Each voice gateway establishes at least two call legs. The incoming call leg is associated with the inbound (source) dial peer, while the outgoing call leg is associated with the outbound (destination) dial peer, as shown in Figure 1-28. Attributes that are defined in a dial peer are applied to that call leg.

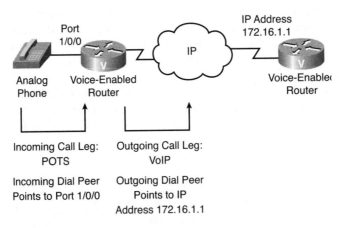

Figure 1-28   *Inbound and Outbound Dial Peers*

Call legs are router-centric. When an inbound call arrives on a gateway, the gateway finds the inbound dial peer and processes its settings. If the settings are acceptable, the gateway finds the outbound dial peer, establishes the outgoing call leg, and the call is switched from the incoming call leg to the outgoing call leg. You need to configure dial peers to enable call routing on a gateway.

Dial Peers

Dial peers are generally classified into POTS dial peers and network dial peers, as described in Table 1-2.

Table 1-2 *Most Prevalent Dial-Peer Types*

Type of Dial Peer	Network Technology
Plain old telephone service (POTS)	Maps a dial string to a specific voice port on the local gateway. The voice port connects the gateway to the PSTN, PBX, or analog telephone.
VoIP	Points to the IP address or DNS name of the destination VoIP device that terminates the call. This mapping applies to VoIP protocols, such as H.323 and SIP.
Multimedia Mail over IP (MMoIP)	The dial peer is mapped to the email address of the SMTP server. This type of dial peer is used for store-and-forward fax (on-ramp and off-ramp faxing).

In Figure 1-29, an analog telephone is connected to the Cisco Unified Communications gateway. The gateway needs two dial peers. The POTS dial-peer configuration includes at least the telephone number of the analog telephone and the voice port to which it is attached. Based on this information, the gateway forwards calls destined to the defined telephone over the specified port.

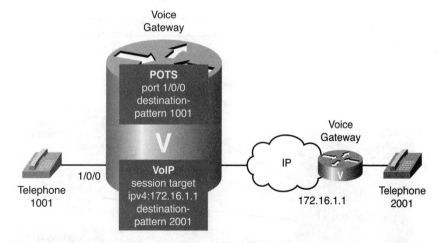

Figure 1-29 *POTS and VoIP Dial Peers*

The VoIP dial peer is connected to the IP network. The VoIP dial-peer configuration includes at least the destination telephone number (or range of numbers) and the next-hop IP address or name used to progress the call further. For call routing to successfully forward calls in both directions, at least these call-routing elements are needed in every voice-processing system:

■ An appropriate POTS dial peer that specifies to which voice port the telephone is attached. This applies only to the edge voice-processing systems.

■ An appropriate VoIP dial peer that specifies the recipient destination address, or at least the address of the next hop.

Dial-peer parameters vary based on the dial-peer type. A VoIP dial peer can point to either an H.323 or SIP device. A Media Gateway Control Protocol (MGCP) device is not an option because of its call agent–centric nature. When Cisco Unified Communications Manager uses MGCP to control the voice gateway, the dial plan is maintained and Cisco Unified Communications Manager makes the routing decisions. The gateway merely receives instructions on how to process the voice circuits.

VoIP dial-peer parameters include coder-decoder (codec), quality of service (QoS), voice activity detection (VAD), dual-tone multifrequency (DTMF) relay, and fax rate.

As shown in Figure 1-30, VoIP dial peers map a dial string to a remote network device. Some examples of these remote network devices are as follows:

■ Cisco Unified Communications Manager cluster

■ Another voice gateway

■ SIP proxy

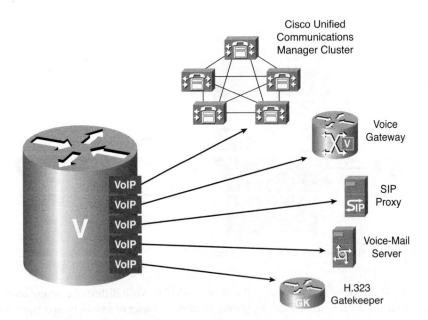

Figure 1-30   *VoIP Dial-Peer Examples*

- Voice-mail server

- H.323 gatekeeper

Call Legs

A comparison of IP packet routing and call-routing principles, as presented in Table 1-3, can be helpful to understand the call-routing process.

Table 1-3 *IP and Call Routing Comparison*

IP Routing	Call Routing
Static or dynamic	Only static
IP routing table	Dial plan
IP route	Dial peer
Hop-by-hop routing, where each router makes an independent decision	Inbound and outbound call legs, where the gateway negotiates VoIP parameters with preceding and next gateways before a call is forwarded
Destination-based routing	Called number, matched by destination pattern, is one of many selection criteria
Longest-match rule	The longest-match rule used for a dial peer's destination pattern exists
Equal paths	Preference can be applied to equal dial peers, or a random selection is made if all criteria are the same
Default route	Possible to have a default route, which often points to a gateway

Because dial peers collectively define where to forward calls, all dial peers together build a dial plan, which is equivalent to the IP routing table. The dial peers are static in nature.

Hop-by-hop call routing builds on the principle of call legs. Before a call-routing decision is made, the gateway must identify the inbound dial peer and process its parameters. This process might involve VoIP parameter negotiation.

The call-routing decision is the selection of the outbound dial peer. This selection is commonly based on the called number when the **destination-pattern** command is used. The selection might be based on other information, and that other criteria might have higher precedence than the called number. When the called number is matched to find the outbound dial peer, the longest-match rule applies.

If more than one dial peer equally matches the dial string, all the matching dial peers are used to form a rotary group. The router attempts to establish the outbound call leg using all the dial peers in the rotary group until one is successful. The selection order within the group can be influenced by configuring a preference value.

A default call route can be configured using special characters when matching the number.

The VoIP gateway is often faced with the task of selecting the best path for a given destination number. Such a requirement arises when the preferred path goes through the IP WAN, and the backup PSTN path should be chosen when the IP WAN is either unavailable or lacks the needed bandwidth resources.

Figure 1-31 illustrates a scenario with two locations connected to the IP WAN and PSTN. When the call goes through the PSTN, its numbers (both calling and called) might have to be manipulated so that they are reachable within the PSTN network. Otherwise, the PSTN switches will not recognize the called number, and the call will fail.

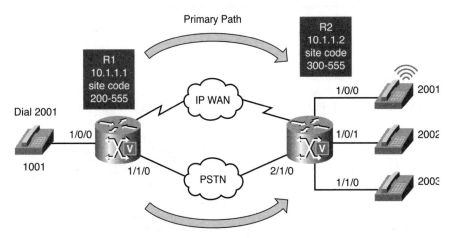

Secondary path, call forwarded to 300 555-2001
(requires digit manipulation for routing through PSTN).

Figure 1-31   *Call Routing with Secondary Path*

Figure 1-32 illustrates the call legs that are processed on a gateway that receives a call from a locally attached telephone and originates a VoIP session.

These call legs are created when the telephone (1001) attached to an R1 gateway dials a telephone number in another location (2001). When a call arrives on R1, the gateway creates an inbound call leg that corresponds to the inbound dial peer, makes a routing decision by finding an outbound dial peer, and creates an outbound call leg by forwarding the call toward the destination. If the routing decision chooses an IP WAN, the outbound call leg will be VoIP; if the routing decision chooses a PSTN, the outbound call leg will be POTS.

Figure 1-33 illustrates the call legs that are processed on the gateway that terminates the VoIP session and forwards the call to the locally attached telephone with extension 2001.

The inbound call leg is created when the call arrives either through the IP WAN or the PSTN network. The gateway makes the routing decision by selecting the outbound dial peer. The outbound call leg corresponds to a POTS dial peer that points to the voice port

1/0/0, where the recipient's telephone is attached. The gateway signals an incoming call on that port, and the telephone rings.

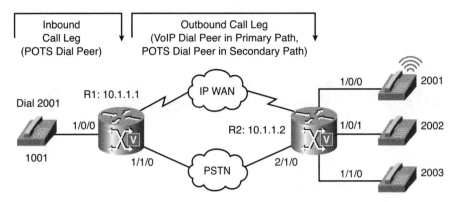

Figure 1-32 *Call Legs—Source Gateway Perspective*

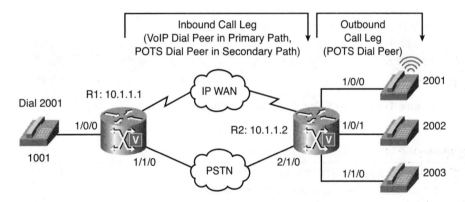

Figure 1-33 *Call Legs—Destination Gateway Perspective*

Configuring POTS Dial Peers

Figure 1-34 illustrates examples of POTS dial peer use.

This section explains how to configure the POTS dial peers that effectively enable call forwarding along the PSTN path. The configuration of the primary VoIP path will be covered later. Also, the digit manipulation requirement is not covered at this time.

Figure 1-35 and Examples 1-1 and 1-2 illustrate the configuration that enables calling from extension 1001 to extension 2001.

Example 1-1 *Router R1's Configuration*

```
R1(config)#dial-peer voice 1 pots
R1(config-dialpeer)#destination-pattern 2001
```

```
R1(config-dialpeer)#forward-digits all
R1(config-dialpeer)#port 1/1/0
```

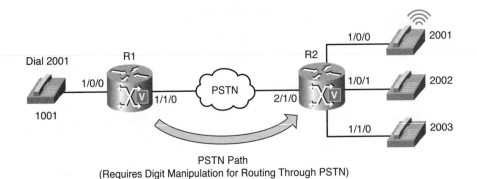

Figure 1-34   *POTS Dial-Peer Example*

Figure 1-35   *POTS Dial-Peer Configuration Example*

Example 1-2   *Router R2's Configuration*

```
R2(config)#dial-peer voice 1 pots
R2(config-dialpeer)#destination-pattern 2001
R2(config-dialpeer)#port 1/0/1
```

The outbound dial-peer type is POTS, because the destination number 2001 is reachable over a POTS voice port 1/1/0. There are two basic parameters that need to be specified on this dial peer: the telephone number and the voice port.

The **destination-pattern** command is used to match the called telephone number. The R1 gateway uses the destination pattern "2001."

The **port** command specifies the respective voice port. In this example, port 1/1/0 defines that the port is on module 1, voice interface card (VIC) slot 1, and voice port 0.

The **forward-digits all** command makes the gateway send the entire called number in the call signal to the next gateway. By default, the explicitly matched digits are discarded when the call is forwarded over an outbound POTS call leg. In this case, the destination pattern "2001" matches explicitly all four digits, so the gateway would not send any digits when forwarding the call through the PSTN. The digit consumption rule applies only to outbound POTS call legs. When a call is forwarded over an outbound VoIP call leg, no digit consumption occurs, by default, and all digits are sent to the next VoIP device.

Examples 1-3 and 1-4 provide the configuration that enables call routing both ways. The R1 gateway has the POTS dial peer 2 that matches extension 1001 and points to the voice port 1/0/0, where a telephone is attached. The R2 gateway, in addition to having the POTS dial peer that points to the attached telephone, has the POTS dial peer 2, which matches the extension 1001 and points toward the PSTN.

Example 1-3   *Router R1's Configuration (Continued)*

```
R1(config)#dial-peer voice 1 pots
R1(config-dialpeer)#destination-pattern 2001
R1(config-dialpeer)#forward-digits all
R1(config-dialpeer)#port 1/1/0
R1(config-dialpeer)#dial-peer voice 2 pots
R1(config-dialpeer)#destination-pattern 1001
R1(config-dialpeer)#port 1/0/0
```

Example 1-4   *Router R2's Configuration (Continued)*

```
R2(config)#dial-peer voice 1 pots
R2(config-dialpeer)#destination-pattern 2001
R2(config-dialpeer)#port 1/0/1
R2(config-dialpeer)#dial-peer voice 2 pots
R2(config-dialpeer)#destination-pattern 1001
R2(config-dialpeer)#forward-digits all
R2(config-dialpeer)#port 2/1/0
```

The **forward-digits all** command is used on both gateways in the dial peers pointing to the PSTN. Without this command, the gateways would discard the explicitly matched digits when sending the call to the PSTN. No digits would be forwarded.

Matching a Dial Peer

In addition to matching a dial peer based on a call's incoming voice port (that is, using the **port** command), you can use the following three commands that match telephone numbers:

```
Router(config-dialpeer)#destination-pattern string
Router(config-dialpeer)#incoming called-number string
Router(config-dialpeer)#answer-address string
```

Two telephone numbers are usually sent with the call: the calling number, known in ISDN as the Automatic Number Identification (ANI), and the called number, referred to as the Dialed Number Identification Service (DNIS). Both numbers can be used to find the inbound and outbound dial peers.

The obvious use of the **destination-pattern** command is to match the outbound dial peer based on the called number. The command is also considered when matching the inbound dial peer, but then the destination pattern string is matched against the calling number.

The **incoming called-number** command is only considered when selecting the inbound dial peer. It matches the original called number.

The **answer-address** command is only considered when selecting the inbound dial peer. It matches the original calling number.

The three string-matching commands, **destination-pattern**, **incoming called-number**, and **answer-address**, have a string parameter. The gateway compares the received numbers with the strings defined in the respective commands. The string might explicitly match the characters in the telephone numbers (0–9, A–D, *, #), and it can contain special regular expressions, as summarized in Table 1-4.

Table 1-4 *Regular Expressions Used to Match Number Strings*

Metacharacter	Description
0–9, A–D,*,#	Standard characters are digits 0–9, letters A–D, the asterisk (*), and the pound sign (#) that appear on dial pads.
Plus sign (+)	As first character, indicates E.164 standard number; otherwise it specifies that the preceding digit occurred one or more times.
Period (.)	Matches any entered digit (used as a wildcard).
Percent sign (%)	Indicates that the preceding digit occurred either zero or more times.
Question mark (?)	Repeats the previous character zero or one time. Press **Ctrl-V** to disable context-sensitive help and enter the ? character.
Circumflex (^)	Indicates a match to the beginning of the string.
Dollar sign ($)	Matches the null string at the end of the string.
T	Timer character. Indicates a variable-length dial string. Makes the router wait until all digits are received before routing call.
Backslash (\)	Followed by a single character, matches that character.
Brackets [ ]	Indicates a range.
Parentheses ( )	Indicates a pattern.

Note The asterisk (*) and pound sign (#) are not considered special characters. They appear on standard touch-tone dial pads and might be used when passing a call to an automated application that requires these characters to signal the use of a special feature. For example, when a user calls an interactive voice response (IVR) system that requires a code for access, the number dialed might be 5551212888#, which would initially dial the telephone number 5551212 and input a code of 888 followed by the pound key to terminate the IVR input query.

Table 1-5 provides examples of number matching.

Table 1-5 *Number-Matching Examples*

Number	Matching Telephone Number(s)
5551234	This pattern matches one telephone number exactly, 5551234. This destination pattern is typically used when there is a single device, such as a telephone or fax machine, connected to a voice port.
^5551234$	This pattern matches the number 5551234 using an explicit match of the beginning and the end of the string.
555123[5-9]	This pattern matches the number range 5551235 through 5551239.
55512[3-4].	This destination pattern matches a seven-digit telephone number where the first five digits are 55512, the sixth digit can be a 3 or 4, and the last digit can be any digit. This destination pattern is used when telephone number ranges are assigned to specific sites. In this example, the destination pattern is used in a small site that does not need more than 30 numbers assigned.
.T	This destination pattern matches any telephone number that has at least one digit and can vary in length from 1 through 32 digits. This destination pattern is used for a dial peer that services a variable-length dial plan for local, national, and international calls. It can also be used as a default destination pattern so that any calls that do not match a more specific pattern will match this pattern and can be directed to an operator.
(200)?5551234	Matches the numbers 2005551234 and 5551234. This expression uses a pattern (200) that can occur zero or one time.
1[2-3]%4	Matches numbers that start with 1, have any number of occurrences of the digit 2 or 3, and end with 4. This expression uses a range [2–3] that can occur zero or more times.

The inbound dial peer determines the call properties for the incoming side of the call. To match inbound call legs to dial peers, the router uses three elements in the call setup message, as illustrated in Figure 1-36, and five configurable dial-peer attributes.

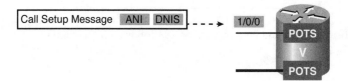

Figure 1-36 *ANI and DNIS Used in Matching Inbound Dial Peer*

The three call setup elements are, in the example of ISDN, as follows:

- **Called number (DNIS):** Specifies the destination, which is derived from the ISDN setup message or channel associated signaling (CAS) DNIS

- **Calling number (ANI):** Denotes the origin, which is derived from the ISDN setup message or CAS ANI

- **Voice port:** Carries the incoming call

The gateway selects an inbound dial peer by matching the information elements in the setup message with the dial-peer attributes. The gateway matches these items in the following order:

Step 1.   Called number with **incoming called-number**.

First, the gateway attempts to match the called number of the call setup request with the configured **incoming called-number** parameter of each dial peer. This attribute has matching priority over the **answer-address** and **destination-pattern** matching. If multiple **incoming called-number** attributes match the DNIS, the longest match wins.

Step 2.   Calling number with **answer-address**.

If no match is found in Step 1, the gateway attempts to match the calling number of the call setup request with the **answer-address** of each dial peer. This attribute might be useful in situations where you want to match calls based on the calling number. If multiple **answer-address** attributes match the ANI, the longest match wins.

Step 3.   Calling number with **destination-pattern**.

If no match is found in Step 2, the gateway attempts to match the calling number of the call setup request to the **destination-pattern** of each dial peer. If multiple **destination-pattern** attributes match the DNIS, the longest match wins.

Step 4.   Voice port (associated with the incoming call setup request) with the configured dial-peer **port** parameter (applicable for inbound POTS call legs).

If no match is found in Step 3, the gateway attempts to match the configured dial-peer **port** parameter to the voice port associated with the incoming call.

If multiple dial peers have the same port configured, the dial peer first added in the configuration is matched.

Step 5. If there is no match, the default dial peer is used. The default dial peer is explained later in this chapter.

Only one condition must be met. The gateway stops searching when a dial-peer match is found.

Figure 1-37 illustrates an example of matching inbound dial peers. When the destination gateway receives the call setup request, it looks for the inbound dial peer. The ANI is 1001; the DNIS is 2001. The **incoming called-number** command has the first precedence and exists in dial peer 3 but does not match the DNIS. The **answer-address** command has the second precedence, exists in dial peer 2, and matches the ANI. Therefore, dial peer 2 is selected as the incoming dial peer.

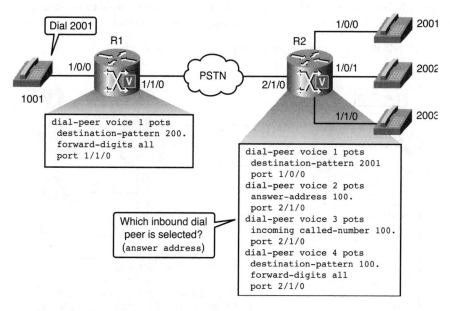

Figure 1-37 *Inbound Dial-Peer Matching Example*

Use the **answer-address** command when matching the geographical region of the caller. This approach is recommended in these situations:

■ Callers from a given country should be directed to the appropriate language-speaking team.

■ Callers from a specific region should be directed to the regional sales staff.

Use the **incoming called-number** command whenever possible. Because all types of call setup messages and signals always include the DNIS information, Cisco recommends using the **incoming called-number** command for inbound dial-peer matching. In particular, the **incoming called-number** command is useful for service selection, such as in these situations:

■ Different numbers are available to reach the sales and technical support departments.

■ Different numbers exist for shipping order, tracking, and cancellation services.

Matching Outbound Dial Peers

When a call setup request arrives on a voice gateway, the gateway uses the incoming dial string to match the destination pattern in the outbound dial peer. Both dial peers—POTS and VoIP—are considered together for outbound dial-peer matching.

Once the outbound dial peer is found, the call setup progresses to the next device along the path. On outbound POTS dial peers, the **port** command is used to forward the call. On outbound VoIP dial peers, the **session target** command is used to forward the call.

Figure 1-38 illustrates an example of outbound dial-peer matching.

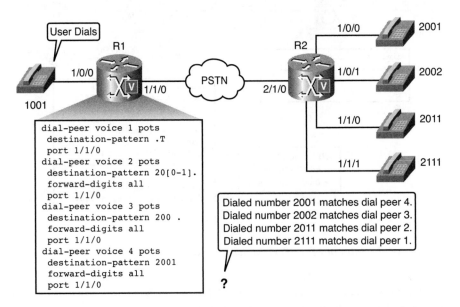

Figure 1-38 *Outbound Dial-Peer Matching Example*

Four calls are made from the telephone with extension 1001:

■ The user dials 2001. The best match is found with dial peer 4.

  The user dials 2002. Dial peer 1 matches that number, but the match is the least specific.

- The user dials 2002. Dial peer 2 matches that number and also a total of 20 numbers (2000 to 2019). Dial peer 3 matches that number and also a total of 10 numbers (2000 to 2009). Dial peer 3 yields the best match.

- The user dials 2011. Dial peers 1 and 2 match the number, with the latter offering the longest match.

- The user dials 2111. Only dial peer 1 matches.

Default Dial Peer

Figure 1-39 depicts a situation in which the call routing works only in one direction. This scenario brings up the question about the inbound dial peers selected on both gateways.

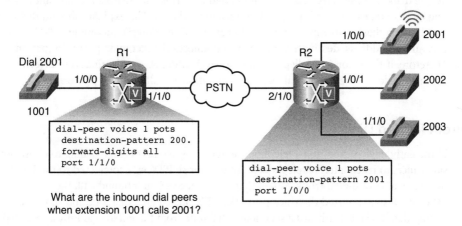

Figure 1-39   *Default Dial-Peer Example*

If no inbound peer can be matched by the defined criteria, the gateway resorts to the default dial peer. The default dial peer is referred to as dial peer 0. Default dial peers are used for inbound matches only. They never match outbound calls. The characteristics of dial peer 0 cannot be changed.

Dial peer 0 for inbound VoIP peers has the following characteristics:

- G.729 and G.711 codecs are supported.

- IP precedence is set to 0.

- VAD is enabled.

- RSVP is not supported.

- Fax-rate service is supported.

Dial peer 0 for inbound POTS peers has the following characteristics:

- No applications are supported.

- No direct inward dialing is supported.

You cannot change the default configuration for dial peer 0. The default dial peer (that is, dial peer 0) cannot negotiate nondefault capabilities, services, and applications, such as DTMF relay or disabled VAD. When the default dial peer is matched on an inbound POTS call leg, there is no default IVR application enabled on the port. As a result, the user gets a dial tone and proceeds to dial digits.

Avoid using dial peer 0. Having the **incoming called-number** parameter configured correctly ensures that the dial peer is always matched with the parameters that you want when placing outbound calls through a gateway. Many problems with calling out through a Cisco IOS gateway are caused by codec, VAD, and DTMF-relay misconfigurations when dial peer 0 is being matched. When the Cisco AS5350, AS5400, or AS5850 Universal Gateway platforms do not explicitly match an incoming dial peer, dial peer 0 is matched and the call is treated as a dial modem call. This call treatment can result in getting modem tones rather than a dial tone for inbound calls. The explicit inbound dial-peer matching on these platforms matches only the first three criteria (**incoming called-number, answer address, destination-pattern**) and ignores the incoming port information. Therefore, if the **incoming called-number, answer-address,** and **destination-pattern** commands do not match, the call is treated as a modem call on these platforms.

Direct Inward Dialing

In the early days of traditional telephony, enterprises used two-stage dialing to allow outside callers to reach internal telephones. An enterprise PBX was connected to the PSTN over an analog or digital trunk. When that trunk received an inbound call, the central office (CO) switch seized the voice port. The PBX presented a dial tone and started collecting digits. The caller heard a secondary dial tone from the enterprise PBX and dialed the number required to reach the internal telephone.

With the invention of direct inward dialing (DID) in the 1970s, one-stage dialing was made possible. With one-stage dialing, the callers enter the entire called-party number, including the number required to reach the internal telephone. They do not hear a secondary dial tone. The PSTN CO switch sends the entire DNIS to the PBX, which forwards the call to the internal telephone.

Voice gateways can use DID if it is enabled on inbound POTS dial peers. It is supported on all digital voice ports and the analog FXS-DID ports. It is not supported on analog Foreign Exchange Station (FXS), Foreign Exchange Office (FXO), or ear and mouth (E&M) voice ports.

Two-Stage Dialing

Figure 1-40 shows the process of two-stage dialing, which is depicted in the following steps:

Step 1.   The user takes the phone off-hook, receives the dial tone, and dials 555.

Step 2.   The PSTN receives the digits and delivers to the destination gateway. The trunk line to the destination gateway is seized by the adjacent CO switch. The destination gateway presents the secondary dial tone and starts collecting digits until it can identify an outbound dial peer. Whether the digits are dialed with irregular intervals by humans or in a regular fashion by telephony equipment that sends the precollected digits, dial-peer matching is done digit by digit. This means that the gateway attempts to match a dial peer after each digit is received.

Step 3.   The user hears the secondary dial tone and dials 2001.

Step 4.   The gateway uses the number 2001 to match the outbound dial peer.

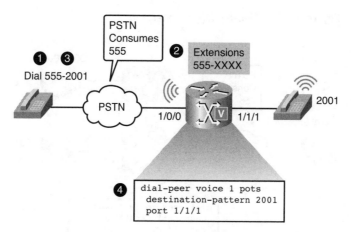

Figure 1-40 *Two-Stage Dialing Example*

The destination gateway signals an incoming call to the telephone on port 1/1/1, and the telephone rings.

A potential issue related to two-stage dialing is presented in Figure 1-41.

The destination gateway uses an incorrectly designed dial plan. Because the destination gateway collects the dialed digits in-band, on a digit-by-digit basis, it matches dial peer 2 before the complete number has been received. The call cannot be delivered to its intended recipient.

To solve the problem of the incorrectly designed dial plan and two-stage dialing, use a wildcard in the destination pattern of dial peer 2, as illustrated in Figure 1-42.

This causes the destination gateway to wait for four digits before making the call-routing decision. With this solution, the call can be delivered to its intended recipient.

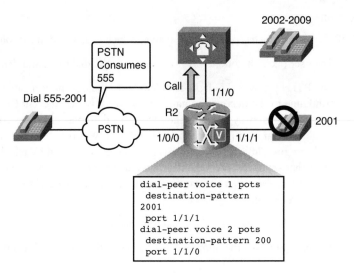

Figure 1-41   *Digit-by-Digit Collection*

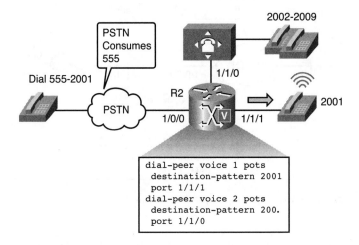

Figure 1-42   *Wildcard Use*

The process of two-stage dialing on a gateway-by-gateway basis is enumerated in Figure 1-43.

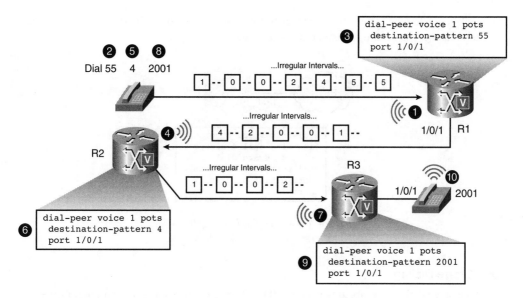

Figure 1-43 *Gateway-by-Gateway Processing*

Figure 1-43 shows the following process:

1. The user takes the phone off-hook and receives the dial tone from local gateway R1.

2. The user dials 55 by entering the digits in irregular intervals.

3. R1 collects the two digits (55), matches the outbound dial peer, and seizes the trunk line 1/0/1 toward R2.

4. R2 presents the second dial tone.

5. The user hears the secondary dial tone and dials 4.

6. R2 matches the outbound dial peer. R2 seizes the trunk line 1/0/1 to R3.

7. R3 presents the third dial tone.

8. The user hears the third dial tone and dials 2001 by entering the digits in irregular intervals.

9. R3 keeps collecting digits until the number 2001 has been received. That number matches the outbound dial peer.

10. R3 signals an incoming call to the voice port 1/0/1. The recipient phone rings.

There are situations in which expected dial strings do not have a set number of digits. In such cases, it is usually best to use variable-length dial peers by configuring the **T** terminator on the dial-peer **destination-pattern** command. When the timer character (**T**) is included at the end of the destination pattern, as illustrated in Figure 1-44, the router collects dialed digits until the interdigit timer expires (10 seconds, by default) or until the termination character (the default is **#**) is dialed.

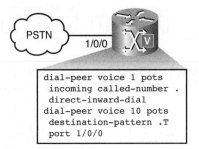

Figure 1-44   *Variable-Length Numbers*

One-Stage Dialing

One-stage dialing is enabled when the DID feature is configured on the inbound POTS dial peer of the destination voice gateway. With one-stage dialing, the destination gateway does not present the dial tone. Therefore, the caller enters the entire number without hearing any secondary dial tone. The PSTN can deliver the called number to the destination gateway in one of two ways:

■ **Over digital interfaces:** The CO switch sends a call setup message that contains the entire DNIS. The DNIS is mapped to the outbound dial peer. The gateway forwards the call directly to the configured destination.

■ **Over analog interfaces (FXS-DID):** The digits are automatically signaled to the destination gateway by the switch, without the requirement of the secondary dial tone.

Figure 1-45 illustrates one-stage dialing.

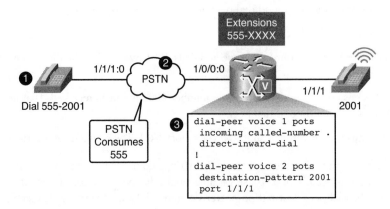

Figure 1-45   *DID Overview*

The following describes the process shown in Figure 1-45:

1.   The user takes the phone off-hook, receives the dial tone, and dials 555-2001.

2.   The PSTN delivers the call to the destination gateway. The destination gateway receives the last four digits of the called number in one call setup message or over an analog FXS DID trunk.

3.   The destination gateway matches the outbound dial peer and signals an incoming call to port 1/1/1. The recipient phone rings.

Figure 1-46 shows how DID manages the problem of incorrectly designed dial plans. The destination gateway is connected to the PSTN over a digital trunk and has the DID feature enabled on the inbound POTS dial peer. Because the PSTN has consumed the first digits from the called number, the destination gateway receives the last four digits in one call setup message. The destination gateway selects dial peer 2 as the best match. The call reaches the intended recipient.

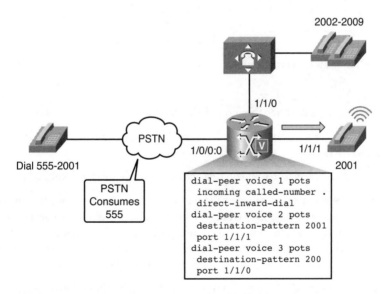

Figure 1-46   *Matching with Complete Called Number*

The process of one-stage dialing on a gateway-by-gateway basis is depicted in Figure 1-47.

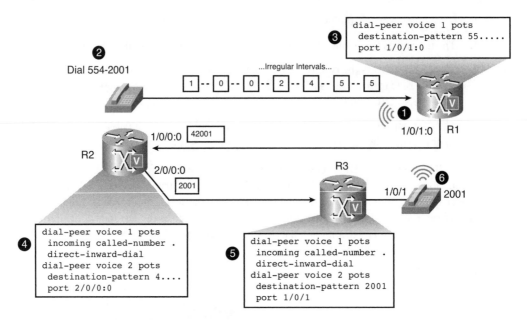

Figure 1-47   *Gateway-by-Gateway Processing*

The following steps describe the process shown in Figure 1-47:

1. The user takes the phone off-hook and receives the dial tone from the local gateway R1.

2. The user dials 554-2001 by entering the digits in irregular intervals.

3. R1 collects the number, matches the outbound dial peer, and finds that the outgoing call leg goes over the digital trunk 1/0/1:0. Because the outgoing voice port is a digital circuit, R1 sends the entire called number in one call setup message. R1 does not forward the first two digits (55) because they are explicitly matched by the destination pattern and are consumed by default (**forward-digits all** is not configured).

4. R2 receives the called number (42001), matches the outbound dial peer 1, and forwards the called number (2001) in a single call setup message over the outgoing digital trunk, to R3. The first digit (4) is consumed through the explicit match by the destination pattern.

5. R3 receives the called number (2001) in a single message and matches the outbound dial peer.

6. R3 signals an incoming call to port 1/0/1, and the recipient phone rings.

Note   If analog trunks were used in this example, the digits would be sent sequentially. The caller would not hear any secondary or tertiary dial tones.

As shown in Figure 1-48, the DID feature is configured using the **direct-inward-dial** command in the incoming dial peer. The inbound dial peer can be matched in various ways. The recommended method to match inbound dial peers is to use the **incoming called-number** command. The figure displays the two most commonly found DID configurations, while the method using the **incoming called-number** command is preferred. Note that the timer character (**T**) is not used in the **incoming called-number** command, although it is used in destination patterns.

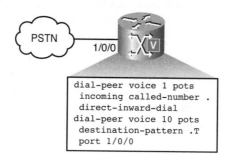

```
dial-peer voice 1 pots
  incoming called-number .
  direct-inward-dial
dial-peer voice 10 pots
  destination-pattern .T
  port 1/0/0
```

Figure 1-48   *Configuring DID*

Following is the explanation of the two strings:

■   The string . (single period) matches any number with at least one digit. It is useful for outbound matching using the **destination-pattern** command, and especially for inbound matching with the **incoming called-number** command.

■   The string **.T** (single period followed by T) matches any number with at least one digit. The timer character matches either the interdigit timeout or the termination character (**#**). The string is useful for outbound matching using the **destination-pattern** command.

Bonus Video   To view a video of the author discussing dial-peer theory and demonstrating dial-peer configuration, navigate to the CVOICE page on the 1ExamAMonth.com website (http://oneexamamonth.com/). The video on dial peers is titled *Dial Peer Pressure*. Additional video tutorials from this website will be recommended later in this book.

Configuration of Voice Ports

Connecting voice devices to a network infrastructure requires an in-depth understanding of the signaling and electrical characteristics specific to each type of interface. Improperly matched electrical components can cause echo and create poor audio quality. Configuring devices for international implementation requires knowledge of country-specific settings. This section examines analog voice ports, analog signaling, and configuration parameters for analog voice ports.

Analog Voice Ports

Voice ports on routers and access servers emulate physical telephony switch connections so that voice calls and their associated signaling can be transferred intact between a packet network and a circuit-switched network or device. For a voice call to occur, certain information must be passed between the telephony devices at either end of the call, such as the on-hook status of the devices, the availability of the line, and whether an incoming call is trying to reach a device. This information is referred to as *signaling*, and to process it properly, the devices at both ends of the call segment, which are directly connected to each other, must use the same type of signaling.

The devices in a packet network must be configured to convey signaling information in a way that a circuit-switched network can understand. They must also be able to understand signaling information that is received from the circuit-switched network. This is accomplished by installing appropriate voice hardware in a router or access server and by configuring the voice ports that connect to telephony devices or the circuit-switched network. Figure 1-49 shows typical examples of how voice ports are used.

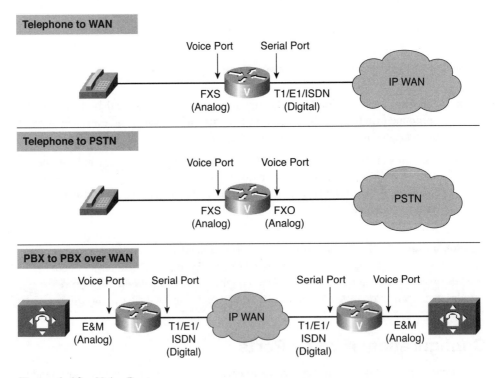

Figure 1-49 *Voice Ports*

Signaling Interfaces

Voice ports on routers and access servers physically connect the router, access server, or call control device to telephony devices such as telephones, fax machines, PBXs, and PSTN central office (CO) switches through signaling interfaces.

These signaling interfaces generate information about things such as

- On-hook status

- Ringing

- Line seizure

The voice port hardware and software of the router need to be configured to transmit and receive the same type of signaling being used by the device they are interfacing with so calls can be exchanged smoothly between a packet network and a circuit-switched network.

The signaling interfaces discussed in the following sections include FXO, FXS, and E&M, which are types of analog interfaces. Digital signaling interfaces include T1, E1, and ISDN. Some digital connections emulate FXO, FXS, and E&M interfaces. It is important to know which signaling method the telephony side of the connection is using and to match the router configuration and voice interface hardware to that signaling method.

Analog Voice Port Interfaces

Analog voice port interfaces connect routers in packet-based networks to analog two-wire or four-wire circuits in telephony networks. Two-wire circuits connect to analog telephone or fax devices, and four-wire circuits connect to PBXs. Connections to the PSTN CO are typically made with digital interfaces. Three types of analog voice interfaces are supported by Cisco gateways, as illustrated in Figure 1-50.

The following is a detailed explanation of each of the three types of analog voice interfaces:

- **FXS:** An FXS interface connects the router or access server to end-user equipment such as telephones, fax machines, or modems. The FXS interface supplies ring, voltage, and dial tone to the station and includes an RJ-11 connector for basic telephone equipment, key sets, and PBXs.

- **FXO:** An FXO interface is used for trunk, or tie-line, connections to a PSTN CO or to a PBX that does not support E&M signaling (when the local telecommunications authority permits). This interface is of value for off-premises station applications. A standard RJ-11 modular telephone cable connects the FXO voice interface card to the PSTN or PBX through a telephone wall outlet.

- **E&M:** Trunk circuits connect telephone switches to one another. They do not connect end-user equipment to the network. The most common form of analog trunk circuit is the E&M interface, which uses special signaling paths that are separate from the trunk audio path to convey information about the calls. The signaling paths are known as the E-lead and the M-lead. E&M connections from routers to telephone switches or to PBXs are preferable to FXS and FXO connections, because E&M provides better answer and disconnect supervision.

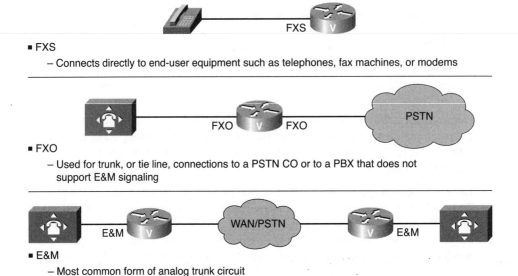

- FXS
  - Connects directly to end-user equipment such as telephones, fax machines, or modems

- FXO
  - Used for trunk, or tie line, connections to a PSTN CO or to a PBX that does not support E&M signaling

- E&M
  - Most common form of analog trunk circuit

Figure 1-50   *Analog Voice Ports*

The name E&M is thought to derive from the phrase Ear and Mouth or rEceive and transMit, although it could also come from Earth and Magneto. The history of these names dates back to the early days of telephony, when the CO side had a key that grounded the E circuit, and the other side had a sounder with an electromagnet attached to a battery. Descriptions such as Ear and Mouth were adopted to help field personnel understand and determine the direction of a signal in a wire.

Like a serial port, an E&M interface has a DTE/DCE type of reference. In the telecommunications world, the trunking side is similar to the DCE and is usually associated with CO functionality. The router acts as this side of the interface. The other side is referred to as the signaling side, like a DTE, and is usually a device such as a PBX.

Note   Depending on how the router is connected to the PSTN, the voice gateway might provide clocking to an attached key system or PBX, because the PSTN has more accurate clocks, and the voice gateway can pass this capability to downstream devices.

Analog Signaling

The human voice generates sound waves, and the telephone converts the sound waves into electrical signals, analogous to sound. Analog signaling is not robust because of line noise. Analog transmissions are boosted by amplifiers because the signal diminishes the farther it travels from the CO. As the signal is boosted, the noise is also boosted, which often causes an unusable connection.

In digital networks, signals are transmitted over great distances and coded, regenerated, and decoded without degradation of quality. Repeaters amplify the signal and clean it to its original condition. Repeaters then determine the original sequence of the signal levels and send the clean signal to the next network destination.

Voice ports on routers and access servers physically connect the router or access server to telephony devices such as telephones, fax machines, PBXs, and PSTN CO switches. These devices might use any of several types of signaling interfaces to generate information about on-hook status, ringing, and line seizure.

Signaling techniques can be placed into one of three categories:

- **Supervisory:** Involves the detection of changes to the status of a loop or trunk. When these changes are detected, the supervisory circuit generates a predetermined response. A circuit (loop) can close to connect a call, for example.

- **Addressing:** Involves passing dialed digits (pulsed or tone) to a PBX or CO. These dialed digits provide the switch with a connection path to another phone or customer premises equipment (CPE).

- **Informational:** Provides audible tones to the user, which indicate certain conditions such as an incoming call or a busy phone.

FXS and FXO Supervisory Signaling

FXS and FXO interfaces indicate on-hook or off-hook status and the seizure of telephone lines by one of two access signaling methods: loop-start or ground-start. The type of access signaling is determined by the type of service from the telephone company's CO. Standard home telephone lines use loop-start, but business telephones can order ground-start lines instead.

Loop-Start

Loop-start, as enumerated in Figure 1-51, is the more common of the access signaling techniques. When a handset is picked up (the telephone goes off-hook), this action closes the 48V circuit that draws current from the telephone company CO and indicates a change in status, which signals the CO to provide a dial tone. An incoming call is signaled from the CO to the called handset by sending a signal in a standard on/off pattern, which causes the telephone to ring. When the called subscriber answers the call, the 48V circuit is closed and the CO turns off the ring voltage. At this point, the two circuits are tied together at the CO.

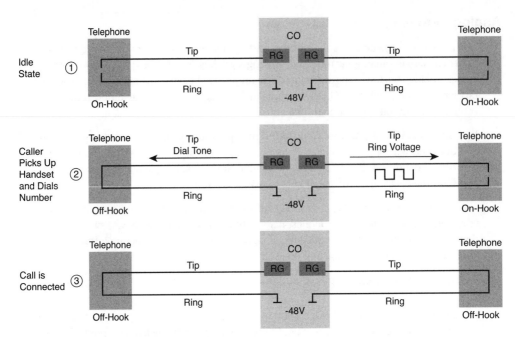

Figure 1-51 *Loop-Start Signaling*

The loop-start signaling process is as follows:

1. In the idle state, the telephone, PBX, or FXO module has an open two-wire loop (tip and ring lines open). It could be a telephone set with the handset on-hook or a PBX or FXO module that generates an open between the tip and ring lines. The CO or FXS waits for a closed loop, which allows current to flow. The CO or FXS has a ring generator connected to the tip line and −48VDC on the ring line.

2. A telephone set, PBX, or FXO module closes the loop between the tip and ring lines. The telephone takes its handset off-hook, or the PBX or FXO module closes a circuit connection. The CO or FXS module detects current flow and then generates a dial tone, which is sent to the telephone set, PBX, or FXO module. This indicates that the customer can start to dial. At the same time, the CO or FXS module seizes the ring line of the telephone, PBX, or FXO module called by superimposing a 20-Hz, 90VAC signal over the −48VDC ring line. This procedure rings the called-party telephone set or signals the PBX or FXS module that there is an incoming call. The CO or FXS module removes this ring after the telephone set, PBX, or FXO module closes the circuit between the tip and ring lines.

3. The telephone set closes the circuit when the called party picks up the handset. The PBX or FXS module closes the circuit when it has an available resource to connect to the called party.

Loop-start has two disadvantages:

- There is no way to prevent the CO and the subscriber from seizing the same line at the same time, a condition known as *glare*. It takes about 4 seconds for the CO switch to cycle through all the lines it must ring. This delay in ringing a phone causes the glare problem, because the CO switch and the telephone set seize a line simultaneously. When this happens, the person who initiated the call is connected to the called party almost instantaneously, with no ring-back tone.

Note   The best way to prevent glare is to use ground-start signaling.

- It does not provide switch-side disconnect supervision for FXO calls. The telephony switch is the connection in the PSTN, another PBX, or key system. This switch expects the FXO interface of the router, which looks like a telephone to the switch, to hang up the calls it receives through its FXO port. However, this function is not built in to the router for received calls. It operates only for calls originating from the FXO port.

These disadvantages are usually not a problem on residential telephones, but they become significant with the higher call volume experienced on business telephones.

Ground-Start

Ground-start signaling, as shown in Figure 1-52, is another supervisory signaling technique, like loop-start, that provides a way to indicate on-hook and off-hook conditions in a voice network. Ground-start signaling is used primarily in switch-to-switch connections. The main difference between ground-start and loop-start signaling is that ground-start requires ground detection to occur in both ends of a connection before the tip and ring loop can be closed.

Ground-start signaling works by using ground and current detectors that allow the network to indicate off-hook or seizure of an incoming call independent of the ringing signal and allow for positive recognition of connects and disconnects. Because ground-start signaling uses a request and/or confirm switch at both ends of the interface, it is preferable over FXOs and other signaling methods on high-usage trunks. For this reason, ground-start signaling is typically used on trunk lines between PBXs and in businesses where call volume on loop-start lines can result in glare.

The ground-start signaling process is as follows:

1. In the idle state, both the tip and ring lines are disconnected from ground. The PBX and FXO constantly monitor the tip line for ground, and the CO and FXS constantly monitor the ring line for ground. The battery (–48VDC) is still connected to the ring line just as in loop-start signaling.

2. A PBX or FXO grounds the ring line to indicate to the CO or FXS that there is an incoming call. The CO or FXS senses the ring ground and then grounds the tip lead to let the PBX or FXO know that it is ready to receive the incoming call.

3. The PBX or FXO senses the tip ground and closes the loop between the tip and ring lines in response. It also removes the ring ground.

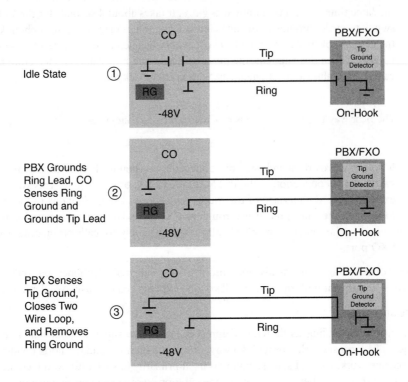

Figure 1-52 *Ground-Start Signaling*

Analog Address Signaling

The dialing phase allows the subscriber to enter a phone number (address) of a telephone at another location. The customer enters this number with either a rotary phone that generates pulses or a touch-tone (push-button) phone that generates tones. Table 1-6 shows the frequency tones generated by DTMF dialing.

Telephones use two different types of address signaling to notify the telephone company where a subscriber calls:

■ Pulse dialing

■ DTMF dialing

These pulses or tones are transmitted to the CO switch across a two-wire twisted-pair cable (tip and ring lines). On the voice gateway, the FXO port sends address signaling to the FXS port. This address indicates the final destination of a call.

Table 1-6 *DTMF Frequencies*

Frequencies	1209	1336	1477
697	1	2	3
770	4	5	6
852	7	8	9
941	*	0	#

Pulses were used by the old rotary phones. These phones had a disk that was rotated to dial a number. As the disk rotated, it opened and closed the circuit a specified number of times based on how far the disk was turned. The exchange equipment counted those circuit interruptions to determine the called number. The duration of open-to-closed times had to be within specifications according to the country you were in.

These days, analog circuits use DTMF tones to indicate the destination address. DTMF assigns a specific tone (consisting of two separate frequencies) to each key on the touchtone telephone dial pad. The combination of these two frequencies notifies the receiving subscriber of the digits dialed.

Informational Signaling

The FXS port provides informational signaling using call progress (CP) tones, as detailed in Table 1-7. These CP tones are audible and are used by the FXS connected device to indicate the status of calls.

Table 1-7 *Network Call Progress Tones*

Tone	Frequency (Hz)	On Time (Sec)	Off Time (Sec)
Dial	350 + 440	Continuous	Continuous
Busy	480 + 620	0.5	0.5
Ring-back, line	440 + 480	2	4
Ring-back, PBX	440 + 480	1	3
Congestion (toll)	480 + 620	0.2	0.3
Reorder (local)	480 + 620	0.3	0.2
Receiver off-hook	1400 + 2060 + 2450 + 2600	0.1	0.1
No such number	200 to 400	Continuous	Continuous

The progress tones listed in Table 1-7 are for North American phone systems. International phone systems can have a completely different set of progress tones. Users should be familiar with most of the following call progress tones:

- **Dial tone:** Indicates that the telephone company is ready to receive digits from the user telephone.

- **Busy tone:** Indicates that a call cannot be completed because the telephone at the remote end is already in use.

- **Ring-back (normal or PBX) tone:** Indicates that the telephone company is attempting to complete a call on behalf of a subscriber.

- **Congestion:** Progress tone is used between switches to indicate that congestion in the long-distance telephone network currently prevents a telephone call from being processed.

- **Reorder:** Tone indicates that all the local telephone circuits are busy and thus prevents a telephone call from being processed.

- **Receiver off-hook:** Tone is the loud ringing that indicates the receiver of a phone is left off-hook for an extended period of time.

- **No such number:** Tone indicates that the number dialed cannot be found in the routing table of a switch.

E&M Signaling

E&M is another signaling technique used mainly between PBXs or other network-to-network telephony switches (Lucent 5 Electronic Switching System [5ESS], Nortel DMS-100, and so on). E&M signaling supports tie-line type facilities or signals between voice switches. Instead of superimposing both voice and signaling on the same wire, E&M uses separate paths, or leads, for each.

There are six distinct physical configurations for the signaling part of the interface. They are Types I–V and Signaling System Direct Current No. 5 (SSDC5). They use different methods to signal on-hook or off-hook status, as shown Table 1-8. Cisco voice implementation supports E&M Types I, II, III, and V.

The following list details the characteristics of each E&M signaling type introduced in Table 1-8:

- **Type I:** Type I signaling is the most common E&M signaling method used in North America. One wire is the E lead, the second wire is the M lead, and the remaining two pairs of wires serve as the audio path. In this arrangement, the PBX supplies power, or battery, for both E and M leads. In the idle (on-hook) state, both the E and M leads are open. The PBX indicates an off-hook by connecting the M lead to the battery. The line side indicates an off-hook by connecting the E lead to ground.

- **Type II:** Type II signaling does not require a common ground between the PBX and the attached device. This type uses four wires for signaling. One wire is the E lead, another wire is the M lead, and the two other wires are signal ground (SG) and signal battery (SB). In Type II, SG and SB are the return paths for the E lead and M lead, respectively. The PBX side indicates an off-hook by connecting the M lead to the SB lead. The line side indicates an off-hook by connecting the E lead to the SG lead.

■ **Type III:** Type III signaling helps prevent electromagnetic interference (EMI) from being interpreted as signaling. In the idle state (on-hook), the E lead is open and the M lead is connected to the SG lead, which is grounded. The PBX side indicates an off-hook by moving the M lead from the SG lead to the SB lead. The line side indicates an off-hook by grounding the E lead.

■ **Type IV:** Type IV also uses four wires for signaling. In the idle state (on-hook), the E and M leads are both open. The PBX side indicates an off-hook by connecting the M lead to the SB lead, which is grounded on the line side. The line side indicates an off-hook by connecting the E lead to the SG lead, which is grounded on the PBX side.

Note   E&M Type IV is not supported on Cisco voice gateways. However, Type IV operates similarly to Type II except for the M-lead operation. On Type IV, the M-lead states are open/ground, compared to Type II, which is open/battery. Type IV can interface with Type II. To use Type IV, you can set the E&M voice port to Type II and perform the necessary M-lead rewiring.

■ Type V: Type V is the most common E&M signaling form used outside of North America. Type V is similar to Type I because two wires are used for signaling (one wire is the E lead and the other wire is the M lead). In the idle (on-hook) state, both the E and M leads are open. The PBX indicates an off-hook by grounding the M lead. The line side indicates an off-hook by grounding the E lead.

■ SSDC5: Similar to Type V, SSDC5 differs in that on- and off-hook states are backward to allow for fail-safe operation. If the line breaks, the interface defaults to off-hook (busy). SSDC5 is most often found in England.

Table 1-8   *E&M Signaling Types*

Type	M-Lead Off-Hook	M-Lead On-Hook	E-Lead Off-Hook	E-Lead On-Hook
I	Battery	Ground	Ground	Open
II	Battery	Open	Ground	Open
III	Loop Current	Ground	Ground	Open
IV	Ground	Open	Ground	Open
V	Ground	Open	Ground	Open
SSDC5	Earth On	Earth Off	Earth On	Earth Off

E&M Physical Interface

The physical E&M interface is an RJ-48 connector that connects to PBX trunk lines, which are classified as either two-wire or four-wire.

Note Two-wire and four-wire refer to the voice wires. A connection might be called a four-wire E&M circuit although it actually has six physical wires (that is, two tip leads, two ring leads, an E lead, and an M lead).

E&M Address Signaling

PBXs built by different manufacturers can indicate on-hook/off-hook status and telephone line seizure on the E&M interface by using any of three types of access signaling:

■ **Immediate-start:** Immediate-start, as illustrated in Figure 1-53, is the simplest method of E&M access signaling. The calling side seizes the line by going off-hook on its E lead, waits for a minimum of 150 ms, and then sends address information as DTMF digits or as dialed pulses. This signaling approach is used for E&M tie trunk interfaces.

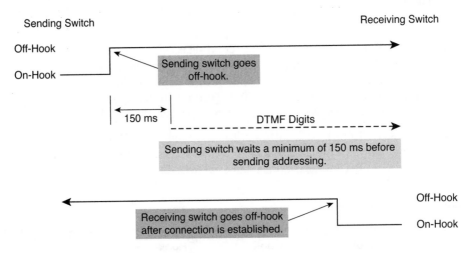

Figure 1-53 *Immediate-Start Signaling*

■ **Wink-start:** Wink-start, as shown in Figure 1-54, is the most commonly used method for E&M access signaling and is the default for E&M voice ports. Wink-start was developed to minimize glare, a condition found in immediate-start E&M, in which both ends attempt to seize a trunk at the same time. In wink-start, the calling side seizes the line by going off-hook on its E lead; it then waits for a short temporary off-hook pulse, or "wink," from the other end on its M lead before sending address information as DTMF digits. The switch interprets the pulse as an indication to proceed and then sends the dialed digits as DTMF or dialed pulses. This signaling is used for E&M tie trunk interfaces. This is the default setting for E&M voice ports.

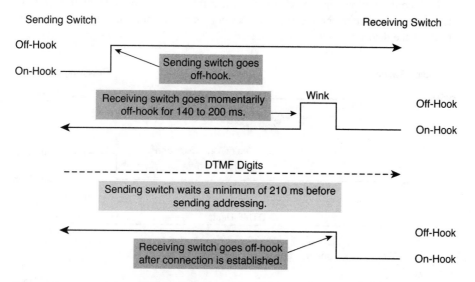

Figure 1-54 *Wink-Start Signaling*

■ **Delay-start:** With delay-start signaling, as depicted in Figure 1-55, the calling station seizes the line by going off-hook on its E lead. After a timed interval, the calling side looks at the status of the called side. If the called side is on-hook, the calling side starts sending information as DTMF digits. Otherwise, the calling side waits until the called side goes on-hook and then starts sending address information. This signaling approach is used for E&M tie trunk interfaces.

Configuring Analog Voice Ports

The three types of analog ports that you learn to configure in this section are

■ FXS

■ FXO

■ E&M

FXS Voice Port Configuration

In North America, the FXS port connection functions with default settings most of the time. The same cannot be said for other countries and continents. Remember, FXS ports look like switches to the edge devices that are connected to them. Therefore, the configuration of the FXS port should emulate the switch configuration of the local PSTN.

For example, consider an international company that has offices in the United States and England. Each PSTN provides signaling that is standard for its own country. In the United

States, the PSTN provides a dial tone that is different from the dial tone in England. The signals that ring incoming calls are different in England. Another instance where the default configuration might be changed is when the connection is a trunk to a PBX or key system. In each of these cases, the FXS port must be configured to match the settings of the device to which it is connected.

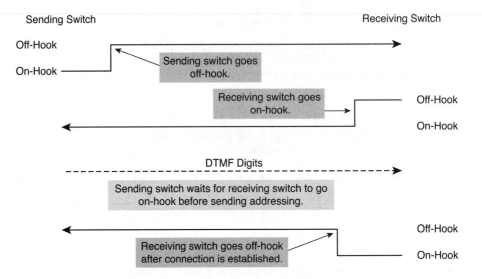

Figure 1-55 *Delay-Start Signaling*

In this example, you have been assigned to configure a voice gateway to route calls to a POTS phone connected to an FXS port on a remote router in Great Britain. Figure 1-56 shows how the British office is configured to enable ground-start signaling on FXS voice port 0/2/0. The call-progress tones are set for Great Britain, and the ring cadence is set for pattern 1.

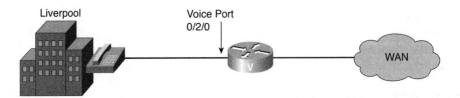

Figure 1-56 *FXS Configuration Topology*

The requirements for your configuration are the following:

■ Configure the voice port to use ground-start signaling.

■ Configure the call-progress tones for Great Britain.

You would then complete the following steps to accomplish the stated objectives:

Step 1.   Enter voice port configuration mode.

```
Router(config)#voice-port slot/port
```

Step 2.   Select the access signaling type to match the telephony connection you are making.

```
Router(config-voiceport)#signal {loopstart | groundstart}
```

Note   If you change signal type, you must execute a **shutdown** and a **no shutdown** command on the voice port.

Step 3.   Select the two-letter locale for the voice call progress tones and other locale-specific parameters to be used on this voice port.

```
Router(config-voiceport)#cptone locale
```

Step 4.   Specify a ring pattern. Each pattern specifies a ring-pulse time and a ring-interval time.

```
Router(config-voiceport)#ring cadence {pattern-number | define pulse interval}
```

Note   The *patternXX* keyword provides preset **ring-cadence** patterns for use on any platform. The **define** keyword allows you to create a custom ring cadence.

Step 5.   Activate the voice port.

```
Router(config-voiceport)#no shutdown
```

Example 1-5 shows the complete FXS voice port configuration.

Example 1-5   *FXS Voice Port Configuration*

```
Router(config)#voice-port 0/2/0
Router(config-voiceport)#signal groundstart
Router(config-voiceport)#cptone GB
Router(config-voiceport)#ring cadence pattern01
Router(config-voiceport)#no shutdown
```

FXO Voice Port Configuration

An FXO trunk is one of the simplest analog trunks available. Because DNIS information can be sent out only to the PSTN, no DID is possible. ANI is supported for inbound calls. Two signaling types exist, loop-start and ground-start, with ground-start being the preferred method.

For example, consider the topology shown in Figure 1-57. Imagine you have been assigned to configure a voice gateway to route calls to and from the PSTN through an FXO port on the router.

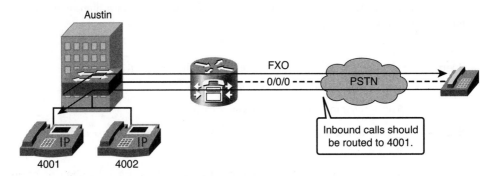

Figure 1-57   *FXO Configuration Topology*

In this scenario, you must set up a private line automatic ringdown (PLAR) connection using an FXO port connected to the PSTN.

The configuration requirements are the following:

■   Configure the voice port to use ground-start signaling.

■   Configure a PLAR connection from a remote location to extension 4001 in Austin.

■   Configure a standard dial peer for inbound and outbound PSTN calls.

Because an FXO trunk does not support DID, two-stage dialing is required for all inbound calls. If all inbound calls should be routed to a specific extension (for example, a front desk), you can use the **connection plar opx** command. In this example, all inbound calls are routed to extension 4001.

You could then complete the following steps to configure the FXO voice port:

Step 1.   Enter voice port configuration mode.

```
Router(config)#voice-port 0/0/0
```

Step 2.   Select the access signaling type to match the telephony connection you are making.

```
Router(config-voiceport)#signal ground-start
```

Step 3.   Specify a PLAR off-premises extension (OPX) connection.

```
Router(config-voiceport)#connection plar opx 4001
```

Note   PLAR is an autodialing mechanism that permanently associates a voice interface with a far-end voice interface, allowing call completion to a specific telephone number or PBX without dialing. When the calling telephone goes off-hook, a predefined network dial peer is automatically matched. This sets up a call to the destination telephone or PBX.

Using the **opx** option, the local voice port provides a local response before the remote voice port receives an answer. On FXO interfaces, the voice port does not answer until the remote side has answered.

Step 4.   Activate the voice port.

```
Router(config-voiceport)#no shutdown
```

Step 5.   Exit voice port configuration mode.

```
Router(config-voiceport)#exit
```

Step 6.   Create a standard dial peer for inbound and outbound PSTN calls.

```
Router(config)#dial-peer voice 90 pots
```

Step 7.   Specify the destination pattern.

```
Router(config-dialpeer)#destination-pattern 9T
```

Note   The T control character indicates that the destination-pattern value is a variable-length dial string. Using this control character enables the router to wait until all digits are received before routing the call.

Step 8.   Specify the voice port associated with this dial peer.

```
Router(config-dialpeer)#port 0/0/0
```

Example 1-6 shows the complete FXO voice port configuration.

Example 1-6 *FXO Voice Port Configuration*

```
Router(config)#voice-port 0/0/0
Router(config-voiceport)#signal groundstart
Router(config-voiceport)#connection plar opx 4001
Router(config)#dial-peer voice 90 pots
Router(config-dialpeer)#destination-pattern 9T
Router(config-dialpeer)#port 0/0/0
```

E&M Voice Port Configuration

Configuring an E&M analog trunk is straightforward. Three key options have to be set:

■   The signaling E&M signaling type

■   Two- or four-wire operation

■   The E&M type

As an example, consider the topology shown in Figure 1-58.

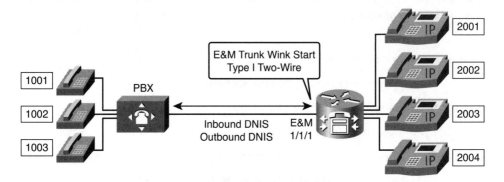

Figure 1-58   *E&M Configuration Topology*

In this example, you have been assigned to configure a voice gateway to work with an existing PBX system according to network requirements. You must set up a voice gateway to interface with a PBX to allow the IP phones to call the POTS phones using a four-digit extension.

The configuration requirements are the following:

■   Configure the voice port to use wink-start signaling.

■   Configure the voice port to use 2-wire operation mode.

■   Configure the voice port to use Type I E&M signaling.

■   Configure a standard dial peer for the POTS phones behind the PBX.

Both sides of the trunk need to have a matching configuration. The following example configuration shows an E&M trunk using wink-start signaling, E&M Type I, and two-wire operation. Because E&M supports inbound and outbound DNIS, DID support is also configured on the corresponding dial peer.

You could complete the following steps to configure the E&M voice port:

Step 1.   Enter voice port configuration mode.

```
Router(config)#voice-port 1/1/1
```

Step 2. Select the access signaling type to match the telephony connection you are making.

```
Router(config-voiceport)#signal wink-start
```

Step 3. Select a specific cabling scheme for the E&M port.

```
Router(config-voiceport)#operation 2-wire
```

Note This command affects only voice traffic. If the wrong cable scheme is specified, the user might get voice traffic in only one direction.

Also, using this command on a voice port changes the operation of both voice ports on a voice port module (VPM) card. The voice port must be shut down and then opened again for the new value to take effect.

Step 4. Specify the type of E&M interface.

```
Router(config-voiceport)#type 1
```

Step 5. Activate the voice port.

```
Router(config-voiceport)#no shutdown
```

Step 6. Exit voice port configuration mode.

```
Router(config-voiceport)#exit
```

Step 7. Create a dial peer for the POTS phones.

```
Router(config)#dial-peer voice 10 pots
```

Step 8. Specify the destination pattern for the POTS phones.

```
Router(config-dialpeer)#destination-pattern 1...
```

Step 9. Specify direct inward dialing.

```
Router(config-dialpeer)#direct-inward-dial
```

Note DID is needed when POTS phones call IP phones. In this case we match the POTS dial peer. This same dial peer is also used to call out to POTS phones.

Step 10. Specify digit forwarding for all digits, so that no digits will be stripped as they are forwarded out of the voice port. By default, only digits matched by wildcard characters in the **destination-pattern** command are forwarded.

```
Router(config-dialpeer)#forward-digits all
```

Step 11. Specify the voice port associated with this dial peer.

```
Router(config-dialpeer)#port 1/1/1
```

Example 1-7 shows the complete E&M voice port configuration.

Example 1-7 *E&M Voice Port Configuration*

```
Router(config)#voice-port 1/1/1
Router(config-voiceport)#signal wink-start
Router(config-voiceport)#operation 2-wire
Router(config-voiceport)#type 1
Router(config-voiceport)#no shutdown
Router(config-voiceport)#exit
Router(config)#dial-peer voice 10 pots
Router(config-dialpeer)#destination-pattern 1...
Router(config-dialpeer)#direct-inward-dial
Router(config-dialpeer)#forward-digits all
Router(config-dialpeer)#port 1/1/1
```

Trunks

Trunks interconnect gateways or PBX systems to other gateways, PBX systems, or the PSTN. A trunk is a single physical or logical interface that contains several physical interfaces and connects to a single destination. This could be a single FXO port that provides a single line connection between a Cisco gateway and an FXS port of small PBX system, a POTS device, or several T1 interfaces with 24 lines each in a Cisco gateway providing PSTN lines to several hundred subscribers.

Trunk ports can be analog or digital and use a variety of signaling protocols. Signaling can be done using either the voice channel (in-band) or an extra dedicated channel (out-of-band). The available features depend on the signaling protocol in use between the devices.

Figure 1-59 illustrates a variety of possible trunk connections.

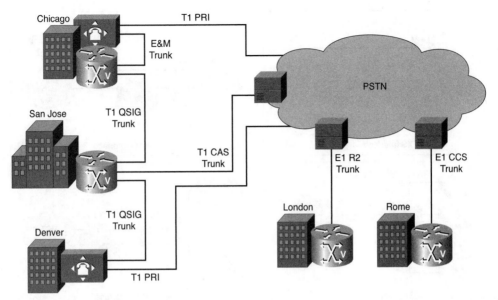

Figure 1-59   *Trunk Connections*

Consider the following characteristics of the trunks depicted in Figure 1-59:

■   If a subscriber at the London site places a call to the PSTN, the gateway uses one voice channel of the E1 R2 trunk interface.

■   If a subscriber of the legacy PBX system at the Chicago site needs to place a call to a subscriber with an IP phone connected to the Chicago gateway, the call will go via the E&M trunk between the legacy PBX and the gateway.

■   The Denver and the Chicago sites are connected to San Jose via Q Signaling (QSIG) to build up a common private numbering plan between those sites. Because Denver's Cisco IP telephony rollout has not started yet, the QSIG trunk is established directly between San Jose's gateway and Denver's legacy PBX.

The following discussion describes features offered by analog trunks. Additionally, you will see how to overcome a caller ID issue often seen with analog trunks and how to support calls coming into a router via an analog trunk (that is, a DID trunk).

Analog Trunks

Because many organizations continue to use analog devices, a requirement to integrate analog circuits with VoIP or IP telephony networks still exists. To implement a Cisco voice gateway into an analog trunk environment, the FXS, FXO, DID, and E&M interfaces are commonly used, as illustrated in Figure 1-60.

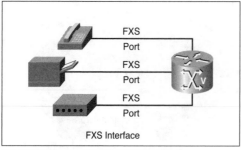
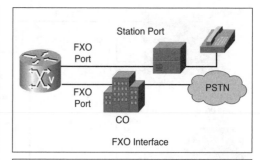
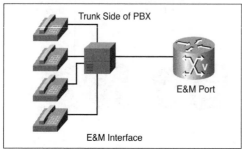
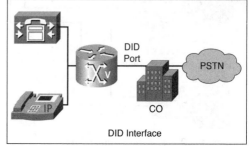

Figure 1-60   *Analog Trunks*

PSTN carriers typically offer analog trunk features that can be supported on home phones. Table 1-9 presents a description of the common analog trunk features.

Figure 1-61 shows a small business voice network connected through a gateway to the PSTN. The voice network supports both analog phones and IP phones. The connection to the PSTN is through an FXO port, and the analog phone is connected to the small business network through an FXS port. The issue in this scenario is how the caller ID is passed to call destinations.

Table 1-9   *Analog Trunk Features*

Feature	Description
Caller ID	Caller ID allows users to see the calling number before answering the phone.
Message waiting	Two methods activate an analog message indicator: • High-DC voltage message waiting indicator (MWI) light and frequency-shift keying (FSK) messaging • Stuttered dial tone for phones without a visual indicator
Call waiting	When a user is on a call and a new call comes in, the user hears an audible tone and can "click over" to the new caller.
Caller ID on call waiting	When a user is on a call, the name of the second caller is announced or the caller ID is shown.

Table 1-9   *Analog Trunk Features*

Feature	Description
Transfer	This feature includes both blind and supervised transfers using the standard established by Bellcore laboratories. The hookflash method is common with analog trunks.
Conference	Conference calls are initiated from an analog phone using hookflash or feature access codes.
Speed dial	A user can set up keys for commonly dialed numbers and dial these numbers directly from an analog phone.
Call forward all	Calls can be forwarded to a number within the dial plan.
Redial	A simple last-number redial can be activated from analog phones.
DID	Direct inward dialing is supported on E&M and FXS DID ports.

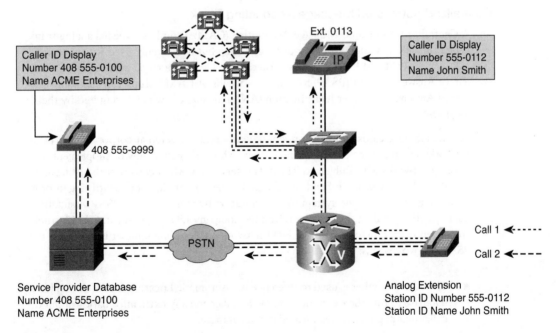

Figure 1-61   *Analog Trunks Example*

This example describes two calls; the first call is to an on-premises destination, and the second call is to an off-premises destination:

- **Call 1:** Call 1 is from the analog phone to another phone on the premises. The FXS port is configured with a station ID name and station ID number. The name is John Smith, and the number is 555-0112. When a call is placed from the analog phone to another phone on the premises, an IP phone in this case, the caller name and number are displayed on the screen of the IP phone.

- **Call 2:** Call 2 is placed from the same analog phone, but the destination is off the premises on the PSTN. The FXO port forwards the station ID name and station ID number to the CO switch. The CO switch discards the station ID name and station ID number and replaces them with information it has configured for this connection.

For inbound calls, the caller ID feature is supported on the FXO port in the gateway. If the gateway is configured for H.323, the caller ID is displayed on the IP phones and on the analog phones (if supported).

Centralized Automated Message Accounting Trunk

A Centralized Automated Message Accounting (CAMA) trunk is a special analog trunk type originally developed for long-distance billing but now mainly used for emergency call services (911 and E911 services). You can use CAMA ports to connect to a Public Safety Answering Point (PSAP) for emergency calls. A CAMA trunk can send only outbound Automatic Number Identification (ANI) information, which is required by the local PSAP.

CAMA interface cards and software configurations are targeted at corporate enterprise networks and at service providers and carriers who are creating new or supplementing existing networks with Enhanced 911 (E911) services. CAMA carries both calling and called numbers by using in-band signaling. This method of carrying identifying information enables the telephone system to send a station ID number to the PSAP via multifrequency (MF) signaling through the telephone company E911 equipment. CAMA trunks are currently used in 80 percent of E911 networks. The calling number is needed at the PSAP for two reasons:

- The calling number is used to reference the Automatic Location Identification (ALI) database to find the exact location of the caller and any extra information about the caller that might have been stored in the database.

■ The calling number is used as a callback number in case the call is disconnected. A number of U.S. states have initiated legislation that requires enterprises to connect directly to the E911 network. The U.S. Federal Communications Commission (FCC) has announced model legislation that extends this requirement to all U.S. states. Enterprises in areas where the PSTN accepts 911 calls on ISDN trunks can use existing Cisco ISDN voice gateway products, because the calling number is an inherent part of ISDN.

Note   You must check local legal requirements when using CAMA.

Calls to emergency services are routed based on the calling number, not the called number. The calling number is checked against a database of emergency service providers that cross-references the service providers for the caller location. When this information is determined, the call is then routed to the proper PSAP, which dispatches services to the caller location.

During the setup of an E911 call, before the audio channel is connected, the calling number is transmitted to each switching point, known as a selective router, via CAMA.

Cisco's VIC2-2FXO and VIC2-4FXO cards support CAMA via software configuration. CAMA support is also available for the Cisco 2800 Series and 3800 Series ISRs. It is common for E911 service providers to require CAMA interfaces to their network.

Figure 1-62 shows a site that has a T1 PRI circuit for normal inbound and outbound PSTN calls. Because the local PSAP requires a dedicated CAMA trunk for emergency (911) calls, all emergency calls are routed using a dial peer pointing to the CAMA trunk.

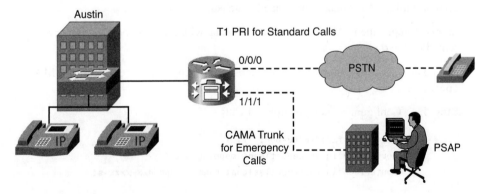

Figure 1-62   *Configuring a CAMA Trunk*

The voice port 1/1/1 is the CAMA trunk. The actual configuration depends on the PSAP requirements. In this case, the digit 1 signals the area code 312. The voice port is then configured for CAMA signaling using the **signal cama** command. Five options exist:

- **KP-0-NXX-XXXX-ST:** Seven-digit ANI transmission. The Numbering Plan Area (NPA), or area code, is implied by the trunk group and is not transmitted.

- **KP-0-NPA-NXX-XXXX-ST:** Ten-digit transmission. The E.164 number is fully transmitted.

- **KP-0-NPA-NXX-XXXX-ST-KP-YYY-YYY-YYYY-ST:** Supports CAMA signaling with ANI/Pseudo ANI (PANI).

- **KP-2-ST:** Default transmission when the CAMA trunk cannot get a corresponding Numbering Plan Digit (NPD) in the lookup table or when the calling number is fewer than ten digits. (NPA digits are not available.)

- **KP-NPD-NXX-XXXX-ST:** Eight-digit ANI transmission, where the NPD is a single MF digit that is expanded into the NPA. The NPD table is preprogrammed in the sending and receiving equipment (on each end of the MF trunk). For example: 0 = 415, 1 = 510, 2 = 650, 3 = 916

  05551234 = (415) 555-1234, 15551234 = (510) 555-1234

  The NPD value range is 0–3.

When you use the NPD format, the area code needs to be associated with a single digit. You can preprogram the NPA into a single MF digit using the **ani mapping** voice port command. The number of NPDs programmed is determined by local policy as well as by the number of NPAs the PSAP serves. Repeat this command until all NPDs are configured or until the NPD maximum range is reached.

In this example, the PSAP expects NPD signaling, with the area code 312 being represented by the digit 1.

You could then complete the following steps to configure the voice port for CAMA operation:

Step 1.   Configure a voice port for 911 calls.

```
Router(config)#voice-port 1/1/1
Router(config-voiceport)#ani mapping 1 312
Router(config-voiceport)#signal cama kp-npd-nxx-xxxx-st
```

Step 2.   Configure a dedicated dial peer to route emergency calls using the CAMA trunk when a user dials 911.

```
Router(config)#dial-peer voice 911 pots
Router(config-dialpeer)#destination-pattern 911
```

```
Router(config-dialpeer)#prefix 911
Router(config-dialpeer)#port 1/1/1
```

Step 3. Configure a dedicated 9911 dial peer to route all emergency calls using the
CAMA trunk when a user dials 9911.

```
Router(config)#dial-peer voice 9911 pots
Router(config-dialpeer)#destination-pattern 9911
Router(config-dialpeer)#prefix 911
Router(config-dialpeer)#port 1/1/1
```

Step 4. Configure a standard PSTN dial peer for all other inbound and outbound
PSTN calls.

```
Router(config)#dial-peer voice 910 pots
Router(config-dialpeer)#destination-pattern 9[2-8]
Router(config-dialpeer)#port 0/0/0:23
```

Example 1-8 shows the complete CAMA trunk configuration.

Example 1-8 *CAMA Trunk Configuration*

```
Router(config)#voice-port 1/1/1
Router(config-voiceport)#ani mapping 1 312
Router(config-voiceport)#signal cama KP-NPD-NXX-XXXX-ST
Router(config)#dial-peer voice 911 pots
Router(config-dialpeer)#destination-pattern 911
Router(config-dialpeer)#prefix 911
Router(config-dialpeer)#port 1/1/1
Router(config)#dial-peer voice 9911 pots
Router(config-dialpeer)#destination-pattern 9911
Router(config-dialpeer)#prefix 911
Router(config-dialpeer)#port 1/1/1
Router(config)#dial-peer voice 910 pots
Router(config-dialpeer)#destination-pattern 9[2-8]
Router(config-dialpeer)#port 0/0/0:23
```

Direct Inward Dialing Trunk

Typically, FXS ports connect to analog phones, but some carriers offer FXS trunks that
support DID. The DID service is offered by telephone companies, and it enables callers to
dial an extension directly on a PBX or a VoIP system (for example, Cisco Unified
Communications Manager and Cisco IOS routers and gateways) without the assistance of
an operator or automated call attendant. This service makes use of DID trunks, which
forward only the last three to five digits of a phone number to the PBX, router, or gateway. For example, a company has phone extensions 555-1000 to 555-1999. A caller dials
555-1234, and the local CO forwards 234 to the PBX or VoIP system. The PBX or VoIP
system then rings extension 234. This entire process is transparent to the caller.

Because an FXS DID trunk can receive only inbound calls, a combination of FXS, DID, and FXO ports is required for inbound and outbound calls. Two signaling types exist, loop-start and ground-start, with ground-start being the preferred method.

Figure 1-63 shows an analog trunk using an FXS DID trunk for inbound calls and a standard FXO trunk for outbound calls.

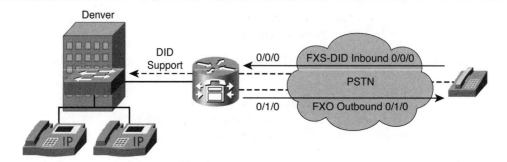

Figure 1-63   *Configuring DID Trunks*

You could then complete the following steps to enable DID signaling on the FXS port:

Step 1.   Configure the FXS port for DID and wink-start.

```
Router(config)#voice-port 0/0/0
Router(config-voiceport)#signal did wink-start
```

Step 2.   Configure the FXO port for ground-start signaling.

```
Router(config)#voice-port 0/1/0
Router(config-voiceport)#signal groundstart
```

Step 3.   Create an inbound dial peer using the FXS DID port. Note that DID is enabled.

```
Router(config)#dial-peer voice 1 pots
Router(config-dialpeer)#incoming called-number .
Router(config-dialpeer)#direct-inward-dial
Router(config-dialpeer)#port 0/0/0
```

Step 4.   Create a standard outbound dial peer using the FXO port.

```
Router(config)#dial-peer voice 910 pots
Router(config-dialpeer)#destination-pattern 9[2-8]
Router(config-dialpeer)#port 0/1/0
```

Example 1-9 shows the complete DID trunk configuration.

Example 1-9 *DID Trunk Configuration*

```
Router(config)#voice-port 0/0/0
Router(config-voiceport)#signal did wink-start
Router(config)#voice-port 0/1/0
Router(config-voiceport)#signal groundstart
Router(config)#dial-peer voice 1 pots
Router(config-dialpeer)#incoming called-number .
Router(config-dialpeer)#direct-inward-dial
Router(config-dialpeer)#port 0/0/0
Router(config)#dial-peer voice 910 pots
Router(config-dialpeer)#destination-pattern 9[2-8]
Router(config-dialpeer)#port 0/1/0
```

Timers and Timing

You can set a number of timers and timing parameters for fine-tuning a voice port. Following are voice port configuration mode commands you can use to set a variety of timing parameters:

- **timeouts initial seconds:** Configures the initial digit timeout value in seconds. This value controls how long the dial tone is presented before the first digit is expected. This timer value typically does not need to be changed.

- **timeouts interdigit** *seconds*: Configures the number of seconds for which the system will wait between caller-entered digits before sending the input to be assessed. If the digits are coming from an automated device, and the dial plan is a variable-length dial plan, you can shorten this timer so the call proceeds without having to wait the full default of 10 seconds for the interdigit timer to expire.

- **timeouts ringing** {*seconds* | **infinity**}: Configures the length of time a caller can continue to let the telephone ring when there is no answer. You can configure this setting to be less than the default of 180 seconds so that you do not tie up a voice port when it is evident the call is not going to be answered.

- **timing digit** *milliseconds*: Configures the DTMF digit signal duration for a specified voice port. You can use this setting to fine-tune a connection to a device that might have trouble recognizing dialed digits. If a user or device dials too quickly, the digit might not be recognized. By changing the timing on the digit timer, you can provide for a shorter or longer DTMF duration.

- **timing interdigit** *milliseconds*: Configures the DTMF interdigit duration for a specified voice port. You can change this setting to accommodate faster or slower dialing characteristics.

- **timing hookflash-input** *milliseconds* and **timing hookflash-output** *milliseconds*: Configure the maximum duration (in milliseconds) of a hookflash indication. Hookflash is an indication by a caller that wants to do something specific with the call, such as transfer the call or place the call on hold. For the **timing hookflash-input** command, if the hookflash lasts longer than the specified limit, the FXS interface processes the indication as on-hook. If you set the value too low, the hookflash might be interpreted as a hang-up. If you set the value too high, the handset has to be left hung up for a longer period to clear the call. For the **timing hookflash-output** command, the setting specifies the duration of the hookflash indication that the gateway generates outbound. You can configure this to match the requirements of the connected device.

Under normal use, these timers do not need to be adjusted. In two instances, these timers can be configured to allow more or less time for a specific function:

■   When ports are connected to a device that does not properly respond to dialed digits or hookflash

■   When the connected device provides automated dialing

Example 1-10 shows a configuration for a home for someone with a disability who might require more time to dial digits. Notice the requirement to allow the telephone to ring, unanswered, for 4 minutes. The configuration enables several timing parameters on a Cisco voice-enabled router voice port 0/1/0. The initial timeout is lengthened to 15 seconds; the interdigit timeout is lengthened to 15 seconds; the ringing timeout is set to 240 seconds; and the **hookflash-in** (that is, the maximum amount of time an on-hook condition will be interpretted as a hookflash) is set to 500 ms.

Example 1-10   *Timers and Timing Configuration*

```
Router(config)#voice-port 0/1/0
Router(config-voiceport)#timeouts initial 15
Router(config-voiceport)#timeouts interdigit 15
Router(config-voiceport)#timeouts ringing 240
Router(config-voiceport)#timing hookflash-in 500
```

Verifying Voice Ports

After physically connecting analog or digital devices to a Cisco voice-enabled router, you might need to issue **show**, **test**, or **debug** commands to verify or troubleshoot your configuration. For example, the following list enumerates six steps to monitor and troubleshoot voice ports:

Step 1.   Pick up the handset of an attached telephony device and check for a dial tone. If there is no dial tone, check the following:

■   Is the plug firmly seated?

■   Is the voice port enabled?

■   Is the voice port recognized by the Cisco IOS?

- Is the router running the correct version of Cisco IOS to recognize the module?

- Is a dial peer configured for that port?

Step 2. If you have a dial tone, dial a DTMF digit. If the dial tone stops when you dial a digit, the voice port is probably configured properly.

Step 3. Use the **show voice port** command to verify that the data configured is correct. If you have trouble connecting a call, and you suspect that the problem is associated with voice port configuration, you can try to resolve the problem by performing Steps 4 through 6.

Step 4. Use the **show voice port** command to make sure the port is enabled. If the port is administratively down, use the **no shutdown** command. If the port was working previously and is not working now, it is possible the port is in a hung state. Use the **shutdown/no shutdown** command sequence to reinitialize the port.

Step 5. If you have configured E&M interfaces, make sure the values associated with your specific PBX setup are correct. Specifically, check for two-wire or four-wire wink-start, immediate-start, or delay-start signaling types, and the E&M interface type. These parameters need to match those set on the PBX for the interface to communicate properly.

Step 6. You must confirm that the voice network module (VNM) (that is, the module in the router that contains the voice ports) is correctly installed. With the device powered down, remove the VNM, and reinsert it to verify the installation. If the device has other slots available, try inserting the VNM into another slot to isolate the problem. Similarly, you can move the voice interface card (VIC) to another VIC slot to determine whether the problem is with the VIC card or with the module slot.

For reference, Table 1-10 lists six **show** commands for verifying the voice port configuration.

Example 1-11 provides sample output for the **show voice port** command.

Table 1-10 *Commands to Verify Voice Ports*

Command	Description
show voice port	Shows all voice port configurations in detail
show voice port slot/subunit/port	Shows one voice port configuration in detail
show voice port summary	Shows all voice port configurations in brief
show voice busyout	Shows all ports configured as busyout
show voice dsp	Shows the status of all DSPs
show controller T1 | E1	Shows the operational status of a controller

Example 1-11   show voice port *Command*

```
Router#show voice port

Foreign Exchange Station 0/0/0 Slot is 0, Sub-unit is 0, Port is 0
 Type of VoicePort is FXS  VIC2-2FXS
 Operation State is DORMANT
 Administrative State is UP
 No Interface Down Failure
 Description is not set
 Noise Regeneration is enabled
 Non Linear Processing is enabled
 Non Linear Mute is disabled
 Non Linear Threshold is -21 dB
 Music On Hold Threshold is Set to -38 dBm
 In Gain is Set to 0 dB
 Out Attenuation is Set to 3 dB
 Echo Cancellation is enabled
 Echo Cancellation NLP mute is disabled
 Echo Cancellation NLP threshold is -21 dB
 Echo Cancel Coverage is set to 64 ms
 Echo Cancel worst case ERL is set to 6 dB
 Playout-delay Mode is set to adaptive
 Playout-delay Nominal is set to 60 ms
```

Example 1-12 provides sample output for the **show voice port summary** command.

Example 1-12   show voice port summary *Command*

```
router#show voice port summary
                                 IN      OUT
PORT       CH  SIG-TYPE   ADMIN OPER STATUS   STATUS   EC
========= == ============ ===== ==== ======== ======== ==
0/0/0      —   fxs-ls     up    dorm on-hook  idle     y
0/0/1      —   fxs-ls     up    dorm on-hook  idle     y
50/0/11    1     efxs     up    dorm on-hook  idle     y
50/0/11    2     efxs     up    dorm on-hook  idle     y
50/0/12    1     efxs     up    dorm on-hook  idle     y
50/0/12    2     efxs     up    dorm on-hook  idle     y
```

For further reference, Table 1-11 provides a series of commands used to test Cisco voice ports. The **test** commands provide the capability to analyze and troubleshoot voice ports on voice-enabled routers. As Table 1-11 shows, you can use five **test** commands to force voice ports into specific states to test the voice port configuration. The **csim start** *dial-string* command simulates a call to any end station for testing purposes.

Table 1-11 test *Commands*

Command	Description
test voice port *port_or_DS0-group_identifier* **detector {m-lead	battery-reversal	ring	tip-ground	ring-ground	ring-trip} {on	off	disable}**	Forces a detector into specific states for testing.
test voice port *port_or_DS0-group_identifier* **inject-tone {local	network} {1000hz	2000hz	200hz	3000hz	300hz	3200hz	3400hz	500hz	quiet	disable}**	Injects a test tone into a voice port. A call must be established on the voice port under test. When you are finished testing, be sure to use the **disable** option to end the test tone.
test voice port *port_or_DS0-group_identifier* **loopback {local	network	disable}**	Performs loopback testing on a voice port. A call must be established on the voice port under test. When you finish the loopback testing, be sure to use the **disable** option to end the forced loopback.
test voice port *port_or_DS0-group_identifier* **relay {e-lead	loop	ring-ground	battery-reversal	power-denial	ring	tip-ground} {on	off	disable}**	Tests relay-related functions on a voice port.
test voice port *port_or_DS0-group_identifier* **switch {fax	disable}**	Forces a voice port into fax or voice mode for testing. If the voice port does not detect fax data, the voice port remains in fax mode for 30 seconds and then reverts automatically to voice mode. After you enter the **test voice port switch fax** command, you can use the **show voice call** command to check whether the voice port is able to operate in fax mode.
csim start *dial-string*	Simulates a call to the specified dial string. This command is most useful when testing dial plans.

Bonus Video   To view a video of the author discussing analog voice port theory and demonstrating analog voice port configuration, navigate to the CVOICE page on the 1ExamAMonth.com website. The video on analog voice ports is entitled *The Secret Life of an Analog Voice Port*. Additional video tutorials from this website will be recommended later in this book.

Digital Voice Ports

Digital voice ports are found at the intersection of a packet voice network and a digital, circuit-switched telephone network. The digital voice port interfaces that connect the router or access server to T1 or E1 lines pass voice data and signaling between the packet network and the circuit-switched network.

Three types of digital voice circuits are supported on Cisco voice gateways:

- **T1:** Uses time-division multiplexing (TDM) to transmit digital data over 24 voice channels using channel associated signaling (CAS).

- **E1:** Uses TDM to transmit digital data over 30 voice channels using either CAS or common channel signaling (CCS).

- **ISDN:** A circuit-switched telephone network system using CCS. Variations of Integrated Services Digital Network (ISDN) circuits include the following:

  - **BRI:** 2 B (Bearer) channels and 1 D (Delta) channel

  - **T1 PRI:** 23 B channels and 1 D channel

  - **E1 PRI:** 30 B channels and 1 D channel

Digital Trunks

Digital trunks connect to the PSTN, to a PBX, or to the WAN and are widely available worldwide. In some areas, CAS trunks are the only connections available. Basic Rate Interface (BRI) and Primary Rate Interface (PRI) trunks are very common when connecting a voice gateway to the PSTN. This section maps out the various digital interfaces and explains how to implement and verify digital trunks.

Digital voice ports interconnect gateways or PBX systems to other gateways, PBX systems, or the PSTN. A trunk is a single physical or logical interface that contains several logical interfaces and connects to a single destination.

There are two aspects to consider when signaling on digital lines. One aspect is the actual information about line and device states that is transmitted, and the second aspect is the method used to transmit the information on the digital lines.

The actual information about line and device states is communicated over digital lines using signaling methods that emulate the methods used in analog circuit-switched networks: Foreign Exchange Station (FXS), Foreign Exchange Office (FXO), and RecEive and TransMit (E&M).

For signaling to pass between a packet network and a circuit-switched network, both networks must use the same type of signaling. The voice ports on Cisco routers and access servers can be configured to match the signaling of most COs and PBXs. Table 1-12 lists some of the common digital circuit options.

The T1, E1, or ISDN lines that connect a telephony network to the digital voice ports on a router or access server contain channels for voice calls. A T1 or ISDN PRI line contains 24 full-duplex channels or time slots, and an E1 line contains 30. The signal on each channel is transmitted at 64 kbps, a standard known as digital signal level 0 (DS0). The channels are known as DS0 channels. The **ds0-group** command creates a logical voice port (a DS0 group) from some or all of the DS0 channels, which allows you to address those channels easily, as a group, using voice port configuration commands.

Table 1-12 *Digital Trunks*

Circuit Option	Comments
T1/E1 CAS E1 R2	Analog signaling over digital T1/E1 Can provide Automatic Number Identification (ANI)
ISDN T1 PRI E1 PRI	More services than CAS Separate data channel (D channel) Common on modern PBXs
PRI NFAS	Multiple ISDN PRI interfaces controlled by a single D channel Backup D channel can be configured
BRI	Mostly for Europe, Middle East, and Africa
QSIG	Created for interoperation of PBXs from different vendors Rich in supplementary services

The method used to transmit the information describes the way that the emulated analog signaling is transmitted over digital lines.

Digital lines use two types of signaling:

- CAS: Takes place within the voice channel itself

- CCS: Sends signaling information over a dedicated channel

Two main types of digital trunks with CAS exist, as illustrated in Figure 1-64:

- **T1 CAS trunk:** This type of circuit allows analog signaling via a digital T1 circuit. Many CAS variants operate over analog and digital interfaces. A common digital interface is used where each grouping of T1 frames (known as a Super Frame or an Extended Super Frame) includes two or four dedicated signaling bits. The type of signaling most commonly used with T1 CAS is E&M signaling. In addition to setting up and tearing down calls, CAS provides the receipt and capture of dialed number identification (DNIS) and ANI information, which are used to support authentication and other functions. The main disadvantage of CAS signaling is its use of user bandwidth to perform these signaling functions.

- **E1 R2 trunk:** R2 signaling is a CAS system developed in the 1960s that is still in use today in Europe, Latin America, Australia, and Asia. R2 signaling exists in several country versions or variants in an international version called Consultative Committee for International Telegraph and Telephone (CCITT-R2). The R2 signaling specifications are contained in ITU-T recommendations Q.400 through Q.490. R2 also provides ANI.

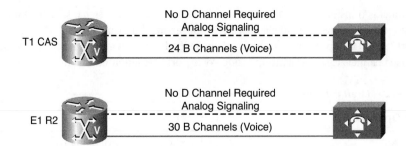

Figure 1-64 *Digital Voice Ports*

T1 CAS

T1s have been around since early voice networks. They were developed as a means of carrying multiple calls across one copper loop. Because the copper loop could carry much more bandwidth than the 4000 Hz required for voice transmission, they first used frequency-division multiplexing (FDM) to transmit 24 calls across a single copper loop. Currently, T1 circuits use TDM to transmit digital data (1s and 0s) instead of the old analog signals.

A single digital voice channel requires 64 kbps of bandwidth. This is calculated using the following formula:

64 kbps = 8000 samples/sec * 8 bits/sample = 64,000 bits/sec

This 64-kbps voice channel is also known as DS0. With 24 voice channels at 64 kbps per channel, a T1 represents 1.536 Mbps of data. Add an additional 8 kbps for framing, and the total speed of a T1 circuit comes to 1.544 Mbps.

T1 CAS uses a digital T1 circuit together with in-band CAS. This is done by using bits in the actual voice channel to transmit signaling information. CAS is sometimes called robbed-bit signaling because user bandwidth is robbed by the network for signaling. A bit is taken from every sixth frame of voice data to communicate on- or off-hook status, wink-start, ground-start, dialed digits, and other information about the call.

T1 CAS uses the same signaling types available for analog trunks: loop-start, ground-start, and E&M variants such as wink-start, delay-start, and immediate-start. There are also various feature groups available when you use E&M. Here are some common feature groups:

- **E&M FG-B:** Inbound and outbound DNIS, inbound ANI (only on Cisco AS5x00)

- **E&M FG-D:** Inbound and outbound DNIS, inbound ANI

- **E&M FG-D EANA:** Inbound and outbound DNIS, outbound ANI

Figure 1-65 shows CAS with the T1 Super Frame (SF) format. The top row of boxes represents a single T1 frame with 24 time slots of 8 bits each. An additional bit is added at the end of each frame that is used to synchronize the SF. A sequence of 12 T1 frames makes up one SF. CAS is implemented by bit-robbing in frames 6 and 12 in this sequence. The bottom row of boxes represents T1 frames 6 and 12. The least significant bit of each voice channel is robbed, leaving 7 bits for voice data.

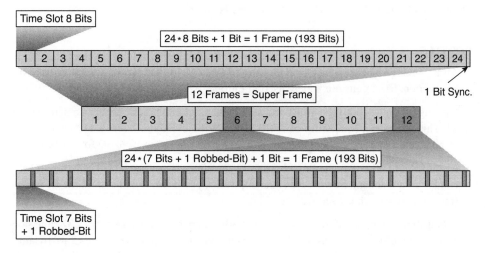

Figure 1-65 *T1 CAS Super Frame Format*

Extended Super Frame (ESF) format, as depicted in Figure 1-66, was developed as an upgrade to SF and is now dominant in public and private networks. Both formats retain the basic frame structure of 1 framing bit followed by 192 data bits. However, ESF repurposes the use of the F bit. In ESF, of the total 8000 F bits used in T1, 2000 are used for framing, 2000 are used for cyclic redundancy check (CRC) for error checking only, and 4000 are used as an intelligent supervisory channel to control functions end to end (such as loopback and error reporting).

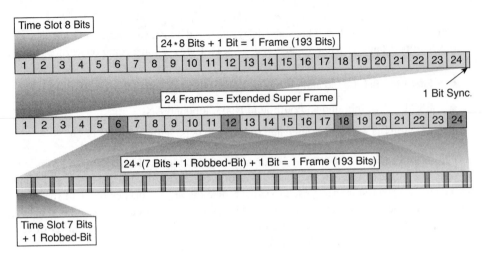

Figure 1-66   *T1 CAS Extended Super Frame Format*

E1 R2 CAS

An E1 circuit is similar to a T1 circuit. It is a TDM circuit that carries several DS0s in one connection. E1 circuits are widely used in Europe, Asia, and Central and South America.

One big difference between an E1 and a T1 is that an E1 bundles 32 time slots instead of 24. This results in a bandwidth of 2.048 Mbps. With an E1, one time slot is used for framing and one is used for signaling. This leaves 30 time slots available for user data.

E1 digital circuits can be deployed using R2 signaling. These trunks are called E1 R2 trunks. To understand how E1 R2 signaling works, you need to understand the E1 multiframe format, which is used with E1 R2.

A multiframe consists of 16 consecutive 256-bit frames. Each frame carries 32 time slots. The first time slot is used exclusively for frame synchronization. Time slots 2 to 16 and 18 to 32 carry the actual voice traffic, and time slot 17 is used for R2 signaling.

The first frame in an E1 multiframe includes the multiframe format information in time slot 17. Frames 2 to 16 include the signaling information, each frame containing the signaling for two voice time slots.

Using this signaling method, E1R2 supports inbound and outbound DNIS and ANI.

Figure 1-67 shows the signaling concept used by E1 R2.

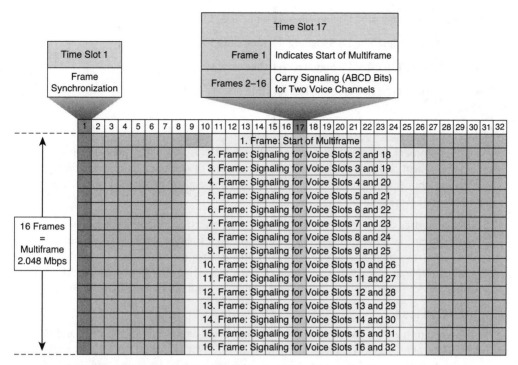

Figure 1-67   *E1 R2 CAS*

Time slot 17 is used for signaling, and each of its frames carries information for two voice time slots. This results in the following frame allocation for signaling:

- 1. Frame, Time slot 17: Declares the multiframe

- 2. Frame, Time slot 17: Signaling for time slots 2 and 18

- 3. Frame, Time slot 17: Signaling for time slots 3 and 19

- 4. Frame, Time slot 17: Signaling for time slots 4 and 20

- 5. Frame, Time slot 17: Signaling for time slots 5 and 21

- 6. Frame, Time slot 17: Signaling for time slots 6 and 22

- 7. Frame, Time slot 17: Signaling for time slots 7 and 23

- 8. Frame, Time slot 17: Signaling for time slots 8 and 24

- 9. Frame, Time slot 17: Signaling for time slots 9 and 25

- 10. Frame, Time slot 17: Signaling for time slots 10 and 26

- 11. Frame, Time slot 17: Signaling for time slots 11 and 27

- 12. Frame, Time slot 17: Signaling for time slots 12 and 28

- 13. Frame, Time slot 17: Signaling for time slots 13 and 29

- 14. Frame, Time slot 17: Signaling for time slots 14 and 30

- 15. Frame, Time slot 17: Signaling for time slots 15 and 31

- 16. Frame, Time slot 17: Signaling for time slots 16 and 32

ISDN

Another protocol used for digital trunks is ISDN. ISDN is a circuit-switched telephone network system designed to allow digital transmission of voice and data over ordinary telephone copper wires, resulting in better quality and higher speeds than are available with the PSTN system.

ISDN comprises digital telephony and data-transport services offered by regional telephone carriers. ISDN involves the digitization of the telephone network, which permits voice, data, text, graphics, music, video, and other source material to be transmitted over existing telephone wires. The emergence of ISDN represents an effort to standardize subscriber services, user/network interfaces, and network and internetwork capabilities.

ISDN Services

In contrast to the CAS and R2 signaling, which provide only DNIS, ISDN offers additional supplementary services such as call waiting and Do Not Disturb (DND). ISDN applications include high-speed image applications (such as Group IV facsimile), additional telephone lines in homes to serve the telecommuting industry, high-speed file transfer, and video conferencing. Voice service is also an application for ISDN.

ISDN Media Types

Cisco routing devices support ISDN BRI and ISDN PRI. Both media types use B channels and D channels. The B channels carry user data. The D channel, in its role as signal carrier for the B channels, directs the CO switch to send incoming calls to particular time slots on the Cisco access server or router. It also identifies the call as a circuit-switched digital call or an analog modem call. Circuit-switched digital calls are relayed directly to the ISDN processor in the router. Analog modem calls are decoded and then sent to the onboard modems. Figure 1-68 illustrates three sample ISDN installation options.

ISDN BRI, referred to as "2 B + D," has the following characteristics:

- Two 64-kbps B channels carry voice or data for a maximum transmission speed of 128 kbps.

- One 16-kbps D channel carries signaling traffic—that is, instructions about how to handle each of the B channels, although it can support user data transmission under certain circumstances.

The D-channel signaling protocol comprises Layers 1 through 3 of the Open Systems Interconnection (OSI) reference model. BRI also provides for framing control and other overhead, bringing its total bit rate to 192 kbps.

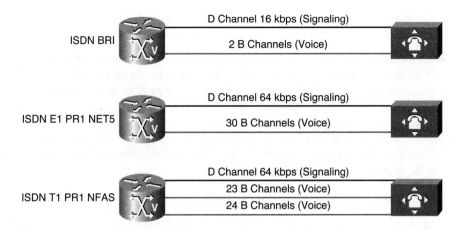

Figure 1-68 *ISDN Installation Options*

The BRI physical layer specification is ITU-T I.430. BRI is very common in Europe and is also available in North America. BRI allows up to two simultaneous calls.

ISDN PRI, referred to as "23 B + D" or "30 B + D," has the following characteristics:

- 23 B channels (in North America and Japan) or 30 B channels (in the rest of the world) carry voice or data, yielding a total bit rate of 1.544 Mbps and 2.048 Mbps, respectively.

- One 64-kbps D channel carries signaling traffic.

The PRI physical layer specification is ITU-T Standards Section I.431.

Note   The PRI interface is economically preferable to BRI, because an interface card supporting PRI is usually already in place on modern PBXs.

Following are worldwide standards for PRI:

- **T1-PRI:** Use this interface to designate North American ISDN PRI with 23 B channels and one CCS channel.

- **E1-PRI:** Use this interface to designate European ISDN PRI with 30 B channels, one CCS channel, and one framing channel.

- **ISDN-PRI Nonfacility Associated Signaling (NFAS):** ISDN NFAS enables a single D channel to control multiple ISDN PRIs on a chassis. This D channel functions as the primary channel with the option of having another D channel in the group as a backup. After you have configured the channelized controllers for ISDN NFAS, you need to configure only the NFAS primary D channel. Its configuration is distributed to all the members of the associated NFAS group. The benefit of PRI NFAS is it frees the

B channel by using a single D channel to control multiple PRI interfaces. One B channel on each additional interface is free to carry other traffic.

- **Fractional PRI:** The term fractional PRI has different meanings in different parts of the world. One meaning indicates multiple PRI groups (B channel and associated D channel) on the same T1/E1 interface. Because an NM-HDV (that is, a Cisco High Density Voice Network Module) supports only a single D channel per T1/E1, the PRI feature does not support this definition of fractional PRI. However, the other version of the term indicates the capability to define a single D channel for each interface with less than 23/30 B channels associated with it. This definition of fractional PRI is supported on Cisco voice gateways.

BRI and PRI Interfaces

Table 1-13 compares the capabilities of BRI and PRI interfaces.

Table 1-13   *BRI and PRI Interfaces*

Capability	BRI	T1 PRI	E1 PRI
B-Channels	2 × 64 kbps	23 × 64 kbps	30 × 64 kbps
D-Channel	1 × 16 kbps	1 × 64 kbps	1 × 64 kbps
Framing	16 kbps	8 kbps	64 kbps
Total Data Rate	160 kbps	1.544 Mbps	2.048 Mbps
Framing	NT, TE Frame	SF, ESF	Multiframe
Line Coding	2B1Q or 4B3T	AMI or B8ZS	HDB3
Country	World	North America, Japan	Europe, Australia

Using ISDN for voice traffic has these benefits:

- ISDN is perfect for G.711 pulse-code modulation (PCM), because each B channel is a full 64 kbps with no robbed bits.

- ISDN has a built-in call control protocol known as ITU-T Q.931.

- ISDN can convey standards-based voice features, such as speed dialing, automated operator services, call waiting, call forwarding, and geographic analysis of customer databases.

- ISDN supports standards-based enhanced dial-up capabilities, such as Group 4 (G4) fax and audio channels.

With ISDN, user data is separated from signaling data. User data, such as the payload from a digitized phone call, goes to a 64-kbps B channel, and signaling data, such as a call setup message, goes to a D channel. A single D channel supports multiple B channels, which is why ISDN service is known as CCS.

ISDN Signaling

ISDN uses Q.921 as its Layer 2 signaling protocol, and Q.931 as its Layer 3 signaling protocol.

Q.921 Layer 2 of the ISDN signaling protocol is also known as Link Access Procedure, D channel (LAPD). LAPD is similar to High-Level Data Link Control (HDLC) and Link Access Procedure, Balanced (LAPB). As the expansion of the LAPD acronym indicates, this layer is used across the D channel to ensure that control and signaling information flows and is received properly. The LAPD frame format is very similar to that of HDLC. Like HDLC, LAPD uses supervisory information and unnumbered frames. The LAPD protocol is formally specified in ITU-T Q.920 and ITU-T Q.921. The Terminal Endpoint Identifier (TEI) field identifies either a single terminal or multiple terminals. A TEI of all 1s indicates a broadcast.

Q.931 Two Layer 3 specifications are used for ISDN signaling: ITU-T I.450 (also known as ITU-T Q.930) and ITU-T I.451 (also known as ITU-T Q.931). Together, these protocols support user-to-user, circuit-switched (the B channels), and packet-switched (the D channel) connections. A variety of call-establishment, call-termination, information, and miscellaneous messages are specified, including SETUP, CONNECT, RELEASE, USER INFORMATION, CANCEL, STATUS, and DISCONNECT. These messages are functionally similar to those provided by the X.25 protocol.

Because ISDN message types might influence the function of a BRI or PRI trunk configuration, you should examine the messages that are part of the Q.931 packet structure and see how ISDN carries out the signaling function.

Nonfacility Associated Signaling

ISDN NFAS, as illustrated in Figure 1-69, allows a single D channel to control multiple PRI interfaces. Use of a single D channel to control multiple PRI interfaces frees one B channel on all other interfaces to carry other traffic. A backup D channel can be configured for use when the primary NFAS D channel fails. When a backup D channel is configured, any hard system failure causes a switchover to the backup D channel, and currently connected calls remain connected.

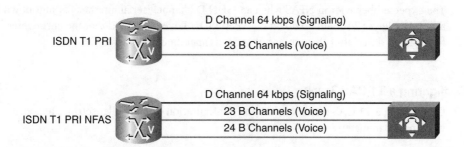

Figure 1-69 *NFAS*

NFAS is supported only with a channelized T1 controller and must be ISDN PRI capable. After the channelized T1 controllers are configured for ISDN PRI, only the NFAS primary D channel must be configured. Its configuration is distributed to all members of the associated NFAS group. Any configuration changes made to the primary D channel will be propagated to all NFAS group members. The primary D-channel interface is the only interface shown after the configuration is written to memory.

The channelized T1 controllers on the router must also be configured for ISDN. The router must connect to either an AT&T 4ESS, Northern Telecom DMS-100 or DMS-250, or National ISDN switch type.

The ISDN switch must be provisioned for NFAS. The primary and backup D channels should be configured on separate T1 controllers. The primary, backup, and B-channel members on the respective controllers should be the same configuration as that configured on the router and ISDN switch. The interface ID assigned to the controllers must match that of the ISDN switch.

You can disable a specified channel or an entire PRI interface, thereby taking it out of service or placing it into one of the other states that is passed in to the switch using the **isdn service** interface configuration command.

In the event that a controller belonging to an NFAS group is shut down, all active calls on the controller that is shut down will be cleared (regardless of whether the controller is set to primary, backup, or none), and one of the following events will occur:

- If the controller that is shut down is configured as the primary, and no backup is configured, all active calls on the group are cleared.

- If the controller that is shut down is configured as the primary, and the active (in service) D channel is the primary, and a backup is configured, the active D channel changes to the backup controller.

- If the controller that is shut down is configured as the primary, and the active D channel is the backup, the active D channel remains as backup controller.

- If the controller that is shut down is configured as the backup, and the active D channel is the backup, the active D channel changes to the primary controller.

The expected behavior in NFAS when an ISDN D channel (serial interface) is shut down is that ISDN Layer 2 should go down but keep ISDN Layer 1 up, and that the entire interface will go down after the number of seconds specified for timer T309.

Configuring a T1 CAS Trunk

Configuring a T1 CAS trunk involves the configuration of controller settings as well as voice port parameters.

Controller Settings

Before configuring a T1 or E1 trunk, you must decide on a variety of parameters for the T1 or E1 digital controller. The following discussions explain the implications of these parameter selections.

Framing Formats   The framing format parameter describes the way bits are robbed from specific frames to be used for signaling purposes. The controller must be configured to use the same framing format as the line from the PBX or CO that connects to the voice port you are configuring.

Digital T1 lines use SF or ESF framing formats. SF provides two-state, continuous supervision signaling, in which bit values of 0 are used to represent on-hook, and bit values of 1 are used to represent off-hook. ESF robs 4 bits instead of 2, yet has little impact on voice quality. ESF is required for 64-kbps operation on DS0 and is recommended for PRI configurations.

E1 lines can be configured for cyclic redundancy check (CRC4) or no cyclic redundancy check, with an optional argument for E1 lines in Australia.

Line Coding   Digital T1/E1 interfaces require that line coding be configured to match that of the PBX or CO that is being connected to the voice port. Line coding defines the type of framing that is used on the line.

T1 line coding methods include alternate mark inversion (AMI) and binary 8-zero substitution (B8ZS). AMI is used on older T1 circuits and references signal transitions with a binary 1, or "mark." B8ZS, a more reliable method, is more popular and is recommended for PRI configurations. B8ZS encodes a sequence of eight zeros in a unique binary sequence, including two line-coding violations at specific bit positions, which are interpreted as a byte containing all zeros.

Supported E1 line coding methods are AMI and high-density bipolar 3 (HDB3), which is a form of zero-suppression line coding.

Clock Sources   Digital T1/E1 interfaces use timers called *clocks* to ensure voice packets are delivered and assembled properly. All interfaces handling the same packets must be configured to use the same source of timing so packets are not lost or delivered late. The timing source that is configured can be external (from the line) or internal to a router's digital interface.

If the timing source is internal, timing derives from the onboard phase lock loop (PLL) chip in the digital voice interface. If the timing source is line (external), timing derives from the PBX or PSTN CO to which the voice port is connected. It is generally preferable to derive timing from the PSTN because its clocks are maintained at an extremely accurate level. This is the default setting for the clocks. When two or more controllers are configured, one should be designated as the primary clock source. It will drive the other controllers.

Consider a couple of examples:

■ **Single voice port providing clocking:** In this scenario, the digital voice hardware is the clock source for the connected device, as shown in Figure 1-70 and Example 1-13. The PLL generates the clock internally and drives the clocking on the line. Generally, this method is useful only when connecting to a PBX, key system, or channel bank. A Cisco VoIP gateway rarely provides clocking to the CO because CO clocking is much more reliable.

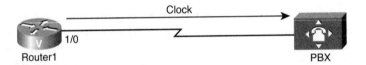

Figure 1-70 *Clock Source Example 1*

Example 1-13 Clock Source Example 1

```
Router1(config)#controller E1 1/0
Router1(config-controller)#framing crc4
Router1(config-controller)#linecoding hdb3
Router1(config-controller)#clock source internal
Router1(config-controller)#ds0-group timeslots 1-15 type e&m-wink-start
```

■ **Single voice port receiving internal clocking:** In this scenario, the digital voice hardware receives clocking from the connected device (CO telephony switch or PBX), as illustrated in Example 1-14 and Figure 1-71. The PLL clocking is driven by the clock reference on the receive (Rx) side of the digital line connection.

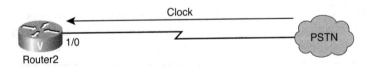

Figure 1-71 *Clock Source Example 2*

Example 1-14 *Clock Source Example 2*

```
Router2(config)#controller T1 1/0
Router2(config-controller)#framing esf
Router2(config-controller)#linecoding ami
Router2(config-controller)#clock source line
Router2(config-controller)#ds0-group timeslots 1-12 type e&m-wink-start
```

Network Clock Timing   Voice systems that pass digitized (PCM) speech rely on the clocking signal being embedded in the received bit stream. This reliance allows connected devices to recover the clock signal from the bit stream and then use this recovered clock signal to ensure that data on different channels keeps the same timing relationship with other channels.

If a common clock source is not used between devices, the binary values in the bit streams might be misinterpreted because the device samples the signal at the wrong moment. For example, if the local timing of a receiving device is using a slightly shorter time period than the timing of the sending device, a string of eight continuous binary 1s might be interpreted as nine continuous 1s. If this data is then re-sent to further downstream devices that use varying timing references, the error could be compounded. By ensuring that each device in the network uses the same clocking signal, you can ensure the integrity of the traffic.

If timing between devices is not maintained, a condition known as clock slip can occur. *Clock slip* is the repetition or deletion of a block of bits in a synchronous bit stream because of a discrepancy in the read and write rates at a buffer.

Slips are caused by the inability of an equipment buffer store (or other mechanisms) to accommodate differences between the phases or frequencies of the incoming and outgoing signals in cases where the timing of the outgoing signal is not derived from that of the incoming signal.

A T1 or E1 interface sends traffic inside repeating bit patterns called *frames*. Each frame is a fixed number of bits, allowing a device to see the start and end of a frame. The receiving device also knows exactly when to expect the end of a frame simply by counting the appropriate number of bits that have come in. Therefore, if the timing between the sending and receiving device is not the same, the receiving device might sample the bit stream at the wrong moment, resulting in an incorrect value being returned.

Even though Cisco IOS can be used to control the clocking on these platforms, the default clocking mode is effectively free running, meaning that the received clock signal from an interface is not connected to the backplane of the router and used for internal synchronization between the rest of the router and its interfaces. The router will use its internal clock source to pass traffic across the backplane and other interfaces.

For data applications, this clocking generally does not present a problem because a packet is buffered in internal memory and is then copied to the transmit buffer of the destination interface. The reading and writing of packets to memory effectively removes the need for any clock synchronization between ports.

Digital voice ports have a different issue. It would appear that unless otherwise configured, Cisco IOS uses the backplane (or internal) clocking to control the reading and writing of data to the digital signal processors (DSP). If a PCM stream comes in on a digital voice port, it will obviously be using the external clocking for the received bit stream. However, this bit stream will not necessarily be using the same reference as the router backplane, meaning the DSPs will possibly misinterpret the data coming in from the controller.

This clocking mismatch is seen on an E1 or T1 controller of the router as a clock slip. The router is using its internal clock source to send traffic out the interface, but the traffic coming into the interface is using a different clock reference. Eventually, the difference in the timing relationship between the transmit and receive signals becomes so great that the controller registers a slip in the received frame.

To eliminate the problem, change the default clocking behavior through Cisco IOS configuration commands. It is absolutely critical to set up the clocking commands properly.

Even though these commands are optional, Cisco strongly recommends you enter them as part of your configuration to ensure proper network clock synchronization:

```
network-clock-participate [slot slot-number | wic wic-slot | aim aim-slot-number]
network-clock-select priority {bri | t1 | e1} slot/port
```

The **network-clock-participate** command allows the router to use the clock from the line via the specified slot, WAN interface card (WIC), or Advanced Integration Module (AIM) and synchronize the onboard clock to the same reference.

If multiple voice WAN interface cards (VWIC) are installed, the commands must be repeated for each installed card. The system clocking can be confirmed using the **show network clocks** command.

DS0 Groups   For digital voice ports, a single command, **ds0-group**, performs the following functions:

■   Defines the T1/E1 channels for compressed voice calls

■   Automatically creates a logical voice port

■   Defines the emulated analog signaling method the router uses to connect to the PBX or PSTN

When you purchase a T1 or E1 connection, make sure that your service provider gives you the appropriate settings.

Bonus Video   To view a video of the author discussing digital voice port theory and another digital voice port demonstrating digital voice port configuration, navigate to the CVOICE page on the 1ExamAMonth.com website. The video on digital voice port theory is entitled *Let's Get D-I-G-I-T-A-L (Theory)*. The video on digital voice port configuration is entitled *Let's Get D-I-G-I-T-A-L (Configuration)*. Additional video tutorials from this website will be recommended later in this book.

VoIP Dial Peers   You must create a digital voice port on the T1 or controller to be able to configure voice port parameters. You must also assign time slots and signaling to the logical voice port through configuration. The first step is to create the T1 or E1 digital voice port with the **ds0-group** *ds0-group-no* **timeslots** *timeslot-list* **type** *signal-type* command.

Note   The **ds0-group** command automatically creates a logical voice port that is numbered as slot/port:ds0-group-no.

The *ds0-group-no* argument identifies the DS0 group (number from 0 to 23 for T1 and from 0 to 30 for E1). This group number is used as part of the logical voice port numbering scheme.

The **timeslots** command allows the user to specify which time slots are part of the DS0 group. The *timeslot-list* argument is a single time slot number, a single range of numbers, or multiple ranges of numbers separated by commas.

The **type** command defines the emulated analog signaling method the router uses to connect to the PBX or PSTN. The type depends on whether the interface is T1 or E1.

To delete a DS0 group, you must first shut down the logical voice port. When the port is in shutdown state, you can remove the DS0 group from the T1 or E1 controller with the **no ds0-group** *ds0-group-no* command.

Figure 1-72 shows how a **ds0-group** command gathers some of the DS0 time slots from a T1 line into a group that becomes a single logical voice port, which can later be addressed as a single entity in voice port configurations. Other DS0 groups for voice can be created from the remaining time slots shown in Figure 1-72, or the time slots can be used for data or serial pass-through.

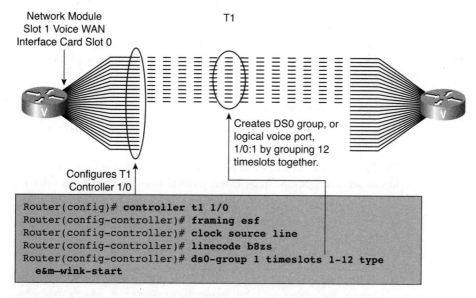

Figure 1-72   *T1 Voice Port Configuration*

T1 CAS Controller Configuration Example   In this example, you have been asked to configure a T1 controller for a voice gateway according to the following network requirements:

- T1

  - Framing = ESF

  - Line code = B8ZS

  - Clock source = PSTN

  - DS0 group = 1 will utilize 12 time slots with E&M wink-start signaling

- Voice Port

  - Call progress tones = US

  - Companding standard = u-law

To configure controller settings for digital T1/E1 voice ports, use the following steps:

Step 1. Enter controller configuration mode.

```
Router(config)#controller {t1 | e1} slot/port
```

Step 2. Select frame type for T1 or E1 line.

T1 lines:

```
Router(config-controller)#framing {sf | esf}
```

E1 lines:

```
Router(config-controller)#framing {crc4 | no-crc4} [Australia]
```

Use this command in configurations in which the router or access server is intended to communicate with T1 or E1 fractional data lines. The service provider determines the framing type that is required for your T1/E1 circuit.

This command does not have a **no** form.

Step 3. Configure the clock source.

```
Router(config-controller)#clock source {line [primary | bits] |
internal | free-running}
```

The **line** keyword specifies that the clock source is derived from the active line rather than from the free-running internal clock. The following rules apply to clock sourcing on the controller ports:

- When both ports are set to line clocking with no primary specification, port 0 is the default primary clock source, and port 1 is the default secondary clock source.

- When both ports are set to line, and one port is set as the primary clock source, the other port is by default the backup or secondary source and is loop-timed.

- If one port is set to clock source line or clock source line primary, and the other is set to clock source internal, the internal port recovers clock from the clock source line port if the clock source line port is up. If it is down, the internal port generates its own clock.

■ If both ports are set to clock source internal, only one clock source exists: internal.

Step 4.   Specify the line coding to use.

T1 lines:

```
Router(config-controller)#linecode {ami | b8zs}
```

E1 lines:

```
Router(config-controller)#linecode {ami | hdb3}
```

Use this command in configurations in which the router or access server must communicate with T1 fractional data lines. The T1 service provider determines which line code type, either **ami** or **b8zs**, is required for your T1 circuit. Likewise, the E1 service provider determines which line code type, either **ami** or **hdb3**, is required for your E1 circuit.

Step 5.   Define the T1 channels for use by compressed voice calls and the signaling method the router uses to connect to the PBX or CO.

```
Router(config-controller)#ds0-group ds0-group-number timeslots
    timeslot-list [service service-type] type {e&m-fgb | e&m-fgd | e&m-
    immediate-start | fgd-eana | fgd-os | fxs-ground-start | fxs-loop-start
    | none | r1-itu | r1-modified | r1-turkey}
```

The **ds0-group** command automatically creates a logical voice port. The resulting logical voice port will be 1/0:1, where 1/0 is the module and slot number and :1 is the *ds0-group-number* argument you assign in this step.

Step 6.   Activate the controller.

```
Router(config-controller)#no shutdown
```

Digital Voice Port Parameters

After setting up the controller, you can configure voice port parameters for that digital voice port. When you specified a **ds0-group**, the system automatically created a logical voice port. You must then enter the voice port configuration mode to configure port-specific parameters. Each voice port you set up in digital voice port configuration is one of the logical voice ports you created with the **ds0-group** command.

Follow these steps to configure basic parameters for digital T1/E1 voice ports:

Step 1.   Enter voice port configuration mode.

```
Router(config)#voice-port slot/port:ds0-group-number
```

Step 2.   Select a two-letter keyword for the voice call progress tones and other locale-specific parameters to be used on this voice port.

```
Router(config-voiceport)#cptone locale
```

Step 3. Specify the companding standard that is used to convert between analog and digital signals.

```
Router(config-voiceport)#compand-type {u-law | a-law}
```

> **Note** This command is used in cases when a DSP is not used, such as local cross-connects, and overwrites the **compand-type** value set by the **cptone** command.

Step 4. Activate the voice port.

```
Router(config-voiceport)#no shutdown
```

Figure 1-73 and Example 1-15 illustrate a complete digital voice port configuration that specifies US as the type of call progress tones to use and u-law as the companding type.

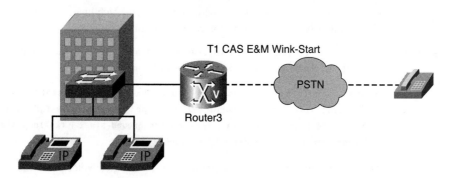

Figure 1-73 *Digital Voice Port Configuration Topology*

Example 1-15 *Digital Voice Port Configuration*

```
Router3(config)#voice-port 1/0:1
Router3(config-voiceport)#cptone US
Router3(config-voiceport)#compand-type u-law
Router3(config-voiceport)#no shutdown
```

Configuring T1 CAS Trunks: Inbound E&M FGD and Outbound FGD EANA Example

Because E&M FGD (that is, Feature Group D) supports only inbound ANI, a deployment requiring both inbound and outbound ANI can combine an E&M FGD and FGD EANA (that is, Exchange Access North American) trunk. The FGD trunk will be used for inbound calls, and the FGD EANA trunk will be used for outbound calls.

In this example, you have been asked to configure a T1 controller for a voice gateway according to the following network requirements:

- T1

  - Framing = ESF

  - Line code = B8ZS

  - Time slots 1–12 should be the FGD trunk

  - Time slots 13–24 should be the FGD EANA trunk

- The voice gateway must support inbound and outbound ANI.

Follow this procedure to configure a T1 CAS digital voice port with inbound and outbound ANI:

Step 1.   Enter controller configuration mode.

```
Router(config)#controller T1 0/0/0
```

Step 2.   Specify the framing format.

```
Router(config-controller)#framing esf
```

Step 3.   Specify line coding.

```
Router(config-controller)#linecode b8zs
```

Step 4.   Configure one DS0 group to use time slots 1 to 12 and E&M feature group-D.

```
Router(config-controller)#ds0-group 0 timeslots 1-12 type e&m-fgd
```

Step 5.   Configure another DS0 group to use time slots 13 through 24 and E&M feature group-D EANA.

```
Router(config-controller)#ds0-group 1 timeslots 13-24 type fgd-eana
```

Note   This creates two voice ports: 0/0/0:0 and 0/0/0:1.

Step 6.   Configure an inbound dial peer using the 0/0/0:0 trunk, which supports inbound ANI:

```
Router(config)#dial-peer voice 1 pots
Router(config-dialpeer)#incoming called-number .
Router(config-dialpeer)#port 0/0/0:0
```

Step 7.   Configure an outbound dial peer using the 0/0/0:1 trunk, which supports outbound ANI:

```
Router(config)#dial-peer voice 90 pots
Router(config-dialpeer)#destination-pattern 9T
Router(config-dialpeer)#port 0/0/0:1
```

Example 1-16 and Figure 1-74 illustrate the configuration previously described.

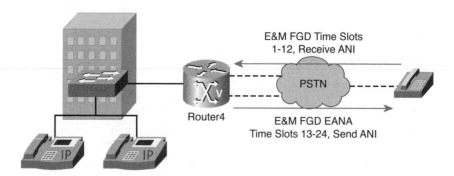

Figure 1-74 *Configuring a T1 CAS Trunk for Inbound and Outbound Calls*

Example 1-16 *T1 CAS Trunk Configuration Example*

```
Router4(config)#controller T1 0/0/0
Router4(config-controller)#framing esf
Router4(config-controller)#linecode b8zs
Router4(config-controller)#ds0-group 0 timeslots 1-12 type e&m-fgd
Router4(config-controller)#ds0-group 1 timeslots 13-24 type fgd-eana
Router4(config)#dial-peer voice 1 pots
Router4(config-dialpeer)#incoming called-number .
Router4(config-dialpeer)#direct-inward-dial
Router4(config-dialpeer)#port 0/0/0:0
Router4(config)#dial-peer voice 90 pots
Router4(config-dialpeer)#destination-pattern 9T
Router4(config-dialpeer)#port 0/0/0:1
```

Configuring an E1 R2 Trunk Example

You use the **ds0-group** controller command to configure E1 R2 trunks as well. The Cisco implementation of R2 signaling has DNIS support enabled by default. If you enable the ANI option, DNIS information is still collected. Specification of the ANI option does not disable the DNIS collection.

In this example, you have been asked to configure an E1 controller for a voice gateway according to the following network requirements:

- E1
  - Framing = CRC4
  - Line code = HDB3

■ Time slots 1–31 should use R2 digital signaling

■ The voice gateway must support inbound and outbound DNIS and ANI.

Follow this procedure to configure an E1 R2 digital voice port with inbound and outbound ANI:

Step 1.   Enter controller configuration mode.

```
Router(config)#controller e1 0/0/0
```

Step 2.   Define the DS0 group.

```
Router(config-controller)#ds0-group 0 timeslots 1-31 type r2-digital
    r2-compelled ani
```

After the DS0 group has been created, you can tune additional parameters using the **cas custom** *ds0-id* command.

Step 3.   Customize E1 R2 signaling parameters.

```
Router(config-controller)#cas-custom 0
```

Use the other **cas-custom** subcommands for further customization required to accommodate a certain PBX or switch.

```
Router(config-ctrl-cas)#country china use-defaults
```

Use this command to specify the local country, regional, and some corporation settings for R2 signaling. Replace the name variable with one of the supported country names. The default country setting is ITU.

Note   Cisco strongly recommends you include the **use-defaults** option, which enables the default settings for a specific country.

Step 4.   Create a dial peer.

```
Router(config)#dial-peer voice 90 pots
Router(config-dialpeer)#destination-pattern 9T
Router(config-dialpeer)#port 0/0/0:0
Router(config-dialpeer)#direct-inward-dial
```

Figure 1-75 and Example 1-17 illustrate the configuration previously described.

Example 1-17   *E1 R2 Trunk Configuration*

```
Router5(config)#controller E1 0/0/0
Router5(config-controller)#ds0-group 0 timeslots 1-31 type r2-digital
    r2-compelled ani
Router5(config-controller)#cas-custom 0
```

```
Router5(config-ctrl-cas)#country china use-defaults
Router5(config)#dial-peer voice 90 pots
Router5(config-dialpeer)#destination-pattern 9T
Router5(config-dialpeer)#direct-inward-dial
Router5(config-dialpeer)#port 0/0/0:0
```

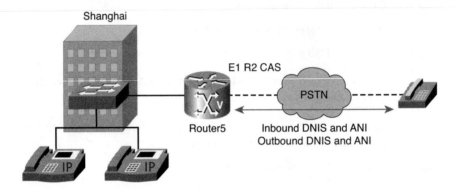

Figure 1-75   *E1 R2 Trunk Configuration Topology*

Configuring an ISDN Trunk

Many PBX vendors support either T1/E1 PRI or BRI connections. In Europe, where ISDN is more popular, many PBX vendors support BRI connections. When designing how the PBX passes voice to the network, you must ensure that the router supports the correct connection. The first step in provisioning ISDN capabilities for T1 or E1 PRI is to enter the basic configuration of the controllers. After the clock source, framing, and line code are configured, ISDN voice functionality requires these configuration commands:

- **isdn switch-type:** Configures the ISDN switch type. You can enter this parameter in global configuration mode or at the interface level. If you configure both, the interface switch type takes precedence over the global switch type. This parameter must match the provider ISDN switch. This setting is required for both BRI and PRI connections.

- **pri-group:** Configures time slots for the ISDN PRI group. T1 allows for time slots 1 through 23 to be configured as B channels, with time slot 24 allocated to the signaling channel (D channel). E1 allows for time slots 1 through 31, with time slot 16 allocated to the D channel. You can configure the PRI group to include all available time slots, or you can configure only a select group of time slots.

- **isdn incoming-voice:** Configures the interface to send all incoming calls to the DSP card for processing.

- **isdn switch-type [primary-qsig | basic-qsig]:** Configures the use of QSIG signaling on the D channel. You typically use this setting when connecting via ISDN to a PBX. The command to enable QSIG signaling is **isdn switch-type primary-qsig** for PRI and **isdn switch-type basic-qsig** for BRI connections.

Example 1-18 and Figure 1-76 show the configuration for a PBX connection to a Cisco voice-enabled router. The connection is configured for QSIG signaling across all 23 time slots.

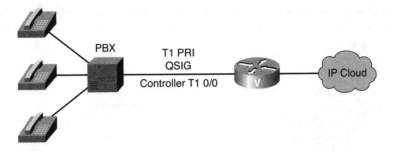

Figure 1-76   *ISDN Example Configuration Topology*

Example 1-18   *ISDN Configuration*

```
Router(config)#isdn switch-type primary-qsig
Router(config)#controller t1 0/0
Router(config-controller)#pri-group timeslots 1-24
Router(config-controller)#interface serial 0/0:23
Router(config-if)#isdn incoming-voice voice
```

The following steps detail the previous configuration:

Step 1.   Specify the CO switch type on the ISDN interface.

```
Router(config)#isdn switch-type primary-qsig
```

You have a choice of configuring the **isdn-switch-type** command to support QSIG at either the global configuration level or at the interface configuration level.

Step 2.   Enter controller configuration mode.

```
Router(config)#controller t1 0/0
```

Step 3.   Create an ISDN PRI group.

```
Router(config-controller)#pri-group timeslots 1-24
```

Step 4.   Enter voice port configuration mode for the D channel. Channel 23 is the D channel, because the channel numbering begins at 0. Therefore, Channel 23 is the 24th channel.

```
Router(config)#interface serial 0/0:23
```

Step 5.   Send incoming calls to DSPs rather than internal modems.

```
Router(config-if)#isdn incoming-voice voice
```

Step 6.   Activate the voice port.

```
Router(config-if)#no shutdown
```

Configuring a BRI Trunk Example

In this example, you have been asked to configure a BRI connection to the PSTN according to the following network requirements. Figure 1-77 presents the topology used in this example.

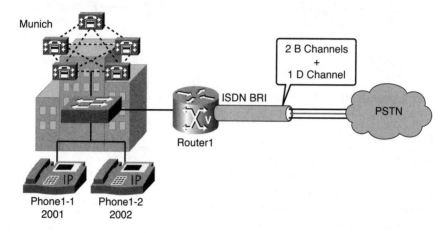

Figure 1-77   *ISDN BRI Example Configuration Topology*

The requirements are as follows:

- Because the ISDN switch is located in Munich, you need to configure the **isdn switch-type** as **basic-net3** for Germany.

- The DSP clocking will be synchronized with the WIC in slot 0.

- Because the possibility exists for the incoming number to be sent digit by digit and not en bloc, you need to configure **isdn overlap-receiving**.

- To define incoming calls as voice-only, configure **isdn incoming-voice voice**. This will send incoming calls to the DSP resources.

- If the current configuration is set to the network-side, use the **isdn protocol-emulate user** command to switch to user-side ISDN. The user-side setting is the default, so it is not shown in the configuration.

Perform these steps to build the BRI trunk to the PSTN:

Step 1.   Configure DSP clocking so it is synchronized with the PSTN clock.

Step 2.   Configure the ISDN switch type according to the country's ISDN implementation.

Step 3. Configure ISDN overlap-receiving for countries with variable-length numbering plans.

Step 4. Configure incoming ISDN calls as voice. The calls will be directly passed to the DSPs.

Step 5. Configure BRI as user-side, if necessary. This is the default, so it does not need to be configured in most circumstances.

Step 6. Reset the interface if necessary, depending on the configuration.

Example 1-19 illustrates the completed configuration.

Example 1-19 *BRI Trunk*

```
Router1#clear interface bri0/0
Router1(config)#network-clock-participate wic 0
Router1(config)#interface bri 0/0
Router1(config-if)#isdn switch-type basic-net3
Router1(config-if)#isdn overlap-receiving
Router1(config-if)#isdn incoming-voice voice
Router1(config-if)#isdn protocol-emulate user
```

Configuring a PRI Trunk Example

In this example, you have been asked to configure a PRI connection to the PSTN according to the following network requirements. Figure 1-78 presents the topology used in this example.

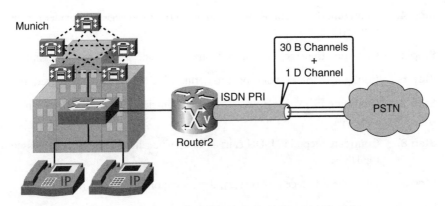

Figure 1-78 *ISDN PRI Example Configuration Topology*

The requirements are as follows:

■ The ISDN switch is located in Munich, Germany. According to the ISDN Switch Type BRI Parameters table, you need to configure the **isdn switch-type** as **primary-net5**.

- The DSP clocking will be synchronized with the WIC in slot 0.

- The line coding for the E1 controller will be **linecoding ami.** (This is not shown in Example 1-20, because this is the default configuration.)

- The framing needs to be defined for the E1 controller. In this case, **crc4** framing will be used. (This is not shown in Example 1-20, because this is the default configuration.)

- The clock source will be set to the PSTN. (This is the default setting, so it is also not shown in the configuration.)

- The logical voice ports need to be created. This is done with the **pri-group timeslots 1-31** command, which defines all 30 B channels as logical voice ports. (Again, this is the default configuration.)

- A variable-length numbering plan needs to be configured. Although the users have a four-digit extension, the switchboard is available via a 0 extension. You therefore configure **overlap-receiving.**

- To define incoming calls as voice-only, you configure **isdn incoming-voice voice.** This will send incoming calls to the DSP resources.

Perform these steps to build the PRI trunk to the PSTN:

Step 1. Configure the ISDN switch type according to the country's ISDN implementation.

Step 2. Configure DSP clocking so it is synchronized with the PSTN clock.

Step 3. Configure the E1 line code. Refer to the local service provider for the correct setting.

Step 4. Configure the E1 frame format. Refer to the local service provider for the correct setting.

Step 5. Configure the clock source to define which side will provide clocking.

Step 6. Configure a logical voice port to define which channels will be used for voice.

Step 7. Configure ISDN overlap-receiving for countries with variable-length numbering plans.

Step 8. Configure incoming ISDN calls as voice. The calls will be directly passed to the DSPs.

Step 9. Reset the interface if necessary, depending on the configuration.

Example 1-20 illustrates the completed configuration.

Example 1-20 *PRI Trunk*

```
Router2(config)#network-clock-participate wic 0
Router2(config)#isdn switch-type primary-net5
Router2(config)#controller e1 0/0/0
```

```
Router2(config-controller)#pri-group timeslots 1-31
Router2(config)#interface Serial0/0/0:15
Router2(config-if)#isdn switch-type primary-net5
Router(config-if)#isdn overlap-receiving
Router2(config-if)#isdn incoming-voice voice
```

Verifying Digital Voice Ports

After configuring the voice ports on your router, perform the following steps to verify proper operation:

Step 1. Pick up the handset of an attached telephony device, and check for a dial tone. Note that current versions of Cisco IOS require a POTS dial peer be configured for the voice port being tested before a dial tone will be heard.

Step 2. If you have a dial tone, check for DTMF detection. If the dial tone stops when you dial a digit, the voice port is probably configured properly.

Step 3. Use the **show voice port summary** command to identify the port numbers of voice interfaces installed in your router.

Step 4. Use the **show voice port** command to verify voice port parameter settings.

Step 5. Use the **show running-config** command to verify the codec complexity setting for digital T1/E1 connections.

Step 6. Use the **show controller** command to verify the digital T1/E1 controller is up and no alarms have been reported, and to display information about clock sources and other controller settings.

Step 7. Use the **show voice dsp** command to display voice-channel configuration information for all DSP channels.

Step 8. Use the **show voice call summary** command to verify the call status for all voice ports.

Step 9. Use the **show call active voice** command to display the contents of the active call table, which shows all the calls currently connected through the router or concentrator.

Step 10. Use the **show call history voice** command to display the contents of the call history table.

Following are some examples of commands used to verify digital port configurations. Example 1-21 shows the output of the **show voice port summary** command. For example, the highlighted portion of the output shows the status of an FXS port.

Example 1-21   show voice port summary *Command*

```
Router#show voice port summary


                                    IN      OUT
PORT    CH SIG-TYPE    ADMIN OPER STATUS   STATUS    EC
======  == ========== ===== ==== ======== ========  ==
0:17    18 fxo-ls      down down idle      on-hook   y
0:18    19 fxo-ls      up   dorm idle      on-hook   y
0:19    20 fxo-ls      up   dorm idle      on-hook   y
0:20    21 fxo-ls      up   dorm idle      on-hook   y
0:21    22 fxo-ls      up   dorm idle      on-hook   y
0:22    23 fxo-ls      up   dorm idle      on-hook   y
0:23    24 e&m-imd     up   dorm idle      idle      y
1/1     -  fxs-ls      up   dorm on-hook   idle      y
1/2     -  fxs-ls      up   dorm on-hook   idle      y
1/3     -  e&m-imd     up   dorm idle      idle      y
1/4     -  e&m-imd     up   dorm idle      idle      y
1/5     -  fxo-ls      up   dorm idle      on-hook   y
1/6     -  fxo-ls      up   dorm idle      on-hook   y
```

Example 1-22 shows the output of the **show voice port** command.

Example 1-22   show voice port *Command*

```
Router#show voice port
DS0 Group 1:0 - 1:0
 Type of VoicePort is CAS
 Operation State is DORMANT
 Administrative State is UP
 No Interface Down Failure
 Description is not set
 Noise Regeneration is enabled
 Non Linear Processing is enabled
 Music On Hold Threshold is Set to -38 dBm
 In Gain is Set to 0 dB
 Out Attenuation is Set to 0 dB
 Echo Cancellation is enabled
 Echo Cancel Coverage is set to 8 ms
 Playout-delay Mode is set to default
 Playout-delay Nominal is set to 60 ms
 Playout-delay Maximum is set to 200 ms
 Connection Mode is normal
 Connection Number is not set
 Initial Time Out is set to 10 s
 Interdigit Time Out is set to 10 s
 Call-Disconnect Time Out is set to 60 s
```

```
Ringing Time Out is set to 180 s
Companding Type is u-law
Region Tone is set for US
Wait Release Time Out is 30 s
Station name None, Station number None


Voice card specific Info Follows:
DS0 channel specific status info:
                                  IN      OUT
    PORT   CH SIG-TYPE   OPER STATUS   STATUS    TIP     RING
```

Example 1-23 shows the output of the **show controller T1** command. You can use this command to verify operation of the controller plus correct framing, line code, and clock source.

Example 1-23   show controller T1 *Command*

```
Router#show controller T1 1/0/0
T1 1/0/0 is up.
  Applique type is Channelized T1
  Cablelength is long gain36 0db
  No alarms detected.
  alarm-trigger is not set
  Framing is ESF, Line Code is B8ZS, Clock Source is Line.
  Data in current interval (180 seconds elapsed):
     0 Line Code Violations, 0 Path Code Violations
     0 Slip Secs, 0 Fr Loss Secs, 0 Line Err Secs, 0 Degraded Mins
     0 Errored Secs, 0 Bursty Err Secs, 0 Severely Err Secs, 0 Unavail Secs
```

Example 1-24 shows the output of the **show voice dsp** command.

Example 1-24   show voice dsp *Command*

```
Router#show voice dsp
TYPE DSP CH CODEC     VERS STATE STATE    RST AI PORT     TS ABORT   TX/RX-PAK-CNT
==== === == ========  ==== ===== =======  === == =======  == =====   ================
C549 007 00 {medium}  3.3  IDLE  idle      0   0 1/0:1     4    0              0/0
                      .13
C549 008 00 {medium}  3.3  IDLE  idle      0   0 1/0:1     5    0              0/0
                      .13
C549 009 00 {medium}  3.3  IDLE  idle      0   0 1/0:1     6    0              0/0
                      .13
C549 010 00 {medium}  3.3  IDLE  idle      0   0 1/0:1     7    0              0/0
                      .13
```

```
C549 011 00 {medium}  3.3 IDLE  idle    0  0 1/0:1   8    0           0/0
                   .13
C549 012 00 {medium}  3.3 IDLE  idle    0  0 1/0:1   9    0           0/0
                   .13
C542 001 01 g711ulaw  3.3 IDLE  idle    0  0 2/0/0        0         512/519
                   .13
C542 002 01 g711ulaw  3.3 IDLE  idle    0  0 2/0/1        0         505/502
                   .13
C542 003 01 g711alaw  3.3 IDLE  idle    0  0 2/1/0        0     28756/28966
                   .13
C542 004 01 g711ulaw  3.3 IDLE  idle    0  0 2/1/1        0         834/8
```

Example 1-25 shows the output of the **show voice call summary** command.

Example 1-25   show voice call summary *Command*

```
Router#show voice call summary

PORT       CODEC    VAD VTSP STATE            VPM STATE
=========  ======== === ==================== =========================
1/0:15.1   g729r8   y   S_CONNECT            S_TSP_CONNECT
1/0:15.2   g729r8   y   S_CONNECT            S_TSP_CONNECT
1/0:15.3   g729r8   y   S_CONNECT            S_TSP_CONNECT
1/0:15.4   g729r8   y   S_CONNECT            S_TSP_CONNECT
1/0:15.5   g729r8   y   S_CONNECT            S_TSP_CONNECT
1/0:15.6   g729r8   y   S_CONNECT            S_TSP_CONNECT
1/0:15.7   g729r8   y   S_CONNECT            S_TSP_CONNECT
1/0:15.8   g729r8   y   S_CONNECT            S_TSP_CONNECT
1/0:15.9   g729r8   y   S_CONNECT            S_TSP_CONNECT
1/0:15.10  g729r8   y   S_CONNECT            S_TSP_CONNECT
1/0:15.11  g729r8   y   S_CONNECT            S_TSP_CONNECT
1/0:15.12  g729r8   y   S_CONNECT            S_TSP_CONNECT
```

Example 1-26 shows the output of the **show call active voice** command.

Example 1-26   show call active voice *Command*

```
Router#show call active voice
GENERIC:
SetupTime=94523746 ms
Index=448
PeerAddress=##73072

PeerSubAddress=
PeerId=70000
```

```
PeerIfIndex=37
LogicalIfIndex=0
ConnectTime=94524043
DisconnectTime=94546241
CallOrigin=1
ChargedUnits=0
InfoType=2
TransmitPackets=6251
TransmitBytes=125020
ReceivePackets=3300
ReceiveBytes=66000
VOIP:
ConnectionId[0x142E62FB 0x5C6705AF 0x0 0x385722B0]
RemoteIPAddress=171.68.235.18

RemoteUDPPort=16580

RoundTripDelay=29 ms
SelectedQoS=best-effort
tx_DtmfRelay=inband-voice
SessionProtocol=cisco
SessionTarget=ipv4:171.68.235.18
OnTimeRvPlayout=63690
GapFillWithSilence=0 ms
GapFillWithPrediction=180 ms
GapFillWithInterpolation=0 ms
GapFillWithRedundancy=0 ms
HiWaterPlayoutDelay=70 ms
LoWaterPlayoutDelay=30 ms
ReceiveDelay=40 ms

LostPackets=0 ms
EarlyPackets=1 ms
LatePackets=18 ms

VAD = disabled

CoderTypeRate=g729r8
CodecBytes=20

cvVoIPCallHistoryIcpif=0

SignalingType=cas
```

Example 1-27 shows the output of the **show call history voice** command.

Example 1-27   show call history voice *Command*

```
Router#show call history voice

GENERIC:
SetupTime=94893250 ms
Index=450
PeerAddress=##52258
PeerSubAddress=
PeerId=50000
PeerIfIndex=35
LogicalIfIndex=0
DisconnectCause=10
DisconnectText=normal call clearing.

ConnectTime=94893780
DisconectTime=95015500
CallOrigin=1

ChargedUnits=0
InfoType=2
TransmitPackets=32258
TransmitBytes=645160
ReceivePackets=20061
ReceiveBytes=401220
VOIP:
ConnectionId[0x142E62FB 0x5C6705B3 0x0 0x388F851C]
RemoteIPAddress=171.68.235.18

RemoteUDPPort=16552

RoundTripDelay=23 ms
SelectedQoS=best-effort
tx_DtmfRelay=inband-voice
SessionProtocol=cisco
SessionTarget=ipv4:171.68.235.18
OnTimeRvPlayout=398000
GapFillWithSilence=0 ms

GapFillWithPrediction=1440 ms
```

```
GapFillWithInterpolation=0 ms
GapFillWithRedundancy=0 ms
HiWaterPlayoutDelay=97 ms
LoWaterPlayoutDelay=30 ms
ReceiveDelay=49 ms
LostPackets=1 ms
EarlyPackets=1 ms

LatePackets=132 ms
VAD = disabled
CoderTypeRate=g729r8

CodecBytes=20
cvVoIPCallHistoryIcpif=0
```

Cross-Connecting a DS0 with an Analog Port

The channel bank feature provides support for the TDM cross-connect functionality between analog voice ports and digital DS0s on the same NM-HD-2VE using CAS, as shown in Figure 1-79. The cross-connect works as a switch between the selected time slots on the T1/E1 CAS trunk and an analog voice interface.

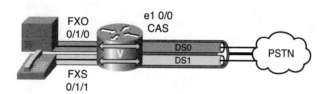

Figure 1-79 *DS0 to Analog Port Crossover Example*

These restrictions apply:

- The configuration for cross-connect must be on the same network module.

- A maximum of four FXS or FXO ports can be cross-connected to a T1 interface.

- A BRI-to-PRI or analog-to-BRI/PRI cross-connect cannot be configured; the only connection for cross-connect is analog-to-T1/E1 CAS (that is, a DS0 group).

- The DS0 group must contain only one time slot. The signaling type of the DS0 group must match that of the analog voice port.

- If the channel bank feature is used for the T1 controller, the rest of the unused DS0 group cannot be used for fractional PRI signaling.

To establish a channel bank (cross-connect) connection between an analog voice port and a T1 DS0, configure the **connect** command in global configuration mode. The parameters of this command include the analog voice port identifier, and the controller identifier with the DS0 number that should be cross-connected. Example 1-28 offers an example of the DS0 to analog port crossover as depicted in Figure 1-78.

Example 1-28 *DS0 to Analog Port Crossover*

```
controller e1 0/0
   ds0-group 0 timeslots 5 type fxs-ground-start
   ds0-group 1 timeslots 8 type e&m-fgd
voice-port 0/0:0
   signal loop-start
   voice-port 0/0:1
   operation 2-wire
   type 1
   signal wink-start
connect connect1 voice-port 0/1/0 e1 0/0 0
connect connect1 voice-port 0/1/1 e1 0/0 1
```

Echo Cancellation

Echo is the sound of your own voice reverberating in the telephone receiver while you are talking. When timed properly, echo is not a problem in a conversation; however, if the echo interval exceeds approximately 25 ms, it can be distracting to the speaker. In the traditional telephony network, echo is generally caused by an impedance mismatch when the four-wire network is converted to the two-wire local loop.

Echo Origin

Figure 1-80 shows an example of a two- to four-wire hybrid circuit. Hybrid echo is caused by an impedance mismatch in the hybrid circuit. This mismatch causes the transmit (Tx) signal to appear on the receive (Rx) signal.

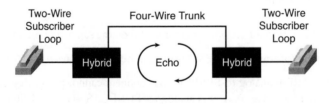

Figure 1-80 *Echo Origin*

The telephone company (telco) usually applies its own port tuning techniques to minimize echo. Echo is constant in a telco environment; however, low delay and low amplitude typically make echo not an issue.

For echo to be a problem, all of the following conditions must exist:

- An analog leakage path between analog Tx and Rx paths

- Sufficient delay in echo return for echo to be perceived as annoying

- Sufficient echo amplitude to be perceived as annoying

Talker Echo

Talker echo occurs when the speech energy of a talker, transmitted down the primary signal path, is coupled into the receiving path from the far end (or tail circuit). Talkers then hear their own voice, delayed by the total echo path delay time. If the echoed signal has sufficient amplitude and delay, the result can be annoying to the customer and can interfere with the normal speech process. Talker echo, as illustrated in Figure 1-81, is usually a direct result of the two- to four-wire conversion that takes place in the PSTN.

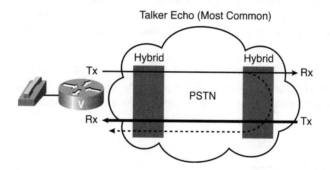

Figure 1-81   *Talker Echo*

Listener Echo

Listener echo occurs at the far end by circulating voice energy, as shown in Figure 1-82. Listener echo is generally caused by the two- and four-wire hybrid transformers (caused by the echo being echoed). The voice of the talker is echoed by the far-end hybrid, and when the echo comes back to the listener, the hybrid on the side of the listener echoes the echo back toward the listener. The effect is that the person listening hears both the talker and an echo of the talker.

Echo Cancellation

An echo canceller is a tool that you can use to control echo. An echo canceller reduces the level of echo that leaks from the Rx path (from the gateway out into the tail circuit) into the Tx path (from the tail circuit into the gateway). From the perspective of the echo canceller in a voice gateway, the Rx signal is a voice that comes across the network from another location. The Tx signal is a mixture of the voice call in the other location and the echo of the original voice, which comes from the tail circuit on the initiating end and is sent to the receiving end.

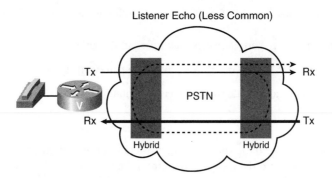

Figure 1-82   *Listener Echo*

Echo cancellers face into the PSTN tail circuit and eliminate echo occurring in the tail circuit. The echo canceller in the originating gateway looks out into the tail circuit. By design, echo cancellers are limited by the total amount of time that they wait for the reflected speech to be received, which is known as an echo tail. The echo tail is normally 32 ms.

Echo cancellation is implemented in the DSP firmware on Cisco voice gateways and is independent of other functions implemented in the DSP, such as the DSP protocol and compression algorithm. In voice packet-based networks, echo cancellers are built into the low-bit-rate codecs and operate on each DSP.

Echo Canceller Operation

An echo canceller removes the echo portion of the signal coming out of the tail circuit and headed into the WAN. To do this, the echo canceller learns the electrical characteristics of the tail circuit and forms its own model of the tail circuit in its memory, and creates an estimated echo signal based on the current and past Rx signal. The echo canceller subtracts the estimated echo from the actual Tx signal coming out of the tail circuit. The quality of the estimation is continuously improved because the echo canceller monitors the estimation error.

Echo Canceller Components

A typical echo canceller includes two components: a convolution processor and a nonlinear processor (NLP), as shown in Figure 1-83.

Metrics used to measure and influence echo cancellation include ERL, ERLE, ACOM, output attenuation, and input gain:

- ERL (echo return loss): Represents the reduction of returning echo (larger is better)

- ERLE (ERL enhancement): Additional echo loss from canceller

- ACOM (A COMbined value) = ERL + ERLE (larger is better)

- Use output attenuation and input gain to tune ERL to at least 6 dB

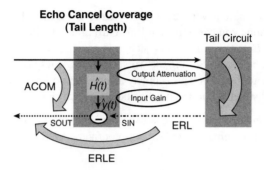

Figure 1-83   *Echo Canceller*

The convolution processor first captures and stores the outgoing signal toward the far-end hybrid. The convolution processor then switches to monitoring mode and, when the echo signal returns, estimates the level of the incoming echo signal, and subtracts the attenuated original voice signal from the echo signal.

The time that it takes to adjust the level of attenuation to the original signal is called the *convergence time*. Because the convergence process requires that the voice signal be stored in memory, the echo canceller has limited coverage of tail circuit delay, normally 64 ms, 96 ms, and up to 128 ms. After convergence, the convolution processor provides about 18 dB of ERLE. Because a typical analog phone circuit provides at least 12 dB of ERL (that is, the echo path loss between the echo canceller and the far-end hybrid), the expected permanent ERL of the converged echo canceller is about 30 dB or greater.

Configuring Echo Cancellation

Echo canceller coverage (also known as tail coverage or tail length) is the length of time that the echo canceller stores its approximation of an echo in memory. An echo canceller can eliminate the maximum echo delay.

The echo canceller faces into a static tail circuit with an input and an output. If a word enters a tail circuit, the echo is a series of delayed and attenuated versions of that word, depending on the number of echo sources and delays associated with them. After a certain period, no signal comes out. This time period is known as the *ringing time* of the tail circuit—the time required for all of the ripples to disperse. To fully eliminate all echoes, the coverage of the echo canceller must be as long as the ringing time of the tail circuit. Use the following command to set the tail coverage. (The available time options and the default value differ per platform and Cisco IOS version.)

```
Router(config-voiceport)#echo-cancel coverage {8 | 16 | 24 | 32 | 48 | 64}
```

To change the threshold at which the gateway will be able to detect echo, use the following command:

```
Router(config-voiceport)#(no) echo-cancel enable
```

For example, if you have a worst-case ERL of 6 (**echo-cancel erl worst-case 6**), when you speak into the phone you can expect at least 6 dB of attenuation on the signal by the time it gets back to the original source (echo). In general, you do not need to change this value from the default of 6. Setting the worst-case ERL does not directly modify the inbound or outbound signals. This is purely a configuration parameter for the echo canceller to help it distinguish between echo and a new signal.

You can disable and re-enable the echo canceller using the **echo-cancel enable** and **no echo-cancel enable** commands in voice port configuration mode. The canceller is enabled by default.

Voice Packets Processing with Codecs and DSPs

Because WAN bandwidth is probably the most expensive component of an enterprise network, network administrators must know how to calculate the total bandwidth required for voice traffic and how to reduce overall bandwidth consumption. This section describes in detail codecs, DSPs, codec complexity, and the bandwidth requirements for VoIP calls. Several variables affecting total bandwidth are explained, as well as how to calculate and reduce total bandwidth consumption.

Codecs

A codec is a device or program capable of performing encoding and decoding on a digital data stream or signal. Various types of codecs are used to encode and decode or compress and decompress data that would otherwise use large amounts of bandwidth on WAN links. Codecs are especially important on lower-speed serial links, where every bit of bandwidth is needed and utilized to ensure network reliability.

One of the most important factors for a network administrator to consider while building voice networks is proper capacity planning. Network administrators must understand how much bandwidth is used for each VoIP call. To understand bandwidth, the administrator must know which codec is being utilized across the WAN link. With a thorough understanding of VoIP bandwidth and codecs, the network administrator can apply capacity planning tools.

Coding techniques are standardized by the ITU. The ITU-T G-series codecs are among the most popular standards for VoIP applications.

Following is a list of codecs supported by Cisco IOS gateways:

■ **G.711:** The international standard for encoding telephone audio on a 64-kbps channel. It is a PCM scheme operating at an 8-kHz sample rate, with 8 bits per sample. With G.711, the encoded voice is already in the correct format for digital voice delivery in the PSTN or through PBXs. It is widely used in the telecommunications field because it improves the signal-to-noise ratio without increasing the amount of data.

There are two subsets of the G.711 codec:

- **mu-law:** Used in North American and Japanese phone networks

- **a-law:** Used in Europe and elsewhere around the world

Both mu-law and a-law subsets use digitized speech carried in 8-bit samples. They use an 8-kHz sampling rate with 64 kbps of bandwidth demand.

- **G.726:** An ITU-T Adaptive Differential Pulse-Code Modulation (ADPCM) coding at 40, 32, 24, and 16 kbps. ADPCM-encoded voice can be interchanged between packet voice, PSTN, and PBX networks if the PBX networks are configured to support ADPCM. The four bit rates associated with G.726 are often referred to by the bit size of a sample, which are 2 bits, 3 bits, 4 bits, and 5 bits, respectively.

- **G.728:** Describes a 16-kbps Low-Delay Code Excited Linear Prediction (LDCELP) variation of CELP voice compression. CELP voice coding must be translated into a public telephony format for delivery to or through the PSTN.

- **G.729:** Uses Conjugate Structure Algebraic Code Excited Linear Prediction (CS-ACELP) compression to code voice into 8-kbps streams. G.729a (that is, G.729 Annex A) requires less computation, but the lower complexity is not without a trade-off because speech quality is marginally worsened. Also, G.729b (that is, G.729 Annex B) adds support for VAD and CNG, to cause G.729 to be more efficient in its bandwidth usage. The features of G.729a and G.729b can be combined into G.729ab. Standard G.729 operates at 8 kbps, but there are extensions that provide 6.4 kbps (Annex D) and 11.8 kbps (Annex E) rates for marginally worse and better speech quality, respectively.

- **G.723:** Describes a dual-rate speech coder for multimedia communications. This compression technique can be used for compressing speech or audio signal components at a very low bit rate as part of the H.324 family of standards. This codec has two bit rates associated with it:

  - **r63:** 6.3 kbps; using 24-byte frames and the MPC-MLQ (Multipulse LPC with Maximum Likelihood Quantization) algorithm

  - **r53:** 5.3 kbps; using 20-byte frames and the ACELP algorithm

The higher bit rate is based on ML-MLQ technology and provides a somewhat higher quality of sound. The lower bit rate is based on CELP and provides system designers with additional flexibility.

- **GSM Full Rate Codec (GSMFR):** Introduced in 1987, the GSMFR speech coder has a frame size of 20 ms and operates at a bit rate of 13 kbps. GSMFR is an RPE-LTP (Regular Pulse Excited–Linear Predictive) coder. To write VoiceXML scripts that can function as the user interface for a simple voice-mail system, the network must support GSMFR codecs. The network messaging must be capable of recording a voice message and depositing the message to an external server for later retrieval. This codec supports the Cisco infrastructure and application partner components required for service providers to deploy unified messaging applications.

■ **Internet Low Bit Rate Codec (iLBC):** Designed for narrowband speech, it results in a payload bit rate of 13.33 kbps for 30-ms frames and 15.20 kbps for 20-ms frames. The algorithm is a version of Block-Independent Linear Predictive Coding, with the choice of data frame lengths of 20 and 30 ms. The encoded blocks have to be encapsulated in a suitable protocol for transport, such as RTP. This codec enables graceful speech quality degradation in the case of lost frames, which occurs in connection with lost or delayed IP packets.

The network administrator should balance the need for voice quality against the cost of bandwidth in the network when choosing codecs. The higher the codec bandwidth, the higher the cost of each call across the network.

Impact of Voice Samples and Packet Size on Bandwidth

Voice sample size is a variable that can affect total bandwidth used. A voice sample is defined as the digital output from a codec's DSP encapsulated into a protocol data unit (PDU). Cisco uses DSPs that output samples based on digitization of 10 milliseconds' worth of audio. Cisco voice equipment encapsulates 20 ms of audio in each PDU by default, regardless of the codec used. You can apply an optional configuration command to vary the number of samples encapsulated. When you encapsulate more samples per PDU, the total bandwidth is reduced. However, encapsulating more samples per PDU comes at the risk of larger PDUs, which can cause variable delay and severe gaps if PDUs are dropped. Table 1-14 demonstrates how the number of packets required to transmit one second of audio varies with voice sample sizes.

Using a simple formula, it is possible for you to determine the number of bytes encapsulated in a PDU based on the codec bandwidth and the sample size (20 ms is the default):

$$Bytes\_per\_Sample = (Sample\_Size * codec\_Bandwidth) / 8$$

If you apply G.711 numbers, the formula reveals the following:

$$Bytes\_per\_Sample = (.020 * 64000) / 8$$
$$Bytes\_per\_Sample = 160$$

Notice from Table 1-14 that the larger the sample size, the larger the packet, and the fewer the encapsulated samples that have to be sent (which reduces bandwidth).

Evaluating Quality of Codecs

There is a saying in the business world that you cannot manage what you cannot measure. Fortunately, multiple measurements are available for the voice quality of various codecs.

Table 1-14 *Impact of Voice Samples*

Codec	Bandwidth (bps)	Sample Size (Bytes)	Packets
G.711	64,000	240	33
G.711	64,000	160	50
G.726r32	32,000	120	33
G.726r32	32,000	80	50
G.726r24	24,000	80	25
G.726r24	24,000	60	33
G.726r16	16,000	80	25
G.726r16	16,000	40	50
G.728	16,000	80	13
G.728	16,000	40	25
G.729	8000	40	25
G.729	8000	20	50
G.723r63	6300	48	16
G.723r63	6300	24	33
G.723r53	5300	40	17
G.723r53	5300	20	33

Mean Opinion Score

Mean opinion score (MOS) is a scoring system for voice quality. An MOS is generated when listeners evaluate prerecorded sentences that are subject to varying conditions, such as compression algorithms. Listeners then assign values to the sentences based on a scale from 1 to 5, where 1 is the worst and 5 is the best.

The test scores are then averaged to a composite score. The test results are subjective, because they are based on the opinions of the listeners. The tests are also relative, because a score of 3.8 from one test cannot be directly compared to a score of 3.8 from another test. Therefore, a baseline for all tests must be established so that the scores can be normalized and compared.

Perceptual Evaluation of Speech Quality

Perceptual Evaluation of Speech Quality (PESQ) is a family of standards comprising a test methodology for automated assessment of the speech quality as experienced by a user of a telephony system. Defined as ITU-T recommendation P.862 (February 2001), it is a worldwide applied industry standard for objective voice quality testing, used by phone manufacturers, network equipment vendors, and telco operators. PESQ can take into account codec errors, filtering errors, jitter problems, and delay problems that are typical in a VoIP network. PESQ scores range from 1 (worst) to 4.5 (best), with 3.8 considered toll quality that can be mapped to MOSs. PESQ replaces its predecessor, Perceptual Speech Quality Measurement (PSQM).

Perceptual Evaluation of Audio Quality

Perceptual Evaluation of Audio Quality (PEAQ) is a standardized algorithm for objectively measuring perceived audio quality, not only speech. Defined as ITU-R recommendation BS.1387, it utilizes software to simulate perceptual properties of the human ear and then integrate multiple model output variables into a single metric. PEAQ characterizes the perceived audio quality as subjects would do in a listening test. PEAQ results principally model MOSs that cover a scale from 1 (bad) to 5 (excellent).

The PEAQ technology is protected by several patents and is available under license, together with the original code for commercial applications. However, free, unvalidated PEAQ model implementations exist.

Test Method Comparison

Table 1-15 summarizes the key features of the described methods: mean opinion score, Perceptual Evaluation of Speech Quality, Perceptual Evaluation of Audio Quality, and the predecessor of PESQ, Perceptual Speech Quality Measurement. In essence, PSQM, PESQ, and PEAQ provide an objective methodology that can be mapped to the subjective MOS model. The current standards, PESQ and PEAQ, include a complete range of factors that would be also considered by a subjective test. PEAQ differs from PESQ mainly in that it is also used to evaluate other audio types.

Table 1-15   *Voice Quality Test Method Comparison*

Feature	MOS	PSQM	PESQ	PEAQ
Test method	Subjective	Objective	Objective	Objective
End-to-end packet loss test	Inconsistent	No	Yes	Yes
End-to-end jitter test	Inconsistent	No	Yes	Yes
Measurement subject	Voice and other audio	Voice	Voice	Voice and other audio

Codec Quality

Table 1-16 provides the average MOSs for most typical codecs. These values represent MOSs under ideal network conditions—no packet loss, low delay, and no jitter. The MOS values measured under heavy network load will differ from the values shown in this table.

Table 1-16   *Codec Quality*

Codec	Bandwidth (kbps)	MOS
G.711	64	4.3
G.726r32	32	3.8
G.726r24	24	3.75
G.726r16	16	3.7
G.728	16	3.75
iLBC	15.2	4.14
GSM Full Rate	13	3.5
G.729	8	3.92
G.729a	8	3.7
G.723r63	6.3	3.7
G.723r53	5.3	3.65

Evaluating Overhead

The packetization period and the related voice payload size affect the raw voice bandwidth. Table 1-17 illustrates the most common codecs with selected packetization periods, payload sizes, packet ratios, and the resulting voice bandwidth, including the overhead introduced by Layer 3 and above. The longer the packetization period is, the larger the sample size is, and the lower the Layer 3+ voice bandwidth is.

Table 1-17   *Evaluating Overhead*

Codec	Packetization Period	Voice Payload	Packets per Second	Layer 3+ Bandwidth per Call
G.711	20 ms	160 byte	50	80 kbps
G.711	30 ms	240 byte	33	74 kbps
G.729	20 ms	20 byte	50	24 kbps
G.729	30 ms	30 byte	33	19 kbps

To compute the total call bandwidth, the additional Layer 2 header must be considered, using the following formula:

BW_per_call = (Voice_payload + L3+_overhead + L2_overhead) * Packet_ratio) * 8 bits/byte

Several factors must be included in calculating the overhead of a VoIP call. Layer 2 and security protocols significantly add to the packet size.

Data-Link Overhead

A significant contributing factor to bandwidth is the Layer 2 protocol that is used to transport VoIP. VoIP alone carries a 40-byte IP, User Datagram Protocol (UDP), and Real-Time Transport Protocol (RTP) header. The larger the Layer 2 overhead, the more bandwidth that is required to transport VoIP:

- **IEEE 802.3 Ethernet:** Carries 18 bytes of overhead: 6 bytes for source MAC, 6 bytes for destination MAC, 2 bytes for type, and 4 bytes for CRC.

- **IEEE 802.1Q Ethernet:** In addition to the 802.3 overhead, there is a 32-bit 802.1Q header that carries, among others, a 12-bit VLAN ID.

- **PPP:** Carries 4 to 8 bytes of overhead. The PPP header includes a 1- to 2-byte flag to indicate the beginning or end of a frame (in successive frames, only one character is used), 0 to 1 address byte, 0 to 1 control byte, 1- to 2-byte protocol field, and 2 bytes for CRC. If both PPP peers agree to perform address and control field compression during Link Control Protocol (LCP) negotiation, the control and address fields are not included. If both PPP peers agree to perform protocol field compression during LCP negotiation, the protocol field is 1 byte.

- **Frame Relay:** Carries 6 bytes of overhead: 2 bytes of header, 2 bytes of trailer (CRC), and 2 bytes of flags.

- **Frame Relay Fragmentation Implementation Agreement (FRF.12):** In addition to the Frame Relay overhead, there is a 2-byte FRF.12 subheader that includes 4 bits of flags and a 12-bit sequence number to facilitate reassembly at the remote end.

IP and Upper Layers Overhead

The IP and transport layers also have overhead to contribute to the size of the packets:

- **IP:** Adds a 20-byte header

- **UDP:** Adds an 8-byte header

- **RTP:** Adds a 12-byte header

VPN Overhead

VPN encapsulation adds additional overhead to the VoIP packets:

- **Encapsulating Security Payload (ESP):** Adds typically a 50- to 57-byte overhead. Two variables affect the ESP overhead: cipher block size and the authentication algorithm. The typical block size is 8 octets, but Advanced Encryption Standard (AES) works with

16-octet block sizes. The block size influences the size of the initialization vector field, which is the same as the block size plus the padding overhead, which can be up to block size minus 1 octet. The authentication algorithm yields different fingerprint sizes:

- Message Digest 5 (MD5): 16 octets

- Secure Hash Algorithm 1 (SHA-1): 20 octets

- Secure Hash Algorithm 192 (SHA-192): 24 octets

- Secure Hash Algorithm 256 (SHA-256): 32 octets

- **Generic Routing Encapsulation (GRE), Layer 2 Tunneling Protocol (L2TP):** Adds a 24-byte header.

- **Multiprotocol Label Switching (MPLS):** Adds a 4-byte header for every label carried in the packet. A label stack might include multiple labels in an MPLS VPN or traffic engineering environment.

Bandwidth Calculation Example

The example calculates the total bandwidth for a G.711 voice call with 50 pps carried over a Frame Relay network.

To compute the total call bandwidth, this formula is used:

Bandwidth_per_call = (Voice_payload + Layer 3_overhead + Layer 2_overhead) * PACKET_ratio) * 8 bits/byte

For the specified call, the bandwidth computes to the following:

Bandwidth_per_call = (160 + 40 + 6) * 50) * 8 bits/byte = 82,400 b/s = 82.4 kbps

Per-Call Bandwidth Using Common Codecs

Table 1-18 includes the total call bandwidth used by the most common codecs. It lists the Layer 3+ bandwidth and the total call bandwidth over 802.3 Ethernet and Frame Relay networks. The Layer 3+ bandwidth takes into account the voice payload and IP, UDP, and RTP overhead. The 802.3 Ethernet and Frame Relay bandwidths consider the additional Layer 2 overhead. The table is produced using the formula introduced earlier.

Table 1-18 *Per-Call Bandwidth*

Codec	Voice Payload	Packets per Second	Only Layer 3+	Call over Frame Relay	Call over 802.3 Ethernet
G.711	160 bytes	50	80 kbps	82.4 kbps	87.2 kbps
G.711	240 bytes	33	74.66 kbps	76.27 kbps	79.47 kbps
G.729	20 bytes	50	24 kbps	26.4 kbps	31.2 kbps
G.729	30 bytes	33	18.66 kbps	20.27 kbps	23.47 kbps

Digital Signal Processors

A DSP is a specialized microprocessor designed specifically for digital signal processing. DSPs enable Cisco platforms to efficiently process digital voice traffic. DSPs on a router provide stream-to-packet signal processing functionality that includes voice compression, echo cancellation, and tone- and voice-activity detection.

A media resource is a software-based or hardware-based entity that performs media-processing functions on the data streams to which it is connected. A few examples are media-processing functions that include mixing multiple streams to create one output stream (conferencing), passing the stream from one connection to another (media termination point), converting the data stream from one compression type to another (transcoding), echo cancellation, signaling, termination of a voice stream from a TDM circuit (coding/decoding), packetization of a stream, and streaming audio (annunciation).

The terms *DSP* and *media resource* are often used interchangeably in some documentation.

The four major functions of DSPs in a voice gateway are as follows:

- **Transcoding:** Transcoding is the direct digital-to-digital conversion from one codec to another. Transcoding compresses and decompresses voice streams to match end-point-device capabilities. Transcoding is required when an incoming voice stream is digitized and compressed (by means of a codec) to save bandwidth, but the local device does not support that type of compression. Ideally, all IP telephony devices would support the same codecs, but this is not the case. Rather, different devices support different codecs.

  Transcoding is processed by DSPs on a DSP farm. Sessions are initiated and managed by Cisco Unified Communications Manager. Cisco Unified Communications Manager also refers to transcoders as hardware MTPs.

  If an application or service can handle only one specific codec type, which is usually G.711, a G.729 call from a remote site must be transcoded to G.711. This can be done only via DSP resources. Because applications and services are often hosted in main sites, DSP transcoding resources are most common in central sites.

- **Voice termination:** Voice termination applies to a call that has two call legs, one leg on a TDM interface and the second leg on a VoIP connection. The TDM leg must be terminated by hardware that performs coding/decoding and packetization of the stream. DSPs perform this termination function. The DSP also provides echo cancellation, voice activity detection, and jitter management at the same time it performs voice termination.

- **Media termination point (MTP):** An MTP is an entity that accepts two full-duplex voice streams using the same codec. It bridges the media streams and allows them to be set up and torn down independently. The streaming data received from the input stream on one connection is passed to the output stream on the other connection, and vice versa. In addition, the MTP can be used to transcode a-law to mu-law and vice versa, or it can be used to bridge two connections that utilize different packetization periods. MTPs are also used to provide further processing of a call, such as RFC 2833 support.

- **Audio conferencing:** In a traditional circuit-switched voice network, all voice traffic goes through a central device (such as a PBX system), which provides audio conferencing services as well. Because IP phones transmit voice traffic directly between phones, a network-based conference bridge is required to facilitate multiparty conferences.

A conference bridge is a resource that joins multiple participants into a single call. It can accept any number of connections for a given conference, up to the maximum number of streams allowed for a single conference on that device. A one-to-one correspondence exists between media streams connected to a conference and participants connected to the conference. The conference bridge mixes the streams together and creates a unique output stream for each connected party. The output stream for a given party is the composite of the streams from all connected parties minus their own input stream. Some conference bridges mix only the three loudest talkers on the conference and distribute that composite stream to each participant (minus their own input stream if they are one of the talkers).

Hardware conference bridges are used in two environments. They can be used to increase the conferencing capacity in a central site without putting an additional load on Cisco Unified Communications Manager servers, which can host software-based conference bridges. More important is the use of hardware conference bridges in remote sites. If no remote-site conference resources are deployed, every conference will be routed to central resources, resulting in sometimes-excessive WAN usage.

In addition, DSP-based conference bridges can mix G.711 and G.729 calls, thus supporting any call-type scenario in multisite environments. In contrast, software-based conference bridges deployed on Cisco Unified Communications Manager servers can mix only G.711 calls.

Hardware Conferencing and Transcoding Resources

Figure 1-84 shows a multisite environment with deployed DSP resources. Router2 in Chicago is offering DSP-based conferencing services to support mixed codec environments and optimal WAN usage.

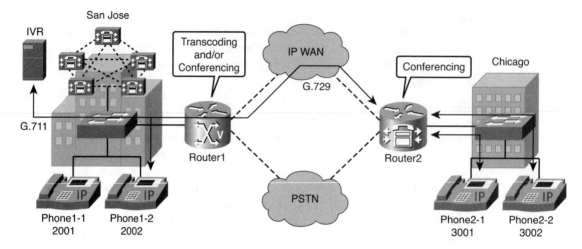

Figure 1-84   *Media Resource Deployment Example*

The central gateway, Router1, offers transcoding and conferencing services. The transcoding resources can be used to transcode G.729 to G.711 and then connect to an application server or even a software-based Cisco Unified Communications Manager conference bridge.

DSP Chip

The DSP chip plays a crucial role in the Cisco Unified Communications system. The DSP chip comes in several form factors, from soldered on to the main board of the Cisco Unified IP phone or gateway, to the modular packet voice DSP module (PVDM). The PVDM can have multiple DSPs on the module.

The type of DSP chip, the number of DSP resources, and the type of codec that is used all factor into the calculation of how many simultaneous calls can be processed.

DSP Modules

Currently, there are two major types of high-density PVDMs: PVDM generation 2 (PVDM2) and PVDM generation 3 (PVDM3). The Cisco 2800 and 3800 Series platforms support only the PVDM2 modules. The Cisco 2900 and 3900 Series platforms support both the PVDM2 and PVDM3 modules. The PVDM3 modules provide higher density (up to four times higher) than the PVDM2s. They also provide improved performance in terms of the number of conference and transcoding sessions supported.

PVDM2 is installed in

- Motherboard PVDM2 slot on Cisco 2800 and 3800 Series ISRs

- Cisco High Density Digital Voice Network Modules (NMHDV2, NM-HDV2-1T1/E1, and NM-HDV2-2T1/E1)

- PVDM2 Adapter for PVDM3 slot on Cisco 2900, 3900 Series ISRs

PVDM3 is installed in

- Motherboard PVDM3 slot on Cisco 2900, 3900 Series ISRs

- Cisco 2901 and 2911 routers have two slots each, Cisco 2921 and 2951 routers have three slots each, and Cisco 3925 and 3945 routers have four slots each.

- Cisco IOS Software Release 15.0.1(M) and later

Table 1-19 lists the major differences between PVDM2 and PVDM3 modules. Each series includes multiple models that differ in the number and capacity of the DSPs that they have on board. The number (8, 16, 32, 64, and so on) in the model name indicates the maximum number of G.711 voice calls that a particular module can support.

Table 1-19 *DSP Module Comparison*

	PVDM2	**PVDM3**
Platform support	Cisco 2800, 3800, 2900, 3900 Series ISRs	Cisco 2900,3900 Series ISRs
Models	PVDM2-8, PVDM2-16, PVDM2-32, PVDM2-48, PVDM2-64*	PVDM3-16, PVDM3-32, PVDM3-64, PVDM3-128, PVDM3-192, PVDM3-256*
Capabilities	Voice/fax	Voice/video (no Cisco Fax Relay)
Resource sharing	Per-module and per-chassis sharing	DSP resources in motherboard slots shared across the chassis backplane
Coexistence	Can coexist on the Cisco 2900 and 3900 Series ISR platforms but PVDM2 cannot be installed directly on the motherboard	

.*Number in the model name identifies the number of supported G.711 channels

All features supported by PVDM2s are supported on PVDM3s, except Cisco Fax Relay, which is no longer supported on PVDM3s. PVDM3 modules have a number of new features, including video support.

The PVDM2 and PVDM3 modules can coexist as long as they are not both installed in the same domain. The motherboard PVDM slots form one domain, and each service module slot forms a separate domain. The motherboard domain can contain either all PVDM2 modules or all PVDM3 modules. A service module domain can contain only PVDM2 modules housed by the NM-HDV2 carrier card. If a mix of PVDM2s and PVDM3s are detected on the motherboard slots, then the PVDM2s will be deactivated, allowing only the PVDM3s to be used actively. If PVDM2s are detected in service module slots and PVDM3s are installed on the motherboard, then both will continue to function in their own domains and coexist.

Codec Complexity

Codec complexity refers to the amount of processing that is required to perform voice compression. Codec complexity affects call density, which is the number of calls that are reconciled on the DSPs. With higher codec complexity, fewer calls can be processed, as illustrated in Table 1-20. A higher codec complexity might be required to support a particular codec or combination of codecs. A lower codec complexity supports the greatest number of voice channels, if the lower complexity is compatible with the particular codecs in use.

Table 1-20 *Media Termination and Transcoding*

	Low Complexity	Medium Complexity	High Complexity
	G.711 and Clear-Channel Codec	G.729A, G.729AB, G.726, G.722, and Fax Relay	G.723.1, G.728, G.729, G.729B, iLBC, and Modem Relay
PVDM2-8	8	4	4
PVDM2-16	16	8	6
PVDM2-32	32	16	12
PVDM2-48	48	24	18
PVDM2-64	64	32	24
PVDM3-16	16	12	10
PVDM3-32	32	21	14
PVDM3-64	64	42	28
PVDM3-128	128	96	60
PVDM3-192	192	138	88

Recommended Usage in Deployment Models

The selection of the appropriate codec depends on the VoIP path that the call takes, as follows:

- **Single-site deployment:** In this deployment model, the VoIP calls are made within the same site. The site consists of LAN or MAN networks where enough bandwidth is available. G.711 and G.722 codecs are recommended to provide the best voice quality. The bandwidth usage of the codec is not a concern within a single site.

- **Multisite WAN with centralized or distributed call signaling and clustering over the WAN:** In these models, intrasite calls should use the same codecs as in single site—G.711 or G.722—as these codecs offer the best voice quality and the bandwidth consumption is not a problem. Intersite calls should use G.729 using any annex type. This codec family consumes very little bandwidth per call and guarantees good voice quality. It is widely supported in the industry, so the interoperability with other vendors is guaranteed.

Packet Voice DSP Module Conferencing

PVDM2 modules offer more flexibility in resource sharing than the PVDM2 modules. The PVDM3 modules have a universal firmware image that allows sharing DSP resources between transcoding, voice, and conference calls. On the PVDM2, you can use the same DSP for voice and transcoding calls, but a different DSP firmware image is required for conference calls. If a PVDM2 DSP is assigned for a conferencing session, it cannot be used for transcoding or voice calls at the same time. Note that conferencing needs a dedicated PVDM2 DSP, but not a dedicated PVDM2 module. For example, the PVDM2-64 contains four DSPs; if you use one of them for conferencing, the other three can be used for other purposes. The number of supported conferences and participants depends on codec complexity. As an example, the PVDM3-256 module supports the following:

- 66 G.711 conferences with 8 participants each

- 6 G.711 conferences with 64 participants each

- 30 G.722 conferences with 8 participants each

- 36 G.729 or G.729A conferences with 8 participants each

- 18 iLBC conferences with 8 participants each

- Up to 32 participants per G.729, G.729A, or G.722 conference

- Up to 16 participants per iLBC conference

DSP Calculator

For easier DSP calculation, a DSP calculator tool is available at the following URL (and requires appropriate login credentials for the Cisco website):

http://cisco-apps.cisco.com/web/applicat/dsprecal/dsp_calc.html

Note   The DSP calculator requires that you log in to Cisco.com with appropriate credentials.

The following example shows how to calculate the required DSPs to deploy the following media resources on a single gateway:

Router model: Cisco 2811

Cisco IOS release: 12.4(6)T

Installed voice interface cards (VIC): Onboard slot 0, VWIC2-1MFT-T1/E1 used as a PRI T1 with 23 voice bearer channels

Number of G.711 calls: 23

Number of transcoding sessions: 8 G.711 to G.729a

Number of conferences: Four mixed-mode conferences

Follow these steps to perform the calculation:

Step 1.   Select the correct router model, in this case Cisco 2811.

Step 2.   Select the correct Cisco IOS release: Mainline Release, T Train Release, or Special Release, as shown in Figure 1-85. In this case, 12.4(6)T is selected. Different Cisco IOS releases might lead to different DSP calculations, because the firmware of a DSP depends on the Cisco IOS version used.

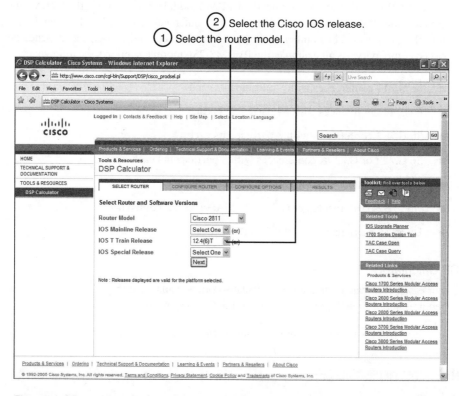

Figure 1-85   *DSP Calculator (Steps 1 and 2)*

Step 3.   Select the appropriate VIC configuration. In this case, VWIC2-1MFT-T1/E1 (T1 voice) is selected, as shown in Figure 1-86. The T1 voice option is necessary because the VWIC2 supports both E1 and T1.

Step 4.   Specify the maximum number of calls for a specific codec or fax configuration. In this case, a full T1 is configured for PRI—that is, 23 G.711 calls, as illustrated in Figure 1-86.

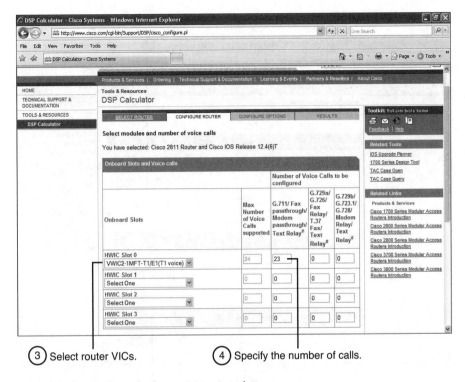

Figure 1-86 *DSP Calculator (Steps 3 and 4)*

Note A full T1 PRI supports only 23 voice channels. A T1 configured for channel associated signaling (CAS) or a T1 configured for Nonfacility Associated Signaling (NFAS) can support as many as 24 voice channels.

Step 5. Specify the number of transcoding sessions with the appropriate codec, as shown in Figure 1-87. In this example, 8 G.711 to G.729a sessions are required.

Step 6. Specify the number of conferences required on the gateway, either single-mode G.711 or mixed-mode conferences, as demonstrated in Figure 1-87.

Step 7. After entering all parameters, you can calculate the required DSP resources. For our example, five C5510 DSPs need to be deployed, as shown in Figure 1-88.

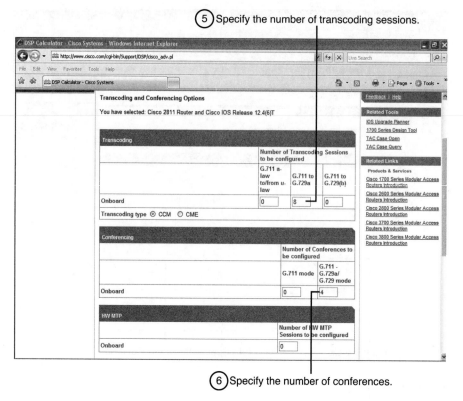

Figure 1-87 *DSP Calculator (Steps 5 and 6)*

Configuring DSPs

The codec complexity can be configured to tell the gateway how many DSP resources to allocate to a voice channel. These settings are available:

- **High complexity:** This option supports any high-complexity codec or a combination of high- and lower-complexity codecs.

- **Medium complexity:** This option supports any medium-complexity codec or a combination of medium- and low-complexity codecs. It offers the greatest number of voice channels, if the lower complexity is compatible with the particular codecs in use. All medium-complexity codecs can also be run in high-complexity mode, but fewer (usually about half) of the channels are available per DSP.

- **Flex:** In this option, more voice channels can be connected (or configured in the case of DS0 groups and PRI groups) to the module than the DSPs can accommodate. If all voice channels should go active simultaneously, the DSPs become oversubscribed, and calls that are unable to allocate a DSP resource fail to connect. This is the default setting.

■ **Secure:** This option supports the Secure Real-Time Transport Protocol (SRTP) package capability for media encryption and authentication. This setting supports the lowest number of selected low- and medium-complexity codecs (G.711 a-law and mu-law, G.729, and G.729A) per DSP.

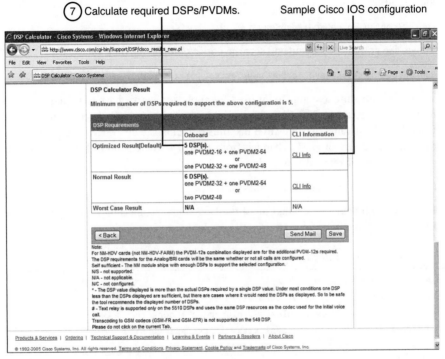

Figure 1-88 *DSP Calculator (Step 7)*

The DSP resources, when installed on a voice gateway, do not have to be configured to support voice termination. In certain situations, it is necessary to fine-tune their operations. For fine-tuning, the **voice-card** *slot* command is used to enter the voice card configuration mode. The voice card corresponds to a service module installed on the gateway.

```
Router(config)#voice-card slot
```

The **dspfarm** command adds a specified voice card to the DSP resource pool. If there are not enough DSPs on the motherboard to terminate the required PRI and CAS channels, you can use the **dspfarm** command under the available voice card (NM-HDV2 or another network module with PVDM2s). The DSPs of that voice card will be added to the shared resource pool. This method allows the termination of PRI and CAS channels, but not analog circuits.

```
Router(config-voicecard)#dspfarm
```

The **codec complexity** command sets the codec complexity on a voice card.

```
Router(config-voicecard)#codec complexity {flex | high | medium | secure}
```

The **codec sub-sample** command is used for applications that have strict requirements for round-trip delay times. This command reduces the G.711 sampling period inside the DSP from the default value of 10 ms to 5 ms, thus reducing the delay. However, this reduces the channel density of G.711 channels from 16 to 14. There is no difference in secure channel density if this mode is enabled.

```
Router(config-voicecard)#codec sub-sample
```

For codec complexity to change, all of the DSP voice channels must be in the idle state. Example 1-29 illustrates a codec complexity configuration.

Example 1-29 *Voice Card Configuration Example*

```
Router(config)#voice-card 1
Router(config-voicecard)#codec complexity ?
     flex Set codec Flex complexity, higher call density.
     high Set codec to high complexity, lower call density.
     medium Set codec to mid range complexity and call density
     secure Set codec complexity to secure.
Router(config-voicecard)#codec complexity flex
Router(config-voicecard)#codec sub-sample
```

When you use the **codec complexity high** command to change codec complexity, the system prompts you to remove all existing DS0 or PRI groups using the specified voice card. Then all DSPs are reset, loaded with the specified firmware image, and released.

The complexity of DSPs can be verified with the **show voice dsp** command, as shown in Example 1-30.

Example 1-30 *Verifying Codec Complexity*

```
HQ-1#show voice dsp

DSP   DSP                 DSPWARE CURR  BOOT                               PAK      TX/RX
TYPE NUM CH CODEC         VERSION STATE STATE   RST AI VOICEPORT TS ABORT  PACK COUNT
==== === == ========      ======= ===== =======  === == ========= == ===== ===========
```

```
- - - - - - - - - - - - - - - - - - - - - - - - - -FLEX VOICE CARD 0 - - - - - - - - - - - - - - - - - - - - - - - - - - -
                           *DSP VOICE CHANNELS*


CURR STATE : (busy)inuse (b-out)busy out (bpend)busyout pending
LEGEND     : (bad)bad    (shut)shutdown  (dpend)download pending


DSP   DSP                 DSPWARE CURR  BOOT                      PAK   TX/RX
TYPE  NUM CH CODEC        VERSION STATE STATE   RST AI VOICEPORT TS ABRT PACK COUNT
===== === == ========= ======= ===== ======= === == ========= == ==== ===========
                           *DSP SIGNALING CHANNELS*
DSP   DSP                 DSPWARE CURR  BOOT                      PAK   TX/RX
TYPE  NUM CH CODEC        VERSION STATE STATE   RST AI VOICEPORT TS ABRT PACK COUNT
===== === == ========= ======= ===== ======= === == ========= == ==== ===========
C5510 002 01 {flex}       8.2.0 alloc idle      0  0 0/2/0     02  0         0/0
C5510 002 02 {flex}       8.2.0 alloc idle      0  0 0/2/1     02  0         0/0
- - - - - - - - - - - - - - - - - - - - - -END OF FLEX VOICE CARD 0 - - - - - - - - - - - - - - - - - - - - - - - - -
```

Configuring Conferencing and Transcoding on Voice Gateways

The configuration of transcoding and conferencing on a voice gateway involves DSP resource requirements, Skinny Client Control Protocol (SCCP) configuration, DSP farm and DSP farm profile configuration, and hardware configurations.

The basic steps for configuring conferencing and transcoding on voice gateway routers are as follows:

Step 1. **Determine DSP resource requirements:** DSPs reside either directly on a voice network module (such as the NM-HD-2VE), on PVDM2s that are installed in a voice network module (such as the NM-HDV2), or on PVDM2s that are installed directly onto the motherboard (such as on the Cisco 2800 and 3800 Series voice gateway routers). You must determine the number of PVDM2s or network modules required to support your conferencing and transcoding services and install the modules on your router.

Step 2. **Enable SCCP:** The Cisco IOS router containing DSP resources communicates with Cisco Unified Communications Manager using SCCP. Therefore, SCCP needs to be enabled and configured on the router.

Step 3. **Configure enhanced conferencing and transcoding:** Configuring conferencing and transcoding on the voice gateway includes the following substeps:

   ■ Enable DSP farm services.

   ■ Configure a DSP farm profile.

   ■ Associate a DSP farm profile to a Cisco Unified Communications Manager group.

   ■ Verify DSP farm configuration.

The remainder of this section explores DSP farm configuration tasks, including both Cisco IOS configuration and Cisco Unified Communications Manager configuration. Examples are provided for each configuration task.

DSP Farms

A DSP farm is the collection of DSP resources available for conferencing, transcoding, and MTP services. DSP farms are configured on the voice gateway and managed by Cisco Unified Communications Manager through SCCP.

The DSP farm can support a combination of transcoding sessions, MTP sessions, and conferences simultaneously. The DSP farm maintains the DSP resource details locally. Cisco Unified Communications Manager requests conferencing or transcoding services from the gateway, which either grants or denies these requests, depending on resource availability. The details of whether DSP resources are used, and which DSP resources are used, are transparent to Cisco Unified Communications Manager.

The DSP farm uses the DSP resources in network modules on Cisco routers to provide voice conferencing, transcoding, and hardware MTP services.

Consider the topology in Figure 1-89. Prior to actual media resource configuration, the DSPs need to be enabled for DSP farm usage. The **dsp services dspfarm** voice card configuration mode command allocates the DSPs to the DSP farm.

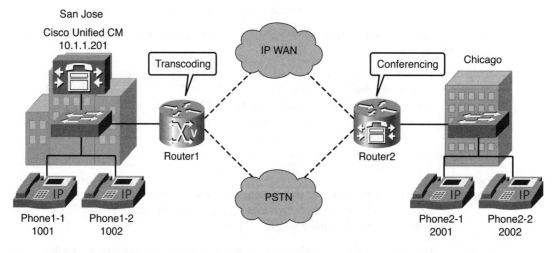

Figure 1-89 *DSP Farm Configuration Topology Example*

These commands are issued on both gateways, Router1 and Router2, as illustrated in Examples 1-31 and 1-32.

Example 1-31 *Allocating DSPs to a DSP Farm on Router1*

```
Router1(config)#voice-card 0
Router1(config-voicecard)#dsp services dspfarm
```

Example 1-32 *Allocating DSPs to a DSP Farm on Router2*

```
Router2(config)#voice-card 0
Router2(config-voicecard)#dsp services dspfarm
```

DSP Profiles

DSP farm profiles are created to allocate DSP farm resources. Under the profile, you select the service type (conference, transcode, MTP), associate an application, and specify service-specific parameters such as codecs and the maximum number of sessions. A DSP farm profile allows you to group DSP resources based on the service type. Applications associated with the profile, such as SCCP, can use the resources allocated under the profile. You can configure multiple profiles for the same service, each of which can register with one Cisco Unified Communications Manager group. The profile ID and service type uniquely identify a profile, allowing the profile to uniquely map to a Cisco Unified Communications Manager group that contains a single pool of Cisco Unified Communications Manager servers.

When the DSPs are ready, the DSP profile is configured using the **dspfarm profile** command. In this example, because transcoding is required on Router1, the **dspfarm profile 1 transcoding** command is used. On Router2, the **dspfarm profile 1 conferencing** command creates a profile for conferencing.

Because both G.711 and G.729 are used in this deployment, multiple codecs are enabled in both the transcoding and conferencing profiles using the **codec** *codec-type* command. Configurations for Router1 and Router2 are provided in Examples 1-33 and 1-34.

Example 1-33 *Creating a DSP Profile on Router1*

```
Router1(config)#dspfarm profile 1 transcode
Router1(config-dspfarm-profile)#codec g711ulaw
Router1(config-dspfarm-profile)#codec g711alaw
Router1(config-dspfarm-profile)#codec g729ar8
Router1(config-dspfarm-profile)#codec g729abr8
Router1(config-dspfarm-profile)#codec g729r8
Router1(config-dspfarm-profile)#maximum sessions 6
Router1(config-dspfarm-profile)#associate application SCCP
Router1(config-dspfarm-profile)#no shutdown
```

Example 1-34 *Creating a DSP Profile on Router2*

```
Router2(config)#dspfarm profile 1 conference
Router2(config-dspfarm-profile)#codec g711ulaw
```

```
Router2(config-dspfarm-profile)#codec g711alaw
Router2(config-dspfarm-profile)#codec g729ar8
Router2(config-dspfarm-profile)#codec g729abr8
Router2(config-dspfarm-profile)#codec g729br8
Router2(config-dspfarm-profile)#maximum sessions 2
Router2(config-dspfarm-profile)#associate application SCCP
Router2(config-dspfarm-profile)#no shutdown
```

Note   Because mixed-mode conferencing is configured, the two configured conferences require a full DSP. If only G.711 would be allowed, a single DSP on a PVDM2 would allow up to eight conferences.

SCCP Configuration

After the profiles are set up, both routers should be configured for SCCP. As a reminder, the SCCP protocol is used for signaling between Cisco Unified Communications Manager and the router containing the DSP resources.

Both routers use their Fast Ethernet 0/1 interface as the SCCP source interface, and the IP address of the primary Cisco Unified Communications Manager is 10.1.1.201. Because Cisco Unified Communications Manager 8.0 is deployed, 7.0+ is specified in the SCCP configuration on each router to ensure full interoperability between the router and Cisco Unified Communications Manager. Note that Cisco IOS 15.1(1)T1 is used in this example. Future Cisco IOS versions might support an 8.0 parameter for the **sccp ccm** command.

After the Cisco Unified Communications Manager servers have been defined, the SCCP groups can be configured. Again, Fast Ethernet 0/1 is used as the source interface for the group, and the previously defined Cisco Unified Communications Manager is associated using the **associate ccm 1 priority 1** command. Note that the San Jose Cisco Unified Communications Manager server references the identifier option previously specified.

Then, the DSP farm profile is associated with the SCCP group using the **associate profile** command. The **register XCODERouter1** option used on Router1 assigns the name XCODERouter1 to the profile. This name will be used when registering with Cisco Unified Communications Manager and will be required when configuring the Cisco Unified Communications Manager to point back to the DSP resource. On Router2, the **register CFBRouter2** option is used, because this profile is a conference bridge.

These commands are issued on both gateways, Router1 and Router2, as illustrated in Examples 1-35 and 1-36.

Example 1-35   *Configuring SCCP on Router1*

```
Router1(config)#sccp local FastEthernet 0/1
Router1(config)#sccp ccm 10.1.1.201 identifier 1 priority 1 version 7.0+
Router1(config)#sccp
```

```
Router1(config)#sccp ccm group 1
Router1(config-sccp-ccm)#bind interface FastEthernet 0/1
Router1(config-sccp-ccm)#associate ccm 1 priority 1
Router1(config-sccp-ccm)#associate profile 1
Router1(config-sccp-ccm)#register XCODERouter1
```

Example 1-36 *Configuring SCCP on Router2*

```
Router2(config)#sccp local FastEthernet 0/1
Router2(config)#sccp ccm 10.1.1.201 identifier 1 priority 1 version 7.0+
Router2(config)#sccp
Router2(config)#sccp ccm group 1
Router2(config-sccp-ccm)#bind interface FastEthernet 0/1
Router2(config-sccp-ccm)#associate ccm 1 priority 1
Router2(config-sccp-ccm)#associate profile 1
Router2(config-sccp-ccm)#register CFBRouter2
```

Unified Communications Manager Configuration

After the Cisco IOS configuration is complete, the media resources need to be added to Cisco Unified Communications Manager.

Continuing with the current example, a conference bridge is defined in the **Media Resource > Conference Bridge** menu option, as shown in Figure 1-90.

Go to Media Resources > Conference Bridge

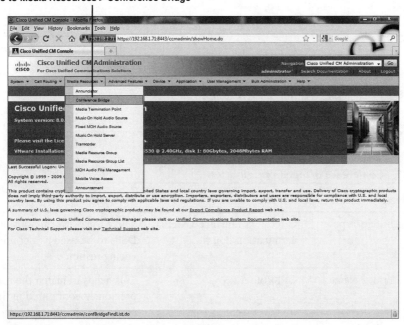

Figure 1-90 *Navigating to the Conference Bridge Configuration Screen*

The newly added conference bridge now needs to be set up. Because the conference bridge is using a PVDM2 deployed on an ISR, the Conference Bridge Type needs to be Cisco IOS Enhanced Conference Bridge, as illustrated in Figure 1-91.

After you select the correct type, specify the parameters described in Table 1-21 and illustrated in Figure 1-92.

Select Cisco IOS Enhanced Conference Bridge
for PVDM2 and PVDM3 deployments.

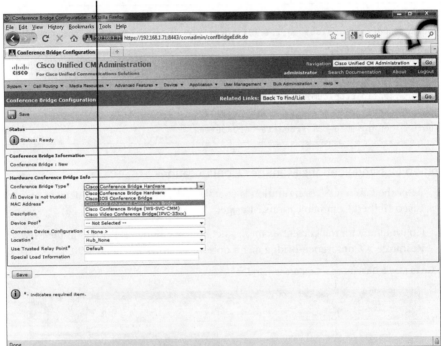

Figure 1-91 *Defining a Conference Bridge Type*

Note For simplicity, the device pool and location are left at their defaults.

Table 1-21 *Conference Bridge Configuration*

Parameter	Value	Description
Conference Bridge Type	Cisco IOS Enhanced Media Termination Point	Select the platform housing the DSPs to be used as a conferencing resource.
Conference Bridge Name	CFBRouter2	This needs to match the name previously configured in the **associate profile** command on the gateway.

Table 1-21 *Conference Bridge Configuration*

Parameter	Value	Description
Description	CFBRouter2	Choose a meaningful description.
Device Pool	Default	Select the correct device pool.
Common Device Configuration	< None >	Optionally select a Common Device Configuration.
Location	< None >	Select the correct location.
Device Security Mode	Non Secure Conference Bridge	Set the conference bridge to either a nonsecure or an encrypted conference bridge.
Use Trusted Relay Point	Default	Optionally select a Trusted Relay Point (TRP), which identifies an MTP or transcoder that is identified as a TRP.

Conference Bridge Name must match the name used in the SCCP group configuration.

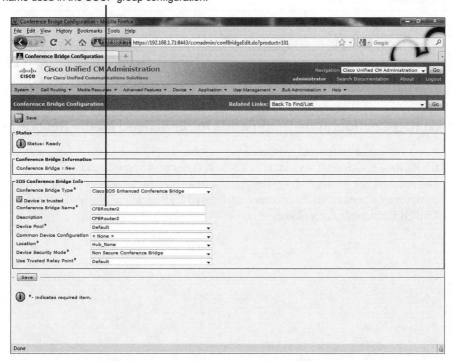

Figure 1-92 *Specifying Conference Bridge Parameters*

To add a transcoding resource, navigate to the **Media Resource > Transcoder** menu option. Because PVDM2s are also used for transcoding, select Cisco IOS Enhanced Media Termination Point as the Transcoder Type. After you select the correct type, specify the parameters as described in Table 1-22 and illustrated in Figure 1-93.

Table 1-22   *Transcoder Configuration*

Parameter	Value	Description
Transcoder Type	Cisco IOS Enhanced Media Termination Point	Select the platform housing the DSPs to be used as a conferencing resource.
Description	XCODERouter1	Choose a meaningful description.
Device Name	XCODERouter1	This needs to match the name previously configured in the **associate profile** command on the Router1 gateway.
Device Pool	Default	Select the correct device pool.
Common Device Configuration	< None >	Optionally select a Common Device Configuration.
Special Load Information	—	This should be left blank.
Trusted Relay Point check box	Unchecked	Check to identify the transcoding resource as a Trusted Relay Point (TRP).

Cisco IOS Configuration Commands for Enhanced Media Resources

As previously demonstrated, you need to configure DSP-based media resources both on the hardware platform (for example, a Cisco IOS router) and on Cisco Unified Communications Manager. For reference, the following discussion details the Cisco IOS configuration commands for making router-based DSP resources available to Cisco Unified Communications Manager.

Device Name must match the name
used in the SCCP group configuration.

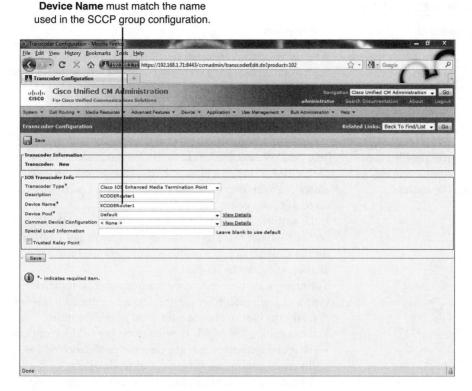

Figure 1-93 *Specifying Transcoder Parameters*

DSP Farm Configuration Commands for Enhanced Media Resources

Prior to creating a DSP farm profile, you need to enable the DSPs for DSP services. You
do this in the respective voice card configuration mode. After you have enabled DSPs for
media resources, you can configure a DSP farm profile for conferencing, transcoding, or
as an MTP. The commands required to perform this initial DSP farm configuration are
provided in Table 1-23.

Table 1-23   *DSP Farm Configuration Commands*

Command	Description
voice-card *slot*	To enter voice card configuration mode and configure a voice card, use the **voice-card** command in global configuration mode.
dsp services dspfarm	The router must be equipped with one or more voice network modules that provide DSP resources. DSP resources are used only if this command is configured for the particular voice card.
dspfarm profile *profile-identifier* {**conference | mtp | transcode**}	To enter DSP farm profile configuration mode and define a profile for DSP farm services, use the **dspfarm profile** command in global configuration mode. To delete a disabled profile, use the **no** form of this command. If the profile is successfully created, the user enters the DSP farm profile configuration mode. Multiple profiles can be configured for the same service. If a profile is active, the user will not be allowed to delete the profile. The profile identifier uniquely identifies a profile. If the service type and profile identifier are not unique, a message is displayed that asks the user to choose a different profile identifier. You can choose the profile type by using one of these options: • To create a conference bridge, use the **conference** option. • To create a transcoder, use the **transcode** option. • To create a media termination point, use the **mtp** option.

Within the DSP farm configuration, you need to specify the supported codecs and maximum number of sessions. This configuration directly affects the number of required DSPs, so ensure that the configuration matches the design specifications.

You also need to associate the DSP farm profile with SCCP. This is done using the **associate application sccp** command. The DSP farm configuration mode commands are provided in Table 1-24.

Table 1-24   *DSP Farm Profile Configuration Mode Commands*

Command	Description
codec {*codec-type* | pass-through}	To specify the codecs supported by a DSP farm profile, use the **codec** command in DSP farm profile configuration mode. To remove the codec, use the **no** form of this command. Depending on the media resource, multiple codecs can be configured. Using higher-complexity codecs, such as G.729, might decrease the number of sessions per DSP. The **pass-through** option is available only for MTPs and is typically used for RSVP-based call admission control.
maximum sessions *number*	To specify the maximum number of sessions supported by a profile, use the **maximum sessions** command in DSP farm profile configuration mode. To reset to the default, use the **no** form of the command. For conferencing, the *number* specifies the number of conferences, not participants.
associate application sccp	To associate the SCCP to the DSP farm profile, use the **associate application** command in DSP farm profile configuration mode. To remove the protocol, use the **no** form of this command. This also requires a correct **sccp group** configuration to work correctly.

SCCP Configuration Commands for Enhanced Media Resources

Configuring enhanced media resources includes the SCCP configuration that will be used to register with Cisco Unified Communications Manager. Global configuration includes the configuration of the individual Cisco Unified Communications Managers, the local SCCP interface used for signaling, and activating SCCP.

The SCCP configuration commands are shown in Table 1-25.

Table 1-25   *SCCP Configuration Commands*

Command	Description
sccp ccm {*ip-address* | *dns*} **identifier** *identifier-number* [**priority** *priority*] [**port** *port-number*] [**version** *version_number*]	To add a Cisco Unified Communications Manager server to the list of available servers and set various parameters, including the IP address or Domain Name System (DNS) name, port number, and version number, use the **sccp ccm** command in global configuration mode. To remove a particular server from the list, use the **no** form of this command. You can configure up to four Cisco Unified Communications Manager servers, a primary and up to three backups, to support DSP farm services. To do this, use the **priority** option, with **1** being the highest priority and **4** being the lowest. To add the Cisco Unified Communications Manager server to a Cisco Unified Communications Manager group, use the **associate ccm** command.
sccp local *interface-type interface-number* [**port** *port-number*]	To select the local interface that SCCP applications (transcoding and conferencing) use to register with Cisco Unified Communications Manager, use the **sccp local** command in global configuration mode. To deselect the interface, use the **no** form of this command. This should be either a LAN interface or a loopback interface and needs to be reachable from Cisco Unified Communications Manager. WAN interfaces should be avoided. The **port** option should be used only if the default port 2000 has been changed on Cisco Unified Communications Manager.
sccp	To enable the SCCP protocol and its related applications (transcoding and conferencing), use the **sccp** command in global configuration mode. To disable the protocol, use the **no** form of this command. SCCP and its related applications (transcoding and conferencing) become enabled only if DSP resources for these applications are configured, DSP farm service is enabled, and the Cisco Unified Communications Manager registration process is completed. The **no** form of this command disables SCCP and its applications by unregistering from the active Cisco Unified Communications Manager, dropping existing connections, and freeing allocated resources.

After globally configuring SCCP, you need to create an SCCP group. An SCCP group references previously configured Cisco Unified Communications Managers and then associates a DSP profile with the group. To bind an SCCP group to a local interface, use the **bind interface** command. Table 1-26 describes these SCCP group configuration commands.

Table 1-26 *SCCP Group Configuration Commands*

Command	Description
sccp ccm group *group_number*	To create a Cisco Communications Manager group and enter SCCP Cisco Unified Communications Manager configuration mode, use the **sccp ccm group** command in global configuration mode. To remove a particular Cisco Unified Communications Manager group, use the **no** form of this command. Use this command to group Cisco Unified Communications Manager servers that are defined with the **sccp ccm** command. You can use the **associate profile** command to associate designated DSP farm profiles so that the DSP services are controlled by the Cisco Unified Communications Manager servers in the group.
associate ccm *identifier-number* **priority** *priority*	To associate a Cisco Unified Communications Manager with a Cisco Communications Manager group and establish its priority within the group, use the **associate ccm** command in the SCCP Cisco Unified Communications Manager configuration mode. To disassociate a Cisco Unified Communications Manager from a Cisco Unified Communications Manager group, use the **no** form of this command. The *identifier-number* references the Cisco Unified Communications Managers that were previously configured using the **sccp ccm** command. You can configure up to four Cisco Unified Communications Manager servers, a primary and up to three backups, to support DSP farm services. To do this, use the **priority** option, with **1** being the highest priority and **4** being the lowest.
associate profile *profile-identifier* **register** *device-name*	To associate a DSP farm profile with a Cisco Unified Communications Manager group, use the **associate profile** command in SCCP Cisco Unified Communications Manager configuration mode. To disassociate a DSP farm profile from a Cisco Unified Communications Manager, use the **no** form of this command. The **profile** option references the identifier of a DSP farm profile configured using the **dspfarm profile** command. The device name must match the name configured in Cisco Unified Communications Manager. Otherwise, the profile is not registered to Cisco Unified Communications Manager. Each profile can be associated to only one Cisco Unified Communications Manager group.

continues

Table 1-26 *SCCP Group Configuration Commands*

Command	Description
bind interface *interface-type interface-number*	To bind an interface to a Cisco Communications Manager group, use the **bind interface** command in SCCP Cisco Unified Communications Manager configuration mode. To unbind the selected interface, use the **no** form of this command. The selected interface is used for all calls that belong to the profiles associated to this Cisco Unified Communications Manager group. If the interface is not selected, it uses the best interface's Cisco IP address in the gateway. Interfaces are selected according to user requirements. If only one group interface exists, configuration is not needed.

Verifying Media Resources

To verify the configuration of a DSP farm profile, use the **show dspfarm profile** command. Example 1-37 shows the DSP farm profile with ID 1 used for conferencing. Also note the "Number of Resource Configured : 2" line, which is set by the **maximum session 2** command.

Example 1-37 show dspfarm profile *Command*

```
Router2#show dspfarm profile 1
Dspfarm Profile Configuration

 Profile ID = 1, Service = CONFERENCING, Resource ID = 1
 Profile Description :
 Profile Admin State : UP
 Profile Operation State : ACTIVE
 Application : SCCP    Status : ASSOCIATED
 Resource Provider : FLEX_DSPRM    Status : UP
 Number of Resource Configured : 2
 Number of Resource Available : 2
 Codec Configuration
 Codec : g711ulaw, Maximum Packetization Period : 30 , Transcoder: Not Required
 Codec : g711alaw, Maximum Packetization Period : 30 , Transcoder: Not Required
 Codec : g729ar8, Maximum Packetization Period : 60 , Transcoder: Not Required
 Codec : g729abr8, Maximum Packetization Period : 60 , Transcoder: Not Required
 Codec : g729r8, Maximum Packetization Period : 60 , Transcoder: Not Required
 Codec : g729br8, Maximum Packetization Period : 60 , Transcoder: Not Required
```

To check the DSP status used for DSP farm profiles, use the **show dspfarm dsp all** command. Example 1-38 shows two available DSPs configured for conferencing.

Example 1-38   show dspfarm dsp all *Command*

```
Router2#show dspfarm dsp all
SLOT DSP VERSION  STATUS CHNL USE   TYPE   RSC_ID BRIDGE_ID PKTS_TXED PKTS_RXED

0    5   1.0.6    UP     N/A  FREE  conf   1      -         -         -
0    5   1.0.6    UP     N/A  FREE  conf   1      -         -         -

Total number of DSPFARM DSP channel(s) 2
```

Summary

The main topics covered in this chapter are the following:

■ Voice gateways support the Cisco Unified Communications architecture by converting voice signals and offering advanced voice features.

■ Call routing involves incoming and outgoing call legs that correspond to inbound and outbound dial peers.

■ Gateways support various interface types: analog with inband signaling (FXO, FXS, FXS-DID, E&M), digital with CAS signaling (T1/E1 CAS), and digital with CCS signaling (T1/E1 PRI, BRI).

■ Voice conversion into VoIP uses codecs with varying complexity and MOS, and is performed by dedicated DSPs.

Chapter Review Questions

The answers to these review questions are in the appendix.

1. Which two of the following VoIP signaling protocols does a Cisco Unified Communications gateway support? (Choose two.)

    a. RTP

    b. SIP

    c. SS7

    d. MGCP

    e. ISDN

2. Which two functionalities differentiate multisite WAN deployment with centralized call processing from multisite deployment with distributed call processing? (Choose two.)

   a. Intersite VoIP signaling

   b. Codecs that should be used in the WAN

   c. PSTN signaling protocol

   d. SRST

   e. The need for DSP resources

3. Which statement describes G.729 Annex B?

   a. It uses higher bandwidth than G.729A.

   b. It uses lower bandwidth than G.729 Annex A.

   c. It is more susceptible to delay, variation, and "tandeming" than G.729 Annex A.

   d. It has higher complexity than G.729 Annex A.

4. Which two functions are performed by a POTS dial peer? (Choose two.)

   a. Providing an address for the edge network or device

   b. Providing a destination address for the edge device that is located across the network

   c. Routing the call across the network

   d. Identifying the specific voice port that connects the edge network or device

   e. Associating the destination address with the next-hop router or destination router, depending on the technology that is used

5. Which special character in a destination pattern string is used as a wildcard?

   a. Asterisk (*)

   b. Pound sign (#)

   c. Comma (,)

   d. Period (.)

6. What happens when no matching dial peer is found for an outbound call leg?

   a. The default dial peer is used.

   b. Dial peer 0 is used.

   c. The POTS dial peer is used.

   d. The call is dropped.

7. Which parameter is configured only for POTS dial peers?

    a. answer-address

    b. destination-pattern

    c. incoming called-number

    d. port

8. What command is used to configure a T1 controller for CAS?

    a. pri-group

    b. bri-group

    c. ds0-group

    d. ds1-group

9. Which condition must occur for echo to become a problem?

    a. Disabled echo canceller

    b. Sufficient voice amplitude

    c. Leakage between transmit (Tx) and receive (Rx) paths

    d. Incorrectly selected tie-line (two-wire versus four-wire)

10. Which two statements describe PVDM2 and PVDM3? (Choose two.)

    a. Both can be installed on router motherboards.

    b. Both can be installed in appropriate PVDM adapters.

    c. Both support voice and video.

    d. Both can be installed in a Cisco 3900 Series Integrated Services Router platform.

Chapter 2

Configuring Basic Voice over IP

After reading this chapter, you should be able to perform the following tasks:

- Describe how VoIP signaling and media transmission differs from traditional voice circuits, and explain how voice is sent over IP networks, including analog-to-digital conversion, coding, packetization, and all variants of RTP.

- Describe the characteristics of H.323 and explain when to use it.

- Describe the characteristics of SIP and explain when to use it.

- Describe the characteristics of MGCP and explain when to use it.

- Discuss special requirements for VoIP call legs, including the need for QoS, fax/modem relay, and DTMF support.

- Describe how to configure dial peers to meet special requirements.

VoIP transmission differs from traditional circuit-switched telephony in the way that the calls are signaled and the voice media is transported through the network. Successful implementation of a VoIP network relies heavily on the correct deployment of VoIP gateway signaling protocols: H.323, Session Initiation Protocol (SIP), and Media Gateway Control Protocol (MGCP). The VoIP network provides special transmission methods for fax, modem, and dual-tone multifrequency (DTMF) tones. This chapter describes the characteristics and implementation of the gateway signaling protocols and explains the configuration of VoIP dial peers to support advanced features such as fax/modem pass-through and relay and DTMF relay.

Voice Coding and Transmission

The inherent characteristics of a converged voice and data IP network present certain challenges to network engineers and administrators in delivering voice traffic correctly. This section describes the challenges of integrating a voice and data network and explains the technologies that enable voice media transmission.

VoIP Overview

VoIP transports voice information over IP networks, which use packet-switched forwarding. This principle differs from the circuit-switched technology of traditional telephone networks, where a channel is set up between the communicating endpoints through the telecommunications infrastructure. Table 2-1 contrasts traditional telephony with VoIP.

Table 2-1   *VoIP and Traditional Telephony Comparison*

	Traditional Telephony	**VoIP**
Transmission technology	Circuit-switched	Packet-switched
Basic signaling functions	Supervisory, address, informational	Supervisory, address, informational
Signaling protocols and methods	Digital: SS7, ISDN, QSIG Analog: loop-start, ground-start, immediate-start, wink-start, delay-start, DTMF, pulse	H.323, SIP, MGCP, SCCP
Transmission method	Dedicated circuit	Bundle of UDP flows

Before a call is established, signaling methods are used to detect an off-hook state, collect a called number, and inform the network about the call. The signaling protocols fulfill similar functions, and must meet additional requirements imposed by the IP-based transmission method—for example, negotiation of VoIP transmission parameters such as codecs.

As introduced in Chapter 1, "Introducing Voice Gateways," and described in more detail later in this chapter, the four VoIP signaling protocols are H.323, Session Initiation Protocol (SIP), Media Gateway Control Protocol (MGCP), and Skinny Client Control Protocol (SCCP). Each protocol is best suited for specific scenarios.

The media is transported over IP networks in Real-time Transport Protocol (RTP) packets that are encapsulated in User Datagram Protocol (UDP) flows. An RTP flow is unidirectional. Therefore, a voice call typically includes two unidirectional RTP flows.

Major Stages of Voice Processing in VoIP

For transmission over an IP network, the voice wavelength must be sampled, quantized, encoded, optionally compressed, and then encapsulated in a VoIP packet, as illustrated in Figure 2-1.

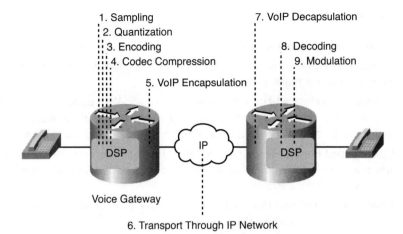

Figure 2-1   *VoIP Call-Processing Stages*

The first four steps are performed by a digital signal processor (DSP) in the originating gateway and are detailed in the following section. The VoIP packets are then delivered to the destination gateway, and the voice information is retrieved from the packet. Finally, a DSP on the terminating gateway decodes the payload and modulates the wavelength to reverse the process performed on the originating gateway.

VoIP Components

Figure 2-2 depicts the basic components of a packet voice network.

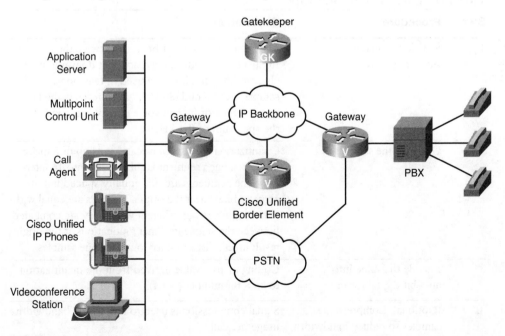

Figure 2-2   *VoIP Components*

The components shown are as follows:

- **Cisco Unified IP Phones:** Provides an IP endpoint for voice communication.

- **Gatekeeper:** Provides call admission control (CAC), bandwidth control and management, and address translation.

- **Gateway:** Provides translation between VoIP and non-VoIP networks such as a public switched telephone network (PSTN). Gateways also provide physical access for local analog and digital voice devices such as telephones, fax machines, key sets, and PBXs.

- **Cisco Unified Border Element (Cisco UBE):** Interconnects two VoIP networks. It acts as a proxy between signaling protocols and can be configured to provide proxy services to the media stream.

- **Multipoint control unit (MCU):** Provides real-time connectivity for participants in multiple locations to attend the same videoconference or meeting.

- **Call agent:** Provides call control for Cisco Unified IP Phones, CAC, bandwidth control and management, and address translation.

- **Application servers:** Provide services such as voice-mail, unified messaging, interactive voice response (IVR), presence information, multimedia conferencing, and others.

- **Videoconference station:** Provides access for end-user participation in videoconferencing. The videoconference station contains a video capture device for video input and a microphone for audio input. The user can view video streams and hear the audio that originates at a remote user station.

Table 2-2 describes the steps to convert voice information to VoIP.

Table 2-2 *Converting Voice to VoIP*

Step	Procedure	Description
1.	Sample the analog signal regularly.	The sampling rate must be at least twice the highest frequency to produce playback that does not appear choppy. The sampling rate used in telephony is 8000 samples per second (8 kHz), which reflects the fact that the bulk of human voice energy is carried in the spectrum of 0-4 kHz.
2.	Quantize the sample.	Quantization consists of a scale made up of 8 major segments. Each segment is subdivided into 16 intervals. The segments are not equally spaced but are actually finest near the origin. Intervals are equal within the segments but different when they are compared between the segments. Finer graduations at the origin result in less distortion for lower volume samples.
3.	Encode the value into an 8-bit digital form.	Coding maps a value derived from the quantization to an 8-bit number (octet).
4.	(Optional) Compress the samples to reduce bandwidth.	Signal compression is used to reduce the bandwidth usage per call.

The first three steps describe the pulse-code modulation (PCM) process, which corresponds to the G.711 codec. Step 4 explains compression that is performed by low-bandwidth codecs, such as G.729, G.728, G.726, or Internet Low Bitrate Codec (iLBC).

Sampling

Sampling, as illustrated in Figure 2-3, is a process that takes readings of the waveform amplitude at regular intervals, by a process called *pulse-amplitude modulation* (PAM). The output is a series of pulses that approximates the analog waveform. For this output to have an acceptable level of quality for the signal to be reconstructed, the sampling rate must be rapid enough.

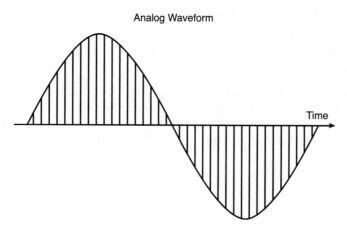

Figure 2-3 *Sampling*

Harry Nyquist developed a mathematical proof about the rate at which a waveform can be sampled and the information that can be recovered from those samples. The Nyquist theorem states that when a signal is instantaneously sampled at the transmitter in regular intervals and has a rate of at least twice the highest channel frequency, the samples will contain sufficient information to allow an accurate reconstruction of the signal at the receiver.

Although the human ear can sense sounds from 20 to 20,000 Hz, speech encompasses sounds from about 200 to 9000 Hz. The telephone channel was designed to operate at frequencies of 300 to 4000 Hz. This economical range offers enough fidelity for voice communications, although higher frequency samples are not transmitted. The removal of higher frequencies leads to issues with sounds such as "s" or "th." The voice frequency of 4000 Hz requires 8000 samples per second; that is, one sample every 125 microseconds.

Quantization

Quantization divides the range of amplitude values that are present in an analog signal sample into a set of discrete steps that are closest in value to the original analog signal. Each step is assigned a unique digital codeword. Quantization matches a PAM signal to a segmented scale. The scale measures the amplitude (height) of the PAM signal and assigns an integer number to define that amplitude.

Figure 2-4 shows quantization in action. In the example, the x-axis represents time, and the y-axis represents the voltage value. The output is a series of pulses that approximates the analog waveform.

The voltage range is divided into 16 segments (0 to 7 positive, and 0 to 7 negative). Starting with segment 0, each segment has less-granular intervals than the previous segment, which reduces the signal-to-noise ratio (SNR) and makes the segment uniform. This segmentation also corresponds closely to the logarithmic behavior of the human ear.

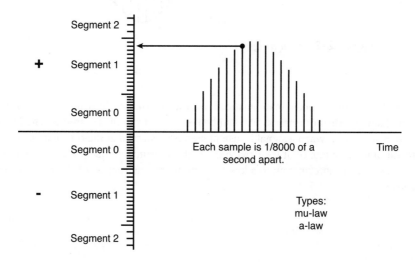

Figure 2-4   *Quantization*

The two principal schemes for generating these samples in electronic communication are *a-law* and *mu-law*. a-law and mu-law are audio compression schemes, defined by ITU-T G.711, that compress 16-bit linear PCM data down to 8 bits of logarithmic data. The a-law standard is primarily used in Europe and the rest of the world, while mu-law is used in North America and Japan.

The similarities between mu-law and a-law include the following:

- Both are linear approximations of the logarithmic input/output relationship.

- Both are implemented using 8-bit codewords (256 levels, one for each quantization interval). Eight-bit codewords allow for a bit rate of 64 kbps. This is calculated by multiplying the sampling rate (twice the input frequency) by the size of the codeword (2 * 4 kHz * 8 bits = 64 kbps).

- Both break a dynamic range into a total of 16 segments:

  - Eight positive and eight negative segments.

  - Each segment is twice the length of the preceding one.

  - Uniform quantization is used within each segment.

- Both use a similar approach to coding the 8-bit word:

  - First bit (MSB) identifies polarity.

  - Bits two, three, and four identify segment.

  - Final four bits quantize the segment.

The differences between mu-law and a-law include the following:

- Different linear approximations lead to different lengths and slopes.

- The numerical assignment of the bit positions in the 8-bit codeword to segments and the quantization levels within segments are different.

- a-law provides a greater dynamic range than mu-law.

- mu-law provides better signal-distortion performance for low-volume signals than a-law.

- a-law requires 13 bits for a uniform PCM equivalent, while mu-law requires 14 bits for a uniform PCM equivalent.

- An international connection must use a-law, and mu-law to a-law conversion is the responsibility of the mu-law country.

Coding

Coding converts an integer base-10 number to a binary number. The output of coding is a binary expression in which each bit is either a 1 (pulse) or a 0 (no pulse). After PAM samples an input analog voice signal, the next step is to encode these samples in preparation for transmission over a telephony network. This process is called *pulse-code modulation* (PCM).

The PCM process, as shown in Figure 2-5, mathematically converts the value obtained from PAM sampling to another binary value within the range –127 to +127. It is at this stage that companding, the process of first compressing an analog signal at the source and then expanding this signal back to its original size when it reaches its destination, is applied. This entire process is generally referred to as PCM coding. A DSP, which is a specialized chip, quickly performs the PCM process.

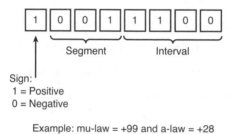

Example: mu-law = +99 and a-law = +28

Figure 2-5 *Coding*

In the United States, Canada, and Japan, mu-law is used. The rest of the world uses a-law. Both mu-law and a-law companding produces PCM values in the range of –127 to +127. Both mu-law and a-law represent a positive sign value with a value of 1, and a negative sign value with a value of 0. This representation is a departure from the "normal" computational use where positive is usually represented by 0.

Of the two methods, a-law appears to be the more logical method, because a PCM value of +127 is represented as 11111111; in other words, a positive sign value (the first bit) followed by a binary value of 127 composed of the segment and interval bits. Similarly, –32 is represented as 00100000. Mu-law operates a bit differently by logically inverting the segment and interval bits. Using mu-law companding, the value of +127 becomes 10000000; in other words, a positive sign value (the first bit) followed by the bit inverse of +127.

Note   When a mu-law country connects with an a-law country, the mu-law end must convert its signal.

Uncompressed digital speech signals are sampled at a rate of 8000 samples per second, with each sample consisting of 8 bits. This corresponds to 64 kbps per call. Multiple algorithms have been developed to allow voice transmission at lower bandwidth consumption. The most common coder-decoder (codec) algorithms are presented in Table 2-3 together with their bandwidth.

Table 2-3 *Compression*

Codec	Bandwidth (kbps)
G.711	64
G.726r32	32
G.726r24	24
G.726r16	16
G.728	16
iLBC (Internet Low Bitrate Codec)	15.2, 13.3
GSM Full Rate (GSM-FR)	13
G.729 (A/B/AB)	8
G.723r63	6.3
G.723r53	5.3

VoIP Packetization

After the voice wavelength is digitized, the DSP collects the digitized data for an amount of time until there is enough data to fill the payload of a single packet.

The example in Figure 2-6 shows how PCM samples are packaged into the payload of a single packet using the G.711 codec. With G.711, either 20 ms or 30 ms worth of voice wavelength is transmitted in a single packet.

20 ms worth of voice wavelength corresponds to 160 samples (at 8000 samples per second, 10 ms would correspond to 80 samples, and 20 ms would be 160 samples). With 20 ms worth of voice wavelength, 50 VoIP packets are transmitted in each direction in 1 second (1 second consists of 50 20-ms intervals: 1 sec / 20 ms = 50).

Similarly, 30 ms worth of voice wavelength corresponds to 240 samples (at 8000 samples per second, 10 ms would equal 80 samples, and 30 ms would be 240 samples). With 30 ms worth of voice, approximately 33 VoIP packets are transmitted in each direction in 1 second (1 second consists of 33.[3] 30-ms intervals: 1 sec / 30 ms = 33.[3]).

Packetization Rate

The length of voice information carried in a single packet affects the payload size, which is referred to in Table 2-4 as the size of collected G.711 samples for a single packet. Before the payloads are transmitted over the IP network, they must be encapsulated in a packet that introduces an additional overhead caused by Open Systems Interconnection (OSI) Layers 3 and above. These headers consume additional bandwidth, in addition to the 64 kbps required for raw voice transmission. The bandwidth overhead depends on packet rate, as shown in Table 2-4.

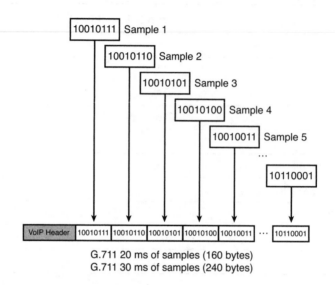

G.711 20 ms of samples (160 bytes)
G.711 30 ms of samples (240 bytes)

Figure 2-6   *PCM (G.711)*

Table 2-4   *Packetization Rate*

	20 ms Voice Length in a Packet	30 ms Voice Length in a Packet	40 ms Voice Length in a Packet	60 ms Voice Length in a Packet	80 ms Voice Length in a Packet
Packetization rate	50 pps	33.3 pps	25 pps	16.7 pps	12.5 pps
Size of collected G.711 samples for a single packet	160 bytes	240 bytes	320 bytes	480 bytes	640 bytes
Uncompressed raw voice bandwidth	64 kbps	64 kbps	64 kbps	64 kbps	64 kbps
Layer 3+ uncompressed VoIP bandwidth	80 kbps	74.7 kbps	72 kbps	69.3 kbps	68 kbps

Codec Operations

Figure 2-7 illustrates the operation of an optional codec algorithm. G.729 is presented in this example. The DSP samples, quantizes, and encodes the analog waveform at the input. The DSP generates one codeword for each 10 ms worth of voice. The codewords are encapsulated in the payload of VoIP packets. A single VoIP packet carries by default 20 ms worth of audio, encapsulating two G.729 codewords in one payload. Another supported packetization rate is 30 ms, in which the VoIP packets are generated every 30 ms and carry three G.729 codewords in each packet.

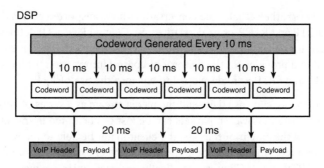

Figure 2-7   *Codec Operations (G.729)*

Packetization and Compression Example

Table 2-5 illustrates the common operation modes of the G.729 codec: 50-pps rate with 20 ms worth of voice wavelength in a single packet, and 33.3-pps rate with 30 ms worth of voice wavelength in a single packet. After compression, the payload size is 20 bytes or 30 bytes, respectively. In both modes, the compressed raw voice bandwidth is 8 kbps, but the Layer 3+ bandwidth depends on the packetization rate, and is 24 kbps and 18.7 kbps, respectively.

Table 2-5   *Example: Packetization Rate*

	20 ms Voice Length in a Packet	30 ms Voice Length in a Packet
Packetization rate	50 pps	33.3 pps
Size of collected, compressed G.729 samples for a single packet	20 bytes	30 bytes
Compressed raw voice bandwidth	8 kbps	8 kbps
Layer 3+ G.729 VoIP bandwidth	24 kbps	18.7 kbps

The call bandwidth can be computed using the following formula:

Bandwidth per Call = (Voice Payload + Layer 3 Overhead + Layer 2 Overhead) * Packets per Second * 8 bits/Byte

The examples shown in Table 2-5 do not consider Layer 2 overhead, which varies based on the packet technology in use.

VoIP Media Transmission

In a VoIP network, the actual voice conversations are transported across the transmission media using RTP and RTCP, or its derivatives, SRTP and cRTP. RTP defines a standardized packet format for delivering audio and video over the Internet. RTCP is a companion protocol to RTP, and provides for the delivery of control information for individual RTP streams. cRTP and SRTP were developed to enhance the use of RTP.

Datagram protocols, such as UDP, send the media stream as a series of small packets. This is simple and efficient; however, packets can be lost or corrupted in transit. Depending on the protocol and the extent of the loss, the client might be able to recover the data with error correction techniques, might interpolate over the missing data, or might suffer a data dropout. RTP and RTCP were specifically designed to stream media over networks. They are both built on top of UDP.

RTP is streamed between two VoIP endpoints, such as H.323 gateways, as illustrated in Figure 2-8.

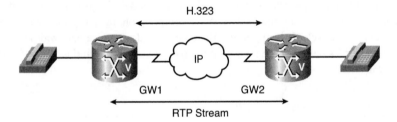

Figure 2-8 *RTP Stream*

The following lists the primary protocols involved in voice media transmission:

■ **Real-time Transport Protocol (RTP):** Delivers the actual audio and video streams over networks

■ **Real-time Transport Control Protocol (RTCP):** Provides out-of-band control information for an RTP flow

■ **Compressed RTP (cRTP):** Compresses IP/UDP/RTP headers on low-speed serial links

■ **Secure RTP (SRTP):** Provides encryption, message authentication and integrity, and replay protection to RTP

The next sections describe each protocol in greater detail.

Real-Time Transport Protocol

RTP, described in RFC 3550, defines a standardized packet format for delivering audio and video over an IP network.

RTP typically runs on top of UDP so that it can use the multiplexing and checksum services of that protocol. RTP applications are typically sensitive to delays; so, UDP is a better choice than the more complex TCP. RTP does not have a standard port on which it communicates. The only standard that it obeys is that UDP communications are done via an even port, and the next higher odd port is used for RTCP communications. Although there are no standards assigned, RTP commonly uses ports 16384 to 32767. The fact that RTP uses a dynamic port range makes it difficult for it to traverse firewalls.

The functions of RTP include the following:

- **Payload type identification**, which identifies the type of payload carried in the packet, such as codec, or media format. This identifier allows the changing of codecs and data formats while the flow is active, as is the case with fax and modem pass-through.

- **Sequence numbering**, which monitors the sequence of arriving packets and is primarily used to detect packet loss. RTP does not request retransmission if a packet is lost.

- **Time stamping**, which is necessary to place the arriving packets in the correct timing order. The dejitter buffer evaluates this parameter when compensating the variable path delay.

RTP supports both unicast and multicast transmission. In addition to the roles of sender and receiver, RTP also defines the roles of translator and mixer to support the multicast requirements. Figure 2-9 depicts the structure of an RTP header.

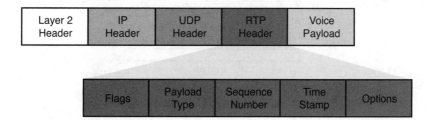

Figure 2-9   *RTP Header*

Real-Time Transport Control Protocol

RTCP, defined in RFC 3550, is a sister protocol of RTP. RTCP provides out-of-band control information for an RTP flow. Although it is used periodically to transmit control packets to participants in a streaming multimedia session, the primary function of RTCP is to provide feedback on the quality of service (QoS) being provided by RTP.

RTCP gathers statistics on a media connection, such as bytes sent, packets sent, lost packets, jitter, feedback, and round-trip delay. Applications use this information to adjust the transmission parameters.

There are several types of RTCP packets: sender report packet, receiver report packet, source description RTCP packet, goodbye RTCP packet, and application-specific RTCP packet.

RTCP provides the following feedback on current network conditions:

■   RTCP provides a mechanism for hosts involved in an RTP session to exchange information about monitoring and controlling the session. RTCP monitors the quality of elements such as packet count, packet loss, delay, and interarrival jitter. RTCP transmits packets as a percentage of session bandwidth, but at a specific rate of at least every 5 seconds.

■   The RTP standard states that the Network Time Protocol (NTP) time stamp is based on synchronized clocks. The corresponding RTP time stamp is randomly generated and based on data packet sampling. Both NTP information and RTP information are included in RTCP packets by the sender of the data.

RTCP provides a separate flow from RTP for transport used by UDP, as shown in Figure 2-10. When a voice stream is assigned UDP port numbers, RTP is typically assigned an even-numbered port and RTCP is assigned the next odd-numbered port. Each voice call has four ports assigned: RTP with RTCP in the transmit direction and RTP with RTCP in the receive direction.

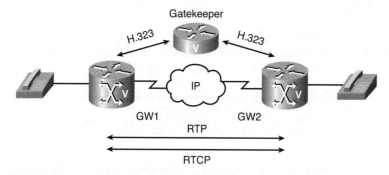

Figure 2-10   *RCTP Flow*

Compressed RTP

The overhead introduced by packet headers is often considerably larger than the voice payload. The overhead consists of an IP (20 octets), UDP (8 octets), and RTP header (12 octets) and amounts to 40 bytes.

cRTP, specified in RFCs 2508, 2509, and 3545, was developed to decrease the size of the IP, UDP, and RTP headers. cRTP maps the IP/UDP/RTP header to 2 bytes (without checksum) or 4 bytes (with checksum).

RTP header compression is supported on point-to-point interfaces, such as serial lines using Frame Relay, High-Level Data Link Control (HDLC), or PPP encapsulation. It is a link-local mechanism that must be enabled on both sides of the link.

cRTP is recommended for slow-speed links less than or equal to 768 kbps, as emphasized in Figure 2-11. On faster links, the bandwidth savings might be offset by an increase in CPU utilization on the router.

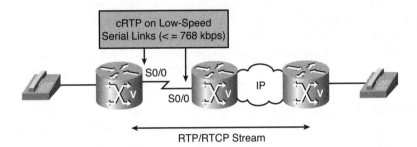

Figure 2-11 *cRTP Flow*

During compression of an RTP stream, a session context is defined. For each context, the session state is established and shared between the compressor and the decompressor. The context state consists of the complete IP/UDP/RTP headers, a few first-order differential values, a link sequence number, a generation number, and a delta coding table. The context state must be synchronized between compressor and decompressor for successful decompression to take place.

After the context state is established, compressed packets might be sent. The compressed header carries pointers to the respective context entities and the difference from the previous packet (delta).

Secure RTP

SRTP, defined in RFC 3711, is designed to provide encryption, message authentication and integrity, and replay protection to the RTP data in both unicast and multicast applications. Figure 2-12 shows an SRTP flow between two voice gateways.

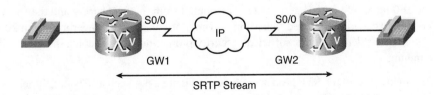

Figure 2-12 *SRTP Flow*

SRTP also has a sister protocol, called Secure RTCP (SRTCP). SRTCP provides the same security-related features to RTCP as those provided by SRTP to RTP. SRTP can be used in conjunction with compressed RTP.

SRTP's security features include encryption, authentication and integrity, and replay protection, as discussed in the following sections.

Encryption

Encryption is the conversion of data into a form, called a *ciphertext*, which cannot be understood by unauthorized people. This feature is also referred to as privacy. It ensures that the conversation content is kept private among the endpoints. If an attacker intercepts the packets, the attacker will not be able to decipher them. Decryption is the process of converting encrypted data back into its original form, so that it can be understood. SRTP uses Advanced Encryption Standard (AES).

Authentication and Integrity

Encryption algorithms do not secure message integrity themselves, allowing the attacker to forge data. SRTP provides the means to ensure packet integrity.

Hashed Message Authentication Code-Secure Hash Algorithm 1 (HMAC-SHA-1) authenticates the message and protects its integrity. Authentication provides the assurance that the VoIP stream is coming from the authentic endpoint, and not someone impersonating the endpoint. This method produces a 160-bit result, which is then truncated to 80 bits to become the authentication tag that is then appended to the packet. The HMAC is calculated over the packet payload and material from the packet header, including the packet sequence number. If an attacker tampers with the packets, the recipients will detect the tampering by verifying the HMAC authenticator.

Replay Protection

SRTP uses sequencing to protect against replay attacks. A replay attack is a form of cryptographic attack, in which the hacker sends outdated information to force some action on the recipient end. To prevent such attacks, the receiver maintains the indices of previously received messages, comparing them with the index of each newly received message and admitting the new message only if it has not been played before. This function relies on the integrity protection that prevents spoofing of message indices.

Secure RTP Packet Format

SRTP differs from RTP only in the encrypted voice payload and the 32-bit SHA-1 authentication tag that is added to the packet. The authentication tag holds the first 32 bits of the 160-bit SHA-1 hash digest that was computed from the RTP header and the encrypted voice payload ("truncated fingerprint"). The shortening of the fingerprint from 20 to 4 bytes is considered to offer sufficient integrity protection while keeping the overhead at a minimum.

The fields used in the RTP header, as shown in Figure 2-13, such as Payload Type, Sequence Number, Time Stamp, and the remaining flags are carried in SRTP packets in cleartext, allowing the same packet processing as with RTP.

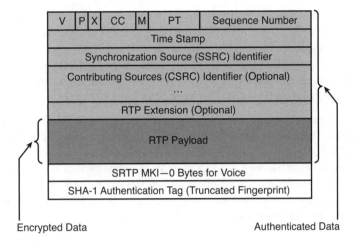

Figure 2-13 *SRTP Packet Format*

The RTP packet header and the RTP payload (encrypted voice) are authenticated. RTP encryption is performed before RTP authentication.

VoIP Media Considerations

VoIP consists of two key components: signaling and media, as depicted in Figure 2-14. The signaling protocols use static port numbers. The default values are H.323 (TCP/UDP port 1720), SIP (TCP/UDP port 5060), MGCP (UDP/2427), SCCP (TCP/2000). Static ports allow the firewalls to easily identify the signaling traffic and either allow or block it, depending on the security policy.

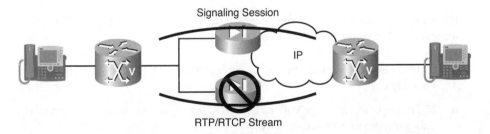

Figure 2-14 *VoIP Signaling and Media Flows*

RTP and RTCP streams use dynamically negotiated UDP port numbers. Static access control list (ACL) filters are not able to selectively allow or block certain media streams.

Stateful firewalls, such as the Cisco Adaptive Security Appliance (ASA), track the RTP port negotiation managed by the signaling protocol and selectively allow the negotiated UDP ports if the preceding signaling session was permitted by the firewall policy. All other ports remain blocked, and only the currently negotiated ports are passed through. This technique works well if the RTP and RTCP sessions flow over the same firewall as the signaling messages. If the paths diverge, the RTP and RTCP streams will be dropped by a firewall, because that firewall has not processed the signaling messages and therefore has not opened the UDP ports. To avoid such problems, the network design should ensure that the media streams take the same path as the signaling.

In intersite communications, the enterprise often secures the traffic exchanged between the locations. The most common VPN technology used in such cases is IP Security (IPsec), with Encapsulating Security Payload (ESP) as the encryption and authentication protocol, as shown in Figure 2-15. ESP provides the same type of security as SRTP. Protecting the voice media using both IPsec and SRTP at the same time is superfluous, because it increases the overhead and consumes computational resources without adding any significant security advantage.

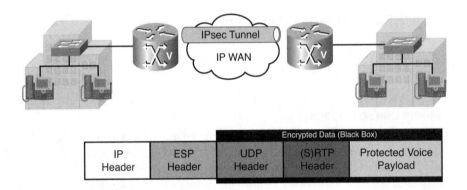

Figure 2-15   *Using IPsec to Protect Voice*

If both security methods (SRTP and IPsec) are deployed in the network, SRTP is typically recommended to secure calls, for these reasons:

■   SRTP creates less overhead than IPsec, thus consuming less bandwidth and improving delay.

■   SRTP can protect all other VoIP calls, such as from roaming users, allowing a more uniform approach to voice security.

Voice Activity Detection

Voice Activity Detection (VAD) is a technology that builds on the nature of human conversation, where one person speaks while others listen. This typical unidirectional conversation is illustrated in Figure 2-16.

VAD classifies VoIP packets into three classes: speech, silence, and unknown. With VAD enabled, speech and unknown packets are sent over the network and silence packets are discarded.

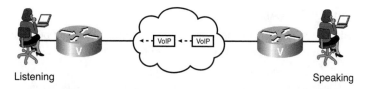

Figure 2-16   *Unidirectional Nature of Human Conversation*

VAD provides a maximum of 35 percent bandwidth savings based on an average volume of more than 24 calls. Bandwidth savings of 35 percent is a subjective figure and does not take into account loud background sounds, differences in languages, and other factors. The savings will vary on every individual voice call or on any specific point measurement.

> **Note**   For the purposes of network design and bandwidth engineering, VAD should not be taken into account, especially on links that will simultaneously carry fewer than 24 voice calls.

Various features, such as music on hold (MOH) and fax, render VAD ineffective. When a network is engineered for the full voice call bandwidth, all savings provided by VAD are available to data applications.

The degradation in voice quality might be noticeable when the initial sounds are chopped off after a period of silence. In such cases, the disabling of VAD usually solves the problem.

Bandwidth Savings

Table 2-6 indicates the bandwidth savings achieved by VAD when transmitting VoIP packets over Frame Relay links. The table compares the raw codec bandwidth (codec speed) with the effective bandwidths, taking into account the entire overhead (Layer 2 and above), with and without VAD.

Table 2-6   *Average Bandwidth Savings for VAD*

Codec	Codec Speed	Sample Size	Frame Relay without VAD	Frame Relay with VAD
G.711	64 kbps	240 bytes	76.3 kbps	49.6 kbps
G.711	64 kbps	160 bytes	82.4 kbps	53.6 kbps
iLBC	13.3 kbps	30 bytes	26.1 kbps	17.0 kbps
iLBC	15.2 kbps	20 bytes	34.4 kbps	22.4 kbps
G.729	8 kbps	30 bytes	20.3 kbps	13.2 kbps
G.729	8 kbps	20 bytes	26.4 kbps	17.2 kbps

Voice Port Settings for VAD

VAD is enabled by default if the negotiated codec supports it. It can be disabled in the dial-peer configuration mode. VAD operation is illustrated in Figure 2-17.

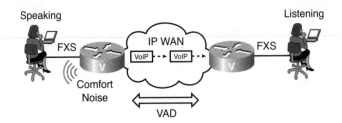

Figure 2-17   *VAD Operation*

Two VAD-related parameters are configured on voice ports: comfort noise generation (CNG) and music threshold.

CNG creates subtle background noise to fill silent gaps during the conversation. If comfort noise is not generated, the resulting silence can fool the caller into thinking the call is disconnected instead of being merely idle. CNG provides locally generated white noise to give the speaker the impression of background noise coming from the other end.

The music threshold specifies the minimal decibel level of music played when calls are put on hold. The music threshold might be tuned to ensure that MOH is correctly interpreted as media and not classified as silence packets.

Voice Signaling Protocols: H.323

H.323 gateways are among the most common Cisco IOS voice gateways within Cisco Unified Communications Manager environments. H.323 gateways are the endpoints on a LAN that provide real-time, two-way communications between H.323 terminals on the LAN and other ITU-T terminals on the network. H.323 gateways can also communicate with other H.323 gateways. Gateways enable H.323 terminals to communicate with terminals that are not H.323 terminals by converting protocols. Gateways are the point where a circuit-switched call is encoded and repackaged into IP packets. Because gateways function as H.323 endpoints, they provide admission control, address lookup and translation, and accounting services.

H.323 Architecture

H.323 is a suite of protocols that ITU defines for multimedia conferences over LANs. It was developed based on ISDN Q.931 as a protocol to provide IP networks with traditional telephony functionality. H.323 is a mature, vendor-neutral protocol that is currently the most widely deployed standards-based voice and videoconferencing standard for packet-switched networks.

H.323 is a peer-to-peer protocol in which each gateway plays an equal part in the signaling process and must maintain its own dial plan to make call forwarding decisions. This characteristic differentiates H.323 from server-client signaling protocols such as MGCP, where the gateway registers on the call agent to receive further instructions. H.323 is supported on all Cisco voice gateways and all Cisco Unified Communications call control platforms.

H.323 describes an infrastructure of terminals, common control components, services, and protocols that is used for multimedia (voice, video, and data) communications.

An H.323 gateway is an optional type of endpoint that provides interoperability between H.323 endpoints and endpoints that are located on a Switched Circuit Network (SCN), such as the PSTN or an enterprise voice network. Ideally, the gateway is transparent to both the H.323 endpoint and the SCN-based endpoint.

H.323 Advantages

There are several advantages to using H.323 gateways as voice gateways:

- **Self-sufficient dial plan per gateway:** It enables processing the call routing locally without relying on a call agent, as is the case with MGCP.

- **Call-routing configuration can be more specific than on Cisco Unified Communications Manager:** Cisco IOS gateways enable translating and matching to the called number and the calling number, which can improve call routing. Cisco Unified Communications Manager matches only the called number. For example, this difference enables call routing from specific callers to a special destination.

- **There is no need for extra call routing configurations that are related to Cisco Unified Survivable Remote Site Telephony (SRST):** Because the call routing configuration is done directly on the gateway, no additional dial plan is required for SRST.

- **Translations can be defined per gateway:** This supports regional requirements such as calling party transformations or special number formats. All incoming and outgoing calls can be translated directly on the gateway to meet the internally used number format.

- **There is no dependency on the Cisco Unified Communications Manager:** Because the configuration is performed on the gateway and the H.323 umbrella is a peer-to-peer protocol, there is no dependence on software versions and feature sets of other signaling components.

- **More voice interface types are supported:** Because the Cisco Unified Communications Manager does not need to control the interface cards within H.323 environments, more interface cards are supported when you use H.323 rather than MGCP.

- **ISDN Nonfacility Associated Signaling (NFAS) is supported:** The H.323 gateway signaling protocol supports NFAS, which MGCP does not.

■ **Enhanced fax support:** Fax support is better on H.323 gateways than on MGCP gateways because H.323 supports T.37 and T.38. An H.323 gateway can route a fax direct inward dialing (DID) number directly to a Foreign Exchange Station (FXS) port on the gateway.

■ **Enhanced call preservation:** Call preservation is useful when a gateway and its communicating peer (typically a Cisco Unified IP Phone) are collocated while the call is signaled over a Cisco Unified Communications Manager resident in another site. When the WAN connectivity fails, the media connection between the gateway and the phone will remain active because of the call preservation enhancements.

H.323 Network Components

Figure 2-18 shows some typical terminal devices in an H.323 network.

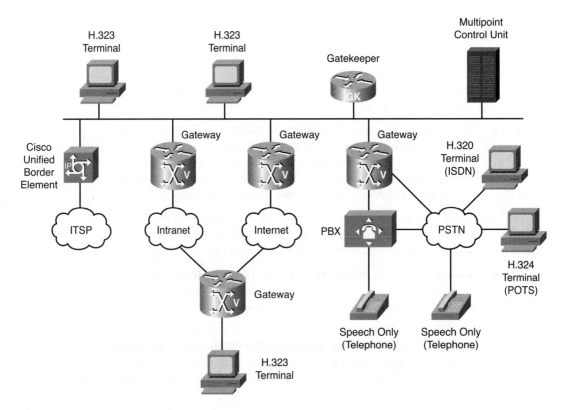

Figure 2-18   *H.323 Devices*

An H.323 network includes the following components:

■ Terminals: H.320 (ISDN), H.323, H.324 (plain old telephone service [POTS])

■ Gateways

■ Gatekeepers

- Multipoint control units

- Cisco Unified Border Element (covered in Chapter 6, "Using Gatekeepers and Cisco Unified Border Elements")

H.323 Terminals

An H.323 terminal is an endpoint that provides real-time voice (and optionally, video and data) communications with another endpoint, such as an H.323 terminal or MCU. The communications consist of control, indications, audio, moving color video pictures, or data between the two terminals. A terminal might provide the following:

- Audio only

- Audio and data

- Audio and video

- Audio, data, and video

The terminal can be a computer-based videoconferencing system or other device.

An H.323 terminal must be capable of transmitting and receiving voice that is encoded with G.711 (a-law and mu-law), and might support other encoded voice formats, such as G.729 and G.723.1.

H.323 Gateways

Figure 2-19 shows a gateway connecting an H.323 device, and a terminal that is not an H.323 terminal, such as an analog telephone. The H.323 device can be an H.323 terminal, MCU, gatekeeper, or another H.323 gateway.

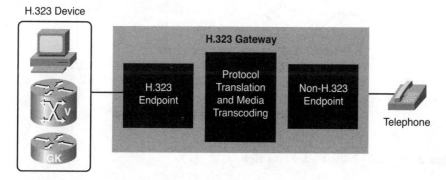

Figure 2-19 *H.323 Gateways*

Gateways allow H.323 devices to communicate with devices that are running other protocols. They provide protocol conversion between the devices that are running different types of protocols. Ideally, the gateway is transparent to both the H.323 endpoint and the non-H.323 endpoint.

An H.323 gateway performs these services:

■   Translation between audio, video, and data formats

■   Conversion between call setup signals and procedures

■   Conversion between communication control signals and procedures

H.323 Gatekeepers

An H.323 gatekeeper, as depicted in Figure 2-20, provides address translation and access control for H.323 terminals, gateways, and MCUs. Gatekeepers are optional nodes that manage endpoints in an H.323 network. The endpoints communicate with the gatekeeper using the Registration, Admission, and Status (RAS) protocol.

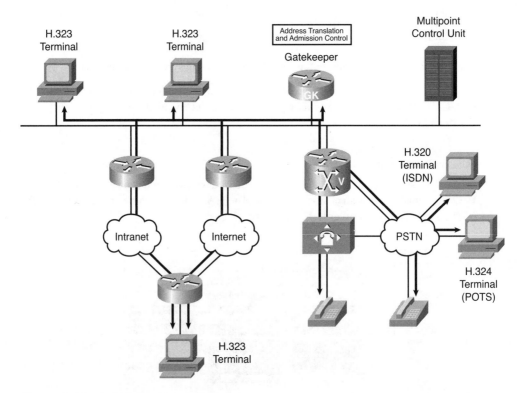

Figure 2-20   *H.323 Gatekeeper Functions*

Endpoints attempt to register with a gatekeeper on startup. When they want to communicate with another endpoint, they request admission to initiate a call. If the gatekeeper decides that the call can proceed, it returns a destination IP address to the originating endpoint. This IP address might not be the actual address of the destination endpoint, but an intermediate address, such as the address of a proxy or a gatekeeper that routes call signaling.

When a gatekeeper is included, it performs these functions:

- **Address translation:** Converts an alias address to an IP address

- **Admission control:** Limits access to network resources based on call bandwidth restrictions

- **Bandwidth control:** Responds to bandwidth requests and modifications

- **Zone management:** Provides services to registered endpoints

The gatekeeper might also perform these functions:

- **Call authorization:** Rejects calls based on authorization failure

- **Bandwidth management:** Limits the number of concurrent accesses to IP internet-work resources (call admission control [CAC])

- **Call management:** Maintains a record of ongoing calls H.323 gatekeepers are covered in more detail in a later module.

H.323 Multipoint Control Units

A multipoint control unit, as shown in Figure 2-21, is an endpoint on the network that allows three or more endpoints to participate in a multipoint conference. It controls and mixes video, audio, and data from endpoints to create a robust multimedia conference. An MCU might also connect two endpoints in a point-to-point conference, which might later develop into a multipoint conference.

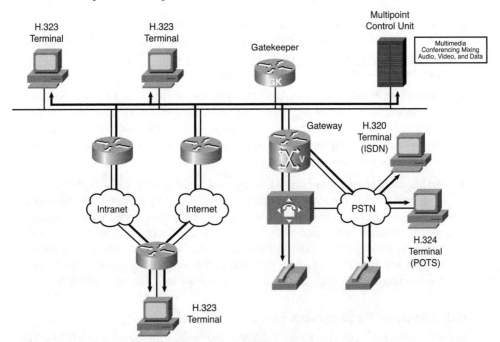

Figure 2-21 *H.323 MCU Functions*

Multipoint conferences rely on a single MCU to coordinate the membership of a conference. Each endpoint has an H.245 control channel connection to the MCU.

Either the MCU or the endpoint initiates the control channel setup. H.323 defines three main types of multipoint conferences: centralized, distributed, and ad hoc, as illustrated in Figure 2-22.

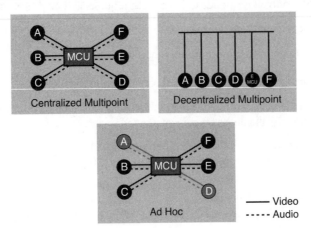

Figure 2-22   *Conference Types*

The three main types of multipoint conferences are

- **Centralized multipoint conference:** The endpoints must have their audio, video, or data channels connected to a multipoint processor (MP). The MP performs mixing and switching of the audio, video, and data, and if the MP supports the capability, each endpoint can operate in a different mode.

- **Distributed multipoint conference:** The endpoints do not have a connection to an MP. Instead, endpoints multicast their audio, video, and data streams to all participants in the conference. Because an MP is not available for switching and mixing, any mixing of the conference streams is a function of the endpoint, and all endpoints must use the same communication parameters.

- **Ad hoc multipoint conference:** An ad hoc multipoint conference is a hybrid situation, in which the audio and video streams are managed by a single MCU, but where one stream relies on multicast (according to the distributed model) and the other uses the MP (as in the centralized model). Any two endpoints in a call can convert their relationship into a point-to-point conference. When the point-to-point conference is created, other endpoints become part of the conference by accepting an invitation from a current participant, or the endpoint can request to join the conference.

H.323 Regional Requirements Example

In the scenario enumerated in Figure 2-23, Maria in Spain with the number 917216111 calls Alice in the United States and Frank in Germany.

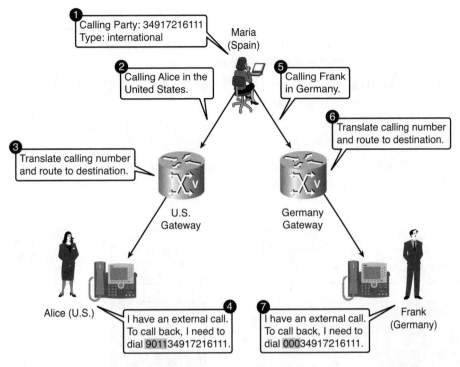

Figure 2-23 *Manipulating Caller ID Information Based on Destination Country*

The procedure enabling Alice and Frank to call back Maria using their missed call list is as follows:

1. When a caller (Maria) in Spain dials an international number, the number sent out as the calling party by the Spanish provider is 34917216111 with "international" as the type of number (TON), because the International Direct Dialing (IDD) prefix for Spain is 34.

2. Maria places a call to Alice in the United States.

3. When the call arrives on the U.S. gateway, the calling party number (34917216111) is translated to meet the common dialing regulations of the United States: 011 is prepended as the international dialing prefix, and a leading 9 is prepended as the access code for external calls from the company network.

4. The missed calls list on Alice's phone displays a call from 901134917216111, and she will be able to reach Maria by using the callback feature.

5. Maria places a call to Frank in Germany. The calling party number for Maria is 34917216111 with the international TON.

6. When the call arrives on the German gateway, the calling party number (34917216111) is translated to meet the dialing regulations of Germany: 00 is prepended as the IDD prefix and a leading 0 is prepended as the access code for external calls from the company network.

7. The missed calls list on Frank's phone displays a call from 00034917216111, and he will be able to reach Maria by using the callback feature.

H.323 Call Flows

Figure 2-24 shows the elements of an H.323 terminal and highlights the protocol infrastructure of an H.323 endpoint.

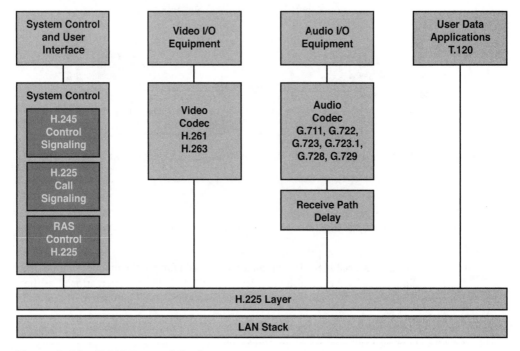

Figure 2-24 *H.323 Protocol Stack*

H.323 is considered an "umbrella protocol" because it defines all aspects of call transmission, from call establishment to capabilities exchange to network resource availability. H.323 defines these protocols:

■ **H.225 for call setup:** The call-signaling function allows an endpoint to create connections with other endpoints. The call-signaling function defines call setup procedures that are based on the ISDN ITU Q.931 protocol, which allows interoperability with the PSTN and Signaling System 7 (SS7).

- **H.225 for Registration, Admission, and Status (RAS) control:** The RAS signaling function uses a separate signaling channel to perform registration, admissions, bandwidth changes, status, and disengage procedures between endpoints and a gatekeeper.

- **H.245 for capabilities exchange:** The H.245 control channel is separate from the call signaling channel and is responsible for these functions:

    - **Logical channel signaling:** Opens and closes the RTP or RTCP media streams.

    - **Capabilities exchange:** Negotiates audio, video, and codec capabilities.

    - **Master or responder determination:** Determines which endpoint is a master and which is a responder. It is used to resolve conflicts during the call.

    - **Mode request:** Requests a change in mode, or capability, of the media stream.

H.323 Slow Start Call Setup

Figure 2-25 shows an H.323 slow start call setup exchange between two gateways.

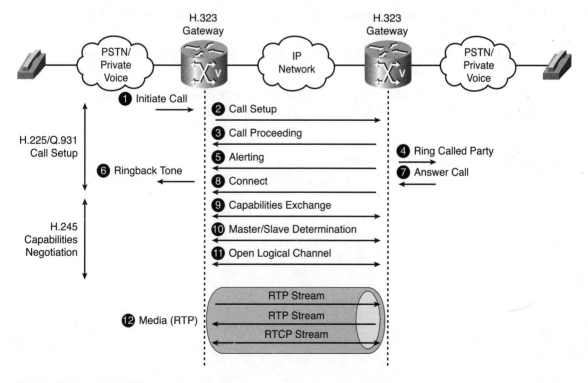

Figure 2-25 *H.323 Slow Start Call Setup*

The same procedure is used when one or both endpoints are H.323 terminals:

1. An endpoint initiates a call.

2. The originating gateway initiates an H.225 session with the terminating gateway on TCP port 1720. The originating gateway determines the terminating gateway address from its local configuration.

3. The terminating gateway acknowledges the Call Setup with the Call Proceeding message.

4. The terminating gateway sends the ringing signal to the recipient telephone.

5. The terminating gateway notifies the originating gateway about the ringing with the Alerting message.

6. The originating gateway signals the ringback tone to the originating endpoint.

7. The recipient takes the phone off-hook.

8. The terminating gateway sends the Connect message to the originating gateway.

9. The endpoints open another channel for the H.245 control function. The H.245 control function negotiates capabilities.

10. The H.245 control function determines the master/slave roles to resolve potential conflicts.

11. The H.245 control function exchanges Open Logical Channel (OLC) messages that describe RTP flows.

12. The gateways start transmitting media over the RTP channels and exchanging call quality statistics using RTCP.

H.323 Slow Start Call Teardown

Figure 2-26 shows an H.323 slow start call termination between two gateways.

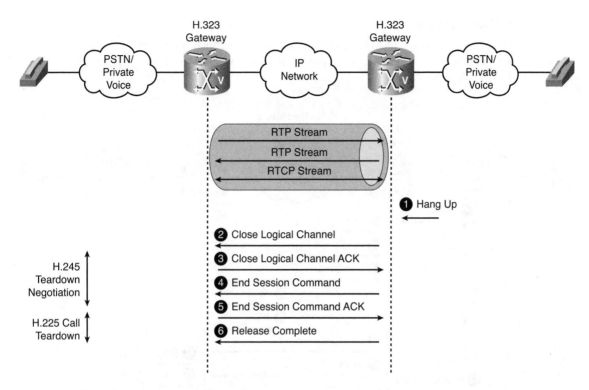

Figure 2-26 *H.323 Slow Start Call Teardown*

The following list describes each step:

1. One communicating party hangs up. This example shows the endpoint behind the terminating gateway, but this procedure would be mirrored if the endpoint behind the originating gateway hung up.

2. The terminating gateway sends the Close Logical Channel message to the originating gateway.

3. The originating gateway acknowledges the message.

4. The terminating gateway sends the End Session Command message to the originating gateway.

5. The originating gateway acknowledges the message.

6. The terminating gateway sends the Release Complete message to the originating gateway.

H.225 RAS Call Setup

Figure 2-27 shows an H.323 basic call setup exchange between two gateways that are registered to a gatekeeper. The same procedure is used when one or both endpoints are H.323 terminals.

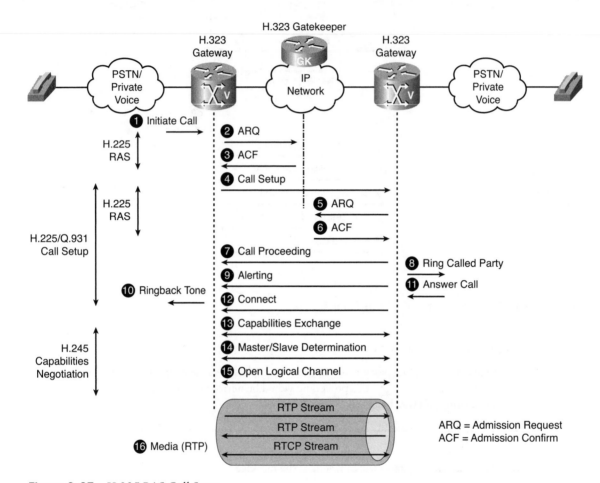

Figure 2-27   *H.225 RAS Call Setup*

The following list describes each step:

1.   An endpoint initiates a call.

2.   The originating gateway initiates an H.225 session with the gatekeeper on registered RAS port TCP/1719. The gatekeeper listens on TCP port 1718 for discovery messages, and the discovery process must be completed before the gateway can send RAS messages to the gatekeeper. The gateway sends the Admission Request (ARQ).

3. The gatekeeper returns the Admission Confirmation (ACF) that includes the IP address of the terminating gateway.

4. The originating gateway initiates an H.225 session with the terminating gateway on port TCP/1720 using the H.225/Q.931 Call Setup message.

5. The terminating gateway sends ARQ to the gatekeeper (TCP/1719) requesting permission to accept the call.

6. The gatekeeper returns ACF to the terminating gateway, granting permission to accept the call.

7. The terminating gateway acknowledges the Call Setup with the Call Proceeding message to the originating gateway.

8. The terminating gateway sends the ringing signal to the recipient telephone.

9. The terminating gateway notifies the originating gateway about the ringing with the Alerting message.

10. The originating gateway signals the ringback tone to the originating endpoint.

11. The recipient takes the phone off-hook.

12. The terminating gateway sends the Connect message to the originating gateway.

13. The endpoints open another channel for the H.245 control function. The H.245 control function first negotiates capabilities.

14. The H.245 control function determines the master/slave roles to resolve potential conflicts.

15. The H.245 control function exchanges Open Logical Channel messages that describe RTP flows.

16. The gateways start transmitting media over the RTP channels and exchanging call quality statistics using RTCP.

H.225 RAS Call Teardown

Figure 2-28 shows an H.323 call termination between two gateways that are registered to a gatekeeper.

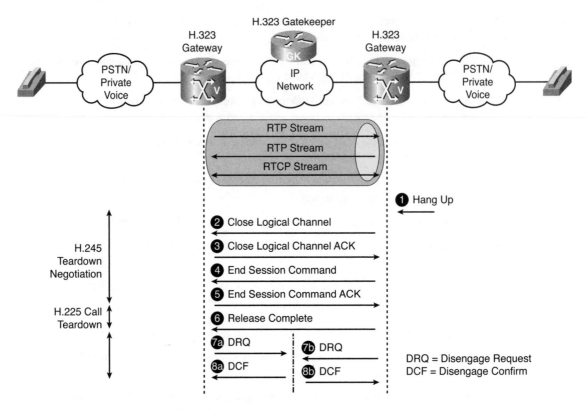

Figure 2-28   *H.225 RAS Call Teardown*

The following list describes each step:

1.   A communicating party hangs up.

2.   The terminating gateway sends the Close Logical Channel message to the originating gateway.

3.   The originating gateway acknowledges the message.

4.   The terminating gateway sends the End Session Command message to the originating gateway.

5.   The originating gateway acknowledges the message.

6.   The terminating gateway sends the Release Complete message to the originating gateway.

7.   Both gateways send Disengage Request (DRQ) messages to the gatekeeper.

8.   The gatekeeper replies to both DRQs with Disengage Confirm (DCF) messages.

Codecs in H.323

The H.245 call control performs three functions when a call is being set up:

- **Capability negotiation:** The most important H.245 function, enables devices to communicate without having prior knowledge of the capabilities of the remote entity. It negotiates audio/video/text codecs, additional parameters such as VAD, and enables real-time data conferencing. The capabilities are offered using Terminal Capabilities Set (TCS) messages, and answered using an Acknowledge, Reject, or Confirm.

- **Master/slave determination:** Occurs after the first TCS message is sent. H.323 attempts to determine which device is the "master" and which is the "slave." The master of a call settles all "disputes" between the two devices. For example, if the slave attempts to open an incompatible media flow, the master takes the action to reject the incompatible flow. The determination principle selects the endpoint with the larger terminal type value as master. There are four terminal types (ordered from the highest to the lowest value): MCU, gatekeeper, gateway, and terminal. If the terminal type values are the same, the master is set to the endpoint with the larger statusDeterminationNumber, which is a random number that is generated by each party, in the range from 0 to $2^{24} - 1$.

- **Logical channel signaling:** Occurs after capabilities are exchanged and master/slave determination is completed. The devices open media flows, referred to as "logical channels." This is done by sending an OLC message that carries the RTP/RTCP ports and receiving an acknowledgment message. Upon receipt of the acknowledgment message, an endpoint might then transmit audio or video to the remote endpoint.

Negotiation in Slow Start Call Setup

Figure 2-29 provides a detailed description of all H.225 and H.245 messages that are exchanged during call setup without a gatekeeper. It shows that the H.245 exchange is triggered by the terminating gateway in Step 9. The capability negotiation and master/slave determination is performed in the first six H.245 messages (Steps 9 through 15). After the capabilities have been confirmed and the master determined, the originating gateway starts the logical channel signaling phase that consists of four messages (Steps 16 through 19). When the OLC messages (with RTP/RTCP port numbers) have been confirmed, the gateways start streaming voice media.

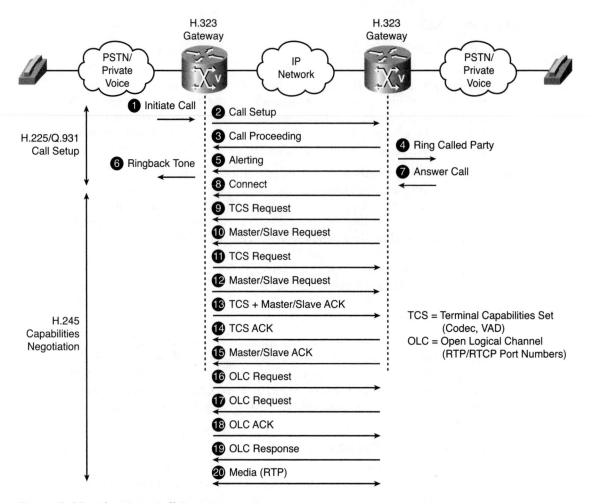

Figure 2-29   *Slow Start Call Setup Negotiation*

H.323 Fast Connect

Figure 2-30 shows an H.323 setup exchange that uses the Fast Connect abbreviated procedure available in H.323 version 2.

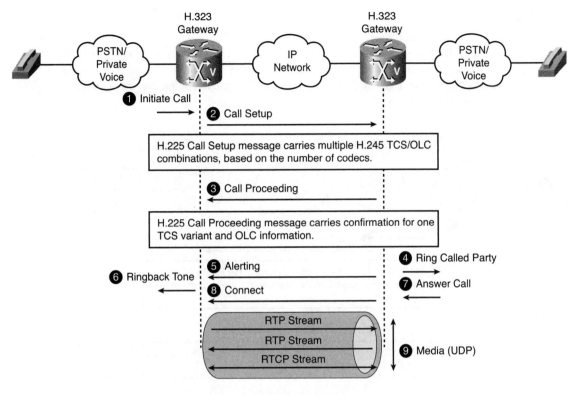

Figure 2-30   *H.225 Fast Connect*

The Fast Connect (Fast Start) procedure reduces the number of round-trip exchanges and achieves the capability exchange and logical channel assignments in one round trip. Fast Connect is widely supported in the industry.

The Fast Connect feature occurs in these steps:

1. An endpoint initiates a call.

2. The originating gateway initiates an H.225 session with the destination gateway on registered TCP port 1720. The Call Setup message is combined with the H.245 control channel and includes a set of capabilities and logical channel descriptions. The number of these proposals depends on the number of codecs that are supported by the originating gateway.

3. The terminating gateway responds using the Call Proceeding message that carries the confirmation for one TCS variant and includes the OLC information about the RTP/RTCP port numbers.

4–9. The remaining H.225 exchange follows the same pattern as in the standard call setup procedure, after which the RTP media and RTCP monitoring channels start.

H.323 Early Media

The Early Media feature, as described by Figure 2-31, builds on the Fast Connect exchange. Both gateways negotiate the capabilities, such as codecs, and the RTP/RTCP port numbers within the first two messages (Call Setup and Call Proceeding). When the Early Media is also negotiated, they open the media channels before any other H.225 messages are exchanged.

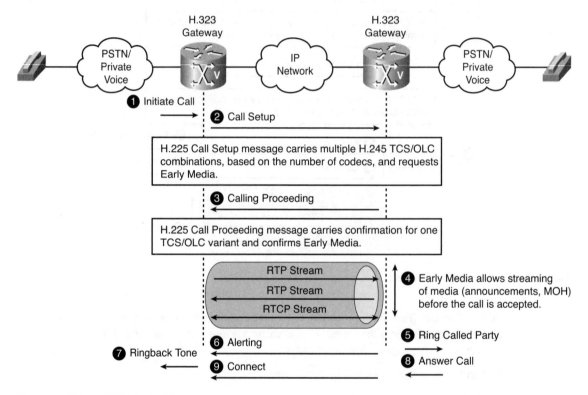

Figure 2-31 *H.323 Early Media*

Early Media allows sending of media from the called party or an application server to the caller, prior to the call being accepted. Early Media is usually sent from the PSTN and carries ringing tones or announcements. If no audio information is available for transmission before the call is accepted, the media streams carry silence.

An example of Early Media is the streaming of announcements that cell phone operators allow their subscribers to customize. When a cell phone owner records their own announcement, it is played whenever the extension is called and the cell phone is ringing. If that call travels over an IP network using H.323 signaling, H.323 Early Media is used.

Configuring H.323 Gateways

A Cisco voice gateway must have at least one VoIP dial peer to act as an H.323 originating gateway. The default protocol of a VoIP dial peer is set to H.323. Therefore, the gateway will use H.323 to signal any calls that are matched by the outbound VoIP dial peer with the default protocol.

A Cisco gateway is, by default, enabled to act as an H.323 terminating gateway. When an H.323 call is received on that gateway, even when no dial peers exist, the gateway tries to use the default dial peer to match the incoming setup request. If VoIP dial peers exist, the gateway tries to find the inbound dial peer using the commands **incoming called-number**, **answer-address**, and **destination-pattern** (in this order).

H.323 service is an integral part of the VoIP service and cannot be controlled separately from the VoIP service. VoIP service is enabled by default and can be disabled by the administrator.

To disable or re-enable the VoIP service, you must enter the voice service voip configuration mode using the **voice service voip** global configuration command. The VoIP services are enabled by default and can be disabled using the **shutdown** command. The **forced** option causes the gateway to immediately terminate all in-progress calls. Disabling the VoIP service affects all VoIP signaling protocols and media transmissions.

The **dial-peer voice** command, as follows, is used to define dial peers, including VoIP dial peers. An H.323 gateway needs VoIP dial peers to make VoIP calls using H.323. The *tag* parameter is a locally significant number.

```
Router(config)#dial-peer voice tag voip
```

H.323 Gateway Configuration Example

Figure 2-32 shows two H.323 gateways that are configured with the dial peers that allow H.323-based calls between two network locations. The VoIP dial peers use H.323 by default. H.323 signaling messages are transported by default over TCP. They use the destination IP address that is specified in the **dial-peer session target** command. The source address is taken from the outgoing interface toward that session target (the routing table points over the outgoing interface to the destination address).

VoIP service is enabled by default, and therefore does not appear in the configuration. It could be disabled using the **shutdown** command in voice service VoIP configuration mode.

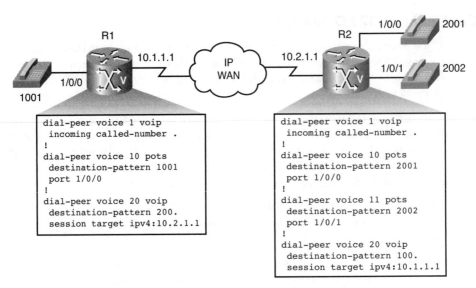

```
dial-peer voice 1 voip
  incoming called-number .
!
dial-peer voice 10 pots
  destination-pattern 1001
  port 1/0/0
!
dial-peer voice 20 voip
  destination-pattern 200.
  session target ipv4:10.2.1.1
```

```
dial-peer voice 1 voip
  incoming called-number .
!
dial-peer voice 10 pots
  destination-pattern 2001
  port 1/0/0
!
dial-peer voice 11 pots
  destination-pattern 2002
  port 1/0/1
!
dial-peer voice 20 voip
  destination-pattern 100.
  session target ipv4:10.1.1.1
```

Figure 2-32   *H.323 Gateway Configuration Example*

Customizing H.323 Gateways

The most common H.323 customization tasks include the following:

- Defining the session transport protocol: TCP or UDP

- Selecting a source IP address by binding the gateway functionality to a network interface

- Tuning H.225 timers

H.323 Session Transport

To customize the H.323 gateway parameters, you enter the voice service VoIP configuration mode using the **voice service voip** global configuration command.

```
Router(config)#voice service voip
```

From the voice service VoIP configuration mode, you can enter H.323 configuration mode using the **h323** command. The **h323** command does not have a default behavior or values. The **no h323** command does not disable the H.323 service but only removes all commands that were previously configured in the H.323 configuration mode.

```
Router(config-voi-serv)#h323
```

You can change the H.323 transport protocol using the **session transport udp** command in the H.323 configuration mode. To change the transport back to the default TCP setting, issue the **no session transport udp** command. UDP session transport allows the shortest call setup time, theoretically in as few as 1.5 round trips. TCP takes longer due to its overhead and acknowledgment exchange, but guarantees packet delivery. UDP might be chosen if communicating with third-party devices with UDP support.

```
Router(config-serv-h323)#session transport udp
```

Idle Connection and H.323 Source IP Address

To tune the H.225 idle call connection timer, use the **h225 timeout tcp call-idle** command in the H.323 configuration mode. The default idle call connection timer is 10 seconds.

```
Router(conf-serv-h323)#h225 timeout tcp call-idle {value | never}
```

To configure the interface binding feature, issue the **h323-gateway voip bind srcaddr** command in the interface configuration mode. It must be the interface with which the H.323 gateway service should be associated. The command points to an IPv4 or IPv6 address of that interface. The address will be used as the source IP address for all outgoing H.323 traffic, including H.225, H.245, and RAS signaling.

```
Router(config-if)#h323-gateway voip bind srcaddr ip-address
```

H.225 Timers

To tune H.225 timers, create an H.323 voice class using the **voice class h323** command. The voice class is identified using a tag. In the H.323 voice class configuration mode, you can tune these timers:

- The **h225 timeout tcp establish** command defines the timeout, after which the H.225 TCP session times out if the gateway does not receive a response. This timeout should be shortened if a backup terminating gateway exists, so that the originating gateway does not have to wait the default 15 seconds before contacting the backup device. A timeout of 3 seconds is recommended if the gateway communicates with a Cisco Unified Communications Manager cluster with multiple redundant servers.

```
Router(config)#voice class h323 h323_class_tag
Router(config-class)#h225 timeout tcp establish value
```

- The **h225 timeout setup** defines the response timeout value for outgoing Call Setup messages. Its default value of 15 seconds works well in most cases.

```
Router(config-class)#h225 timeout setup value
Router(config-dial-peer)#voice-class h323 h323_voice_class_tag
```

Finally, the H.323 voice class must be associated with dial peers. This association is configured with the **voice-class h323** command.

H.323 Gateway Tuning Example

Figure 2-33 shows the configuration of these features:

- **Interface binding:** The gateway uses the 10.1.1.1 address for all outgoing H.323 packets. The gateway uses two redundant WAN interfaces, and the interface binding decouples H.323 signaling from the physical path.

- **Transport protocol:** The transport protocol is set to TCP. This command will not show in the configuration, because it is the default setting.

- **H.225 TCP establish timeout:** The TCP establish timeout is shortened to 3 seconds to speed up fallback to the backup gateway if the primary fails. The primary gateway (10.2.1.1) is reached over the dial peer 1 with the best preference 0 (not shown because it is the default value). The dial peer 2 with preference 1 points to the secondary gateway 10.3.1.1.

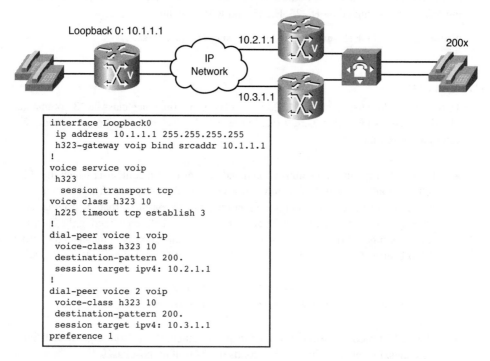

```
interface Loopback0
 ip address 10.1.1.1 255.255.255.255
 h323-gateway voip bind srcaddr 10.1.1.1
!
voice service voip
 h323
  session transport tcp
voice class h323 10
 h225 timeout tcp establish 3
!
dial-peer voice 1 voip
 voice-class h323 10
 destination-pattern 200.
 session target ipv4: 10.2.1.1
!
dial-peer voice 2 voip
 voice-class h323 10
 destination-pattern 200.
 session target ipv4: 10.3.1.1
 preference 1
```

Figure 2-33 *H.323 Gateway Tuning Example*

Verifying H.323 Gateways

Use the **show gateway** command to verify that the H.323 gateway is operational and to display the current status of the gateway.

The sample output provided in Example 2-1 shows the report that appears when a gateway is not registered with a gatekeeper.

Example 2-1 *H.323 DTMF Configuration Example*

```
Router#show gateway
H.323 ITU-T Version: 4.0 H323 Stack Version: 0.1
H.323 service is up
This gateway is not registered to any gatekeeper
Alias list (CLI configured) is empty
Alias list (last RCF) is empty
H323 resource thresholding is Disabled
```

Voice Signaling Protocols: SIP

Session Initiation Protocol (SIP) is one of the most important voice signaling protocols within service provider VoIP networks and is supported by most IP telephony system vendors. As such, it is an ideal protocol for interconnecting different VoIP systems and networks. An understanding of the features and functions of SIP components, and the relationships that the components establish with each other, is important in implementing a scalable, resilient, and secure SIP environment. This section describes how to configure SIP and explores the features and functions of the SIP environment, including its components, how these components interact, and how to accommodate scalability and survivability.

SIP Architecture

The Internet Engineering Task Force (IETF) developed SIP as an alternative to H.323. SIP is a common standard that is based on the logic of the World Wide Web and very simple to implement. It is widely used with gateways and proxy servers within service provider networks for internal and end-customer signaling. Like other VoIP protocols, SIP is designed to address the functions of signaling and session management within a packet telephony network.

SIP operates on the principle of session invitations that are based on an HTTP-like request and response transaction model. Each transaction consists of a request that invokes a particular method, or function, on the server and at least one response. Through invitations, SIP initiates sessions or invites participants into established sessions. Descriptions of these sessions are advertised by any one of several means, including the Session Announcement Protocol (SAP) defined in RFC 2974. SAP incorporates a session description according to the Session Description Protocol (SDP) defined in RFC 2327.

SIP uses other IETF protocols to define other aspects of VoIP and multimedia sessions; for example, URLs for addressing, Domain Name System (DNS) for service location, and Telephony Routing over IP (TRIP) for call routing.

SIP is a peer-to-peer protocol where Internet endpoints (called user agents [UAs]) initiate sessions, similar to an H.323 peer. The UAs discover each other and agree on a session that they would like to share. For locating session participants and other functions, SIP enables the creation of an infrastructure of network hosts (called proxy servers) to which user agents can send registrations, invitations to sessions, and other requests. SIP is an agile, general-purpose tool for creating, modifying, and terminating sessions, which works independently of underlying transport protocols and without depending on the type of session that is being established.

Unlike H.323, SIP uses ASCII text-based messages to communicate. Therefore, it allows for easy troubleshooting by analyzing the signaling content.

Signaling and Deployment

SIP supports five methods of establishing and terminating multimedia communications, which result in the following capabilities:

- **Determines the location of the target endpoint:** SIP supports address resolution, name mapping, and call redirection.

- **Determines the media capabilities of the target endpoint:** SIP determines the lowest level of common services between the endpoints through SDP. Conferences are established using only the media capabilities that can be supported by all endpoints.

- **Determines the availability of the target endpoint:** If a call cannot be completed because the target endpoint is unavailable, SIP determines whether the called party is connected to a call already or did not answer in the allotted number of rings. SIP then returns a message indicating why the target endpoint was unavailable.

- **Establishes a session between the originating and target endpoints:** If the call can be completed, SIP establishes a session between the endpoints. SIP also supports midcall changes, such as the addition of another endpoint to the conference or the changing of a media characteristic or codec.

- **Manages the transfer and termination of calls:** SIP supports the transfer of calls from one endpoint to another. During a call transfer, SIP simply establishes a session between the transferee and a new endpoint (specified by the transferring party) and terminates the session between the transferee and the transferring party.

SIP Architecture Components

As illustrated in Figure 2-34, SIP is a peer-to-peer protocol.

As previously mentioned, the peers in a session are called user agents. A UA can function in one of these two roles:

- **User agent client (UAC):** A client application that initiates a SIP request

- **User agent server (UAS):** A server application that contacts the user when a SIP invitation is received and then returns a response on behalf of the user to the invitation originator

Typically, a UA can function as a UAC or a UAS during a session, but not both in the same session. Whether the endpoint functions as a UAC or a UAS depends on the UA that initiated the request; the UAC initiates the session and the UAS terminates the session.

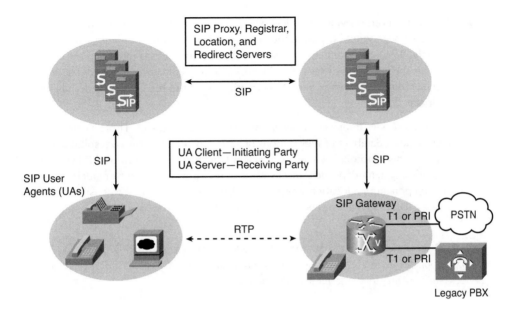

Figure 2-34 *SIP Architecture Components*

From an architectural standpoint, the physical components of a SIP network are grouped into these two categories:

■ **Clients (endpoints)**

   ■ **Phone:** An IP telephone acts as a UAS or UAC on a session-by-session basis.

   ■ **Gateway:** A gateway acts as a UAS or UAC and provides call control support. Like in H.323, SIP gateways provide many services, the most common being a translation function between SIP endpoints and other device types, such as PSTN destinations.

■ **Servers:** Registrar, proxy, redirect, and location

SIP Servers

The different server roles in the SIP environment have these characteristics:

■ **Registrar server:** Receives requests from UACs for registration of their current location. Registrar servers are often located near or even collocated with other network servers, most often a location server.

■ **Proxy server:** An intermediate component that receives SIP requests from a client and then forwards the requests on behalf of the client to the next SIP server in the network. The next server can be another proxy server or a UAS. Proxy servers can provide functions such as authentication, authorization, network access control, routing, reliable request transmissions, and security.

- **Redirect server:** Provides the client with information about the next hop or hops that a message should take, and then the client contacts the next-hop server or UAS directly. When the redirect server sends a redirect message to the client, the client resends the invitation to the server identified in the redirection message. The client can be redirected either to another network server or to the UAS in the terminating endpoint.

- **Location server:** Implements mechanisms to resolve addresses. These mechanisms can include a database of registrations or access to commonly used resolution tools such as Finger protocol, whois, Lightweight Directory Access Protocol (LDAP), or operating system–dependent mechanisms. A registrar server can be modeled as one subcomponent of a location server; the registrar server is partly responsible for populating a database that is associated with the location server.

Note   SIP servers can interact with other application services, such as LDAP servers, a database application, or an XML application. These application services provide back-end services, such as directory, authentication, and billing services.

SIP Architecture Examples

As shown in Figure 2-35, Cisco Unified Communications implementations can deploy SIP on the following products:

- Cisco Unified Communications Manager

- Cisco Unified Communications Manager Business Edition

- Cisco Unified Communications Manager Express

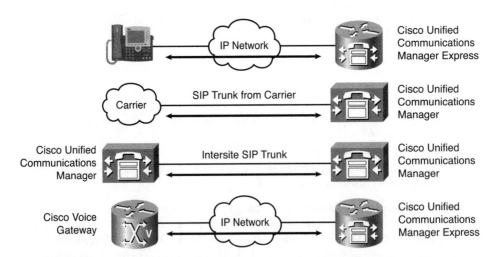

Figure 2-35   *SIP Architecture Examples*

- Cisco Smart Business Communications System

- Cisco voice gateways

- Cisco Unified IP Phones running SIP firmware, which register on a Cisco Unified Communications Manager or Cisco Unified Communications Manager Express

- Cisco Unified IP Phones running SIP firmware and connecting directly to an Internet telephony service provider (ITSP)

- SIP trunks to a carrier, and between corporate offices

SIP Call Flows

Figure 2-36 depicts the direct call setup and teardown between two SIP gateways.

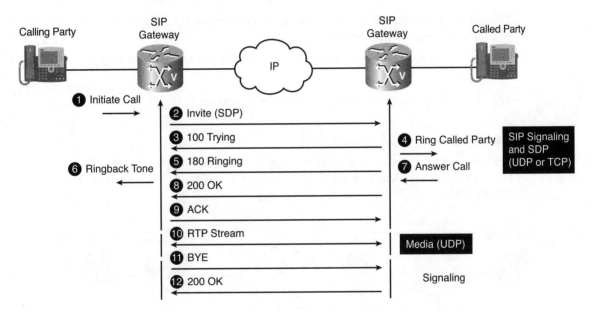

Figure 2-36   *Direct Call Setup*

When a UAC recognizes the address of a terminating endpoint from cached information, or has the capacity to resolve it by some internal mechanism, the UAC might initiate direct (UAC-to-UAS) call setup procedures. If a UAC recognizes the destination UAS, the client communicates directly with the server. In situations in which the client is unable to establish a direct relationship, the client solicits the assistance of a network server.

Direct call setup proceeds as follows:

1. Endpoint initiates a call.

2. The originating UAC sends an invitation (INVITE) to the UAS of the recipient. The message includes an endpoint description of the UAC and the SDP description of the supported media parameters.

3. The UAS of the recipient responds to the INVITE message using the 100 Trying message.

4. The terminating gateway sends the ringing signal to the recipient telephone.

5. The recipient UAS informs the UAC about the ring signal with the Ringing message.

6. The originating gateway sends the ringback tone to the caller telephone.

7. The called telephone is taken off-hook.

8. If the UAS of the recipient determines that the call parameters are acceptable, it responds positively to the originator UAC using the 200 OK message.

9. The originating UAC issues an acknowledgment (ACK) to the UAS.

10. At this point, the UAC and UAS have all the information that is required to establish RTP sessions between them.

11. One of participants terminates the call. Its UA sends the BYE message to the other UA.

12. The BYE message is confirmed by the 200 OK message.

SIP Call Setup Using Proxy Server

The proxy server procedure, as diagramed in Figure 2-37, is transparent to a UAC. The proxy server intercepts and forwards an invitation to the destination UAS on behalf of the originator.

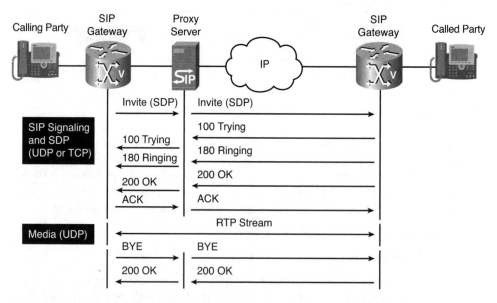

Figure 2-37   *SIP Call Setup Using Proxy Server*

A proxy server responds to the issues of the direct method by centralizing control and management of call setup and providing a more dynamic and up-to-date address resolution capability. The benefit to the UAC is that it does not need to learn the coordinates of the destination UAS, yet it can still communicate with the destination UAS. The disadvantages of this method include an increase in the signaling and the dependency on the proxy server. If the proxy server fails, the UAC is incapable of establishing its own sessions.

Note   Although the proxy server acts on behalf of a UA for call setup, the UAs establish RTP sessions directly with each other.

SIP Call Setup Using Redirect Server

A redirect server is programmed to discover a path to the destination. Instead of forwarding the INVITE to the destination, the redirect server reports back to a UA with the destination coordinates that the UA should try next. The operation of a SIP redirect server is pictured in Figure 2-38.

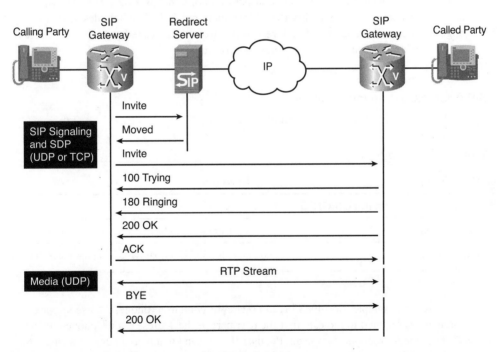

Figure 2-38   *SIP Call Setup Using Redirect Server*

A redirect server implements many of the features of the proxy server. In the redirect server scenario, fewer messages are exchanged than in the case of the proxy server. The UAC has a heavier workload because it must initiate the subsequent invitation.

When a redirect server is used, the call setup procedure starts when the originating UAC sends an INVITE to the redirect server. The redirect server, if required, consults the location server to determine the path to the recipient and its IP address. The redirect server returns a "moved" response to the originating UAC with the IP address obtained from the location server. The originating UAC acknowledges the redirection and continues as described in the direct call setup procedure.

SIP Addressing

SIP addresses use Internet URLs. Their general form is name@domain. An address in SIP is defined in the syntax with "sip:" or "sips:" (for secure SIP connections) as the URL type. The URLs identify the originator, the current destination, the final recipient, and any contact party. When two UAs communicate directly with each other, the current destination and final recipient URLs are the same. However, the current destination and the final recipient are different if a proxy or redirect server is used.

To obtain the IP address of a SIP UAS or a network server, a UAC performs address resolution of a user identifier. An address consists of an optional user ID, a host description, and optional parameters to qualify the address more precisely. The host description might be a domain name or an IP address. A password is associated with the user ID, and a port number is associated with the host description.

SIP Addressing Variants Example

Table 2-7 provides examples of SIP addresses.

Table 2-7   *SIP Address Types*

Address Type	Example
Fully qualified domain name (FQDN)	sip:jdoe@cisco.com
E.164 (PSTN) address	sip:14085551234@gateway.com;user=phone
Mixed format	sip:14085551234;password=changeme@10.1.1.1

In the second example, sip:14085551234@gateway.com; user=phone, the user=phone parameter is required to indicate that the user part of the address is a telephone number. Without the user=phone parameter, the user ID is taken literally as a numeric string. The 14085559876 in the URL sip:14085559876@10.1.1.1 is an example of a numeric user ID. In the same example, the password changeme is defined for the user.

Address Registration

A SIP address is acquired in several ways: by interacting with a user, by caching information from an earlier session, or by interacting with a network server. The network servers must recognize the endpoints in the network. This knowledge is abstracted to reside in a location server and is dynamically acquired by its registrar server.

To contribute to this dynamic knowledge, an endpoint registers its user addresses with a registrar server. Figure 2-39 illustrates a voice register mode request to a registrar server. When the registration is complete, the information about the UAC is entered into the location database, and the proxy server will be able to provide the endpoint address when other endpoints wish to contact it, as depicted in Figure 2-39.

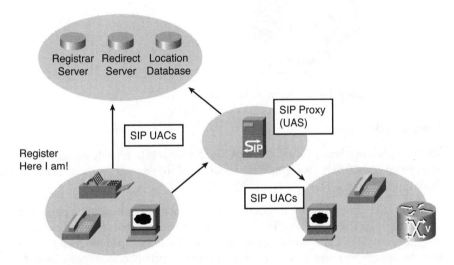

Figure 2-39   *Address Registration*

Address Resolution

When an endpoint attempts to communicate, it must resolve the IP address of the destination endpoint that is based on its address in the fully qualified domain name (FQDN), E.164, or mixed address format. To resolve an address, a UA uses a variety of internal mechanisms, such as a local host table and DNS lookup, or more commonly, it leaves that responsibility to the proxy server. The proxy server uses any of the tools available to a UA or interacts with the location server. In Figure 2-40, the SIP proxy server interacts with a location server to derive the location of the end device in question. Once the IP address of the destination endpoint is established, the SIP proxy forwards the call to the destination device, or the redirect server responds to the initiating endpoint with the address of the destination party.

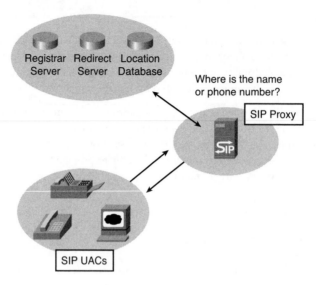

Figure 2-40   *Address Resolution*

Codecs in SIP

SIP leverages a number of other standards-based protocols to provide a large set of features based on relatively simple mechanisms. One of the relevant protocols is the Session Description Protocol (SDP).

SDP is an IETF-based format for describing streaming media initialization parameters in an ASCII string. SDP is intended for describing multimedia communication sessions for the purposes of session announcement, session invitation, and parameter negotiation. SDP does not deliver media itself but is used for negotiation between endpoints of media type, format, and all associated properties. The set of properties and parameters is often called a *session profile*. SDP is designed to be extensible to support new media types and formats.

SIP leverages SDP to negotiate the type of media (audio, video), the transport protocol (RTP or UDP ports), and the format of media (audio and video codecs). The initiating endpoint can provide a list of capabilities, while the first offer is the default (highest priority) proposal. The destination endpoint selects an offer that matches its capabilities and keeps the complete list of common capabilities in case the capabilities should be changed midcall.

SIP uses the Offer/Answer model for establishing SIP sessions. An Offer is contained in the SDP fields that are sent in the body of a SIP message. The Offer defines the media characteristics that are supported by the device (media streams, codecs, directional attributes, IP address, and ports to use). The device receiving the Offer sends an Answer in the SDP fields of its SIP response, with its corresponding matching media streams and codec, whether accepted or not, and the IP address and port on which it wants to receive the media streams.

Example 2-2 and Example 2-3 present two SDP examples.

Example 2-2   *Audio, RTP/49100, G.711 mu-law*

```
v=0
o=bjoe +1-201-555-1212 IN IP4
host1.cisco.com
s=Example1
t=0 0
c=IN IP4 192.168.1.1
m=audio 49100 RTP/AVP 0
```

Example 2-3   *Audio, RTP/3456, G.729 Most Preferred, G.711 mu-law Second Choice,*
G.711 a-law Third Choice

```
v=0
o=asmith 13015556789 IN IP4 cisco.com
s=Example2
t=0 0
c=IN IP4 10.234.1.1
m=audio 3456 RTP/AVP 18 0 8
```

Table 2-8 explains the parameters in the preceding examples.

Table 2-8   *SDP Examples*

Field	Description
Version	v=0
Origin	o=<username> <session id> <version> <network type> <address type> <address>
Session Name	s=<session name>
Times	t=<start time> <stop time>
Connection Data	c=<network type> <address type> <connection address>
Media	m=<media> <port> <transport> <media format list>
Audio Video Profile (AVP) Codes	0: G.711 mu-law 8: G.711 a-law 3:GSM codec 18:G.729

SDP content varies depending on the message type.

Delayed Offer

There are two ways to exchange the SDP Offer and Answer messages. These methods are commonly known as *Delayed Offer* and *Early Offer*, and support for both methods by user agent client/servers is a mandatory requirement of the SIP specification. In the simplest terms, an initial SIP Invite that is sent with SDP in the message body defines an Early Offer, whereas an initial SIP Invite without SDP in the message body defines a Delayed Offer.

In a Delayed Offer, as illustrated in Figure 2-41, the session initiator does not send its capabilities in the initial Invite but waits for the called device to send its capabilities first (for example, the list of codecs supported by the called device, thus allowing the calling device to choose the codec to be used for the session).

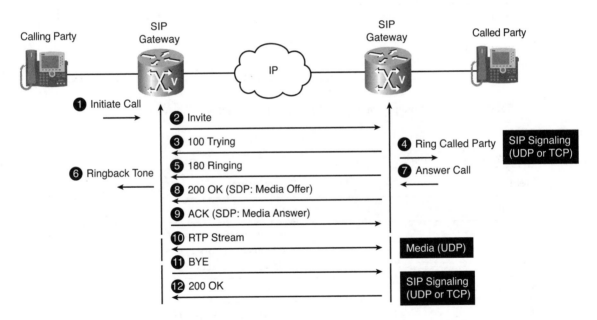

Figure 2-41   *Delayed Offer*

The Delayed Offer is recommended for SIP trunks because it enables the ITSPs to provide their capabilities first. The Cisco Unified Communications Manager allows the administrator to select the offer method. Cisco gateways support both methods but originating gateways default to Early Offer.

Early Offer

In an Early Offer, as depicted in Figure 2-42, the session initiator (calling device) sends its capabilities (including supported codecs) in the SDP contained in the initial Invite. This method allows the called device to choose its preferred codec for the session. Early Offer is the default method that is used by a Cisco voice gateway acting as the originating gateway.

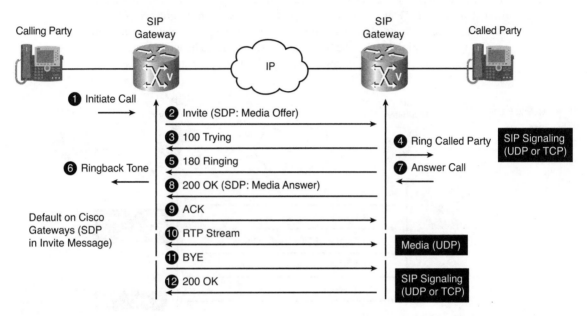

Figure 2-42   *Early Offer*

Early Media

SIP Early Media was originally defined in RFC 3960 as a facility for PSTN interworking.

Early Media allows the sending of media from the called party or an application server to the caller, even before the call is accepted. The most common reasons for using Early Media include the following:

■ The called device might want to establish an Early Media RTP path to reduce the effects of audio cut-through delay (clipping) for calls experiencing long signaling delays or to provide a network-based voice message to the caller.

■ The calling device might want to establish an Early Media RTP path to access a DTMF or voice-driven IVR system.

Cisco gateways support Early Media for both Early Offer and Delayed Offer calls.

If no media is available for streaming at this early stage, the Early Media channels carry silence. VAD, if negotiated, would in that case prevent bandwidth consumption by dropping silence packets.

With Early Offer (default on Cisco gateways), the SDP offer is carried in the INVITE message. In Early Media with Delayed Offer, both messages can transport the initial SDP offer: 183 Session Progress response or 180 Ringing response. 183 Session Progress is stipulated by the IETF and is more common. The 183 Session Progress response, as illustrated in Figure 2-43, indicates that information about the call state is present in the message body media information. The SDP media response is exchanged in an additional pre-ACK message, after which the endpoints can establish the RTP streams.

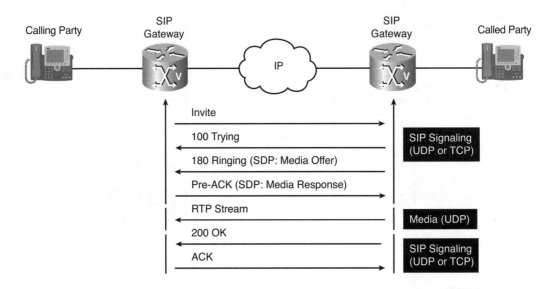

Figure 2-43 *Early Media—183 Session Progress Option*

To facilitate Early Media with Delayed Offer, the IETF draft allows the use of other messages than the 183 Session Progress response. Some implementations use the 180 Ringing response to send the initial SDP media offer. The 180 Ringing message is a provisional or informational response that is used to indicate that the INVITE message has been received by the user agent and that alerting is taking place. Cisco gateways support both 180 and 183 methods to negotiate Early Media.

Cisco gateways, by default, process a 180 Ringing response with SDP in the same manner as a 183 Session Progress response; that is, the SDP is assumed to be an indication that the far end would send Early Media. This behavior can be changed so that a gateway ignores the presence or absence of SDP in 180 messages, as shown in Figure 2-44, and as a result, treats all 180 messages in a uniform manner.

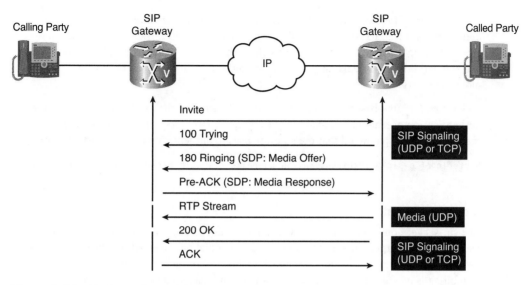

Figure 2-44 *Early Media—180 Ringing Option*

Configuring Basic SIP

A SIP configuration consists of two parts: the SIP UA and the VoIP dial peers that select SIP as the session protocol.

The basic UAC configuration includes the following:

■ Authentication parameters: username and password

■ SIP servers (registrar and proxy)

SIP dial peers have these two basic parameters that are specific to SIP:

■ Session protocol

■ Session target

User Agent Configuration

To configure SIP user agent parameters, enter SIP UA configuration mode using the **sip-ua** command.

```
Router(config)#sip-ua
```

The **registrar** command enables the gateway to register E.164 numbers on behalf of analog telephone voice ports (Foreign Exchange Station [FXS]), IP phone virtual voice ports (enhanced FXS [EFXS]), and Skinny Client Control Protocol (SCCP) phones with an external SIP proxy or SIP registrar. It defines the IP address of the registrar server.

```
Router(config-sip-ua)#registrar {dhcp | [index] registrar-address[:port]
```

The registrar address can be obtained via DHCP. The *registrar-index* option allows the configuration of up to six registrars that can be used concurrently for redundancy and load-balancing purposes. Further options allow the use of Secure SIP, TCP transport, and the definition of a registrar pair (primary and secondary) instead of multiple indexed servers.

To enable username-based message digest authentication of the user agent, configure the **authentication username** command in UA configuration mode. This command defines the username and password that the gateway uses to authenticate on the registrar server.

```
Router(config-sip-ua)#authentication username username password [0 | 7] password
```

Dial-Peer Configuration

The **sip-server** command is a time-saving method. If you use this command, you can also use the **session target sip-server** command on each dial peer instead of repeatedly entering the SIP server interface address for each dial peer. Configuring a SIP server as a session target is useful if the gateway acts as a UAC and makes calls over a SIP proxy. Multiple dial peers can reference the same proxy server.

```
Router(config-sip-ua)#sip-server {dns:host-name | ipv4:ipv4-address | ipv6:[ipv6-
  address][:port-num]}
Router(config-dial-peer)#session target sip-server
```

The **session protocol sipv2** command enables a dial peer to use SIP version 2 as the signaling protocol for a particular dial peer. The default value is H.323.

```
Router(config-dial-peer)#session protocol sipv2
```

Basic SIP Configuration Example

Figure 2-45 and Example 2-4 show a voice gateway, and its configuration, that communicates via SIP with two external SIP servers.

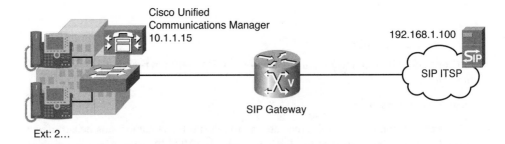

Figure 2-45 *Basic SIP Configuration Example—Topology*

Example 2-4 *Basic SIP Configuration Example—Configuration*

```
sip-ua
  authentication username JDoe password secret
  registrar 10.1.1.15
  sip-server 10.1.1.15
!
dial-peer voice 2001 voip
  destination-pattern 2...
  session protocol sipv2
  session target sip-server
!
dial-peer voice 2002 voip
  destination-pattern 9T
  session target ipv4:192.168.1.100
  session protocol sipv2
```

In this example, a Cisco Unified Communications Manager and is communicating with a SIP service that is operated by an ITSP. The Cisco Unified Communications Manager (with IP address 10.1.1.15) includes two collocated components: SIP registrar and SIP proxy. The SIP UA refers to the registrar component using the **registrar** command and references the proxy component using the **sip-server** command. The UA configured on the gateway uses the dial peer 2001 to match the destination patterns 2... and connect to the SIP proxy running on the Cisco Unified Communications Manager (the **session target sip-server** command points to the address set with the **sip-server** command in **sip-ua** configuration mode). The gateway will register on the Communications Manager using the credentials that are defined in the **authentication** command.

For all other destinations that use the prefix 9 to represent the outside world, the dial peer 2002 points via SIP version 2 to the ITSP SIP proxy.

Configuring SIP ISDN Support

SIP can be configured for various ISDN features. The most relevant ISDN functions that apply to most situations are as follows:

■ ISDN calling name display

■ Blocking caller ID when privacy exists

■ Substituting the calling number for the display name, if the display name is unavailable

Calling Name Display

In ISDN networks, caller ID (sometimes called calling line ID [CLID] or incoming calling line identification [ICLID]) is a service that is offered by a central office (CO) to supply calling party information to subscribers. Caller ID allows the calling party number and name to appear on a device such as a telephone display, as shown in Figure 2-46.

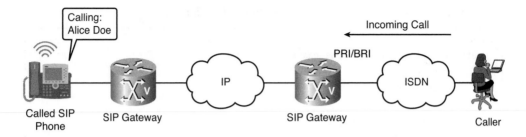

Figure 2-46   *Caller ID Display*

ISDN messages signal call control and are composed of information elements that specify screening and presentation indicators. ISDN messages and their information elements are passed in Generic Transparency Descriptor (GTD) format. GTD enables transport of signaling data in a standard format across network components and applications. The standard format enables other devices to scan and interpret the data. The SIP network extracts the calling name from the GTD format and sends the calling name information to the SIP endpoint.

Calling Name Display Commands

When an ISDN subscriber places a call to a SIP endpoint, the subscriber calling number is by default supplied to the SIP endpoint and appears on the display when the call comes in. The calling name is typically not forwarded by default. Two commands are needed to enable the calling name display:

- **signaling forward:** This command is issued in the voice service VoIP configuration mode. It specifies whether the originating gateway forwards the signaling payload to the terminating gateway. Keywords are as follows:

    - **none:** Prevents the gateway from passing the signaling payload to the terminating gateway

    - **unconditional:** Forwards the signaling payload received in the originating gateway to the terminating gateway, even if the attached external route server has modified the GTD payload

    ```
    Router(conf-voi-serv)#signaling forward {none | unconditional}
    ```

- **isdn supp-service name calling:** This command is issued in the configuration mode of the serial interface that is created on a channelized E1/T1 controller. The command sets the calling name display parameters that are sent out an ISDN serial interface.

    ```
    Router(config-if)#isdn supp-service name calling
    ```

Calling Name Display Configuration

Figure 2-47 shows how to configure the calling name display feature on a voice gateway that is connected to the PSTN via a T1 channelized controller using ISDN PRI signaling. The serial interface and the voice service VoIP are configured to unconditionally forward the signaling information that results in the calling name being displayed on the SIP end-point when a call arrives.

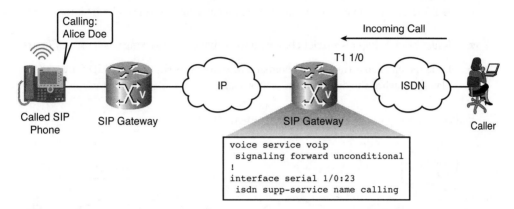

Figure 2-47 *Calling Name Display Configuration*

Blocking and Substituting Caller ID

The caller ID information is private information. In ISDN, there is a private setting that can be set to protect this information. However, when SIP gets the caller ID information, it does not hide the private information. Rather, it just sets a field to reflect that it is private and not to display it on a caller ID display, as shown in Figure 2-48. But the data is still viewable in the SIP message requests.

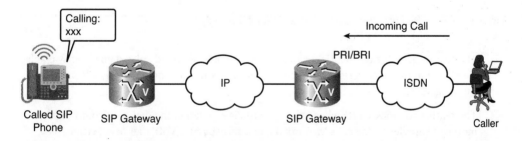

Figure 2-48 *Blocking and Substituting Caller ID*

The block option allows the gateway to delete the caller ID information from the SIP message requests so that it cannot be read on the network.

The substitution option is helpful if there is no Display Name field but there is a number and the presentation is not prohibited. In that case it copies the number into the Display Name field, so that the number is displayed on the caller ID display of the recipient. The Cisco gateway omits the Display Name field if no display information is received.

Blocking and Substituting Caller ID Commands

The **clid strip pi-restrict** and **clid substitute name** commands can each be issued from within voice service VoIP configuration mode or from within dial-peer configuration mode. These two commands are used for blocking and substituting caller ID information:

■ Issue the **clid strip pi-restrict** command to enable CLID blocking when privacy exists.

■ Issue the **clid substitute name** command to enable substitution of CLID for the display name when the display name is unavailable.

Figure 2-49 shows an example with two features enabled.

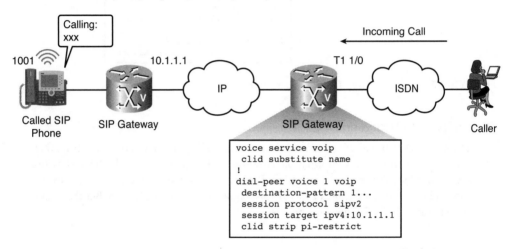

Figure 2-49   *Blocking and Substituting Caller ID Example*

The feature to substitute CLID for the display name when the display name is unavailable is enabled in the voice service VoIP configuration mode and applies to all calls processed by the gateway.

The feature to block CLID when privacy exists is enabled in the dial-peer configuration mode and applies to the calls forwarded using this specific VoIP dial-peer setting.

Configuring SIP SRTP Support

SIP offers two methods to secure voice communications:

■ **SIP secure (SIPS):** Offers signaling authentication and encryption using the Transport Layer Security (TLS) protocol. When TLS is used, the cryptographic parameters that are required to successfully negotiate Secure Real-Time Transport Protocol (SRTP) rely on the cryptographic attribute in the SDP. To ensure the integrity of cryptographic parameters across a network, SRTP uses the SIPS schema.

■ **SRTP:** Offers media authentication (Hashed Message Authentication Code-Secure hash Algorithm 1 [HMAC-SHA-1]) and encryption (Advanced Encryption Standard [AES]) to secure the media flow between two SIP endpoints. Typically, SRTP is used in combination with SIPS, although SIPS is no longer required for SRTP in Cisco IOS Release 12.4(22)T and later. Calls established with SIP (and not SIPS) can still successfully negotiate SRTP. In such cases, the signaling should be protected using a different protocol, such as IPsec.

Table 2-9 shows various combinations of the SIPS and SRTP settings. The second combination (SIPS disabled, SRTP enabled) results in varying behavior, depending on the Cisco IOS release. With Cisco IOS Release 12.4(22)T and later, the signaling is in cleartext and the media is encrypted. With earlier releases, the calls either fall back to RTP or fail, depending on the **securertp fallback** command.

Table 2-9   *SIP SRTP Support*

SIPS (TLS)	SRTP	Description
On	On	Signaling and media are secure.
Off	On	Signaling is insecure or secured with other methods. Media is secure with Cisco IOS Release 12.4(22)T and later. Media falls back to RTP or fails in earlier versions.
On	Off	Media insecure (RTP only).
Off	Off	Signaling and media insecure.

SIPS Global and Dial-Peer Commands

SIPS functionality was introduced in Cisco IOS Release 12.4(15)T. You can configure secure signaling on both a global level (in SIP mode) and on an individual dial-peer basis. To configure SIPS globally, you must first enter the voice service VoIP configuration mode (with the **voice service voip** command) and then the SIP configuration mode (**sip** command). To enable SIPS, issue the **url sips** command.

```
Router(config)#voice service voip
Router(conf-voi-serv)#sip
Router(conf-serv-sip)#url sips
```

The dial-peer setting overwrites the global setting, which is useful when disabling SIPS on selected dial peers when SIPS is enabled globally. To configure SIPS for a dial peer, from dial-peer configuration mode you enter the command **voice-class sip url sips**.

```
Router(conf-dial-peer)#voice-class sip url sips
```

SRTP Global and Dial-Peer Commands

SRTP was introduced in Cisco IOS Release 12.4(15)T. You can configure the secure media transport on both a global level (in SIP configuration mode) and on an individual dial-peer basis. To configure SRTP globally, you must first enter the voice service VoIP configuration mode (**voice service voip** command) and then issue the **securertp** command. The **securertp fallback** command can then be issued to allow a call to use RTP (that is, without security) if the other endpoint does not support SRTP.

```
Router(config)#voice service voip
Router(conf-voi-serv)#securertp
Router(conf-voi-serv)#securertp fallback
```

The dial-peer setting overwrites the global setting. To configure SRTP for a dial peer, you first enter the **voice-class sip** command from the dial-peer configuration mode.

```
Router(conf-dial-peer)#voice-class sip
Router(conf-dial-peer)#securertp
Router(conf-dial-peer)#securertp fallback
```

SIPS and SRTP Configuration Example

Figure 2-50 shows the configuration of two voice gateways that are configured for SIPS and SRTP. The gateway on the left has the settings configured globally, while the right gateway is configured on a specific dial peer. Both support fallback to RTP in case SRTP is not supported by the other endpoint.

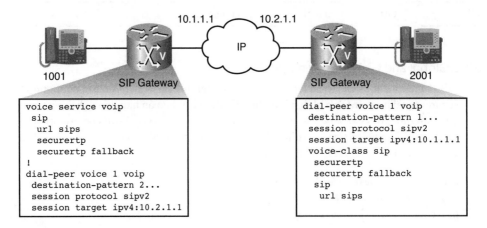

Figure 2-50 *SIPS and SRTP Configuration Example*

Customizing SIP Gateways

The most common SIP customization tasks include the following:

- Defining the session transport protocol: TCP, TCP-TLS, or UDP. This setting can be applied in global SIP, dial-peer, or UA configuration mode.

- Selecting a source IP address by binding the gateway functionality to a network interface. This option is available only in global SIP configuration mode.

- Tuning SIP timers. These parameters are tunable in UA configuration mode.

- Disabling Early Media cut-through treatment for SIP 180 Ringing messages.

SIP Transport

The configuration of SIP session transport refers to two aspects of signaling:

- **Outbound signaling:** Default is UDP. The transport for outgoing SIP messages can be configured globally, in SIP configuration mode, and in the dial-peer configuration mode. The **system** option in the dial-peer configuration mode applies the global option to a specific dial peer and is used as a time saver. Instead of configuring a non-UDP option repeatedly for each dial peer, you can configure the global setting and apply it to the required dial peers. The **system** option issued in dial-peer configuration mode refers to the SIP session protocol option configured in SIP user agent (that is, **sip-ua**) configuration mode. The **tcp tls** option causes SIP messages to use the TLS over TCP transport, while the **udp** option causes SIP messages to be sent using UDP.

  ```
  Router(conf-voi-serv)#session transport {system | tcp tls | udp}
  ```

  or

  ```
  Router(conf-dial-peer)#session transport {system | tcp tls | udp}
  ```

- **Inbound signaling:** This option is configured in the SIP UA configuration mode. It specifies the transport methods accepted for receiving inbound calls. The default is to accept all three transports: UDP, TCP, and TCP TLS, on port 5060.

  ```
  Router(conf-sip-ua)#transport {top tls | udp}
  ```

SIP Source IP Address

The interface binding feature sets the IP address for outgoing SIP-related traffic. To configure the interface binding feature, issue the **bind** command in the global SIP configuration mode. You have the option to bind either signaling, media, or both, using the **control**, **media**, and **all** keywords. The command points to an interface and specifies its IPv4 or IPv6 address that should be used as the source IP address for outgoing traffic.

```
Router(conf-voi-serv)#bind {control | media | all} source-interface interface-id
 [ipv4-address ipv4-address | ipv6-address ipv6-address]
```

To tune SIP timers, you must enter SIP UA configuration mode and issue the **timers** command, followed by appropriate command options.

SIP UA Timers

The default values of SIP timers work well in most environments and should not be changed unless the administrator identifies a specific requirement. These timers can be set in the SIP UA configuration mode:

- **Connect:** Time (in ms) to wait for a 200 response to an ACK request. Range is from 100 to 1000. The default is 500.

- **Disconnect:** Time (in ms) to wait for a 200 response to a BYE request. Range is from 100 to 1000. The default is 500.

- **Expires:** Time (in ms) for which an INVITE request is valid. Range is from 60000 to 300000. The default is 180000.

- **Hold:** Time (in minutes) to wait before disconnecting a held call by sending a BYE request. Range is from 15 to 2880 minutes. The default is 2880.

- **Notify:** Time (in ms) to wait before retransmitting a Notify message. Range is from 100 to 1000. The default is 500.

- **Refer:** Time (in ms) to wait before retransmitting a Refer request. Range is from 100 to 1000. The default is 500.

- **Register:** Time (in ms) to wait before retransmitting a Register request. Range is from 100 to 1000. The default is 500.

- **Trying:** Time (in ms) to wait for a 100 response to an INVITE request. Range is from 100 to 1000. The default is 500.

SIP Early Media

The SIP Enhanced 180 Provisional Response Handling feature provides the ability to enable or disable Early Media cut-through on Cisco IOS gateways for SIP 180 response messages. This feature allows you to specify whether 180 messages with SDP are handled in the same way as 183 responses with SDP. The 180 Ringing message is a provisional or informational response that is used to indicate that the INVITE message has been received by the user agent and that alerting is taking place. The 183 Session Progress response indicates that information about the call state is present in the message body media information. Both 180 and 183 messages might contain SDP, which allow an Early Media session to be established prior to the call being answered.

By default, Cisco gateways handle a 180 Ringing response with SDP in the same manner as a 183 Session Progress response; that is, the SDP is assumed to be an indication that the far end would send Early Media. Cisco gateways handle a 180 response without SDP by providing local ringback, rather than Early Media cut-through. This feature provides the capability to ignore the presence or absence of SDP in 180 messages and, as a result, treat all 180 messages in a uniform manner. The **disable-early-media 180** command, issued in sip-ua configuration mode, allows specifying which call treatment, Early Media, or local ringback is provided for 180 responses with SDP. The treatments of various combinations of response message types and SIP handling statuses are presented in Table 2-10.

Table 2-10   *SIP Early Media Treatment*

Response Message	SIP Handling Status	Treatment
180 response with SDP	Enabled (default)	Early media cut-through
180 response with SDP	Disabled	Local ringback
180 response without SDP	Not affected	Local ringback
183 response with SDP	Not affected (default enabled)	Early media cut-through

Gateway-to-Gateway Configuration Example

Figure 2-51 shows two voice gateways that signal calls via SIP. Both gateways source the signaling and media traffic from the IP addresses configured on their respective Loopback 0 interfaces. Both gateways use TCP as the transport protocol for outbound signaling. The dial peer 1 on R1 refers to the system setting that is configured in the SIP mode. The dial peer 1 on R2 has the transport that is configured in its dial-peer settings. If dial peer 1 on R1 would not have the **session transport system** command, it would signal calls to R2 using UDP transport. R2 would accept that traffic, because the supported transports for inbound signaling are configured in **sip-ua** configuration mode and, by default, include all three options: UDP, TCP, and TCP TLS. SIP 180 Ringing responses carrying SDP media offers are ignored.

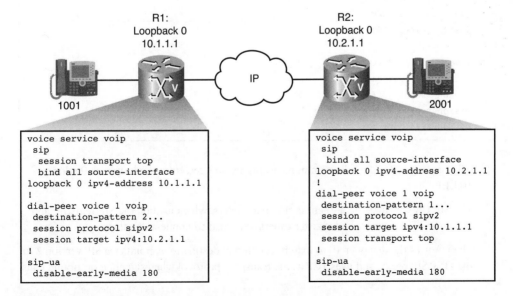

```
R1:
Loopback 0
10.1.1.1

              1001                    IP

voice service voip
 sip
  session transport top
  bind all source-interface
loopback 0 ipv4-address 10.1.1.1
!
dial-peer voice 1 voip
 destination-pattern 2...
 session protocol sipv2
 session target ipv4:10.2.1.1
!
sip-ua
 disable-early-media 180
```

```
R2:
Loopback 0
10.2.1.1

                                     2001

voice service voip
 sip
  bind all source-interface
loopback 0 ipv4-address 10.2.1.1
!
dial-peer voice 1 voip
 destination-pattern 1...
 session protocol sipv2
 session target ipv4:10.1.1.1
 session transport top
!
sip-ua
 disable-early-media 180
```

Figure 2-51   *Gateway-to-Gateway Configuration Example*

UA Example

The topology shown in Figure 2-52 depicts a voice gateway that communicates via SIP with an external SIP server operated by an ITSP. Example 2-5 shows the corresponding user agent configuration.

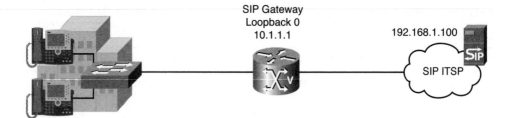

Figure 2-52   *User Agent Configuration Example—Topology*

Example 2-5   *User Agent Configuration Example—Configuration*

```
voice service voip
  sip
    bind all source-interface loopback0 ipv4-address 10.1.1.1
!
sip-ua
  authentication username JDoe password secret
  registrar 10.1.1.15 expires 3600
  sip-server 10.1.1.15
  timers connect 1000
  timers register 300
!
dial-peer voice 10 voip
  destination-pattern 9T
  session target ipv4:192.168.1.100
  session protocol sipv2
  session transport top
```

All outgoing SIP and media communications are sourced from the loopback 0 address 10.1.1.1.

The SIP UA specifies the authentication parameters, which include the SIP registrar and SIP proxy. The connect and register timers are tuned to nondefault values.

The UA uses the dial peer 10 to match all external destinations, points via SIP version 2 to the ITSP SIP proxy, and uses TCP as the transport protocol when signaling outbound calls.

Verifying SIP Gateways

The **show** commands listed in Table 2-11 allow you to examine the status of SIP components and to troubleshoot.

Table 2-11 show sip-ua *Command Overview*

Command	Description
show sip-ua service	Displays the status of the SIP service
show sip-ua status	Displays the status of the SIP UA
show sip-ua register status	Displays the status of E.164 numbers that a SIP gateway has registered with an external primary SIP registrar
show sip-ua timers	Displays SIP UA timers
show sip-ua connections	Displays active SIP UA connections
show sip-ua calls	Displays active SIP UA calls
show sip-ua statistics	Displays SIP traffic statistics

Some of the **show** commands presented in Table 2-11 are general-purpose SIP UA verification commands, while other commands focus on the verification of SIP UA registration status and SIP UA call information.

SIP UA General Verification

The **show sip-ua service** command, as demonstrated in Example 2-6, displays the status of SIP call service on a SIP gateway. The sip-ua service is up when the VoIP service has not been shut down in the voice service VoIP configuration mode. By default, VoIP service is enabled, and therefore SIP service is up.

Example 2-6 *SIP UA General Verification Examples*

```
Router#show sip-ua service
SIP Service is up

Router#show sip-ua status
SIP User Agent Status
SIP User Agent for UDP : ENABLED
SIP User Agent for TCP : ENABLED
SIP User Agent for TLS over TCP : ENABLED
SIP User Agent bind status(signaling): ENABLED 10.1.250.101
SIP User Agent bind status(media): DISABLED
SIP early-media for 180 responses with SDP: ENABLED
```

```
...
SDP application configuration:
 Version line (v=) required
 Owner line (o=) required
 Timespec line (t=) required
 Media supported: audio video image
 Network types supported: IN
 Address types supported: IP4 IP6
 Transport types supported: RTP/AVP udptl
```

The **show sip-ua status** command, also demonstrated in Example 2-6, displays the status
for the SIP user agent. It shows which transports are accepted for incoming calls. This
output shows the default setting, which is to accept UDP, TCP, and TCP TLS. Next, the
interface binding information is displayed. In this case, the signaling traffic is sourced
from the address 10.1.250.101, and the media will be sourced from the outgoing interface
IP address. The command informs about the gateway support for SIP Early Media using
180 Ringing responses with SDP. It is enabled by default. The **show sip-ua status** command reports the required and supported SDP options.

SIP UA Registration Status

The **show sip-ua register status** command, as demonstrated in Example 2-7, displays the
status of E.164 numbers that a SIP gateway has registered with an external SIP registrar
server. SIP gateways can register E.164 numbers on behalf of analog telephone voice
ports (FXS), IP phone virtual voice ports (EFXS), and SCCP phones with an external SIP
proxy or SIP registrar. The command **show sip-ua register status** is only for outbound
registration, so if there are no SCCP phones or FXS dial peers to register, there is no output when the command is run. In this example, some endpoints are attached to the SIP
gateway, but they have not been registered with an external SIP registrar.

Example 2-7   *SIP UA Registration Status and Timers Examples*

```
Router#show sip-ua register status

Line peer expires(sec) registered

4001 20001 596 no

4002 20002 596 no

5100 1 596 no
9998 2 596 no

Router#show sip-ua timers
```

```
SIP UA Timer Values (millisecs)
trying 500, expires 180000, connect 500, disconnect 500
comet 500, prack 500, rel1xx 500, notify 500
refer 500, register 500
```

The **show sip-ua timers** command displays the current settings for the SIP UA timers. In Example 2-7, the command output shows the default values of the timers.

SIP UA Call Information

The **show sip-ua calls** command, the output of which is seen in Example 2-8, displays active UAC and UAS calls and their parameters. The output includes information about IPv6, Resource Reservation Protocol (RSVP), and media forking (splitting the media session in multiple sessions) for each call on the device and for all media streams associated with the calls. There can be any number of media streams associated with a call, of which typically only one is active. A call can include up to three active media streams if the call is media-forked.

Example 2-8 *SIP UA Call Information Example*

```
Router#show sip-ua calls
SIP UAC CALL INFO
    Number of SIP User Agent Client(UAC) calls: 0

SIP UAS CALL INFO
Call 1
SIP Call ID        :D215F304-7B5A11DC-8005EA1A-6A8F4AD@10.10.10.2
    State of the call      : STATE_ACTIVE (7)
    Calling Number         : 2818902001
    Called Number          : 1003
    Source IP Address (Sig ) : 10.10.10.1
    Destn SIP Req Addr:Port  : 10.10.10.2:5060
    Destn SIP Resp Addr:Port : 10.10.10.2:56884
    Destination Name         : 10.10.10.2
Number of Media Streams : 1
    Number of Active Streams: 1
      Media Stream 1
      State of the stream      : STREAM_ACTIVE
      Stream Call ID           : 1
      Stream Type              : voice-only (0)
      Negotiated Codec         : g729r8 (20 bytes)
      Codec Payload Type       : 18
      Negotiated Dtmf-relay    : inband-voice
      Media Source IP Addr:Port : 10.10.10.1:18050
      Media Dest IP Addr:Port   : 10.10.10.2:16522
      ...
```

SIP Debugging Overview

The **debug** commands listed here are valuable when examining the status of SIP components and troubleshooting:

- **debug ccsip:** This command has various options, as follows:
    - **debug ccsip all:** This command enables all **ccsip**-type debugging. This **debug** command is very active; you should use it sparingly in a live network.
    - **debug ccsip calls:** This command displays all SIP call details as they are updated in the SIP call control block. You can use this **debug** command to monitor call records for suspicious clearing causes.
    - **debug ccsip errors:** This command traces all errors that are encountered by the SIP subsystem.
    - **debug ccsip events:** This command traces events, such as call setups, connections, and disconnections. An **events** version of a **debug** command is often the best place to start because detailed debugs provide much useful information.
    - **debug ccsip info:** This command enables tracing of general SIP security parameter index (SPI) information, including verification that call redirection is disabled.
    - **debug ccsip media:** This command enables tracing of SIP media streams.
    - **debug ccsip messages:** This command shows the headers of SIP messages that are exchanged between a client and a server.
    - **debug ccsip preauth:** This command enables diagnostic reporting of authentication, authorization, and accounting (AAA) for SIP calls.
    - **debug ccsip states:** This command displays the SIP states and state changes for sessions within the SIP subsystem.
    - **debug ccsip transport:** This command enables tracing of the SIP transport handler and the TCP or UDP process.
- **debug voip ccapi inout:** This command shows every interaction with the call control application programming interface (API) on both the telephone interface and on the VoIP side. By monitoring the output, you can follow the progress of a call from the inbound interface or VoIP peer to the outbound side of the call. This **debug** command is very active; you should use it sparingly in a live network.
- **debug voip ccapi protoheaders:** This command displays messages that are sent between the originating and terminating gateways. If no headers are being received by the terminating gateway, verify that the **header-passing** command is enabled on the originating gateway.

Examining the INVITE Message

Example 2-9 shows the output of the **debug ccsip** messages command. It shows the beginning of a SIP INVITE message being sent from the endpoint with address 166.34.245.230 to the endpoint with address 166.34.245.231. This example includes the description of the message originator, the intended recipient, and, among other parameters, the content type, which is application/sdp. The SDP description of the media capabilities is truncated in this output.

Example 2-9   *INVITE Message*

```
Router#debug ccsip messages
INVITE sip:3660210@166.34.245.231;user=phone;phone-context=unknown
SIP/2.0
Via: SIP/2.0/UDP 166.34.245.230:55820
From: "3660110" <sip:3660110@166.34.245.230>
To: <sip:3660210@166.34.245.231;user=phone;phone-context=unknown>
...
Content-Type: application/sdp
v=0
o=CiscoSystemsSIP-GW-UserAgent 4629 354 IN IP4 55.1.1.42
s=SIP Call
c=IN IP4 55.1.1.42
t=0 0
m=audio 18978 RTP/AVP 0 100
c=IN IP4 10.1.1.42
a=rtpmap:0 PCMU/8000
a=rtpmap:100 X-NSE/8000
```

Examining the 200 OK Message

Example 2-10 shows the output of the **debug ccsip messages** command. It shows a SIP 200 OK message being sent in response to an earlier SIP INVITE message. The INVITE message was sent from 166.34.245.230 to 166.34.245.231, and this address set is retained in the 200 OK message, with the addition of the Contact field that defines the originator of the 200 OK message (166.34.245.231). The content of the 200 OK message includes, among other parameters, the content type, which is application/sdp. The second part of the output shows the SDP description of the media. The media endpoint (the device that responds with the 200 OK message) is 166.34.245.231. It will use UDP/RTP port 20224. The AVP is 0, which means the call will use G.711 mu-law.

Example 2-10   *200 OK Message*

```
Router#debug ccsip messages

SIP/2.0 200 OK
Via: SIP/2.0/UDP 166.34.245.230:55820
```

```
From: "3660110" <sip:3660110@166.34.245.230>
To: <sip:3660210@166.34.245.231;user=phone;phonecontext=
unknown>;tag=27DBC6D8-1357
Date: Mon, 08 Mar 1993 22:45:12 GMT
Call-ID: ABBAE7AF-823100E2-0-1CD274BC@172.18.192.194
Timestamp: 731427554
Server: Cisco VoIP Gateway/ IOS 12.x/ SIP enabled
Contact: <sip:36602105060;user=phone>

CSeq: 101 INVITE
Content-Type: application/sdp
Content-Length: 138


v=0
o=CiscoSystemsSIP-GW-UserAgent 1193 7927 IN IP4 166.34.245.231
s=SIP Call
t=0 0
c=IN IP4 166.34.245.231
m=audio 20224 RTP/AVP 0
```

Examining the BYE Message

Example 2-11 shows the output of the **debug ccsip** messages command. It shows the BYE message that is sent when a call participant terminates the call.

Example 2-11   *BYE Message*

```
Router#debug ccsip messages

BYE sip:36601105060;user=phone SIP/2.0
Via: SIP/2.0/UDP 166.34.245.231:53600
From: <sip:3660210@166.34.245.231;user=phone;phonecontext=
unknown>;tag=27DBC6D8-1357
To: "3660110" <sip:3660110@166.34.245.230>
Date: Mon, 08 Mar 1993 22:45:14 GMT
Call-ID: ABBAE7AF-823100E2-0-1CD274BC@172.18.192.194
User-Agent: Cisco VoIP Gateway/ IOS 12.x/ SIP enabled
Max-Forwards: 6
Timestamp: 731612717
CSeq: 101 BYE
Content-Length: 0
```

Voice Signaling Protocols: MGCP

MGCP enables the remote control and management of voice and data communications devices at the edge of multiservice IP packet networks. Because of its centralized architecture, MGCP overcomes the distributed configuration and administration problems inherent in the use of protocols such as H.323. This section describes how to configure MGCP on a gateway and describes the features and functions of the MGCP environment.

MGCP Overview

MGCP is a protocol used within a distributed VoIP system. MGCP is defined in RFC 3435, which obsoletes an earlier definition in RFC 2705. Another protocol used for the same purpose is Megaco, a coproduction of IETF (RFC 3525) and ITU (Recommendation H.248-1). Both protocols follow the guidelines of the API Media Gateway Control Protocol Architecture and Requirements at RFC 2805.

These IETF standards describe MGCP as a centralized device control protocol with simple endpoints. The MGCP protocol allows a central control component, or call agent, to remotely control various devices. This protocol is referred to as a stimulus protocol, because the endpoints and gateways cannot function alone. MGCP incorporates the IETF SDP to describe the type of session to initiate.

MGCP is an extension of the earlier version of Simple Gateway Control Protocol (SGCP) and supports SGCP functionality in addition to several enhancements. Systems using SGCP can easily migrate to MGCP, and MGCP commands are available to enable SGCP capabilities.

MGCP is a plaintext protocol that uses a server-to-client relationship between the call agent and the gateway to fully control the gateway and its associated ports. The plaintext commands are sent to gateways from the call agent using UDP port 2427. Port 2727 is used to send messages from the gateways to the call agent.

An MGCP gateway handles translation between audio signals and a packet network. Gateways interact with a call agent (CA), also called a Media Gateway Controller (MGC), that performs signal and call processing on gateway calls. In the MGCP configurations that Cisco IOS supports, a gateway can be a Cisco router, access server, or cable modem, and the CA is a server from a third-party vendor.

Configuration commands for MGCP define the path between the call agent and the gateway, the type of gateway, and the type of calls handled by the gateway.

MGCP uses endpoints and connections to construct a call. Endpoints are sources or destinations for data and can be physical or logical locations in a device. Connections can be point-to-point or multipoint.

Similar to SGCP, MGCP uses UDP for establishing audio connections over IP networks. However, MGCP also uses "hairpinning" to return a call to the PSTN when the packet network is not available.

MGCP Advantages

There are several advantages to using MGCP controlled gateways as voice gateways:

- **Alternative dial tone for VoIP environments:** Deregulation in the telecommunications industry gives Competitive Local-Exchange Carriers (CLECs) opportunities to provide toll-bypass from the Incumbent Local-Exchange Carriers (ILECs) by means of VoIP. MGCP enables a VoIP system to control call setup and teardown and Custom Local Area Subscriber Services (CLASS) features for less-sophisticated gateways.

- **Simplified configuration for static VoIP network dial peers:** When you use MGCP as the call agent in a VoIP environment, you need not configure static VoIP network dial peers. The MGCP call agent provides functions similar to VoIP network dial peers.

- **Migration paths:** Systems using earlier versions of the protocol can easily migrate to MGCP.

- **Centralized dial plan configured on Cisco Unified Communications Manager:** A centralized dial plan configuration on Cisco UBE enables you to handle and manage the entire dial plan configuration on Cisco Unified Communications Manager cluster within a multisite network. This simplifies the management and troubleshooting of a company telephone network.

- **Centralized gateway configuration on Cisco Unified Communications Manager:** As in the case of the dial plan, centralized gateway configurations for all gateways are managed via one central configuration page, which simplifies the management and troubleshooting of a company telephony network.

Note   Some network management tools do not work correctly when performing the configuration via Cisco Unified Communications Manager. In such cases, you might need to manually configure the gateway for MGCP without using the config download functionality.

- Simple Cisco IOS gateway configuration: Because the gateway configuration is mostly done on Cisco Unified Communications Manager, far fewer Cisco IOS router commands are necessary to bring up the gateway, as compared to any other gateway type.

- **Supports Q Signaling (QSIG) supplementary services with Cisco Unified Communications Manager:** With the support of QSIG supplementary services, MGCP is a protocol you can use to interconnect a Cisco Unified Communications Manager environment with a traditional PBX.

MGCP Architecture

The distributed system is composed of a call agent (or MGC), at least one media gateway (MG) that performs the conversion of media signals between circuits and packets, and at least one signaling gateway (SG) when connected to the PSTN.

MGCP defines a number of components and concepts. You should understand the relationships between components and how the components use the concepts to implement a working MGCP environment.

The following components are used in an MGCP environment:

■ **Endpoints:** Represent the point of interconnection between a packet network and a traditional telephone network.

■ **Gateways:** Handle the translation of audio between an SCN and a packet network. The media gateway uses MGCP to report events (such as off-hook or dialed digits) to a call agent.

■ **Call agent:** Exercises control over the operation of a gateway. The call agent uses MGCP to tell the gateway:

   ■ What events should be reported to the call agent

   ■ How endpoints should be connected

   ■ What signals should be implemented on endpoints

MGCP also allows the call agent to audit the current state of endpoints on a gateway.

Figure 2-53 shows an MGCP environment with all three components.

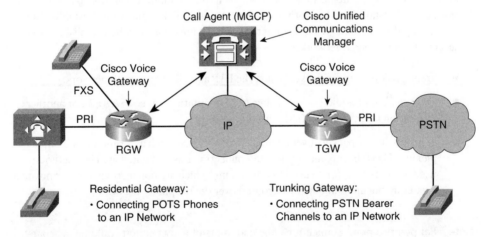

Figure 2-53 *MGCP Components*

Cisco voice gateways can act as MGCP gateways, and Cisco Unified Communications Manager acts as an MGCP call agent.

MGCP Gateways

Using Cisco IOS Software, voice gateways can be configured as MGCP gateways. Cisco Unified Communications Manager acts as an MGCP call agent, controlling the setting up and tearing down of connections between the endpoints in a VoIP network and endpoints in the PSTN, while managing all dial-plan-related configuration elements.

In the case of MGCP, calls are routed via route patterns using Cisco Unified Communications Manager, not by dial peers on the gateway. The gateway voice ports must be configured for proper signaling.

MGCP supports both residential and trunking gateways:

- **Trunking gateway (TGW):** Provides an interface between PSTN trunks and a VoIP network. A trunk can be a DS0, a T1, or an E1 line. Examples of TGWs include access servers and routers.

- **Residential gateway (RGW):** Provides an interface between analog (RJ-11) calls from a telephone and a VoIP network. The interfaces on a residential gateway might terminate a POTS connection to a phone, a key system, or a PBX. Examples of RGWs include cable modems and Cisco 2600 Series routers.

MGCP gateway connections can be point-to-point or multipoint. A point-to-point connection is an association between two endpoints with the purpose of transmitting data between these endpoints. Data transfer between these endpoints can take place after this association is established for both endpoints. A multipoint connection is established by connecting the endpoint to a multipoint session. Connections can be established over several types of bearer networks:

- Transmission of audio packets using the RTP and UDP over an IP network.

- Transmission of audio packets using ATM adaptation Layer 2 (AAL2), or another adaptation layer, over an ATM network.

- Transmission of packets over an internal connection, such as a time-division multiplexing (TDM) backplane or the interconnection bus of a gateway. This method is used, in particular, for "hairpin" connections, which are connections that terminate in a gateway but are immediately rerouted over the telephony network.

Note   For point-to-point connections, the endpoints of a connection could be in separate gateways or in the same gateway.

Creating a call connection involves a series of signals and events that describes the connection process. Each event causes signal messages to be sent to the call agent, and associated commands are sent back. That information might include indicators such as the off-hook event that triggers a dial-tone signal. These events and signals are specific to the type of endpoint that is involved in the call. MGCP groups these events and signals into packages.

MGCP Call Agents

A call agent, or MGC, represents the central controller in an MGCP environment, as depicted in Figure 2-54.

Figure 2-54 *MGCP Call Agent*

A call agent exercises control over the operation of a gateway and its associated end-points by requesting that a gateway observe and report events. In response to the events, the call agent instructs the endpoint what signal, if any, the endpoint should send to the attached telephone equipment. This requires a call agent to recognize each endpoint type it supports and the signaling characteristics of each physical and logical interface that is attached to a gateway.

A call agent uses its directory of endpoints and the relationship each endpoint has with the dial plan to determine appropriate call routing. Call agents initiate all VoIP call legs.

Basic MGCP Concepts

The basic MGCP concepts are as follows:

- **MGCP calls and connections:** Allow end-to-end calls to be established by connecting two or more endpoints

- **MGCP control commands:** Fundamental MGCP concept that allows a call agent to provide instructions for a gateway

- **Package types:** Fundamental MGCP concept that allows a gateway to determine the call destination

MGCP Calls and Connections

End-to-end calls are established by connecting two or more endpoints. To establish a call, the call agent instructs the gateway that is associated with each endpoint to make a connection with a specific endpoint or an endpoint of a particular type. The gateway returns the session parameters of its connection to the call agent, which in turn sends these session parameters to the other gateway. With this method, each gateway acquires the necessary session parameters to establish RTP sessions between the endpoints. All connections that are associated with the same call will share a common Call ID and the same media stream. Figure 2-55 illustrates the setup and teardown of an MGCP call.

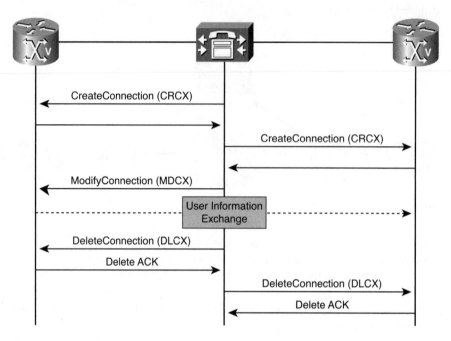

Figure 2-55 *Calls and Connections*

At the conclusion of a call, the call agent sends a DeleteConnection (DLCX) request to each gateway.

MGCP Control Commands

MGCP packets are unlike what you find in many other protocols. Usually wrapped in UDP port 2427, the MGCP datagrams are formatted with white space, much like you would expect to find in TCP protocols. An MGCP packet is either a command or a response.

A call agent uses control messages to direct its gateways and their operational behavior. Gateways use the control messages in responding to requests from a call agent and notifying the call agent of events and abnormal behavior.

There are eight command verbs. Two verbs are used by a call agent to query the state of a media gateway:

- **AuditEndpoint (AUEP):** This message requests the status of an endpoint. The call agent issues the command.

- **AuditConnection (AUCX):** This message requests the status of a connection. The call agent issues the command.

Three verbs are used by a call agent to manage an RTP connection on a media gateway. (A media gateway can also send a DLCX when it needs to delete a connection for its self-management.)

- **CreateConnection (CRCX):** This message instructs the gateway to establish a connection with an endpoint. The call agent issues the command.

- **DeleteConnection (DLCX):** This message informs the recipient to delete a connection. The call agent or the gateway can issue the command. The gateway or the call agent issues the command to advise that it no longer has the resources required to sustain the call.

- **ModifyConnection (MDCX):** This message instructs the gateway to update its connection parameters for a previously established connection. The call agent issues the command.

One verb is used by a call agent to request notification of events on the media gateway and to request a media gateway to apply signals:

- **NotificationRequest (RQNT):** This message instructs the gateway to watch for events on an endpoint and specifies the action to take when they occur. The call agent issues the command.

One verb is used by a media gateway to indicate to the call agent that it has detected an event for which the call agent had previously requested notification (via the RQNT command verb):

- **Notify (NTFY):** This message informs the call agent of an event for which notification was requested. The gateway issues the command.

One verb is used by a media gateway to indicate to the call agent that it is in the process of restarting:

- **RestartInProgress (RSIP):** This message notifies the call agent that the gateway and its endpoints are removed from service or are being placed back in service. The gateway issues the message.

Package Types

A call connection involves a series of events and signals, such as off-hook status, a ringing signal, or a signal to play an announcement, that are specific to the type of endpoint involved in the call.

MGCP groups these events and signals into packages. A trunk package, for example, is a group of events and signals relevant to a trunking gateway. An announcement package is a group of events and signals relevant to an announcement server. These packages are enabled by using the **mgcp package-capability** command. Table 2-12 lists some of the available package types and their descriptions.

Table 2-12   *Selected Package Types*

Package	Description
line-package	Package or residential lines; default for residential gateways
trunk-package	Events and signals for trunk lines; default for trunking gateways
as-package	Announcement server package
script-package	Events and signals for script loading
srtp-package	Secure RTP (SRTP) package; the default is disabled
dt-package	Events and signals for immediate-start, DTMF, and dial-pulse trunks
dtmf-package	Events and signals for DTMF relay
fxr-package	Events and signals for fax transmissions
gm-package	Events and signals for several types of endpoints, such as trunking gateways, access gateways, or residential gateways
md-package	Provides support for Feature Group D (FGD) Exchange Access North American (EANA) protocol signaling
ms-package	Events and signals for wink-start and immediate-start DID and Direct Outward Dialing (DOD), basic R1, and FGD Terminating Protocol

MGCP Call Flows

Figure 2-56 illustrates a dialog between a call agent and two gateways.

Although the gateways in this example are both residential gateways, the principles of operation listed here are the same for other gateway types:

1. The call agent sends a RQNT to each gateway. Because they are residential gateways, the request instructs the gateways to wait for an off-hook transition (event). When the off-hook transition event occurs, the call agent instructs the gateways to supply dial tone (signal). The call agent asks the gateway to monitor for other events as well. By providing a digit map in the request, the call agent can have the gateway collect digits before it notifies the call agent.

2. The gateways respond to the request. At this point, the gateways and the call agent wait for a triggering event.

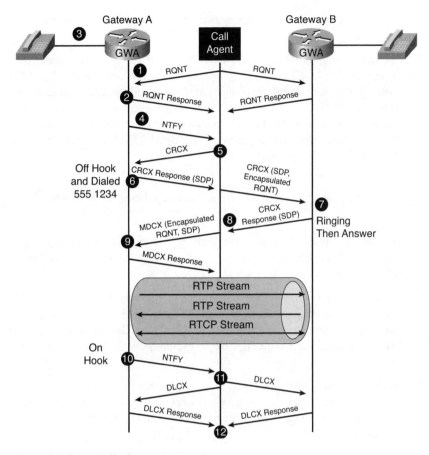

Figure 2-56 *Call Flows*

3. A user on Gateway A goes off-hook. As instructed by the call agent in its earlier request, the gateway provides a dial tone. Because the gateway is provided with a digit map, it begins to collect digits (as they are dialed) until either a match is made or no match is possible. For the remainder of this example, assume that the digits match a digit map entry.

4. Gateway A sends a NTFY to the call agent to advise the call agent that a requested event was observed. The NTFY identifies the endpoint, the event, and in this case the dialed digits.

5. After confirming that a call is possible based on the dialed digits, the call agent instructs Gateway A to CRCX with its endpoint.

6. The gateway responds with a session description if it is able to accommodate the connection. The session description identifies at least the IP address and UDP port for use in a subsequent RTP session. The gateway does not have a

session description for the remote side of the call, and the connection enters a wait state.

7. The call agent prepares and sends a CRCX to Gateway B. In the request, the call agent provides the session description obtained from Gateway A. The CRCX is targeted to a single endpoint, if only one endpoint is capable of handling the call, or to any one of a set of endpoints. The call agent also embeds a RQNT that instructs the gateway about the signals and events it should now consider relevant. In this example, in which the gateway is residential, the signal requests ringing and the event is an off-hook transition.

Note   The interaction between Gateway B and its attached user has been simplified.

8. Gateway B responds to the request with its session description. Notice that Gateway B has both session descriptions and recognizes how to establish its RTP sessions.

9. The call agent relays the session description to Gateway A in an MDCX. This request might contain an encapsulated NTFY request that describes the relevant signals and events at this stage of the call setup. Now Gateway A and Gateway B have the required session descriptions to establish the RTP sessions over which the audio travels.

10. At the conclusion of the call, one of the endpoints recognizes an on-hook transition. In the example, the user on Gateway A hangs up. Because the call agent requested the gateways to notify in such an event, Gateway A notifies the call agent.

11. The call agent sends a DLCX request to each gateway.

12. The gateways delete the connections and respond.

Configuring MGCP Gateways

Configuring MGCP on a gateway depends on what type of gateway you are configuring. Residential gateway configuration is done in dial-peer configuration mode, whereas a trunking gateway is configured under the controller interface.

Note   After configuring the gateway, the gateway must be added to the call agent.

To configure MGCP on a gateway, perform the tasks in the following sections.

MGCP Residential Gateway Configuration Example

MGCP is invoked with the **mgcp** command. If the call agent expects the gateway to use the default port (UDP 2427), the **mgcp** command is used without any parameters. If the call agent requires a different port, the port must be configured as a parameter in the **mgcp** command; for example, **mgcp 5036** would tell the gateway to use port 5036 instead of the default port.

You can perform the following steps to configure an RGW:

Step 1.   Initiate the MGCP application.

Step 2.   Specify the call agent's IP address or domain name, port, and gateway control service type.

At least one **mgcp call-agent** command is required after the **mgcp** command. The command identifies the call agent by an IP address or a hostname. Using a hostname adds a measure of fault tolerance in a network that has multiple call agents. When the gateway asks the DNS for the IP address of the call agent, the DNS might provide more than one address, in which case the gateway can use either one. If multiple instances of the **mgcp call-agent** command are configured, the gateway uses the first call agent to respond.

Step 3.   Set up the dial peer for a voice port:

■ Specify the MGCP application to run on the voice port.

■ Specify the voice port to bind with MGCP.

When the parameters of the MGCP gateway are configured, the active voice ports (endpoints) are associated with MGCP. Dial peer 1, in Example 2-12, illustrates an **application mgcpapp** subcommand. This command binds a voice port (for example, 1/0/0) to MGCP. Also, notice that the dial peer does not have a destination pattern. A destination pattern is not used because the relationship between the dial number and the port is maintained by the call agent.

Step 4.   (Optional) Specify the event packages that are supported on the residential gateway. The default package is line-package.

The configuration example in Example 2-12 and Figure 2-57 illustrates the commands required to configure an MGCP residential gateway, including the commands to identify the packages that the gateway expects the call agent to use when it communicates with the gateway.

Example 2-12 *MGCP Residential Gateway Configuration*

```
Router(config)#ccm-manager mgcp
Router(config)#mgcp
Router(config-mgcp)#mgcp call-agent 172.20.5.20 service-type mgcp
Router(config)#dial-peer voice 1 pots
Router(config-dialpeer)#application mgcpapp
```

```
Router(config-dialpeer)#port 1/0/0
Router(config)#dial-peer voice 2 pots
Router(config-dialpeer)#application mgcpapp
Router(config-dialpeer)#port 1/0/1
Router(config-dialpeer)#exit
Router(config)#mgcp package-capability dtmf-package
Router(config)#mgcp package-capability gm-package
Router(config)#mgcp package-capability line-package
Router(config)#mgcp package-capability rtp-package
Router(config)#mgcp default-package line-package
```

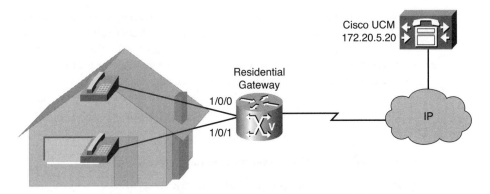

Figure 2-57 *MGCP Residential Gateway Topology*

Configuring an MGCP Trunk Gateway Example

Figure 2-58 and Example 2-13 illustrate commands for configuring an MGCP trunk gateway.

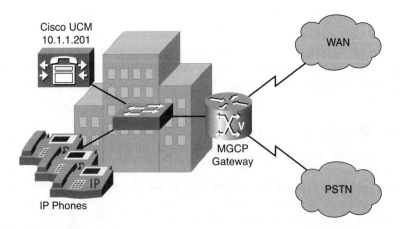

Figure 2-58 *MGCP Trunk Gateway Topology*

Example 2-13 *MGCP Trunk Gateway Configuration Example*

```
Router(config)#ccm-manager mgcp
Router(config)#mgcp 4000
Router(config)#mgcp call-agent 10.1.1.201 4000
Router(config)#controller t1 0/1/0
Router(config-controller)#framing esf
Router(config-controller)#clock source internal
Router(config-controller)#ds0-group 1 timeslots 1-24 type none service mgcp
Router(config)#controller t1 0/1/1
Router(config-controller)#framing esf
Router(config-controller)#clock source internal
Router(config-controller)#ds0-group 1 timeslots 1-24 type none service mgcp
```

Instead of using the **application mgcpapp** command in a dial peer, a trunk endpoint identifies its association with MGCP using the **service mgcp** parameter in the **ds0-group** controller subcommand. As always in MGCP, the call agent maintains the relationship between the endpoint (in this case, a digital trunk) and its address.

You can complete the following steps to configure a trunking gateway:

Step 1. Initiate the MGCP application.

> **Note** The **ccm-manager mgcp** command is required only if the call agent is a Cisco Unified Communications Manager.

Step 2. Specify the call agent's IP address or domain name, the port, and the gateway control service type.

Step 3. Specify the controller number of the T1 trunk to be used for analog calls and enter controller configuration mode.

Step 4. Configure the channelized T1 time slots to accept the analog calls and use the MGCP service.

Step 5. (Optional) Specify the event packages that are supported on the trunking gateway. The default is trunk-package.

Configuring Fax Relay with MGCP Gateways

Figure 2-59 and Example 2-14 show an MGCP configuration of a voice gateway that is configured for T.38 fax support.

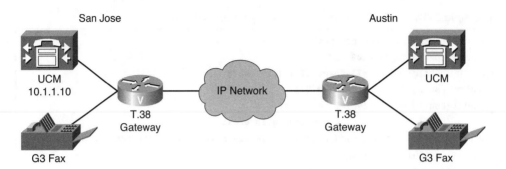

Figure 2-59 *Fax Pass-Through and Relay with MGCP Gateways Topology*

Example 2-14 *Fax Pass-Through and Relay with MGCP Gateways Example*

```
Router(config)#ccm-manager mgcp
Router(config)#no ccm-manager fax protocol cisco
Router(config)#mgcp
Router(config)#mgcp call-agent 10.1.1.10 service-type mgcp version 0.1
Router(config)#mgcp package-capability fxr-package
Router(config)#mgcp package-capability rtp-package
Router(config)#mgcp fax rate 14400
Router(config)#mgcp timer 300
Router(config)#mgcp fax-relay sg3-to-g3
```

This scenario requires a company's headquarters in San Jose to be able to fax to its Austin office using MGCP. As a network administrator, your responsibility is to configure the gateway to meet the requirements of the network.

Requirements dictate that you:

■ Configure a call agent to work with the gateway.

■ Disable Cisco Fax Relay.

■ Enable MGCP on the gateways.

■ Specify additional MGCP package capabilities.

■ Specify the maximum fax rate allowed for MGCP.

■ Adjust the Named Signaling Event (NSE) timers for network conditions.

■ Configure the fax machines to negotiate down to G3 speeds.

The following steps describe how to configure fax pass-through with MGCP gateways:

Step 1.   Enable the gateway to communicate with Cisco Unified Communications Manager through the MGCP.

```
Router(config)#ccm-manager mgcp
```

This command enables the gateway to communicate with Cisco Unified Communications Manager (UCM) through MGCP. This command also enables control agent redundancy when a backup UCM server is available.

Step 2.   Disable the Cisco Fax Relay protocol.

```
Router(config)#no ccm-manager fax protocol cisco
```

Step 3.   Allocate resources for the MGCP.

```
Router(config)#mgcp [port]
```

The *port* option specifies the UDP port for the MGCP gateway. The UDP port range is from 1025 through 65535. The default is UDP port 2427.

Step 4.   Specify the address and protocol of the call agent for MGCP.

```
Router(config)#mgcp call-agent {host-name | ip-address} [port]
   [service-type type [version protocol-version]]
```

Step 5.   Specify the FXR package for fax transmissions.

```
Router(config)#mgcp package-capability package
```

Events specified in the MGCP messages from the call agent must belong to one of the supported packages. Otherwise, connection requests are refused by the gateway.

By default, certain packages are configured as supported on each platform type. Using this command, you can configure additional package capability only for packages that are supported by your call agent. You can also disable support for a package with the **no** form of this command. Enter each package you want to add as a separate command.

Step 6.   Define the maximum fax rate for MGCP T.38 sessions.

```
Router(config)#mgcp fax rate [2400 | 4800 | 7200 | 9600 | 12000 | 14400
   | voice]
```

Step 7.   Define the timeout period for awaiting NSE responses from the dial peer.

```
Router(config)#mgcp timer {receive-rtcp timer | net-cont-test timer |
   nse-response t38 timer}
```

The **nse-response t38** option sets the timer for awaiting T.38 NSE responses. This timer is configured to tell the terminating gateway how long to wait for an NSE from a peer gateway. The NSE from the peer gateway can either acknowledge the switch and its readiness to accept packets or indicate that it cannot accept T.38 packets.

Step 8.   Allow SG3 fax machines to operate at G3 speeds in fax relay mode.

```
Router(config)#mgcp fax-relay sg3-to-g3
```

When this command is entered, the DSP fax relay firmware suppresses the V.8 call menu (CM) tone, and the fax machines negotiate down to G3 speeds for a fax stream.

Verifying MGCP

Several **show** and **debug** commands provide support for verifying and troubleshooting MGCP. You should be familiar with the information provided from each command and how this information can help you.

Use the output of the **show mgcp** command, an example of which is provided in Example 2-15, to verify the status of a router's MGCP parameters. You should see the IP address of the UCM server that you use (10.1.1.101, in this example) and the port you are using for MGCP. You should also see the administrative and operational states as ACTIVE. All other parameters are left at their default behavior in this example. Also highlighted in the example are the packages supported by the gateway.

Example 2-15   show mgcp *Command*

```
router#show mgcp
MGCP Admin State ACTIVE, Oper State ACTIVE - Cause Code NONE
MGCP call-agent: 10.1.1.101 4000 Initial protocol service is MGCP 0.1
MGCP validate call-agent source-ipaddr DISABLED
MGCP validate domain name DISABLED
MGCP block-newcalls DISABLED
MGCP send SGCP RSIP: forced/restart/graceful/disconnected DISABLED
MGCP quarantine mode discard/step
MGCP quarantine of persistent events is ENABLED
MGCP dtmf-relay for VoIP is SDP controlled
MGCP dtmf-relay for voAAL2 is SDP controlled
MGCP voip modem passthrough disabled
MGCP voaal2 modem passthrough disabled
MGCP voip tremolo modem relay: Disabled
MGCP T.38 Named Signalling Event (NSE) response timer: 200
MGCP Network (IP/AAL2) Continuity Test timer: 200
MGCP 'RTP stream loss' timer: 5
MGCP request timeout 500
MGCP maximum exponential request timeout 4000
MGCP gateway port: 4000, MGCP maximum waiting delay 3000
MGCP restart delay 0, MGCP vad DISABLED
MGCP rtrcac DISABLED
MGCP system resource check DISABLED
MGCP xpc-codec: DISABLED, MGCP persistent hookflash: DISABLED
MGCP persistent offhook: ENABLED, MGCP persistent onhook: DISABLED
```

```
MGCP piggyback msg ENABLED, MGCP endpoint offset DISABLED
MGCP simple-sdp DISABLED
MGCP undotted-notation DISABLED
MGCP codec type g711ulaw, MGCP packetization period 20
MGCP JB threshold lwm 30, MGCP JB threshold hwm 150
MGCP LAT threshold lwm 150, MGCP LAT threshold hwm 300
MGCP PL threshold lwm 1000, MGCP PL threshold hwm 10000
MGCP CL threshold lwm 1000, MGCP CL threshold hwm 10000
MGCP playout mode is adaptive 60, 40, 200 in msec
MGCP Fax Playout Buffer is 300 in msec
MGCP media (RTP) dscp: ef, MGCP signaling dscp: af31
MGCP default package: trunk-package
MGCP supported packages: gm-package dtmf-package trunk-package line-package
                         hs-package atm-package ms-package dt-package mo-package
                         res-package mt-package fxr-package md-package
MGCP Digit Map matching order: shortest match
SGCP Digit Map matching order: always left-to-right
MGCP VoAAL2 ignore-lco-codec DISABLED
```

The **show ccm-manager** command verifies the active and redundant configured Cisco CallManager servers. It also indicates whether the gateway is currently registered with Cisco Unified Communications Manager. Example 2-16 illustrates sample output from the command.

Example 2-16   show ccm-manager *Command*

```
router#show ccm-manager
MGCP Domain Name: cisco-voice-01
Priority        Status                     Host
=============================================================
Primary         Registered                 10.89.129.211
First Backup    None
Second Backup   None


Current active Call Manager: 10.89.129.211
Backhaul/Redundant link port: 2428
Failover Interval: 30 seconds
Keepalive Interval: 15 seconds
Last keepalive sent: 5w1d (elapsed time: 00:00:04)
Last MGCP traffic time: 5w1d (elapsed time: 00:00:04)
Last failover time: None
Switchback mode: Graceful
MGCP Fallback mode: Not Selected
Last MGCP Fallback start time: 00:00:00
```

```
Last MGCP Fallback end time: 00:00:00

Configuration Error History:
```

The **show mgcp** endpoint command displays a list of the voice ports that are configured for MGCP. Example 2-17 illustrates sample output from the command.

Example 2-17   show mgcp endpoint *Command*

```
router#show mgcp endpoint

Interface T1 0/1/0


                ENDPOINT-NAME    V-PORT        SIG-TYPE    ADMIN
        S0/SU1/ds1-0/1@HQ-1      0/1/0:1          none      up
        S0/SU1/ds1-0/2@HQ-1      0/1/0:1          none      up
        S0/SU1/ds1-0/3@HQ-1      0/1/0:1          none      up
        S0/SU1/ds1-0/4@HQ-1      0/1/0:1          none      up
        S0/SU1/ds1-0/5@HQ-1      0/1/0:1          none      up
        S0/SU1/ds1-0/6@HQ-1      0/1/0:1          none      up
        S0/SU1/ds1-0/7@HQ-1      0/1/0:1          none      up
        S0/SU1/ds1-0/8@HQ-1      0/1/0:1          none      up
        S0/SU1/ds1-0/9@HQ-1      0/1/0:1          none      up
        S0/SU1/ds1-0/10@HQ-1     0/1/0:1          none      up
```

The **show mgcp statistics** command displays a count of the successful and unsuccessful control commands, as shown in Example 2-18. You should investigate a high unsuccessful count.

Example 2-18   show mgcp statistics *Command*

```
router#show mgcp statistics

UDP pkts rx 8, tx 9
Unrecognized rx pkts 0, MGCP message parsing errors 0
Duplicate MGCP ack tx 0, Invalid versions count 0
CreateConn rx 4, successful 0, failed 0
DeleteConn rx 2, successful 2, failed 0
ModifyConn rx 4, successful 4, failed 0
DeleteConn tx 0, successful 0, failed 0
NotifyRequest rx 0, successful 4, failed 0
AuditConnection rx 0, successful 0, failed 0
AuditEndpoint rx 0, successful 0, failed 0
RestartInProgress tx 1, successful 1, failed 0
```

```
Notify tx 0, successful 0, failed 0
ACK tx 8, NACK tx 0
ACK rx 0, NACK rx 0
IP address based Call Agents statistics:
IP address 10.24.167.3, Total msg rx 8, successful 8, failed 0
```

Debug Commands

The following **debug** commands are useful for monitoring and troubleshooting MGCP:

- **debug voip ccapi inout:** This command shows every interaction with the call control API on the telephone interface and the VoIP side. Watching the output allows users to follow the progress of a call from the inbound interface or VoIP peer to the outbound side of the call. This **debug** command is very active. Therefore, you should use it sparingly in a live network.

- **debug mgcp [all | errors | events | packets | parser]:** This command reports all **mgcp** command activity. You should use this **debug** command to trace the MGCP request and responses.

VoIP Quality Considerations

The inherent characteristics of a converged voice and data IP network cause network engineers and administrators to face certain challenges in delivering voice traffic correctly. This section describes the challenges of integrating a voice and data network and offers solutions for avoiding problems when designing a VoIP network for optimal voice quality.

IP Networking and Audio Clarity

Because of the nature of IP networking, voice packets sent via IP are subject to certain transmission problems. Conditions present in the network might introduce problems such as echo, jitter, or delay. These problems must be addressed with QoS mechanisms.

The clarity (that is, the "cleanliness" and "crispness") of the audio signal is of utmost importance. The listener must be able to recognize the identity and sense the mood of the speaker. The following factors can affect clarity:

- **Fidelity:** The degree to which a system, or a portion of a system, accurately reproduces at its output the essential characteristics of the signal impressed upon its input, or the result of a prescribed operation on the signal impressed upon its input (definition from the Alliance for Telecommunications Industry Solutions [ATIS]). The bandwidth of the transmission medium almost always limits the total bandwidth of the spoken voice. Human speech typically requires a bandwidth from 100 to 10,000 Hz, although 90 percent of speech intelligence is contained between 100 and 3000 Hz.

- **Echo:** A result of electrical impedance mismatches in the transmission path. Echo is always present, even in traditional telephony networks, but at a level that cannot be detected by the human ear. The two components that affect echo are amplitude (loudness of the echo) and delay (the time between the spoken voice and the echoed sound). You can control echo using suppressors or cancellers.

- **Jitter:** Variation in the arrival of coded speech packets at the far end of a VoIP network. The varying arrival time of the packets can cause gaps in the re-creation and playback of the voice signal. These gaps are undesirable and annoy the listener. Delay is induced in the network by variation in the routes of individual packets, contention, or congestion. You can resolve variable delay by using dejitter buffers.

- **Delay:** The time between the spoken voice and the arrival of the electronically delivered voice at the far end. Delay results from multiple factors, including distance (propagation delay), coding, compression, serialization, and buffers.

- **Packet loss:** Voice packets might be dropped under various conditions such as an unstable network, network congestion, or too much variable delay in the network. Lost voice packets are not recoverable, resulting in gaps in the conversation that are perceptible to the user.

- **Side tone:** The purposeful design of the telephone that allows the speakers to hear their spoken audio in the earpiece. Without side tone, the speaker is left with the impression that the telephone instrument is not working.

- **Background noise:** The low-volume audio that is heard from the far-end connection. Certain bandwidth-saving technologies, such as VAD, can eliminate background noise altogether. When this technology is implemented, the speaker audio path is open to the listener, while the listener audio path is closed to the speaker. The effect of VAD is often that speakers think the connection is broken because they hear nothing from the other end. Therefore, VAD is often combined with comfort noise generation (CNG) to prevent the illusion that the call has been disconnected.

Jitter

Jitter is defined as a variation in the arrival of received packets. On the sending side, packets are sent in a continuous stream with the packets spaced evenly. Because of network congestion, improper queuing, or configuration errors, this steady stream can become uneven because the delay between each packet varies instead of remaining constant, as displayed in Figure 2-60.

When a router receives a VoIP audio stream, it must compensate for the jitter that is encountered. The mechanism that handles this function is the play out delay buffer, or dejitter buffer. The play out delay buffer must buffer these packets and then play them out in a steady stream to the DSPs to be converted back to an analog audio stream. The play out delay buffer, however, affects overall absolute delay.

When a conversation is subjected to jitter, the results can be clearly heard. If the talker says, "Watson, come here. I want you," the listener might hear, "Wat....s...on.......come here, I......wa......nt.........y......ou." The variable arrival of the packets at the receiving end causes the speech to be delayed and garbled.

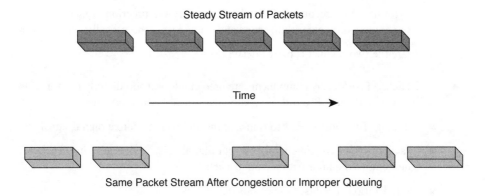

Figure 2-60 *Jitter in IP Networks*

Delay

Overall or absolute delay can affect VoIP. You might have experienced delay in a telephone conversation with someone on a different continent. The delays can cause entire words in the conversation to be cut off and can therefore be very frustrating. Figure 2-61 illustrates various areas in the network that can introduce delay.

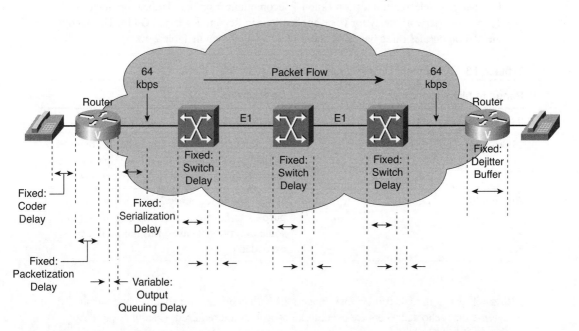

Figure 2-61 *Sources of Delay*

When you design a network that transports voice over packet, frame, or cell infrastructures, it is important to understand and account for the predictable delay components in the network. You must also correctly account for all potential delays to ensure overall network performance is acceptable. Overall voice quality is a function of many factors, including the compression algorithm, errors and frame loss, echo cancellation, and delay.

Following are the two distinct types of delay:

- **Fixed delay:** Fixed-delay components are predictable and add directly to overall delay on the connection. Fixed-delay components include the following:

  - **Coding:** The time it takes to translate the audio signal into a digital signal

  - **Packetization:** The time it takes to put digital voice information into packets and remove the information from packets

  - **Serialization:** The insertion of bits onto a link

  - **Propagation:** The time it takes a packet to traverse a link

- **Variable delay:** Variable delays arise from queuing delays in the egress trunk buffers that are located on the serial port connected to the WAN. These buffers create variable delays, called jitter, across the network.

Acceptable Delay

International Telecommunication Union Telecommunication Standardization Sector (ITU-T) specifies network delay for voice applications in Recommendation G.114. This recommendation defines three bands of one-way delay, as shown in Table 2-13.

Table 2-13 *Acceptable Delay: G.114*

Range in Milliseconds	Description
0 to 150	Acceptable for most user applications.
150 to 400	Acceptable, provided administrators are aware of the transmission time and its impact on the transmission quality of user applications.
Above 400	Unacceptable for general network planning purposes. (However, it is recognized that in some exceptional cases, this limit will be exceeded.)

Note This recommendation is for connections with echo that are adequately controlled, implying that echo cancellers are used. Echo cancellers are required when one-way delay exceeds 25 ms (G.131).

The G.114 recommendation is oriented toward national telecommunications administrations and, therefore, is more stringent than recommendations that would normally be applied in private voice networks. When the location and business needs of end users are well known to a network designer, more delay might prove acceptable. For private networks, a 200-ms delay is a reasonable goal and a 250-ms delay is a limit. This goal is what Cisco Systems proposes as reasonable as long as excessive jitter does not affect voice quality. However, all networks must be engineered so the maximum expected voice connection delay is known and minimized.

The G.114 recommendation is for one-way delay only and does not account for round-trip delay. Network design engineers must consider both variable and fixed delays. Variable delays include queuing and network delays, and fixed delays include coding, packetization, serialization, and dejitter buffer delays. Table 2-14 offers a sample delay budget calculation.

Table 2-14 *Delay Budget Calculations*

Delay Type	Fixed (ms)	Variable (ms)
Coder delay	18	
Packetization delay	30	
Queuing and buffering		8
Serialization (64 kbps)	5	
Network delay (public frame)	40	25
Dejitter buffer	45	
Total	138	33

Packet Loss

Lost data packets are recoverable if the endpoints can request retransmission. Lost voice packets, as depicted in Figure 2-62, are not recoverable, because the audio must be played out in real time and retransmission is not an option.

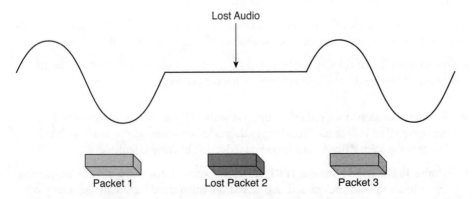

Figure 2-62 *Effect of Packet Loss*

Voice packets might be dropped under the following conditions:

- The network is unstable (flapping links).

- The network is congested.

- Too much variable delay exists in the network, because packets might arrive too late to be admitted into an interface's dejitter buffer.

Packet loss causes voice clipping and skips. As a result, the listener hears gaps in the conversation, as shown in Figure 2-62. The industry-standard codec algorithms that are used in Cisco DSPs correct for 20 ms to 50 ms of lost voice through the use of Packet Loss Concealment (PLC) algorithms. PLC intelligently analyzes missing packets and generates a reasonable replacement packet to improve the voice quality. Cisco VoIP technology uses 20-ms samples of voice payload per VoIP packet by default. Effective codec correction algorithms require that only a single packet can be lost at any given time. If more packets are lost, the listener experiences gaps.

If a conversation experiences packet loss, the effect is immediately heard. If the talker says, "Watson, come here. I want you," the listener might hear, "Wat——, come here, ———you."

VoIP and QoS

Real-time applications, such as voice applications, have different characteristics and requirements from those of traditional data applications. Because they are real-time based, voice applications tolerate minimal variation in the amount of delay affecting delivery of their voice packets. Voice traffic is also intolerant of packet loss and jitter, both of which unacceptably degrade the quality of the voice transmission delivered to the recipient end user. To effectively transport voice traffic over IP, mechanisms are required that ensure reliable delivery of voice packets. Cisco IOS QoS features collectively embody these techniques, offering the means to provide priority service that meets the stringent requirements of voice packet delivery.

The QoS components for Cisco Unified Communications are provided through the IP traffic management, queuing, and shaping capabilities of a Cisco IP network infrastructure.

Following are a few of the Cisco IOS features that address the requirements of end-to-end QoS and service differentiation for voice packet delivery:

- **Header compression:** Used in conjunction with RTP and TCP, it compresses the extensive RTP or TCP header, resulting in decreased consumption of available bandwidth for voice traffic. A corresponding reduction in delay is realized.

- **Frame Relay Traffic Shaping (FRTS):** Delays excess traffic using a buffer or queuing mechanism to hold packets and shape the flow when the data rate of the source is higher than expected.

- **FRF.12:** Ensures predictability for voice traffic, aiming to provide better throughput on low-speed Frame Relay links by interleaving delay-sensitive voice traffic on one virtual circuit (VC) with fragments of a long frame on another VC utilizing the same interface.

- **Public Switched Telephone Network (PSTN) Fallback:** Provides a mechanism to monitor congestion in the IP network and either redirect calls to the PSTN or reject calls based on the network congestion.

- **IP RTP Priority and Frame Relay IP RTP Priority:** Provides a strict priority queuing scheme that allows delay-sensitive data, such as voice, to be dequeued and sent before packets when other queues are dequeued. These features are especially useful on slow-speed WAN links, including Frame Relay, Multilink PPP [MLP], and T1 ATM links. It works with weighted fair queuing (WFQ) and class-based WFQ (CBWFQ).

- **IP to ATM Class of Service (CoS):** Includes a feature suite that maps QoS characteristics between IP and ATM. Offers differential service classes across the entire WAN, not just the routed portion. Gives mission-critical applications exceptional service during periods of high network usage and congestion.

- **Low Latency Queuing (LLQ):** Provides strict priority queuing. This feature enables you to configure the priority status for a class within CBWFQ and is not limited to UDP port numbers, as is IP RTP Priority.

- **MLP:** Allows large packets to be multilink encapsulated and fragmented so they are small enough to satisfy the delay requirements of real-time traffic. MLP also provides a special transmit queue for smaller, delay-sensitive packets, enabling them to be sent earlier than other flows.

- **Resource Reservation Protocol (RSVP):** Supports the reservation of resources across an IP network, allowing end systems to request QoS guarantees from the network. For networks supporting VoIP, RSVP (in conjunction with features that provide queuing, traffic shaping, and voice call signaling) can provide call admission control (CAC) for voice traffic. Cisco also provides RSVP support for LLQ and Frame Relay.

QoS at its essence is managed unfairness. For example, bandwidth management can be a zero-sum game, where some applications might be given preferential treatment, to the detriment of other applications. So, VoIP network designers should strategically use QoS mechanisms to help protect voice traffic from other traffic types, while not starving out those other traffic types. QoS is discussed is much more detail in Chapter 7, "Introducing Quality of Service," and Chapter 8, 'Configuring QoS Mechanisms."

Objectives of QoS

To ensure VoIP is an acceptable replacement for standard PSTN telephony services, customers must receive the same consistently high quality of voice transmission they receive with basic telephone services. Like other real-time applications, VoIP is extremely sensitive to issues related to bandwidth and delay. To ensure VoIP transmissions are intelligible to the receiver, voice packets cannot be dropped, excessively delayed, or be subject to variations in delay (jitter). A successful VoIP deployment must provide an acceptable level of voice quality by meeting VoIP traffic requirements for issues related to bandwidth, latency, and jitter.

QoS refers to the ability of a network to provide improved service to selected network traffic over various underlying technologies including Frame Relay, ATM, Ethernet and 802.1 networks, SONET, and IP-routed networks. VoIP guarantees high-quality voice transmission only if the signaling and audio channel packets have priority over other kinds of network traffic.

In particular, QoS features provide improved and more predictable network service by implementing the following services:

■ **Support guaranteed bandwidth:** Designing the network so the necessary bandwidth is always available to support voice and data traffic

■ **Improve loss characteristics:** Designing the Frame Relay network, for example, so discard eligibility is not a factor for frames containing voice, keeping voice below the committed information rate (CIR)

■ **Avoid and manage network congestion:** Ensuring the LAN and WAN infrastructure can support the volume of data traffic and voice calls

■ **Shape network traffic:** Using Cisco traffic-shaping tools to ensure smooth and consistent delivery of frames to the WAN

■ **Set traffic priorities across the network:** Marking voice traffic as priority and queuing it first

Using QoS to Improve Voice Quality

Voice features that provide QoS are deployed at different points in the network and designed for use with other QoS features to achieve specific goals, such as minimization of jitter and delay.

Cisco IOS Software includes a complete set of features for delivering QoS throughout the network. Although a complete survey of QoS features is beyond the scope of this book, Cisco's recommended QoS mechanism for VoIP queuing, in a router's output interface, is LLQ.

LLQ provides strict priority queuing (PQ) in conjunction with CBWFQ. LLQ configures the priority status for a class within CBWFQ, in which voice packets receive priority over all other traffic.

For example, consider Figure 2-63. Whereas web traffic receives at least 128 kbps of bandwidth (if the web traffic needs that much bandwidth), voice traffic receives 256 kbps of "priority" bandwidth (if the voice traffic needs that much bandwidth), meaning the voice traffic is transmitted first, ahead of the web traffic. However, the voice traffic will not starve out the other traffic types, because the voice traffic is also limited to consuming no more than 256 kbps.

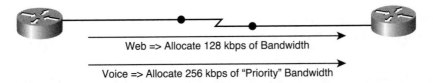

Figure 2-63 *Low Latency Queuing Example*

Transporting Modulated Data over IP Networks

An IP, or packet-switched, network enables data to be sent in packets to remote locations. The data is assembled by a packet assembler/disassembler (PAD) into individual packets of data, involving a process of segmentation or subdivision of larger sets of data as specified by the native protocol of the sending device. Each packet has a unique identifier that makes it independent and has its own destination address. Because the packet is unique and independent, it can traverse the network in a stream of packets and use different routes. This has some implications for fax transmissions that use data packets rather than using an analog signal over a circuit-switched network.

Differences from Fax Transmission in the PSTN

In IP networks, individual packets that are part of the same data transmission might follow different physical paths of varying lengths. They can also experience varying levels of propagation delay and delay that is caused by being held in packet buffers awaiting the availability of a subsequent circuit. The packets can also arrive in an order different from the order in which they entered the network. The destination node of the network uses the identifiers and addresses in the packet sequencing information to reassemble the packets into the correct sequence.

Fax transmissions are designed to operate across a 64-kbps PCM-encoded voice circuit, but in packet networks, the 64-kbps stream is often compressed into a much smaller data rate by passing it through a DSP. The codecs normally used to compress a voice stream in a DSP are designed to compress and decompress human speech, not fax or modem tones. For this reason, faxes and modems are rarely used in a VoIP network without some kind of relay or pass-through mechanism in place.

Fax Services over IP Networks

There are three conceptual methods of carrying fax-machine-to-fax-machine communications across packet networks:

- **Fax relay:** The T.30 fax from the PSTN is demodulated at the sending gateway. The demodulated fax content is enveloped into packets, sent over the network, and re-modulated into T.30 fax at the receiving end.

> **Note**   Cisco IOS supports two types of fax relay: T.38 fax relay and Cisco Fax Relay (which is proprietary).

- Fax pass-through: Modulated fax information from the PSTN is passed in-band, end-to-end over a voice speech path in an IP network. There are two pass-through techniques:

  - The configured voice codec is used for the fax transmission. This technique works only when the configured codec is G.711 with no VAD and no echo cancellation (EC) or when the configured codec is a clear-channel codec or G.726/32. Low-bit-rate codecs cannot be used for fax transmissions.

  - The gateway dynamically changes the codec from the codec configured for voice to G.711 with no VAD and no EC for the duration of the fax session. This method is specifically referred to as "codec up speed" or "fax pass-through with up speed."

- **Store-and-forward fax:** Breaks the fax process into distinct sending and receiving processes and allows fax messages to be stored between those processes. Store-and-forward fax is based on the ITU-T T.37 standard, and it also enables fax transmissions to be received from or delivered to computers rather than fax machines.

Understanding Fax/Modem Pass-Through, Relay, and Store and Forward

Several features are available to overcome the issues involved with carrying fax and modem signals across an IP network:

- Fax and modem pass-through

- Fax and modem relay

- Fax store and forward

Fax Pass-Through

Fax pass-through, as illustrated in Figure 2-64, is the simplest technique for sending fax over IP networks, but it is not the default, nor is it the most desirable method of supporting fax over IP. T.38 fax relay provides a more reliable and error-free method of sending faxes over an IP network, but some third-party H.323 and SIP implementations do not support T.38 fax relay. These same implementations often support fax pass-through.

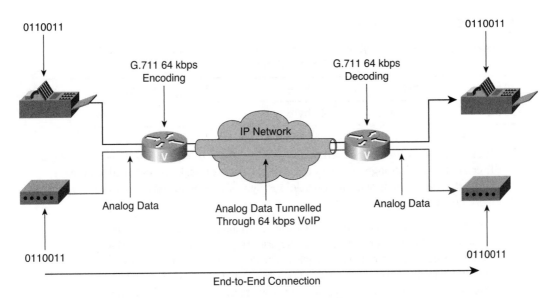

Figure 2-64 *Fax and Modem Pass-Through Topology*

Fax pass-through is the state of the channel after the fax up-speed process has occurred. In fax pass-through mode, gateways do not distinguish a fax call from a voice call. Fax communication between the two fax machines is carried in its entirety in-band over a voice call. When using fax pass-through with up speed, the gateways are to some extent aware of the fax call. Although relay mechanisms are not employed, with up speed, the gateways recognize a called terminal identification fax tone, automatically change the voice codec to G.711 if necessary (thus the designation up speed), and turn off EC and VAD for the duration of the call.

Fax pass-through is also known as voice-band data by the ITU. Voice-band data refers to the transport of fax or modem signals over a voice channel through a packet network with an coding appropriate for fax or modem signals. The minimum set of coders for voice-band data mode is G.711 mu-law and a-law with VAD disabled.

Fax pass-through takes place when incoming T.30 fax data is not demodulated or compressed for its transit through the packet network. The two endpoints (fax machines or modems) communicate directly to each other over a transparent IP connection. The gateway does not distinguish fax calls from voice calls.

With pass-through, the fax traffic is carried between the two gateways in RTP packets using an uncompressed format resembling the G.711 codec. This method of transporting fax traffic takes a constant 64-kbps (payload) stream plus its IP overhead end-to-end for the duration of the call. IP overhead is 16 kbps for normal voice traffic, but when switching to pass-through, the packetization period is reduced from 20 ms to 10 ms. Table 2-15 compares a G.711 VoIP call that uses 20-ms packetization with a G.711 fax pass-through call that uses 10-ms packetization.

Table 2-15 *G.711 Packetization Periods*

Packetization	G.711 Payload	Overhead for Layers 3 and 4	Packet Size	Bit Rate
10 ms	80 byte	40 byte	120 byte	96 kbps
20 ms	160 byte	40 byte	200 byte	80 kbps

Packet redundancy might be used to mitigate the effects of packet loss in the IP network. Even so, fax pass-through remains susceptible to packet loss, jitter, and latency in the IP network. The two endpoints must be clocked synchronously for this type of transport to work predictably.

Performance might become an issue. To attempt to mitigate packet loss in the network, redundant coding (1X, or one repeat of the original packet) is used, which doubles the amount of data transferred in each packet. The doubling of packets imposes a limitation on the total number of ports that can run fax pass-through at one time. One fax pass-through session with redundancy needs as much bandwidth as two G.711 calls without VAD.

Fax pass-through does not support the switch from G.Clear to G.711. If fax pass-through and the G.Clear codec are both configured, the gateway cannot detect the fax tone.

Fax pass-through is supported under these call control protocols:

- H.323

- SIP

- Media Gateway Control Protocol (MGCP)

Modem Pass-Through

Modem pass-through over VoIP provides the transport of modem signals through a packet network by using PCM-encoded packets. It is based on the same logic as fax pass-through: An analog voice stream is encoded into G.711, passed through the network, and decoded back to analog signals at the far end.

The following factors need to be considered when determining whether to use modem pass-through:

- Modem pass-through does not support the switch from G.Clear to G.711.

- VAD and echo cancellation need to be disabled.

- Modem pass-through over VoIP performs these functions:

    - Represses processing functions like compression, echo cancellation, high-pass filter, and VAD

    - Issues redundant packets to protect against random packet drops

    - Provides static jitter buffers of 200 ms to protect against clock skew

- Discriminates modem signals from voice and fax signals, indicating the detection of the modem signal across the connection, and placing the connection in a state that transports the signal across the network with the least amount of distortion

- Reliably maintains a modem connection across the packet network for a long duration under normal network conditions

Fax Relay

Cisco Fax Relay is the oldest method of supporting fax on Cisco IOS gateways and has been supported since Cisco IOS Release 11.3. Cisco Fax Relay uses RTP as the method of transport. In Cisco Fax Relay mode, gateways terminate T.30 fax signaling by spoofing a virtual fax machine to the locally attached fax machine. The gateways use a Cisco-proprietary fax relay RTP-based protocol to communicate between themselves.

Unlike fax pass-through, fax relay, as depicted in Figure 2-65, demodulates the fax bits at the local gateway, sends the information across the voice network using the fax relay protocol, and then remodulates the bits back into tones at the far gateway. The fax machines on either end are sending and receiving tones and are not aware that a demodulation/modulation fax relay process is occurring.

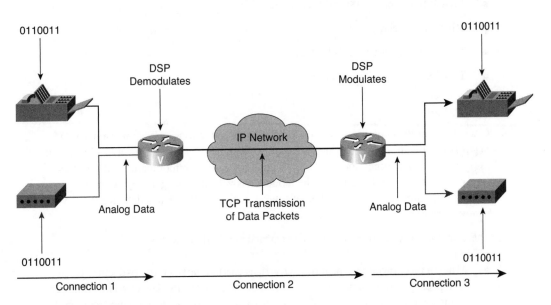

Figure 2-65 *Fax and Modem Relay Topology*

The default method for fax transmission on Cisco IOS gateways is Cisco Fax Relay. This is an RTP-based transmission method that uses proprietary signaling and coding mechanisms.

The mechanism for Cisco Fax Relay is the same for calls that are controlled by SIP, MGCP, and H.323 call control protocols. Cisco provides two methods for fax relay:

■ **Cisco Fax Relay:** A Cisco-proprietary method, and the default on most platforms if a fax method is not explicitly configured.

■ **T.38 fax relay:** A method based on the ITU-T T.38 standard. It is real-time fax transmission (that is, two fax machines communicating with each other as if there were a direct phone line between them). T.38 fax relay is configured by using a few additional commands on gateway dial peers that have already been defined and configured for VoIP calls.

The T.38 fax relay feature can be configured for H.323, SIP, and MGCP call control protocols. For H.323 and SIP networks, the only configuration tasks that differ are those involving the configuration of VoIP dial peers.

T.38 is an ITU-T standards-based method and protocol for fax relay. Data is packetized and encapsulated according to the T.38 standard. T.38 fax relay has the following features:

■ Fax relay PLC

■ MGCP-based fax (T.38) and DTMF relay

■ SIP T.38 fax relay

■ T.38 fax relay for the T.37/T.38 fax gateway

■ T.38 fax relay for VoIP H.323

Modem Relay

Cisco Modem Relay provides support for modem connections across traditional TDM networks. Modem relay demodulates a modem signal at one voice gateway and passes it as packet data to another voice gateway, where the signal is remodulated and sent to a receiving modem. On detection of the modem answer tone, the gateways switch into modem pass-through mode and then, if the call menu (CM) signal is detected, the two gateways switch into modem relay mode.

There are two ways to transport modem traffic over VoIP networks:

■ **Modem pass-through:** The modem traffic is carried between the two gateways in RTP packets, using an uncompressed voice codec, G.711 mu-law or a-law. Although modem pass-through remains susceptible to packet loss, jitter, and latency in the IP network, packet redundancy can be used to mitigate the effects of packet loss in the IP network.

■ **Modem relay:** The modem signals are demodulated at one gateway, converted to digital form, and carried in the Simple Packet Relay Transport (SPRT) protocol. SPRT is a protocol running over UDP packets to the other gateway, where the modem signal is re-created, remodulated, and passed to the receiving modem.

In this implementation, the call starts out as a voice call, switches into modem pass-through mode, and then into modem relay mode.

Modem relay significantly reduces the effects that dropped packets, latency, and jitter have on the modem session. Compared to modem pass-through, it also reduces the amount of bandwidth used.

Modem relay includes these features:

- Modem tone detection and signaling
- Relay switchover
- Payload redundancy
- Dynamic and static jitter buffers
- Gateway-controlled modem relay

Consider the modem relay characteristics in the following sections.

Modem Tone Detection and Signaling

Modem relay supports V.34 modulation and the V.42 error correction and link layer protocol with maximum transfer rates of up to 33.6 kbps. It forces higher-rate modems to train down to the supported rates. Signaling support includes SIP, MGCP, and H.323:

- For MGCP and SIP, during the call setup, gateways negotiate these items:
  - To use or not use the modem relay mode
  - To use or not use the gateway exchange identification (XID)
  - The value of the payload type for Named Signaling Event (NSE) packets
- For H.323, the gateways negotiate these items:
  - To use or not use the modem relay mode
  - To use or not use the gateway XID

Relay Switchover

When the gateways detect a data modem, both the originating gateway and the terminating gateway switch to modem pass-through mode by performing these actions:

- Switching to the G.711 codec
- Disabling the high-pass filter
- Disabling VAD
- Using special jitter buffer management algorithms
- Disabling the echo canceller upon detection of a modem phase reversal tone

At the end of the modem call, the voice ports revert to the previous configuration, and the DSPs switch back to the state they were in before the switchover. You can configure the codec by using the **g711alaw** or **g711ulaw** option of the **codec** command.

Payload Redundancy

You can enable payload redundancy so the modem pass-through over VoIP switchover causes the gateway to send redundant packets. Redundancy can be enabled in one or both of the gateways. When only a single gateway is configured for redundancy, the other gateway receives the packets correctly, but does not produce redundant packets. When redundancy is enabled, 10-ms sample-sized packets are sent. When redundancy is disabled, 20-ms sample-sized packets are sent.

Note By default, the modem relay over VoIP capability and redundancy are disabled.

Dynamic and Static Jitter Buffers

When gateways detect a data modem, both the originating gateway and the terminating gateway switch from dynamic jitter buffers to static jitter buffers of 200-ms depth. The switch from dynamic to static is designed to compensate for PSTN clocking differences at the originating and terminating gateways. When the modem call is concluded, the voice ports revert to dynamic jitter buffers.

Gateway-Controlled Modem Relay

Beginning with Cisco IOS Release 12.4(4)T, Cisco supports gateway-controlled negotiation parameters for modem relay. This new feature is a nonnegotiated, bearer-switched mode for modem transport that does not involve call agent–assisted negotiation during the call setup. Instead, the negotiation parameters are configured directly on the gateway. These gateway-controlled negotiation parameters use NSEs to indicate the switchover from voice, to voice-band data, to modem relay.

Upon detecting a 2100-Hz tone, the terminating gateway sends an NSE 192 to the originating gateway and switches over to modem pass-through. The terminating gateway also sends an NSE 199 to indicate modem relay. If this event is recognized by the originating gateway, the call occurs as modem relay. If the event is not recognized, the call occurs as modem pass-through.

Because Cisco Modem Relay uses configured parameters, it removes the signaling dependency from the call agent and allows modem relay support independent of call control. Cisco Modem Relay can be deployed over any call agent that is capable of setting up a voice connection between gateways, including Cisco Unified Communications Manager, Cisco Unified Communications Manager Express, and the Cisco BTS and PGW soft switches.

The gateway-controlled modem relay parameters are enabled by default when Cisco modem relay is configured. Interestingly, when Cisco Modem Relay is configured, gateway XID parameter negotiation is always enabled. Gateway XID parameters are negotiated using the SPRT protocol.

Store-and-Forward Fax

The transmitting gateway is referred to as an *on-ramp gateway*, and the terminating gateway is referred to as an *off-ramp* gateway. Figure 2-66 illustrates the operation of on-ramp and off-ramp gateways.

On-ramp receives faxes that are delivered as e-mail attachments.

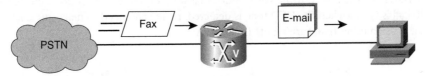

Off-ramp sends standard e-mail messages that are delivered as faxes.

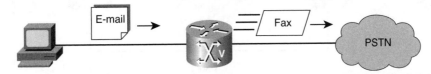

Figure 2-66 *Store-and-Forward Fax Topology*

The following are some of the basic characteristics of on- and off-ramp faxing:

- **On-ramp faxing:** A voice gateway that handles incoming calls from a standard fax machine or the PSTN converts a traditional G3 fax to an email message with a Tagged Image File Format (TIFF) attachment. The fax email message and attachment are handled by an email server while traversing the packet network and can be stored for later delivery or delivered immediately to a PC or to an off-ramp gateway.

- **Off-ramp faxing:** A voice gateway that handles calls going out from the network to a fax machine or the PSTN converts a fax email with a TIFF attachment into a traditional fax format that can be delivered to a standard fax machine or the PSTN.

On-ramp and off-ramp faxing processes can be combined on a single gateway, or they can occur on separate gateways. Store-and-forward fax uses two different IVR applications for on-ramp and off-ramp functionality. The applications are implemented in two Toolkit Command Language (TCL) scripts that you can download from Cisco.com.

The basic functionality of store-and-forward fax is facilitated through Simple Mail Transfer Protocol (SMTP), with additional functionality that provides confirmation of delivery using existing SMTP mechanisms, such as Extended Simple Mail Transfer Protocol (ESMTP).

Gateway Signaling Protocols and Fax Pass-Through and Relay

Figure 2-67 illustrates a fax pass-through operation. When a terminating gateway (TGW) detects a called terminal identification (CED) tone from a called fax machine, the TGW exchanges the voice codec that was negotiated during the voice call setup for a G.711 codec and turns off EC and VAD. This switchover is communicated to the originating gateway (OGW), which allows the fax machines to transfer modem signals as though they were traversing the PSTN. If the voice codec that was configured and negotiated for the VoIP call is G.711 when the CED tone is detected, there is no need to make any changes to the session other than turning off EC and VAD.

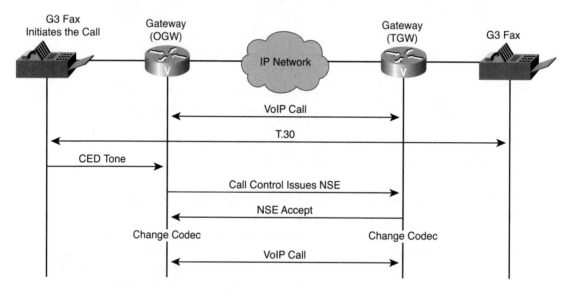

Figure 2-67   *Fax Pass-Through Operation*

If pass-through is supported, these events occur:

1. For the duration of the call, the DSP listens for the 2100-Hz CED tone to detect a fax or modem on the line.

2. If the CED tone is heard, an internal event is generated to alert the call control stack that a fax or modem changeover is required.

3. The call control stack on the OGW instructs the DSP to send an NSE to the TGW, informing the TGW of the request to carry out a codec change.

4. If the TGW supports NSEs, it responds to the OGW instruction and loads the new codec. The fax machines are able to communicate on an end-to-end basis with no further intervention by the voice gateways.

Control of fax pass-through is achieved through NSEs that are sent in the RTP stream. NSEs are a Cisco-proprietary version of IETF-standard named telephony events (NTEs), which are specially marked data packets used to digitally convey telephony signaling tones and events. NSEs use different event values than NTEs use and are generally sent with RTP payload type 100, whereas NTEs use RTP payload type 101. NSEs and NTEs provide a more reliable way to communicate tones and events using a single packet rather than a series of in-band packets that can be corrupted or partially lost.

Fax pass-through and fax pass-through with up speed use peer-to-peer NSEs within the RTP stream or bearer stream to coordinate codec switchover and the disabling of EC and VAD. Redundant packets can be sent to improve reliability when the probability of packet loss is high.

When a DSP is put into voice mode at the beginning of a VoIP call, the DSP is informed by the call control stack whether or not the control protocol can support pass-through.

Cisco Fax Relay

Figure 2-68 illustrates the operation of Cisco Fax Relay.

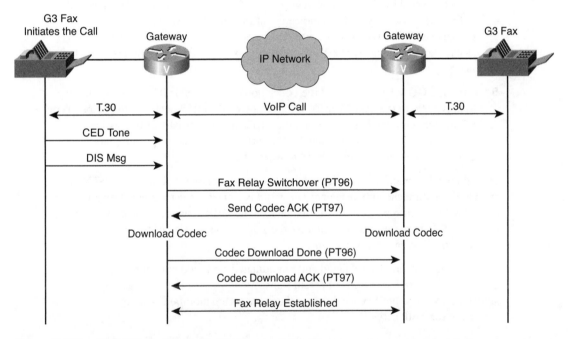

Figure 2-68 *Cisco Fax Relay Operation*

When a DSP is put into voice mode at the beginning of a VoIP call, the DSP is informed by the call control stack whether fax relay is supported and, if it is supported, whether it is Cisco Fax Relay or T.38 fax relay. If Cisco Fax Relay is supported, the following events occur:

1. Initially, a VoIP call is established as if it were a normal speech call. Call control procedures are followed, and the DSP is put into voice mode, after which human speech is expected to be received and processed.

2. At anytime during the life of the call, if a fax answer or calling tone (ANSam [modified ANSwer tone] or CED) is heard, the DSP does not interfere with the speech processing. The ANSam or CED tone causes a switch to modem pass-through, if enabled, to allow the tone to pass cleanly to the remote fax.

3. A normal fax machine, after generating a CED or hearing a CNG (CalliNG) tone, sends a DIS (digital identification signal) message with the capabilities of the fax machine. The DSP in the Cisco IOS gateway attached to the fax machine that generated the DIS message (normally the TGW) detects the High-Level Data Link Control (HDLC) flag sequence at the start of the DIS message and initiates fax relay switchover. The DSP also triggers an internal event to notify the call control stack that fax switchover is required. The call control stack then instructs the DSP to change the RTP payload type to 96 and to send this payload type to the OGW.

4. When the DSP on the OGW receives an RTP packet with the payload type set to 96, it triggers an event to inform its own call control stack that a fax changeover has been requested by the remote gateway. The OGW then sends an RTP packet to the TGW with payload type 97 to indicate that the OGW has started the fax changeover. When the TGW receives the payload type 97 packet, the packet serves as an acknowledgement. The TGW starts the fax codec download and is ready for fax relay.

5. After the OGW has completed the codec download, it sends RTP packets with payload type 96 to the TGW. The TGW responds with an RTP packet with payload type 97, and fax relay can begin between the two gateways. As part of the fax codec download, other parameters such as VAD, jitter buffers, and echo cancellation are changed to suit the different characteristics of a fax call.

During fax relay operation, the T.30 analog fax signals are received from the PSTN or from a directly attached fax machine. The T.30 fax signals are demodulated by a DSP on the gateway and then packetized and sent across the VoIP network as data. The TGW decodes the data stream and remodulates the T.30 analog fax signals to be sent to the PSTN or to a destination fax machine.

The messages that are demodulated and remodulated are predominantly the phase B, phase D, and phase E messages of a T.30 transaction. Most of the messages are passed across without any interference, but certain messages are modified according to the constraints of the VoIP network.

During phase B, fax machines interrogate each other's capabilities. They expect to communicate with each other across a 64-kbps PSTN circuit, and they attempt to make best use of the available bandwidth and circuit quality of a 64-kbps voice path. However, in a VoIP network, the fax machines do not have a 64-kbps PSTN circuit available. The bandwidth per call is probably less than 64 kbps, and the circuit is not considered a clear circuit.

Because transmission paths in VoIP networks are more limited than in the PSTN, the Cisco IOS CLI is used to adjust fax settings on the VoIP dial peer. The adjusted fax settings restrict the facilities that are available to fax machines across the VoIP call leg and are also used to modify values in DIS and NSF messages that are received from fax machines.

H.323 T.38 Fax Relay

Figure 2-69 illustrates an H.323 T.38 relay operation. The T.38 fax relay feature provides an ITU-T standards-based method and protocols for fax relay.

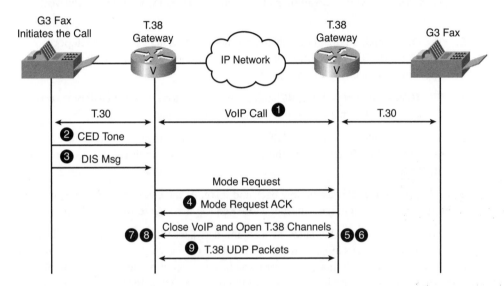

Figure 2-69 *H.323 Fax Relay Operation*

Data is packetized and encapsulated according to the T.38 standard. The coding of the packet headers and the mechanism to switch from VoIP mode to fax relay mode are clearly defined in the specification. Annexes to the basic specification include details for operation under SIP and H.323 call control protocols.

Figure 2-69 shows the H.245 message flow:

1. Initially, a VoIP call is established as if it were a normal speech call. Call control procedures are followed, and the DSP is put into voice mode, after which human speech is expected to be received and processed.

2. At anytime during the life of the call, if a fax answer or calling tone (ANSam or CED) is heard, the DSP does not interfere with the speech processing. The ANSam or CED tone causes a switch to modem pass-through, if enabled, to allow the tone to pass cleanly to the remote fax.

3. A normal fax machine, after generating a CED or hearing a CNG, sends a DIS message with the capabilities of the fax machine. The DSP in the Cisco IOS gateway attached to the fax machine that generated the DIS message (normally the TGW)

detects the HDLC flag sequence at the start of the DIS message and initiates fax relay switchover. The DSP also triggers an internal event to notify the call control stack that fax switchover is required. The call control stack then instructs the DSP to change the RTP payload type to 96 and to send this payload type to the OGW.

4.   The detecting TGW sends a ModeRequest message to the OGW, and the OGW responds with a ModeRequestAck.

5.   The OGW sends a closeLogicalChannel message to close its VoIP UDP port, and the TGW responds with a closeLogicalChannelAck message while it closes the VoIP port.

6.   The OGW sends an openLogicalChannel message that indicates to which port to send the T.38 UDP information on the OGW, and the TGW responds with an openLogicalChannelAck message.

7.   The TGW sends a closeLogicalChannel message to close its VoIP UDP port, and the OGW responds with a closeLogicalChannelAck message.

8.   The TGW sends an openLogicalChannel message that indicates to which port to send the T.38 UDP stream, and the OGW responds with an openLogicalChannelAck message.

9.   T.38-encoded UDP packets flow back and forth. At the end of the fax transmission, either gateway can initiate another ModeRequest message to return to VoIP mode.

T.38 fax relay uses data redundancy to accommodate packet loss. During T.38 call establishment, voice gateways indicate the level of packet redundancy they incorporate in their transmission of fax UDP transport layer packets. The level of redundancy (the number of times the packet is repeated) can be configured on Cisco IOS gateways.

The T.38 Annex B standard defines the mechanism that is used to switch over from voice mode to T.38 fax mode during a call. The capability to support T.38 must be indicated during the initial VoIP call setup. If the DSP on the gateway is capable of supporting T.38 mode, this information is indicated during the H.245 negotiation procedures as part of the regular H.323 VoIP call setup.

After the VoIP call setup is completed, the DSP continues to listen for a fax tone. When a fax tone is heard, the DSP signals the receipt of the fax tone to the call control layer, which then initiates fax changeover as specified in the T.38 Annex B procedures.

SIP T.38 Fax Relay

Figure 2-70 illustrates a SIP T.38 relay operation. When the call control protocol is SIP, T.38 Annex D procedures are used for the changeover from VoIP to fax mode during a call.

Initially, a normal VoIP call is established using SIP INVITE messages. The DSP needs to be informed that it can support T.38 mode while it is put into voice mode. Then, during the call, when the DSP detects fax HDLC flags, it signals the detection of the flags to the call control layer, and the call control layer initiates a SIP INVITE message mid-call to signal the desire to change the media stream.

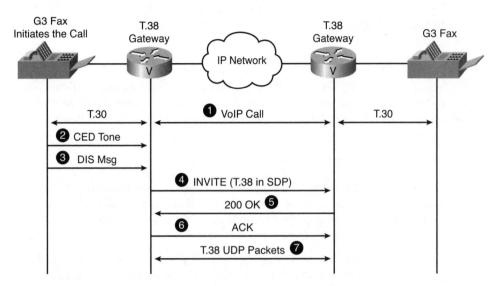

Figure 2-70   *SIP T.38 Fax Relay Operation*

The SIP T.38 fax relay call flow is as follows:

1.   Initially, a VoIP call is established as if it were a normal speech call. Call control procedures are followed, and the DSP is put into voice mode, after which human speech is expected to be received and processed.

2.   At anytime during the life of the call, if a fax answer or calling tone (ANSam or CED) is heard, the DSP does not interfere with the speech processing. The ANSam or CED tone causes a switch to modem pass-through, if enabled, to allow the tone to pass cleanly to the remote fax.

3.   A normal fax machine, after generating a CED or hearing a CNG, sends a DIS message with the capabilities of the fax machine. The DSP in the Cisco IOS gateway attached to the fax machine that generated the DIS message (normally the TGW) detects the HDLC flag sequence at the start of the DIS message and initiates fax relay switchover. The DSP also triggers an internal event to notify the call control stack that fax switchover is required. The call control stack then instructs the DSP to change the RTP payload type to 96 and to send this payload type to the OGW.

4.   The TGW detects a fax V.21 flag sequence and sends an INVITE message with T.38 details in the SDP field to the OGW or to the SIP proxy server, depending on the network topology.

5.   The OGW receives the INVITE message and sends back a 200 OK message.

6. The TGW acknowledges the 200 OK message and sends an ACK message directly to the OGW.

7. The OGW starts sending T.38 UDP packets instead of VoIP UDP packets across the same ports. At the end of the fax transmission, another INVITE message can be sent to return to VoIP mode.

MGCP T.38 Fax Relay

The MGCP T.38 fax relay feature conforms to ITU-T T.38, "Procedures for real-time Group 3 (G3) facsimile communication over IP networks," which determines procedures for real-time facsimile communication in various External Gateway Control Protocol (XGCP) applications.

MGCP T.38 fax relay provides two modes of implementation:

■ **Gateway-controlled mode:** Gateways negotiate fax relay transmission by exchanging capability information in SDP messages. Transmission of SDP messages is transparent to the call agent. Gateway-controlled mode allows the use of an MGCP-based T.38 fax without the necessity of upgrading the call agent software to support the feature.

■ **Call agent–controlled mode:** Call agents use MGCP messaging to instruct gateways to process fax traffic. For MGCP T.38 fax relay, call agents can also instruct gateways to revert to gateway-controlled mode if the call agent is unable to handle the fax control messaging traffic, as is the case in overloaded or congested networks.

MGCP-based T.38 fax relay enables interworking between the T.38 application that already exists on Cisco gateways and the MGCP applications on call agents.

Following is the call flow for an MGCP-based T.38 fax relay:

1. A call is initially established as a voice call.

2. The gateways advertise capabilities in an SDP exchange during connection establishment.

3. If both gateways do not support T.38 fax relay, fax pass-through is used for fax transmission. If both gateways support T.38, they attempt to switch to T.38 upon fax tone detection. The existing audio channel is used for T.38 fax relay, and the existing connection port is reused to minimize delay. If failure occurs at some point during the switch to T.38, the call reverts to the original settings it had as a voice call. If this failure occurs, a fallback to fax pass-through is not supported.

4. Upon completion of the fax image transfer, the connection remains established and reverts to a voice call using the previously designated codec, unless the call agent instructs the gateways to do otherwise.

A fax relay MGCP event allows the gateway to notify the call agent of the status (start, stop, or failure) of T.38 processing for the connection. This event is sent in both call agent–controlled and gateway-controlled modes.

Gateway-Controlled MGCP T.38 Fax Relay

In gateway-controlled mode, a call agent uses the *fx:* extension of the local connection option (LCO) to instruct a gateway how to process a call. Gateways do not need instruction from the call agent to switch to T.38 mode. This mode is used if the call agent has not been upgraded to support T.38 and MGCP interworking, or if the call agent does not want to manage fax calls. Gateway-controlled mode can also be used to bypass the message delay overhead caused by call agent handling (for example, to meet time requirements for switchover to T.38 mode). If the call agent does not specify the mode to the gateway, the gateway defaults to gateway-controlled mode.

In gateway-controlled mode, the gateways exchange NSEs by performing these steps:

1. Instruct the peer gateway to switch to T.38 for a fax transmission.

2. Either acknowledge the switch and the readiness of the gateway to accept T.38 packets or indicate that the gateway cannot accept T.38 packets.

Call Agent–Controlled MGCP T.38 Fax Relay

In CA-controlled mode, the call agent can instruct the gateway to switch to T.38 for a call. In Cisco IOS Release 12.3(1) and later releases, CA-controlled mode enables T.38 fax relay interworking between H.323 gateways and MGCP gateways and between two MGCP gateways under the control of a call agent. This feature supersedes previous methods for CA-controlled fax relay and introduces these gateway capabilities:

■   The capability to accept the MGCP FXR package, to receive the fxr prefix in commands from the call agent, and to send the fxr prefix in notifications to the call agent.

■   The capability to accept a new port when switching from voice to fax transmission during a call. This new capability allows successful T.38 CA-controlled fax communications between H.323 and MGCP gateways in those situations in which the H.323 gateway assigns a new port when changing a call from voice to fax. New ports are assigned in H.323 gateways using images from Cisco IOS Release 12.2(2)T through Cisco IOS Release 12.2(7.5)T. MGCP gateways in MGCP-to-MGCP fax calls reuse the same port, but CA-controlled T.38 fax relay enables MGCP gateways to handle both situations, either switching to a new port or reusing the same port, as directed by the call agent.

DTMF Support

A dual-tone multifrequency (DTMF) tone is the tone generated on a touchtone phone when keypad digits are pressed. Gateways send these tones in the RTP stream by default. This default behavior is fine when the voice stream is sent uncompressed, but problems arise when sending voice across slower WAN links using compression algorithms, as illustrated in Figure 2-71.

During a call, DTMF digits might be entered to access IVR systems, such as voice-mail or automated banking services. Although DTMF is usually transported accurately when using high-bit-rate voice codecs such as G.711, low-bit-rate codecs such as G.729 and

G.723.1 are highly optimized for voice patterns and tend to distort DTMF tones. As a result, IVR systems might not correctly recognize the tones.

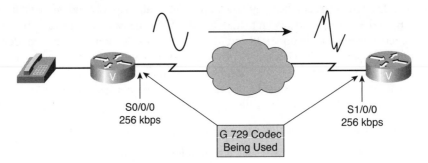

Figure 2-71 *Need for DTMF Support*

DTMF relay solves the problem of DTMF distortion by transporting DTMF tones "out-of-band," or separate from the RTP voice stream.

H.323 DTMF Support

Cisco gateways currently support four methods of DTMF relay using H.323:

■ **Cisco proprietary:** DTMF tones are sent in the same RTP channel as voice data. However, the DTMF tones are encoded differently from the voice samples and are identified as payload type 121, which enables the receiver to identify them as DTMF tones. This method requires the use of Cisco gateways at both the originating and terminating endpoints of the H.323 call.

■ **H.245 Alphanumeric:** Separates the DTMF digits from the voice stream and sends them through the H.245 signaling channel instead of through the RTP channel. The tones are transported in H.245 User Input Indication messages. The H.245 signaling channel is a reliable channel, so the packets that transport the DTMF tones are guaranteed to be delivered. This method does not send tone length information.

■ **H.245 Signal:** This method does pass along tone length information, thereby addressing a potential problem with the alphanumeric method. This method is optional on H.323 gateways.

Note All H.323 Version 2 compliant systems are required to support the **h245-alphanumeric** method, whereas support of the **h245-signal** method is optional.

■ NTE: Transports DTMF tones in RTP packets according to section 3 of RFC 2833. RFC 2833 defines formats of NTE RTP packets used to transport DTMF digits, hookflash, and other telephony events between two peer endpoints. With the NTE method, the endpoints perform per-call negotiation of the DTMF relay method. They also negotiate to determine the payload type value for the NTE RTP packets. As a result, DTMF tones are communicated via RTP packets, using an RTP payload type that prevents the tones from being compressed via the codec being used to encode the voice traffic.

MGCP DTMF Support

The four current implementations of MGCP-based DTMF relay include

- **Cisco proprietary:** DSPs on the gateways send and receive DTMF digits in-band in the voice RTP stream but code them differently so they can be identified by the receiver as DTMF tones.

- **NSE:** Conforms to RFC 2833 to provide a standardized method of DTMF transport using NTEs in RTP packets. RFC 2833 support is standards-based and allows greater interoperability with other gateways and call agents.

- **NTE:** Provides for two modes of implementation:

  - **Gateway-controlled mode:** In gateway-controlled mode, the gateways negotiate DTMF transmission by exchanging capability information in SDP messages. That transmission is transparent to the call agent. Gateway-controlled mode allows the use of the DTMF relay feature without upgrading the call agent software to support the feature.

  - **Call agent–controlled mode:** In CA-controlled mode, call agents use MGCP messaging to instruct gateways to process DTMF traffic.

- **Out-of-band:** Sends the tones as signals to Cisco Unified Communications Manager out-of-band over the control channel. Cisco Unified Communications Manager interprets the signals and passes them on.

SIP DTMF Support

SIP gateways can use Cisco-proprietary Notify-based out-of-band DTMF relay. In addition, Notify-based out-of-band DTMF relay can be used by analog phones attached to analog voice ports on the router.

Notify-based out-of-band DTMF relay sends messages bidirectionally between the originating and terminating gateways for a DTMF event during a call. If multiple DTMF relay mechanisms are enabled on a SIP dial peer and are negotiated successfully, Notify-based out-of-band DTMF relay takes precedence.

The originating gateway sends an Invite message with a SIP Call-Info header to indicate the use of Notify-based out-of-band DTMF relay. The terminating gateway acknowledges the message with an 18x or 200 Response message, also using the Call-Info header. Whenever a DTMF event occurs, the gateway sends a SIP Notify message for that event after the SIP Invite and 18x or 200 Response messages negotiate the Notify-based out-of-band DTMF relay mechanism. In response, the gateway expects to receive a 200 OK message. The Notify-based out-of-band DTMF relay mechanism is similar to the DTMF message format described in RFC 2833.

Customization of Dial Peers

Support for fax, modem, and DTMF transmission often requires extra dial-peer configuration. Therefore, this section reviews basic configuration and describes the required customization procedures to support these non-voice transmissions.

Configuration Components of VoIP Dial Peer

Figure 2-72 illustrates the key components of VoIP dial-peer configuration. The second dial peer on each gateway is used to match incoming VoIP calls. The VoIP dial peers 2000 and 1000 are configured to forward calls to the remote location, respectively. For call forwarding, the VoIP dial peer uses the **destination-pattern** and the **session target** commands. For matching inbound VoIP dial peers, the priority of matching is defined in this order: **incoming called-number**, **answer-address**, and **destination-pattern**.

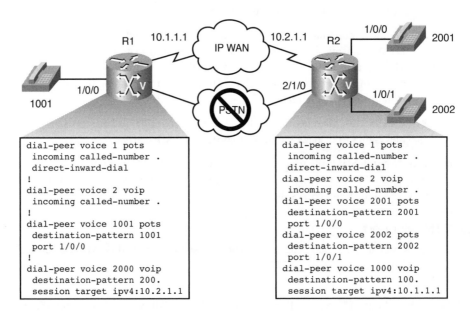

Figure 2-72 *VoIP Dial-Peer Configuration Example*

VoIP Dial-Peer Characteristics

Consider the following aspects when you configure VoIP dial peers:

- **Signaling protocol:** H.323 is the default setting. The protocol can be changed to SIPv2. MGCP control can only be configured for POTS dial peers; it is not available for VoIP.

- **Source IP address:** By default, the source IP address is defined by the IP layer. The routing table defines the outgoing interface to reach a defined session target. The outgoing interface address is used as the source address for both signaling and media. This behavior can be modified by interface binding, using the **h323-gateway voip bind srcaddr** command for H.323 (interface mode) or the **bind** command for SIP (SIP mode).

- **Digit consumption:** Unlike POTS dial peers, VoIP dial peers do not consume any digits.

- **Session target:** The target of the VoIP session can be set to an IP address, DNS name, gatekeeper (RAS), or SIP server. It is configured with the **session target** command.

- **Inbound dial-peer matching:** Performed with these commands, in this order: **incoming called-number**, **answer-address**, **destination-pattern**, and **port**. If no inbound dial peer is matched, the default peer is tried. The default peer has these parameters: any codec, no DTMF relay, IP precedence, VAD enabled. If these parameters cannot be negotiated (for example, if the originating gateway has VAD disabled), the call fails.

- **Outbound dial-peer matching:** The most explicit match of the **destination-pattern** command.

- **Direct inward dialing (DID):** Not applicable to VoIP dial peers; available for inbound POTS dial peers only.

Configuring DTMF Relay

DTMF relay methods for SIP and H.323 are configured in the dial-peer configuration mode, using the **dtmf-relay** command. If this command is not configured, the DTMF tones are disabled and sent in-band. That is, they are left in the audio stream. The **dtmf-relay** command specifies how an H.323 or SIP gateway relays DTMF tones between telephony interfaces and an IP network. The complete command syntax is as follows:

```
Router(config-dial-peer)#dtmf-relay {[cisco-rtp] [h245-alphanumeric] [h245-
   signal] [rtp-nte [digit-drop]] [sip-notify]}
```

Although all shown options are available when configuring a VoIP dial peer, only some of them are applicable, depending on which signaling protocol is used. The options are as follows:

- **cisco-rtp** (H.323 only): Forwards DTMF tones using Real-Time Transport Protocol (RTP) with a Cisco-proprietary payload type

- **h245-alphanumeric** (H.323 only): Forwards DTMF tones by using the H.245 "alphanumeric" user input indication method; supports tones from 0 to 9, *, #, and from A to D

- **h245-signal** (H.323 only): Forwards DTMF tones by using the H.245 "signal" user input indication method; supports tones from 0 to 9, *, #, and from A to D

- **rtp-nte** (H.323 and SIP): Forwards DTMF tones by using RTP with the named telephony event (NTE) payload type

- **digit-drop** (H.323 and SIP): Passes digits out-of-band and drops in-band digits; only available when the **rtp-nte** keyword is configured

- **sip-notify** (SIP only): Forwards DTMF tones using SIP Notify messages; available only if the VoIP dial peer is configured for SIP

DTMF Relay Configuration Example

Figure 2-73 illustrates an example of how the DTMF relay methods are configured and negotiated in H.323 and SIP.

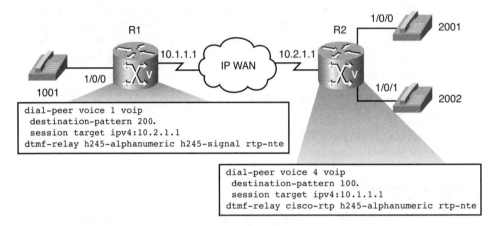

```
dial-peer voice 1 voip
 destination-pattern 200.
 session target ipv4:10.2.1.1
dtmf-relay h245-alphanumeric h245-signal rtp-nte
```

```
dial-peer voice 4 voip
 destination-pattern 100.
 session target ipv4:10.1.1.1
dtmf-relay cisco-rtp h245-alphanumeric rtp-nte
```

Figure 2-73   *DTMF Relay Configuration Example*

H.323 is used for signaling and is the default protocol. During the capabilities negotiation in the H.245 phase, the gateways exchange the supported DTMF relay methods. In this example, both gateways support **h245-alphanumeric** and **rtp-nte** methods. Because **h245-alphanumeric** is the higher-priority choice, it is selected for all calls between the gateways. When a digit is pressed on an endpoint telephone, it will be signaled as an H.245 message, instead of transmission in the RTP flow.

Configuring Fax/Modem Support

The support for fax can be defined using the following commands:

- **fax protocol:** This command specifies if fax pass-through or Cisco Fax Relay is negotiated, and defines pass-through settings.

- **fax protocol t38:** This command specifies if T.38 fax relay is negotiated and defines its settings. This command overwrites the **fax protocol** command, if issued in the same mode.

- **fax rate:** This command can throttle down fax transmission speed.

- **fax-relay:** This command enables Super Group 3 (SG3) fax machines to negotiate down to G3 speeds.

Cisco Fax Relay and Fax Pass-Through

The **fax protocol** command is available globally (in voice service VoIP configuration mode), and for a specific dial peer (dial-peer configuration mode). It enables either Cisco Fax Relay or fax pass-through. The enabled option will be negotiated with the remote gateway before it can be used. When fax pass-through is selected, the upspeed codec options are G.711 mu-law and G.711 a-law.

```
Router(conf-voi-serv)#fax protocol {cisco | none | pass-through {g711ulaw |
  g711alaw}}
```

or

```
Router(conf-dial-peer)#fax protocol {cisco | none | system | pass-through
  {g711ulaw | g711alaw}}
```

The dial-peer setting takes precedence over the global setting. The global setting defaults to Cisco fax relay, while the dial-peer setting defaults to the global setting.

T.38 Fax Relay Configuration

The **fax protocol t38** command is available globally (in voice service VoIP configuration mode) and for a specific dial peer (dial-peer configuration mode). It overwrites the **fax protocol** command, if issued in the same mode, because T.38 fax relay is mutually exclusive with Cisco fax relay or pass-through. The dial-peer setting takes precedence over the global setting.

```
Router(conf-voi-serv)#fax protocol t38 [nse [force]] [ls-redundancy value [hs-
  redundancy value]] [fallback {cisco | none | pass-through {g711ulaw | g711alaw}}]
```

or

```
Router(conf-dial-peer)#fax protocol t38 [nse [force]] [ls-redundancy value [hs-
  redundancy value]] [fallback {cisco | none | pass-through {g711ulaw | g711alaw}}]
```

The options are the following:

- **nse:** Uses Named Signaling Events (NSEs) to switch to T.38 fax relay. The **force** keyword uses NSEs unconditionally and is used for interoperability between H.323 or SIP, and MGCP.

- **ls-redundancy:** Specifies the number of redundant T.38 fax packets to be sent for the low-speed V.21-based T.30 fax machine protocol. The range is from 0 to 7, the default is 0.

- **hs-redundancy:** Specifies the number of redundant T.38 fax packets to be sent for high-speed V.17, V.27, V.29, T.4, or T.6. The range is from 0 to 3, where the default is 0.

- **fallback:** A fallback mode is used to transfer a fax across a VoIP network if T.38 fax relay could not be successfully negotiated at the time of the fax transfer.

- **cisco:** As fallback option, Cisco proprietary fax relay.

- **pass-through:** As fallback option, fax pass-through with either G.711 mu-law or a-law upspeed codec.

Fax Relay Speed Configuration

The **fax rate** command can be configured for a specific dial peer (in dial-peer configuration mode).

```
Router(conf-dial-peer)#fax rate {2400 | 4800 | 7200 | 9600 | 12000 | 14400}
  {disable | voice} [bytes milliseconds]
```

The **disable** option disables fax relay transmission capability. The **voice** option selects the highest possible transmission speed that is allowed by the codec rate.

The values for this command apply only to the fax transmission speed and do not affect the quality of the fax itself. The higher transmission speed values (14,400 bps) provide a faster transmission speed but monopolize a significantly large portion of the available bandwidth. The lower transmission speed values (2400 bps) provide a slower transmission speed and use a relatively smaller portion of the available bandwidth.

The fax call is not compressed using the **ip rtp header-compression** command, because Simple Packet Relay Transport (SPRT) over UDP is being used instead of RTP. For example, a 9600-bps fax call takes approximately 24 kbps.

Fax Relay SG3 Support Configuration

The **fax-relay** command is also used to disable fax relay Error Correction Mode (ECM). The command is configured globally (in voice service VoIP configuration mode) or in dial-peer configuration mode. The dial-peer mode has the **system** keyword to refer to the global setting.

```
Router(conf-voi-serv)#fax-relay {ans-disable | ecm disable | sg3-to-g3}
```

or

```
Router(conf-dial-peer)#fax-relay {ans-disable | ecm disable | sg3-to-g3 [system]}
```

The **ans-disable** option suppresses answer (ANS) tones from originating SG3 fax machines so that these machines can operate at G3 speeds using fax relay.

The **ecm disable** option disables fax relay ECM.

The **sg3-to-g3** option allows SG3 machines to negotiate down to G3 speeds using fax relay.

If the **fax-relay** command is not configured, modem upspeed can occur when ANS tones are detected, fax relay ECM is enabled, and SG3-to-SG3 fax relay communication is not supported. The fax communications will probably fail.

Fax Support Configuration Example

Figure 2-74 shows two gateways with dial peers configured for fax support. R2 is configured for T.38 fax relay with a fallback option to Cisco fax relay. R1 uses the default fax protocol setting, which is Cisco Fax Relay. Cisco Fax Relay is negotiated between the gateways when a fax transmission occurs. R2 throttles down to 7200 bps, so the lowest common value is 4800 bps (fax rate of R1). Both gateways are configured to support SG3 fax machines so that they will negotiate the transmission speed down to G3.

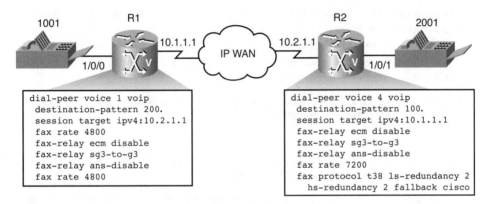

```
dial-peer voice 1 voip
  destination-pattern 200.
  session target ipv4:10.2.1.1
  fax rate 4800
  fax-relay ecm disable
  fax-relay sg3-to-g3
  fax-relay ans-disable
  fax rate 4800
```

```
dial-peer voice 4 voip
  destination-pattern 100.
  session target ipv4:10.1.1.1
  fax-relay ecm disable
  fax-relay sg3-to-g3
  fax-relay ans-disable
  fax rate 7200
  fax protocol t38 ls-redundancy 2
    hs-redundancy 2 fallback cisco
```

Figure 2-74 *Fax Support Configuration Example*

Configuring Modem Support

Modem pass-through and relay are configured using three commands:

- **modem passthrough:** This command enables modem pass-through.

- **modem relay:** This command enables modem pass-through or relay, depending on the negotiation results. It removes the **modem passthrough** command, if configured in the same mode.

- **modem relay gateway-xid:** This command configures additional modem relay parameters, such as compression.

Modem Pass-Through

Modem pass-through can be configured globally (in voice service VoIP configuration mode) or in dial-peer configuration mode using the **modem pass-through** command. The **system** option is available in the dial-peer mode and references the global setting. The **nse** option defines that NSEs are used to communicate codec switchover between gateways, with the optional specification of the payload type. If the payload type is configured explicitly, it must be set to the same value on both the originating and terminating gateways. The **codec** option defines the upspeed codec. The **redundancy** option enables a single repetition of packets to improve reliability by protecting against packet loss.

```
Router(conf-voi-serv)#modem passthrough {nse [payload-type number] codec
  {g711ulaw | g711alaw} [redundancy]
```

or

```
Router(conf-dial-peer)#modem passthrough {system | nse [payload-type number]
  codec {g711ulaw | g711alaw} [redundancy]
```

Modem Relay

The **modem relay** command enables modem pass-through or relay, depending on the negotiation results. It removes the **modem passthrough** command, if configured in the same mode. Modem relay can be configured globally (in voice service VoIP configuration mode) or in dial-peer configuration mode. The **system** option is available in the dial-peer mode and references the global setting.

```
Router(conf-voi-serv)#modem relay {nse [payload-type number] codec {g711alaw |
  g711ulaw} [redundancy]} gw-controlled
```

or

```
Router(conf-dial-peer)#modem relay {nse [payload-type number] codec {g711alaw |
  g711ulaw} [redundancy] | system} gw-controlled
```

The **nse** option defines that NSEs are used to communicate codec switchover between gateways, with the optional specification of the NSE payload type. Range varies by platform, and is typically from 98 to 117. If the payload type is configured explicitly, it must be set to the same value on both the originating and terminating gateways. The **codec** option defines the upspeed codec, which is used when pass-through is negotiated and relay is not. The **redundancy** option enables a single repetition of packets when pass-through is negotiated and relay is not. The **gw-controlled** option selects the gateway-configured method for establishing modem relay parameters.

Modem Relay Compression

The **modem relay gateway-xid** command configures in-band negotiation of compression parameters between two VoIP gateways. This setting can be configured globally (in voice service VoIP configuration mode) or in dial-peer configuration mode. The dial-peer setting has higher precedence than the global setting. The command is enabled when the **modem relay** command is configured.

```
Router(conf-voi-serv)#modem relay gateway-xid [compress {backward | both | forward
  | no}] [dictionary value] [string-length value]}
```

or

```
Router(conf-dial-peer)#modem relay gateway-xid [compress {backward | both |
  forward | no}] [dictionary value] [string-length value]}
```

The **compress** option specifies the direction in which data flow is compressed. For normal operations, compression should be enabled in both directions. This is the default setting. Forward compression is used on the originating gateway to reduce the amount of data that is sent toward the terminating gateway. Backward compression is the ability of the terminating gateway to correctly interpret the compressed data that is received from the originating gateway. Forward compression on one gateway must be matched by backward compression on the peer gateway. The **backward** parameter enables compression only in the backward direction. The **forward** parameter enables compression only in the forward direction. The **no** parameter disables compression in both directions.

The **dictionary** and **string-length** options define the V.42 bis parameters that specify the compression algorithm characteristics. The range is from 512 to 2048 and 16 to 32, respectively. Defaults are 1024 and 32, respectively. Modems might support values higher than these ranges. A value acceptable to both sides is negotiated during modem call setup.

Modem Pass-Through and Modem Relay Interaction

Cisco Modem Relay is a nonnegotiated, bearer-switched mode for modem transport that does not involve call agent–assisted negotiation during the call setup. Instead, the negotiation parameters are configured directly on the gateway. These gateway-controlled negotiation parameters use NSEs to indicate the switchover from voice, to voice-band data, to modem relay.

Upon detecting a 2100-Hz tone, the terminating gateway sends an NSE 192 to the originating gateway and switches over to modem pass-through. The terminating gateway also sends an NSE 199 to indicate modem relay. If this event is recognized by the originating gateway, the call occurs as modem relay. If the event is not recognized, the call occurs as modem pass-through.

In case of MGCP signaling, because modem relay has been configured locally on the gateways, it removes the signaling dependency from the call agent and allows modem relay support independent of call control. The gateway-controlled modem relay parameters are enabled by default when Cisco Modem Relay is configured, and when Cisco Modem Relay is configured, gateway exchange identification (XID) parameter negotiation is always enabled. Gateway XID parameters are negotiated using the SPRT protocol.

Modem Support Configuration Example

Figure 2-75 shows two gateways that are configured to support modem transmission over an IP network. R1 is configured for pass-through while R2 is configured for modem relay and pass-through. Both gateways agree on modem pass-through with the upspeed codec set to G.711 mu-law. Redundant packets will be sent only in one direction—from R1 to R2.

Configuring Codecs

Cisco voice gateways offer the option to define a list of codecs to be used for negotiation of VoIP capabilities.

A codec list is configured as a codec voice class using the **voice class** command and identified using a *class-tag*.

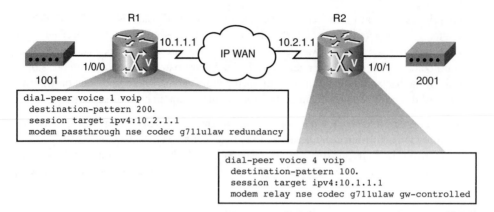

```
dial-peer voice 1 voip
 destination-pattern 200.
 session target ipv4:10.2.1.1
 modem passthrough nse codec g711ulaw redundancy
```

```
dial-peer voice 4 voip
 destination-pattern 100.
 session target ipv4:10.1.1.1
 modem relay nse codec g711ulaw gw-controlled
```

Figure 2-75 *Modem Support Configuration Example*

```
Router(config)#voice class codec class_tag
```

The **codec voice class** command allows the configuration of a prioritized list of codecs and their parameters. The **preference** value represents the priority of a given codec type.

```
Router(config-class)#codec preference value codec-type [mode frame-size][bytes
  payload-size]
```

The **mode** and **frame-size** parameter apply to Internet Low Bitrate Codec (iLBC) and signifies the following:

- **20:** 20-ms frames for 15.2-kbps bit rate (default)

- **30:** 30-ms frames for 13.33-kbps bit rate

The **payload-size** parameter defines the voice payload of each frame. The available values depend on the selected codec type.

Codec-Related Dial-Peer Configuration

The codec settings are applied to VoIP dial peers in either of two ways:

```
Router(config-class)#voice-class codec class_tag
```

or

```
Router(config-dial-peer)#codec {codec [bytes payload-size] | transparent} [fixed-
  bytes]
```

- The **voice-class codec** command applies a list of codecs that are configured with the **voice class codec** command. This option enables multiple codec types for the given dial peer.

- The **codec** command specifies a single codec to be used by the given dial peer. The default is G729r8, 20-byte payload. The options for the single codec include the following:

  - **payload-size:** Voice payload of each frame; available values depend on the codec type.

  - **transparent:** Enables codec capabilities to be passed transparently between endpoints in a Cisco Unified Border Element.

  - **fixed-bytes:** Codec byte size is fixed and nonnegotiable.

Codec Configuration Example

In Figure 2-76, two gateways negotiate calls using H.323. When R1 signals a call, it offers a large set of supported codecs, configured using the **voice-class codec** command. When R2 receives the call setup request, it matches the inbound dial peer. In this example, the inbound dial peer is dial peer 4, which supports only the default codec G.729r8 with 20-byte payload. If dial peer 4 did not exist on R2, R2 would match the default dial peer (dial peer 0). Because the default dial peer supports all codecs, R2 would select the first codec in the offered proposal (G.711 a-law).

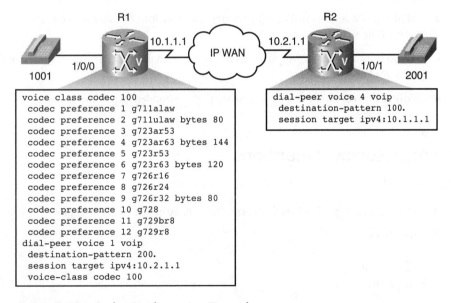

Figure 2-76 *Codec Configuration Example*

Limiting Concurrent Calls

The total number of either incoming or outgoing connections can be limited on a per-dial-peer basis. This feature is typically used to define the number of connections that are used simultaneously to send or receive fax mail, for off-ramp store-and-forward fax functions. The limit is configured using the **max-conn** command in the dial-peer configuration mode. By default, no limit is imposed.

```
Router(config-dial-peer)#max-conn number
```

Summary

The main topics covered in this chapter are the following:

- VoIP transmission requires the sampling, coding, and packetization of the original audio waveform.

- Gateways using peer-to-peer signaling protocols (H.323, SIP) build the dial plan using the dial peers.

- SIP is an RFC-based signaling protocol with open architecture that allows flexibility and extensibility.

- MGCP gateways forward calls by receiving instructions from a call agent and responding to its requests.

- Audio transmission quality depends on factors such as delay, jitter, packet loss, and available bandwidth.

- VoIP dial peers can be configured to support fax/modem pass-through, relay, and DTMF relay.

Chapter Review Questions

The answers to these review questions are in the appendix.

1. By default, a single VoIP packet carries how many milliseconds of audio?

    a. 10 ms

    b. 20 ms

    c. 30 ms

    d. 40 ms

2. What is a function of RTP?

    a. Call multiplexing

    b. Encryption

   c. Payload identification

   d. Replay protection

3. Which two tasks are performed by the RAS signaling function of H.225? (Choose two.)

   a. Conducts bandwidth changes

   b. Transports audio messages between endpoints

   c. Conducts disengage procedures between endpoints and a gatekeeper

   d. Allows endpoints to create connections between call agents

   e. Defines call setup procedures that are based on ISDN call setup

4. Which configuration is required to activate an H.323 gateway on a Cisco router (if it is not already enabled)?

   a. **gateway** in interface configuration mode

   b. Setting the gateway source IP address

   c. Binding the gateway functionality to an interface

   d. **gateway** in global configuration mode

5. Which of the following are types of SIP servers? (Choose four.)

   a. Registrar

   b. Gateway

   c. Redirect

   d. Location

   e. Proxy

   f. Database

   g. Relocation

6. What is one disadvantage of the SIP direct call setup method?

   a. It relies on cached information, which might be out of date.

   b. It uses more bandwidth, because it requires more messaging.

   c. It must learn the coordinates of the destination UA.

   d. It needs the assistance of a network server.

7. Which protocol does MGCP use to describe the type of initiated session?

   a. SIP

   b. Cisco Discovery Protocol

   c. SDP

   d. MGC

8. Which two MGCP messages can be issued by a gateway? (Choose two.)

   a. AuditConnection

   b. NotificationRequest

   c. CreateConnection

   d. DeleteConnection

   e. RestartInProgress

9. Which of the following QoS mechanisms provides strict priority queuing?

   a. FRF.12

   b. LLQ

   c. cRTP

   d. CB-WFQ

   e. CB-Policing

10. What happens when gateways fail to negotiate a common DTMF relay method?

   a. DTMF tones are dropped.

   b. DTMF tones are left in-band.

   c. DTMF tones are left out-of-band.

   d. DTMF tones are carried asymmetrically, using the method that is preferred by each gateway.

Chapter 3

Supporting Cisco IP Phones with Cisco Unified Communications Manager Express

After reading this chapter, you should be able to perform the following tasks:

■ Describe the functions and operation of Cisco Unified Communications Manager Express.

■ Describe all components required to support endpoints by Cisco Unified Communications Manager Express, and explain how to configure them.

■ Describe Cisco Unified Communications Manager Express endpoint configuration elements, such as phones and directory numbers.

This chapter describes the basic functionality of Cisco Unified Communications Manager Express (CUCME). This information includes the configuration of specific network components and services necessary for the proper functioning of CUCME.

The chapter also describes features for a basic Cisco Unified Communications Manager Express system. The endpoints that are supported by Cisco Unified Communications Manager Express include Cisco IP Phones running either Skinny Client Control Protocol (SCCP) or Session Initiation Protocol (SIP). The chapter describes different types of endpoints, their models, and capabilities.

Finally, this chapter explains how to configure the systemwide and endpoint-specific components of Cisco Unified Communications Manager Express. Special attention is given to the various types of directory numbers, which play a key role in making calls.

Introducing Cisco Unified Communications Manager Express

Cisco Unified Communications Manager Express provides call processing for Cisco IP Phones for small-office or branch-office environments. It enables the large portfolio of Cisco Integrated Services Routers to deliver unified communications features that are commonly used by business users to meet voice and video communications requirements of the small or medium-sized office.

This section introduces the key features and functionality of Cisco Unified Communications Manager Express and explains what is required to deploy it on Cisco IOS routers.

Fundamentals of Cisco Unified Communications Manager Express

Cisco Unified Communications Manager Express extends enterprise telephony features and functions to packet telephony network devices. These packet telephony network devices include Cisco IP Phones, media-processing devices, VoIP gateways, and multimedia applications.

Cisco Unified Communications Manager Express provides these functions:

- **Call processing:** Call processing refers to the complete process of routing, originating, and terminating calls, including any billing and statistical collection processes.

- **Signaling and device control:** Cisco Unified Communications Manager Express signals calls between endpoints and directs devices such as phones, gateways, and conference bridges to establish and tear down streaming connections.

- **Dial plan administration:** The dial plan is a set of dial peers that Cisco Unified Communications Manager Express uses to determine call routing. Cisco Unified Communications Manager Express provides the ability to create scalable dial plans.

- **Phone feature administration:** Cisco Unified Communications Manager Express offers services such as hold, transfer, forward, conference, speed dial, last-number redial, Call Park, and other features to Cisco IP Phones and gateways.

- **Directory services:** Cisco Unified Communications Manager Express stores user- and phone-related data in the NVRAM of a Cisco IOS router.

- **Direct access to gateway features and modules:** Cisco Unified Communications Manager Express runs on a Cisco IOS router and has direct access to the digital signal processor (DSP) resources and modules that are installed in it.

While CUCME acts as a call processing solution, keep in mind that CUCME is only one of Cisco's call processing solutions.

Cisco Unified Communications Manager Express Positioning

Cisco offers four product options for call processing, as follows:

- **Cisco Smart Business Communications System:** This product runs on the Cisco Unified Communications 500 Series for Small Business platform and supports up to 104 users.

- **Cisco Unified Communications Manager Express:** This platform runs on the Cisco Integrated Services Routers (that is, ISR and ISR2) and offers support for as many as 365 users.

- **Cisco Unified Communications Manager Business Edition:** This software product runs on Cisco 7800 Series Media Convergence Servers and supports up to 500 users.

- **Cisco Unified Communications Manager:** This software product runs on Cisco 7800 Series Media Convergence Servers or a Cisco Unified Computing System. The Cisco Unified Computing System reduces the number of devices that must be purchased, cabled, configured, powered, cooled, and secured. The solution delivers end-to-end optimization for virtualized environments while retaining the ability to support traditional operating system and application stacks in physical environments. It is well suited for the largest Cisco Unified Communications Manager deployments, for as many as 30,000 users per cluster.

Cisco Unified Communications Manager Express Deployment Models

Architecturally, CUCME can be deployed in either a single-site or a multisite deployment.

Single-Site Deployment

Single-site deployments, an example of which is provided in Figure 3-1, use the public switched telephone network (PSTN) communications for all offsite voice traffic. One Cisco Unified Communications Manager Express site supports as many as 365 Cisco IP Phones. If a Cisco Unity Express module is installed in the router, voice-mail service is also available.

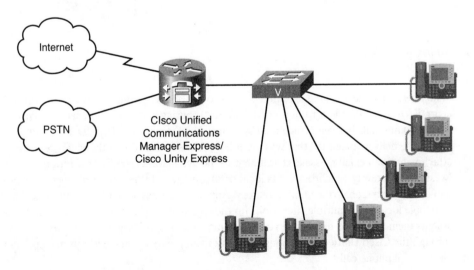

Figure 3-1   *Single-Site CUCME Deployment*

Multisite Deployment

Multisite deployments place VoIP calls between sites, as shown in Figure 3-2. When the H.323 protocol is used for communications between clusters, an H.323 gatekeeper can be used for call routing and call admission control (CAC). Remote sites can be Cisco Unified Communications Manger clusters or Cisco Unified Communications Manager Express sites.

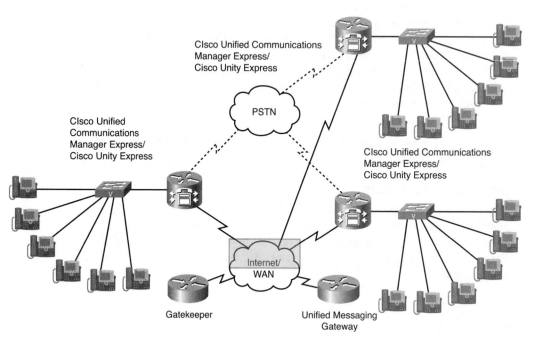

Figure 3-2 *Multisite Deployment*

When voice-mail networking is required, a Cisco Unified Messaging Gateway provides a centralized Voice Profile for Internet Mail (VPIM) routing and resolution service. This service routes calls between voice-mail systems using Simple Mail Transfer Protocol (SMTP) to deliver voice mail that was recorded at the source, adding the message as an attachment to an email message that is sent to the destination. The Cisco Unified Messaging Gateway synchronizes its local database with all the registered voice-mail systems to create a global voice-mail directory. Any user wishing to send the same voice mail to people located in multiple sites looks up the recipients in the global directory and assigns them as needed to a single voice-mail message. The message is then relayed through the Cisco Unified Messaging Gateway to all the recipients, without placing a single external phone call.

Cisco Unified Communications Manager Express Key Features and Benefits

Cisco Unified Communications Manager Express allows small- to medium-sized businesses and autonomous small enterprise branch offices to deploy voice, data, and IP telephony on a single platform, therefore streamlining operations and lowering network costs. Cisco Unified Communications Manager Express is ideal for customers who have data connectivity requirements and have a need for a telephony solution in the same office. Whether offered through the managed service offerings of a service provider or purchased directly by a corporation, Cisco Unified Communications Manager Express offers most of the core telephony features required in a small office, and many advanced features not available with traditional telephony solutions. The ability to deliver IP telephony and data routing using a single converged solution allows customers to optimize their operations and maintenance costs, resulting in a very cost-effective solution that meets office needs.

Because the solution is based on Cisco IOS Software, it builds on convergent networks that include content networking, video, quality of service (QoS), firewall, and XML services.

Administration and management are accomplished through either the familiar Cisco IOS Software command-line interface (CLI) or a web-based GUI.

Phone Features

The following are high-level phone features of Cisco Unified Communications Manager Express:

- Support for the complete line of Cisco single-line and multiline IP phones

- Support for analog phones and fax machines on the Cisco Unified Communications Manager Express router analog voice ports and on the Cisco Analog Telephone Adaptor 186 (ATA 186)

- Media encryption using Secure Real-Time Transport Protocol (SRTP)

- Cisco Extension Mobility

- XML services on Cisco IP Phones—XML-based directory services

- Call handling:

    - On-hook dialing

    - Speed dial and last-number redial

    - Call transfer—consultative and blind

    - Call hold and call retrieve

    - Call pickup of on-hold calls

- Call waiting
- Tone on hold and tone on transfer for internal calls

- Local directory lookup
- Configurable ring types
- Do Not Disturb (DND) feature to divert calls directly to voice mail
- Single Number Reach (SNR): Calls to an enterprise number simultaneously ring a desk set and a cell phone and can be answered at either. Calls can be switched from a cell phone to an IP phone with one button press. The desk phone number can be sent as caller ID instead of the original calling number.

System Features

The following are high-level system features of Cisco Unified Communications Manager Express:

- Multiple administration methods:
  - CLI
  - Web-based embedded GUI for moves, adds, and changes
  - Cisco Configuration Professional (CCP), an administrator tool that helps reduce configuration time
- Cisco Unified Survivable Remote Site Telephony (SRST): Telephony backup services to ensure that a branch office has continuous telephony service. Cisco Unified Communications Manager Express takes over the role of the Cisco Unified Communications Manager during an IP connectivity loss.
- Signaling encryption.
- Hardware and software conferencing capabilities.
- Music on hold (MOH): When a call is placed on hold, that call can receive MOH from the router's flash or from an external source.
- Paging.
- Intercom.
- Distinctive ringing—internal versus external.
- International language support.
- Cisco Unified IP Interactive Voice Response (IVR) Auto Attendant.
- Class of restriction to restrict calling capabilities.
- Computer Telephony Integration (CTI) support with Cisco Telephony Application Programming Interface (TAPI) Lite.
- Call Detail Record (CDR) generation via RADIUS.

Trunk Features

The following are high-level trunk features of Cisco Unified Communications Manager Express:

- Direct Inward Dialing (DID) and Direct Outward Dialing (DOD)

- Basic Rate Interface (BRI) and Primary Rate Interface (PRI) support

- Caller identification display and blocking, calling name display, and Automatic Number Identification (ANI) support

- Analog: Foreign Exchange Office (FXO), DID

- Digital trunk support: T1 and E1

- WAN link support: Frame Relay, ATM, Multilink PPP (MLP), and DSL

- Network calls using H.323

- Dedicated trunk mapping to phone button

- H.323 to Session Initiation Protocol (SIP) call routing to Cisco Unity Express

- RFC 2833 support over SIP trunks

- Transcoding

Voice-Mail Features

The following are high-level voice-mail features for Cisco Unified Communications Manager Express:

- Integration with Cisco Unity voice mail

- Integration with Cisco Unity Express voice mail

- Third-party voice-mail integration—H.323, analog dual-tone multifrequency (DTMF)

- Integration with Cisco Unified Messaging Gateway—routing of voice-mail messages and exchanging subscriber and directory information within a unified messaging network

- Voice-mail enhancements for Cisco IP Phones—fast voice-mail access, message waiting indicator (MWI)

Cisco Unified Communications Manager Express Supported Platforms

Cisco Unified Communications Manager Express supports a variety of Cisco platforms, including Cisco 1861 Integrated Services Router and Cisco 2800, 2900, 3800, and 3900 Series Integrated Services Routers. Figure 3-3 shows a few platform examples.

Cisco 1861 Series Router

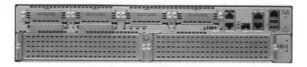

Cisco 2900 Series Router

Cisco 3900 Series Router

Figure 3-3   *Examples of Supported Platforms*

Note   Cisco 2900 and 3900 Series Integrated Services Routers are referred to as Generation 2 (G2) router platforms.

These platforms have varying levels of scalability, as discussed in the following sections.

Cisco Integrated Services Routers Scalability

Some platforms support a higher number of phones in SRST mode than in Cisco Unified Communications Manager Express mode. SRST mode is enabled only during WAN failures, when branch phones lose IP connectivity to the Cisco Unified Communications Manager cluster and fall back to the local SRST gateway. Table 3-1 contrasts the number of supported IP phones for various ISR router models, both for SRST operation and for CUCME operation.

Table 3-1 *Scalability of ISR Routers*

Router Model	Phones Supported in SRST Mode	Phones Supported by CUCME
Cisco 1861	15	15
Cisco 2801	25	25
Cisco 2811	35	35
Cisco 2821	50	50
Cisco 2851	100	100
Cisco 3825	350	175
Cisco 3845	730	250

Cisco Integrated Services Routers Generation 2 Scalability

Cisco 3925 and 3945 platforms support a higher number of phones in SRST mode than in regular Cisco Unified Communications Manager Express mode, as shown in Table 3-2.

For more information pertaining to the scalability of these platforms, visit the following URLs:

- **Cisco Unified SRST:**
  www.cisco.com/en/US/docs/voice_ip_comm/cusrst/requirements/guide/srs80spc.html (for SRST 8.0)

- **Cisco Unified Communications Manager Express:**
  www.cisco.com/en/US/docs/voice_ip_comm/cucme/requirements/guide/cme85spc.htm.html (for CUCME 8.5).

The modularity of both series enables integration with additional gateway features.

Table 3-2 *Scalability of ISR2 Routers*

Router Model	Phones Supported in SRST Mode	Phones Supported by CUCME
Cisco 2901	35	35
Cisco 2911	50	50
Cisco 2921	100	100
Cisco 2951	250	150
Cisco 3925/3925E	1100	250/400
Cisco 3945/3945E	1200	350/450

Memory Requirements

Table 3-3 lists the memory that is required by each CUCME platform. The number of supported phones represents the highest number on the given platform. If a lower number of phones is needed in an enterprise environment, the router might perform well with less RAM, but the provided memory figures are highly recommended.

Table 3-3   *Memory Requirements*

Router Model	Number of IP Phones Supported for CUCME	RAM (MB)	Flash (MB)
Cisco 1861	25	256	128
Cisco 2801	25	256	128
Cisco 2811	35	256	128
Cisco 2821	50	256	128
Cisco 2901	42	512	256
Cisco 2911	58	512	256
Cisco 2921	110	512	256
Cisco 2951	165	512	256
Cisco 3825	175	384	128
Cisco 3845	150	384	128
Cisco 3925	250	1024	512
Cisco 3925E	400	1024	512
Cisco 3945	350	1024	512
Cisco 3945E	450	1024	512

Cisco Integrated Services Routers Licensing and Software

Cisco Unified Communications Manager Express uses the right-to-use licensing approach, in which the CUCME feature license entitles an enterprise to use the feature. This license is based on the number of endpoints to be deployed. Each Cisco IP Phone or Cisco ATA port requires a Cisco Unified Communications Manager Express seat license.

The following are the requirements for a CUCME release on a supported router:

- Cisco IOS Software Release 15.0.1M or greater
- IP voice feature set for Cisco IOS Software
- The appropriate amount of flash memory and RAM in the router

You need to download and configure additional files if you want to use the optional GUI or Cisco Configuration Professional. Also, you need to download and install the firmware files for the models of phones that you choose to deploy with Cisco Unified Communications Manager Express. You can retrieve these files from Cisco.com, with appropriate login credentials.

Cisco Integrated Services Routers Generation 2 Licensing Model

Cisco Generation 2 platforms (Cisco 2900 and 3900 Series Integrated Services Routers) introduce a new licensing approach that uses license-based software activation. A universal Cisco IOS image is combined with multiple package options. The new CUCME and SRST bundles for the G2 routers provide the entry level for 25 user seats across all platforms. The bundles include unified communications technology packets, flash, and DRAM. Currently, the software activation license approach is not yet implemented for Cisco Unified Communications Manager Express or SRST. For these features, the old-style, owner-based, right-to-use licensing approach is still in place. The licensing for Cisco Unified Communications Manager Express and SRST is interchangeable within the same number of user counts, for investment protection purposes. Licenses can be transformed from a Cisco Integrated Services Router–based platform into a Cisco Integrated Services Router G2–based platform.

Figure 3-4 illustrates the difference between Cisco Integrated Services Router–based and Cisco Integrated Services Router G2–based licensing. The Cisco Integrated Services Router license includes two components: the platform-related CUCME or SRST feature license, and the per-seat feature license (either Cisco Unified Communications Manager Express or SRST). The Cisco Integrated Services Router G2 package is related to the Cisco 2900 or 3900 Series and includes three components.

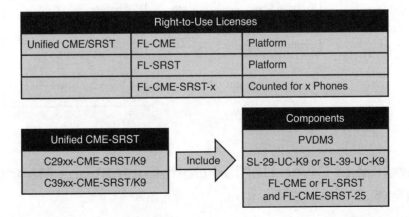

Figure 3-4 *ISR2 Licensing*

- Packet voice DSP module (PVDM) license.

- Cisco Unified Communications license.

- License to use either Cisco Unified Communications Manager Express or SRST, in-cluding 25 user seats. Additional per-seat licenses must be purchased separately.

Cisco Unified Communications Manager Express Operation

Figure 3-5 illustrates the operation of Cisco Unified Communications Manager Express running on a voice gateway that is connected to the PSTN over a digital trunk. It has multiple Cisco IP Phones registered to it. The registered phones can make calls to each other. The calls are signaled by exchanging messages between the phones and the CUCME, but the media flows directly between the phones. The gateway routes calls to external destinations over the dial peer that uses the T1 channelized controller. When making and receiving calls to and from the PSTN, the gateway typically performs digit manipulation in the calling (ANI) and called numbers (Dialed Number Identification Service [DNIS]). With this approach, numbers are made routable in the PSTN and are shortened to internal numbers within the enterprise network.

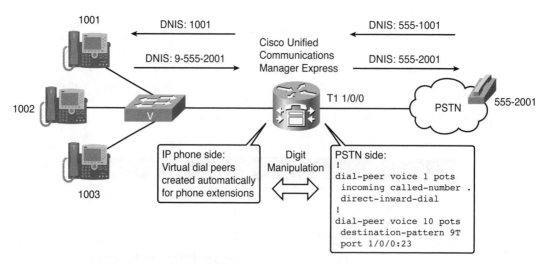

Figure 3-5   *Call to and from PSTN*

Operation of Cisco Unified Communications Manager Express

It is important to be able to distinguish between various Cisco Unified Communications end-user devices that you might encounter during the course of deploying and administering a Cisco Unified Communications network. In addition, understanding the boot and registration communication between a Cisco IP Phone and a Cisco Unified

Communications Manager Express is critical for understanding normal voice network operations and for troubleshooting. This section introduces the endpoints supported by Cisco Unified Communications Manager Express and describes their features.

Overview of Cisco Unified Communications Manager Express Endpoints

A variety of endpoints, including Cisco products as well as third-party products, can be used with Cisco Unified Communications Manager Express. The endpoints include Cisco IP Phones, analog station gateways (which allow analog phones to interact with CUCME), and video endpoints.

Cisco Unified Communications Manager Express supports two protocols used by for endpoints: Skinny Client Control Protocol (SCCP) and Session Initiation Protocol (SIP).

Endpoint Signaling Protocols

From a feature support perspective, the protocols can be categorized into three groups:

- **SCCP:** SCCP is a Cisco-proprietary protocol and typically is used only by Cisco Unified IP endpoints. SCCP offers a large set of telephony features, most of which are supported on all Cisco IP Phone models.

- **Standard SIP:** Cisco Unified Communications Manager Express supports standards-based SIP endpoints. The number of standardized telephony features, however, is limited compared to feature-rich SCCP.

- **Cisco Unified Communications Manager Express SIP support for Cisco IP Phones:** When Cisco Unified Communications Manager Express interacts with Cisco IP Phones using the SIP protocol, many features are supported in addition to the standard feature set of SIP. CUCME supports similar features for Cisco IP Phones supported with SCCP, but the number of features that are supported depends on the particular model of Cisco IP Phone.

Endpoint Capabilities

Cisco IP Phones cover a wide range of types, from simple, display-less, entry-level phones to upper-level phones with high-resolution, color, touchscreen displays. Differences in hardware-related capabilities include the following:

- **Screen:** Different models have screens with different resolution, size, color, and touchscreen capabilities.

- **Codec support:** All Cisco IP Phones support G.711 and G.729 codecs. High-end models also support Internet Low Bitrate Codec (iLBC) and wideband codecs for superior voice quality.

- **LAN:** Most IP phones have a PC port, so that a PC can be connected to the network without requiring its own wall socket, in-house cabling, and physical switch port. Different phone models support different speeds on the PC port and on the IP phone switch port (the port that is connected to a LAN switch).

- **Navigation and feature buttons:** The number of IP phone buttons, softkeys, and other buttons also differs per phone model. There are also differences in the type of navigation clusters (two-way or four-way).

- **Speakerphone and headset support:** Some IP phones offer speakerphone and headset support.

- **Number of lines:** The number of lines also differs per phone model.

- **Other features:** Some IP phones provide other special features such as video, Wi-Fi support, or dedicated support for use in conference rooms (for example, enhanced speakerphone capabilities, including the option to connect multiple microphones).

Basic Cisco IP Phone Models

Basic Cisco IP Phones include these models:

- **Cisco Unified IP Phones 7906 and 7911:** These phones fill the communications needs of cubicle, retail, classroom, or manufacturing workers, or anyone who conducts low-to-moderate telephone traffic. Four dynamic softkeys guide users through core business features and functions, while a pixel-based display combines standard features, calling information, and XML services. Both phones offer numerous important security features, plus the choice of IEEE 802.3af Power over Ethernet (PoE), Cisco inline power, or local power through an optional power adapter. Figure 3-6 shows a Cisco Unified IP Phone 7906G.

Figure 3-6   *Cisco Unified IP Phone 7906G*

■ **Cisco Unified Wireless IP Phone 7921:** This wireless phone supports a variety of features that are accessible as long as the phone is associated with a wireless access point. Figure 3-7 shows a Cisco Unified Wireless IP Phone 7921G.

Figure 3-7   *Cisco Unified Wireless IP Phone 7921G*

■ **Cisco Unified IP Phone 7931:** This phone meets the communications needs of retail, commercial, and manufacturing workers, plus anyone with moderate telephone traffic and specific call requirements. Dedicated hold, redial, and transfer keys facilitate call handling in a retail environment. Illuminated mute and speakerphone keys give an indication of speaker status. A pixel-based display with a white backlight makes calling information easy to see. Figure 3-8 shows a Cisco Unified IP Phone 7931G.

Midrange Cisco IP Phones

Midrange Cisco Unified IP Phones 7940, 7941, 7942, 7960, 7961, and 7962 address the communications needs of a transaction-type worker. They provide two or four programmable line and feature keys, plus a high-quality speakerphone. These phone models have four dynamic softkeys that guide users through call features and functions. A built-in headset port and an integrated Ethernet switch are standard with these phones. The phones also include audio controls for the full-duplex, hands-free speakerphone, handset, and headset. Figure 3-9 shows a Cisco Unified IP Phone 7942G.

Cisco Unified IP Phones 7941 and 7961 have lighted line keys, and Cisco Unified IP Phones 7942 and 7962, the latter of which is shown in Figure 3-10, add support for the high-fidelity wideband codec.

Figure 3-8   *Cisco Unified IP Phone 7931G*

Figure 3-9   *Cisco Unified IP Phone 7942G*

Note   For a detailed list of features per phone model, refer to the data sheets of the Cisco IP Phone 7900 Series products.

Figure 3-10   *Cisco Unified IP Phone 7962G*

Upper-End Cisco IP Phones

Upper-end Cisco Unified IP Phones 7945, 7965, 7970, 7971, 7975, and 8961 demonstrate the latest advances in VoIP telephony, including wideband audio support, backlit color displays, and an integrated Gigabit Ethernet port. They address the needs of executives and transaction-type workers with significant phone traffic, and the needs of those working with bandwidth-intensive applications on collocated PCs. Figure 3-11 shows an example of a Cisco Unified IP Phone 7975G.

These IP phones include a large, backlit, color display for access to communication information, and features such as date and time, calling party name, calling party number, digits dialed, and presence information. They also accommodate XML applications that take advantage of the display. The phones provide direct access to at least two or as many as eight telephone lines (or combination of lines, speed dials, and direct access to telephony features), four or five interactive softkeys that guide you through call features and functions, and a four-way (plus Select key) navigation cluster. A hands-free speakerphone and handset that is designed for high-fidelity wideband audio are standard, as is a built-in headset connection. Figure 3-12 shows two versions of the Cisco Unified 8961G IP Phone.

Note   For a detailed list of features per phone model, refer to the data sheets of the Cisco IP Phone 7900 Series products.

Figure 3-11 *Cisco Unified IP Phone 7975G*

Figure 3-12 *Cisco Unified IP Phone 8961G Versions*

Video-Enabled Cisco IP Phones

Cisco offers a range of video-enabled Cisco IP Phones that includes the following models:

■ **Cisco Unified IP Phone 7985:** This is a personal desktop videophone for the Cisco Unified Communications solution. Offering a productivity-enhancing tool that makes instant, face-to-face communication possible, the Cisco Unified IP Phone 7985 has a video call camera, LCD screen, speaker, keypad, and handset incorporated into one unit, as shown in Figure 3-13.

Figure 3-13   *Cisco Unified IP Phone 7985G*

■ **Cisco Unified IP Phone 9951:** This advanced collaborative media endpoint provides voice, video, applications, and accessories. Highlights include interactive video with support from the Cisco Unified Video Camera, high-definition voice, a high-resolution color display, Gigabit Ethernet, and a new ergonomic design and user interface. Accessories, sold separately, include a color Cisco Unified IP Color Key Expansion Module and the Cisco Unified Video Camera. Figure 3-14 shows an example of this phone.

■ **Cisco Unified IP Phone 9971:** This is an advanced collaborative media endpoint with extended features, such as interactive multiparty video, high-resolution color touchscreen display, and desktop Wi-Fi connectivity. Figure 3-15 shows an example.

Conference Stations

Cisco Unified IP Conference Stations include the following models:

■ **Cisco Unified IP Conference Station 7936:** This conference station combines state-of-the-art speakerphone conferencing technologies with award-winning Cisco voice communications technologies. The net result is a conference room phone that offers superior voice and microphone quality, with simplified wiring and administrative cost benefits. A full-featured, IP-based, hands-free conference station, the new Cisco Unified IP Conference Station 7936 is designed for use on desktops, in conference rooms, and in executive suites. Figure 3-16 shows the Cisco Unified IP Phone 7936.

Figure 3-14   *Cisco Unified IP Phone 9951*

Figure 3-15   *Cisco Unified IP Phone 9971*

Figure 3-16   *Cisco Unified IP Phone 7936*

■ **Cisco Unified IP Conference Station (CS) 7937:** This conference station, shown in Figure 3-17, offers many improvements over the Cisco Unified IP Conference Station 7936, such as the following:

  ■ Superior wideband acoustics with the support of the G.722 wideband codec

  ■ Support for PoE or the Cisco Power Cube 3

  ■ Expanded room coverage of up to 30 by 40 feet (10 by 13 meters) with the optional external microphone kit

Figure 3-17   *Cisco Unified IP Conference Station 7937G*

Identifying Cisco Unified Communications Manager Express Endpoint Requirements

Cisco IP Phones provide the following features:

- **CDP:** Cisco IP Phones exchange Cisco Discovery Protocol (CDP) messages like almost all other Cisco network products. They listen to messages sent by Cisco Catalyst switches. In this way, a Cisco Catalyst switch can indirectly configure the LAN configuration of the phone, including the voice VLAN and Class of Service (CoS) priority marking for traffic that is received from an attached PC. The CDP messages that are sent by the Cisco IP Phones are important when Cisco Unified Video Advantage is used. Cisco Unified Video Advantage is a solution in which the phones interact with video hardware and software that is installed on the PC.

- **DHCP:** Cisco IP Phones can have a static IP configuration that is entered at the IP phone, or use DHCP to obtain IP addresses that are assigned from a DHCP server.

- **MAC address–based device identification:** Cisco IP Phones are identified by a device ID, which is based on the MAC address of the IP phone. This allows the device to be moved between subnets and simplifies DHCP configuration, because no specific IP address is required for an individual phone.

- **TFTP:** Cisco IP Phone configuration does not take place individually at the phone, but is retrieved from CUCME. Cisco Unified Communications Manager Express generates device-specific configuration files and makes them available for download from one or more TFTP servers. Cisco IP Phones learn the IP address of the TFTP server via DHCP, and then load the appropriate configuration file automatically as part of their boot sequence. The phones can be powered over their Ethernet cabling from any PoE-compliant LAN switch, such as a Cisco Catalyst switch. This eliminates the need for extra power adapters and cabling on the user desk.

- **PC port (optional):** Cisco IP Phones allow PCs to be connected to a phone's PC port and then share the uplink toward the switch. By using a voice VLAN feature of Cisco Catalyst switches and Cisco IP Phones, the phone and a PC can be separated into different VLANs on a single access port at a LAN switch.

Phone Startup Process

When connected to the network, a Cisco IP Phone goes through a standard startup process consisting of several steps. Depending on your specific network configuration, all of these steps might not occur on your Cisco IP Phone.

Figure 3-18 illustrates the first four steps of the startup process, described here:

1. **Obtaining power from the switch:** The Cisco IP Phone obtains power from the switch, if PoE is used. Alternatively, the Cisco IP Phone can be powered by wall power or an inline power injector.

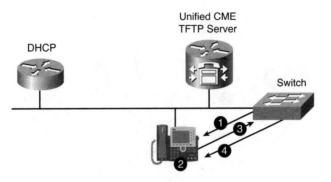

Figure 3-18 *IP Phone Startup Process: Steps 1–4*

2. **Loading the stored phone image:** The Cisco IP Phone has nonvolatile flash memory in which the phone firmware image is stored. At startup, the phone runs a bootstrap loader that loads the phone image from flash memory. Using this image, the phone initializes its software and hardware.

3. **Configuring voice VLAN (IP Phone):** Cisco IP Phones can use 802.1Q VLAN tagging to differentiate voice traffic from data traffic of a PC attached to the phone's PC port. The voice VLAN ID can be configured locally at the Cisco IP Phone or at the Cisco Catalyst switch. If no voice VLAN is configured locally, the Cisco IP Phone requests the voice VLAN ID by sending out a CDP message that includes a VoIP VLAN Query. This message also includes the required power for the phone model used. This allows the switch to possibly reduce the supplied power to match a Cisco IP Phone's real power demand.

4. **Configuring voice VLAN (switch):** If a voice VLAN ID is configured on the switch, it responds to the received message and informs the Cisco IP Phone about the voice VLAN ID by also sending out a CDP message. If no voice VLAN is configured on the switch, it will not respond with a CDP message. In this case, the Cisco IP Phone typically sends out two more CDP messages asking for the voice VLAN ID before it continues the boot process. This results in longer boot times if no voice VLAN is configured on the switch. The **switchport voice vlan untagged** command instructs the switch to respond with a CDP message in order to speed up the phone boot process.

Figure 3-19 illustrates Steps 5 and 6 of the startup process, described here:

5. **Obtaining an IP address:** If the Cisco IP Phone uses DHCP to obtain an IP address, the phone queries the DHCP server to obtain an IP address. DHCP also informs the Cisco IP Phone about how to reach the TFTP server (DHCP option 150). If DHCP is not used in your network, a static IP address and TFTP server address must be locally assigned to each Cisco IP Phone. If the DHCP server does not respond, the Cisco IP Phone uses the last-used configuration stored in NVRAM.

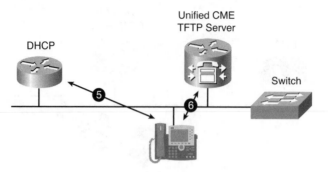

Figure 3-19 *IP Phone Startup Process: Steps 5–6*

6. **Requesting the configuration file:** The Cisco IP Phone requests various files from the TFTP server. The first file it tries to download is the Certificate Trust List (CTLSEP<MAC>.tlv), which is used only if cryptographic features are enabled in Cisco Unified Communications Manager Express. The Cisco IP Phone next requests its individual configuration file (SEP<MAC>.cnf.xml), which is present on the TFTP server only if the phone is already configured as an SCCP device in CUCME. If this file is not available, the Cisco IP Phone tries to download the SIP-based configuration file (SIP<MAC>.cnf).

Figure 3-20 shows Steps 7 and 8 of the startup process, described here:

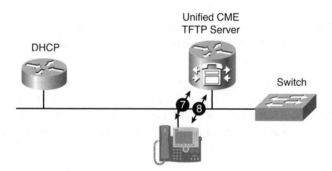

Figure 3-20 *IP Phone Startup Process: Steps 7–8*

7. **Requesting the default configuration file:** If the TFTP server responds with a File not Found error message to the previous request for configuration files, the Cisco IP Phone requests the XMLDefault.cnf.xml file. Like the individual configuration file, this file contains a prioritized list of as many as three call processing nodes and the Phone-Load-Version that is to be used for each phone model.

8. **Checking the Phone Load:** Once the Cisco IP Phone receives either the individual or the default configuration file, it compares its local Load-Version with the one specified in the configuration file. If they are different, the phone downloads the new load from the TFTP server and reboots.

Figure 3-21 shows Steps 9 and 10 of the startup process, described here:

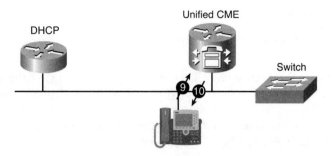

Figure 3-21   *IP Phone Startup Process: Steps 9–10*

9. **Registering on Cisco Unified Communications Manager Express:** The Cisco IP Phone attempts to register with the highest-priority call processing node on the list.

10. **Configuring Final Parameters via SCCP:** If the phone is already configured as an SCCP phone in Cisco Unified Communications Manager Express, it successfully registers and is instructed by SCCP messages to set up the display layout. The display layout includes attributes such as directory numbers, softkey buttons, and speed dials.

    Figure 3-22 shows the last step of the startup process, described here:

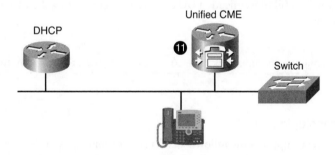

Figure 3-22   *IP Phone Startup Process: Step 11*

11. If the Cisco IP Phone is not yet configured and receives the list of call processing nodes from the default configuration file, the following options are possible:

    ■ **Auto Registration enabled:** After the Cisco IP Phone tries to register with a call processing node, CUCME dynamically creates an individual configuration file for this phone and requests it to reboot. After reboot, the phone successfully registers.

    ■ **Auto Registration disabled:** Cisco Unified Communications Manager Express will not allow registration. The Cisco IP Phone displays a Registration Rejected message on the phone display.

Power over Ethernet

Most Cisco IP Phone models are capable of using the following three options for power:

- **Power over Ethernet:** With PoE, the phone plugs into a data jack that connects to a switch, and a user PC in turn connects to an IP phone. With power-sourcing equipment (PSE), such as Cisco Catalyst PoE-capable modular and fixed-configuration switches, power is inserted into the Ethernet cable to power devices such as an IP phone or IEEE 802.11 wireless access point.

- **Midspan power injection:** Because some switches do not support PoE, a midspan power source might be used instead. This midspan device sits between a LAN switch and a powered device and inserts power on an Ethernet cable to the powered device. A major technical difference between the midspan and inline power mechanism is that power is delivered on the spare pairs (pins 4, 5, 7, and 8). An example of midspan PSE is a Cisco Unified IP Phone Power Injector.

Note   More information about the Cisco Unified IP Phone Power Injector can be found in the document Cisco Unified IP Phone Power Injector at www.cisco.com/en/US/partner/products/ps6951/index.html. (Requires login with appropriate credentials.)

- Wall power: Wall power needs a DC converter for connecting the Cisco IP Phone to a wall outlet.

Note   An external power supply for a Cisco IP Phone is ordered separately from the phone itself.

Two PoE Technologies

Cisco equipment supports the following two types of inline power delivery:

- **Cisco original implementation of PoE:** Cisco was the first to develop PoE. The original Cisco prestandard implementation supports the following features:
  - Provides –48VDC at up to 6.3 to 7.7 W per port over data pins 1, 2, 3, and 6.
  - Supports most Cisco devices (IP Phones and wireless access points).
  - Uses a Cisco-proprietary method to determine if an attached device requires power. Power is delivered only to devices that require power.

- **802.3af PoE:** Since the first deployment of PoE, Cisco has been driving the evolution of this technology toward standardization by working with the IEEE and member vendors to create a standards-based means of providing power from an Ethernet switch port. The 802.3af committee has ratified this capability. The 802.3af standard supports the following features:

■ Specifies –48VDC at up to 15.4 W per port over data pins 1, 2, 3, and 6 or the spare pins 4, 5, 7, and 8 (a PSE can use one or the other, but not both). Cisco Catalyst generally provides 802.3af PoE using the data pins.

■ Enables a new range of Ethernet-powered devices that consume additional power.

■ Standardizes the method of determining whether an attached device requires power. Power is delivered only to devices that require power. This type has several optional elements, such as power classification, where powered devices can optionally support a signature that defines their maximum power requirement. PSE that supports power classification reads this signature and budgets the correct amount of power per powered device, which will likely be significantly less than the maximum allowed power.

Without power classification defined, the switch reserves the full 15.4 W of power for every device. This behavior might result in oversubscription of the available power supplies. So, that some devices might not be powered even though there is sufficient power available.

Power classification defines these five classes:

■ **0 (default):** 15.4 W reserved

■ **1:** 4 W

■ **2:** 7 W

■ **3:** 15.4 W

■ **4:** Reserved for future expansion

All Cisco 802.3af–compliant switches support power classification.

The Cisco Power Calculator is an online tool that enables you to calculate the power supply requirements for a specific PoE configuration. The Cisco Power Calculator is available to registered Cisco.com users at http://tools.cisco.com/cpc/LU.cpc.

Cisco Prestandard Device Detection

When a switch port that is configured for inline power detects a connected device, the switch sends an Ethernet Fast Link Pulse (FLP) to the device, as illustrated in Figure 3-23. The Cisco IP Phone loops the FLP back to the switch to indicate its inline power capability. The switch then delivers −48VDC PoE (inline) power to the phone or other endpoint.

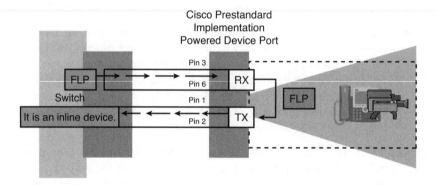

Figure 3-23 *Cisco Prestandard Device Detection*

IEEE 802.3af Device Detection

The Cisco Catalyst switch detects a powered device by applying a voltage in the range of −2.8V to −10V on the cable and then looks for a 25-kOhm signature resistor, as depicted in Figure 3-24. Compliant powered devices must support this resistance method. If the appropriate resistance is found, the Cisco Catalyst switch delivers power.

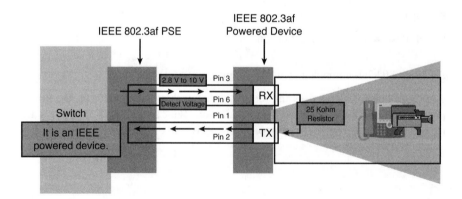

Figure 3-24 *IEEE 802.3af Device Detection*

Cisco Catalyst Switch: Configuring PoE

Use the **power inline** command in interface configuration mode to enable inline power for a specific interface. The powered device-discovery algorithm is operational in the **auto** mode. The powered device-discovery algorithm is disabled in the **never** mode.

Other modes exist for allocating power, depending on the version of Cisco IOS Software—for example, the ability to allocate power on a per-port basis with the **allocation** *milliwatt* mode.

```
Router(config-if)#power inline {auto | never}
```

> **Note** The Cisco Catalyst 6500 Series Switches can run either Cisco Catalyst operating system software or native Cisco IOS Software if the switch supervisor engine has a Multilayer Switch Feature Card (MSFC). Otherwise, these switches can run only Cisco Catalyst software. The Cisco Catalyst 4500 and 4000 Series Switches can also run Cisco Catalyst software or native Cisco IOS Software, depending on the supervisor engine. Generally, late edition supervisor engines run native Cisco IOS Software; however, the product documentation should be checked to determine the supervisor engine and the operating system that is supported on a specific model.

Use the **show power inline** command to display a view of the power that is allocated on Cisco Catalyst switches. Sample output is provided in Example 3-1. The switch shows the default allocated power as 10 W in addition to the inline power status of every port.

Example 3-1 show power inline *Command*

```
Switch#show power inline
Interface       Admin   Oper    Power ( mWatt )   Device
..........      .....   ....    ...............   .......
FastEthernet9/1 auto    on      6300              Cisco 6500 IP Phone
FastEthernet9/2 auto    on      6300              Cisco 6500 IP Phone
FastEthernet9/3 auto    off     0                 n/a
```

VLAN Infrastructure

Many models of Cisco IP Phones contain an integrated three-port 100/1000 switch. The ports provide dedicated connections to these devices:

- Port 0 is an internal 100/1000 interface that carries the Cisco IP Phone traffic.

- Port 1 connects to a PC or other device.

- Port 2 connects to the access switch or other network devices. Inline power can be obtained at port 2.

The voice VLAN feature allows voice traffic from an attached IP phone and data traffic from a daisy-chained PC to be transmitted on different VLANs. This capability provides flexibility and simplicity in IP address allocation and the prioritization of voice over data.

If CDP is enabled on the switch port, a switch instructs an attached Cisco IP Phone to treat the Layer 2 CoS priority value of the attached PC in one of the following ways (based on the extended priority that is configured on the switch port):

■ **Trusted:** The Cisco IP Phone allows the PC to send IEEE 802.3 frames (with no CoS priority value) as well as IEEE 802.1p frames with any CoS priority value.

■ **Untrusted (default):** The Cisco IP Phone changes the CoS priority value to 0 if the PC uses 802.1p.

■ **Configured CoS priority level:** The Cisco IP Phone sets an 802.1p header with a CoS priority value of x if the PC uses 802.1p with a different CoS priority level than x, or if the PC did not use 802.1p at all but sent 802.3 frames.

The traffic that a Cisco IP Phone sends is trusted. It can be one of the following:

■ **802.1Q:** In the voice VLAN, tagged with a Layer 2 CoS priority value

■ **802.1p:** In the access VLAN, tagged with a Layer 2 CoS priority value

■ **Untagged:** In the access VLAN, untagged with no Layer 2 CoS priority value

If CDP is enabled on the switch port, a switch instructs the Cisco IP Phone to use one of the three listed options, based on the **voice vlan** command.

Voice VLAN Support

There are various methods of configuring a Cisco Catalyst switch to support voice traffic, including the following:

■ Single-VLAN access port

■ Multi-VLAN access port

■ Trunk port

Various factors have to be considered, including the following:

■ Security

■ Cisco IP Phones/other IP phones/IP softphones (IP softphone is used here as a generic term for all software-based IP phones that are installed on a workstation)

■ Spanning tree

■ QoS

Single-VLAN Access Port

A single-VLAN access port, as illustrated in Figure 3-25, is the default state when an IP phone is connected to an unconfigured Cisco Catalyst switch. It is typically used for IP phones other than Cisco, IP softphones, or when Cisco IP Phones or other Cisco voice devices do not support PCs to be connected to them.

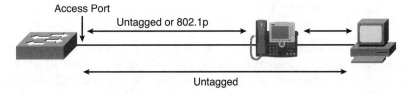

Figure 3-25   *Single-VLAN Access Port*

When using the port for such a device, the access VLAN ID should be the ID of the voice VLAN (that is, the VLAN containing the phones). If a softphone is used on a PC, the device itself (that is, the PC) cannot be in different VLANs per application (phone software versus data applications). Therefore, the access port is usually configured for the data VLAN, and the IP address (or subnet) of the PC is allowed to access VLANs with voice devices.

If a Cisco IP Phone has a PC attached, it is not recommended to put both into the same VLAN, because voice and data services should be separated.

Features of a single-VLAN access port include the following:

■   It can be configured as a secure port.

■   It allows physical separation of voice and data traffic using different physical ports.

■   It works with both Cisco IP Phones and other IP phones.

■   The IP phone can use 802.1p (with VLAN ID set to 0) for CoS.

Switches other than Cisco switches are typically configured in this way, because they do not usually support the voice VLAN feature.

Multi-VLAN Access Port

All Cisco Catalyst switches support multi-VLAN access ports, as shown in Figure 3-26. All data devices typically reside on data VLANs in the traditional switched scenario. A separate voice VLAN might be needed when combining the voice network into the data network.

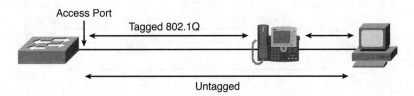

Figure 3-26   *Multi-VLAN Access Port*

The placement of nondata devices, such as IP phones, in a voice VLAN makes it easier for customers to automate the process of deploying IP phones. IP phones boot and reside in a voice VLAN if a switch is configured to support them, just as data devices boot and reside in an access (data) VLAN. An IP phone communicates with a switch via CDP when it powers up. The switch provides the IP phone with an appropriate VLAN ID.

You can implement multiple VLANs on the same port by configuring an access port. A tagging mechanism distinguishes among VLANs on the same port. 802.1Q is the IEEE standard for tagging frames with a VLAN ID number. An IP phone sends tagged 802.1Q frames. A PC sends untagged frames, and a switch puts the frame into the configured access VLAN. When the switch receives a frame, from the network, that is destined for the PC, it removes the access VLAN tag before forwarding the untagged frame to the PC.

The following are some advantages of implementing dual VLANs:

- A multi-VLAN access port can be configured as a secure port.

- A voice VLAN ID is discovered using CDP, or it is configured on the IP phone.

- Dual VLANs allow for the scalability of a network, from an addressing perspective. IP subnets usually have more than 50 percent (often more than 80 percent) of their IP addresses allocated. A separate VLAN (separate IP subnet) to carry voice traffic allows the introduction of many new devices, such as IP phones, into a network without extensive modifications to the IP addressing scheme.

- Dual VLANs allow for the logical separation of data and voice traffic, which allows a network to process these two traffic types individually.

- Implementing dual VLANs allows you to connect two devices that are in different VLANs to a single switch port.

Trunk Port

Rather than a dual-VLAN access port, you can use a trunk port for connecting a switch to an IP phone, as depicted in Figure 3-27. Because a Cisco Catalyst switch supports multi-VLAN access ports, a trunk port is not commonly used to connect a switch to a Cisco IP Phone. However, a trunk port can also be a way to connect a Cisco IP Phone to a switch other than a Cisco switch. Some of the first Cisco switches supported voice VLAN features, allowing the voice VLAN ID to be used by a phone via CDP only on trunk ports.

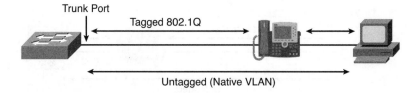

Figure 3-27   *Trunk Port*

When an 802.1Q trunk port is used, frames of the native VLAN are always transmitted untagged and should be received untagged. In other words, a PC, which usually does not send 802.1Q frames but rather untagged Ethernet frames, is part of the native VLAN, while a Cisco IP Phone tags its frames with 802.1Q. However, a PC could send and receive tagged frames and thus access all VLANs that are configured in the switch.

Some of the considerations when implementing a trunk port to support Cisco IP Phones are as follows:

■ On some end of life (EOL) Cisco Catalyst switches, PortFast cannot be enabled on a trunk port.

■ The port cannot be configured as a secure port.

■ The PC can access all VLANs if it supports 802.1Q.

Ethernet Frame Types Generated by Cisco IP Phones

Based on the switch port configuration that is used to connect a Cisco IP Phone, the following Ethernet frame types, as shown in Figure 3-28, are present:

■ **Single-VLAN access port:** If the switch port is configured as a single-VLAN access port only, standard Ethernet V2 frames will be generated by a Cisco IP Phone and a Cisco Catalyst switch for voice traffic. There is no VLAN ID nor CoS information present within the transmitted frames. CoS classification can be configured on the switch.

■ **Multi-VLAN access port and trunk port:** Both port types will cause a Cisco IP Phone and a Cisco Catalyst switch to generate standard-based 802.1Q frames to tag voice VLAN traffic accordingly. Because 802.1Q includes 802.1p, CoS markings are included in these frame types.

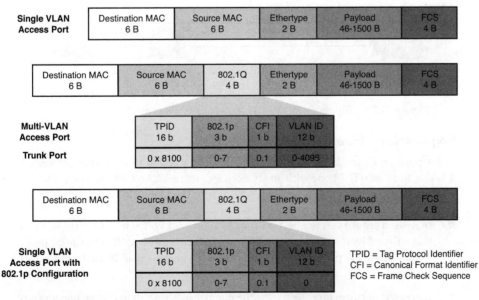

Figure 3-28 *Ethernet Frame Types Generated by Cisco IP Phones*

If the switch port is configured as a multi-VLAN access port, only voice VLAN–tagged frames and untagged frames (native VLAN for data traffic) are present. In a trunk port configuration, tagged frames for other VLANs that might be configured on the switch will also be sent out on the switch port. This can be prevented by specifying allowed VLANs.

■ **Single-VLAN access port with 802.1p configuration:** In a single-VLAN access port with additional 802.1p CoS configuration, standard 802.1Q framing will be used. The difference between the framing of a multi-VLAN access port or a trunk port and a single-VLAN access port with 802.1p configuration is that the latter will always use 0 for the VLAN ID.

Blocking PC VLAN Access at IP Phones

When a PC is connected to an IP phone, as shown in Figure 3-29, there are two primary security issues:

■ If the switch port is configured as a trunk, the PC has access to all VLANs.

■ If the switch port is configured as an access port, the PC has access to the voice VLAN.

The reason for this is that, by default, an IP phone forwards all frames that are received from a switch to a PC and vice versa. You can configure Cisco IP Phones to block access by the PC to the voice VLAN. If configured, the IP phone will not forward frames that are tagged with the voice VLAN ID. This configuration solves PC VLAN access issues with dual-VLAN access ports, because the PC is limited to using the access VLAN (untagged frames).

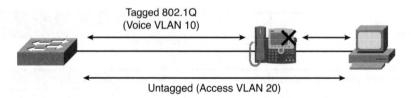

Tagged 802.1Q
(Voice VLAN 10)

Untagged (Access VLAN 20)

Figure 3-29   *Blocking PC VLAN Access at IP Phones*

Limiting VLANs on Trunk Ports at the Switch

Trunk ports on Cisco Catalyst switches should be configured to allow only the necessary VLANs. In a Cisco IP Phone with an attached PC, these VLANs are the voice VLAN and the native VLAN. Denying all other VLANs provides the following advantages:

■ **Increased security:** It is a best practice to allow on a switch port only those VLANs that are used by the connecting end devices. Access to voice VLANs can be prevented only by IP phone configuration but is supported on all IP phone models with PC ports.

■ **Increased performance:** Reducing the number of VLANs cuts down unnecessary broadcast traffic.

■ **Increased stability:** Limiting the number of VLANs also minimizes potential Spanning Tree Protocol (STP) issues and increases network stability.

Configuring Voice VLAN in Access Ports Using Cisco IOS Software

Example 3-2 shows the configuration of a single-VLAN access port. The switch is configured to transmit CDP frames to enable a Cisco IP Phone to transmit voice traffic in 802.1p frames that are tagged with VLAN ID 0 and a Layer 2 CoS value. The switch puts the 802.1p voice traffic into the configured access VLAN, VLAN 261, which is used for voice traffic.

Example 3-2 *Single-VLAN Access Port*

```
Switch(config)#interface FastEthernet0/1
Switch(config-if)#switchport mode access
Switch(config-if)#switchport voice vlan dot1p
Switch(config-if)#switchport access vlan 261
```

Example 3-3 shows a multi-VLAN access port configuration in which the voice traffic is sent to VLAN 261, and the data is using the access VLAN 262.

Example 3-3 *Multi-VLAN Access Port*

```
Switch(config)#interface FastEthernet0/1
Switch (config-if)#switchport mode access
Switch (config-if)#switchport voice vlan 261
Switch (config-if)#switchport access vlan 262
```

Note   The multi-VLAN access port is the recommended configuration for Cisco IP Phones that have a PC port.

The Cisco Catalyst switch voice interface commands used in Example 3-3 are detailed in Table 3-4.

Configuring Trunk Ports Using Cisco IOS Software

Use the commands shown in Example 3-4 to configure the trunk interface of a switch. In the example, VLAN 261 is used for voice traffic; VLAN 262, which is also the native VLAN, is used for data traffic. All other VLANs are blocked from the trunk interface.

Table 3-4 *Cisco Catalyst Switch Voice Interface Commands for Access Ports*

Command	Description
switchport mode access	Configures the switch port to be an access (nontrunking) port.
spanning-tree portfast	Causes a port to enter the spanning-tree forwarding state immediately, bypassing the listening and learning states. You can use PortFast on switch ports that are connected to a single workstation or server (as opposed to another switch or network device) to allow those devices to connect to the network immediately. This command is automatically added to the interface's configuration after you specify a voice VLAN.
switchport access vlan *data_VLAN_ID*	Configures the interface as a static access port with the access VLAN ID (262 in this example); the range is 1–4094.
switchport voice vlan {*voice_vlan_ID* | **dot1p** | **none** | **untagged**}	When configuring the way in which the Cisco IP Phone transmits voice traffic, note the following syntax information: • Enter a voice VLAN ID to send CDP v2 packets that configure the Cisco IP Phone to transmit voice traffic in 802.1Q frames that are tagged with the voice VLAN ID and a Layer 2 CoS value (the default is 5). Valid VLAN IDs are from 1 to 4094. The switch puts the 802.1Q voice traffic into the voice VLAN. • Enter the **dot1p** keyword to send CDP v2 packets that configure a Cisco IP Phone to transmit voice traffic in 802.1p frames that are tagged with VLAN ID 0 and a Layer 2 CoS value (the default is 5 for voice traffic and 3 for voice control traffic). The switch puts the 802.1p voice traffic into an access VLAN. • Enter the **untagged** keyword to send CDP v2 packets that configure a Cisco IP Phone to transmit untagged voice traffic. The switch puts the untagged voice traffic into the access VLAN. • Enter the **none** keyword to allow a Cisco IP Phone to use its own configuration and transmit untagged voice traffic. The switch puts the untagged voice traffic into the access VLAN.

Example 3-4 *Configuring Trunk Ports Using Cisco IOS Software*

```
Switch(config)#interface FastEthernet0/1
Switch(config-if)#switchport trunk encapsulation dot1q
Switch(config-if)#switchport mode trunk
Switch(config-if)#switchport trunk native vlan 262
Switch(config-if)#switchport voice vlan 261
Switch(config-if)#spanning-tree portfast trunk
Switch(config-if)#switchport trunk allowed vlan261,262
```

Note   The native VLAN does not have to be explicitly permitted in the allowed VLAN list.

The Cisco Catalyst switch voice interface commands used in Example 3-4 are detailed in Table 3-5.

Table 3-5   *Cisco Catalyst Switch Voice Interface Commands for Trunk Ports*

Command	Description
switchport mode trunk	Configures a switch port to be a trunk port.
switchport trunk encapsulation dot1q	Configures a switch port trunk encapsulation to 802.1Q instead of leaving it as autodetect.
switchport trunk native vlan *VLAN-ID*	Configures an interface's native VLAN. When you use an 802.1Q trunk port, all frames are tagged except those on the VLAN that are configured as the native VLAN for the port. Frames on the native VLAN are always transmitted untagged and are normally received untagged.
spanning-tree portfast trunk	Causes a trunk port to transition to the Spanning Tree Protocol active state almost immediately, bypassing the listening and learning states. You can use the **portfast** command on switch ports that are connected to a single workstation or server (as opposed to another switch or network device) to allow those devices to connect to the network immediately.
switchport trunk allowed vlan *VLAN-ID*	Specifies the VLANs allowed on a trunk port.

Verifying Voice VLAN Configuration

You can verify voice VLAN configuration on Cisco Catalyst switches using the **show interface** *interface_id* **switchport** command.

Example 3-5 shows that interface Fa0/4 is configured as an access port with access VLAN 262 and voice VLAN 261. Also, this port is using the default native VLAN ID of 1.

Example 3-5   *Verifying Voice VLAN Configuration*

```
Switch#show interfaces fa0/4 switchport
Name: Fa0/4
Switchport: Enabled
Administrative Mode: static access
```

```
Operational Mode: static access
Administrative Trunking Encapsulation: negotiate
Operational Trunking Encapsulation: native
Negotiation of Trunking: Off
Access Mode VLAN: 262 (VLAN0262)
Trunking Native Mode VLAN: 1 (default)
Voice VLAN: 261 (VLAN0261)
...
```

IP Addressing and DHCP

Cisco IP Phones require network IP addresses. The IP addresses assigned to the phones should be assigned from separate subnets for easier manageability and security, as shown in Figure 3-30.

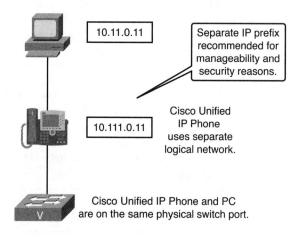

Figure 3-30   *Voice Segment Addressing*

In most scenarios, the following guidelines should be followed when deploying IP addresses:

- Existing IP address subnets should be used for data devices (PCs, workstations, servers).

- DHCP should be used to assign IP addresses to Cisco IP Phones.

- Separate IP subnets should be used for phones, if available in the existing address space.

- Private address space (defined in RFC 1918), such as the 10.0.0.0 network, can be used for the voice VLAN if other subnets are not available.

Several actions might be required when configuring DHCP. These actions include the configuration of a DHCP pool (along with various DHCP parameters), the configuration of an IEEE 802.1Q trunk (to support a router-on-a-stick topology), and configuring DHCP relay (to allow a DHCPDISCOVERY broadcast to cross a router boundary).

DHCP Parameters

When DHCP is used to dynamically assign IP parameters to a Cisco IP Phone, a DHCP server can be implemented either on CUCME, another Cisco IOS router, or any DHCP server in the network. The DHCP scope must include a range of IP addresses with the subnet mask, the default gateway, and the address(es) of the TFTP server(s), which are carried using option 150 (for IP addresses) or option 66 (for DNS names). Optionally, the DHCP scope can also specify the DNS server addresses.

The following messages are involved in a DHCP exchange:

- **DHCPDISCOVER:** By default, a Cisco IP Phone (DHCP client) sends a DHCPDIS-COVER request to the 255.255.255.255 broadcast address on the acquired voice VLAN.

- **DHCPOFFER:** A server assigns a free IP address with the remaining required parameters for the scope. An offer is sent to the DHCP client (the phone) using the broadcast address 255.255.255.255.

- **DHCP Settings Initialized:** The phone takes the values, received from the DHCP response, and applies them to the IP stack of the IP phone, and then sends a Gratuitous ARP to normalize the ARP cache for other devices on the network.

- **Configuration Requested From TFTP server:** The phone uses the value, typically received in option 150, to retrieve a configuration file from the TFTP server. The Cisco Unified Communications Manager Express router is typically the TFTP server, although an external TFTP server can be used alternatively.

Router Configuration with an IEEE 802.1Q Trunk

Figure 3-31 illustrates a Cisco IOS router that acts as DHCP server and has an interface that is configured for 802.1Q trunking necessary to support voice and data VLANs. The DHCP server is configured with two scopes: for the phone subnet (Phones) and for the PC subnet (data). The Phones scope uses the command **option 150 ip 10.111.0.1** to indicate the TFTP server IP address. In this example, the TFTP server address is a local interface address, which is common for CUCME deployments. DHCP, TFTP, and Cisco Unified Communications Manager Express could either run on the same Cisco IOS router or be distributed. The router has two interfaces that correspond to the 802.1Q tags of the voice and data VLANs.

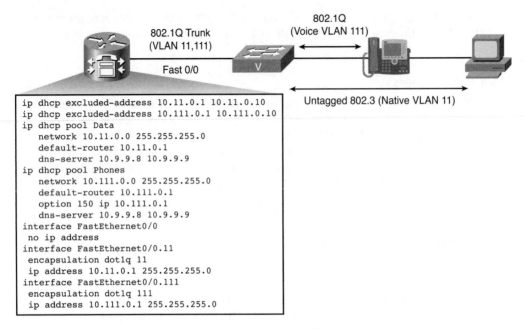

```
ip dhcp excluded-address 10.11.0.1 10.11.0.10
ip dhcp excluded-address 10.111.0.1 10.111.0.10
ip dhcp pool Data
   network 10.11.0.0 255.255.255.0
   default-router 10.11.0.1
   dns-server 10.9.9.8 10.9.9.9
ip dhcp pool Phones
   network 10.111.0.0 255.255.255.0
   default-router 10.111.0.1
   option 150 ip 10.111.0.1
   dns-server 10.9.9.8 10.9.9.9
interface FastEthernet0/0
 no ip address
interface FastEthernet0/0.11
 encapsulation dot1q 11
 ip address 10.11.0.1 255.255.255.0
interface FastEthernet0/0.111
 encapsulation dot1q 111
 ip address 10.111.0.1 255.255.255.0
```

Figure 3-31 *Router Configuration with an IEEE 802.1Q Trunk*

Router Configuration with Cisco EtherSwitch Network Module

Figure 3-32 shows a router with an installed Cisco EtherSwitch module. With integrated switch components on the router, Layer 3 interfaces are defined using the **interface vlan** command. The VLANs are then applied to the physical ports using the **switchport** command, because they are used on Cisco IOS switches. The DHCP configuration is omitted, because it is identical to the previous example.

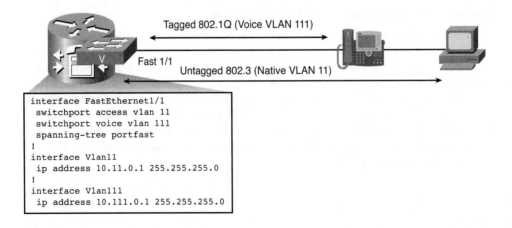

```
interface FastEthernet1/1
 switchport access vlan 11
 switchport voice vlan 111
 spanning-tree portfast
!
interface Vlan11
 ip address 10.11.0.1 255.255.255.0
!
interface Vlan111
 ip address 10.111.0.1 255.255.255.0
```

Figure 3-32 *Router Configuration with an IEEE 802.1Q Trunk*

DHCP Relay Configuration

The DHCP relay agent is a device that relays DHCP messages between clients and servers on different IP networks. It is a Cisco IOS router that "listens" to DHCP client messages being broadcast on the subnet and relays them to the configured DHCP server. The DHCP server then sends responses using the DHCP relay agent back to the DHCP client. The DHCP relay agent saves the administrator the effort of installing and running a DHCP server on each subnet.

Figure 3-33 shows a Cisco IOS router that has the voice and data VLANs directly attached to it. It acts as the DHCP relay agent for the voice and data subnets and has the **ip helper-address** command configured on the respective voice and data interfaces. The **ip helper-address** command points to the DHCP server and is necessary to convert the DHCP broadcasts to unicasts sent to a DHCP server. The DHCP server has pools that are configured for two subnets (voice and data).

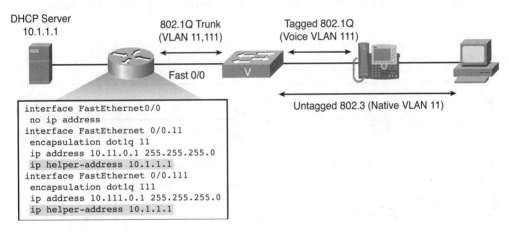

Figure 3-33 *DHCP Relay Configuration*

Network Time Protocol

The time clock should be synchronized in all components of the Cisco Unified Communications network. Time accuracy is needed for a number of aspects, such as the following:

- **Phone display:** Cisco IP Phones display the time as it is received from Cisco Unified Communications Manager Express.

- **Call lists:** Cisco IP Phones list the missed, received, and placed calls, including the time that the call occurred.

- **Voice mail:** Voice-mail systems provide the time when the message was left.

- **Reporting and troubleshooting:** Reporting data is typically collected on central systems that order the information based on the time that an event is received. Such data is marked with time stamps for future use. The time stamps must be reliable and accurate for effective troubleshooting and monitoring.

■ **Billing:** Call Detail Records (CDR) are used to report information about the calls. This data can be sent to billing applications.

NTP is a widespread Internet Engineering Task Force (IETF) standard that supports a hierarchy of clock sources that vary in the level of trust. Trusted servers are typically highly available systems that are equipped with extremely reliable clocks, such as atomic sources. NTP is strongly recommended to be used instead of the internal router clock, which can drift. NTP synchronizes the Cisco Unified Communications Manager Express router to a single clock on the network, known as the master clock.

Figure 3-34 shows the CUCME router in the Pacific Standard time zone with daylight saving time turned on. The router is set to synchronize its system time to the external time servers 10.1.1.1 and 10.2.2.2, while the former server is the preferred NTP source.

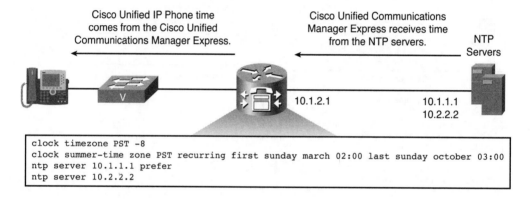

```
clock timezone PST -8
clock summer-time zone PST recurring first sunday march 02:00 last sunday october 03:00
ntp server 10.1.1.1 prefer
ntp server 10.2.2.2
```

Figure 3-34 *NTP Configuration Example*

Endpoint Firmware and Configuration

The TFTP server has device-specific and generic configuration files. A configuration file includes parameters for connecting to Cisco Unified Communications Manager Express and information about which image load a phone should be running.

As shown in Figure 3-35, the phone first requests the CTLSEP<MAC>.tlv file that contains a certificate trust list not covered in this course. Then it requests its MAC-address-specific SCCP/SIP configuration file: first SEP<MAC>.cnf.xml and then SIP<MAC>.cnf. If the TFTP server does not respond, the IP phone falls back to the last-used configuration stored in NVRAM. If the phone is new, this file will not be found, because the phone is not currently configured in the CUCME database. In that case, the TFTP server responds without providing the device-specific configuration file. The phone then requests the generic XMLDefault.cnf.xml file.

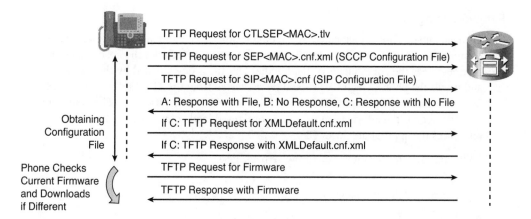

Figure 3-35 *Downloading Phone Configuration*

The phone requests the .loads file, if one was specified in the configuration file (specific or default), to see what image the phone should be running. If the .loads file specifies an image that is different from the image that is stored in the phone NVRAM, the phone attempts to obtain the new image from a TFTP server. If an image is downloaded and verified successfully, the phone reboots to load the new image and then to register to the primary Cisco Unified Communications Express system.

Downloading Firmware

The **tftp-server** *location:filename* command allows the file, specified using the location and filename parameters, to be downloaded using TFTP. For Cisco Unified Communications Manager Express, you must configure the firmware files that will be downloaded by endpoints to be available through TFTP.

Example 3-6 shows how to configure the TFTP service for the files belonging to the SIP firmware package of Cisco Unified IP Phones 7945 and 7965 version 9.0.

Example 3-6 *Making Firmware Files Available from Flash via TFTP*

```
Router(config)#tftp-server flash:apps45.9-0-2ES2.sbn
Router(config)#tftp-server flash:cnu45.9-0-2ES2.sbn
Router(config)#tftp-server flash:cvm45sip.9-0-2ES2.sbn
Router(config)#tftp-server flash:dsp45.9-0-2ES2.sbn
Router(config)#tftp-server flash:jar45sip.9-0-2ES2.sbn
Router(config)#tftp-server flash:SIP45.9-0-2SR1S.loads
Router(config)#tftp-server flash:term45.default.loads
Router(config)#tftp-server flash:term65.default.loads
```

Firmware Images

Firmware images are implemented as file bundles that contain multiple images for various components of the Cisco IP Phone. The firmware package includes the .loads loader file that describes the components of the bundle. This file is downloaded by the phone first and it tells the phone which files should be requested from the TFTP server. The phone learns the name of the appropriate .loads file from the configuration file. The configuration file obtains the information from the configured **load** command. The **load** command references the appropriate .loads file.

Following are a few examples of firmware packages:

■ cmterm-7945_7965-sip.9-0-2SR1 (SIP, 7945/65, v9.0)

■ cmterm-7945_7965-sccp.9-0-2SR1 (SCCP, 7945/65, v9.0).

Setting Up Cisco Unified Communications Manager Express in an SCCP Environment

Setting up a Cisco Unified Communications Manager Express system manually involves using the CLI. This type of setup enables you to leverage existing knowledge of Cisco IOS Software to implement Cisco Unified Communications Manager Express functions. You can view, back up, and restore the configuration using a simple text file. Manual setup can save time and effort when you use it for multisite deployments, because you change only the settings that are different on each site.

The **telephony-service** command enters the configuration mode for systemwide parameters for SCCP IP phones in CUCME.

```
Router(config)#telephony-service
```

The **protocol mode** command is used to configure SCCP phones in IPv4-only, IPv6-only, or dual-stack mode. For dual-stack mode, the user can configure the preferred family, IPv4 or IPv6. For a specific mode, the user is free to configure any address and the system will not hide or restrict any commands on the router. On a per-call basis, and based on the configured mode, SCCP phones choose the right address for communication.

```
Router(config-telephony)#protocol mode {ipv4 | ipv6 | dual-stack [preference {ipv4
 | ipv6}]}
```

For example, if the DNS reply has both IPv4 and IPv6 addresses and the configured mode is IPv6-only (or IPv4-only), the system discards all IPv4 (or IPv6) addresses and tries the IPv6 (or IPv4) addresses in the order in which they were received in the DNS reply. If the configured mode is **dual-stack**, the system first tries the addresses of the preferred family in the order in which they were received in the DNS reply. If all the addresses fail, the system tries addresses of the other family.

Configuring Source IP Address and Firmware Association

The **ip source-address** command enables a router to receive messages from Cisco IP Phones through the specified IP address and port. A Cisco Unified Communications Manager Express router cannot communicate with Cisco Unified Communications Manager Express phones if the IP address of the port to which they attempt to attach is not configured. The Cisco Unified Communications Manager Express router can receive messages from IPv6-enabled or IPv4-enabled IP phones or from phones in dual-stack (both IPv6 and IPv4) mode. The default SCCP port is 2000. The configured IP address might or might not be the same as the TFTP server address. The **secondary** option allows the configuration of the second CUCME router with which phones can register if the primary Cisco Unified Communications Manager Express router fails. The **strict-match** keyword instructs the router to reject IP phone registration attempts if the IP server address used by the phone does not match the source address.

```
Router(config-telephony)#ip source-address {ipv4_address | ipv6_address} port]
 [secondary {ipv4_address | ipv6_address} [rehome seconds]] [any-match | strict-
 match]
```

The **load** command updates the Cisco Unified Communications Manager Express configuration file for the specified type of Cisco IP Phone to add the name of the firmware file to be loaded by a particular phone type. The firmware filename also provides the version number for the phone firmware that is in the file. A separate **load** command is needed for each type of phone.

```
Router(config-telephony)#load model firmware-file
```

The following list shows the supported phone models for which you can use the **load** command:

- **7902:** Cisco Unified IP Phone 7902G model

- **7905:** Cisco Unified IP Phone 7905G model

- **7906:** Cisco Unified IP Phone 7906G model

- **7910:** Cisco Unified IP Phone 7910G+SW model

- **7911:** Cisco Unified IP Phone 7911G model

- **7912:** Cisco Unified IP Phone 7912G model

- **7914:** Cisco Unified IP Phone 7914 Expansion Module

- **7920:** Cisco Unified Wireless IP Phone 7920 model

- **7921:** Cisco Unified Wireless IP Phone 7921G model

- **7931:** Cisco Unified IP Phone 7931G model

- **7935:** Cisco Unified IP Conference Station 7935 model

- **7936:** Cisco Unified IP Conference Station 7936 model

- **7960-7940:** Cisco Unified 7960G and 7940G models

- **7941:** Cisco Unified IP Phone 7941G model

- **7941GE:** Cisco Unified IP Phone 7941G-GE model

- **7942:** Cisco Unified IP Phone 7942G model

- **7945:** Cisco Unified IP Phone 7945G model

- **7961:** Cisco Unified IP Phone 7961G model

- **7961GE:** Cisco Unified IP Phone 7961G-GE model

- **7962:** Cisco Unified IP Phone 7962G model

- **7965:** Cisco Unified IP Phone 7965G model

- **7970:** Cisco Unified IP Phone 7970G model

- **7971G-GE:** Cisco Unified IP Phone 7971G-GE model

- **7975:** Cisco Unified IP Phone 7975G model

- **7985:** Cisco Unified Video IP Phone 7985G model

- **ATA:** Cisco ATA 186 and 188 Analog Telephone Adapters

Note Do not use the file suffix when using the **load** command.

Enabling SCCP Endpoints

An SCCP endpoint is defined within CUCME as an *ephone* (that is, the CUCME entity representing an Ethernet phone). The maximum number of ephones depends on the hardware platform of Cisco Unified Communications Manager Express. The **max-ephones** command is set to 0 by default to conserve system memory. If you set this value above the required number of directory numbers, the router reserves system memory that it could use for other functions. Use the **max-ephone ?** command in telephony-service configuration mode to determine the maximum number of ephones supported by the hardware. Set the value within the range that complies with the license.

```
Router(config-telephony)#max-ephones maximum-ephones
```

Before any directory numbers can be created for SCCP endpoints, the **max-dn** command must be configured in the telephony-service configuration mode. The maximum number of directory numbers depends on the hardware platform of Cisco Unified Communications Manager Express.

```
Router(config-telephony)#max-dn maximum-ephone-dns
```

The **max-dn** command is set to 0 by default to conserve system memory. If this value is set above the required number of directory numbers, the router reserves system memory that it could use for other functions.

The command **max-dn ?** helps to determine the maximum allowed number of *ephone-dns* (that is, CUCME entities representing directory numbers of ephones) that the hardware supports. As with ephones, you should set the maximum value of ephone-dns within the range that complies with the license.

Locale Parameters

You can customize the CUCME system with the local language used on the Cisco IP Phone display, as well as the call progress indicators and ring cadence that the phone uses. This customization allows users to hear and interact with the system using the language and audible cues familiar to them.

You can set the language that the phone displays and the call progress tones and ring cadences that the phone uses to one of several ISO 3166 codes that indicate specific languages and geographic regions. The **user-locale** command specifies the language that the Cisco IP Phone displays, and the **network-locale** command specifies the set of call progress tones and ring cadences that the phone uses.

```
Router(config-telephony)#user-locale [index] language-code
Router(config-telephony)#network-locale [index] language-code
```

The *index* command allows the configuration of multiple user and network locale settings. User/network-locale 0 always holds the default setting that is used for all SCCP phones that are not assigned alternative locales. The system default is US (United States), unless a different locale is designated as the default.

To apply alternative locales to different phones, you can use the **cnf-files** command to specify per-phone configuration files. When you use per-phone configuration files, the configuration file of the phone automatically uses the default locales in user locale 0 and network locale 0. You can override this default for individual ephones by assigning locale tags to the alternative language codes that you want to use.

Date and Time Parameters

You can also modify the format in which the phone displays the date and time to the format that is typical for the location of the installation. You can use the **date-format** and **time-format** commands to configure the date and time format on a systemwide basis for all SCCP phones.

```
Router(config-telephony)#date-format {mm-dd-yy | dd-mm-yy | yy-dd-mm | yy-mm-dd}
Router(config-telephony)#time-format {12 | 24}
```

The following is a list of typical date formats that are supported by the **date-format** command:

- **dd-mm-yy:** Sets the date to dd-mm-yy format

- **mm-dd-yy:** Sets the date to mm-dd-yy format

- **yy-dd-mm:** Sets the date to yy-dd-mm format

- **yy-mm-dd:** Sets the date to yy-mm-dd format

The following is a list of typical time formats that are supported:

- **12:** Sets the time to 12-hour (a.m. and p.m.) format

- **24:** Sets the time to 24-hour format

Parameter Tuning

The keepalive time interval determines how frequently keepalives are sent between Cisco IP Phones and a Cisco Unified Communications Manager Express router. If a Cisco Unified Communications Manager Express router fails to receive three successive keepalive messages, it considers the phone to be out of service until the phone re-registers.

The default setting for the keepalives is 30 seconds. To change this interval, use the **keepalive** command in telephony-service configuration mode.

```
Router(config-telephony)#keepalive seconds
```

Adjusting the keepalive determines how quickly a failure is detected. To detect a failure more quickly than 90 seconds, change the keepalive to a number lower than 30.

Note   It might be useful to adjust the keepalive to a higher value when phones register across a WAN link, to conserve bandwidth.

The **codec** command selects the default codec for SCCP IP phones in CUCME. The default codec is G.711 mu-law, but it can be changed to G.722-64k. The telephone firmware version on a Cisco IP Phone must support the specified codec. If this command is configured, and a phone does not support the specified codec, the default codec for that phone is G.711 mu-law.

```
Router(config-telephony)#codec {g711-ulaw | g722-64k}
```

Generating Configuration Files for SCCP Endpoints

The **create cnf-files** command in telephony-service configuration mode builds the XML configuration files required for provisioning SCCP phones in Cisco Unified Communications Manager Express. The command writes the files to the location specified with the **cnf-file location** command.

```
Router(config-telephony)#create cnf-files
```

The **cnf-file {perphonetype | perphone}** command in telephony-service configuration mode affects how many configuration files are generated using the **create cnf-files** command.

```
Router(config-telephony)#cnf-file {perphonetype | perphone}
```

Three options exist:

- **persystem:** All phones use a single configuration file. This command is the default behavior and therefore CUCME does not need this command. The default user and network locale in a single configuration file are applied to all phones in the Cisco Unified Communications Manager Express system.

- **perphonetype:** Creates separate configuration files for each phone type. For example, all Cisco 7965 IP Phones use XMLDefault7965.cnf.xml, and all Cisco 7975 IP Phones use XMLDefault7975.cnf.xml. All phones of the same type use the same configuration file, which is generated using the default user or network locale. This option is not supported if the **cnf-file** location is configured for **system**.

- **perphone:** Creates a separate configuration file for each phone by MAC address; for example, SEP123456789.cnf.xml. The configuration file for a phone is generated with the default user and network locale unless a different user and network locale are applied to the phone using an ephone template. This option is not supported if the location option is **system**.

The **cnf-file location** command in telephony-service configuration mode specifies a storage location for phone configuration files. The default is that a single phone configuration file (**persystem**) is stored in system memory and is used by all phones.

```
Router(config-telephony)#cnf-file location {flash: | slot0: | tftp tftp-url}
```

Any one of these locations can be configured to store configuration files:

- **system:** This is the default. When the system is the storage location, there can be only one default configuration file, and it is used for all phones in the system. All phones, therefore, use the same user locale and network locale.

- **flash or slot 0:** When flash or slot 0 memory on the router is the storage location, you can create additional configuration files that can be applied per phone type or per individual phone. Up to five user-defined user and network locales can be used in these configuration files. The generation of configuration files on flash or slot 0 can take up to a minute, depending on the number of files being generated.

- **tftp:** When an external TFTP server is the storage location, you can create additional configuration files that can be applied per phone type or per individual phone. Up to five user-defined user and network locales can be used in these configuration files. TFTP does not support file deletion. When configuration files are updated, they overwrite any existing configuration files with the same name. If you change the configuration file location, files are not deleted from the TFTP server.

Cisco Unified Communications Manager Express SCCP Environment Example

Figure 3-36 shows a configuration example of systemwide SCCP parameters.

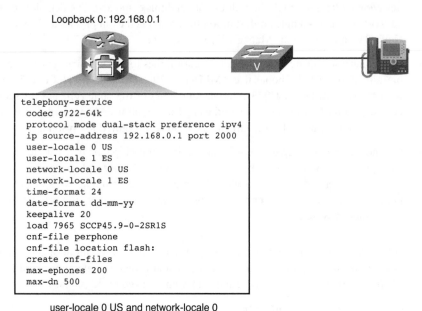

Loopback 0: 192.168.0.1

```
telephony-service
 codec g722-64k
 protocol mode dual-stack preference ipv4
 ip source-address 192.168.0.1 port 2000
 user-locale 0 US
 user-locale 1 ES
 network-locale 0 US
 network-locale 1 ES
 time-format 24
 date-format dd-mm-yy
 keepalive 20
 load 7965 SCCP45.9-0-2SR1S
 cnf-file perphone
 cnf-file location flash:
 create cnf-files
 max-ephones 200
 max-dn 500
```

user-locale 0 US and network-locale 0
US do not appear in the configuration.

Figure 3-36 *Cisco Unified Communications Manager Express SCCP Environment Example*

Setting Up Cisco Unified Communications Manager Express in a SIP Environment

To configure Cisco Unified Communications Manager Express to support SIP endpoints, you need to enter the voice service VoIP configuration mode with the **voice service voip** command and allow calls between SIP endpoints, using the **allow-connections sip to sip** command.

```
Router(config)#voice service voip
Router(conf-voi-serv)#allow-connections sip to sip
```

Further global SIP configuration is applied in the SIP mode. To enter the SIP configuration mode, enter the **sip** command in the voice service VoIP configuration mode. The SIP registrar server can be enabled using the **registrar server** command.

```
Router(conf-voi-serv)#sip
Router(conf-serv-sip)#registrar server
```

The **bind** command in SIP configuration mode binds the source address for SIP signaling or media packets to the IPv4 or IPv6 address of a specific interface. The binding of signaling traffic (**control** option) is relevant for CUCME support of SIP endpoints, because media streams are terminated directly on the SIP endpoints. This command is required if Cisco Unified Communications Manager Express should not use the IP layer to determine the source IP address for SIP communications. If configured, it must match the **source-address** command configured in the voice register global configuration mode.

```
Router(conf-serv-sip)#bind {control | media | all} source-interface
```

Configuring Cisco Unified Communications Manager Express for SIP

The **voice register global** command is used to set provisioning parameters for all supported SIP phones in a Cisco Unified Communications Manager Express system.

```
Router(config)#voice register global
```

The **mode cme** command enables Cisco Unified Communications Manager Express on the router for configuration purposes. It should be issued before configuring SIP phones in CUCME to ensure that all required commands are available in the configuration mode. The default setting is that the router is enabled only for Cisco SIP Survivable Remote Site Telephony (SRST) but not for SIP-based Cisco Unified Communications Manager Express.

```
Router(config-register-global)#mode cme
```

Configuring Source IP Address and Associating Firmware

The **source-address** command in voice register global or cme configuration mode sets the source address for communication with Cisco Unified Communications Manager Express SIP endpoints. This command is required if Cisco Unified Communications Manager Express should not use the IP layer to determine the source IP address. If configured, it must match the **bind control** *source-interface* command in SIP configuration mode.

```
Router(config-register-global)#source-address ip-address [port port]
```

The **load** command updates the configuration file for the specified phone type to add the name of the correct firmware file that the phone should load. This filename also provides the version number for the phone firmware that is in the file. Later, whenever a phone is started up or rebooted, the phone reads the configuration file to determine the name of the firmware file that it should load and then looks for that firmware file on a TFTP server. A separate **load** command is needed for each type of phone.

```
Router(config-register-global)#load model firmware-file
```

For most Cisco IP Phones (including Cisco Unified IP Phones 7961, 7965, 7970, 7971, and 7975) there are multiple firmware files. For these phones, use the TERMnn.x-y-x-w.loads or SIPnn.x-y-x-w.loads firmware filename for the **load** command, without the .loads file extension. For such phones, you do not configure the **load** command for any firmware file other than the TERM.loads or SIP.loads firmware file. In addition to the

load command, use the **tftpserver** command to enable TFTP access to the file by Cisco IP Phones. The file extensions are required when using the **tftp-server** command.

Enabling SIP Endpoints

The **max-pool** command that is configured in the voice register global configuration mode limits the number of SIP phones (referred to as *voice register pools*) available in a CUCME system. The command is platform-specific, and the default value is 0.

```
Router(config-register-global)#max-pool max-phones
```

The **max-dn** command that is configured in the voice register global configuration mode limits the number of SIP phone directory numbers available in a Cisco Unified Communications Manager Express system. The command is platform-specific. The default value is 0. You can increase the number of allowable extensions to the maximum, but after the maximum allowable number is configured, you cannot reduce the limit without rebooting the router. You cannot reduce the number of allowable extensions without removing the already configured directory numbers with dn-tags that have a higher number than the maximum number to be configured.

```
Router(config-register-global)#max-dn max-directory-numbers
```

Locale Parameters

The locale parameters for a Cisco Unified Communications Manager Express SIP environment are configured identically to the SCCP environment, but in the voice register global configuration mode.

A CUCME system can be customized with the local language on the display of SIP-based phones. The call progress indicators and cadence can also be adjusted for SIP endpoints.

The **user-locale** command specifies the language that the Cisco IP Phone will display. The **network-locale** command specifies the set of call progress tones and cadences that the phone will use.

```
Router(config-register-global)#user-locale [index] language-code
Router(config-register-global)#network-locale [index] language-code
```

The *index* allows the configuration of multiple user and network locale settings. User/network-locale 0 always holds the default setting that is used for all SIP phones that are not assigned alternative locales. The system default is US (United States), unless a different locale is designated as the default.

Date and Time Parameters

The date and time parameters for the Cisco Unified Communications Manager Express SIP environment are configured similarly to the SCCP environment, but they are applied in voice register global configuration mode. The **date-format** and **time-format** commands are used to configure the date and time format on a systemwide basis for all SIP phones.

```
Router(config-register-global)#date-format {M/D/Y | D/M/Y | Y/D/M | Y/M/D | YY/M/D}
Router(config-register-global)#time-format {12 | 24}
```

The **timezone** command defines the time zone of the Cisco Unified Communications Manager Express system. Context-sensitive help can be used to determine an appropriate number to use with the **timezone** command.

```
Router(config-register-global)#timezone number
```

NTP and DST Parameters

The **ntp-server** command specifies the IP address of the NTP server that is used by SIP phones in a CUCME system. It causes all SIP phones to be synchronized to the specified NTP server.

```
Router(config-register-global)#ntp-server ip-address [mode {anycast |
  directedbroadcast | multicast | unicast}]
```

The **dst auto-adjust** command enables the DST adjustment of system time. It is enabled by default with the default DST time period.

```
Router(config-register-global)#dst auto-adjust
```

The **dst start/stop** command is used to define the DST period. It is required only if it differs from the default setting.

```
Router(config-register-global)#dst {start | stop} month [day day-of-month | week
week-number | day day-of-week] time hour:minutes
```

Generating Configuration Files for SIP Endpoints

The configuration files for SIP endpoints are referred to as *configuration profiles*. To generate the configuration profiles for SIP phones, use the **create profile** command in voice register global configuration mode. This command generates configuration files that are used for provisioning SIP phones and writes these files to the location specified with the **tftp-path** command. After a change to the SIP configuration files, it might be necessary to issue the **no create profile** command to delete an existing file, followed by the **create profile** command to re-create the file, including the changes just made.

```
Router(config-register-global)#create profile
```

The **tftp-path** command defines the directory to which the configuration profiles are written. The default directory is system memory (system:/cme/sipphone/).

```
Router(config-register-global)#tftp-path {flash: | slot0: | tftp://url}
```

The **file text** command declares that the configuration profiles are written as ASCII text files.

```
Router(config-register-global)#file text
```

Cisco Unified Communications Manager Express SIP Environment Example

Figure 3-37 provides a configuration example of systemwide Cisco Unified Communications Manager Express SIP parameters.

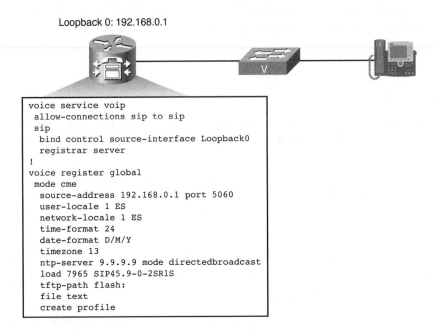

```
voice service voip
 allow-connections sip to sip
 sip
  bind control source-interface Loopback0
  registrar server
!
voice register global
 mode cme
  source-address 192.168.0.1 port 5060
  user-locale 1 ES
  network-locale 1 ES
  time-format 24
  date-format D/M/Y
  timezone 13
  ntp-server 9.9.9.9 mode directedbroadcast
  load 7965 SIP45.9-0-2SR1S
  tftp-path flash:
  file text
  create profile
```

Figure 3-37　*Cisco Unified Communications Manager Express SIP Environment Example*

Configuration of Cisco Unified Communications Manager Express

This section describes how to configure the Skinny Client Control Protocol (SCCP) and Session Initiation Protocol (SIP) endpoints in Cisco Unified Communications Manager Express. SCCP endpoints are defined as the Ethernet phones (ephones) and have SCCP directory numbers (ephone-dns) associated with them. The SIP endpoints are defined as voice register pools and have SIP directory numbers (voice register directory numbers) associated with them. This section discusses the various types of directory numbers available for Cisco IP Phones using either SCCP or SIP.

Directory Numbers and Phones in Cisco Unified Communications Manager Express

A phone represents the configuration and settings of the physical IP phone and is associated with a physical device by MAC address. A phone is configured as an SCCP *ephone*, or *Ethernet phone*, or a *voice register pool* for SIP. The phone can be either a Cisco IP

Phone or an analog phone. Each phone has a unique tag, or sequence number, to identify it during configuration.

A directory number, also known as an *ephone-dn* for SCCP or a *voice register dn* for SIP, is the software configuration in Cisco Unified Communications Manager Express that represents the line connecting a voice channel to a phone. A directory number has one or more extensions or telephone numbers associated with it to allow call connections to be made. Each directory number has a unique dn tag, or sequence number, to identify it during configuration. Directory numbers are assigned to line buttons on phones. One virtual voice port and one or more dial peers are automatically created for each directory number (one dial peer for each telephone number associated with the directory number) when the phone registers in CUCME.

Table 3-6 contrasts CUCME's phone and directory number entities.

Table 3-6   *Phones and Directory Numbers*

Feature	Phone	Directory Number
Name (SCCP)	Ephone	ephone-dn
Name (SIP)	Voice register pool	voice register dn
What it is	Phone as represented in Cisco Unified Communications Manager Express configuration.	Software configuration that represents the line connecting a voice channel to a phone.
Identifier	tag (sequence number)	dn-tag (sequence number)
Number of entities	Number of registered endpoints.	Number of simultaneous calls (each directory number represents a virtual voice port in the router).
Association	Phone can have one or more directory numbers associated with it.	Directory number can have one or more telephone numbers associated with it.
Binding	Phone MAC address ties the software configuration to the hardware.	Directory numbers are assigned to line buttons on phones.
Impact on dial plan	None.	For each directory number, one virtual voice port and one or more dial peers are created.

Directory Number Types

The number of directory numbers affects the number of simultaneous calls, because each directory number represents a virtual voice port in the router. A directory number is the basic building block of a Cisco Unified Communications Manager Express system. Six types of directory numbers can be combined in different ways for different call coverage situations. The selection of the type depends on the specific enterprise requirements. For example, to keep the number of directory numbers low and provide service to a large number of people, shared directory numbers are useful. To have a limited quantity of extension numbers and a large quantity of simultaneous calls, two or more directory numbers with the same telephone number can be created.

As illustrated in Figure 3-38, the directory numbers that are supported by CUCME can belong to any of these types:

- Single-line directory number (SCCP or SIP)

- Dual-line directory number (SCCP only)

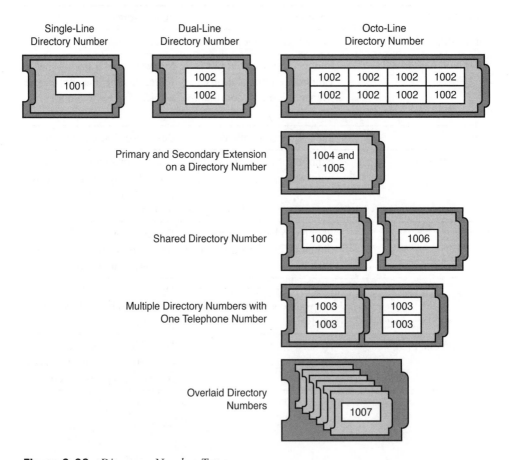

Figure 3-38 *Directory Number Types*

- Octo-line directory number (SCCP only)

- Dual-number (SCCP or SIP)

- Shared-line—nonexclusive (SIP only)

- Shared-line—exclusive (SCCP only)

- Two directory numbers with one telephone number (SCCP or SIP)

- Overlaid directory numbers (SCCP only)

Single- and Dual-Line Directory Numbers

A single-line directory number, as depicted in Figure 3-39, has the following characteristics:

- Supports one call at a time using one phone line button. A single-line directory number in SCCP has one telephone number associated with it. In SIP, it can have as many as ten telephone numbers associated with it.

- Ideal for lines dedicated to intercom, paging, message waiting indicator (MWI), loopback, and music on hold (MOH) feed sources.

- Can be combined with dual-line directory numbers on the same phone.

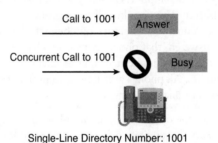

Single-Line Directory Number: 1001

Figure 3-39 *Single-Line Directory Number*

A dual-line directory number, as demonstrated in Figure 3-40, has the following characteristics:

- One voice port with two channels.

- Supported on Cisco IP Phones running SCCP, but not supported for SIP.

- Can make two call connections at the same time using one phone line button. A dual-line directory number has two channels for separate call connections.

- Can have one number or two numbers (primary and secondary) associated with it.

- Should be used for a directory number that needs to use one line button for features such as call waiting, call transfer, or conferencing.

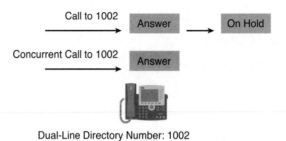

Dual-Line Directory Number: 1002

Figure 3-40   *Dual-Line Directory Number*

Figures 3-39 and 3-40 demonstrate the difference between the single- and dual-line directory numbers when a second call is placed to them. The single-line directory number accommodates only one call and rejects the second, while the dual-line directory number can answer both, place one call on hold, and take further actions, such as call transfer and call conference.

Octo-Line Directory Number

An octo-line directory number supports as many as eight active calls, both incoming and outgoing, on a single button. The octo-line directory numbers are supported only on SCCP endpoints. Unlike a dual-line directory number, which is shared exclusively among phones (after a call is answered, that phone owns both channels of the dual-line directory number), an octo-line directory number can split its channels among other phones that share the directory number. All phones are allowed to initiate or receive calls on the idle channels of the shared octo-line directory number.

Figure 3-41 demonstrates the operation of an octo-line directory number. Because octo-line directory numbers do not require a different ephone-dn for each active call, one octo-line directory number can process multiple calls. Multiple incoming calls to an octo-line directory number ring simultaneously. The ringing stops when a phone answers a call. When phones share an octo-line directory number, incoming calls ring on phones without active calls, and these phones can answer. Phones with an active call hear the call-waiting tone whenever a subsequent call arrives during an active conversation.

After a phone answers an incoming call, the answering phone is in the connected state. Other phones that share the octo-line directory number are in the remote-in-use state.

After a connected call on an octo-line directory number is put on hold, any phone that shares this directory number can pick up the held call. If a phone user is in the process of initiating a call transfer or creating a conference, the call is locked and other phones that share the octo-line directory number cannot steal the call.

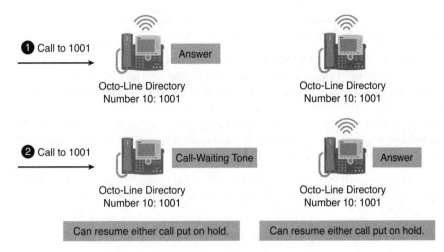

Figure 3-41 *Octo-Line Directory Number*

Nonexclusive Shared-Line Directory Number

Cisco Unified Communications Manager Express supports SIP shared lines to allow multiple phones to share a common directory number, as shown in Figure 3-42. All phones sharing a directory number can initiate and receive calls at the same time. Calls to the shared line ring simultaneously on all phones without active calls. Any of these phones can answer the incoming calls. The ringing stops on all phones when a phone answers the call. The connected phones hear the call-waiting tone on incoming calls to the shared line number.

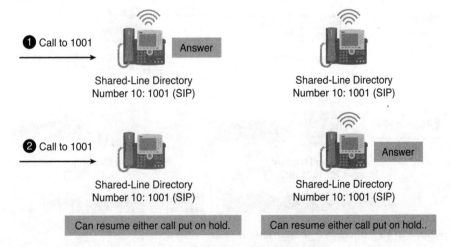

Figure 3-42 *Nonexclusive Shared-Line Directory Number*

The phone that answers an incoming call is in the connected state. Other phones that share the directory number are in the remote-in-use state. The first user that answers the call on the shared line is connected to the caller, and the remaining users see the call information and status of the shared line.

Calls on a shared line can be put on hold like calls on a nonshared line. When a call is placed on hold, other phones with the shared-line directory number receive a hold notification so that all phones sharing the line are aware of the held call. Any shared-line phone user can resume the held call. If the call is placed on hold as part of a conference or call transfer operation, the resume is not allowed. The ID of the held call is used by other shared-line members to resume the call. Notifications are sent to all associated phones when a held call is resumed on a shared line.

Shared lines support up to 16 calls. Cisco Unified Communications Manager Express rejects any new call that exceeds the configured limit.

Exclusive Shared-Line Directory Number

An exclusive shared-line directory number, as depicted in Figure 3-43, has the following characteristics:

- Supported by SCCP endpoints only

- Line appears on two different phones but uses the same directory number

- Can make one call at a time; that call appears on both phones

- Should be used when you want the capability to answer or pick up a call at more than one phone

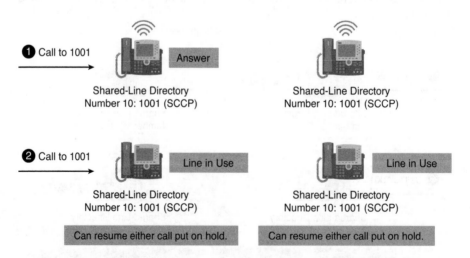

Figure 3-43 *Exclusive Shared-Line Directory Number*

Because this directory number is shared exclusively among phones, if the directory number is connected to a call on one phone, that directory number is unavailable for calls on any other phone. If a call is placed on hold on one phone, it can be retrieved on the second phone. This is like having a single-line phone in your house with multiple extensions. An incoming call can be answered from any phone on which the number appears, and it can be picked up from hold on any phone on which the number appears.

Multiple Directory Numbers with One Telephone Number

Multiple directory numbers with one telephone number have the following characteristics:

- Same telephone number that is combined with multiple separate virtual voice ports supports multiple separate call connections

- Can be dual-line (SCCP only) or single-line directory numbers

- Can appear on the same phone on different buttons or on different phones

- Suitable for making more calls while using fewer numbers

As shown in Figure 3-44, the situation of multiple-directory-numbers-with-one-number is different from the situation of an exclusive shared line (SCCP), which also has multiple buttons with one number but has only one directory number for all of them. An SCCP shared directory number has the same call connection at all the buttons on which the shared directory number appears. If a call on an SCCP shared directory number is answered on one phone and then placed on hold, the call can be retrieved from another phone on which the shared directory number appears. But when there are two directory numbers with one telephone number, a call connection appears only on the phone and button at which the call is placed or received.

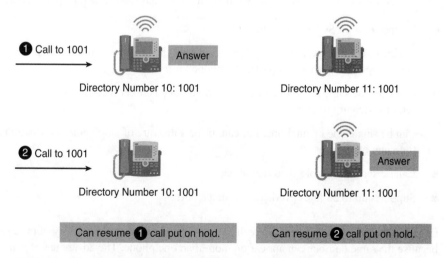

Figure 3-44 *Multiple Directory Numbers with One Telephone Number*

Multiple-Number Directory Number

A multiple-number directory number, as illustrated in Figure 3-45, has the following characteristics:

- Maximum of two telephone numbers (primary and secondary) for SCCP endpoints

- Maximum of ten telephone numbers for SIP endpoints

- Maximum of one call at a time if it is a single-line directory number

- Maximum of two calls at a time if it is a dual-line directory number (SCCP only)

- Useful for different numbers for the same button without using more than one directory number

Call to 1001 or 1002

Answer

Directory Number 10: 1001, 1002

Figure 3-45 *Multiple-Number Directory Number*

Overlaid Directory Number

An overlaid directory number, as shown in Figure 3-46, has the following characteristics:

- Is supported for SCCP endpoints only

- Is a member of an overlay set, which includes all the directory numbers that have been assigned together to a particular phone button

- Can have the same telephone or extension number as other members of the overlay set, or different numbers

- Can be single-line or dual-line, but cannot be a mixture of single-line and dual-line in the same overlay set

- Can be shared on more than one phone

- Supports up to 25 lines overlaid on a single button

Overlaid directory numbers provide call coverage similar to shared directory numbers, because the same number can appear on more than one phone. The advantage of using two directory numbers in an overlay arrangement rather than as a simple shared line is that a call to the number on one phone does not block the use of the same number on the other phone, which would happen if it were a shared directory number.

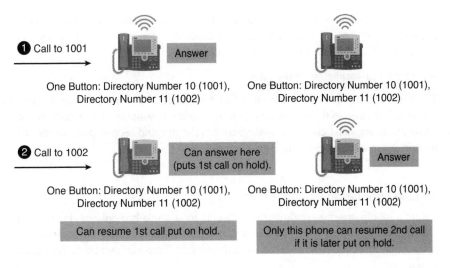

Figure 3-46 *Overlaid Directory Number*

Creating Directory Numbers for SCCP Phones

The **ephone-dn** *dn-tag* global configuration command creates an ephone-dn, which builds one virtual voice port. The *dn-tag* parameter must contain a unique number for a new ephone-dn or an existing number if you are modifying a current ephone-dn. If you want to assign the ephone-dn to an extension and a phone line, the ephone-dn needs to be able to accept two calls on the same line at the same time. Use the keyword **dual-line** or **octo-line** at the end for these special types of directory numbers. If you do not configure either option, the directory number is a single-line directory number.

```
Router(config)#ephone-dn dn-tag [dual-line | octo-line]
```

The **number** command defines a valid number for an ephone-dn that is to be assigned to an SCCP phone. The **secondary** keyword allows you to associate a second telephone number with an ephone-dn so that it can be called by dialing either the main or secondary phone number.

```
Router(config-ephone-dn)#number number [secondary number] [no-reg [both |
  primary]]
```

The **no-reg** keyword causes an E.164 number in the dial peer to not register with a gatekeeper. If you do not specify **both** or **primary** after the **no-reg** keyword, only the secondary number does not register.

A number normally contains only numeric characters that allow it to be dialed from any telephone keypad. However, in certain cases such as intercom numbers, which are normally dialed only by the router, you can insert alphabetic characters into the number to prevent phone users from dialing it and using the intercom function without authorization. A number can also contain one or more periods (.) as wildcard characters that will match any dialed number in that position. For example, 51.. rings when any four-digit number starting with 51 is dialed.

The **name** command is used to provide caller ID for calls originating from a directory number. This command also generates local directory information that is accessed by using the Directories button on a Cisco IP Phone.

```
Router(config-ephone-dn)#name name
```

The **name** argument combination must match the order that is specified in the **directory** command (defined in telephony-service mode): either first-name-first or last-name-first. The name string must contain a space between the first and second parts of the string (that is, "first last" or "last first").

Single-Line Ephone-dn Configuration

Figure 3-47 illustrates a configuration example for a single-line ephone-dn. The single-line ephone-dn creates one virtual port that supports only one channel at a time. It does not support the call-waiting feature, and therefore call transfer and conferencing are not possible.

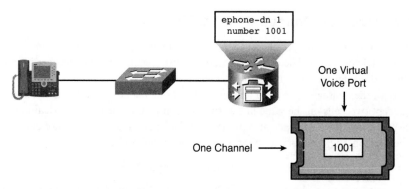

Figure 3-47 *Single-Line Ephone-dn Configuration*

Dual-Line Ephone-dn Configuration

Figure 3-48 illustrates a configuration example for a dual-line ephone-dn. The dual-line ephone-dn creates one virtual port that supports two channels. It supports the call-waiting feature that enables call transfer and conferencing. Dual-line ephone-dns are not recommended for scenarios in which the second channel is never used, such as for intercoms, paging, MWI, call parking slots, and MOH sources.

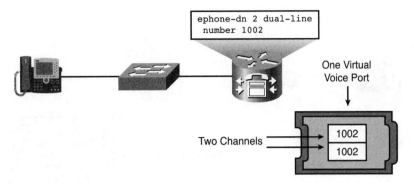

Figure 3-48   *Dual-Line Ephone-dn Configuration*

Octo-Line Ephone-dn Configuration

Figure 3-49 illustrates a configuration example for an octo-line ephone-dn. The octo-line ephone-dn creates one virtual port that supports eight channels. The octo-line is useful when call coverage is implemented to ensure that calls are delivered to their intended destinations.

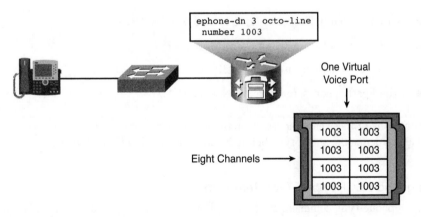

Figure 3-49   *Octo-Line Ephone-dn Configuration*

Dual-Number Ephone-dn Configuration

Figure 3-50 illustrates a configuration example for a dual-line ephone-dn with two telephone numbers configured. With SCCP, two is the maximum number of telephone numbers that can be associated with one directory number. Calls to either number ring on this directory number and can be answered on it. The number of concurrent calls depends on the type of the ephone-dn.

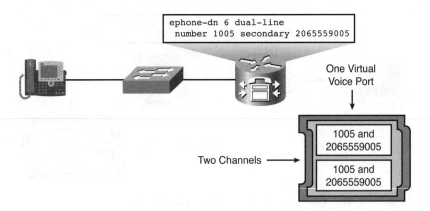

```
ephone-dn 6 dual-line
  number 1005 secondary 2065559005
```

One Virtual
Voice Port

Two Channels →

1005 and
2065559005

1005 and
2065559005

Figure 3-50 *Dual-Number Ephone-dn Configuration*

Configuring SCCP Phone-Type Templates

Cisco Unified Communications Manager Express classifies various endpoints by their phone type. Most phone types are predefined and can be referenced when configuring the devices. The following phone types are not predefined within Cisco Unified Communications Manager Express:

- Cisco Unified IP Phones 6901, 6911, and Wireless 7925

- Cisco Unified IP Phone Expansion Modules 7915 and 7916

- Conference station: Cisco Unified IP Conference Station 7937G

- Third-party phones: for example, Nokia E61

When any of these endpoints exist in the network, the phone-type templates should be used to define the phone type before it can be assigned to the endpoints.

Configuring SCCP Phone-Type Templates

The **ephone-type** command creates an ephone-type template. It defines a unique label that identifies the type of phone. The label is any alphanumeric string with a maximum of 32 characters.

```
Router(config)#ephone-type phone-type [addon]
```

The **addon** option indicates that the phone type is an add-on module, such as a Cisco Unified IP Phone Expansion Module 7915.

The **device-id** command specifies the device ID of the type of phone being added with the ephone-type template. If this command is set to the default value of 0, the ephone-type is invalid. The device IDs are preconfigured to these values:

- **227:** Cisco Unified IP Phone Expansion Module 7915 with 12 buttons

- **228:** Cisco Unified IP Phone Expansion Module 7915 with 24 buttons

- **229:** Cisco Unified IP Phone Expansion Module 7916 with 12 buttons

- **230:** Cisco Unified IP Phone Expansion Module 7916 with 24 buttons

- **376:** Nokia E61

- **484:** Cisco Unified Wireless IP Phone 7925

- **431:** Cisco Unified IP Conference Station 7937G

```
Router(config-ephone-type)#device-id number
```

The **device-name** command is an optional command that allows the definition of a name.

```
Router(config-ephone-type)#device-name name
```

The **device type**, **num-buttons**, and **max-presentation** commands are used to configure the device type, number of buttons, and number of call presentation lines that are supported by a phone type.

```
Router(config-ephone-type)#device-type phone-type
Router(config-ephone-type)#num-buttons number
Router(config-ephone-type)#max-presentation number
```

These values are predetermined by Cisco Unified Communications Manager Express and are presented in Table 3-7.

Table 3-7   *Supported Device Options*

Supported Device	device-id	device-type	num-buttons	max-presentation
Cisco Unified IP Phone Expansion Module 7915 with 12 buttons	227	7915	12	0 (default)
Cisco Unified IP Phone Expansion Module 7915 with 24 buttons	228	7915	24	0
Cisco Unified IP Phone Expansion Module 7916 with 12 buttons	229	7916	12	0
Cisco Unified IP Phone Expansion Module 7916 with 24 buttons	230	7916	24	0
Cisco Unified Wireless IP Phone 7925	484	7925	6	4
Cisco Unified IP Conference Station 7937G	431	7937	1	6
Nokia E61	376	E61	1	1

Ephone Template for Conference Station 7937G Configuration Example

Example 3-7 shows a sample template that defines the ephone type for a Cisco Unified IP Conference Station 7937G, which is shown in Figure 3-51. The type is then referenced by the SCCP device configuration.

Example 3-7   *Conference Station Type Defined with an ephone-type Template*

```
Router#show running-config
...OUTPUT OMITTED...
ephone-type Conference7937
 device-id 431
 device-name Conference Station 7937G
 device-type 7937
 num-buttons 1
 max-presentation 6
!
ephone 1
 mac-address 001C.821C.ED23
 type Conference7937
...OUTPUT OMITTED...
```

Figure 3-51   *Cisco Unified IP Conference Station 7937G*

Creating SCCP Phones

The **ephone** command is used to create or modify an ephone. This command enters the ephone configuration mode, where ephone-specific commands are issued.

```
Router(config)#ephone phone-tag
```

The **mac-address** command associates the MAC address of the endpoint with the endpoint. It specifies 12 hexadecimal characters in groups of four separated by periods; for example, 0000.0c12.3456.

```
Router(config-ephone)#mac-address mac-address
```

Configuring the SCCP Ephone Type

The **type** command in ephone or ephone-template configuration mode is used to assign a phone type to an SCCP phone. It is not mandatory for ephone operations, but it affects the configuration file that is created for the defined endpoints and the default configuration file that is generic to all phone types. In combination with the **load** command, it defines the firmware image that should be used by a specific phone model.

```
Router(config-ephone)#type phone-type [addon 1 module-type [2 module-type]]
```

The **addon** option informs the router that an expansion module is added to the phone and defines the type of the module.

The phone types are preconfigured within Cisco Unified Communications Manager Express to the values shown in Table 3-8. Additional phone types can be defined using the ephone-type templates. If the **type** command is applied both to the ephone-type template and to the ephone, the value that is set in ephone configuration mode has priority.

The *phone-type* and *module-type* parameters are provided in Table 3-8.

Table 3-8 *phone-type and module-type Parameters*

phone-type Parameters	module-type Parameters
12SP, 7902, 7905, 7910, 7911, 7912, 7920, 7921, 7925, 7931, 7935, 7936, 7937, 7940, 7941, 7941GE, 7942, 7945, 7960, 7961, 7961GE, 7962, 7965, 7970, 7971, 7975, 7985, anl (analog), ata (Cisco ATA-186 or ATA-188), bri (SCCP gateway), vgc-phone (VG248 analog phone emulation)	7914, 7915-12, 7915-24, 7916-12, 7916-24

Configuring SCCP Ephone Buttons

The **button** command allows a line button to have one or more ephone-dns assigned to it. The **button-number** parameter represents the physical phone button, with the top button being "1."

```
Router(config-ephone)#button button-number{separator}dn-tag [,dn-tag...] ...
   [[button-number{separator}dn-tag] [,dn-tag...]]
```

The *separator* parameter is a single character that defines the properties of the button:

- **: (colon):** Normal ring. For incoming calls, the phone produces audible ringing, a flashing icon on the phone display, and a flashing red light on the handset.

- **b:** Beep but no ring. The audible ring is suppressed for incoming calls, but call-waiting beeps are allowed. The visual cues are the same as those described for a normal ring.

- **f:** Feature ring. This option differentiates incoming calls on a special line from incoming calls on other lines. The feature ring cadence is a triple pulse, as opposed to a single pulse for normal internal calls and a double pulse for normal external calls.

- **m:** Monitor mode for a shared line. A visible indicator shows if the shared line is in use.

- **o:** Overlay line without call waiting. Multiple ephone-dns share a single button, up to a maximum of ten on a button. The *dn-tag* argument can contain a maximum of ten individual dn-tag values, separated by commas.

- **c:** Overlay line with call waiting. Multiple ephone-dns share a single button, with a maximum of ten on a button. The *dn-tag* argument can contain a maximum of ten individual dn-tag values, separated by commas.

- **s:** Silent ring. The audible ring and the call-waiting beep are suppressed for incoming calls. The visual cues are the same as those described for a normal ring.

- **w:** Watch mode for all lines on the phone for which this directory number is the primary line. Visible line status indicates whether a watched phone is idle or not.

- **x:** Creates an overlay rollover button. When the overlay button specified in this command is occupied by an active call, a second call to one of its ephone-dns will appear on this button. This button is also known as an overlay expansion button.

Configuring Ephone Preferred Codec

The **codec** command is used to change the default G.711 mu-law codec to a less bandwidth-intensive codec, such as G.729 (8 kb/s) or Internet Low Bitrate Codec (iLBC). The firmware version of a telephone must support the specified codec. If a codec is specified by using this command and a phone does not support the preferred codec, the phone will use the global codec as specified by using the **codec** command in telephony-service configuration mode. If the global codec is not supported, the phone will use G.711 mu-law.

```
Router(config-ephone)#codec {g711ulaw | g722r64 | g729r8 [dspfarm-assist] | ilbc}
```

For calls to phones that are not in the same CUCME system (such as VoIP calls), the codec is negotiated based on the protocol that is used for the call (such as H.323). For calls to other phones in the same Cisco Unified Communications Manager Express system, an IP phone that is configured to use G.729 will always have its calls set up using G.729.

When you use the **codec** command without the **dspfarm-assist** keyword, you affect only calls between two phones on the CUCME router (such as between an IP phone and another IP phone or between an IP phone and a Foreign Exchange Station [FXS] analog phone). The command has no effect on a call that is directed through a VoIP dial peer unless you use the **dspfarm-assist** keyword.

When you use a low-bandwidth codec with the **dspfarm-assist** option, and the router is in a VoIP call or conference that requires G.711, the digital signal processor (DSP) farm resources are used to convert G.711 to the low-bandwidth codec. Adequate DSP resources must be appropriately configured.

The benefit of the **dspfarm-assist** keyword is that it allows calls to use the G.729r8 codec, which saves network bandwidth. The disadvantage is the use of DSP resources that might be required for other applications.

Basic Ephone Configuration Example

Figure 3-52 demonstrates how to create ephone-dn 7 and assign it to ephone 1. The ephone-dn is configured as dual-line and is assigned to line button 1 on the Cisco IP Phone with the MAC address of 000F.2470.F8F8. The phone type is 7965.

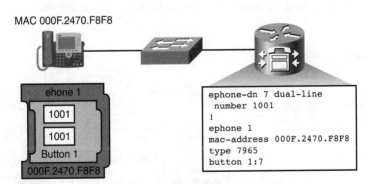

Figure 3-52 *Basic Ephone Configuration Example*

Multiple Ephone Configuration Example

When there are multiple physical devices, the number of ephones must match the number of devices. Then each ephone has one or more ephone-dns that are assigned to line buttons on the physical device. Figure 3-53 shows three ephones with one ephone-dn that is assigned to each of them. Two phones use a normal ring while the third ephone uses the feature ring.

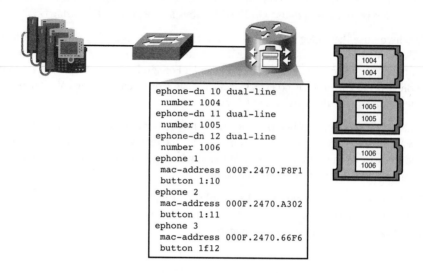

```
ephone-dn 10 dual-line
 number 1004
ephone-dn 11 dual-line
 number 1005
ephone-dn 12 dual-line
 number 1006
ephone 1
 mac-address 000F.2470.F8F1
 button 1:10
ephone 2
 mac-address 000F.2470.A302
 button 1:11
ephone 3
 mac-address 000F.2470.66F6
 button 1f12
```

Figure 3-53 *Multiple Ephone Configuration Example*

Multiple Directory Numbers Configuration Example

In Figure 3-54, multiple ephone-dns are assigned to the ephone buttons.

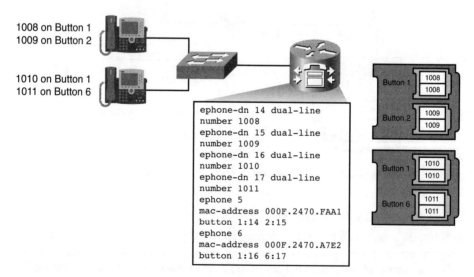

1008 on Button 1
1009 on Button 2

1010 on Button 1
1011 on Button 6

```
ephone-dn 14 dual-line
number 1008
ephone-dn 15 dual-line
number 1009
ephone-dn 16 dual-line
number 1010
ephone-dn 17 dual-line
number 1011
ephone 5
mac-address 000F.2470.FAA1
button 1:14 2:15
ephone 6
mac-address 000F.2470.A7E2
button 1:16 6:17
```

Figure 3-54 *Multiple Directory Numbers Configuration Example*

Shared Directory Number Configuration Example

Figure 3-55 shows a sample configuration for shared directory number in an environment with SCCP endpoints.

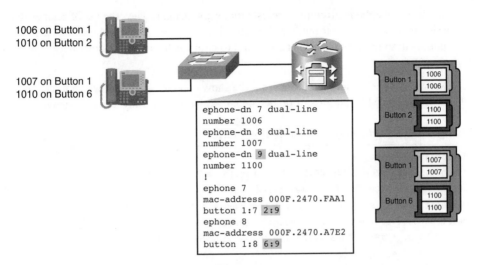

1006 on Button 1
1010 on Button 2

1007 on Button 1
1010 on Button 6

```
ephone-dn 7 dual-line
number 1006
ephone-dn 8 dual-line
number 1007
ephone-dn 9 dual-line
number 1100
!
ephone 7
mac-address 000F.2470.FAA1
button 1:7 2:9
ephone 8
mac-address 000F.2470.A7E2
button 1:8 6:9
```

Button 1 1006 / 1006
Button 2 1100 / 1100

Button 1 1007 / 1007
Button 6 1100 / 1100

Figure 3-55   *Shared Directory Number Configuration Example*

The exclusive (SCCP) shared ephone-dn has the following characteristics:

■   It appears on two different phones, but uses the same ephone-dn and number.

■   If the ephone-dn is connected to a call on one phone, that ephone-dn is unavailable for other calls on the second phone, because the phones share the same ephone-dn. The active call appears on both phones.

■   You should use shared ephone-dns when you want the ability to answer or pick up a call at more than one phone.

■   Both phones ring when a call arrives at the ephone-dn, but only one phone can pick up a call, which ensures privacy.

■   When a call is placed on hold, either phone can retrieve it.

Controlling Automatic Registration

The **auto-reg-ephone** command allows automatic registration, in which Cisco Unified Communications Manager Express allocates an ephone slot to any ephone that connects to it, regardless of whether the ephone appears in the configuration or not. The auto-registration is enabled by default.

```
Router(config-telephony)#auto-reg-ephone
```

The **no** form of this command blocks the automatic registration of ephones whose MAC addresses are not explicitly listed in the configuration. When automatic registration is blocked, Cisco Unified Communications Manager Express records the MAC addresses of phones that attempt to register but cannot because they are blocked.

Use the **show ephone attempted-registrations** command to view the list of phones that have attempted to register but have been blocked. Use the **clear telephony-service ephone-attempted-registrations** command to clear the list of phones that have attempted to register.

Example 3-8 shows sample output from the **show ephone** command, which indicates an ephone with a MAC address of 0024.C445.4B48 has successfully auto-registered.

Example 3-8 *Confirming Automatic Registration*

```
Router#show ephone
ephone-1[0] Mac:0024.C445.4B48 TCP socket:[1] activeLine:0 whisperLine:0
REGISTERED in SCCP ver 17/17 max_streams=5
mediaActive:0 whisper_mediaActive:0 startMedia:0 offhook:0 ringing:0
reset:0 reset_sent:0 paging 0 debug:0 caps:9
IP:10.1.4.21 * 18443 7965 keepalive 0 max_line 6 available_line 6
Preferred Codec: g711ulaw
Lpcor Type: none
```

Partially Automated Endpoint Deployment

The **auto assign** command in telephony-service configuration mode assigns ephone-dn tags to SCCP phones as they register for service with CUCME. This command enables you to assign ranges of ephone-dn tags according to the physical phone type. You can use multiple **auto assign** commands to provide discontinuous ranges and to support multiple types of IP phones. You can assign overlapping ephone-dn ranges so that the ranges map to more than one type of phone. If there are not enough available ephone-dns in the automatic assignment set, some phones will not receive ephone-dns.

```
Router(config-telephony)#auto assign start-dn to stop-dn [type phone-type]
    [cfw number timeout seconds]
```

If you do not specify a type in the **auto assign** command, the values in that range are assigned to phones of any type. If you do assign a phone type to a specific range, the available ephone-dns in that range are used first. The **cfw** and **timeout** keywords set the Call Forward Busy (CFB) number and timeout values on all phones that automatically register.

The ephone-dn tags that the system automatically assigns must have at least a primary number defined. All of the ephone-dns in a single automatic assignment set must be of the same kind (either single-line or dual-line). Automatic assignment cannot create shared lines.

Note   The **auto assign** command grants telephony service to any endpoint that attempts to register. A network should be secured against unauthorized access by unknown phones.

Partially Automated Deployment Example

In Example 3-9, four **auto assign** commands declare different ranges of ephone-dn tags. The system will assign any Cisco Unified IP Phone 7961 the lowest unassigned ephone-dn from 1 to 10. The system will assign any Cisco Unified IP Phone 7965 the lowest unassigned ephone-dn from 11 to 20, and the system will assign any Cisco Unified IP Phone 7975 the lowest unassigned ephone-dn from 21 to 40.

Example 3-9   *Partially Automated Deployment Example*

```
Router#show running-config
...OUTPUT OMITTED...
telephony-service
 auto assign 1 to 10 type 7961
 auto assign 11 to 20 type 7965
 auto assign 21 to 40 type 7975
 auto assign 41 to 50
!
ephone-dn 1 dual-line
 number 1000
...OUTPUT OMITTED...
```

The directory numbers from the generic range of 41 to 50 will be assigned to the specified endpoints if they cannot be assigned an ephone-dn in the assigned range and to all unspecified models of Cisco IP Phones.

Creating Directory Numbers for SIP Phones

After the **max-dn** value is set to a nondefault value, to enable the required number of SIP endpoints, the **voice register dn** command can be used to create directory numbers for SIP IP phones directly connected in Cisco Unified Communications Manager Express. The command defines a directory number for a phone line, intercom line, voice-mail port, or an MWI. The command also enters the voice register dn configuration mode, in which further parameters are set.

```
Router(config)#voice register dn dn-tag
```

The **number** command defines a valid number for an extension that is to be assigned to a SIP phone. This command should be used before any other commands in voice register dn configuration mode.

```
Router(config-register-dn)#number number
```

A number normally contains only numeric characters, which allows users to dial the number from any telephone keypad. However, in certain cases, such as the numbers for intercom extensions, the numbers can include alphabetic characters that can only be dialed internally from a Cisco Unified Communications Manager Express router and not from telephone keypads. When alphabetic characters are included in a number, the extension can be dialed by a router for intercom calls but not by unauthorized individuals from other phones.

The **shared-line** command enables a shared line on an individual SIP phone directory number. The **max-calls** option defines the maximum number of active calls (in the range 2–16) allowed on the shared line. If the **shared-line** command is not applied to a directory number, it does not allow sharing by default. If the **shared-line** command is configured without the **max-calls** keyword, the directory number supports a maximum of two concurrent calls.

```
Router(config-register-dn)#shared-line [max-calls number-of-calls]
```

Voice Register Directory Number Configuration Example

Figure 3-56 illustrates how to configure a single-line directory number for SIP endpoints. The **voice register dn** command creates one virtual port that supports a single voice channel. This configuration is useful for SIP phones, intercoms, MOH feeds, and MWI lines.

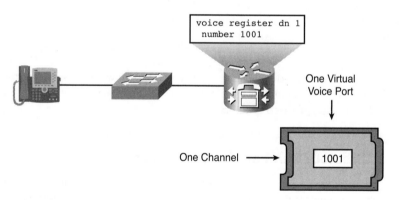

Figure 3-56   *Voice Register Directory Number Configuration Example*

Creating SIP Phones

After the **max-pool** value is set to a nondefault value, to enable the required number of SIP endpoints in Cisco Unified Communications Manager, the **voice register pool** command can be used to create the SIP endpoints. The command enters the voice register pool configuration mode, in which further parameters are set.

```
Router(config)#voice register pool pool-tag
Router(config-register-pool)#id {network address mask mask | ip address mask mask |
  mac address}
```

The **id** command explicitly identifies a locally available individual Cisco SIP IP phone in the voice register pool configuration mode. This command must be used before any other commands in the voice register pool configuration mode. This command offers a degree of authentication, which is required to accept registrations, based on the following criteria:

- Verification of the local Layer 2 MAC address using the router Address Resolution Protocol (ARP) cache. When the **mac** *address* keyword and argument are used, the phone must be in the same subnet as that of the router LAN interface, so that the MAC address of the phone is visible in the router ARP cache.

- Verification of the known single static IP address (or DHCP dynamic IP address within a specific subnet) of the SIP phone.

Configuring SIP Phones

The **type** command in voice register pool configuration mode defines a phone type for a SIP phone. The setting is required for CUCME to write the correct firmware specification into the configuration profile. The appropriate firmware is found based on the phone type and the **load** command, which is set in the voice register global configuration mode.

```
Router(config-register-pool)#type phone-type
```

The **number** command in voice register pool configuration mode indicates the E.164 phone numbers that are permitted by the registrar in the register message from the SIP phone. The keywords and arguments of this command allow for more explicit setting of user preferences regarding what number patterns should match the voice register pool. The tag identifies the telephone number when there are multiple number commands (one to ten numbers are allowed). The optional **preference** defines the preference order. Range is 0 through 10, while the highest preference is 0. The **huntstop** option stops hunting if the dial peer is busy.

```
Router(config-register-pool)#number tag {number-pattern [preference value]
  [huntstop] | dn dn-tag}
```

Tuning SIP Phones

The **username** command in voice register global configuration mode sets authentication credentials for a SIP phone. It is used when authentication is required by the Cisco Unified Communications Manager.

```
Router(config-register-pool)#username username password string
```

The optional **dtmf-relay** command in voice register global configuration mode defines the dual-tone multifrequency (DTMF) relay methods that are supported by a SIP endpoint. This list of methods is advertised by an endpoint when negotiating DTMF relay. By default, the DTMF tones are transported within a Real-time Transport Protocol (RTP) stream.

```
Router(config-register-pool)#dtmf-relay {[cisco-rtp] [rtp-nte] [sip-notify]}
```

The optional **codec** command defines the preferred codec used by a SIP endpoint. The default codec is G.729. The default codec of SIP endpoints differs from the default codec on SCCP endpoints (G.711 mu-law). An SCCP and a SIP endpoint that are registered to the same Cisco Unified Communications Manager Express communicate using the G.729 codec, if both endpoints use default codec values.

```
Router(config-register-pool)#codec g711alaw | g711ulaw | g722-64K | g729r8 | ilbc
```

Shared Directory Number Configuration Example

Figure 3-57 illustrates the configuration of a directory number shared by two SIP endpoints. The shared line supports a maximum of six concurrent calls, so even more endpoints could be assigned to this directory number. The nonexclusive nature of the shared line indicates that the endpoints can make or receive independent calls. After a call is placed on hold, it can be retrieved by any phone that participates in the sharing.

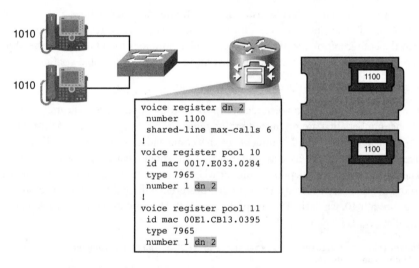

Figure 3-57 *Shared Directory Number Configuration Example*

Configuring Cisco IP Communicator Support

Cisco IP Communicator, as shown in Figure 3-58, is a Microsoft Windows–based softphone application that allows the use of a PC to make voice and video calls (where video calls require the addition of Cisco Unified Video Advantage software and a video camera attached to the PC running the Cisco Unified Video Advantage software). Offering the latest in IP communications technology, it is easy to acquire, deploy, and use. With a USB headset or USB speakerphone and Cisco IP Communicator, the users can access their corporate phone number and voice mail.

To deploy Cisco IP Communicator, you first need to download installation software from Cisco.com with appropriate login credentials and installed as prompted by the installation wizard.

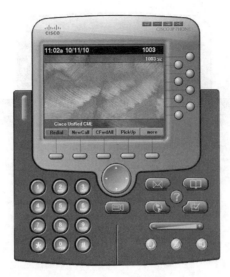

Figure 3-58 *Cisco IP Communicator*

Configuring Cisco IP Communicator

For interoperability with Cisco Unified Communications Manager Express, Cisco IP Communicator needs the setting of a TFTP server address. To set the TFTP address, navigate to **Menu > Preferences**, select the **Use These TFTP Servers** option on the Network tab, as shown on the left in Figure 3-59, and configure the primary and, optionally, secondary TFTP server address.

The preferred codec that is used by Cisco IP Communicator is G.711 mu-law. In an environment with scarce bandwidth, the preferred codec can be set to G.729 by checking the **Optimize for Low Bandwidth** check box on the Audio tab, as shown on the right in Figure 3-59.

Managing Cisco Unified Communications Manager Express Endpoints

When one or more phones that are associated with a Cisco Unified Communications Manager Express router are reconfigured, they must be rebooted to apply the new settings. One of two commands can be used to reboot the phones:

- **reset:** The **reset** command performs a hard reboot that is similar to a power-off, power-on sequence. It reboots the phone and updates the phone with information from a DHCP server and TFTP server. This command takes significantly longer to process than the **restart** command when you are updating multiple phones, but you must use the **reset** command after updating firmware, user locale, network locale, or URL parameters.

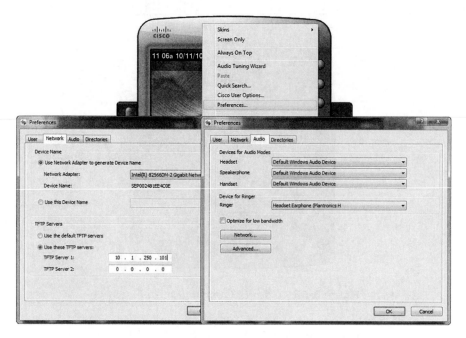

Figure 3-59   *Cisco IP Communicator Preferences*

■ **restart:** The **restart** command performs a soft reboot by simply rebooting the phone without contacting a DHCP or TFTP server. You can use the **restart** command for simple button, line, or speed-dial changes.

Rebooting Commands

The phones can be reset or restarted globally (telephony-service configuration mode or voice register global configuration mode, respectively) or individually (ephone configuration mode or voice register pool configuration mode, respectively).

```
Router(config-register-global)#reset {all [time-interval] | cancel | mac-address |
  sequence-all}
```

or

```
Router(config-register-global)#restart {all [time-interval] | mac-address}
```

An individual reboot affects only a single device. A global reboot can specify the MAC address of the phone to be rebooted and allows a sequential reboot of phones over time. The time interval (in seconds) defines the time between consecutive phone resets. The interval defaults to 15 seconds.

```
Router(config-register-pool)#reset
```

or

```
Router(config-ephone)#reset
```

```
Router(config-register-pool)#restart
```

or

```
Router(config-ephone)#restart
```

Verifying Cisco Unified Communications Manager Express Endpoints

The troubleshooting of endpoints commonly follows the same logical path that endpoints take to register. The general sequence is defined by these steps, although some steps might not be relevant in a given environment:

- **Verify the VLAN ID:** The endpoint uses CDP to obtain a voice VLAN from an attached switch. Use the **Settings** button on the Cisco IP Phone to check the VLAN configuration.

- **Verify Phone IP addressing:** DHCP typically provides the IP parameters. Use the **Settings** button on the phone to check the IP-related settings.

- **Verify Phone TFTP server:** A Cisco IP Phone receives the IP address of a TFTP server via DHCP. The TFTP server's IP address can be viewed from the phone's **IPv4 Configuration** screen.

- **Verify firmware files in flash memory:** Check and verify that the correct firmware files are in the flash memory of the CUCME router. This information is relevant for TFTP operations.

- **Debug the TFTP server:** Ensure that the Cisco Unified Communications Manager Express router is correctly providing the firmware and XML files via TFTP.

- **Verify the firmware installation on the phones:** Use the **Settings** button on the phone to check the firmware that the phone uses. The **debug ephone register** command in CUCME also displays which firmware is being installed.

- **Verify SCCP Endpoint Registration:** The **show ephone** command can be used to display successful registration of an SCCP endpoint.

- **Verify SIP Endpoint Registration:** The **show voice register all** command can be used to display successful registration of an SCCP endpoint.

- **Verify SCCP Registration Process:** The **debug ephone register** command can be used to display the SCCP registration process.

- **Verify SIP Registration Process:** The **debug voice register events** command can be used to display the SIP registration process.

- **Verifying Endpoint-Related Dial-Peers:** The **show dial-peer voice summary** command and the **show dial-peer voice** *tag* command can be used to display dial-peer information.

Verifying Phone VLAN ID

The VLAN ID received via CDP from the switch can be viewed on the Cisco IP Phone by pressing the **Settings** button and navigating to **Network Configuration > Operational VLAN Id**, as shown in Figure 3-60.

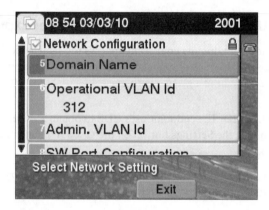

Figure 3-60 *Cisco IP Communicator Voice VLAN ID*

A variety of configuration parameters are accessible from within the Cisco IP Phone's configuration menus.

Verifying Phone IP Parameters

IP parameters that are received via DHCP from the DHCP server can be viewed on the Cisco IP Phone by pressing the **Settings** button, navigating to **Network Configuration > IPv4 Configuration**, and examining the IP Address, Subnet Mask, and Default Router settings, as shown in Figure 3-61.

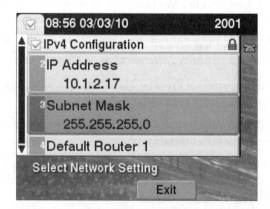

Figure 3-61 *Cisco IP Communicator IP Parameters*

Verifying Phone TFTP Server

An TFTP server's IP address that is received via DHCP option 150 from a DHCP server can be viewed on a Cisco IP Phone by pressing the **Settings** button, navigating to **Network Configuration > IPv4 Configuration**, and examining the TFTP Server 1 setting, as shown in Figure 3-62.

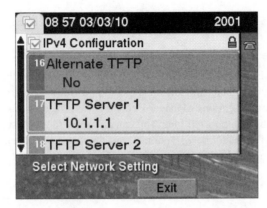

Figure 3-62   *Cisco IP Communicator TFTP Server*

Verifying Firmware Files

The **show flash** command displays the contents of flash memory. Flash memory must contain the firmware files that are necessary for the Cisco IP Phone models that are deployed. Many other files can be in flash as well, depending on other configurations.

Example 3-10 shows that an SCCP firmware image for Cisco 7945 and 7965 IP Phones resides in the SCCP folder in the flash memory. A SIP firmware image for Cisco 7945 and 7965 IP Phones resides in the main directory of the flash memory.

Example 3-10   *Verifying Firmware Files with the* **show flash** *Command*

```
Router#show flash
4 4594326 Feb 26 2010 13:14:50 sccp/apps45.9-0-2ES2.sbn
5 531472 Feb 26 2010 13:17:04 sccp/cnu45.9-0-2ES2.sbn
6 2160038 Feb 26 2010 13:52:46 sccp/cvm45sccp.9-0-2ES2.sbn
7 343039 Feb 26 2010 13:55:02 sccp/dsp45.9-0-2ES2.sbn
8 1883455 Feb 26 2010 14:01:12 sccp/jar45sccp.9-0-2ES2.sbn
9 642 Feb 26 2010 14:14:30 sccp/SCCP45.9-0-2SR1S.loads
10 642 Feb 26 2010 14:14:44 sccp/term45.default.loads
11 642 Feb 26 2010 14:15:00 sccp/term65.default.loads
12 69 Feb 26 2010 20:07:24 syncinfo.xml
13 4594326 Feb 25 2010 16:59:28 apps45.9-0-2ES2.sbn
14 531472 Feb 25 2010 16:59:56 cnu45.9-0-2ES2.sbn
15 2582685 Feb 25 2010 17:01:00 cvm45sip.9-0-2ES2.sbn
```

```
16 343039 Feb 25 2010 17:01:22 dsp45.9-0-2ES2.sbn
17 1885438 Feb 25 2010 17:01:54 jar45sip.9-0-2ES2.sbn
18 642 Feb 25 2010 17:02:12 SIP45.9-0-2SR1S.loads
19 642 Feb 25 2010 17:02:32 term45.default.loads
20 642 Feb 25 2010 17:02:54 term65.default.loads
21 1947 Feb 26 2010 20:07:24 SIPDefault.cnf
...
```

Verifying TFTP Operation

The **debug tftp events** command enables you to view output regarding files that are provided by a TFTP server. You can view files, including firmware files, which are specific to Cisco Unified Communications Manager Express to see whether the CUCME router is using out-of-date or unsupported files. You can also view the XML files for configured IP phones, the XML files for new IP phones, and the locale files. Example 3-11 provides sample output from the **debug tftp events** command.

Example 3-11   *Verifying TFTP Operation*

```
Router#debug tftp events
Feb 26 16:37:44.849: TFTP: Looking for SEP0024C4455233.cnf.xml
Feb 26 16:37:44.853: TFTP: Opened flash:/SEP0024C4455233.cnf.xml, fd 10,
Feb 26 16:37:45.397: TFTP: Finished flash:/SEP0024C4455233.cnf.xml
Feb 26 16:37:59.658: TFTP: Looking for SIP45.9-0-2SR1S.loads
Feb 26 16:37:59.658: TFTP: Opened flash:SIP45.9-0-2SR1S.loads, fd 10
Feb 26 16:37:59.826: TFTP: Finished flash:SIP45.9-0-2SR1S.loads
Feb 26 16:38:00.890: TFTP: Looking for jar45sip.9-0-2ES2.sbn
Feb 26 16:38:00.894: TFTP: Opened flash:jar45sip.9-0-2ES2.sbn, fd 10,
Feb 26 16:43:35.630: TFTP: Finished flash:jar45sip.9-0-2ES2.sbn, time 00:05:34
Feb 26 16:43:40.970: TFTP: Looking for cnu45.9-0-2ES2.sbn
Feb 26 16:43:40.974: TFTP: Opened flash:cnu45.9-0-2ES2.sbn, fd 10, size 531472
Feb 26 16:45:21.349: TFTP: Finished flash:cnu45.9-0-2ES2.sbn, time 00:01:40
Feb 26 16:45:23.277: TFTP: Looking for apps45.9-0-2ES2.sbn
Feb 26 16:45:23.277: TFTP: Opened flash:apps45.9-0-2ES2.sbn, fd 10,
Feb 26 16:59:04.014: TFTP: Finished flash:apps45.9-0-2ES2.sbn, time 00:13:40
Feb 26 16:59:15.999: TFTP: Looking for dsp45.9-0-2ES2.sbn
Feb 26 16:59:16.003: TFTP: Opened flash:dsp45.9-0-2ES2.sbn, fd 10, size 343039
```

Verifying Phone Firmware

An IP phone's currently loaded firmware image can be viewed on a Cisco IP Phone by pressing the **Settings** button, selecting **Model Information**, and examining the Load File information, as shown in Figure 3-63.

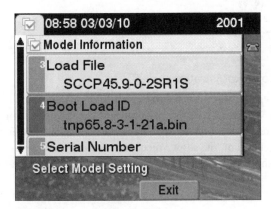

Figure 3-63   *Cisco IP Communicator Load File*

Verifying SCCP Endpoint Registration

The **show ephone** command is used to verify if the phones have registered with a Cisco Unified Communications Manager Express router. A status of "registered" indicates that the phone has successfully registered. A status of "deceased" indicates that there has been a problem with keepalives, and a status of "unregistered" indicates that a connection was closed normally. The command displays the IP addresses and directory numbers that are assigned to endpoints. Sample output from the **show ephone** command is provided in Example 3-12.

Example 3-12   *Verifying SCCP Endpoint Registration with the **show ephone** Command*

```
Router#show ephone
ephone-1[0] Mac:0024.C445.5233 TCP socket:[1] activeLine:0 whisperLine:0
    REGISTERED in SCCP ver 19/17 max_streams=5
mediaActive:0 whisper_mediaActive:0 startMedia:0 offhook:0 ringing:0 reset:0
    reset_sent:0 paging 0 debug:0 caps:9
IP:10.1.2.13 * 53150 7965 keepalive 211 max_line 6 available_line 6
button 1: cw:1 ccw:(0 0)
    dn 1 number 2001 CH1 IDLE CH2 IDLE
button 2: cw:1 ccw:(0 0)
    dn 3 number 2011 CH1 IDLE CH2 IDLE
Preferred Codec: g711ulaw
Lpcor Type: none
ephone-2[1] Mac:0024.C445.4B7F TCP socket:[2] activeLine:0 whisperLine:0
```

```
  REGISTERED in SCCP ver 19/17 max_streams=5
mediaActive:0 whisper_mediaActive:0 startMedia:0 offhook:0 ringing:0 reset:0
reset_sent:0 paging 0 debug:0 caps:9
IP:10.1.2.12 * 50439 7965 keepalive 211 max_line 6 available_line 6
button 1: cw:1 ccw:(0 0)
   dn 2 number 2002 CH1 IDLE CH2 IDLE
Preferred Codec: g711ulaw
```

Verifying SIP Endpoint Registration

The **show voice register all** command displays all SIP-related Cisco Unified Communications Manager Express configurations and register information. This information includes the registration status of all endpoints (voice register pools). To display the status of a single endpoint, the **show voice register pool** command can be used. Sample output from the **show voice register all** command is provided in Example 3-13.

Example 3-13 *Verifying SIP Endpoint Registration with the* show voice register all *Command*

```
Router#show voice register all
...
VOICE REGISTER POOL
===================
Pool Tag 1
Config:
  Mac address is 0024.C445.5233
  Type is 7965
  Number list 1 : DN 1
...
  active primary line is: 1010
  contact IP address: 10.1.2.18 port 5060
Dialpeers created:
dial-peer voice 40001 voip
 destination-pattern 1010
 session target ipv4:10.1.2.18:5060
 session protocol sipv2
Statistics:
  Active registrations : 3
  Total SIP phones registered: 1
  Total Registration Statistics
    Registration requests : 3
    Registration success : 3
```

Verifying the SCCP Registration Process

The **debug ephone register** command is used to debug the SCCP registration process on CUCME. After you have entered the **debug ephone register** command, you might reset the phone and look for the Skinny StationAlarmMessage text in the debug output, which should appear during the phone reregistration process. The **Load =** *parameter* should appear in the display a few lines after the Skinny StationAlarmMessage output, followed by an abbreviated version name that corresponds to the correct firmware filename. Sample output from the **debug ephone register** command is provided in Example 3-14.

Example 3-14   *Verifying SCCP Registration with the* **debug ephone register** *Command*

```
Router#debug ephone register
Mar 2 15:16:57.582: New Skinny socket accepted [1] (2 active)
Mar 2 15:16:57.582: sin_family 2, sin_port 49692, in_addr 10.90.0.11
Mar 2 15:16:57.582: skinny_add_socket 1 10.90.0.11 49692
Mar 2 15:16:57.766: %IPPHONE-6-REG_ALARM: 20: Name=SEP000F2470F8F8
   Load=3.2(2.14) Last=Phone-Keypad
Mar 2 15:16:57.766: Skinny StationAlarmMessage on socket [1] 10.90.0.11
   SEP000F2470F8F8
Mar 2 15:16:57.766: 20: Name=SEP000F2470F8F8 Load=3.2(2.14) Last=Phone-Keypad
Mar 2 15:16:57.766: ephone-(1)[1] StationRegisterMessage (1/2/2) from
   10.90.0.11
Mar 2 15:16:57.766: ephone-(1)[1] Register StationIdentifier DeviceName
SEP000F2470F8F8
Mar 2 15:16:57.766: ephone-(1)[1] StationIdentifier Instance 1 deviceType 7
Mar 2 15:16:57.766: ephone-1[-1]:stationIpAddr 10.90.0.11
Mar 2 15:16:57.766: ephone-1[1]:phone SEP000F2470F8F8 re-associate OK on
   socket [1]
Mar 2 15:16:57.766: %IPPHONE-6-REGISTER: ephone-1:SEP000F2470F8F8
   IP:10.90.0.11 has registered.
Mar 2 15:16:57.766: Phone 0 socket 1
Mar 2 15:16:57.766: Skinny Local IP address = 10.95.0.1 on port 2000
Mar 2 15:16:57.766: Skinny Phone IP address = 10.90.0.11 49692
Mar 2 15:16:57.766: ephone-1[1]:Date Format M/D/Y
...
```

Verifying the SIP Registration Process

The **debug voice register events** command is used to debug the SIP registration process on Cisco Unified Communications Manager Express. Example 3-15 presents only a part of the output generated by the command. It includes information about the endpoint IP address (10.1.2.11), the pool tag (1), the dn tag (1), and the telephone number (1010).

Example 3-15   *Verifying SIP Registration with the* **debug voice register events** *Command*

```
Router#debug voice register events
Feb 26 20:18:12.143: VOICE_REG_POOL: Register request for (1010) from
   (10.1.2.11)
*Feb 26 20:18:12.143: VOICE_REG_POOL: Contact matches pool 1 number list 1
*Feb 26 20:18:12.143: VOICE_REG_POOL: key(1010) contact(10.1.2.11) add to
   contact table
*Feb 26 20:18:12.143: VOICE_REG_POOL: key(1010) exists in contact table
*Feb 26 20:18:12.143: VOICE_REG_POOL: contact(10.1.2.11) added to contact table
*Feb 26 20:18:12.147: VOICE_REG_POOL pool->tag(1), dn->tag(1), submask(1)
*Feb 26 20:18:12.147: VOICE_REG_POOL: Creating param container for dial-peer
   40002.VOICE_REG_POOL pool->tag(1), dn->tag(1), submask(1)
VOICE_REG_POOL pool_tag(1), dn_tag(1)
*Feb 26 20:18:12.151: VOICE_REG_POOL: Created dial-peer entry of type 0
*Feb 26 20:18:12.151: VOICE_REG_POOL: Registration successful for 1010,
   registration id is 5
*Feb 26 20:18:12.151: VOICE_REG_POOL: Pool[1]: service-control (reset type: 2)
   message sent to sip:1010@10.1.2.18
*Feb 26 20:18:12.151: VOICE_REG_POOL: Contact matches pool 1 number list 1
```

Verifying Endpoint-Related Dial Peers

The **show dial-peer voice summary** command displays a summary of dial peers in the system. The list includes SCCP endpoint and SIP endpoint dial peers. The SCCP-related dial peers have tags in the range starting with 20001 and are shown as plain old telephone service (POTS) dial peers. The SIP-related dial peers have tags in the range starting with 40001 and are marked as VoIP dial peers. Specific information about a given dial peer can be displayed using the **show dial-peer voice** command with the relevant dial-peer tag.

Sample output from the **show dial-peer voice summary** command is shown in Example 3-16.

Example 3-16   *Viewing Summary Information for Dial Peers*

```
Router#show dial-peer voice summary
dial-peer hunt 0
            AD                              PRE PASS           OUT
TAG TYPE   MIN  OPER PREFIX DEST-PATTERN FER THRU SESS-TARGET STAT PORT KEEP.
20001 pots up   up          1001$        0                         50/0/1
20002 pots up   up          1002$        0                         50/0/2
40001 voip up   up          1010         0 syst ipv4:10.1.2.18:5060
```

Example 3-17 offers sample output from the **show dial-peer voice** command.

Example 3-17 *Verifying Detailed Information for Dial Peers*

```
Router#show dial-peer voice 20001
peer type = voice, system default peer = FALSE, information type = voice,
        description = `',
        tag = 20001, destination-pattern = `1001$',
        voice reg type = 0, corresponding tag = 0,
        allow watch = FALSE
        answer-address = `', preference=0,
        CLID Restriction = None
        CLID Network Number = `'
        CLID Second Number sent
        CLID Override RDNIS = disabled,
        rtp-ssrc mux = system
        source carrier-id = `', target carrier-id = `',
...
```

Summary

The main topics covered in this chapter are the following:

■ You were introduced to the components comprising Cisco Unified Communications Manager Express (CUCME), along with an overview of CUCME operation.

■ Endpoint (for example, Cisco IP Phone) requirements were examined. These requirements included such topics as: power, VLAN assignment, and IP address assignment.

■ CUCME configuration syntax was presented, along with a collection of examples. The primary configuration for CUCME is performed under telephony-service configuration mode. However, individual endpoints configuration focuses on **ephone-dn** and **ephone** syntax.

Chapter Review Questions

The answers to these review questions are in the appendix.

1. What is the key difference between Cisco Unified Communications Manager Express (CUCME) and other Cisco Unified Communications Manager platforms?

    a. CUCME provides additional features.

    b. CUCME is collocated with a voice gateway.

    c. CUCME offers a management CLI.

    d. CUCME includes a voice-mail system.

2. Identify four Cisco Unified Communications call processing options. (Choose four.)

   a. Cisco Smart Business Communications System

   b. Cisco Unified Communications Manager Express

   c. Cisco Unified Communications Manager Business Edition

   d. Cisco Unified Secure Enterprise CallManager

   e. Cisco Unified Communications Manager

   f. Cisco Smart Communications ASA

3. How does Cisco Unified Communications Manager Express provide reachability of its registered endpoints to external callers?

   a. It intercepts signaling exchanges and forwards the appropriate call setup requests to its endpoints.

   b. It registers the numbers on a voice gateway that is in the voice path.

   c. It distributes the endpoint numbers among neighboring gateways.

   d. It automatically creates virtual dial peers that appear in a gateway's dial plan.

4. What are two differences between Cisco prestandard PoE and IEEE 802.3af? (Choose two.)

   a. Cisco prestandard PoE uses Fast Link Pulses.

   b. IEEE 802.3af delivers power only to devices that require it.

   c. Cisco devices require Cisco prestandard PoE.

   d. Pins that are used in Cisco prestandard PoE (1, 2, 3, 6) are incompatible with IEEE 802.3af.

   e. Cisco prestandard PoE does not classify power levels.

5. When does a phone request a firmware image?

   a. If it does not receive its specific configuration file SEP<MAC>.cnf.xml

   b. If it receives the generic configuration file XMLDefault.cnf.xml with a setting that is different from the current image

   c. If it receives its specific configuration file with the required image information embedded in it

   d. If the generic configuration file is missing and the specific file is received

6. What are two types of ephone-dns available in a Cisco Unified Communications Manager Express system? (Choose two.)

   a. Single-line ephone-dn

   b. Secondary and tertiary extension on one ephone-dn

   c. Shared ephone

   d. Overlay ephone-dn

7. DHCP option _____ is used in telephony environments with a Cisco Unified Communications Manager platform to direct the booting phones to the IP address of a TFTP server.

   a. 50

   b. 66

   c. 150

   d. 160

8. Which command creates an ephone-dn that builds one virtual voice port?

   a. Router(config-telephony)#**ephone-dn** *dn-tag*

   b. Router(config-telephony)#**number** *dn-number*

   c. Router(config)#**ephone-dn** *dn-tag*

   d. Router(config)#**ephone-dn** *dn-number*

9. Which two phone types should be created using the SCCP phone template? (Choose two.)

   a. Cisco Unified IP Conference Station 7937G

   b. Cisco Unified Wireless IP Phone 7925

   c. Cisco Unified IP Phone 7961

   d. Cisco Unified IP Phone 7965

   e. Cisco Unified IP Phone 7975

10. Which of the following performs a hard reboot, similar to a power-off, power-on sequence?

   a. restart

   b. reset

   c. reload

   d. **restart, reset,** or **reload**

   e. Either **restart** or **reset**

Chapter 4

Introducing Dial Plans

After reading this chapter, you should be able to perform the following tasks:

- Describe the characteristics and requirements of a numbering plan.

- Explain the components of a dial plan and their functions.

Dial plans are essential for any Cisco Unified Communications deployment. Whether you are implementing single-site or multisite deployments, having a thorough understanding of dial plans and the knowledge of how to implement them on Cisco IOS gateways is essential for any engineer who designs and implements a Cisco Unified Communications network. This chapter describes the characteristics of a dial plan and associated components (for example, a numbering plan).

Numbering Plan Fundamentals

To integrate VoIP networks into existing voice networks, you should have the skills and knowledge to implement call routing and design an appropriate numbering plan. A scalable numbering plan establishes the baseline for a comprehensive, scalable, and logical dial plan.

This section describes call-routing principles, discusses attributes of numbering plans for voice networks, addresses the challenges of designing these plans, and identifies methods of implementing numbering plans.

Introducing Numbering Plans

A *numbering plan* is a numbering scheme used in telecommunications to allocate telephone number ranges to countries, regions, areas, and exchanges, and to nonfixed telephone networks such as mobile phone networks. A numbering plan defines rules for assigning numbers to a device.

Types of numbering plans include the following:

- **Private numbering plans:** Private numbering plans are used to address endpoints and applications within private networks. Private numbering plans are not required to adhere to any specific format and can be created to accommodate the needs of a network. Because most private telephone networks connect to the PSTN at some point in a design, it is good practice to plan a private numbering plan to coincide with publicly assigned number ranges. Number translation might be required when connecting private voice networks to the PSTN.

- **Public or PSTN numbering plans:** PSTN or public numbering plans are unique to the country in which they are implemented. The most common PSTN numbering plans are explained in this section.

Different regions of the globe have different numbering plans. However, all of these national numbering plans must adhere to the international E.164 standard. As an example, the E.164 standard stipulates than no phone number can be longer than 15 digits.

North American Numbering Plan

The North American Numbering Plan (NANP) is an integrated telephone numbering plan that serves 19 North American countries that share its resources. Developed in 1947 and first implemented in 1951 by AT&T, the NANP simplifies and facilitates the direct dialing of long-distance calls. The countries that use the NANP include the United States and its territories, Canada, Bermuda, Anguilla, Antigua and Barbuda, the Bahamas, Barbados, the British Virgin Islands, the Cayman Islands, Dominica, the Dominican Republic, Grenada, Jamaica, Montserrat, St. Kitts and Nevis, St. Lucia, St. Vincent and the Grenadines, Trinidad and Tobago, and Turks and Caicos Islands.

NANP numbers are ten-digit numbers, usually formatted as NXX-NXX-XXXX, in which N is any digit from 2 through 9 and X is any digit from 0 through 9. This structure is depicted in Figure 4-1.

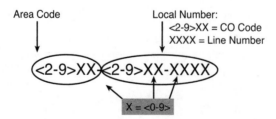

Figure 4-1   *North American Numbering Plan*

The first three digits of an NANP number (NXX) are called the Numbering Plan Area (NPA) code, often called the area code. The second three digits (NXX) are called the central office (CO) code, switched code, or prefix. The final four digits (XXXX) are called the line number or station number. The North American Numbering Plan Administration (NANPA) administers the NANP.

NANP Numbering Assignments

An area served by the NANP is divided into smaller areas, each identified by a three-digit NPA code, or area code. There are 800 possible combinations of area codes with the NXX format. However, some of these combinations are not available or have been reserved for special purposes, as shown in Table 4-1.

Table 4-1 *NANP Numbering Codes*

Reserved Code	Purpose
Easily Recognizable Codes (ERC)	When the second and third digits of an area code are the same, that code is called an ERC. These codes designate special use, such as toll-free service (for example, 800, 866, 877, or 888).
Automatic Number Identification (ANI) II digits	ANI II digits are two-digit pairs sent with an originating telephone number as part of the signaling that takes place during the setup phase of a call. These digits identify the type of originating station.
Carrier Identification Codes (CIC)	CICs are used to route and bill calls in the PSTN. CICs are four-digit codes in the format XXXX, where X is any digit from 0 through 9. There are separate CIC pools for different feature groups, such as line-side and trunk-side access.
International dialing	You dial 011 before the country code and the specific destination number to signal that you are placing an international call.
Long distance	The first 1 dialed defines a toll call within the NANP.
In-state long-distance or local call	A ten-digit number might be either a toll call within a common region or, in many larger markets, a local call if the area code is the same as the source.
Seven-digit number (<2–9>XX-XXXX)	A seven-digit number defines a local call. Some larger areas use ten-digit numbers instead of seven-digit numbers to define local calls. Notice that the first digit is in the range 2 through 9, while the remaining digits (as represented by X) can be any number in the range of 0 through 9.

Eight N11 codes, called *service codes*, are not used as area codes. These are three-digit codes in the N11 format, as shown in Table 4-2.

Table 4-2   *N11 Code Assignments*

N11 Code	Purpose
211	Community information and referral services (United States)
311	Nonemergency police and other governmental services (United States)
411	Local directory assistance
511	Traffic and transportation information (United States); reserved (Canada)
611	Repair service
711	Telecommunications relay services (TRS)
811	Business office
911	Emergency

In some U.S. states, N11 codes that are not assigned nationally can be assigned locally, if the local assignments can be withdrawn promptly if a national assignment is made. There are no industry guidelines for the assignment of N11 codes.

Additional NANP reserved area codes include the following:

- **456-<2–9>XX-XXXX numbers:** These codes identify carrier-specific services by providing carrier identification within the dialed digits. The prefix following 456, <2–9>XX, identifies the carrier. Use of these numbers enables the proper routing of inbound international calls, destined for these services into, and between, NANP area countries.

- **555-01XX line numbers:** These numbers are fictitious telephone numbers that can be used, for example, in the film industry, for educational purposes, and for various types of demonstrations. If anyone dials one of these numbers, it does not cause a nuisance to any actual person.

- **800-XXXX through 855-XXXX line numbers:** These numbers are in the format 800-855- XXXX and provide access to PSTN services for deaf, hard-of-hearing, or speech-impaired persons. Such services include Telecommunications Relay Service (TRS) and message relay service.

- **900-<2–9>XX-XXXX numbers:** These codes are for premium services, with the cost of each 900 call billed to the calling party. 900-<2–9>XX codes, each subsuming a block of 10,000 numbers, are assigned to service providers who provide and typically bill for premium services. These service providers, in turn, assign individual numbers to their customers.

European Telephony Numbering Space

The European Telephony Numbering Space (ETNS) is a European numbering space that is parallel to the existing national numbering spaces and is used to provision pan-European services. A pan-European service is an international service that can be invoked from at least two European countries.

The European Telecommunications Office (ETO) Administrative Council supervises the telecommunications work of the European Radiocommunications Office (ERO). This supervision includes the establishment, detailing, and change of ETNS conventions and the designation of European Service Identification (ESI) for new ETNS services.

The main objective of ETNS is to allow effective numbering for European international services for which national numbers might not be adequate and global numbers might not be available. The designation of a new European country code, 388, allows European international companies, services, and individuals to obtain a single European number for accessing their services.

Four ETNS services are now available: Public Service Application, Customer Service Application, Corporate Networks, and Personal Numbering. An ESI code is designated for each ETNS service. The one-digit code follows the European Country Code 388 and European Service Code 3 (3883), as shown in Table 4-3.

Figure 4-2 shows the structure of a standard international number. The initial part that is known as the ESI consists of the country code and group identification code that identifies the ETNS (3883), followed by a European Service Code that identifies a particular ETNS service. The European Subscriber Number is the number that is assigned to a customer in the context of the specific service. The maximum length of a European Subscriber Number is 15 digits; for example, 3883 X XXXXXXXXX.

Table 4-3 *ETNS Service and ESI Codes*

ETNS Service	ESI
Public Service Application	3883 1
Customer Service Application	3883 3
Corporate Networks	3883 5
Personal Numbering	3883 7

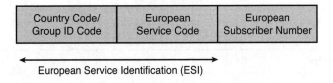

Figure 4-2 *European Numbering Structure*

Fixed and Variable-Length Numbering Plan Comparison

A fixed numbering plan, such as found in North America, features fixed-length area codes and local numbers. An open numbering plan, as found in countries that have not yet standardized on numbering plans, features variance in the length of the area code or the local number, or both.

A numbering plan can specify parameters such as the following:

- **Country code:** A country code is used to reach the particular telephone system for each country or special service.

- **Area code:** An area code is typically used to route calls to a particular city, region, or special service. Depending on the region, it might also be referred to as a Numbering Plan Area, subscriber trunk dialing code, national destination code, or routing code.

- **Subscriber number:** A subscriber number represents the specific telephone number to be dialed, but does not include the country code, area code (if applicable), international prefix, or trunk prefix.

- **Trunk prefix:** A trunk prefix refers to the initial digits to be dialed in a domestic call, prior to the area code and the subscriber number.

- **International prefix:** An international prefix is the code dialed prior to an international number (the country code, the area code if any, and then the subscriber number).

Table 4-4 contrasts the NANP and a variable-length numbering plan (Germany's numbering plan in this example).

Table 4-4 *Fixed and Variable-Length Numbering Plan Comparison*

Components	Fixed Numbering Plan	Variable-Length Numbering Plan
Example	NANP	Germany
Country code	1	49
Area code	Three digits	Two to four digits
Subscriber number	Three-digit exchange code + four-digit station code	Five to eight digits
Access code	9 (commonly used but not required)	0
International prefix	011	00 or +

E.164 Addressing

E.164, as illustrated in Figure 4-3, is an international numbering plan for public telephone systems in which each assigned number contains a one-, two-, or three-digit country code (CC) that is followed by a national destination code (NDC) and then by a subscriber number (SN). An E.164 number can have as many as 15 digits. The ITU originally developed the E.164 plan.

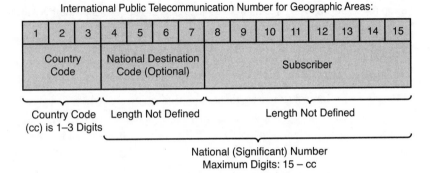

Figure 4-3 *E.164 Address Structure*

In the E.164 plan, each address is unique worldwide. With as many as 15 digits possible in a number, there are 100 trillion possible E.164 phone numbers. This makes it possible, in theory, to direct-dial from any conventional phone set to any other conventional phone set in the world by dialing no more than 15 single digits.

Most telephone numbers belong to the E.164 numbering plan, although this does not include internal private automatic branch exchange (PABX) extensions.

The E.164 numbering plan for telephone numbers includes the following plans:

- Country calling codes

- Regional numbering plans, such as the following:

  - ETNS

  - NANP

- Various national numbering plans, such as the U.K. National Numbering Scheme

Scalable Numbering Plans

Scalable telephony networks require well-designed, hierarchical telephone numbering plans. A hierarchical design has these five advantages:

- **Simplified provisioning:** Ability to easily add new numbers and modify existing numbers

- **Simplified routing:** Keeps local calls local and uses a specialized number key, such as an area code, for long-distance calls

- **Summarization:** Allows the grouping of numbers in number ranges

- **Scalability:** Leaves space for future growth

- **Management:** Control from a single management point

When designing a numbering plan, consider these four attributes to allow smooth implementation:

- Minimal impact on existing systems

- Minimal impact on users of the system

- Minimal translation configuration

- Consideration of anticipated growth

Although a non-overlapping numbering plan is usually preferable to an overlapping numbering plan, both plans can be configured to be scalable.

Non-Overlapping Numbering Plan

A dial plan can be designed so that all extensions within the system are reached in a uniform way. That is, a fixed quantity of digits is used to reach a given extension from any on-net origination point. Uniform dialing is desirable because of its simplicity. A user does not have to remember different ways to dial a number when calling from various on-net locations.

Figure 4-4 shows an example of a four-digit uniform dial plan, described here:

- The 0xxx and 9xxx number ranges are excluded due to off-net access code use and operator dialing. In such a system, where 9 and 0 are reserved codes, no other extensions can start with 0 or 9.

- Site A has been assigned the range 1xxx, allowing for as many as 1000 extensions.

- Site B has been assigned the range 2xxx, allowing for as many as 1000 extensions.

- Sites C and D were each assigned 500 numbers from the 4xxx range.

- The ranges 6xxx, 7xxx, and 8xxx are reserved for future use.

After a given quantity of digits has been selected, and the requisite ranges have been excluded (for example, ranges beginning with 9 or 0), the remaining dialing space has to be divided between all sites. Most systems require that two ranges be excluded, thus leaving eight different possibilities for the leading digit of the dial range. The table in Figure 4-4 is an example of the distribution of dialing space for a typical four-digit uniform dial plan.

Location	Range	Description
	0xxx, 9xxx	Reserved
Site A	1xxx	Site A Extensions
Site B	2xxx	Site B Extensions
Site C	4[0–4]xx	Site C Extensions
Site D	4[5–9]xx	Site D Extensions
	[6–8]xxx	Available for Future Needs

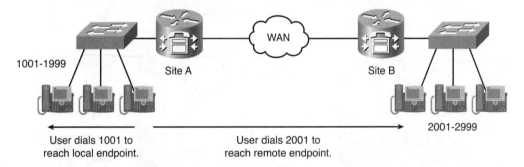

Figure 4-4 *Non-Overlapping Numbering Plan*

Scalable Non-Overlapping Numbering Plan Considerations

In a non-overlapping numbering plan, all extensions can be addressed using the same number of digits, making the call routing simple and making the network easily manageable. The same number length is used to route the call to an internal user and a remote user.

The disadvantage of the non-overlapping numbering plan is that it is often impractical in real life. It requires a centralized numbering approach and a careful design from the very beginning.

Overlapping Numbering Plans

In Figure 4-5, Site A endpoints use directory numbers 1001 through 1099, 3000 through 3157, and 3365 through 3985. At Site B, 1001 through 1099 and 3158 through 3364 are implemented. Site C uses ranges 1001 through 1099 and 3986 through 3999. There are two issues with these directory numbers: 1001 through 1099 overlap. These directory numbers exist at all three sites, so they are not unique throughout the complete deployment. In addition, the poor structure of splitting the range 3000 through 3999 requires many entries in call-routing tables, because the ranges cannot be summarized by one or a few entries.

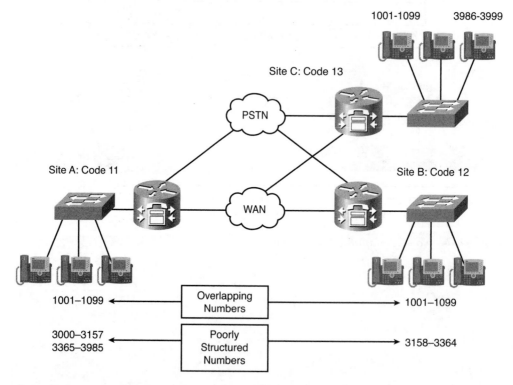

Figure 4-5 *Overlapping and Poorly Structured Numbering Plan*

A sampling of ways to solve overlapping and poorly structured directory number problems includes the following:

- Redesign the directory number ranges to ensure non-overlapping, well-structured directory numbers.

- Use an intersite access code and a site code that will be prepended to a directory number to create unique dialable numbers. For example, you could use an intersite code of 8, assigning Site A the site code 81, Site B the site code 82, and Site C the site code 83.

- Do not assign direct inward dialing (DID) numbers. Instead, publish a single number, and use a receptionist or auto-attendant.

Overlapping Numbering Plan Example

Figure 4-6 illustrates the most common solution to the overlap problem in numbering plans.

Location	Range	Site Code	Intersite Prefix
Site A	1xxx	11	8
Site B	1xxx	12	8
Site C	1xxx	13	8
Site D	2xxx	14	8

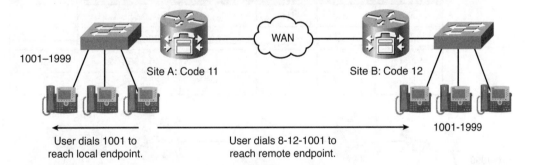

Figure 4-6 *Overlapping Numbering Plan Example*

The principle of site-code dialing introduces an intersite prefix (8, in this example) and a site code (1x, in this example) that must be prepended when dialing an internal extension in another site. With this solution, a Site A user dials a four-digit number starting with 1 to reach a local extension, and enters a seven-digit number starting with 8 to reach an endpoint in a remote site. The intersite prefix and the site code that are used in this scenario show sample values and can be set differently according to enterprise requirements. For example, the intersite prefix is commonly set to 8 and the access code to 9 in an NANP region, while the intersite prefix is typically 9 and the access code 0 in Europe.

Scalable Overlapping Numbering Plan Considerations

The site-code dialing solution of the overlap issue in numbering plans is useful in real life, as it allows a decentralized approach to the numbering effort. Even various departments within an organization can manage their own addressing space, and the site codes can interconnect them into a manageable unified communications network. Site code dialing does not require a careful design from the beginning and can be implemented as the enterprise grows.

Internal extensions should not start with the intersite prefix (for example, 8), because such entries could cause ambiguity in the dial plan. The intersite prefix notifies the call-routing device that the call is destined for a remote location and therefore should not overlap with any internal number.

Private and Public Numbering Plan Integration

Figure 4-7 illustrates an enterprise with four locations in the NANP region.

Location	Range	Site Code	Intersite Prefix	PSTN DID Range	Access Code
Site A	1xxx	11	8	200-555-1xxx	9
Site B	1xxx	12	8	300-555-3xxx	9
Site C	1xxx	13	8	400-555-1234	9
Site D	2xxx	14	8	500-555-22xx	9

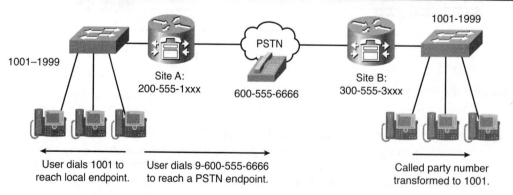

Figure 4-7   *Private and Public Numbering Plan*

Site-code dialing has been designed to allow calls between the enterprise locations. Each site has a trunk connection to the PSTN, with the PSTN DID range provided by the telephone company (telco) operator. Sites A and B have DID ranges that allow public addressing of each internal extension. Site C has a single DID number with an interactive voice response (IVR) solution that prompts the callers for the number of the internal extension for forwarding inbound calls to the intended callee. The DID range of Site D covers some internal extensions and must be combined with an IVR to provide inbound connectivity to others.

Access code 9 identifies a call that is destined to an external PSTN recipient. In this example, internal users dial 9-600-555-6666 to reach the PSTN endpoint.

The following are a few challenges that you might face with numbering plan integration:

■ **Varying number lengths:** Within the IP network, consideration is given to varying number lengths that exist outside the IP network. Local, long-distance, and international dialing from within the IP network might require digit manipulation.

■ **Necessity of prefixes or area codes:** It can be necessary to strip or add area codes, or prepend or replace prefixes. Rerouting calls from the IP network to the PSTN for failure recovery can require extra digits.

Private and Public Numbering Plan Integration Functions

The three basic features, as illustrated in Figure 4-8, that are provided by the integrated private and public numbering plans include the following.

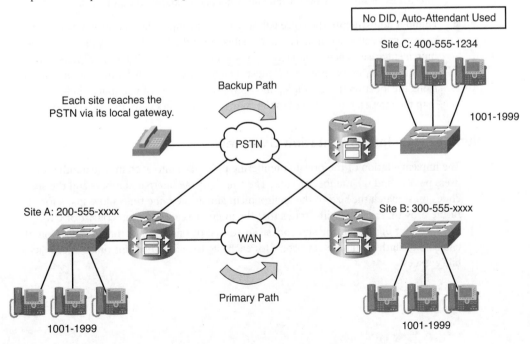

Figure 4-8 *Private and Public Numbering Plan Integration Functions*

- **Reachability to external PSTN destinations:** Internal users get access to external destinations over a gateway, which acts like a junction between the private and public addressing scheme.

- **Auto-attendant:** An IVR system is required to provide connectivity to internal extensions when a sufficient DID range is not available.

- **PSTN acts a backup path in case the IP WAN fails or becomes congested:** In such cases, the gateways redirect the intersite calls over the PSTN to provide uninterrupted service.

Private and Public Numbering Plan Integration Considerations

When integrating private and public numbering plans, give special consideration to these aspects:

- **No ambiguity with the internal and intersite dialing:** The prepended access code should uniquely identify all calls that should break out to the PSTN.

- **Path selection transparent to the user:** Users dial site codes to reach remote locations, and the intersite calls select the IP network as the primary path. If the IP WAN is unavailable, the call should be redirected over the PSTN. The user does not need to take any action for the secondary path to be chosen.

- **Auto-attendant for non-DID numbers:** When the DID range does not cover all internal extensions, an auto-attendant is needed to allow inbound calls.

- **Number adjustment:** The voice gateway needs to adjust the calling and called numbers when a call is set up between the sites or via the PSTN. One manipulation requirement arises when an intersite call is rerouted over the PSTN. The intersite prefix and site code (for example, 8-12) must then be replaced with a public number identifying the location (for example, 300-555). Another type of manipulation is needed to map the internal ranges to DID scopes, for example, 1xxx through 0-555-3xxx.

Number Plan Implementation Overview

The implementation of the private numbering plan takes into account the number of users per site and the number of sites. The length of the internal numbers and the site codes must match the size of the environment and at the same time allow space for future growth. Figure 4-9 illustrates that the internal extensions can consist of two, three, or four digits, and the site codes can consist of one, two, or three digits. Note that extension length should be consistent for each site to avoid interdigit timeout or reachability issues.

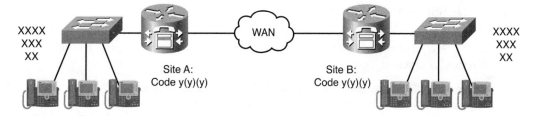

Figure 4-9   *Private Number Plan Implementation*

Call routing to local endpoints is achieved automatically, because the registering end-points have virtual dial peers that are associated with them. The dial peers ensure that calls are routed to the registered phones based on their directory numbers.

Call routing to remote locations is enabled by VoIP dial peers that describe the primary path over an IP WAN.

Private Number Plan Implementation Example

Figure 4-10 shows the enterprise has one large site (Site A) with 7000 users and several smaller sites with less than 700 users each. The codes for all sites are two-digit numbers (21 through 40). The internal extensions in the large site are four digits long (1001–7999), while the extensions in the smaller sites are three digits long (101–799). To implement the dial plan, VoIP dial peers are configured with destination patterns that match seven-digit numbers in the large site and six-digit numbers in the remaining sites, starting with the intersite prefix 8.

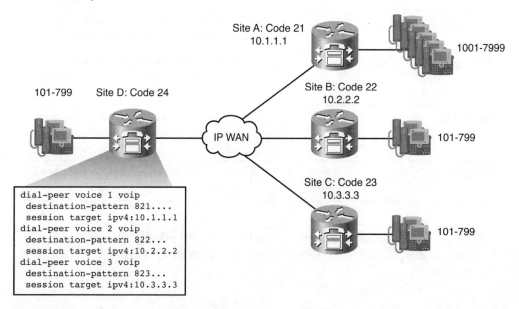

Figure 4-10   *Private Number Plan Implementation Example*

Public Number Plan Implementation

The enterprise does not design its public numbering plan. It is imposed by the telco operator. The enterprise might influence the size of the DID range, which is often related to a financial decision.

Gateways provide a mapping between the DID and the internal number ranges. For example, the PSTN DID range 200-555-3xxx can be easily converted to 1xxx and back when calls traverse the gateway. Complex mapping formulas (for example, mapping of 200-555-3xxx to 1xxx + 50) are too complex to implement and should be avoided.

Call Routing Overview

The most relevant properties of call routing can be compared to the characteristics of IP packet routing, as shown in Table 4-5.

Table 4-5   *Call Routing Refresher*

IP Routing	Call Routing
Static or dynamic	Only static.
IP routing table	Dial plan.
IP route	Dial peer.
Hop-by-hop routing, where each router makes an independent decision	Inbound and outbound call legs. The gateway negotiates VoIP parameters with preceding and next gateways before a call is forwarded.
Destination-based routing	Called number, matched by **destination-pattern**, is one of many selection criteria.
Most explicit match rule	The most explicit match rule for **destination-pattern** exists, but other criteria are also considered.
Equal paths	Preference can be applied to equal dial peers. If all criteria are the same, a random selection is made.
Default route	Possible. Often points at external gateway or gatekeeper.

The entries that define where to forward calls are the dial peers. All dial peers together build the dial plan, which is equivalent to the IP routing table. The dial peers are static in nature.

Hop-by-hop call routing builds on the principle of call legs. Before a call-routing decision is made, the gateway must identify the inbound dial peer and process its parameters. This process might involve VoIP parameter negotiation.

A call-routing decision is the selection of the outbound dial peer. This selection is commonly based on the called number, when the **destination-pattern** command is used. The selection might be based on other information, and that other criteria might have higher precedence than the called number. When the called number is matched to find the outbound dial peer, the longest match rule applies.

If more than one dial peer equally matches the dial string, all of the matching dial peers are used to form a so-called rotary group. The router attempts to place the outbound call leg using all of the dial peers in the rotary group until one is successful. The selection order within the group can be influenced by configuring a preference value.

A default call route can be configured using special characters when matching the number.

Call Routing Example

The voice gateways in this example are faced with the task of selecting the best path for a given destination number. Such a requirement arises when the preferred path goes through an IP WAN. A backup PSTN path should be chosen when an IP WAN is either unavailable or lacks the needed bandwidth resources.

Figure 4-11 illustrates a scenario with two locations that are connected to an IP WAN and PSTN. When the call goes through the PSTN, its numbers (both calling and called) have to be manipulated so that they are reachable within the PSTN. Otherwise, the PSTN switches will not recognize the called number, and the call will fail.

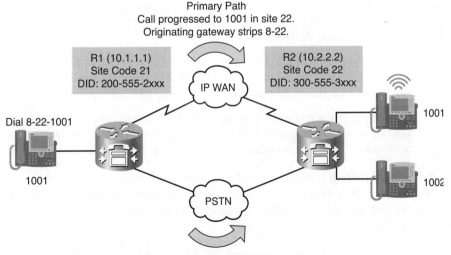

Figure 4-11 *Call Routing Example*

Dial Plan Components

A dial plan is the central part of any telephony solution and defines how calls are routed and interconnected. A dial plan consists of various components, which can be used in various combinations. This section describes the components of a dial plan and how they are used on Cisco IOS gateways.

Defining Dial Plans

Although most people are not acquainted with dial plans by name, they use them daily. A dial plan describes the process of determining how many and which digits are necessary for call routing. If dialed digits match a defined pattern of numbers, the call can processed and forwarded.

Designing dial plans requires knowledge of the network topology, dialing patterns, and traffic routing requirements. There are no dynamic routing protocols for E.164 telephony addresses. VoIP dial plans are statically configured on gateway and gatekeeper platforms.

A dial plan consists of these components:

- **Endpoint addressing (numbering plan):** Assigning directory numbers to all endpoints and applications (such as voice-mail systems, auto attendants, and conferencing systems) enables you to access internal and external destinations.

- **Call routing and path selection:** Multiple paths can lead to the same destination. A secondary path can be selected when a primary path is not available. For example, a call can be transparently rerouted over the PSTN during an IP WAN failure.

- **Digit manipulation:** Manipulation of numbers before routing a call might be required (for example, when a call is rerouted over the PSTN). This can occur before or after the routing decision.

- **Calling privileges:** Different privileges can be assigned to various devices, granting or denying access to certain destinations. For example, lobby phones might reach only internal destinations, while executive phones could have unrestricted PSTN access.

- **Call coverage:** You can create special groups of devices to manage incoming calls for a certain service according to different rules (top-down, circular hunt, longest idle, or broadcast). This also ensures that calls are not dropped without being answered.

While these dial plan components can be implemented using a Cisco Unified Communications Manager server, the focus in this book is on implementing these dial plan components on a Cisco IOS router acting as a call agent.

Dial Plan Implementation

Cisco IOS gateways, including Cisco Unified Communications Manager Express and Cisco Unified Survivable Remote Site Telephony (SRST), support all dial plan components. Table 4-6 provides an overview of the methods that Cisco IOS gateways use to implement dial plans.

Table 4-6   *Dial Plan Implementation*

Dial Plan Component	Cisco IOS Gateway
Endpoint addressing	POTS dial peers for FXS ports, ephone-dn, and voice register directory number
Call routing and path selection	Dial peers
Digit manipulation	**voice translation profile, prefix, digit-strip, forward-digits**, and **num-exp**
Calling privileges	Class of Restriction (COR) names and lists
Call coverage	Call hunt, hunt groups, call pickup, call waiting, call forwarding, overlaid directory numbers

Dial Plan Requirements

Figure 4-12 shows a typical dial plan scenario. Calls can be routed via either an IP WAN link or a PSTN link, and routing should work for inbound and outbound PSTN calls, intrasite calls, and intersite calls.

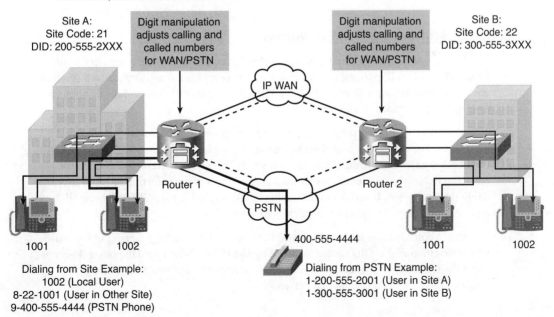

Figure 4-12   *Dial Plan Requirements*

The dial plan defines the rules that govern how a user reaches any destination. Definitions include the following:

- **Extension dialing:** Determines how many digits must be dialed to reach an extension

- **Extension addressing:** Determines how many digits are used to identify extensions

- **Dialing privileges:** Allows or disallows certain types of calls

- **Path selection:** Selects one path from several parallel paths

- **Automated selection of alternate paths in case of network congestion:** For example, using a local carrier for international calls if the preferred international carrier is unavailable

- **Blocking of certain numbers:** Prevents unwarranted high-cost calls

- **Transformation of the called-party number: Allows appropriate digits (that is, DNIS digits) to be presented to the PSTN or a call agent**

- **Transformation of the calling-party number:** Allows appropriate caller-ID information (that is, ANI information) to be presented to a called party

A dial plan suitable for an IP telephony system is not fundamentally different from a dial plan that is designed for a traditional telephony system. However, an IP-based system presents additional possibilities. In an IP environment, telephony users in separate sites can be included in one unified IP-based system. These additional possibilities presented by IP-based systems require you to think about dial plans in new ways.

Endpoint Addressing Considerations

Reachability of internal destinations is provided by assigning directory numbers to all endpoints (such as IP phones, fax machines, and analog phones) and applications (such as voice-mail systems, auto-attendants, and conferencing systems). An example of number assignment is provided in Figure 4-13.

The number of dialable extensions determines the quantity of digits needed to dial extensions. For example, a four-digit abbreviated dial plan cannot accommodate more than 10,000 extensions (from 0000 through 9999). If 0 and 9 are reserved as operator code and external access code, respectively, the number range is further reduced to 8000 (1000 through 8999). If direct inward dialing (DID) is enabled for PSTN calls, the DID numbers are mapped to internal directory numbers.

The most common issue with endpoint addressing is related to the mapping of internal extensions to available DID ranges assigned by the PSTN. When the DID range does not cover the entire internal address scope, an auto-attendant can be used to route calls between the PSTN and the internal network.

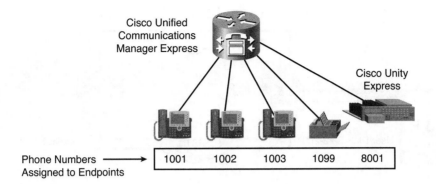

Cisco Unified
Communications
Manager Express

Cisco Unity
Express

Phone Numbers ⟶
Assigned to Endpoints

| 1001 | 1002 | 1003 | 1099 | 8001 |

Figure 4-13   *Endpoint Addressing*

One of the biggest challenges when creating an endpoint addressing scheme for a multi-site installation is to design a flexible and scalable dial plan that has no impact on the end user. The existing overlapping directory numbers present a typical issue that must be addressed.

Endpoint addressing is primarily managed by a call agent, such as Cisco Unified Communications Manager or Cisco Unified Communications Manager Express.

Call Routing and Path Selection

Call routing and path selection are the dial plan components that define where and how calls should be routed or interconnected. Call routing usually depends on the called number (that is, destination-based call routing is usually performed). This is similar to IP routing, which also relies on destination-based routing. Multiple paths to the same destination might exist, especially in multisite environments (for example, a path using an IP connection or a path using a PSTN connection). Path selection helps you decide which of the available paths should be used.

A voice gateway might be involved with call routing and path selection, depending on the protocol and design that is used. For example, an H.323 gateway will at least route the call between the call leg that points to the call handler and the call leg that points to the PSTN. When a Cisco IOS gateway performs call routing and path selection, the key components that are used are dial peers.

In Figure 4-14, if a user dials an extension number in another location (8-22-2001), the call should be sent over the IP WAN. If the WAN path is unavailable (due to network failure, insufficient bandwidth, or no response), the call should use the local PSTN gateway as a backup and send the call through the PSTN.

For PSTN-routed calls, digit manipulation should be configured on the gateway to transform the internal numbers to E.164 numbers that can be used in the PSTN.

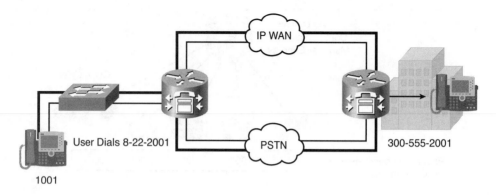

User Dials 8-22-2001

1001

300-555-2001

Figure 4-14 *Path Selection Example*

PSTN Dial Plan Requirements

A PSTN dial plan has three key requirements:

- **Inbound call routing:** Incoming calls from the PSTN must be routed correctly to their final destination, which might be a directly attached phone or endpoints that are managed by Cisco Unified Communications Manager or Cisco Unified Communications Manager Express. This inbound call routing also includes digit manipulation to ensure that an incoming called number matches the pattern expected by the final destination.

- **Outbound call routing:** Outgoing calls to the PSTN must be routed to the voice interfaces of the gateway (for example, a T1/E1 or a Foreign Exchange Office [FXO] connection). As with inbound calls, outbound calls might also require digit manipulation to modify a called number according to PSTN requirements. This outbound call routing usually includes stripping of any PSTN access code that might be included in the original called number.

- **Correct PSTN calling-party number presentation:** An often-neglected aspect is the correct calling number presentation for both inbound and outbound PSTN calls. The calling number for inbound PSTN calls is often left untouched, which might have a negative impact on the end-user experience. The calling number that is presented to the end user should include the PSTN access code and any other identifiers that are required by the PSTN to successfully place a call using that calling number (for example, using the missed calls directory).

Inbound PSTN Calls

Figure 4-15 shows how gateways manage inbound PSTN calls.

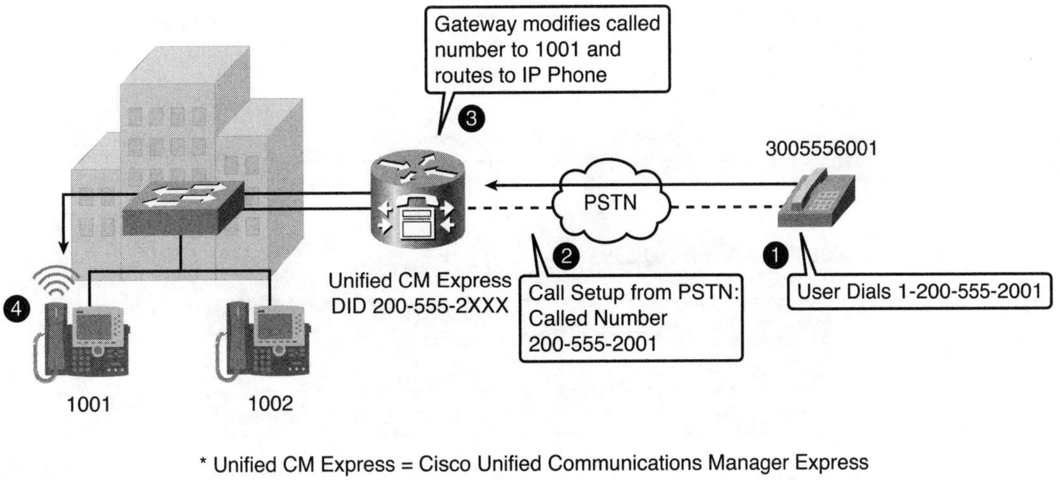

Gateway modifies called number to 1001 and routes to IP Phone

③

3005556001

PSTN

②

①

Unified CM Express DID 200-555-2XXX

Call Setup from PSTN: Called Number 200-555-2001

User Dials 1-200-555-2001

④

1001   1002

* Unified CM Express = Cisco Unified Communications Manager Express

Figure 4-15 *Inbound PSTN Calls*

The site consists of a Cisco Unified Communications Manager Express system with end-points registered to it, connected to the PSTN over a digital trunk. The DID range of the PSTN trunk is 2005552XXX, and phones use the extension range 1XXX. The processing of an inbound PSTN call occurs in these steps:

1. A PSTN user places a call to 1-200-555-2001 (that is, an endpoint with internal extension 1001).

2. The call setup message is received by the gateway with a called number of 200-555-2001.

3. The gateway modifies the called number to 1001 and routes the call to the voice port that was created when a Cisco Unified IP Phone registered with Cisco Unified Communications Manager Express.

4. The phone rings.

Figure 4-16 provides a description of the required number manipulation when a gateway receives an inbound PSTN call.

Both the called and calling numbers must be transformed:

■ The called number can be converted from the public E.164 format to the internal number used for internal dialing. This transformation ensures that the call matches the outbound dial peer that is automatically created at endpoint registration. Directory numbers are commonly configured with their internal extensions.

■ The calling number must be presented to the callee in a way that allows callback. Because access codes are commonly used to reach external destinations, a calling number forwarded to the destination should include an access code. Optionally, some region-specific prefixes might have to be added, such as the long-distance prefix in the NANP region, 1.

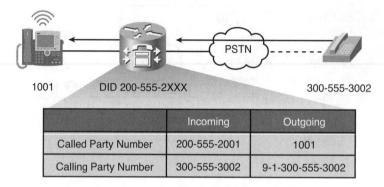

	Incoming	Outgoing
Called Party Number	200-555-2001	1001
Calling Party Number	300-555-3002	9-1-300-555-3002

Figure 4-16   *Numbers in Inbound PSTN Calls*

Outbound PSTN Calls

Figure 4-17 shows the call flow for an outbound call.

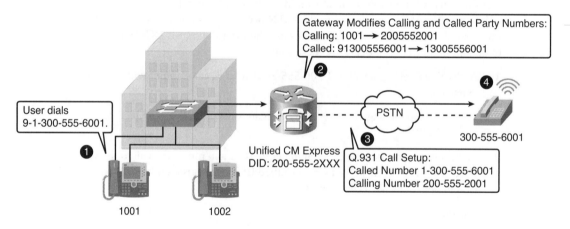

Figure 4-17   *Outbound PSTN Calls*

The site consists of a Cisco Unified Communications Manager Express system with end-points registered to it, connected to the PSTN over a digital trunk. The access code is 9. The processing of an outbound PSTN call occurs in these steps:

1. A user places a call to 9-1-300-555-6001 from the phone with extension 1001.

2. The gateway accepts the call and modifies the called number to 1-300-555-6001, stripping off the PSTN access code 9. The gateway also modifies the calling number to 200-555-2001 by prefixing the area code and local code and mapping the four-digit extension to the DID range.

3. The gateway sends out a call setup message with the called number set to 1-300-555-6001 and the calling number set to 200-555-2001.

4. The PSTN subscriber telephone at 300-555-6001 rings.

Figure 4-18 summarizes the requirements for number manipulation when a gateway processes an outbound PSTN call.

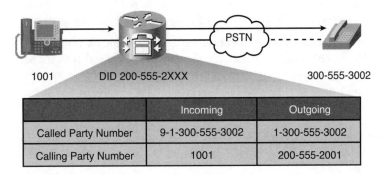

	Incoming	Outgoing
Called Party Number	9-1-300-555-3002	1-300-555-3002
Calling Party Number	1001	200-555-2001

Figure 4-18 *Numbers in Outbound PSTN Calls*

Both the called and calling numbers must be transformed as follows:

- The called number processing involves the stripping of the access code. Optionally, some region-specific prefixes might have to be added, such as the long-distance prefix in the NANP region, 1.

- The calling number must be converted from the internal extension to the public E.164 format. If the outgoing calling number is not configured on the gateway, the telco operator sets the value to the subscriber number, but this setting might be inaccurate if a DID range is available. For example, the calling number for a call originating from 1002 would be set to 222-555-2000. Setting the calling number is considered a good practice and ensures proper callback functionality.

ISDN Dial Plan Requirements

The type of number (TON) or nature of address indicator (NAI) parameter indicates the scope of the address value, such as whether it is an international number (including the country code) a "national," or domestic number (without country code), and other formats such as "local" format (without an area code). It is relevant for E.164 (regular telephone) numbers.

The TON is carried in ISDN-based environments. Voice gateways must consider the TON when transforming the called and calling numbers for ISDN calls.

ISDN networks impose new number manipulation needs, in addition to the typical requirements for PSTN calls:

- **Correct PSTN inbound ANI presentation, depending on TON:** Some ISDN networks present the inbound ANI as the shortest dialable number combined with the TON. This treatment of the ANI can be a potential problem, because simply prefixing the PSTN access code might not result in an ANI that can be called back. A potential problem can be solved by proper digit manipulation on gateways.

- **Correct PSTN outbound ANI presentation, depending on TON:** Some ISDN networks and PBXs might expect a certain numbering plan and TON for both DNIS and ANI. Using incorrect flags might result in incomplete calls or an incorrect DNIS and ANI presentation. Digit manipulation can be used to solve these issues.

Note   The calling-party number in ISDN is called *Automatic Number Identification* (ANI). The called-party number in ISDN is referred to as *Dialed Number Identification Service* (DNIS).

In Figure 4-19, three different calls are received at the voice gateway. The first call is received from the local area with a subscriber TON and a seven-digit number. This number only needs to be prefixed with access code 9. The second call, received with a national TON and ten digits, is modified by adding access code 9 and the long-distance number 1, all of which are required for placing calls back to the source of the call. The third call is received from oversees with an international TON. For this call, the access code 9 and 011 must be added to the received number, as a prefix to the country code.

Digit Manipulation

Digit manipulation is closely related to call routing and path selection. Digit manipulation is performed for inbound calls to achieve these goals:

- Adjust the called-party number to match internally used patterns
- Present the calling-party number as a dialable number

Digit manipulation is implemented for outbound calls to ensure the following:

- Called number satisfies the internal or PSTN requirements
- Calling number is dialable and provides callback if sufficient PSTN DID is available

Digit manipulation is covered in Chapter 5, "Implementing Dial Plans."

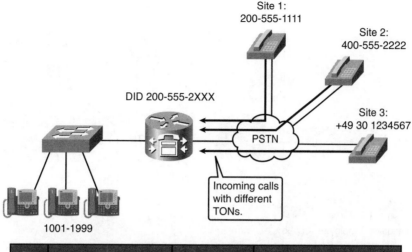

Site	TON	ANI	Required ANI Transformation
1	Subscriber	555-1111	9-555-1111
2	National	400-555-2222	9-1-400-555-2222
3	International	49-30-1234567	9-011-49-30-1234567

Figure 4-19 *Inbound ISDN Calls*

Calling Privileges

Calling privileges are equivalent to firewalls in networking. They define call permissions by specifying which users can dial given destinations. The two most common areas of deploying calling privileges are as follows:

■ Policy-defined rules to reach special endpoints. For example, manager extensions cannot be reached from a lobby phone.

■ Billing-related rules that are deployed to control telephony charges. Common examples include the blocking of costly service numbers and restricting international calls.

Calling privileges are referred to as a "Class of Service," but should not be confused with the Layer 2 class of service (CoS) that describes quality of service (QoS) treatment of traffic on Layer 2 switches.

Figure 4-20 illustrates the typical deployment of calling privileges. The internal endpoints are classified into three roles: executive, employee, and lobby. Each role has a set of dialable PSTN destinations that is associated with it. The executives can dial any PSTN number, the employees are allowed to dial any external numbers except international destinations, and the lobby phones permit the dialing of local numbers only.

The deployment of calling privileges is covered in Chapter 5.

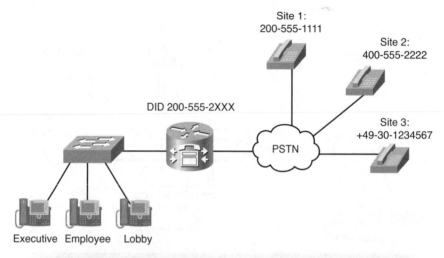

User	Call Permission
Executive	Site 1 (Local), Site 2 (Long Distance), Site 3 (International)
Employee	Site 1 (Local), Site 2 (Long Distance)
Lobby	Site 1 (Local)

Figure 4-20 *Calling Privileges Example*

Call Coverage

Call coverage features are used to ensure that all incoming calls to Cisco Unified Communications Manager Express are answered by someone, regardless of whether the called number is busy or does not answer.

Call coverage can be deployed for two different scopes:

■ **Individual users:** Features such as call waiting and call forwarding increase the chance of a call being answered by giving it another chance for a connection if the dialed user cannot manage the call.

■ **User groups:** Features such as call pickup, call hunt, hunt groups, and overlaid directory numbers provide different ways to distribute the incoming calls to multiple numbers and have them answered by available endpoints.

Call Coverage Features

Cisco voice gateways provide various call coverage features:

■ **Call forwarding:** Calls are automatically diverted to a designated number on busy, no answer, all calls, or only during night-service hours.

- **Call hunt:** The system automatically searches for an available directory number from a matching group of directory numbers until the call is answered or the hunt is stopped.

- **Call pickup:** Calls to unstaffed phones can be answered by other phone users using a softkey or by dialing a short code.

- **Call waiting:** Calls to busy numbers are presented to phone users, giving them the option to answer or let them be forwarded.

- **Basic automatic call distribution (B-ACD):** Calls to a pilot number are automatically answered by an interactive application that presents callers with a menu of choices before sending them to a queue for a hunt group.

- **Hunt groups:** Calls are forwarded through a pool of agents until answered or sent to a final number.

- **Overlaid ephone-dn:** Calls to several numbers can be answered by a single agent or multiple agents.

Summary

The main topics covered in this chapter are the following:

- Public and private numbering plans were contrasted, along with the characteristics and requirements of each.

- You were introduced to the components of dial plans and their functions. These components include endpoint addressing, call routing and path selection, digit manipulation, calling privileges, and call coverage.

Chapter Review Questions

The answers to these review questions are in the appendix.

1. Which dial plan component is responsible for choosing the appropriate path for a call?

   a. Endpoint addressing

   b. Call routing and path selection

   c. Call coverage and path selection

   d. Calling privileges

2. What is the dial plan component called endpoint addressing responsible for assigning to the endpoints?

   a. IP addresses

   b. E.164 addresses

   c. Gateways

   d. Directory numbers

3. Which option implements call routing and path selection on Cisco IOS gateways?

   a. Call-routing tables

   b. Dialer maps

   c. Dial peers

   d. Route patterns

4. What is one way to implement call coverage?

   a. COR

   b. Pilot numbers

   c. Digit manipulation

   d. Endpoint addressing

5. Which of the following are characteristics of a scalable dial plan? (Choose three.)

   a. Backup paths

   b. Full digit manipulation

   c. Hierarchical numbering plan

   d. Dial plan logic distribution

   e. Granularity

   f. High availability

6. Which of the following options are key requirements for a PSTN dial plan? (Choose three.)

   a. Internal call routing

   b. Inbound call routing

   c. Outbound call routing

   d. Correct PSTN ANI presentation

   e. Internet call routing

7. What might some ISDN networks and PBXs expect along with a certain numbering plan for both DNIS and ANI?

   a. ToS

   b. TON

   c. QoS

   d. CoS

8. Which command should be used to display information for all voice dial peers?

   a. show dial-peer voice summary

   b. show dial-peer voice all

   c. show dial-peer summary

   d. show dial-peer all

9. Which function best describes a numbering plan?

   a. Determines routes between source and destination

   b. Defines a telephone number of a voice endpoint or application

   c. Performs digit manipulation when sending calls to the PSTN

   d. Performs least-cost routing for VoIP calls

10. Which worldwide prefix scheme was developed by the ITU to standardize numbering plans?

   a. E.164

   b. G.114

   c. G.164

   d. E.114

Chapter 5

Implementing Dial Plans

After reading this chapter, you should be able to perform the following tasks:

- Describe how to configure a gateway for digit manipulation.

- Explain how to configure a gateway to perform path selection.

- Describe how to configure calling privileges on a voice gateway.

Although a Cisco Unified Communications Manager (UCM) server can perform digit manipulation, perform path selection, and enforce calling privileges (for example, through the use of partitions and calling search spaces), voice-enabled Cisco IOS gateways can perform similar functions. In fact, Cisco IOS gateways have even more granular control of call routing, as compared to UCM (for example, being able to route a call based on caller ID information). This chapter demonstrates a variety of approaches to manipulate numbers on Cisco IOS gateways. Additionally, path selection is discussed, and you will learn how to use the Class of Restriction (COR) feature to implement calling restrictions on dial peers.

Configuring Digit Manipulation

At times, you might need to manipulate the digits of the telephone numbers that come into and go out of your voice gateway. You might need to remove site codes for intersite calls or add area codes and other digits for routing calls through the PSTN. This section covers digit manipulation and digit manipulation tools.

Digit Collection and Consumption

If an endpoint sends dialed digits one-by-one, Cisco Unified Communications Manager Express starts digit analysis immediately upon receiving the first digit. With each additional digit that is received, Cisco Unified Communications Manager Express can reduce the list of potential matches (that is, the call-routing table entries that match the digits that have been received so far). After a single entry, such as the directory number 1001 in Figure 5-1, is matched, the so-called current match is used and the call is sent to the corresponding device.

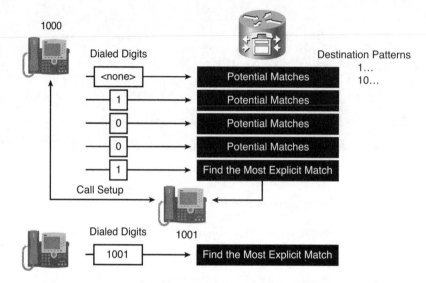

Figure 5-1 *Digit Collection Methods—Digit-by-Digit and En Block*

> **Note**   Cisco Unified Communications Manager Express does not always receive dialed digits one-by-one. Skinny Client Control Protocol (SCCP) phones always send digit-by-digit. Session Initiation Protocol (SIP) phones can use either en bloc dialing, to send the whole dialed string at once, or Keypad Markup Language (KPML), to send digit-by-digit. If digits are received en bloc, the whole received dial string is checked at once against the dial plan.

Cisco Unified Communications Manager Express Addressing Method

Table 5-1 shows the addressing methods that Cisco Unified Communications Manager Express supports for different devices.

With SIP, en bloc dialing or KPML can be used. With en bloc dialing, the whole dialed string is sent in a single SIP Invite message. KPML allows digits to be sent one-by-one. SIP dial rules are processed inside the SIP phone. Therefore, a SIP phone can detect invalid numbers and play a reorder tone, without sending any signaling messages to Cisco Unified Communications Manager Express. If dialed digits match an entry of a SIP dial rule, the dialed string is sent in a single SIP Invite message to Cisco Unified Communications Manager Express. If Cisco Unified Communications Manager Express requires more digits, KPML can be used to send the remaining digits one-by-one, from the SIP phone to Cisco Unified Communications Manager Express.

Table 5-1 *Cisco Unified Communications Manager Express Addressing Method*

Device	Signaling Protocol	Addressing Method
IP phone	SCCP	Digit-by-digit or En bloc (Type B phones only)
IP phone	SIP	En bloc or KPML (Type B phones only) or SIP dial rules
Gateway	MGCP/SIP/H.323	En bloc or Overlap sending and receiving (ISDN PRI only)

ISDN PRIs can be configured for overlap sending and receiving, allowing digits to be sent or received one-by-one over an ISDN PRI.

User Input on SCCP Phones

Whether a number is signaled digit-by-digit or en bloc depends not only on the configured signaling protocol but also on the phone model (Type A or Type B) that is used and on how the phone number is dialed. Examples of Type A phones include Cisco Unified IP Phones 7940 and 7960, while examples of Type B phones include Cisco Unified IP Phones 7941, 7942, 7945, 7961, 7962, 7965, 7970, and 7970.

For Cisco SCCP IP phones, the following rules apply:

- Type A IP phones support only digit-by-digit signaling.

- Type B IP phones support digit-by-digit signaling as well as en bloc signaling.

  - En bloc dialing is used when a call is placed by the user entering the number while the phone is on-hook and then pressing the Dial softkey. Calls that are set up via call list entries or speed dials also use en bloc signaling.

  - En bloc dialing, which is enabled by default, can be disabled via the product-specific Enbloc Dialing configuration parameter from the Phone Configuration page.

  - Digit-by-digit dialing is used whenever the number is dialed after the phone is put off-hook.

Note The dialing behavior might vary based on the phone load version that is used.

SCCP Digit Collection

As depicted in Figure 5-2, an SCCP endpoint detects all user events and individually relays them to the Cisco Unified Communications Manager Express. A user who goes off-hook and then dials 1000 would trigger five individual signaling events from the phone to the gateway. All the resulting feedback that is provided to the user, such as screen messages, playing dial tone, secondary dial tone, ringback, and reorder tone, are commands that are issued by the Cisco Unified Communications Manager Express to the phone in response to the dial plan configuration.

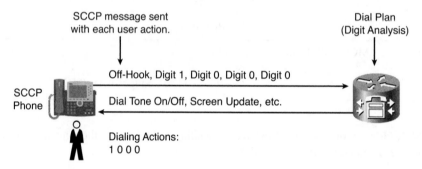

Figure 5-2   *SCCP Digit Collection*

It is neither required nor possible to configure dial plan information on Cisco Unified IP Phones running SCCP. All dial plan functionality is contained in the Cisco Unified Communications Manager Express system, including the recognition of dialing patterns as user input is collected.

If a user dials a pattern that is denied by Cisco Unified Communications Manager Express, a reorder tone is played to the user when that pattern becomes the best match in Cisco Unified Communications Manager Express digit analysis. For instance, if all calls to 92000 are denied, a reorder tone would be sent to the user phone as soon as the user dials 92000.

SIP Digit Collection (Simple Phones)

With en bloc number reporting, a phone accumulates all user input events until the user presses either the # key or the Dial softkey. This function is similar to the Dial button used on many mobile phones.

For example, consider Figure 5-3. A user making a call to extension 1000 would have to press 1, 0, 0, and 0 followed by the Dial softkey or the # key. The phone would then send a SIP Invite message to Cisco Unified Communications Manager Express to indicate that a call to extension 1000 is requested. As a call reaches a gateway, it is subjected to the dial plan, including all the class of service and call-routing logic.

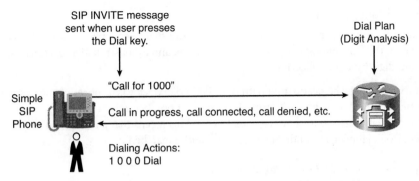

Figure 5-3 *SIP Digit Collection (Simple Phones)*

SIP Digit Collection (Enhanced Phones)

Type B SIP phones offer functionality that is based on KPML to report user activities. Each one of the user input events generates its own KPML-based message to Cisco Unified Communications Manager Express. From the standpoint of relaying each user action immediately to Cisco Unified Communications Manager Express, this mode of operation is similar to that of phones running SCCP.

Every user key press triggers a SIP NOTIFY message to Cisco Unified Communications Manager to report a KPML event corresponding to the key pressed by the user. This messaging enables Cisco Unified Communications Manager Express digit analysis to recognize partial patterns as they are composed by the user, and to provide appropriate feedback such as an immediate reorder tone if an invalid number is being dialed.

In contrast to Type A IP phones running SIP, Type B SIP phones have no Dial key to indicate the end of user input. In Figure 5-4, a user dialing 1000 would be provided call progress indication (either a ringback tone or reorder tone) after dialing the last 0 and without having to press the Dial key. This behavior is consistent with the user interface on phones running the SCCP protocol.

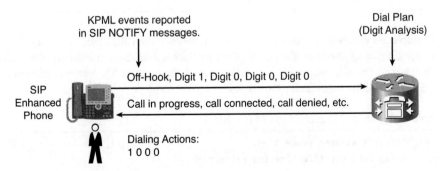

Figure 5-4 *SIP Digit Collection (Enhanced Phones)*

Dial-Peer Management

Examples 5-1, 5-2, and 5-3 demonstrate the impact that overlapping destination patterns have on the call-routing decision. The first two examples illustrate dial-peer management using digit-by-digit collection.

In Example 5-1, the destination pattern (555) in dial peer 1 is a subset of the destination pattern (555....) in dial peer 2. With digit-by-digit number collection, the router matches one digit at a time against available dial peers. This means that an exact match will always occur on dial peer 1, and dial peer 2 will never be matched.

Example 5-1 *Dialed Digits 5550124 (One-by-One)*

```
Router(config)#dial-peer voice 1 voip
Router(config-dial-peer)#destination-pattern 555
Router(config-dial-peer)#session target ipv4:10.18.0.1
Router(config-dial-peer)#exit
Router(config)#dial-peer voice 2 voip
Router(config-dial-peer)#destination-pattern 5550124
Router(config-dial-peer)#session target ipv4:10.18.0.2
```

In Example 5-2, the length of the destination patterns in both dial peers is the same. Dial peer 2 has a more specific value than dial peer 1, so it will be matched first. If the path to IP address 10.18.0.2 is unavailable, dial peer 1 will be used.

Example 5-2 *Dialed Digits 5550124 (One-by-One Continued)*

```
Router(config)#dial-peer voice 1 voip
Router(config-dial-peer)#destination-pattern 555....
Router(config-dial-peer)#session target ipv4:10.18.0.1
Router(config-dial-peer)#exit
Router(config)#dial-peer voice 2 voip
Router(config-dial-peer)#destination-pattern 5550124
Router(config-dial-peer)#session target ipv4:10.18.0.2
```

Example 5-3 examines the dial-peer management when the called number has been received en block. Because the entire called number is available immediately, the second dial peer will match, because it offers the most explicit match. The entire called number (5550124) will be forwarded to the session target.

Example 5-3 *Dialed Digits 5550124 (En Bloc)*

```
Router(config)#dial-peer voice 1 voip
Router(config-dial-peer)#destination-pattern 555
Router(config-dial-peer)#session target ipv4:10.18.0.1
Router(config-dial-peer)#exit
```

```
Router(config)#dial-peer voice 2 voip
Router(config-dial-peer)#destination-pattern 5550124
Router(config-dial-peer)#session target ipv4:10.18.0.2
```

Digit Manipulation

Digit manipulation is the task of adding or subtracting digits from the original dialed number to accommodate user dialing habits (for example, the habit of prepending an area code to a seven-digit dial string) or gateway needs. Digit manipulation incorporates adding, subtracting, and changing telephone numbers. For example, you might need to add the area code to a call that will be routed out to the PSTN or remove a site code from an intersite call with the same company. You can manipulate called numbers, calling numbers, and redirected numbers, as well as the number type. You can apply digit manipulation to incoming or outgoing calls or to all calls globally. You can manipulate digits before or after matching a dial peer.

Because the call agent performs digit manipulation in a Media Gateway Control Protocol (MGCP) network, digit manipulation might be performed only on H.323 and Session Initiation Protocol (SIP) gateways.

Digit manipulation is an important aspect of any dial plan, and various tools exist on Cisco IOS gateways to perform this task, including the following:

- **Basic digit manipulation:** Digit manipulation covers a spectrum of possibilities, including prepending digits, stripping digits, or changing specific digits. Examples are

  - The **digit-strip** command is a dial-peer command that strips off the matched digits in a destination pattern of a dial peer. The **digit-strip** command is supported on plain old telephone service (POTS) dial peers only. Digit stripping occurs after the outbound dial peer is matched and before any digits are sent out. The called number is manipulated using digit stripping. Digit stripping is enabled by default on POTS dial peers.

  - The **forward-digits** {*num-digits* | **all** | **extra**} command is a dial-peer command that specifies how many matched digits should be forwarded. To specify which digits to forward for voice calls, use the **forward-digits** command in dial-peer configuration mode. To specify that any digits not matching the **destination-pattern** are not to be forwarded, use the **no** form of this command. This command applies only to POTS dial peers. Forwarded digits are always right-justified so that extra leading digits are stripped. The **destination-pattern** includes both explicit digits and wildcards if present. Digit forwarding occurs after the outbound dial peer is matched and before any digits are sent out. The called number is manipulated using digit forwarding.

  - The **prefix** command is a dial-peer command that prefixes the specified digits to the number forwarded by the dial peer. Use this command to specify a prefix for a specific dial peer. When an outgoing call is initiated to this dial peer, the prefix string value is sent to the telephony interface first, before the telephone number, associated with the dial peer. If you want to configure different prefixes for dialed numbers on the same interface, you need to configure different dial peers. This command is applicable only to POTS dial peers. This command also applies to off-ramp store-and-forward fax functions. Digit prefixing occurs after the outbound dial peer is matched and before any digits are sent out. The called number is manipulated using digit prefixing.

■   The **num-exp** command is a global command that applies to all calls and performs a match-and-replace operation to inflate or deflate numbers. This command is typically used for short dials and site codes. Number expansion occurs prior to matching a dial peer. The called number is manipulated using number expansion. For example, a four-digit number could be used by an employee to call a co-worker. That four-digit number could then be translated to that co-worker's home phone number and forwarded out to the PSTN.

■   The **clid** command can be used to modify the calling line ID (CLID, and also known as caller ID); for example, to restrict caller ID information. CLID manipulation occurs after the outbound dial peer is matched and before any digits are sent out. The calling number and name are manipulated using CLID manipulation.

■ **Voice translation rules and profiles:** Voice translation rules and profiles are the most powerful Cisco IOS tools you can use to perform digit manipulation. Using regular expressions, a numbering plan, and Type of Number (TON) matching, you can make nearly any possible modification. The only drawback is the complex syntax. Thus, voice translation rules are often combined with simpler mechanisms.

The order of operation in digit manipulation follows the call through the gateway, as shown in Figure 5-5. For inbound POTS calls, rules configured on the voice port are applied first, followed by the incoming dial peer, and then the outgoing dial peer. For inbound Voice over IP (VoIP) calls, global voice translation profiles are applied first, followed by the incoming dial peer, and then the outgoing dial peer. Note the **num-exp** command is applied globally before any dial-peer matching.

When possible, you should use a single method of accomplishing the required digit manipulations. For example, do not use both the **forward-digits** and the **prefix** commands in a dial-peer configuration.

It is possible to use all the digit manipulation methods in a gateway. A single dial peer can be configured with prefixes, voice translation rules, and **clid** commands. A call can be modified by the voice port, number expansion, inbound dial-peer, and outbound dial-peer configuration commands in single or multiple gateways. Understanding the order of operation in digit manipulation is important not only for configuration and test purposes, but also for assisting in troubleshooting.

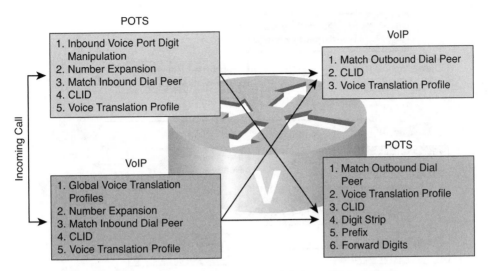

Figure 5-5 *Digit Manipulation Order of Operations*

Digit Stripping

Digit stripping strips any outbound digits that explicitly match the destination pattern of a particular dial peer. By default, POTS dial peers strip any outbound digits that explicitly match their destination pattern, whereas VoIP dial peers transmit all digits in the called number. For example, given a destination pattern of 5551..., the number transmitted to the PSTN would contain the last three digits. The first four digits, 5551, would be stripped because they explicitly match the destination pattern.

In Figure 5-6, users dial 9 to reach an outside number. If the configured destination pattern is 9T, the 9 is matched and stripped from the called number sent to the PSTN. On the other hand, you might have a dial peer for an emergency number, such as 911 in the United States. If the destination pattern is 911, you would not want the numbers stripped when they are explicitly matched. In this case, you could use the **no digit-strip** command to disable the automatic digit stripping function. This allows the router to match digits and pass them to the telephony interface. Figure 5-6 shows an example of this behavior.

Digit Forwarding

If you need more control over the digits that are being transmitted to the PSTN, you can use digit forwarding. Digit forwarding specifies the number of digits that must be forwarded to the telephony interface, regardless of whether they match explicitly or with wildcards. When a specific number of digits are configured for forwarding, the count is right-justified. For example, in Figure 5-7, the POTS dial peer has a destination pattern configured to match all extensions in the 1000 range. By default, only the last three digits are forwarded to the PBX that is connected to the specified voice port. If the PBX needs all four digits to route the call, you could use the **forward-digits 4** or **forward-digits all** command so that the appropriate number of digits are forwarded.

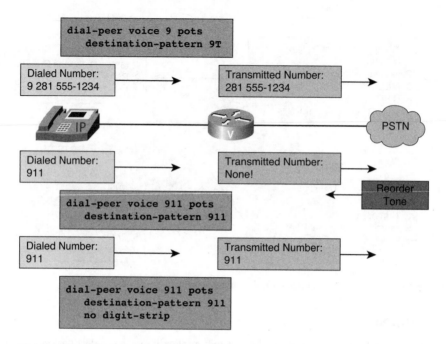

Figure 5-6 *Digit Stripping Example*

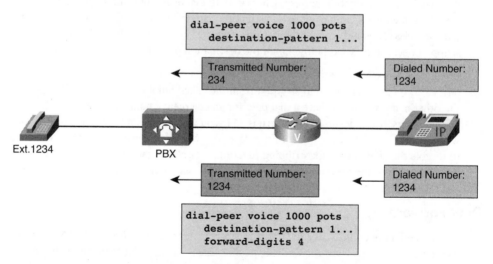

Figure 5-7 *Digit Forwarding Example*

Note   Digit forwarding applies only to POTS dial peers.

Digit Prefixing

Digit prefixing adds digits to the front of a dial string before it is forwarded to a telephony interface. Use the **prefix** command when the dialed digits leaving the router must be changed from the dialed digits that had originally matched the dial peer. For example, consider Figure 5-8. A call is dialed using a four-digit extension, such as 2123, but the call needs to be routed to the PSTN, which requires ten-digit dialing. If the four-digit extension matches the last four digits of the actual PSTN number, you can use the **prefix 5125552** command to prepend the seven additional digits needed for the PSTN to route the call to 512 555-2123. After the POTS dial peer is matched with the destination pattern of 2123, the **prefix** command prepends the additional digits and the string "5125552123" is sent out of the voice port to the PSTN.

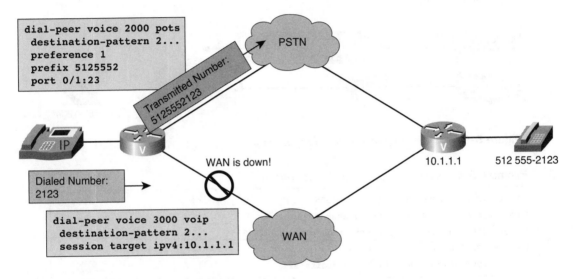

Figure 5-8 *Digit Prefixing Example*

Number Expansion

Number expansion is an alternative method of adding digits to outgoing calls. Whereas prefixing is applied to a single dial peer, number expansion is applied globally to all calls, not just to calls matching a single designated dial peer.

The **num-exp** global command expands a partial telephone number into a full telephone number or replaces one number with another. The number expansion table manipulates the called number. Because number expansion occurs before the outbound dial peer is matched, for the call to be successful you must configure the outbound dial peer with the expanded number in the destination pattern instead of the original number. The number expansion table becomes useful when the PSTN changes the dialing requirements from seven-digit dialing to ten-digit dialing. In this scenario, you can do one of the following:

- Make all the users dial all ten digits to match the new POTS dial peer that is pointing to the PSTN.

- Allow the users to continue dialing the seven-digit number as they have before, but expand the number to include the area code before the ten-digit outbound dial peer is matched.

Consider Figure 5-9 and Example 5-4. Using the number expansion feature, a caller is using a seven-digit dial string. However, the number expansion feature configured in the router prepends the area code of 281 to the dial string. This ten-digit dial string is then passed to the PSTN.

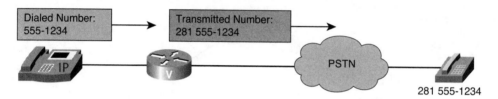

Figure 5-9 *Number Expansion Topology Example*

Example 5-4 *Number Expansion Configuration*

```
Router(config)#num-exp 5551... 2815551...
Router(config)#dial-peer voice 2000 pots
Router(config-dial-peer)#destination-pattern   2815551...
Router(config-dial-peer)#port 0/1:23
Router(config-dial-peer)#forward-digits all
```

Note You can use the **show num-exp** command to view the configured number expansion table. You can use the **show dialplan number** *string* command to confirm the presence of a valid dial peer to match the newly expanded number.

Simple Digit Manipulation for POTS Dial Peers Example

Figure 5-10 shows the operation of simple digit manipulation for POTS dial peers.

A user dials 9 1 312 555-0123, and the call is handled by the **dial-peer voice 9 pots** command on the H.323 gateway. Depending on the commands, the Dialed Number Information Service (DNIS) information will be modified differently:

- If the **no digit-strip** command is used, the DNIS will be 913125550123. No digits are modified.

- If the **digit-strip** command is used, which is the default on all POTS dial peers, the matched 9 will be stripped off, resulting in a DNIS of 13125550123.

- If the **forward-digits 4** command is used, only the last four digits will be forwarded, resulting in a DNIS of 0123.

- If the **prefix 9** and **digit-strip** commands are used in combination, the 9 is first stripped off and then prefixed again, resulting in a DNIS of 913125550123.

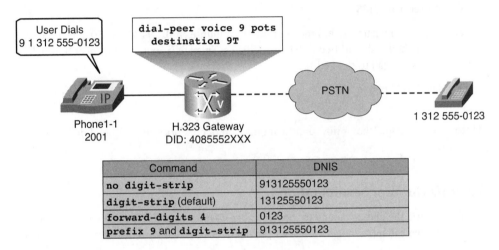

Command	DNIS
`no digit-strip`	913125550123
`digit-strip` (default)	13125550123
`forward-digits 4`	0123
`prefix 9` and `digit-strip`	913125550123

Figure 5-10 *Simple Digit Manipulation for a POTS Dial Peer*

Number Expansion Example

Figure 5-11 and Example 5-5 show how the **num-exp** command defines short dials.

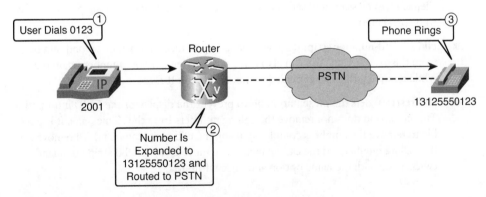

Figure 5-11 *Digit Manipulation with Number Expansion*

Example 5-5 *Digit Manipulation with Number Expansion Configuration*

```
Router(config)#num-exp 0... 913125550...
Router(config)#dial-peer voice 9 pots
Router(config-dial-peer)#destination 9T
```

If a user dials 0123, the call should be routed to DNIS 913125550123:

1. A user dials 0123.

2. Because the gateway has the configuration **num-exp 0... 913125550...**, DNIS 0123 is matched and modified to 913125550123. This DNIS matches dial peer 9, which routes the call to the PSTN.

3. The PSTN phone rings.

Note   This example shows how digit manipulation occurs prior to outbound dial-peer matching.

Caller ID Number Manipulation

You can use the **clid** command to modify caller ID information. The CLID message can include two calling numbers: one "user provided, unscreened" and one "network provided."

CLID Commands

Following are some of the **clid** commands:

- **clid network-number** *number*: Sets the network-provided number in the Information Element (IE) message and sets the presentation bit to allow the calling-party number to be presented.

- **clid second-number strip:** Removes the user-provided number, or second number, from this IE message. You can also leave the existing network number unaltered while removing the user-provided number from the IE.

- **clid restrict:** Sets the presentation bit to prevent the display of the CLID information. This command does not remove the calling numbers from the IE message. It is possible to remove the numbers completely using the **clid strip** command. To remove both the calling number and the calling name, you must enter the **clid strip** command twice: once with the name option and once without.

Station ID Commands

You can use the **station-id** command to control the caller ID information sent by an FXS or FXO port. The information specified with this command shows up as the caller ID of the device connected to the FXS port. This command is often used on FXS ports connected to fax machines that make on-net calls, as illustrated in Figure 5-12 and Example 5-6.

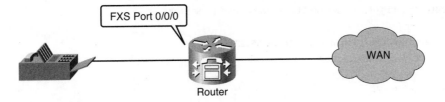

Figure 5-12   *Caller ID Number Manipulation*

Example 5-6   *Caller ID Number Manipulation Example*

```
Router(config)#voice-port 0/0/0
Router(config-voiceport)#station-id name HQ Fax
Router(config-voiceport)#station-id number 7135551003
```

Following are some of the **station-id** commands:

- **station-id name** *string*: Specifies the name sent in the CLID information
- **station-id number** *number*: Specifies the number sent in the CLID information

Displaying Caller ID Information

Sometimes, it is useful to display the CLID information that will be sent. Use the **show dialplan number** *number* command to determine what CLID information will be sent in an IE message. Example 5-7 shows the dial-plan information with no CLID commands applied.

Example 5-7   show dialplan number *Command—First Example*

```
Router#show dialplan number 914085551234
Macro Exp.: 914085551234
VoiceEncapPeer91
        peer type = voice, information type = voice,
        description = '',
        tag = 91, destination-pattern = '91..........',
        answer-address = '', preference=0,
        CLID Restriction = None
        CLID Network Number = ''
        CLID Second Number sent
        CLID Override RDNIS = disabled,
        source carrier-id = '', target carrier-id = '',
        source trunk-group-label = '',  target trunk-group-label = '', numbering
         Type = 'unknown'
```

Example 5-8 shows the result of adding a **clid network-number** command to the dial peer.

Example 5-8 show dialplan number *Command—Second Example*

```
Router(config-dial-peer)#clid network-number 5551234


Router#show dialplan number 914085551234
Macro Exp.: 914085551234


VoiceEncapPeer91
        peer type = voice, information type = voice,
        description = '',
        tag = 91, destination-pattern = '91..........',
        answer-address = '', preference=0,
        CLID Restriction = None
        CLID Network Number = '5551234'
        CLID Second Number sent
        CLID Override RDNIS = disabled,
        source carrier-id = '', target carrier-id = '',
        source trunk-group-label = '',  target trunk-group-label = '', numbering
          Type = 'unknown'
```

Example 5-9 shows the result of using the **clid strip** command.

Example 5-9 show dialplan number *Command—Third Example*

```
Router(config-dial-peer)#clid strip


Router#show dialplan number 914085551234
Macro Exp.: 914085551234


VoiceEncapPeer91
        peer type = voice, information type = voice,
        description = '',
        tag = 91, destination-pattern = '91..........',
        answer-address = '', preference=0,
        CLID Restriction = clid strip
        CLID Network Number = ''
        CLID Second Number sent
        CLID Override RDNIS = disabled,
        source carrier-id = '', target carrier-id = '',
        source trunk-group-label = '',  target trunk-group-label = '', numbering
          Type = 'unknown'
```

Voice Translation Rules and Profiles

Number translation occurs several times during the call-routing process. In both the originating and terminating gateways, the incoming call is translated before an inbound dial peer is matched, before an outbound dial peer is matched, and before a call request is set up. Your dial plan should account for these translation steps when translation rules are defined.

Digit translation is a two-step configuration process. First, the translation rule is defined at the global level. Then, the rule is applied at the dial-peer level either as inbound or outbound translation on either the called or calling number. Translation rules also convert a telephone number into a different number before the call is matched to an inbound dial peer or before the outbound dial peer forwards the call. For example, an employee might dial a five-digit extension to reach another employee of the same company at another site. If the call is routed through the PSTN to reach the other site, the originating gateway might use translation rules to convert the five-digit extension into the ten-digit format that is recognized by the central office (CO) switch.

A translation rule might manipulate a calling-party number (Automatic Number Identification [ANI]) or a called-party number (DNIS) for incoming, outgoing, and redirected calls within voice-enabled gateways.

You can also use translation rules to change the numbering type for a call. For example, some gateways might tag a number with more than 11 digits as an international number, even when the user must dial 9 to reach an outside line. In this case, the number that is tagged as an international number needs to be translated into a national number, without the 9, before it is sent to the PSTN.

Voice translation rules might define up to 15 rules that include Stream Editor (SED)-like expressions (that is, similar to expressions used with the UNIX SED utility) for processing the call translation. A maximum of 128 translation rules are supported. These translation rules are grouped into profiles that are referenced by trunk groups, dial peers, source IP groups, voice ports, and interfaces.

The voice translation rules are associated with a voice translation profile, which can reference up to three voice translation rules:

- A voice translation rule that is used to manipulate the called number (that is, the DNIS)

- A voice translation rule that is used to manipulate the calling number (that is, the ANI)

- A voice translation rule that is used to manipulate the redirected called number (that is, the Redirected Dialed Number Identification Service [RDNIS])

The resulting voice translation profile can be attached to these:

- VoIP dial peers

- Voice ports

- Any inbound VoIP call

- A specific range of source IP addresses in VoIP calls

- A trunk group

- A T1/E1 controller that is used for Nonfacility Associated Signaling (NFAS) trunks

- Survivable Remote Site Telephony (SRST)

Each of these can reference two voice translation profiles: one for incoming calls and one for outgoing calls. You can use the **voice translation-rule** command to create the definition of a translation rule.

Figure 5-13 illustrates the concept of voice translation profiles and rules. Each voice translation rule can have up to 15 individual subrules. The voice translation rule is then referenced by a voice translation profile for called, calling, and redirected called numbers. Note that the same voice translation rule can be referenced by multiple voice translation profiles. Up to 128 voice translation rules are supported in a Cisco IOS gateway.

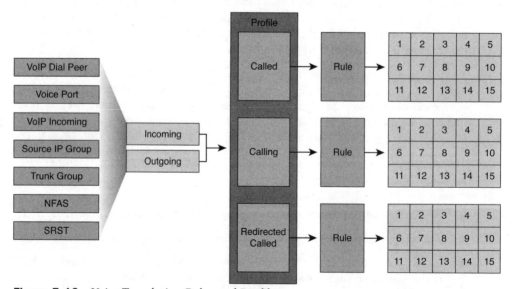

Figure 5-13   *Voice Translation Rules and Profiles*

Note   Although you can have up to 15 subrules within a voice translation rule, the first matching rule will be applied, and no further subrules will be considered.

Voice translation rules use regular expressions for match-and-replace operations. The syntax is very similar to the UNIX SED tool. Table 5-2 describes the most important regular expressions available.

Table 5-2 *Regular Expressions for Voice Translation Rules*

Voice Translation Rule Character	Description
^	Match the expression at the start of the line.
$	Match the expression at the end of the line.
/	Delimiter that marks the start and end of both the matching and replacement strings.
\	Escape the special meaning of the next character.
-	Indicate a range when not in the first/last position. Used with the [and] characters.
[list]	Match a single character in a list.
[^list]	Do not match a single character specified in the list.
.	Match any single character.
*	Repeat the previous regular expression (regex) zero or more times.
+	Repeat the previous regular expression one or more times.
?	Repeat the previous regular expression zero or one time (use Ctrl-V to enter in Cisco IOS, because Cisco IOS interprets a ? character as a request for context-sensitive help).
()	Group regular expressions.

Understanding Regular Expressions in Translation Rules

It is important that you understand how regular expressions are used in translation rules. When the router evaluates a translation rule, it is really only performing a "match this" and "change to this" operation on the regex.

Consider the following example, as illustrated in Figure 5-14.

To further illustrate the configuration of translation rules, consider the following:

- This rule will be used to change the outgoing DNIS to a ten-digit number for routing across the PSTN. The rule will be applied outgoing on an interface, port, or dial peer.

```
Router(config)#voice translation-rule 1
Router(cfg-translation-rule)#rule 1 /1.../ /4085551.../
```

■ This rule will be used to change the incoming ANI to a four-digit number after routing across the PSTN. The rule will be applied incoming on an interface, port, or dial peer.

```
Router(config)#voice translation-rule 2
Router(cfg-translation-rule)#rule 1 /4085551... / /1.../
```

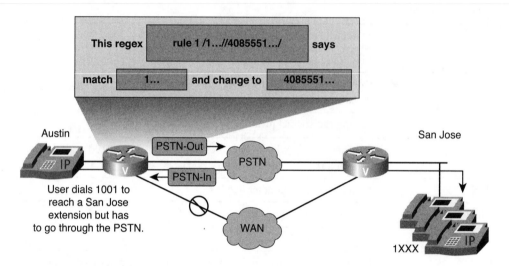

Figure 5-14 *Regular Expressions in Translation Rules*

Table 5-3 illustrates the match-and-replace rules for these rules.

Table 5-3 *Match-and-Replace Table*

Rule	Match This	Change To
/1.../ /4085551.../	1...	4085551...
/408553.../ /1.../	/4085551.../	/1.../

What if you needed to prepend a 9 to all outgoing calls? It would not be feasible to use individual translation rules for each number because of the number of rules needed. For example:

```
rule 1 /4085550100/ /94085550100/
rule 2 /4085550101/ /94085550101/
rule 3 /4085550102/ /94085550102/
```

The solution would be to use variables, as shown in Figure 5-15. Translation rule expressions can be divided into sections by using an escape character to create variables. The regex escape character is the \ symbol.

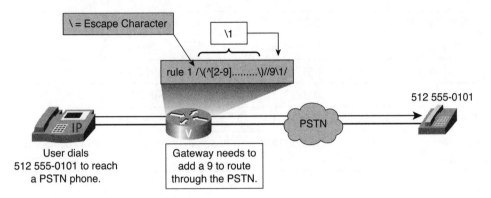

Figure 5-15 *Prepending Digits*

You might use the following translation rule to prepend a 9 to outgoing calls for routing through the PSTN:

```
rule 1 /\(^[2-9].........\)/ /9\1/
```

This rule would prepend a 9 to whatever was matched in the first set of parentheses (\1); in other words, replace \1 with ^[2-9]......... and add a 9 to the beginning.

Search and Replace with Voice Translation Rules Example

Table 5-4 shows how voice translation rules perform search-and-replace operations that use voice translation rules.

The example illustrated in Figure 5-16 shows a complex search-and-replace operation in which this rule is configured:

```
rule 1 /\(9\)\([^10].*\)/ /\11408\2/
```

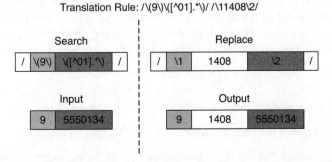

Figure 5-16 *Voice Translation Rule Search and Replace*

Table 5-4 *Examples of Voice Translation Rules*

Rule	Input String	Output String
/^9/ //	914085550123	14085550123
/^2001/ /3001/	2001	3001
/^[23].../ /4000/	2025 or 3051	4000
/^2.../ /801&/	2001	8012001
/^2.../ /801\0/	2001	8012001
/\(9\)\([^10].*\)/ /\11408\2/	95551234	914085551234
/.*/ /91&/ type national national	3125552001 type national	913125552001 type national

This example would be good for prepending a long-distance 1 and an area code to a dialed number exiting the network via the PSTN and accessing a long-distance subscriber. The user would be dialing a 9 plus seven digits to access outside numbers.

This is how the operation proceeds if the input string 95550134 is used:

- The 9 is reinserted using the \1.

- It is followed by the digits 1408.

- Then 5550134 follows, which is referenced by the \2.

- The resulting string is 914085550134.

Note The first set of parentheses is referenced as \1 and the second set as \2.

Voice Translation Profiles

Voice translation profiles introduce a new scheme to translate numbers. The older translation rules are to be gradually phased out of Cisco IOS. Cisco strongly recommends you use only one scheme of translation rules. If you mix the old and new schemes, you could have unforeseen results. Central to the new scheme is the capability to perform regular expression matches and replace substrings. The SED utility is used to translate numbers.

You can define these types of call numbers in a translation profile:

- **called:** Defines the translation profile rule for the called number

- **calling:** Defines the translation profile rule for the calling number

- **redirect-called:** Defines the translation profile rule for the redirect-called number

Each type of call number in the profile can have different translation rules.

After a translation profile is defined, it can be referenced by the following:

- **Trunk group:** Two different translation profiles can be defined in a trunk group to perform number translation for incoming and outgoing POTS calls. If an outgoing translation profile is defined in a trunk group, the number translation is done while the outgoing call is set up.

- **Source IP group:** A translation profile can be defined in a source IP group to perform number translation for incoming VoIP calls.

- **Dial peer:** Two different translation profiles can be defined in a dial peer to perform number translation for incoming and outgoing calls.

- **Voice port:** The translation profile can be defined in a voice port to perform number translation for incoming and outgoing POTS calls. If a voice port is also a trunk group member, the incoming translation profile of a voice port overrides the translation profile of a trunk group.

- **NFAS interface:** The translation profile can be defined for an NFAS interface through the **translation-profile** command from the global **voice service pots** configuration to perform the number translation for incoming and outgoing NFAS calls. This translation profile has a higher precedence than the translation profile of a voice port and trunk group in case a channel also belongs to a voice port and/or trunk group with the translation profile defined.

- **VoIP incoming:** The translation profile can be defined globally for all incoming VoIP (H.323/SIP) calls to perform number translation. If an incoming H.323/SIP call is associated with a source IP group with a translation profile defined, the translation profile of the source IP group overrides the global translation profile for incoming VoIP calls.

Note that voice translation profiles are most commonly assigned to voice ports or dial peers.

Translation Profile Processing

The order in which translation profiles are processed depends on where the profile is applied. Table 5-5 indicates the order in which voice translation profiles will be processed.

Table 5-5 *Translation Profile Order*

Applied	Processing Order	
	Inbound	**Outbound**
Voice port/NFAS	1	4
Trunk group/source IP	2	3
Global	3	1
Dial peer	4	2

Voice Translation Profile Search-and-Replace Example

The example illustrated in Figure 5-17 shows a search-and-replace voice translation profile.

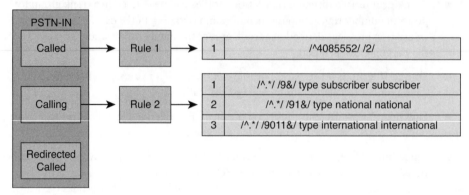

Figure 5-17   *Voice Translation Profile Search-and-Replace Example*

A voice translation profile is required to perform these manipulations:

■ The incoming DNIS 4085552XXX should be modified to 2XXX.

■ The incoming ANI should be prefixed with the appropriate PSTN access code and identifier:

   ■ **Local calls:** Prefix 9

   ■ **National calls:** Prefix 91

   ■ **International calls:** Prefix 9011

Following are the steps you take to configure the translation profile:

Step 1.   Create a translation rule to manipulate the called (DNIS) number.

```
Router(config)#voice translation-rule 1
Router(cfg-translation-rule)#rule 1 /^4085552/ /2/
```

Step 2.   Create a translation rule to manipulate the calling (ANI) number.

```
Router(config)#voice translation-rule 2
Router(cfg-translation-rule)#rule 1 /^.*/ /9&/ type subscriber
   subscriber
Router(cfg-translation-rule)#rule 2 /^.*/ /91&/ type national
   national
Router(cfg-translation-rule)#rule 3 /^.*/ /9011&/ type international
   international
```

Step 3.   Apply the rules to a translation profile.

```
Router(config)#voice translation-profile pstn-in
Router(cfg-translation-profile)#translate called 1
Router(cfg-translation-profile)#translate calling 2
```

Step 4.   Include the translation profile within a dial-peer definition.

```
Router(config)#dial-peer voice 111 POTS
Router(config-dial-peer)#translation-profile incoming pstn-in
```

Example 5-10 shows the complete configuration, which was previously described.

Example 5-10 *Voice Profile Example*

```
Router(config)#voice translation-rule 1
Router(cfg-translation-rule)#rule 1 /^4085552/ /2/
Router(cfg-translation-rule)#exit
Router(config)#voice translation-rule 2
Router(cfg-translation-rule)#rule 1 /^.*/ /9&/ type subscriber subscriber
Router(cfg-translation-rule)#rule 2 /^.*/ /91&/ type national national
Router(cfg-translation-rule)#rule 3 /^.*/ /9011&/ type international
  international
Router(cfg-translation-rule)#exit
Router(config)#voice translation-profile pstn-in
Router(cfg-translation-profile)#translate called 1
Router(cfg-translation-profile)#translate calling 2
```

The following procedure describes an inbound PSTN call example:

Step 1.   A PSTN user dials 1 408 555-2001 from 312 555-0123.

Step 2.   The gateway accepts the call and modifies the DNIS and ANI. The rule
/^4085552/ /2/ modifies the DNIS to 2001, and the rule /^.*/ /91&/ type
national national modifies the ANI to 913125550123.

Step 3.   The phone rings.

Voice Translation Profile Call Blocking Example

The following example, illustrated in Figure 5-18, shows a voice translation profile used
for call blocking. The only option for call blocking is in the incoming direction. From the
perspective of the gateway, the incoming direction can be either of these:

- Incoming from a telephony device directly attached to a voice port on the gateway toward the gateway itself

- Incoming by way of an inbound VoIP call from a peer gateway

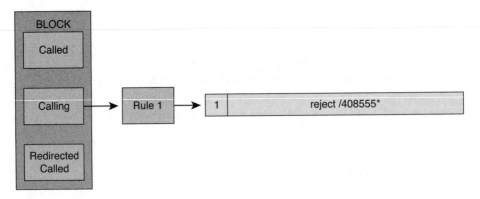

Figure 5-18   *Voice Translation Profile Call Blocking Example*

Following are the steps you take to configure call blocking:

Step 1.   Define a translation rule with a **reject** keyword.

```
Router(config)#voice translation-rule 1
Router(cfg-translation-rule)#rule 1 reject /408555*/
```

Step 2.   Apply the rule to a translation profile for calling numbers.

```
Router(config)#voice translation-profile block
Router(cfg-translation-profile)#translate calling 1
```

Step 3.   Include the translation profile within a dial-peer definition.

```
Router(config)#dial-peer voice 111 POTS
Router(config-dial-peer)#call-block translation-profile incoming block
Router(config-dial-peer)#call-block disconnect-cause incoming invalid-
number
```

In this call blocking example, the gateway blocks any incoming call that successfully matches inbound dial peer 111 and has a calling number that starts with 408555. A component of the **call block** command is the capability to return a disconnect cause. These values include **call-reject**, **invalid-number**, **unassigned-number**, and **user-busy**. When dial peer 111 matches a dialed string starting with 408555, it rejects the call and returns a disconnect cause of "invalid number" to the source of the call.

Example 5-11 shows the complete configuration, which was previously described.

Example 5-11 *Call Blocking Example*

```
Router(config)#voice translation-rule 1
Router(cfg-translation-rule)#rule 1 reject /408555*/
Router(cfg-translation-rule)#exit
Router(config)#voice translation-profile block
Router(cfg-translation-profile)#translate calling 1
Router(cfg-translation-profile)#exit
Router(config)#dial-peer voice 111 pots
Router(config-dial-peer)#call-block translation-profile incoming block
Router(config-dial-peer)#call-block disconnect-cause incoming invalid-number
```

Voice Translation Profiles Versus the dialplan-pattern Command

You can use voice translation profiles to replace the Cisco Unified Survivable Remote Site Telephony (Cisco SRST) and CUCME **dialplan-pattern** command. The **dialplan-pattern** command maps ephone-dns (that is, directory numbers assigned to IP phones in a CUCME environment) to inbound direct-inward dialing (DID) numbers. This mapping is done by dynamically creating a new dial peer that has the DID number of a phone as the destination pattern. This dial peer is also used for outbound calls to present the correct ANI and can be used to register the full DID number of an ephone with a gatekeeper.

Although this technique works for ephone-dns, other devices such as FXS ports and voice-mail pilots are not covered. At the same time, the **dialplan-pattern** command also increases the number of dial peers, which makes troubleshooting more complex.

To solve this problem, voice translation profiles can be used to fully replace the **dialplan-pattern** command, but other interactions need to be considered, such as gatekeeper registration issues.

Cisco Unified Communications Manager Express with dialplan-pattern Example

The topology shown in Figure 5-19 and the corresponding configuration in Example 5-12 show the caveats for the **dialplan-pattern** command.

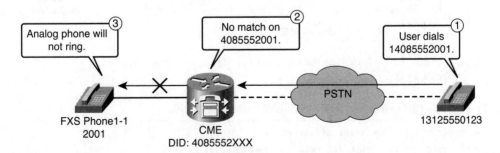

Figure 5-19 *CUCME with* **dialplan-pattern**

Example 5-12 dialplan-pattern *Command Example*

```
Router(config)#telephony-service
Router(config-telephony)#dialplan-pattern 1 4085552... extension-length 4
Router(config-telephony)#exit
Router(config)#dial-peer voice 2001 pots
Router(config-dial-peer)#destination-pattern 2001
Router(config-dial-peer)#port 1/0/0
```

The **dialplan-pattern** command dynamically creates another dial peer for each ephone-dn. Other devices, such as analog phones that are connected to FXS ports, are not covered. Thus, the analog phone dial peer still has a pattern of 2001.

The call flow example in Figure 5-19 illustrates the problem:

1. A PSTN user dials 1 408 555-2001.

2. The call is routed to Cisco Unified Communications Manager Express, which has a DID range of 4085552XXX. No match is found for DNIS 4085552001 because the dial peer has the pattern 2001.

3. The analog phone will not ring.

Cisco Unified Communications Manager Express with Voice Translation Profiles Example

The topology in Figure 5-20 and the corresponding configuration in Example 5-13 show how Cisco Unified Communications Manager Express is configured to use a voice translation profile instead of the **dialplan-pattern** command.

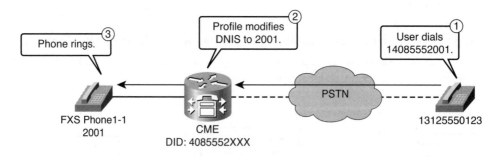

Figure 5-20 *Cisco Unified Communications Manager Express with Voice Translation Profiles*

Example 5-13 voice translation-profile *Command Example*

```
Router(config)#voice translation-rule 1
Router(cfg-translation-rule)#rule 1 /^4085552/ /2/
Router(cfg-translation-rule)#exit
```

```
Router(config)#voice translation-profile pstn-in
Router(cfg-translation-profile)#translate called 1
Router(config)#exit
Router(config-voice-port)#voice-port 0/0/0:23
Router(config-voice-port)#translation-profile incoming pstn-in
Router(config-voice-port)#dial-peer voice 2001 pots
Router(config-voice-port)#destination-pattern 2001
Router(config-voice-port)#port 1/0/0
```

Again, the hypothetical situation is repeated, but this time voice translation profiles are used.

Following are the steps in the successful call flow:

1. A PSTN user dials 1 408 555-2001.

2. The call is routed to Cisco Unified Communications Manager Express, which has a DID range of 4085552XXX. The voice translation profile modifies the DNIS to 2001, which matches the dial peer of Phone1-1.

3. The analog phone rings.

Note Depending on the deployment, using voice translation profiles instead of the **dialplan-pattern** command might be the preferred solution. With gatekeepers, using the **dialplan-pattern** command often leads to less-complex configurations, and thus a configuration with voice translation profiles combined with the **dialplan-pattern** command might be a better solution.

Verifying Voice Translation Rules

To test the functionality of a translation rule, use the **test voice translation-rule** command. The syntax is as follows:

```
Router#test voice translation-rule number input-test-string [type
 match-type [type match-type [plan match-type]]
```

This command applies the specified voice translation rule on the entered test string. Example 5-14 provides sample outputs from this command, given a voice translation rule configuration.

Example 5-14 test voice translation-rule *Command*

```
Router(config)#voice translation-rule 5
Router(cfg-translation-rule)#rule 1 /^201/ /102/
Router(cfg-translation-rule)#end
Router#test voice translation-rule 5 2015550101
```

```
Matched with rule 5
Original number:2015550101   Translated number:1025550101
Original number type: none    Translated number type: none
Original number plan: none    Translated number plan: none
```

The **show voice translation-rule** and **show voice translation-profile** commands can also be useful. Example 5-15 shows how to verify configured translation rules and profiles.

Example 5-15   show voice translation-rule *and* show voice translation-profile *Commands*

```
Router#show voice translation-rule 1
Translation-rule tag: 1


        Rule 1:
        Match pattern: ^555\(....\)
        Replace pattern: 444\1
        Match type: none              Replace type: none
        Match plan: none              Replace plan: none


        Rule 2:
        Match pattern: 777
        Replace pattern: 888
        Match type: national          Replace type: unknown
        Match plan: any               Replace plan: isdn

Router#show voice translation-profile
Translation Profile: mytranslation
        Rule for Calling number:
        Rule for Called number: 1
        Rule for Redirect number:
```

Configuring Digit Manipulation

The example illustrated in Figure 5-21 configures digit manipulation to meet the following network requirements.

- Sites should be able to call a remote site using just the extensions for that site.

- The PSTN should be used as a backup in case the WAN link is down or congested.

- Users should be able to contact 911 emergency services.

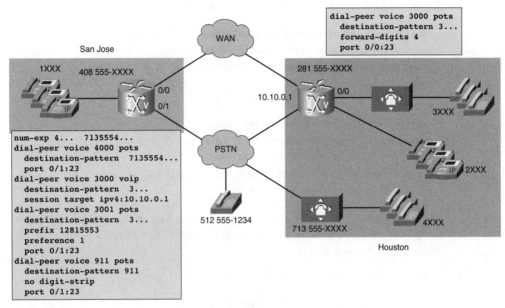

Figure 5-21   *Configuring Basic Digit Manipulation*

The following procedure illustrates how to implement digit manipulation.

- Configure the San Jose gateway to expand the dialed number when calling the 713 area code.

```
Router(config)#num-exp 4... 7135554...
Router(config)#dial-peer voice 4000 pots
Router(config-dial-peer)#destination-pattern 7135554...
Router(config-dial-peer)#port 0/1:23
```

Using the **num-exp** command in this example, the extension number 4... is expanded to 7135554... before an outbound dial peer is matched. For example, the user dials 4001, but the outbound dial peer 4000 is configured to match 7135554001.

- Configure the San Jose gateway to send all digits when a user dials 911.

```
Router(config)#dial-peer voice 911 pots
Router(config-dial-peer)#destination-pattern 911
```

```
Router(config-dial-peer)#no digit-strip
Router(config-dial-peer)#port 0/1:23
```

In this example, all three digits are required to process the call through the PSTN. You can use the **no digit-strip** command to send the appropriate three digits to the PSTN.

■ Configure a route to the 281 area code via the WAN.

```
Router(config)#dial-peer voice 3000 voip
Router(config-dial-peer)#destination pattern 3...
Router(config-dial-peer)#session target ipv4:10.10.0.1
```

■ Configure a PSTN backup to the 281 area code.

```
Router(config)#dial-peer voice 3001 pots
Router(config-dial-peer)#destination pattern 3...
Router(config-dial-peer)#prefix 12815553
Router(config-dial-peer)#preference 1
Router(config-dial-peer)#port 0/1:23
```

In this example, all ten digits are required to process the call through the PSTN. Use the **prefix** command to send the prefix numbers 2815553 before forwarding the three wildcard-matched digits.

■ Configure digit forwarding at the Houston gateway.

```
Router(config)#dial-peer voice 3000 pots
Router(config-dial-peer)#destination pattern 3...
Router(config-dial-peer)#forward-digits 4
Router(config-dial-peer)#port 0/0:23
```

In this example, using the **forward-digits** command allows the PBX to receive the proper number of digits to route the call to the appropriate extension.

Consider another example, as illustrated in Figure 5-22 and Example 5-16.

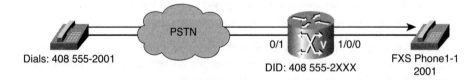

Figure 5-22   *Configuring Translation Rules*

Example 5-16 *Configuring Voice Translation Rules*

```
Router(config)#voice translation-rule 1
Router(cfg-translation-rule)#rule 1 /^4085552/ /2/
Router(cfg-translation-rule)#exit
Router(config)#voice translation-profile pstn-in
Router(cfg-translation-profile)#translate called 1
Router(cfg-translation-profile)#exit
Router(config)#voice-port 0/1:23
Router(config-voiceport)#translation-profile incoming pstn-in
Router(config-voiceport)#exit
Router(config)#dial-peer voice 2001 pots
Router(config-dial-peer)#destination-pattern 2001
Router(config-dial-peer)#port 1/0/0
```

This example shows how to configure digit manipulation using translation rules and profiles to allow an analog phone connected to an FXS port to be able to receive calls from the PSTN.

The following steps show how to configure digit manipulation to meet network requirements.

Step 1.   Configure a search-and-replace translation rule.

```
Router(config)#voice translation-rule 1
Router(cfg-translation-rule)#rule 1 /^4085552/ /2/
```

There are two types of rules:

Match-and-replace rule:

rule *precedence* */match-pattern/* */replace-pattern/* [**type** {*match-type*
  replace-type} [**plan** {*match-type replace-type*}]]

Reject rule:

rule *precedence* **reject** */match-pattern/* [**type** *match-type* [**plan** *match-type*]]

Step 2.   Create a voice translation profile and bind to it the translation rule created in Step 1.

```
Router(config)#voice translation-profile pstn-in
Router(cfg-translation-profile)#translate called 1
```

Note   To specify a translation profile for all incoming VoIP calls, use the **voip-incoming translation-profile** command in global configuration mode. To delete the profile, use the **no** form of this command.

Step 3.   Bind the translation profile to a voice port.

```
Router(config)#voice-port 0/1:23
Router(config-voiceport)#translation-profile incoming pstn-in
```

Step 4.   Configure the dial peer to match the appropriate extension of an analog phone.

```
Router(config)#dial-peer voice 2001 pots
Router(config-dial-peer)#destination-pattern 2001
Router(config-dial-peer)#port 1/0/0
```

In the sample configuration using the **translation-rule** command, the rule is defined to translate 4085552 into 2. The translation profile "pstn-in" notifies the router to translate incoming called numbers. It is applied as an inbound translation to the voice port that connects to the PSTN. The sample configuration replaces the inbound DNIS number and covers inbound and outbound routing of any dial peers.

Configuring Path Selection

Path selection is one of the most important aspects of a well-designed VoIP system. High availability is desirable, so there is usually more than one path for a call to take to its final destination. Multiple paths provide several benefits, including redundancy in case of a link failure or insufficient resources on that link and a reduction in toll costs of a call. This section introduces you to path selection strategies and tools.

Call Routing and Path Selection

The call-routing logic on Cisco IOS routers using the H.323 protocol relies on the dial-peer construct. Dial peers are similar to static routes. They define where calls originate and terminate and what path the calls take through the network. Dial peers are used to identify call source and destination endpoints and to define the characteristics applied to each call leg in a call connection. Attributes within the dial peer determine which dialed digits the router collects and forwards to telephony devices.

One of the keys to understanding call routing with dial peers is the concept of incoming versus outgoing call legs and, consequently, of incoming versus outgoing dial peers. Each call passing through a Cisco IOS router is considered to have two call legs, one entering the router and one exiting the router. The call leg entering the router is the incoming call leg, whereas the call leg exiting the router is the outgoing call leg.

Call legs can be of two main types:

■   Traditional time-division multiplexing (TDM) telephony call legs that connect a router to the PSTN, analog phones, or PBXs

■   IP call legs that connect a router to other gateways, gatekeepers, or Cisco UCM servers

Dial peers are also of two main types, according to the type of call leg with which they are associated:

- POTS dial peers, associated with traditional TDM telephony call legs

- VoIP dial peers, associated with IP call legs

Dial-Peer Matching

Routers must match the correct inbound and outbound dial peers to successfully complete a call. For all calls going through the router, Cisco IOS associates one dial peer to each call leg.

Figure 5-23 shows the following examples of different types of calls going through a Cisco IOS router:

- Call 1 is from another H.323 gateway across an IP network to a traditional PBX connected to the router (for example, via a PRI interface). For this call, an incoming VoIP dial peer and an outgoing POTS dial peer are selected.

- Call 2 is from an analog phone connected to an FXS port on the router to a UCM cluster across an IP network. For this call, an incoming POTS dial peer and an outgoing VoIP dial peer are selected by the router.

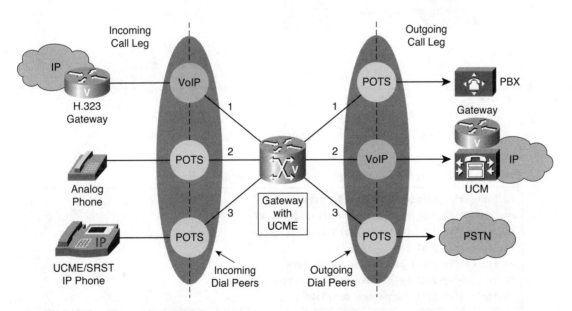

Figure 5-23 *Matching Dial Peers*

■   Call 3 is from an IP phone controlled by Cisco Unified CME or SRST to a PSTN in-
    terface on the router (for example, a PRI interface). For this call, an automatically gen-
    erated POTS dial peer (corresponding to the ephone configured on the router) and an
    outgoing POTS dial peer are selected.

It is important to understand that a Cisco IOS gateway performs dial-peer matching every
time it receives called-party information. For en bloc signaling, this is straightforward.
Specifically, the called-party information is used to find the best dial peer.

For digit-by-digit signaling, such as PSTNs with overlap sending and receiving, Cisco
Unified CME and SRST ephones, and FXS ports, the gateway performs dial-peer matching each time a digit is received.

For example, dial peers are configured on a gateway, as illustrated in Figure 5-24 and
Example 5-17.

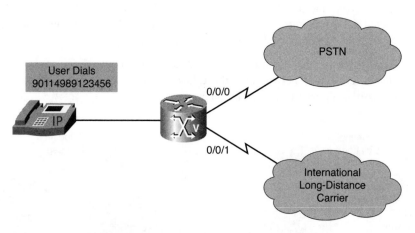

Figure 5-24   *Digit-by-Digit Signaling*

Example 5-17   *Digit-by-Digit Signaling Configuration*

```
Router(config)#dial-peer voice 90 pots
Router(config-dial-peer)#destination-pattern 9T
Router(config-dial-peer)#port 0/0/0:23
Router(config-dial-peer)#exit
Router(config)#dial-peer voice 90110 pots
Router(config-dial-peer)#destination-pattern 9011T
Router(config-dial-peer)#port 0/0/1:23
```

The following steps describe what occurs during the call in this example:

1.   A user wants to call the international number 90114989123456 and starts to dial.

2.   Because the first digit received is a 9, the gateway performs dial-peer matching.

3. Dial-peer 90 is matched, and any further digits are collected by the control character **T** that indicates the **destination-pattern** value is a variable-length dial string.

4. The user finishes dialing, and the call is routed using dial peer 90. Dial peer 90110 will never be considered.

For en bloc signaling, the DNIS is used, so the process is as follows:

1. A user wants to call the international number 90114989123456 and starts to dial.

2. Because en bloc signaling is enabled, the gateway continues to collect digits until the interdigit timeout value is exceeded.

3. The user finishes dialing, and the call is routed using dial peer 90110.

When matching the destination pattern, the Cisco IOS gateway performs a left-aligned match (that is, the pattern is matched with the beginning of the received string).

In the scenario illustrated in Figure 5-25 and Example 5-18, both dial peers match three digits when 555-1234 is the called number.

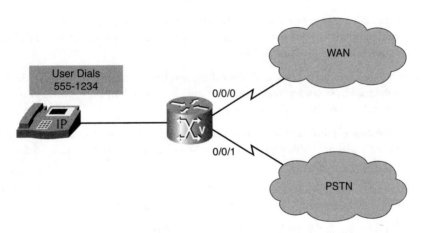

Figure 5-25 *Destination Pattern Matching*

Example 5-18 *Destination Pattern Matching Configuration*

```
Router(config)#dial-peer voice 1 pots
Router(config-dial-peer)#destination-pattern 555
Router(config-dial-peer)#port 0/0/0:23
Router(config-dial-peer)#exit
Router(config)#dial-peer voice 2 pots
Router(config-dial-peer)#destination-pattern 555....
Router(config-dial-peer)#port 0/0/1:23
```

If the first three digits of the called number are 555, dial peer 1 will be matched because it explicitly matches the called number. The rest of the digits will not be processed.

Matching to Inbound and Outbound Dial Peers

When a Cisco IOS gateway routes a call, the inbound and outbound dial peers need to be matched. The gateway will search through all dial peers and apply matching criteria. After a dial peer has been matched, the gateway selects it as the inbound or outbound dial peer.

To match incoming call legs to incoming dial peers, the router selects a dial peer by matching the information elements in the setup message (called number/DNIS and calling number/ANI) with four configurable dial-peer attributes.

Inbound Dial-Peer Matching

Inbound dial-peer matching is prioritized as follows:

1.   If the called number (that is, the DNIS) matches with the **incoming called-number** configuration on a dial peer, this dial peer will be selected as the inbound dial peer. No further matching is performed.

2.   If no dial peer has been found, the calling number (that is, the ANI) is checked. If the **answer-address** configuration of a dial peer is matched, this dial peer will be selected, and no further matching is performed.

3.   If the calling number (the ANI) matches with the **destination-pattern** configuration of a dial peer, this dial peer will be selected, and no further matching is performed.

4.   If none of the previous attempts was successful and the call is inbound on a POTS port, a dial peer with a matching voice port configuration is searched.

5.   If still no match is found, the default dial peer 0 is used.

> **Note** Default dial-peer matching is not desirable because default call characteristics might not be what you want.

The router needs to match only one of these conditions. It is not necessary for all the attributes to be configured in the dial peer or that every attribute match the call setup information. The router stops searching as soon as one dial peer is matched, and the call is routed according to the configured dial-peer attributes. Even if other dial peers exist that would match, only the first match is used.

Note   A typical misconception about inbound dial-peer matching is that the **session-target** of a dial peer is used. This is not true. Instead, use the **incoming called-number** or **answer-address** command to ensure that the correct inbound dial peer is selected.

Outbound Dial-Peer Matching

How the router selects an outbound dial peer depends on whether DID is configured in the inbound POTS dial peer:

■   If DID is not configured in the inbound POTS dial peer, the router collects the incoming dialed string digit-by-digit and compares these digits to configured destination patterns. After an inbound dial peer is matched, the gateway plays a second dial tone to the caller and waits for the caller to enter additional digits. This is referred to as *two-stage dialing*. As soon as a dial peer fully matches the destination pattern, the router immediately routes the call using the configured attributes in the matching dial peer.

■   If DID is configured in the inbound POTS dial peer, the router uses the full incoming dial string to match the destination pattern in the outbound dial peer. This is known as *one-stage dialing*. With DID, the setup message contains all the digits necessary to route a call, so no additional digit collection is required. If more than one dial peer matches the dial string, all the matching dial peers are used to form a hunt group. The router attempts to place the outbound call leg using all of the dial peers in the hunt group until one is successful.

Outbound dial-peer matching is prioritized as follows by default:

1.   The gateway searches through all dial peers and tries to match the called number (the DNIS) with the **destination-pattern** configuration. The dial peer with the closest match is selected.

2.   If multiple equal matches are found, the dial peer with the lowest-preference configuration wins.

3.   If equal preferences are found, a random dial peer is selected.

Dial-Peer Call Routing and Path Selection Commands

Table 5-6 shows commands used to configure ANI and DNIS matching on dial peers.

Table 5-7 shows commands used to configure direct-inward-dial, dial-peer preferences, and outbound status checks.

Table 5-6　*ANI and DNIS Matching on Dial Peers*

Command	Description
destination-pattern [+]*string*[T]	Use this command in dial-peer configuration mode to specify either the prefix or the full E.164 telephone number to be used for a dial peer. To disable the configured prefix or telephone number, use the **no** form of this command. The following characters can be used: • Asterisk (*) and pound sign (#) that appear on standard touch-tone dial pads. • Comma (,), which inserts a pause between digits. • Period (.), which matches any entered digit. (This character is used as a wildcard.) • Percent sign (%), which indicates that the preceding digit occurred zero or more times, similar to the wildcard usage. • Plus sign (+), which indicates that the preceding digit occurred one or more times. **Note:** This plus sign has a different purpose than the plus sign in front of a digit string, which is used to indicate that the string is an E.164 standard number. • Circumflex (^), which indicates a match to the beginning of the string. • Dollar sign ($), which matches the null string at the end of the input string. • Backslash symbol (\), which is followed by a single character and matches that character; can be used with a single character with no other significance (matching that character). • Question mark (?), which indicates that the preceding digit occurred zero or one times. • Brackets ([ ]), which indicate a range (a sequence of characters enclosed in the brackets); only numeric characters from 0 to 9 are allowed in the range. • Parentheses (( )), which indicate a pattern and are the same as the regular expression rule.

Table 5-6   *ANI and DNIS Matching on Dial Peers*

Command	Description
incoming called-number [+]*string*[T]	Use this command in dial-peer configuration mode to specify a digit string that can be matched by an incoming call to associate the call with a dial peer. To reset to the default, use the **no** form of this command.
answer-address [+]*string*[T]	Use this command in dial-peer configuration mode to specify the full E.164 telephone number to be used to identify the dial peer of an incoming call. To disable the configured telephone number, use the **no** form of this command.

Table 5-7   *Direct-Inward-Dial and Dial-Peer Matching Commands*

Command	Description
direct-inward-dial	Use this command in dial-peer configuration mode to enable the DID call treatment for an incoming called number. When this feature is enabled, the incoming call is treated as if the digits were received from the DID trunk. The called number is used to select the outgoing dial peer. No dial tone is presented to the caller.
preference *value*	Use this command in dial-peer configuration mode to indicate the preferred order of a dial peer within a hunt group. The *value* variable can be a value in the range of 0 through 10. To remove the preference, use the **no** form of this command. The default is 0 and is not displayed in a configuration.
no dial-peer outbound status-check pots	Use this command in privileged EXEC mode to check the status of outbound POTS dial peers during call setup and to disallow, for that call, any dial peers whose status is down. This might be required on some ISDN links where the CO ISDN switch activates the ISDN layer only if activity is detected on the link.

Matching Dial Peers in a Hunt Group

By default, dial peers in a hunt group are selected according to the following criteria, in the order listed:

1. **Longest match in phone number:** This method selects the destination pattern that matches the greatest number of dialed digits. For example, if one dial peer is configured with a dial string of 345.... and a second dial peer is configured with 3456789, the router would first select 3456789 because it has the longest explicit match of the two dial peers.

2. **Explicit preference:** This method uses the priority configured with the **preference** dial-peer command. The lower the preference number, the higher the priority. The highest priority is given to the dial peer with preference order 0. If the same preference is defined in multiple dial peers with the same destination pattern, a dial peer is selected randomly.

3. **Random selection:** In this method, all destination patterns are weighted equally.

You can change this default selection order or choose different methods for hunting dial peers by using the **dial-peer hunt** global configuration command. Dial-peer hunt options include the following:

- **0:** Longest match in phone number, explicit preference, random selection; the default hunt order number

- **1:** Longest match in phone number, explicit preference, least recent use

- **2:** Explicit preference, longest match in phone number, random selection

- **3:** Explicit preference, longest match in phone number, least recent use

- **4:** Least recent use, longest match in phone number, explicit preference

- **5:** Least recent use, explicit preference, longest match in phone number

- **6:** Random selection

- **7:** Least recent use

H.323 Dial-Peer Configuration Best Practices

To illustrate best practice procedures when configuring H.323 dial peers on a Cisco IOS router, consider Figure 5-26 and the corresponding dial-peer configuration shown in Example 5-19. In the example, dial peer 1 is used to route calls according to their DNIS, and dial peers 100 and 101 are used to route calls to the primary UCM server, unless it has lost connectivity, and then to use the backup, or secondary, UCM server.

Example 5-19 *Best Practice Dial-Peer Configuration*

```
Router(config)#dial-peer voice 1 pots
Router(config-dial-peer)#incoming called-number .
```

```
Router(config-dial-peer)#direct-inward-dial
Router(config-dial-peer)#exit
Router(config)#dial-peer voice 100 voip
Router(config-dial-peer)#preference 1
Router(config-dial-peer)#destination-pattern 1...
Router(config-dial-peer)#session target ipv4:10.10.10.2
Router(config-dial-peer)#exit
Router(config)#dial-peer voice 101 voip
Router(config-dial-peer)#preference 2
Router(config-dial-peer)#destination-pattern 1...
Router(config-dial-peer)#session target ipv4:10.10.10.3
```

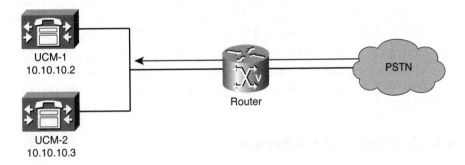

Figure 5-26   *Dial-Peer Best Practice Sample Topology*

The previous figure and example illustrate the following best practice procedures:

■ To ensure that incoming PSTN calls are directly routed to their destination based on the DNIS information, create a default POTS dial peer with the **direct-inward-dial** attribute.

Note   This should be the first POTS dial peer that you configure on the gateway. It should be the only dial peer that contains a "." for the destination pattern and direct inward dial. It should not contain a port number.

■ When using the router as an H.323 gateway connected to a Cisco UCM cluster, provide redundancy by configuring at least two VoIP dial peers with the same destination pattern pointing to two different UCM servers. Use the **preference** attribute to select the priority order between primary and secondary UCM servers.

Path Selection Strategies

When remote sites are involved, different path selection strategies are required. Multisite dial plans include all the requirements of a single-site dial plan, as well as the following requirements:

- **Site-code dialing:** A typical requirement is the support of site-code dialing. Site-code dialing allows users to place an intersite call by dialing a site code that is typically three to four digits long followed by the actual extension of the remote site user. Call routing and path selection can support this by using digit manipulation to prefix and strip off site codes where necessary.

- **Toll-bypass:** Toll-bypass uses the WAN link for call routing to avoid PSTN charges for intersite calls. This includes call routing and path selection for the actual call-routing process, including fallback PSTN routing in case the WAN link fails. Again, digit manipulation is also required to ensure proper number formatting.

- **TEHO:** Tail-End Hop-Off (TEHO) is similar to toll-bypass but extends the WAN usage for PSTN calls as well. The PSTN breakout should be as close as possible to the final PSTN destination to decrease phone charges. The same requirements exist as with toll-bypass.

Site-Code Dialing and Toll-Bypass

When you use site-code dialing, each site is assigned with a unique site code. For example, a network with three sites could have the site codes 801, 802, and 803. If a user wants to place a call to a remote site user, the dialed number would be the site code followed by the actual extension. This form of abbreviated dialing greatly improves the end-user experience because of shorter dialable numbers.

The calling-party number, also referred to as ANI, needs to include the appropriate site code. This allows called users to call back directly using their missed-calls and received-calls directory. You can use digit manipulation to support this as well.

You might also use site-code dialing to solve issues with overlapping numbering plans. Because all extensions of a site are prefixed with a unique site code, an overlapping numbering plan (where extensions in multiple sites overlap) can be turned into a unique numbering plan.

Toll-Bypass Example

The example illustrated in Figure 5-27 and Example 5-20 shows the concepts of call routing and path selection in a toll-bypass scenario.

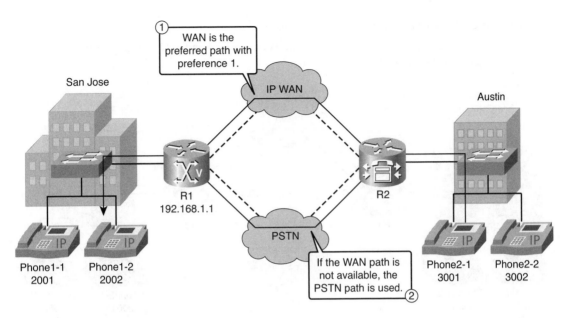

Figure 5-27   *Toll-Bypass Topology Example*

Example 5-20   *Toll-Bypass Configuration Example*

```
R2(config)#dial-peer voice 21 voip
R2(config-dial-peer)#destination-pattern 2...
R2(config-dial-peer)#preference 1
R2(config-dial-peer)#session-target ipv4:192.168.1.1
R2(config-dial-peer)#exit
R2(config)#dial-peer voice 22 pots
R2(config-dial-peer)#destination-pattern 2...
R2(config-dial-peer)#prefix 14085552
R2(config-dial-peer)#preference 2
R2(config-dial-peer)#port 0/0/0:23
```

Figure 5-27 shows a scenario with two sites, San Jose and Austin. The Austin Cisco Unified CME gateway is configured to route calls to San Jose primarily over the WAN, and if the WAN link fails, the PSTN link should be used.

The first dial-peer configuration is used to route calls that match the **destination-pattern 2...** command to San Jose using the IP WAN. Because the dial peer is configured with a preference of **1**, it is preferred over the PSTN dial peer with a preference of **2**.

The second dial-peer configuration is used to route calls that match the **destination-pattern 2...** command to San Jose using the PSTN. The preference of **2** makes this dial peer inferior to dial peer 21 with a preference of **1**.

Site-Code Dialing and Toll-Bypass Example

The example illustrated in Figure 5-28 and Examples 5-21 and 5-22 shows a scenario for site-code dialing and toll-bypass.

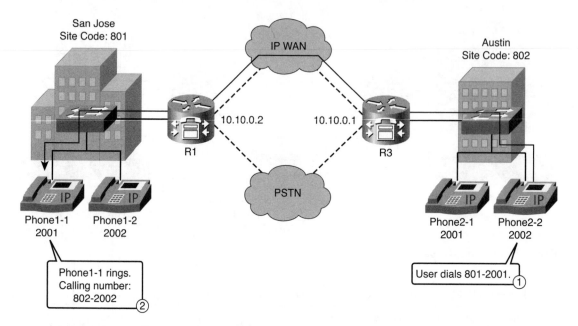

Figure 5-28   *Site-Code Dialing and Toll-Bypass Topology Example*

Example 5-21   *Site-Code Dialing and Toll-Bypass Example—R1's Configuration*

```
R1(config)#dial-peer voice 802 voip
R1(config-dial-peer)#destination-pattern 802....
R1(config-dial-peer)#session target ipv4:10.10.0.1
```

Example 5-22   *Site-Code Dialing and Toll-Bypass Example—R3's Configuration*

```
R3(config)#dial-peer voice 801 voip
R3(config-dial-peer)#destination-pattern 801....
R3(config-dial-peer)#session target ipv4:10.10.0.2
```

Figure 5-28 shows a sample scenario for site-code dialing combined with toll-bypass. San Jose has the site code 801, and Austin uses the site code 802. Also note that both sites use extensions in the range of 2XXX. This is a typical overlapping numbering plan. Following is the process the call goes through in this example:

1.   A user in Austin wants to place a call to Phone1-1. Because Phone1-1 resides in San Jose and has the site code 801, the user dials 801-2001 (that is, the site code 801 followed by the extension 2001).

2. The call is routed over the IP WAN link to San Jose. Phone1-1 rings and displays the calling number 802-2002 (that is, the site code 802 of Austin followed by the extension of Phone2-2, which is 2002).

Tail-End Hop-Off

Tail-End Hop-Off (TEHO) extends the concept of toll-bypass. Instead of only routing intersite calls over an IP WAN link, TEHO also uses the IP WAN link for PSTN calls. The goal is to route a call using the IP WAN as close to the final PSTN destination as possible. As with toll-bypass, PSTN fallback should always be possible in case the IP WAN link fails.

Note   Some countries do not allow TEHO. When implementing TEHO, ensure that the deployment complies with national legal requirements.

TEHO Example

Figure 5-29 shows the TEHO scenario for this example.

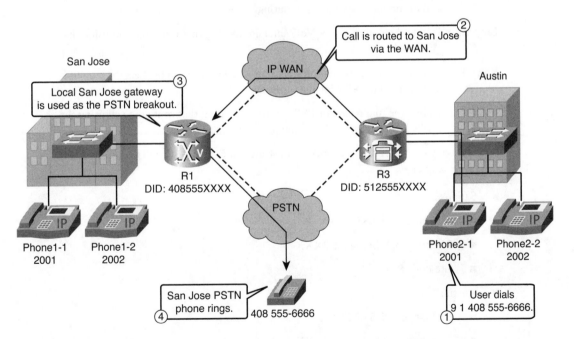

Figure 5-29   *TEHO Scenario*

Here is the process the call goes through:

1. Phone2-1 dials 9 1 408 555-6666 (that is, it places a call to a PSTN phone located in San Jose).

2. The call is routed to San Jose using the IP WAN link.

3. The local San Jose voice gateway is used to route the call as a local call to the San Jose PSTN.

4. The San Jose PSTN phone rings.

Configuring Site-Code Dialing and Toll-Bypass

To demonstrate the configuration of site-code dialing and toll-bypass, the following example walks through a configuration that meets these requirements:

■ All calls from Austin to San Jose should be routed using the WAN link if possible. If the WAN link fails, the PSTN link should be used.

■ Site codes must be used for intersite dialing.

Follow these steps to configure site-code dialing and toll-bypass:

Step 1. Configure voice translation rules and voice translation profiles for inbound and outbound VoIP intersite routing.

Step 2. Define the dial peers for VoIP intersite routing that route the call using the WAN link.

Step 3. Configure voice translation rules and voice translation profiles for inbound and outbound PSTN intersite routing.

Step 4. Define the dial peers for PSTN intersite routing that route the call using the PSTN link in case the WAN link is not available.

The following configuration scenario, as illustrated in Figure 5-30, will be used throughout this example:

■ San Jose:

■ DID range 408 555-2XXX

■ Directory number range 2XXX

■ Site code 801

■ Austin:

■ DID range 312 555-2XXX

■ Directory number range 2XXX

■ Site code 802

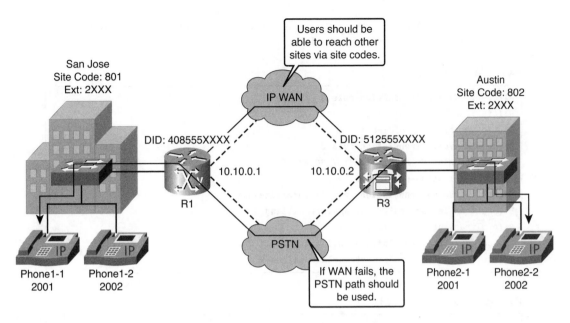

Figure 5-30 *Site-Code Dialing and Toll-Bypass Topology Example*

Step 1: Create Translation Rules and Profiles

To create translation rules and profiles for intersite routing and path selection via the WAN, you can use the following procedure.

For each site:

Step 1.   Create a rule that prefixes the site code to the calling number.

Step 2.   Create a rule that strips off the site code from the called number.

Step 3.   Create a voice translation profile to prefix the site code to the outbound calling-party number.

Step 4.   Create a voice translation profile to strip off the site code from the inbound called-party number.

Examples 5-23 and 5-24 provide the resulting configurations on the San Jose router (that is, R1) and the Austin router (that is, R3).

Example 5-23 *Step 1: R1*

```
R1(config)#voice translation-rule 1
R1(cfg-translation-rule)#rule 1 /^2/ /8012/
R1(cfg-translation-rule)#exit
R1(config)#voice translation-rule 2
R1(cfg-translation-rule)#rule 1 /^8012/ /2/
R1(cfg-translation-rule)#exit
R1(config)#voice translation-profile intersite-out
R1(cfg-translation-profile)#translate calling 1
R1(cfg-translation-profile)#exit
R1(config)#voice translation-profile intersite-in
R1(cfg-translation-profile)#translate called 2
```

Example 5-24 *Step 1: R3*

```
R3(config)#voice translation-rule 1
R3(cfg-translation-rule)#rule 1 /^2/ /8022/
R3(cfg-translation-rule)#exit
R3(config)#voice translation-rule 2
R3(cfg-translation-rule)#rule 1 /^8022/ /2/
R3(cfg-translation-rule)#exit
R3(config)#voice translation-profile intersite-out
R3(cfg-translation-profile)#translate calling 1
R3(cfg-translation-profile)#exit
R3(config)#voice translation-profile intersite-in
R3(cfg-translation-profile)#translate called 2
```

Step 2: Define VoIP Dial Peers

After you configure the voice translation profiles for VoIP routing, you need to define the VoIP dial peers for intersite routing via the WAN. Examples 5-25 and 5-26 provide the configurations for this example.

Example 5-25 *Step 2: R1*

```
R1(config)#dial-peer voice 8021 voip
R1(config-dial-peer)#destination-pattern 8022...
R1(config-dial-peer)#session-target ipv4:10.10.0.2
R1(config-dial-peer)#translation-profile incoming intersite-in
R1(config-dial-peer)#translation-profile outgoing  intersite-out
```

Example 5-26 *Step 2: R3*

```
R3(config)#dial-peer voice 8011 voip
R3(config-dial-peer)#destination-pattern 8012...
R3(config-dial-peer)#session-target ipv4:10.10.0.1
R3(config-dial-peer)#translation-profile incoming intersite-in
R3(config-dial-peer)#translation-profile outgoing intersite-out
```

Note   The same dial peer is used for both inbound and outbound call routing.

Step 3: Add Support for PSTN Fallback

To support PSTN fallback routing in case the WAN link fails, you need to configure an additional voice translation rule and profile:

- This voice translation rule replaces the 801 site code with the PSTN dialable number, 1408555:

  ```
  R3(config)#voice translation-rule 3
  R3(cfg-translation-rule)#rule 1 /^8012/ /14085552/
  ```

- To modify the called number for outbound calls to a PSTN routable format, use the following voice translation profile configuration:

  ```
  R3(config)#voice translation-profile 801PSTN
  R3(cfg-translation- profile)#translate called 3
  ```

Examples 5-27 and 5-28 show the resulting configurations for the San Jose and Austin routers in this example.

Example 5-27 *Step 3: R1*

```
R1(config)#voice translation-rule 3
R1(cfg-translation-rule)#rule 1 /^8022/ /15125552/
R1(cfg-translation-rule)#exit
R1(config)#voice translation-profile 802PSTN
R1(cfg-translation-profile)#translate called 3
```

Example 5-28 *Step 3: R3*

```
R3(config)#voice translation-rule 3
R3(cfg-translation-rule)#rule 1 /^8012/ /14085552/
R3(cfg-translation-rule)#exit
```

```
R3(config)#voice translation-profile 801PSTN
R3(cfg-translation-profile)#translate called 3
```

Step 4: Create a Dial Peer for PSTN Fallback

Finally, you create the PSTN fallback dial peer. Examples 5-29 and 5-30 show these configurations for this example.

Example 5-29   *Step 4: R1*

```
R1(config)#dial-peer voice 8022 pots
R1(config-dial-peer)#destination-pattern 8022...
R1(config-dial-peer)#port 0/0/0:23
R1(config-dial-peer)#preference 1
R1(config-dial-peer)#translation-profile outgoing 802PSTN
```

Example 5-30   *Step 4: R3*

```
R3(config)#dial-peer voice 8012 pots
R3(config-dial-peer)#destination-pattern 8012...
R3(config-dial-peer)#port 0/0/0:23
R3(config-dial-peer)#preference 1
R3(config-dial-peer)#translation-profile outgoing 801PSTN
```

Note   The PSTN dial peer has a preference of 1, so it is the last dial peer that will be used when routing a call to San Jose. The called number will be translated into the PSTN routable format of 1408555XXXX after the dial peer has been matched.

Outbound Site-Code Dialing Example

To illustrate an outbound site-code dialing call flow, consider the topology presented in Figure 5-31 and its corresponding configuration in Example 5-31.

Example 5-31   *Outbound Site-Code Dialing Configuration Example*

```
R3(config)#voice translation-rule 1
R3(cfg-translation-rule)#rule 1 /^2/ /8022/
R3(cfg-translation-rule)#exit
R3(config)#voice translation-profile intersite-out
R3(cfg-translation-profile)#translate calling 1
R3(cfg-translation-profile)#exit
R3(config)#dial-peer voice 8010 voip
R3(config-dial-peer)#destination-pattern 8012...
R3(config-dial-peer)#session-target ipv4:10.10.0.1
```

```
R3(config-dial-peer)#translation-profile outgoing intersite-out
R3(config-dial-peer)#exit
R3(config)#voice translation-rule 3
R3(cfg-translation-rule)#rule 1 /^8012/ /14085552/
R3(cfg-translation-rule)#exit
R3(config)#voice translation-profile 801PSTN
R3(cfg-translation-profile)#translate called 3
R3(cfg-translation-profile)#exit
R3(config)#dial-peer voice 8011 pots
R3(config-dial-peer)#destination-pattern 8012...
R3(config-dial-peer)#preference 1
R3(config-dial-peer)#port 0/0/0:23
R3(config-dial-peer)#translation-profile outgoing 801PSTN
```

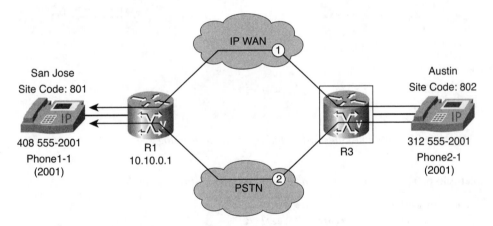

Figure 5-31 *Outbound Site-Code Dialing Topology Example*

Following are the specific steps that are involved in this example:

1. Phone2-1 in Austin dials 801-2001 (that is, it places a call to San Jose Phone1-1). The incoming called number, or DNIS, is 801-2001 and the calling number, or ANI, is 2001. The called number matches two dial peers: 8010 and 8011. Dial peer 8011 is matched because it has the best preference, and the **translation-profile outgoing intersite-out** command is applied because this is an outbound call. Thus, the call is routed to San Jose with DNIS 8012001 and ANI 8022001.

2. If the WAN fails, the call will be routed using dial peer 8011 with preference 1 configured. The translation-profile 801 PSTN is used, which modifies the DNIS to 14085552001 (that is, the call can be routed by the PSTN to San Jose). Note that the ANI is modified using the global voice translation profiles configured on the voice port, which are used for all PSTN calls.

Note In addition to the digit manipulation used for site-code dialing, global voice translation profiles configured on the voice port are used.

Inbound Site-Code Dialing Example

To illustrate an inbound site-code dialing call flow, consider the topology presented in Figure 5-32 and its corresponding configuration in Example 5-32.

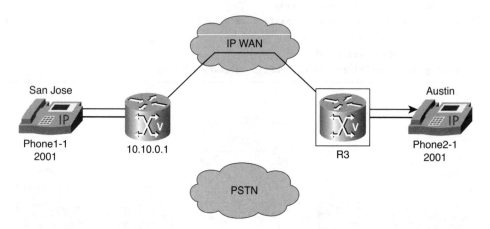

Figure 5-32 *Inbound Site-Code Dialing Example Topology*

Example 5-32 *Inbound Site-Code Dialing Configuration Example*

```
R3(config)#voice translation-rule 2
R3(cfg-translation-rule)#rule 1 /^8022/ /2/
R3(cfg-translation-rule)#exit
R3(config)#voice translation-profile intersite-in
R3(cfg-translation-profile)#translate called 2
R3(cfg-translation-profile)#exit
R3(config)#dial-peer voice 8010 voip
R3(config)#destination-pattern 8012...
R3(config)#session-target ipv4:10.10.0.1
R3(config)#translation-profile incoming intersite-in
```

The same VoIP dial peers can be used for both inbound and outbound calls. Because the gateway in San Jose is also configured to prefix the site code to the calling number for calls to Austin, the inbound calling number to Austin matches the destination pattern of the San Jose dial peers. The inbound translation profile then strips off the Austin 802 site code from the inbound called number, and the call can be routed to Phone2-1 in Austin.

Configuring TEHO

You can complete the following tasks to configure TEHO:

Step 1. Define the VoIP outbound digit manipulation.

Step 2. Define the outbound VoIP dial peer.

Step 3. Define the outbound POTS dial peer.

To illustrate the configuration of TEHO, consider the scenario whose topology is presented in Figure 5-33.

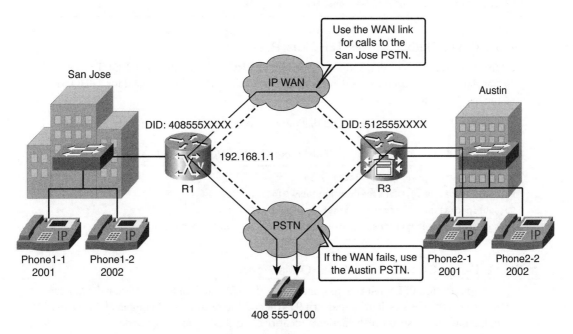

Figure 5-33 *TEHO Configuration Scenario Topology*

The design requirements for this scenario are as follows:

■ San Jose: Local PSTN numbering range: 408XXXXXXX

■ Austin: Local PSTN numbering range: 512XXXXXXX

All calls from Austin to the San Jose PSTN should be routed using the WAN link if possible. If the WAN link fails, the PSTN link should be used.

To ensure that the correct ANI is presented for TEHO calls, a SJC-TEHO-OUT voice translation profile should be configured and attached to both dial peers used for TEHO to the San Jose site.

Step 1: Define VoIP Outbound Digit Manipulation for TEHO

Example 5-33 shows the configuration to define digit manipulation for TEHO on router R3 in this scenario.

Example 5-33 *Step 1: Defining VoIP Outbound Digit Manipulation for TEHO*

```
R3(config)#voice translation-rule 10
R3(cfg-translation-rule)#rule 1 /^2/ /15125552/
R3(cfg-translation-rule)#exit
R3(config)#voice translation-profile SJC-TEHO-OUT
R3(cfg-translation- profile)#translate calling 10
```

Step 2: Define Outbound VoIP TEHO Dial Peer

To ensure that the correct ANI is presented for TEHO calls, an SJC-TEHO-OUT voice translation profile is configured and attached to both VoIP dial peers used for TEHO to the San Jose site.

Example 5-34 defines an outbound dial peer on router R3 that routes calls to San Jose.

Example 5-34 *Step 2: Defining an Outbound VoIP TEHO Dial Peer*

```
R3(config)#dial-peer voice 914081 voip
R3(config-dial-peer)#destination-pattern 91408.......
R3(config-dial-peer)#session-target ipv4:192.168.1.1
R3(config-dial-peer)#translation-profile outgoing SJC-TEHO-OUT
```

Step 3: Define Outbound POTS TEHO Dial Peer

To support pure PSTN fallback routing in case the WAN link fails, an additional dial peer is configured. The **destination-pattern 91408** and the **prefix 1408** commands, as shown in Example 5-35, strip off the national identifier and the San Jose area code.

Example 5-35 *Step 3: Defining an Outbound POTS TEHO Dial Peer*

```
R3(config)#dial-peer voice 914083 pots
R3(config-dial-peer)#destination-pattern 91408.......
R3(config-dial-peer)#prefix 1408
R3(config-dial-peer)#preference 1
R3(config-dial-peer)#port 0/0/0:23
```

Note The **prefix** command could also be replaced by the **forward-digits** command or a voice translation profile.

Complete TEHO Configuration

As a reference, Example 5-36 provides the full TEHO configuration on router R3.

Example 5-36 *TEHO Complete Configuration*

```
R3#show running-config
... OUTPUT OMITTED ...
voice translation-rule 10
 rule 1 /^2/ /13125552/
voice translation-profile SJC-TEHO-OUT
 translate calling 10
dial-peer voice 914081 voip
 destination-pattern 91408.......
 session-target ipv4:192.168.1.1
 translation-profile outgoing SJC-TEHO-OUT
dial-peer voice 914083 pots
 destination-pattern 91408.......
 prefix 1408
 preference 1
 port 0/0/0:23
... OUTPUT OMITTED ...
```

Implementing Calling Privileges on Cisco IOS Gateways

Calling privileges on Cisco IOS gateways are dial plan components that define the types of calls that a phone, or group of phones, is able to place. This section describes the concept of calling privileges and how they can be implemented on Cisco IOS gateways using Class of Restriction (COR).

Calling Privileges

COR is a Cisco voice gateway feature that enables Class of Service (CoS), or calling privileges, to be assigned. It is most commonly used with Cisco Unified SRST and Cisco Unified CME but can be applied to any dial peer.

The COR feature provides the capability to deny certain call attempts based on the incoming and outgoing CORs provisioned on the dial peers.

COR is used to specify which incoming dial peer can use which outgoing dial peer to make a call. Each dial peer can be provisioned with an incoming and an outgoing COR list. COR functionality provides the capability to deny certain call attempts on the basis of the incoming and outgoing CORs that are provisioned on the dial peers. This functionality provides flexibility in network design, allows users to block calls (for example, calls to 900 numbers), and applies different restrictions to call attempts from different originators.

Figure 5-34 shows a route plan consisting of multiple PSTN dial peers, ready for COR.

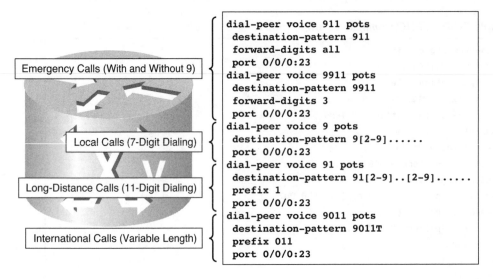

```
dial-peer voice 911 pots
 destination-pattern 911
 forward-digits all
 port 0/0/0:23
dial-peer voice 9911 pots
 destination-pattern 9911
 forward-digits 3
 port 0/0/0:23
dial-peer voice 9 pots
 destination-pattern 9[2-9]......
 port 0/0/0:23
dial-peer voice 91 pots
 destination-pattern 91[2-9]..[2-9]......
 prefix 1
 port 0/0/0:23
dial-peer voice 9011 pots
 destination-pattern 9011T
 prefix 011
 port 0/0/0:23
```

Emergency Calls (With and Without 9)

Local Calls (7-Digit Dialing)

Long-Distance Calls (11-Digit Dialing)

International Calls (Variable Length)

Figure 5-34 *Calling Privileges*

The 911 dial peer is used for emergency calls to the PSTN. Notice the **forward-digits all** command, which sends all matched digits (911 in this case) to the PSTN. Without this command, the dial peer would be matched, but no digits would be sent to the PSTN because of the default **digit-strip** command.

The 9911 dial peer is also used for emergency calls, but this time it also includes the PSTN access code 9. Note that only three digits are sent to the PSTN using the **forward-digits 3** command, because the PSTN access code 9 must not be included in the call setup.

The 9 dial peer is used for PSTN local calls for seven-digit dialing in the United States.

The 91 dial peer is used for PSTN national or long-distance calls for 11-digit dialing in the United States. Because the exactly matched digits are 91, the national identifier 1 needs to be prefixed. This is done using the **prefix 1** command.

The 9011 dial peer is used for PSTN variable-length international calls from the United States. Because 9011 will be stripped because of the **digit-strip** setting, the **prefix 011** command is used to prefix the correct international identifier to the called number.

Understanding COR on Cisco IOS Gateways

The fundamental mechanism at the center of the COR functionality relies on the definition of incoming and outgoing COR lists. Each COR list is defined to include a number of members, which are tags previously defined within Cisco IOS. Multiple CORs are defined, and COR lists are configured that contain these CORs. Each COR list is then assigned to dial peers as an incoming or outgoing COR list.

When a call goes through the router, an incoming dial peer and an outgoing dial peer are selected based on the Cisco IOS dial-peer routing logic. If COR lists are associated with the selected dial peers, the following additional check is performed before extending the call:

- If the COR applied on an incoming dial peer (for incoming calls) is a superset of or equal to the COR applied to the outgoing dial peer (for outgoing calls), the call goes through.

- If the COR applied on an incoming dial peer (for incoming calls) is *not* a superset of or equal to the COR applied to the outgoing dial peer (for outgoing calls), the call is rejected.

Note   *Incoming* and *outgoing* are terms used with respect to the voice ports. For example, if you hook up a phone to one of the FXS ports of a router and try to make a call from that phone, it is an incoming call for the router/voice port. Similarly, if you make a call to that FXS phone, it is an outgoing call.

If no COR list statements are applied to some dial peers, the following properties apply:

- When no incoming COR list is configured on a dial peer, the default incoming COR list is used. The default incoming COR list has the highest possible priority, and it therefore allows this dial peer to access all other dial peers, regardless of their outgoing COR list.

- When no outgoing COR list is configured on a dial peer, the default outgoing COR list is used. The default outgoing COR list has the lowest possible priority, and it therefore allows all other dial peers to access this dial peer, regardless of their incoming COR list.

COR Behavior Example

Figure 5-35 shows the behavior of COR.

The VoIP dial peer is associated with the c1 incoming COR list, with members A, B, and C. You can think of members of the incoming COR list as "keys."

The first POTS dial peer has a destination pattern of 1... and is associated with the c2 outgoing COR list, with members A and B. The second POTS dial peer has a destination pattern of 2.. and is associated with the c3 outgoing COR list, with members A, B, and D. You can think of members of the outgoing COR lists as "locks."

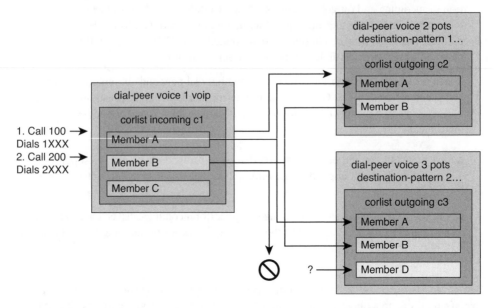

Figure 5-35 *COR Behavior*

For the call to succeed, the incoming COR list of the incoming dial peer must have all the "keys" needed to open all the "locks" of the outgoing COR list of the outgoing dial peer.

In the example shown in Figure 5-35, a first VoIP call with destination 100 is received by the router. The Cisco IOS call-routing logic matches the incoming call leg with the VoIP dial peer and the outgoing call leg with the first POTS dial peer. The COR logic is then applied. Because the c1 incoming COR list has all the keys needed for the c2 outgoing COR list locks (A and B), the call succeeds.

A second VoIP call with destination 200 is then received by the router. The Cisco IOS call-routing logic matches the incoming call leg with the VoIP dial peer and the outgoing call leg with the second POTS dial peer. The COR logic is then applied. Because the c1 incoming COR list is missing one "key" for the c3 outgoing COR list (D), the call is rejected.

Calling privileges on Cisco IOS gateways use two components, as illustrated in Figure 5-36.

When a call is routed, the gateway checks the COR list of the inbound dial peer and the COR list of the outbound dial peer. Table 5-8 reviews the various COR results, which depend on the COR lists applied, or not applied, to incoming and/or outgoing dial peers.

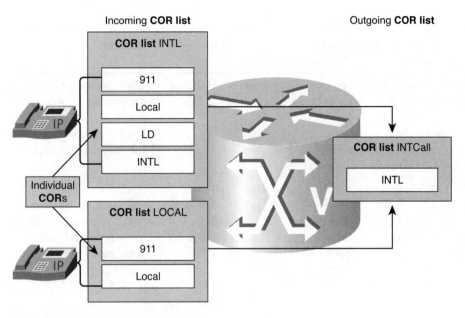

Figure 5-36   *COR Components*

Table 5-8   *Call Routing with Corlists*

Corlist on Incoming Dial Peer	Corlist on Outgoing Dial Peer	Result	Reason
No COR.	No COR.	Call succeeds.	COR is not involved.
No COR.	Corlist applied for outgoing calls.	Call succeeds.	The incoming dial peer, by default, has the highest COR priority when no COR is applied. Therefore, if you apply no COR for an incoming call leg to a dial peer, this dial peer can make calls out of any other dial peer, regardless of the COR configuration on the outgoing dial peer.
The COR list applied for incoming calls.	No COR.	Call succeeds.	The outgoing dial peer, by default, has the lowest priority. Because there are some COR configurations for incoming calls on the incoming, originating dial peer, it is a superset of the outgoing call COR configurations on the outgoing, terminating dial peer.

Table 5-8 *Call Routing with Corlists*

Corlist on Incoming Dial Peer	Corlist on Outgoing Dial Peer	Result	Reason
The COR list applied for incoming calls. (Superset of COR lists applied for outgoing calls on the outgoing dial peer.)	The COR list applied for outgoing calls. (Subset of COR lists applied for incoming calls on the incoming dial peer.)	Call succeeds.	The COR list for incoming calls on the incoming dial peer is a superset of COR lists for outgoing calls on the outgoing dial peer.
The COR list applied for incoming calls. (Subset of COR lists applied for outgoing dial peer.)	The COR list applied for outgoing calls. (Superset of COR lists applied for incoming calls on the incoming dial peer.)	Call cannot be completed using this outgoing dial peer.	Corlists for incoming calls on the incoming dial peer are not a super set of COR lists for outgoing calls on the outgoing dial peer.

COR Example

Figure 5-37 illustrates the concept of COR on Cisco IOS gateways.

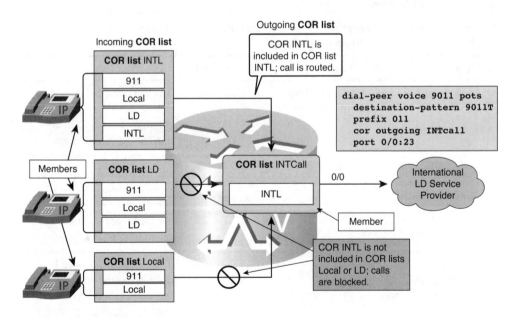

Figure 5-37 *COR Example*

A typical application of COR is to define a COR name for the number that an outgoing dial peer serves, then define a list that contains only that COR name, and assign that list as COR list outgoing for this outgoing dial peer. For example, the dial peer with destination pattern 9011T can have a COR list outgoing that contains COR INTL, as shown in Figure 5-37.

In this example, four CORs are defined:

- 911

- Local

- LD

- INTL

The four CORs are used to create three incoming COR lists that will be assigned to phones and users:

- **Local:** This COR list contains the CORs 911 and Local. This list will allow users to place emergency calls and local PSTN calls.

- **LD:** This COR list contains the CORs 911, Local, and LD. This COR list will allow users to place emergency calls, local calls, and long-distance PSTN calls.

- **INTL:** This COR list contains the CORs 911, Local, LD, and INTL. This COR list will allow users to place any PSTN call.

A COR list will be assigned to an outgoing POTS dial peer used to route international calls to the international long-distance service provider:

- **INTLCall:** This COR list contains the COR INTL and will be used for outbound INTL PSTN calls.

When a call is routed using the incoming COR list INTL and is matched against the outgoing COR list INTLCall, the call succeeds because COR INTL is included in the COR list INTL.

When a call is routed using the incoming COR list Local and is matched against the outgoing COR list INTLCall, the call is blocked because COR INTL is not included in the COR list Local.

Understanding COR for SRST and CME

When you use COR with SRST and Cisco Unified CME, a COR list cannot be simply bound to all dial peers, because one call leg will be represented by dynamic dial peers derived from ephones.

For Cisco Unified CME, the COR list is directly assigned to the appropriate ephone-dn and will then be included in the dynamic ephone dial peer. Both inbound and outbound COR lists can be applied. An inbound COR list on an ephone restricts the destination to which a user can dial, whereas an outbound COR list defines who can call a user.

For standard SRST, ephones are not statically configured on the Cisco IOS gateway. Instead, the gateway pulls the configuration from the phone and dynamically creates corresponding ephones. To assign a COR list in SRST mode, a COR list is matched to a range of directory numbers in global SRST configuration mode.

Note   COR is not limited to Cisco Unified CME or SRST. COR can be applied to any inbound and outbound dial peer on a Cisco IOS gateway.

Figure 5-38 shows a sample configuration for Cisco Unified CME and SRST.

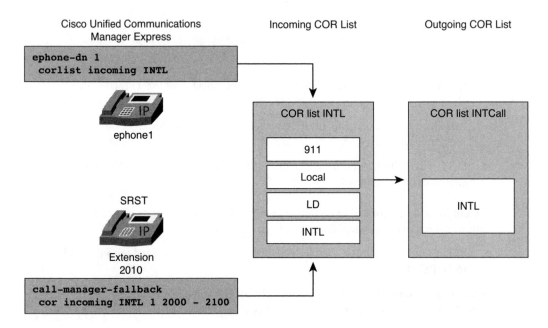

Figure 5-38   *COR and SRST and Cisco Unified CME Example*

This Cisco Unified CME configuration assigns the incoming COR list INTL to ephone 1:

```
Router(config)#ephone-dn 1
Router(config-ephone-dn)#corlist incoming INTL
```

This SRST configuration assigns the incoming COR list INTL to all phones with the DN 2000 through 2010:

```
Router(config)#call-manager-fallback
Router(config-cm-fallback)#cor incoming INTL 1 2000 - 2010
```

> **Note** The number that precedes the directory number range in the SRST configuration is the corlist tag. Up to 20 tags can be configured (that is, up to 20 different corlists can be used for SRST ephones).

Configuring COR for Cisco Unified Communications Manager Express

In the example described in this section, you are required to configure COR for Cisco Unified CME according to the following network requirements. For this example, three calling privilege classes are required:

- **Local:** This class should allow emergency and local calls.

- **Long Distance:** This class should allow emergency, local, and long-distance calls.

- **International:** This class should allow emergency, local, long-distance, and international calls.

> **Note** No standard naming conventions exist for the privilege classes. Ensure that you choose a descriptive name.

You can use the following steps to configure COR for Cisco Unified CME:

Step 1. Define the four individual "tags" (CORs) to be used as COR list members with the command **dial-peer cor custom**.

Step 2. Define the COR lists that will be assigned "outgoing" to the PSTN dial peers with the command **dial-peer cor list** *corlist-name*.

Step 3. Define the COR lists that will be assigned "incoming" from the local dial peers with the command **dial-peer cor list** *corlist-name*.

Step 4. Associate COR lists with existing VoIP or POTS PSTN dial peers by using the command **corlist {incoming | outgoing}** *corlist-name* within the dial-peer configuration.

Step 5. Assign the COR lists for user privileges to the corresponding ephone-dns.

The topology shown in Figure 5-39 will be used throughout the configuration steps in this scenario. Notice that the Chicago site is handled by a Cisco Unified CME router.

Step 1: Define COR Labels

The first step is to define the individual CORs.

Four COR labels will be defined:

- **911:** Allows calls to emergency 911
- **local:** Allows local calls only

■ **ld:** Allows long-distance calls

■ **intl:** Allows international calls

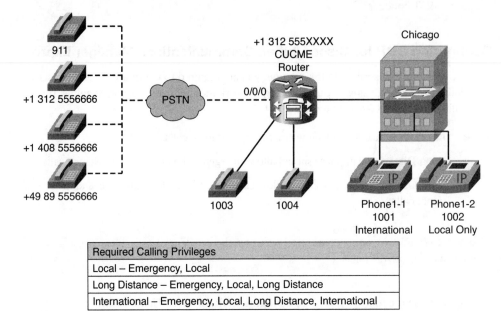

Figure 5-39 *COR CUCME Scenario Topology*

You can use the following procedure to configure these four CORs.

Step 1. Use the **dial-peer cor custom** command to enter COR configuration mode.

```
Router(config)#dial-peer cor custom
```

Step 2. Use the **name** command in COR configuration mode to create the named CORs.

```
Router(config-dp-cor)#name 911
Router(config-dp-cor)#name local
Router(config-dp-cor)#name ld
Router(config-dp-cor)#name intl
```

Step 2: Configure Outbound Corlists

After you define the CORs, you can configure the incoming and outgoing COR lists.

Four outgoing COR lists will be defined:

■ **911call:** Allows calls to emergency 911

■ **localcall:** Allows local calls only

- **ldcall:** Allows long-distance calls

- **intlcall:** Allows international calls

The following configuration defines the COR lists used for the outbound PSTN dial peers. Note that each COR list contains a single COR member.

Step 1.   Define a COR list name for 911 calls.

```
Router(config)#dial-peer cor list 911call
```

Step 2.   Add members to dial-peer COR lists. The member needs to reference a previously configured COR tag.

```
Router(config-dp-corlist)#member 911
```

Step 3.   Repeat Steps 1 and 2 for the other outgoing COR lists.

```
Router(config)#dial-peer cor list localcall
Router(config-dp-corlist)#member local
Router(config)#dial-peer cor list ldcall
Router(config-dp-corlist)#member ld
Router(config)#dial-peer cor list intlcall
Router(config-dp-corlist)#member intl
```

Step 3: Configure Inbound Corlists

After the configuration of the outbound dial peers is complete, you can configure the inbound dial peer. The incoming COR lists will later be assigned to the ephones and inbound dial peers used for attached phones.

Four incoming COR lists will be defined:

- **911:** Allows 911 calls only

  Member is 911.

- **local:** Allows 911 and local calls only

  Members are 911 and local.

- **ld:** Allows 911, local, and long-distance calls

  Members are 911, local, and ld.

- **intl:** Allows 911, local, long-distance, and international calls

  Members are 911, local, ld, and intl.

The following steps define the four inbound COR lists:

Step 1.   The following configuration creates a COR list that corresponds to the calling privilege allowing only emergency calls:

```
Router(config)#dial-peer cor list 911
Router(config-dp-corlist)#member 911
```

Step 2.   The following configuration creates a COR list that corresponds to the calling privilege allowing only emergency and local calls:

```
Router(config)#dial-peer cor list local
Router(config-dp-corlist)#member 911
Router(config-dp-corlist)#member local
```

Step 3.   The following configuration creates a COR list that corresponds to the calling privilege allowing emergency, local, and long-distance calls:

```
Router(config)#dial-peer cor list ld
Router(config-dp-corlist)#member 911
Router(config-dp-corlist)#member local
Router(config-dp-corlist)#member ld
```

Step 4.   The following configuration defines the COR list that corresponds to the calling privilege allowing emergency, local, long-distance, and international calls:

```
Router(config)#dial-peer cor list intl
Router(config-dp-corlist)#member 911
Router(config-dp-corlist)#member local
Router(config-dp-corlist)#member ld
Router(config-dp-corlist)#member intl
```

Step 4: Assign Corlists to PSTN Dial Peers

You can then define the corresponding outbound dial peers using the PSTN COR lists. Note that each of the dial peers is configured with the corresponding outgoing COR list:

- Dial peer 911 has the outgoing 911call COR list.

- Dial peer 9911 has the outgoing 911call COR list.

- Dial peer 9 has the outgoing localcall COR list.

- Dial peer 91 has the outgoing ldcall COR list.

- Dial peer 9011 has the outgoing intlcall COR list.

The following configuration shows the complete dial-peer configuration, including correct destination patterns, digit prefixing, and COR list configuration.

Step 1.   Enter dial-peer configuration mode.

```
Router(config)#dial-peer voice 911 pots
Router(config-dial-peer)#destination-pattern 911
Router(config-dial-peer)#forward-digits all
```

Step 2.   Specify the COR list to be used when a specified dial peer acts as the incoming or outgoing dial peer. The COR list name needs to reference a previously configured COR list.

```
Router(config-dial-peer)#corlist outgoing 911call
Router(config-dial-peer)#port 0/0/0:23
```

Step 3.   Repeat Steps 1 and 2 for the remaining dial peers.

```
Router(config)#dial-peer voice 9911 pots
Router(config-dial-peer)#destination-pattern 9911
Router(config-dial-peer)#forward-digits 3
Router(config-dial-peer)#corlist outgoing 911call
Router(config-dial-peer)#port 0/0/0:23
Router(config)#dial-peer voice 9 pots
Router(config-dial-peer)#destination-pattern 9[2-9]......
Router(config-dial-peer)#corlist outgoing localcall
Router(config-dial-peer)#port 0/0/0:23
Router(config)#dial-peer voice 91 pots
Router(config-dial-peer)#destination-pattern 91[2-9]..[2-9]......
Router(config-dial-peer)#prefix 1
Router(config-dial-peer)#corlist outgoing ldcall
Router(config-dial-peer)#port 0/0/0:23
Router(config)#dial-peer voice 9011 pots
Router(config-dial-peer)#destination-pattern 9011T
Router(config-dial-peer)#prefix 011
Router(config-dial-peer)#corlist outgoing intlcall
Router(config-dial-peer)#port 0/0/0:23
```

Step 5: Assign Corlists to Incoming Dial Peers and Ephone-dns

After the configuration of the outbound dial peers is complete, you can assign COR lists to incoming dial peers and ephone-dns, as shown in Example 5-37.

Example 5-37   *Assign Corlists to Incoming Dial Peers and Ephone-dns*

```
Router#show running-config
... OUTPUT OMMITTED ...
dial-peer voice 1003 pots
 destination-pattern 1003$
 port 1/0/0
 corlist incoming local
 corlist incoming 911
dial-peer voice 1004 pots
 destination-pattern 1004$
 port 1/0/1
 corlist incoming 911
 corlist incoming local
 corlist incoming ld
 corlist incoming intl
ephone-dn 1
```

```
 corlist incoming intl
ephone-dn 2
 corlist incoming local
... OUTPUT OMMITTED ...
```

This configuration is deployed for the ephones:

Step 1.   Assign a COR list for each ephone-dn.

Step 2.   Assign COR lists to dial peers for the attached phones.

Configuring COR for SRST

The example illustrated in Figure 5-40 and Example 5-38 shows how to configure COR for SRST.

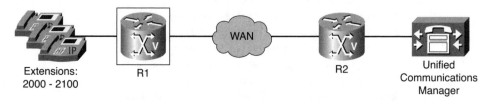

Figure 5-40   *COR SRST Scenario Topology*

Example 5-38   *SRST COR Configuration*

```
R1(config)#call-manager-fallback
R1(config-cm-fallback)#cor incoming INTL 1 2000 - 2100
```

To configure COR for SRST, use the **cor** command in SRST configuration mode.

You can have up to 20 COR lists for each incoming and outgoing call. A default COR is assigned to directory numbers that do not match any COR list numbers or number ranges. An assigned COR is invoked for the dial peers and created for each directory number automatically during Communications Manager fallback registration.

When assigning an incoming or outgoing COR list to SRST ephones, COR lists can be assigned to a specific directory number range (as the following syntax illustrates) or a default COR list can be applied.

```
Router(config)#call-manager-fallback
Router(config-cm-fallback)#cor incoming intl 1 2000 - 2100
```

The syntax of the **cor** command issued in call-manager-fallback configuration mode is

cor {**incoming** | **outgoing**} *cor-list-name* [*cor-list-number starting-number - ending-number* | **default**]

The following is an explanation of the syntax:

- **incoming:** The COR list to be used by incoming dial peers.

- **outgoing:** The COR list to be used by outgoing dial peers.

- *cor-list-name*: The COR list name.

- *cor-list-number*: The COR list identifier. The maximum number of COR lists that can be created is 20, comprising incoming or outgoing dial peers. The first six COR lists are applied to a range of directory numbers. The directory numbers that do not have a COR configuration are assigned to the default COR list, provided a default COR list has been defined.

- *starting-number - ending-number*: The directory number range, such as 2000–2025.

- **default:** Instructs the router to use an existing default COR list.

Verifying COR

You can use the **show dial-peer cor** command to display COR lists and members, as demonstrated in Example 5-39.

Example 5-39   show dial-peer cor *Command*

```
Router#show dial-peer cor

Class of Restriction
  name: 911
  name: local
  name: ld
  name: intl

COR list <911call>
  member: 911

COR list <localcall>
  member: local

COR list <ldcall>
  member: ld

COR list <intlcall>
  member: intl
```

Summary

The main topics covered in this chapter are the following:

- Digit manipulation is the task of adding or subtracting digits from the original dialed number to accommodate user dialing habits or gateway needs.

- Digit stripping strips any outbound digits that explicitly match the destination pattern of a particular dial peer.

- Digit forwarding specifies the number of digits that must be forwarded to a telephony interface.

- Digit prefixing adds digits to the front of the dial string before it is forwarded to a telephony interface.

- Number expansion is applied globally to all calls, not just to calls matching a single designated dial peer.

- By default, when a terminating router matches a dial string to an outbound POTS dial peer, the router strips off the left-justified digits that explicitly match the destination pattern.

- You can use the **clid** command to modify caller ID information.

- You can use voice translation profiles to replace the Cisco Unified CME **dialplan-pattern** command.

- Configuring digit manipulation might require the use of basic commands as well as translation rules and profiles.

- The call-routing logic on Cisco IOS routers using the H.323 protocol relies on the dial-peer construct.

- Routers must match the correct inbound and outbound dial peers to successfully complete a call.

- Dial peers in a hunt group are selected according to criteria such as longest match, explicit preference, or random selection.

- Best practices include a default POTS dial peer and redundant Cisco UCM.

- When remote sites are involved, different path selection strategies are required, including site-code dialing, toll-bypass, and TEHO.

- Site-code dialing uses the concept of prefixing a site code in front of the actual extension and can be combined with toll-bypass to route calls over a WAN link instead of a PSTN connection.

- TEHO extends the concept of toll-bypass by routing calls over a WAN to the closest PSTN breakout to avoid costly long-distance and international phone charges.

- Site-code configuration requires that each site be assigned a unique site code.

- TEHO configuration requires that all calls be routed over the WAN unless the WAN is down.

- Calling privileges are used within a dial plan to define the destination a user is allowed to call.

- Calling privileges are implemented on Cisco IOS gateways using the Class of Restriction (COR) feature.

- For Cisco Unified CME, a COR list is directly assigned to an appropriate ephone. To assign a COR list in SRST mode, a COR list is matched to a range of directory numbers in call-manager-fallback configuration mode.

- Configuring COR includes configuring named CORs and COR lists, and assigning COR lists to dial peers, ephones, or SRST.

Chapter Review Questions

The answers to these review questions are in the appendix.

1. By default, _____ dial peers strip any outbound digits that explicitly match their destination pattern.

   a. PSTN

   b. WAN

   c. POTS

   d. VoIP

2. Which digit manipulation option is applied globally?

   a. number expansion

   b. digit prefixing

   c. digit forwarding

   d. digit stripping

3. Select a rule that would search and replace a ten-digit number with the internal 2XXX extension.

   a. rule 1 /^2/ /4085552/

   b. rule 1 /2/ /^4085552/

   c. rule 1 /4085552/ /^2/

   d. rule 1 /^4085552/ /2/

4. In Cisco IOS, which of the following is associated to each dial peer?

    a. call leg

    b. translation rule

    c. translation profile

    d. interface

5. One best practice is to create a default POTS dial peer with the **direct-inward-dial** attribute using the __ wildcard as the destination pattern.

    a. *

    b. #

    c. ^

    d. .

6. _____ is an easy way to overcome the problem of overlapping directory numbers.

    a. Site-code dialing

    b. Technology prefixes

    c. TEHO

    d. Toll-bypass

7. Instead of only routing intersite calls over an IP WAN link, _____ also uses the IP WAN link for PSTN calls.

    a. site-code dialing

    b. technology prefixes

    c. TEHO

    d. toll-bypass

8. Which of the following is defined to include a number of members that were previously defined?

    a. dial peer

    b. cortags

    c. dial tags

    d. corlist

9. In Cisco Unified CME, COR lists are directly assigned to what?

   a. ephone

   b. ephone-dn

   c. dial-peer

   d. member

10. Which command is used to display COR lists and members?

    a. show cor

    b. show dial-peer cor

    c. show dial-peer

    d. show corlist

Chapter 6

Using Gatekeepers and Cisco Unified Border Elements

After reading this chapter, you should be able to perform the following tasks:

- Describe Cisco IOS gatekeeper functionality.

- Configure gatekeepers for device registration, address resolution, and call routing.

- Implement gatekeeper-based CAC.

- Describe Cisco Unified Border Element (Cisco UBE) functions and features and how a Cisco UBE is used in current enterprise environments.

- Implement a Cisco UBE router to provide protocol interworking.

Gatekeepers play a major part in medium-sized and large H.323 VoIP network solutions. Gatekeepers allow for dial-plan scalability and reduce the need to manage global dial plans locally. This chapter describes the functions of a gatekeeper and explains how to configure gatekeepers to interoperate with gateways.

Also, this module gives an overview of the Cisco Unified Border Element (Cisco UBE) and describes how to implement a Cisco UBE within an enterprise network. A Cisco UBE has the ability to interconnect voice and VoIP networks, offering protocol interworking, address hiding, and security services.

Gatekeeper Fundamentals

This section reviews the functions and roles of gatekeepers. Also, this section discusses in depth the Registration, Admission, and Status (RAS) signaling sequencing between gateways and gatekeepers.

Gatekeeper Responsibilities

A gatekeeper is an H.323 entity on a network that provides services such as address translation and network access control for H.323 terminals, gateways, and multipoint control units (MCU). The primary functions of a gatekeeper are admission control, zone management, and E.164 address translation. Gatekeepers are logically separated from H.323 endpoints and are optional devices in an H.323 network environment.

These optional gatekeepers can manage endpoints in an H.323 network. The endpoints communicate with the gatekeeper using the RAS protocol.

Note The ITU-T specifies that although a gatekeeper is an optional device in H.323 networks, if a network does include a gatekeeper, all H.323 endpoints should use it.

Gatekeepers have mandatory and optional responsibilities. The mandatory responsibilities include the following:

■ **Address resolution:** Calls originating within an H.323 network might use an alias to address the destination terminal. Calls originating outside the H.323 network and received by a gateway can use an E.164 telephone number to address the destination terminal. The gatekeeper must be able to resolve the alias or the E.164 telephone number into the network address for the destination terminal. The destination endpoint can be reached using the network address on the H.323 network. The translation is done using a translation table that is updated with registration messages.

■ **Admission control:** The gatekeeper can control the admission of the endpoints into an H.323 network. It uses these RAS messages to achieve this: Admission Request (ARQ), Admission Confirmation (ACF), and Admission Reject (ARJ). Admissions control might also be a null function that admits all requests.

■ **Bandwidth control:** The gatekeeper manages endpoint bandwidth requirements. When registering with a gatekeeper, an endpoint specifies its preferred codec. During H.245 negotiation, a different codec might be required. These RAS messages are used to control this codec negotiation: Bandwidth Request (BRQ), Bandwidth Confirmation (BCF), and Bandwidth Reject (BRJ).

■ **Zone management:** A gatekeeper is required to provide address translation, admission control, and bandwidth control for terminals, gateways, and MCUs located within its zone of control.

All of these gatekeeper-required roles are configurable. The following are optional responsibilities a gatekeeper can provide:

■ **Call authorization:** With this option, the gatekeeper can restrict access to certain endpoints or gateways based on policies, such as time of day.

■ **Call management:** With this option, the gatekeeper maintains active call information and uses it to indicate busy endpoints or to redirect calls.

■ **Bandwidth management:** With this option, the gatekeeper can reject admission when the required bandwidth is not available.

Figure 6-1 provides a sample topology illustrating the interaction between gatekeepers and other H.323 network components.

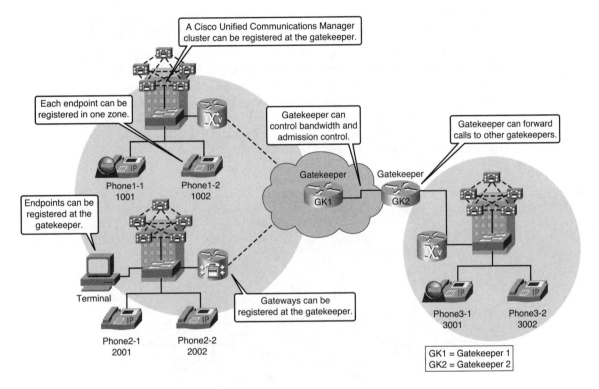

Figure 6-1   *Interaction of Gatekeepers with H.323 Network Components*

Endpoints attempt to register with a gatekeeper on startup. When they want to communicate with another endpoint, they request admission to initiate a call using a symbolic alias for the destination endpoint, such as an E.164 address or an email address. If the gatekeeper decides that the call can proceed, it returns a destination IP address to the originating endpoint. This IP address might not be the actual address of the destination endpoint, but rather might be an intermediate address, such as the address of a proxy or a gatekeeper that routes call signaling. A Cisco IOS gatekeeper provides H.323 call management, including admission control, bandwidth management, and routing services for calls in the network.

Gatekeeper Signaling

Gatekeepers use RAS for signaling. RAS is a subset of the H.225 signaling protocol. This signaling uses User Data Protocol (UDP). Signaling messages between gateways are H.225 call control, setup, or signaling messages.

H.225 call control signaling is used to set up connections between H.323 endpoints. The ITU H.225 recommendation specifies the use and support of Q.931 signaling messages. If no gatekeeper is present, H.225 messages are exchanged directly between endpoints.

As shown in Figure 6-2, after call signaling is set up between gateways, H.245 is negotiated. H.245, a control signaling protocol in the H.323 multimedia communication architecture, is for the exchange of end-to-end H.245 messages between communicating H.323 endpoints. The H.245 call control messages are carried over H.245 control channels. The H.245 control channel is the logical channel 0 and is permanently open, unlike the media channels. The messages carried include messages to exchange capabilities of terminals and to open and close logical channels.

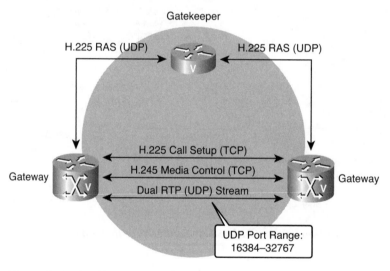

Figure 6-2 *Gatekeeper Signaling*

After a connection has been set up via the call signaling procedure, the H.245 call control protocol is used to resolve the call media type and establish the media flow before the call can be established. It also manages the call after it has been established.

As the call is set up between gateways, all other port assignments are dynamically negotiated, as in the following examples:

- RTP ports are negotiated from the lowest number.

- The H.245 TCP port is negotiated during H.225 signaling for a standard H.323 connection.

- The RTP UDP port range is 16384–32767.

RAS Messages

Gatekeepers communicate through the RAS channel using different types of RAS messages. Table 6-1 shows common RAS signal messages, which are initiated by a gateway or gatekeeper.

Table 6-1   *RAS Message Types*

Category of RAS Message	RAS Message
Gatekeeper Discovery	Gatekeeper Request (GRQ) Gatekeeper Confirmation (GCF) Gatekeeper Reject (GRJ)
Terminal and Gateway Registration	Registration Request (RRQ) Registration Confirmation (RCF) Registration Reject (RRJ)
Terminal and Gateway Unregistration	Unregistration Request (URQ) Unregistration Confirmation (UCF) Unregistration Reject (URJ)
Resource Availability	Resource Availability Indicator (RAI) Resource Availability Confirmation (RAC)
Bandwidth	Bandwidth Request (BRQ) Bandwidth Confirmation (BCF) Bandwidth Reject (BRJ)
Location	Location Request (LRQ) Location Confirmation (LCF) Location Reject (LRJ)
Call Admission	Admission Request (ARQ) Admission Confirmation (ACF) Admission Reject (ARJ)
Disengage	Disengage Request (DRQ) Disengage Confirmation (DCF) Disengage Rejection (DRJ)
Request in Progress	Request in Progress (RIP)
Status	Info Request (IRQ) Info Request Response (IRR) Info_Request_Acknowledge (IACK) Info_Request_Neg_Acknowledge (INAK) Information Confirm (ICF)

RAS message types include those listed here:

- **Gatekeeper Discovery messages:** An endpoint unicasts or multicasts a gatekeeper discovery request. The GRQ message requests that any gatekeeper receiving it respond with a GCF message granting it permission to register. The GRJ message is a rejection of this request, indicating the requesting endpoint should seek another gatekeeper.

  - **Gatekeeper Request (GRQ):** Message sent by an endpoint to a gatekeeper.

  - **Gatekeeper Confirmation (GCF):** Reply from a gatekeeper to an endpoint indicating the transport address of the gatekeeper RAS channel.

  - **Gatekeeper Reject (GRJ):** Reply from a gatekeeper to an endpoint rejecting the request from the endpoint for registration. The GRJ message usually occurs because of a gateway or gatekeeper configuration error.

- **Terminal and Gateway Registration messages:** The RRQ message is a request to register from a terminal to a gatekeeper. If the gatekeeper responds with an RCF message, the terminal uses the responding gatekeeper for future calls. If the gatekeeper responds with an RRJ message, the terminal must seek another gatekeeper with which to register.

  - **Registration Request (RRQ):** Sent from an endpoint to a gatekeeper RAS channel address. Included in this message is the technology prefix, if configured.

  - **Registration Confirmation (RCF):** Reply from the gatekeeper confirming endpoint registration.

  - **Registration Reject (RRJ):** Reply from the gatekeeper rejecting endpoint registration.

- **Terminal and Gateway Unregistration messages:** The URQ message requests the association between a terminal and a gatekeeper be broken. Note the URQ request is bidirectional (that is, a gatekeeper can request a terminal to consider itself unregistered, and a terminal can inform a gatekeeper it is revoking a previous registration).

  - **Unregistration Request (URQ):** Sent from an endpoint or a gatekeeper to cancel registration.

  - **Unregistration Confirmation (UCF):** Sent from an endpoint or a gatekeeper to confirm an unregistration.

  - **Unregistration Reject (URJ):** Indicates that an endpoint was not preregistered with a gatekeeper.

- **Call Admission messages:** The ARQ message requests an endpoint be allowed access to a packet-based network by a gatekeeper. The request identifies the terminating endpoint and the bandwidth required. The gatekeeper either grants the request with an ACF message or denies it with an ARJ message.

- **Admission Request (ARQ):** An attempt by an endpoint to initiate a call.

- **Admission Confirmation (ACF):** An authorization by the gatekeeper to admit the call. This message contains the IP address of the terminating gateway or gatekeeper and enables the originating gateway to initiate call control signaling procedures.

- **Admission Reject (ARJ):** Denies the request from the endpoint to gain access to the network for this particular call if the endpoint is unknown or inadequate bandwidth is available.

- **Location messages:** These are commonly used between interzone gatekeepers to get the IP addresses of different zone endpoints.

  - **Location Request (LRQ):** Sent by a gatekeeper to the directory gatekeeper to request the contact information for one or more E.164 addresses. An LRQ is sent directly to a gatekeeper if one is known, or it is multicast to the gatekeeper discovery multicast address.

  - **Location Confirmation (LCF):** Sent by a responding gatekeeper, it contains the call signaling channel or RAS channel address (IP address) of itself or the requested endpoint. It uses the requested endpoint address when directed endpoint call signaling is used.

  - **Location Reject (LRJ):** Sent by gatekeepers that received an LRQ for a requested endpoint that is not registered or that has unavailable resources.

- **Status messages:** Used to communicate gateway status information to the gatekeeper.

  - **Information Request (IRQ):** Sent from a gatekeeper to an endpoint requesting status.

  - **Information Confirm (ICF):** Sent from an endpoint to a gatekeeper to confirm the status.

  - **Information Request Response (IRR):** Sent from an endpoint to a gatekeeper in response to an IRQ. This message is also sent from an endpoint to a gatekeeper if the gatekeeper requests periodic status updates. Gateways use the IRR to inform the gatekeeper about active calls.

  - **Info_Request_Acknowledge (IACK):** Used by the gatekeeper to respond to IRR messages.

  - **Info_Request_Neg_Acknowledge (INAK):** Used by the gatekeeper to respond to IRR messages.

- **Bandwidth messages:** An endpoint sends a BRQ to its gatekeeper to request an adjustment in call bandwidth. The gatekeeper either grants the request with a BCF message or denies it with a BRJ message.

  - **Bandwidth Request (BRQ):** Sent by an endpoint to a gatekeeper requesting an increase or decrease in call bandwidth.

- **Bandwidth Confirmation (BCF):** Sent by a gatekeeper confirming acceptance of a bandwidth request.

- **Bandwidth Reject (BRJ):** Sent by a gatekeeper rejecting a bandwidth request.

- **Resource Availability messages:** An RAI message is a notification from a gateway to a gatekeeper of its current call capacity for each H-series protocol and data rate for that protocol. Upon receiving an RAI message, a gatekeeper responds with a RAC message to acknowledge its reception.

    - **Resource Availability Indicator (RAI):** Used by gateways to inform the gatekeeper whether resources are available in the gateway to take on additional calls.

    - **Resource Availability Confirmation (RAC):** Notification from the gatekeeper to the gateway acknowledging receipt of an RAI message.

    - **Request in Progress (RIP):** The gatekeeper sends out a RIP message to an endpoint or gateway to prevent call failures, caused by RAS message timeouts during gatekeeper call processing. A gateway receiving an RIP message knows to continue to wait for a gatekeeper response.

- **Disengage messages:** When a call is disconnected, a variety of disconnect messages can be exchanged between an endpoint or gateway and a gatekeeper.

    - **Disengage Request (DRQ):** Notification sent from an endpoint or gateway to its gatekeeper, or vice versa.

    - **Disengage Confirmation (DCF):** A notification sent from a gatekeeper to a gateway or endpoint confirming a DRQ, or vice versa.

    - **Disengage Rejection (DRJ):** A notification sent from a gatekeeper rejecting a DRQ from an endpoint or gateway. Note that if a DRQ is sent from a gatekeeper to an endpoint, the DRQ message forces a call to be dropped. Such a request will not be refused.

Gatekeeper Discovery

Endpoints attempt to discover a gatekeeper, and consequently, the zone of which they are members, by using the RAS message protocol. The protocol supports a discovery message that can be sent via multicast or unicast, as depicted in Figure 6-3.

The initial signaling from a gateway to a gatekeeper is done through H.225 RAS. Gateways can discover their gatekeepers through one of these two processes:

- Unicast discovery:

    - Uses UDP port 1718.

    - In this process, endpoints are configured with the gatekeeper IP address and can attempt registration immediately.

    - The gatekeeper replies with a GCF or GRJ message.

- Multicast discovery:

  - Uses UDP multicast address 224.0.1.41.

  - Autodiscovery enables an endpoint to discover its gatekeeper through a multi-cast message. Because endpoints do not have to be statically configured for gatekeepers, this method has less administrative overhead.

  - A gatekeeper replies with a GCF or GRJ message.

Note   A Cisco IOS gatekeeper always replies to a GRQ with a GCF or GRJ message. It never remains silent.

- A gatekeeper can be configured to respond to specific subnets.

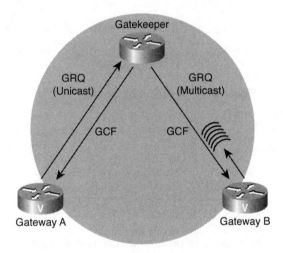

Figure 6-3   *Gatekeeper Discovery*

The GRQ message requests any gatekeeper receiving it to respond with a GCF message granting it permission to register. The GRJ message is a rejection of this request, indicating that the requesting endpoint should seek another gatekeeper.

If a gateway requests an explicit gatekeeper name, only that gatekeeper will respond. Otherwise, the first gatekeeper to respond becomes the gatekeeper of that gateway. If a gatekeeper is not available, the gateway periodically attempts to rediscover a gatekeeper. If the gateway-discovered gatekeeper has gone offline, it stops accepting new calls, and the gateway attempts to rediscover a gatekeeper. Active calls are not affected by this process because the RTP streams are directly between the phones.

Registration Request

The RRQ message is a request from a terminal or a gateway to a gatekeeper to register, as shown in Figure 6-4.

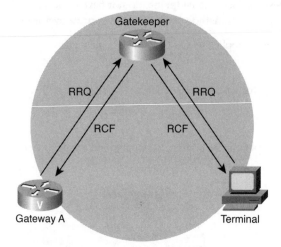

Figure 6-4   *Registration Request*

If the gatekeeper responds with an RCF message, the terminal uses the responding gatekeeper for future calls. If the gatekeeper responds with an RRJ message, the terminal must seek another gatekeeper with which to register.

An H.323 gateway learns of a gatekeeper by using a static configuration or dynamic discovery. Static configuration simply means configuring the gatekeeper's IP address on an interface used for H.323 signaling.

The following is an example of the information used to register an H.323 ID or an E.164 address:

■   **H323 ID:** gatewayname@domain.com

■   **E.164 address:** 4085551212

Lightweight Registration

Prior to H.323 version 2, Cisco gateways reregistered with the gatekeeper every 30 seconds. Each registration renewal used the same process as the initial registration, even though the gateway was already registered with the gatekeeper. This behavior generated considerable overhead at the gatekeeper. H.323 version 2 defines a lightweight registration procedure that still requires the full registration process for initial registration, but uses an abbreviated renewal procedure to update the gatekeeper and minimize overhead.

Lightweight registration, as illustrated in Figure 6-5, requires each endpoint to specify a Time to Live (TTL) value in its RRQ message. If the endpoint does not indicate a TTL, the gatekeeper assigns one and sends it to the gateway in the RCF message. When a gate-keeper receives an RRQ message with a TTL value, it returns an updated TTL timer value in an RCF message to the endpoint. Shortly before the TTL timer expires, the endpoint sends an RRQ message with the Keepalive field set to True, which refreshes the existing registration. No configuration changes are permitted during a lightweight registration, so all fields are ignored other than the endpoint identifier, gatekeeper identifier, tokens, and TTL. With H.323 version 1, endpoints cannot process the TTL field in the RCF. The gate-keeper probes the endpoint with IRQs for a predetermined grace period to learn if the endpoint is still alive.

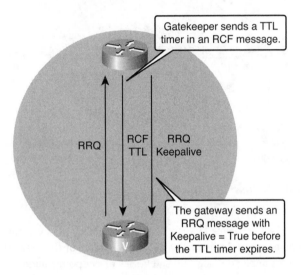

Figure 6-5 *Lightweight Registration*

Admission Request

Figure 6-6 shows an ARQ. Before the call is set up, Gateway A sends an ARQ to the gate-keeper. The gatekeeper checks the status of the called party and sends either an ACF message or an ARJ message. In this case the gatekeeper sends an ACF message. Typically, the H.225 call setup occurs directly between the two gateways.

Admission messages between endpoints and gatekeepers provide the basis for CAC and bandwidth control. Gatekeepers authorize access to H.323 networks by confirming or rejecting an ARQ.

Admission Request Message Failures

It might not be clear from the RAS ARJ message why the message was rejected. The fol-lowing are some basic ARJ messages that might be returned and the reasons why these messages occur:

■ **calledPartyNotRegistered:** This message is returned because the called party either was never registered or has not renewed its registration with a keepalive RRQ.

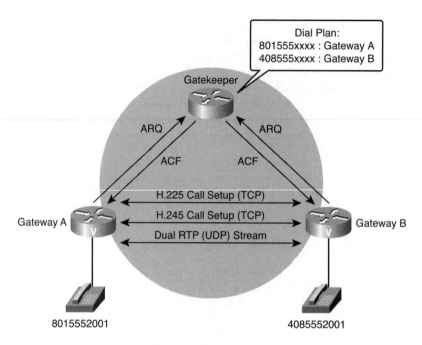

Figure 6-6   *Admission Request*

- **invalidPermission:** The call violates some proprietary policy within the gatekeeper. These policies are typically set by the administrator of the network or by the gatekeeper. For example, only certain categories of endpoints might be allowed to use gateway services.

- **requestDenied:** The gatekeeper performs zone bandwidth management, and the bandwidth required for this call would exceed the bandwidth limit of the zone.

- **undefinedReason:** This message is used only if none of the other reasons are appropriate.

- **callerNotRegistered:** The endpoint asking for permission to be admitted to the call is not registered with the gatekeeper from which it is asking permission.

- **routeCallToGatekeeper:** The registered endpoint has been sent a setup message from an unregistered endpoint, and the gatekeeper wants to route the call signaling channel.

- **invalidEndpointIdentifier:** The endpoint identifier in the ARQ is not the one the gatekeeper assigned to this endpoint in the preceding RCF.

- **resourceUnavailable:** This message indicates that the gatekeeper does not have the resources, such as memory or administrated capacity, to permit the call. It could possibly also be used in reference to the remote endpoint, meaning the endpoint is unavailable. However, another reason might be more appropriate, such as the call capacity has been exceeded, which would return a exceedsCallCapacity message.

- **securityDenial:** This message refers to the tokens or cryptoTokens fields. For example, failed authentication, lack of authorization (permission), failed integrity, or the received crypto parameters are not acceptable or understood. This message might also be used when the password or shared secret is invalid or not available, the endpoint is not allowed to use a service, a replay was detected, an integrity violation was detected, the digital signature was incorrect, or the certificate expired.

- **qosControlNotSupported:** The endpoint specified a transport quality of service (QoS) of gatekeeperControlled in its ARQ, but the gatekeeper cannot or will not provide QoS for this call.

- **incompleteAddress:** This is used for "overlapped sending." If there is insufficient addressing information in the ARQ, the gatekeeper responds with this message. This message indicates the endpoint should send another ARQ when more addressing information is available.

- **routeCallToSCN:** This message means the endpoint is to redirect the call to a specified telephone number on the Switched Circuit Network (SCN) or public switched telephone network (PSTN). This is used only if the ARQ was from an ingress gateway, where ARQ.terminalType.gateway was present and answerCall was False.

- **aliasesInconsistent:** The ARQdestinationInfo contained multiple aliases that identify different registered endpoints. This is distinct from destinationInfo containing one or more aliases identifying the same endpoint plus additional aliases that the gatekeeper cannot resolve.

- **exceedsCallCapacity:** This message was formerly callCapacityExceeded. It signifies that the destination endpoint does not have the capacity to accept the call.

- **undefinedReason:** This message is used only if none of the other reasons are appropriate.

Information Request

A gatekeeper periodically sends an IRQ to each registered endpoint to verify it still exists, as illustrated in Figure 6-7. To limit traffic, the IRQ is sent only if the endpoint does not send some other RAS traffic within a certain interval. If an IRR is not received after an IRQ is sent, the registration is aged out of the system.

Note   In addition, during calls, endpoints are instructed to send periodic unsolicited IRRs to report their call state. Cisco endpoints (proxies and gateways) send IRRs whenever a state transition exists, so that accounting information is accurate.

Whenever an IRR is sent, the age tags on the registration information for the endpoint are refreshed. In addition, if the IRR contains Cisco accounting information in its nonStandardData field, this information is used to generate authentication, authorization, and accounting (AAA) transactions.

Gatekeeper

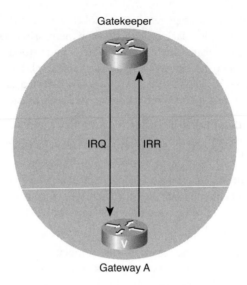

IRQ   IRR

Gateway A

Figure 6-7   *Information Request*

To ensure that accounting is as accurate and simple as possible, the gatekeeper confirms IRRs from Cisco gateways and proxies by sending an ICF. If the gateway or proxy does not receive the ICF, the IRR should be re-sent.

The RAS Status messages include IRQ, IRR, IACK, and INAK.

Location Request

An H.323 LRQ message is sent by a gatekeeper to another gatekeeper to request information about a terminating endpoint.

The second gatekeeper determines the appropriate endpoint on the basis of the information contained in the LRQ message. However, sometimes all the terminating endpoints are busy servicing other calls, and none are available. If you configure the **lrq reject-resource-low** command, the second gatekeeper rejects the LRQ if no terminating endpoints are available. If the command is not configured, the second gatekeeper allocates and returns a terminating endpoint address to the sending gatekeeper even if all the terminating endpoints are busy.

Note   The gatekeeper sends out an RIP message to an endpoint or gateway to prevent call failures, caused by RAS message timeouts during gatekeeper call processing. A gateway receiving an RIP message knows to continue to wait for a gatekeeper response.

Gatekeeper Signaling: LRQ Sequential

For gatekeeper redundancy and load-sharing features, you can configure multiple gate-keepers to service the same zone or technology prefix by sending LRQs to two or more gatekeepers. The LRQs are sent either sequentially to the gatekeepers or to all gatekeepers at the same time (blast).

Sequential forwarding of LRQs is the default forwarding mode. With sequential LRQ forwarding, the originating gatekeeper forwards an LRQ to the first gatekeeper in the matching list. The originating gatekeeper then waits for a response before sending an LRQ to the next gatekeeper on the list. If the originating gatekeeper receives an LCF while waiting, it terminates the LRQ forwarding process.

If you have multiple matching prefix zones, you might want to consider using sequential LRQ forwarding instead of blast LRQ forwarding. With sequential forwarding, you can configure which routes are primary, secondary, and tertiary.

Figure 6-8 shows three gatekeepers to which Gatekeeper A can point. Gatekeeper A, whose configuration is provided in Example 6-1, sends an LRQ first to Gatekeeper B. Gatekeeper B sends a reply as either an LCF or an LRJ to Gatekeeper A. If Gatekeeper B returns an LCF to Gatekeeper A, the LRQ forwarding process will be terminated. If Gatekeeper B returns an LRJ to Gatekeeper A, then Gatekeeper A sends an LRQ to Gatekeeper C. Gatekeeper C returns either an LCF or LRJ to Gatekeeper A. Then Gatekeeper A either terminates the LRQ forwarding process or starts the LRQ process again with Gatekeeper D.

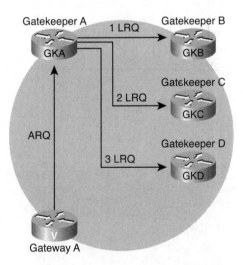

Figure 6-8   *Sequential LRQ*

Example 6-1   *Sequential LRQ Configuration*

```
GKA(config)#gatekeeper
GKA(config-gk)#zone local GKA cisco.com
GKA(config-gk)#zone remote GKB cisco.com
GKA(config-gk)#zone remote GKC cisco.com
GKA(config-gk)#zone remote GKD cisco.com
GKA(config-gk)#zone prefix GKB 1408555.... seq
GKA(config-gk)#zone prefix GKC 1408555.... seq
GKA(config-gk)#zone prefix GKD 1408555.... seq
```

Notice the **zone prefix** commands at the bottom of the router output. Because sequence is the default method for LRQ forwarding, the option **seq** does not need to be included, and sequential LRQ forwarding will take place.

Note   With sequential LRQs, there is a fixed timer when LRQs are sent. Even if Gatekeeper A gets an LRJ back immediately from Gatekeeper B, it waits a fixed amount of time before sending the next LRQ to Gatekeeper C and Gatekeeper D. You can speed up this process by using the **lrq lrj immediate-advance** command.

Gatekeeper Signaling: LRQ Blast

In Figure 6-9 and Example 6-2, when blast LRQ is used, Gatekeeper A simultaneously sends LRQs to all three gatekeepers that match the zone prefix.

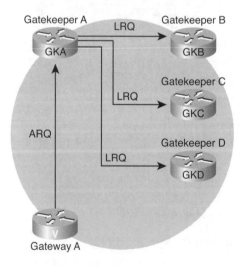

Figure 6-9   *Blast LRQ*

Example 6-2 *Blast LRQ Configuration*

```
GKA(config)#gatekeeper
GKA(config-gk)#zone local GKA cisco.com
GKA(config-gk)#zone remote GKB cisco.com
GKA(config-gk)#zone remote GKC cisco.com
GKA(config-gk)#zone remote GKD cisco.com
GKA(config-gk)#zone prefix GKB 1408555.... blast
GKA(config-gk)#zone prefix GKC 1408555.... blast
GKA(config-gk)#zone prefix GKD 1408555.... blast
```

If all three reply with a positive confirmation (that is, an LCF), Gatekeeper A chooses which one to use. Gatekeeper A can tailor the choice by using the **cost** and **priority** keywords at the end of the **zone remote** statement as follows:

```
GKA(config-gk)#zone remote GKB cisco.com cost 50 priority 50
GKA(config-gk)#zone remote GKC cisco.com cost 51 priority 49
GKA(config-gk)#zone remote GKD Cisco.com cost 52 priority 48
```

The **cost** and **priority** command options need to be examined carefully for correct operation. The default cost is 50, in the range 1–100. In the example, you see that the three gatekeepers have costs of 50, 51, and 52. This means Gatekeeper B has a lower cost than Gatekeeper C, and Gatekeeper C has a lower cost than Gatekeeper D. Therefore, Gatekeeper B will be selected first, and then Gatekeeper C, and finally Gatekeeper D.

The priority can also be set, where a higher priority takes precedence over a lower priority. The default for this option is also 50 in the range 1–100. In the example, the gatekeepers with a higher cost also have a lower priority. When each of the gatekeepers returns an LCF to Gatekeeper A, a decision as to which gatekeeper the call should be forwarded to can be made based on either cost or priority.

You can assign cost and priority values independently of each other. You might choose to assign only a cost or a priority to a specific gatekeeper. If the values you assign to a specific gatekeeper are higher or lower than the default values, and there are other gatekeepers that are using default values for cost and priority, call routing might take these unexpected paths. In the following syntax, the **blast** option has been added to the **zone prefix** commands:

```
GKA(config-gk)#zone prefix GKB 1408555.... blast
GKA(config-gk)#zone prefix GKC 1408555.... blast
GKA(config-gk)#zone prefix GKD 1408555.... blast
```

The **blast** option is an important part of the configuration that is often overlooked. The **blast** option allows Gatekeeper A to simultaneously send LRQs to Gatekeeper B, Gatekeeper C, and Gatekeeper D. If the **blast** command option is omitted, the gatekeeper uses the default method, which is to choose the gatekeeper based on sequence.

To summarize, Gatekeeper A receives an ARQ from a gateway for 1408555xxxx. Gatekeeper A then blasts LRQs to all gatekeepers, which in this case are Gatekeeper B, Gatekeeper C, and Gatekeeper D. Gatekeeper A uses the cost and priority values to evaluate the received LCFs to determine where the call should be forwarded. In this case, if all the downstream gatekeepers respond with LCFs, Gatekeeper A uses the priority and cost values and chooses Gatekeeper B as the gatekeeper to which to forward the call.

H.225 RAS Intrazone Call Setup

In the example shown in Figure 6-10, both endpoints have registered with the same gatekeeper.

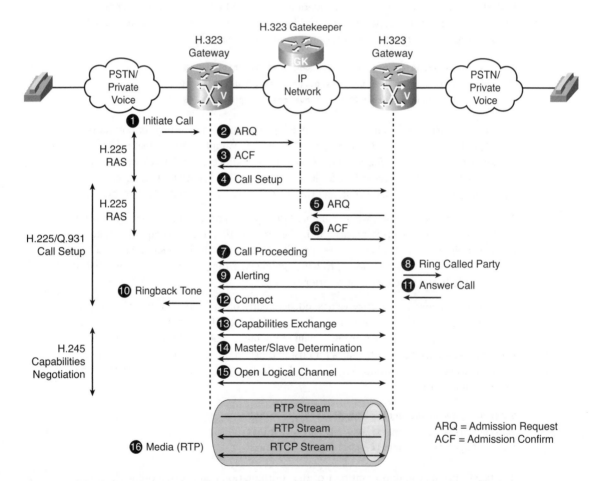

Figure 6-10   *H.225 RAS Intrazone Call Setup*

Call flow with a gatekeeper proceeds as follows:

1. A call is initiated. At this point, both the originating gateway and the terminating gateway have located and registered with the gatekeeper.

2. The originating gateway sends an ARQ to the gatekeeper to initiate the procedure. The gateway is configured with the domain or address of the gatekeeper.

3. The gatekeeper responds to the ARQ with an ACF. In the confirmation, the gatekeeper provides the IP address of the terminating gateway.

4. The originating gateway initiates a basic call setup to the terminating gateway.

5. Before the terminating gateway accepts the call, it sends an ARQ to the gatekeeper to request permission.

6. The gatekeeper responds affirmatively using an ACF message.

7–16. The call setup continues as a regular H.323 call, as described in Chapter 2, "Configuring Basic Voice over IP."

During this procedure, if the gatekeeper responds to either endpoint with an ARJ to the ARQ, the endpoint that receives the rejection terminates the procedure.

H.225 RAS Interzone Call Setup

In Figure 6-11, the gateways belong to different zones and are registered with different gatekeepers.

The call setup procedure involves these messages:

1. A call is initiated.

2. The originating gateway sends an ARQ to its gatekeeper (GK1) requesting permission to proceed and asking for the session parameters for the terminating gateway.

3. GK1 determines from its configuration that the terminating gateway is associated with GK2. GK1 sends an LRQ to GK2.

4. GK2 determines the IP address of the terminating gateway and sends it back in an LCF.

5. If GK1 considers the call acceptable for security and bandwidth reasons, it maps the LCF to an ARQ and sends the Admission Confirmation (ACF) to the originating gateway.

6. The originating gateway initiates a call setup to the terminating gateway.

7. The terminating gateway acknowledges the receipt of the call setup using the Call Proceeding message.

8. Before accepting the incoming call, the terminating gateway sends an ARQ to GK2 requesting permission to accept the incoming call.

9. GK2 admits the call and responds with an ACF.

10–17. The call setup continues as a regular H.323 call, as described in Chapter 2.

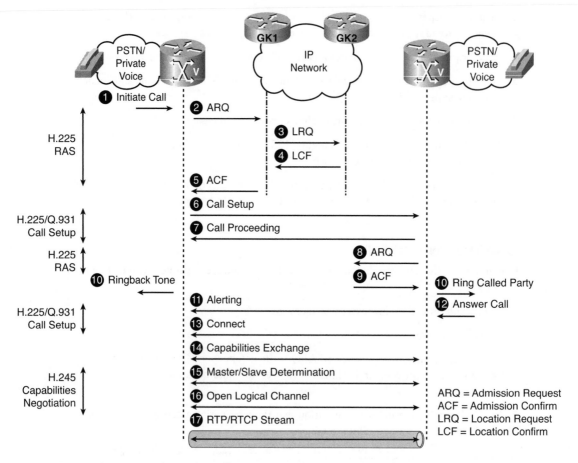

Figure 6-11 *H.225 RAS Interzone Call Setup*

Zones

A zone is defined as the set of H.323 nodes controlled by a single logical gatekeeper. Gatekeepers that coexist on a network might be configured so that they register endpoints from different subnets. There can be only one active gatekeeper per zone. These zones can overlay subnets, and one gatekeeper can manage gateways in one or more of these subnets.

Endpoints attempt to discover a gatekeeper, and consequently, the zone of which they are members, by using the RAS message protocol. The protocol supports a discovery message that might be sent using multicast or unicast.

If the message is sent via multicast, the endpoint registers nondeterministically with the first gatekeeper that responds to the message. To enforce predictable behavior, where endpoints on certain subnets are assigned to specific gatekeepers, the **zone subnet** command can be used to define the subnets that constitute a given gatekeeper zone. Any endpoint on a subnet that is not enabled for the gatekeeper is not accepted as a member of that gatekeeper zone. If the gatekeeper receives a discovery message from such an endpoint, it sends an explicit reject message.

Zone Prefixes

A zone prefix is the part of the called number that identifies the destination zone for a call. Zone prefixes are usually used to associate an area code to a configured zone, and they serve the same purpose as the domain names in the H.323-ID address space.

The Cisco IOS gatekeeper determines whether a call is routed to a remote zone or handled locally. To illustrate, consider the example given in Figure 6-12 and Example 6-3. According to this configuration excerpt, gatekeeper Corp-GK forwards 408....... calls to the San Jose gateway. Calls to area code 281 are handled locally.

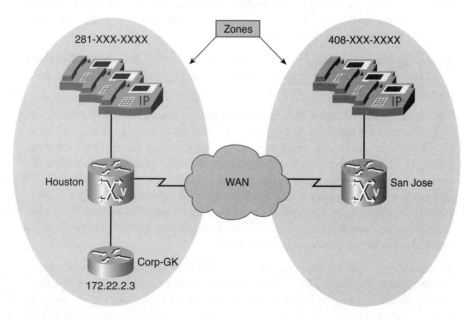

Figure 6-12   *Zone Prefix*

Example 6-3   *Zone Prefix Configuration*

```
GK-A(config)#gatekeeper
GK-A(config-gk)#zone local Houston cisco.com 172.22.2.3 1719
GK-A(config-gk)#zone local SanJose cisco.com
GK-A(config-gk)#zone prefix Houston 281.......
GK-A(config-gk)#zone prefix SanJose 408.......
```

When the San Jose gateway receives the request, the gatekeeper must resolve the address so the call can be sent to its final destination. An H.323 endpoint with that E.164 address might be registered with the San Jose gateway, in which case the San Jose gateway returns the IP address for that endpoint. However, it is possible the E.164 address belongs to a non-H.323 device (for example, a telephone or an H.320 terminal). Because non-H.323 devices do not register with gatekeepers, the San Jose gateway cannot resolve the address. The gatekeeper must be able to select a gateway that can be used to reach the non-H.323 device. This is where the technology prefixes (or "gateway-type prefixes") become useful.

Technology Prefixes

A technology prefix is an optional H.323 standards-based feature that is supported by Cisco gateways and gatekeepers and enables more flexibility in call routing within an H.323 VoIP network. Technology prefixes are used to group gateways by type (such as voice or video) or class or define a pool of gateways.

Technology prefixes are used to separately identify gateways that support different types of services, such as video calls versus voice calls, where the gatekeeper can use this information to correspondingly route traffic to appropriate gateways.

The network administrator selects technology prefixes (tech-prefixes) to denote different types or classes of gateways. The gateways are then configured to register with their gatekeepers with these prefixes. For example, voice gateways can register with **tech-prefix 1#**, H.320 gateways with **tech-prefix 2#**, and voice-mail gateways with **tech-prefix 3#**. More than one gateway can register with the same gateway-type prefix. When this happens, the gatekeeper makes a random selection among gateways of the same type. If the callers know the type of device they are trying to reach, they can include the technology prefix in the destination address to indicate the type of gateway to use to get to the destination, as illustrated in Figure 6-13.

For example, if a caller knows that address 2125551111 belongs to a regular telephone, the destination address of 1#2125551111 can be used, where 1# indicates that the address should be resolved by a voice gateway. When the voice gateway receives the call for 1#2125551111, it strips off the technology prefix and bridges the next leg of the call to the telephone at 2125551111.

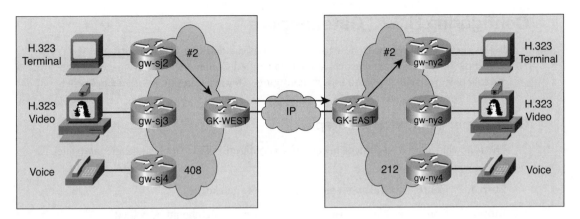

Figure 6-13   *Technology Prefixes*

Cisco IOS gatekeepers use technology prefixes to route calls when no E.164 addresses registered (by a gateway) match the called number. In fact, this is a common scenario because most Cisco IOS gateways can register either their H.323 ID or destination patterns. Cisco Unified Communications Manager Express and Cisco Unified Survivable Remote Site Telephony (SRST) can register their Ethernet phone's directory numbers (ephone-dns) at the gatekeeper. Without E.164 addresses registered, the Cisco IOS gatekeeper relies on these two options to make the call-routing decision:

■   With the technology prefix matches option, the Cisco IOS gatekeeper uses the technology prefix appended in the called number to select the destination gateway or zone.

■   With the default technology prefixes option, the Cisco IOS gatekeeper assigns a default gateway or gateways for routing unresolved call addresses. This assignment is based on the registered technology prefix of the gateways.

The gatekeeper uses a default technology prefix for routing all calls that do not have a technology prefix or for gateways that do not have a technology prefix defined. That remote gatekeeper then matches the technology prefix to decide which of its gateways to hop off. The zone prefix determines the routing to a zone just as the technology prefix determines the gateway in that zone.

If the majority of calls hop off on a particular type of gateway, the gatekeeper can be configured to use that type of gateway as the default type so callers no longer have to prepend a technology prefix on the address. For example, if you use mostly voice gateways in your network, and you have configured all your voice gateways to register with a technology prefix of 1#, you can configure your gatekeeper to use 1#* (that is, a 1# followed by zero or more characters) gateways as the default:

```
Router(config-gk)#gw-type-prefix 1#* default-technology
```

Configuring H.323 Gatekeepers

In this section, you will learn how to configure basic gatekeeper functionality. You will learn how to configure gatekeepers and Cisco Unified Communications Manager to operate together. You will also learn how to configure gateways to register with a gatekeeper.

Gatekeeper Configuration Steps

The following are the basic steps necessary to configure a Cisco IOS gatekeeper and gateway:

Step 1.   Configure local and remote zones on the gatekeeper.

Step 2.   Configure zone prefixes for all zones where calls should be routed.

Step 3.   Configure technology prefixes to provide more flexibility in call routing.

Step 4.   Configure gateways to use H.323 gatekeepers.

Step 5.   Configure dial peers.

Figure 6-14 shows a common topology where a single device (which in this scenario is a gatekeeper) manages multiple zones. Only one gatekeeper can control a zone at any time. The San Jose gateway is registered with the gatekeeper in the San Jose zone, and the Houston gateway is registered in the Houston zone with the Houston gatekeeper. The gatekeeper is responsible for call resolution, call admission control (CAC), and other features previously described in this chapter. After the call setup, the IP phones (which in this case are Phone1-1 and Phone2-2) are directly connected.

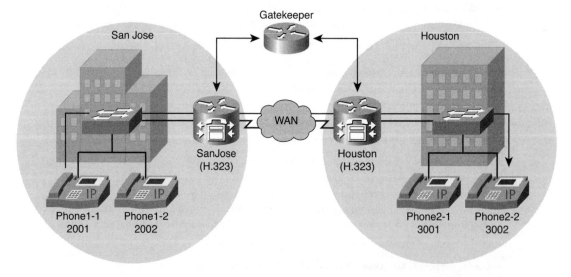

Figure 6-14   *Single Gatekeeper—Multizone Configuration Scenario*

Gateway Selection Process

The gatekeeper maintains a separate gateway list, ordered by priority, for each of its zone prefixes. If a gateway does not have an assigned priority for a zone prefix, it defaults to priority 5, which is the median. To explicitly bar the use of a gateway for a zone prefix, the gateway must be defined as having a priority 0 for that zone prefix.

When selecting gateways, the gatekeeper identifies a target pool of gateways by performing a longest zone prefix match. Then it selects from the target pool according to priorities and resource availability. If all high-priority gateways are busy, a low-priority gateway might be selected.

Cisco H.323 version 2 software improves the gateway selection process as follows:

- When more than one gateway is registered in a zone, the updated **zone prefix** command allows selection priorities to be assigned to these gateways on the basis of the dialed prefix.

- Gateway resource reporting allows the gateway to notify the gatekeeper when H.323 resources are getting low. The gatekeeper uses this information to determine which gateway to use to complete a call.

Configuration Considerations

When configuring a gatekeeper, keep the following in mind:

- Multiple local zones can be defined. The gatekeeper manages all configured local zones. Intrazone behavior is between the gatekeeper and the endpoints and gateways within a specific zone. A gatekeeper can support more than one zone. Even though there is a single gatekeeper per local zone, the communications between zones are considered to be interzone. So, the same gatekeeper can support both intrazone and interzone communications.

- Only one RAS IP argument can be defined for all local zones. You cannot configure each zone to use a different RAS IP address. If you define this IP address in the first zone definition, you can omit it for all subsequent zones that automatically pick up this address. If you set it in a subsequent **zone local** command, it also changes the RAS IP address of all previously configured local zones. After the IP address is defined, you can change it by reissuing any **zone local** command with a different RAS IP address.

- You cannot remove a local zone if there are endpoints or gateways registered in it. To remove the local zone, first shut down the gatekeeper, which forces the endpoints, gateways, and the local zone to unregister.

- Multiple logical gatekeepers control the multiple zones on the same Cisco IOS platform.

- The maximum number of local zones defined in a gatekeeper should not exceed 100.

Basic Gatekeeper Configuration Commands

Table 6-2 shows basic gatekeeper configuration commands.

Table 6-2 *Basic Gatekeeper Configuration Commands*

Command	Purpose
Router(config)#**gatekeeper**	Enters gatekeeper configuration mode.
Router(config-gk)#**zone local** *gatekeeper-name domain-name* [*ras-ip-address*] [**invia** *inbound_gatekeeper* | **outvia** *outbound_gatekeeper* [**enable-intrazone**]]	Specifies a zone controlled by a gatekeeper. • *gatekeeper-name*: Specifies the zone name. This is usually the fully qualified domain name of the gatekeeper. • *domain-name*: Specifies the domain name served by this gatekeeper. • *ras-ip-address*: (Optional) Specifies the IP address of one of the interfaces on the gatekeeper. When the gatekeeper responds to gatekeeper discovery messages, it signals the endpoint or gateway to use this address in future communications. • **invia** *inbound_gatekeeper*: Specifies the gatekeeper used for calls entering this zone. • **outvia** *outbound_gatekeeper*: Specifies the gatekeeper used for calls leaving this zone. • **enable-intrazone**: Forces all intrazone calls to use the via gatekeeper.
Router(config-gk)#**zone remote** *other-gatekeeper-name other-domain-name other-gatekeeper-ip-address* [*port-number*] [**cost** *cost-value* [**priority** *priority-value*]] [*foreign-domain*] [**invia** *inbound_gatekeeper*] | [**outvia** *outbound_gatekeeper*]	Statically specifies a remote zone if domain name service (DNS) is unavailable or undesirable. • *other-gatekeeper-name*: Name of the remote gatekeeper. • *other-gatekeeper-name*: Name of remote gatekeeper's domain. • *other-gatekeeper-ip-address*: IP address of the remote gatekeeper. • *port-number*: (Optional) RAS signaling port number for the remote zone. The range is 1–65535. If the value is not set, the default is the well-known RAS port number of 1719. • **cost** *cost-value*: (Optional) Cost of the zone. The range is 1–100. The default is 50. • **priority** *priority-value*: (Optional) Priority of the zone. The range is 1–100. The default is 50. • *foreign-domain*: (Optional) The cluster is in a different administrative domain. • **invia** *inbound_gatekeeper*: Specifies the gatekeeper for calls entering this zone. • **outvia** *outbound_gatekeeper*: Specifies the gatekeeper for calls leaving this zone.

Table 6-2 *Basic Gatekeeper Configuration Commands*

Command	Purpose
Router(config-gk)#**zone prefix** *gatekeeper-name e164-prefix* [**blast** | **seq**] [**gw-priority** *priority gw-alias* [*gw-alias*, ...]]	Adds a prefix to the gatekeeper zone list. The optional **blast** and **seq** parameters are for fault-tolerant gatekeeper networks. • *gatekeeper-name*: Name of a local or remote gatekeeper, which must have been defined by using the **zone local** or **zone remote** command. • *e164-prefix*: E.164 prefix in standard form followed by dots (.). Each dot represents a number in the E.164 address. • **blast**: (Optional) If you list multiple hop-offs, this indicates that the LRQs should be sent simultaneously to the gatekeepers based on the order in which they were listed. The default is **seq**. • **seq**: (Optional) If you list multiple hop-offs, this indicates that the LRQs should be sent sequentially to the gatekeepers based on the order in which they were listed. • **gw-priority** *priority gw-alias*: (Optional) Defines how the gatekeeper selects gateways in its local zone for calls to numbers beginning with the specified e164-prefix. The range is 0–10, where 0 prevents the gatekeeper from using the gateway's gw-alias for that prefix, and 10 places the highest priority on the gateway's gw-alias. The default is **5**.

Table 6-2   *Basic Gatekeeper Configuration Commands*

Command	Purpose
Router(config-gk)#**gw-type-prefix** *type-prefix* [[**hopoff** *gkid1*] [**hopoff** *gkid2*] [**hopoff** *gkidn*] [**seq** | **blast**]] [**default-technology**] [[**gw ipaddr** *ipaddr* [*port*]]]	Configures a technology prefix in the gatekeeper. Technology prefixes can be configured either on a gatekeeper or directly on a gateway. When using special flags (**hopoff** or **default-technology**), configure the prefix on the gatekeeper and on the gateway. • *type-prefix*: A technology prefix is recognized and is stripped before checking for the zone prefix. • **hopoff** *gkid*: (Optional) Use this option to specify the gatekeeper where the call is to hop off, regardless of the zone prefix in the destination address. The **gkid** argument refers to a gatekeeper previously configured using the **zone local** and/or **zone remote** command. • **seq** | **blast**: (Optional) If you list multiple hop-offs, this indicates that the LRQs should be sent sequentially or simultaneously (**blast**) to the gatekeepers according to the order in which they were listed. • **default-technology**: (Optional) Gateways registering with this prefix option are used as the default for routing any addresses that are otherwise unresolved. • **gw ipaddr** *ipaddr* [*port*]: (Optional) Use this option to indicate the gateway is incapable of registering technology prefixes. When it registers, it adds the gateway to the group for this gateway type prefix, just as if it had sent the technology prefix in its registration.
Router(config-gk)#**no shutdown**	Brings a gatekeeper online.

Configuring Gatekeeper Zones

The scenario presented in Example 6-4 and Figure 6-15 shows the basic steps to configure gatekeepers managing two local zones.

Example 6-4   *Zone Configuration Example*

```
GK1(config)#gatekeeper
GK1(config-gk)#zone local SanJose cisco.com 10.1.1.10
GK1(config-gk)#zone local Houston cisco.com enable-intrazone
GK1(config-gk)#zone remote Austin cisco.com 10.1.1.12
GK1(config-gk)#no shutdown
```

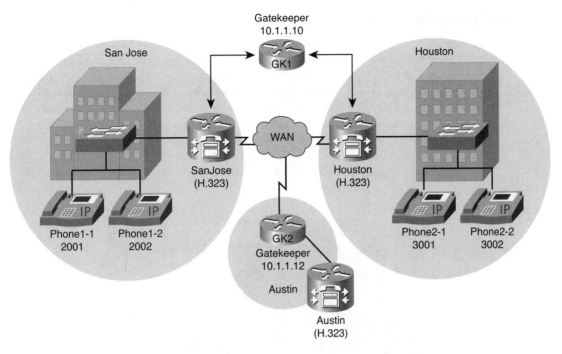

Figure 6-15 *Configuring Zones*

The gatekeeper is configured for the two zones: San Jose and Houston.

You can use the following procedure to configure zones on a gatekeeper:

Step 1.   Enter gatekeeper configuration mode.

```
GK1(config)#gatekeeper
```

Step 2.   Specify local zones to be controlled by the gatekeeper.

```
GK1(config-gk)#zone local SanJose cisco.com 10.1.1.10
GK1(config-gk)#zone local Houston cisco.com enable-intrazone
```

Note   Setting the IP address for one local zone makes it the address used for all local zones.

Step 3.   Specify a remote gatekeeper to which the local gatekeeper can send Location Requests (LRQ).

```
GK1(config-gk)#zone remote Austin cisco.com 10.1.1.12
```

Step 4.   Activate the gatekeeper.

```
GK1(config-gk)#no shutdown
```

Configuring Zone Prefixes

A zone prefix is a string of numbers that is used to associate a gateway to a dialed number in a zone. In Figure 6-16 and Example 6-5, the gatekeeper supports the 2... and 3... zone prefixes. The four digits are used by the gatekeeper for resolving the addresses. The San Jose and Houston sites use these digits for dialing between the sites. The gateways in each zone register with either 2 or 3 at the gatekeeper. This allows the gatekeeper to route the calls for a specific number range to the correct zone and gateway. Instead of using 2... and 3... for the zone prefix configuration, you could use 2* and 3* for the prefixes. The * symbol defines an endless number of digits. For example, a call to 24, 22224444, 2123, or 299999999999 would be routed to the designated gateway.

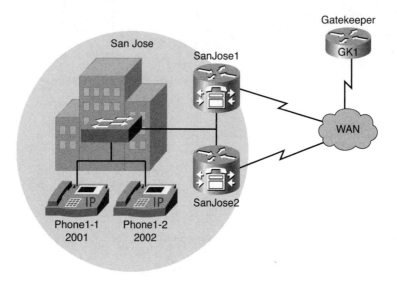

Figure 6-16   *Configuring Zone Prefixes*

Example 6-5   *Zone Prefix Configuration Example*

```
GK1(config)#gatekeeper
GK1(config)#zone local SanJose cisco.com 10.1.1.10
GK1(config)#zone local Houston cisco.com
GK1(config)#zone prefix SanJose 2... gw-priority 5 SanJose1
GK1(config)#zone prefix SanJose 2... gw-priority 10 SanJose2
GK1(config)#no shutdown
```

You can complete the following steps to configure zone prefixes on a gatekeeper:

Step 1.   Enter gatekeeper configuration mode.

```
GK1(config)#gatekeeper
```

Step 2.   Add a prefix to the gatekeeper zone list.

```
GK1(config-gk)#zone prefix SanJose 2... gw-priority 5 SanJose1
GK1(config-gk)#zone prefix SanJose 2... gw-priority 10 SanJose2
```

Configuring Technology Prefixes

To enable the gatekeeper to select the appropriate hop-off gateway, use the **gw-type-prefix** command to configure technology or gateway-type prefixes. Select technology prefixes to denote different types or classes of gateways. The gateways are then configured to register with their gatekeepers using these technology prefixes.

As an example, Example 6-6 and Figure 6-17 illustrate a sample technology prefix configuration, with 99# being used as a voice gateway technology prefix and 1# being used as a default technology prefix.

Example 6-6   *Technology Prefix Configuration Example*

```
GK1(config)#gatekeeper
GK1(config-gk)#zone local SanJose cisco.com 10.1.1.10
GK1(config-gk)#zone local Houston cisco.com
GK1(config-gk)#zone prefix SanJose 2... gw-priority 10 SanJose
GK1(config-gk)#zone prefix Houston 3... gw-priority 10 Houston
GK1(config-gk)#gw-type-prefix 99#* gw ipaddr 192.168.1.1 1720
GK1(config-gk)#gw-type-prefix 1#* default-technology
GK1(config-gk)#no shutdown
```

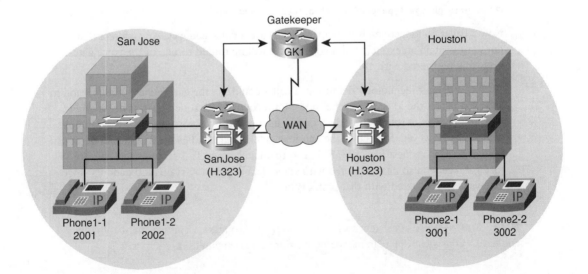

Figure 6-17   *Configuring Technology Prefixes*

As an additional example, voice gateways might register with a technology prefix of 1#, and H.320 gateways might register with a technology prefix of 2#. If several gateways of the same type exist, configure them to register with the same prefix type. By having them register with the same prefix type, the gatekeeper treats the gateways as a pool out of which a random selection is made whenever a call for that prefix type arrives.

Callers will need to know the technology prefixes that are defined and the type of device they are trying to reach. This enables them to prepend the appropriate technology prefix to the destination address for the type of gateway needed to reach the destination.

If the callers know the type of device they are trying to reach, they can include the technology prefix in the destination address to indicate the type of gateway to use to get to the destination. For example, if a caller knows that address 2125551111 belongs to a regular telephone, the destination address of 99#2125551111 can be used, where 99# indicates the address should be resolved by a voice gateway. When the voice gateway receives the call for 99#2125551111, it strips off the technology prefix and bridges the next leg of the call to the telephone at 2125551111.

Additionally, when you use the **gw-type-prefix** command, you can define a specific gateway-type prefix as the default gateway type to be used for addresses that cannot be resolved. This also forces a technology prefix to always hop off in a particular zone.

If the majority of calls hop off on a particular type of gateway, you can configure the gatekeeper to use that type of gateway as the default type so that callers no longer have to prepend a technology prefix on the address. For example, if voice gateways are mostly used in a network, and all voice gateways have been configured to register with technology prefix 1#, the gatekeeper can be configured to use 1# gateways as the default technology if this command is entered:

```
GK1(config-gk)#gw-type-prefix 1#* default-technology
```

Now a caller no longer needs to prepend 1# to use a voice gateway. Any address that does not contain an explicit technology prefix will be routed to one of the voice gateways that registered with 1#.

With this default technology definition, a caller could ask the gatekeeper for admission to 2125551111. If the local gatekeeper does not recognize the zone prefix as belonging to any remote zone, it routes the call to one of its local (1#) voice gateways so the call hops off locally. However, if it knows the San Jose gatekeeper handles the 212 area code, it can send a location request for 2125551111 to that gatekeeper. This requires that the San Jose gatekeeper also be configured with some default gateway-type prefix and its voice gateways be registered with that prefix type.

Note   You must use consistent technology prefixes throughout a gatekeeper deployment and have a consistent dial plan mapped out prior to implementation.

Configuring Gateways to Use H.323 Gatekeepers

The following are the configuration steps for registering a gateway on a gatekeeper:

Step 1.   Enable the gateway process on the router.

Step 2.   Configure interface commands for H.323 registration at the gatekeeper.

Step 3.   Configure the dial peers that are pointing to the gatekeeper.

Step 4.   If necessary, prevent ephone-dn and dial-peer registration at the gatekeeper.

Example 6-7 and Figure 6-18 show the configuration for a gateway registering with a gatekeeper.

Example 6-7   *H.323 Gateway Configuration*

```
Houston#show running-config
gateway
!
interface Loopback 0
 ip address 192.168.1.3 255.255.255.0
 h323-gateway voip interface
 h323-gateway voip bind srcaddr 192.168.1.3
 h323-gateway voip id GK1 ipaddr 192.168.1.15 1719 priority 1
 h323-gateway voip h323-id Houston
 h323-gateway voip tech-prefix 1#
```

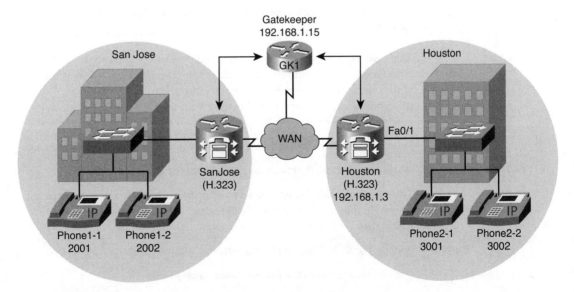

Figure 6-18   *Configuring Gateways to Use H.323 Gatekeepers*

You can use the following steps to configure gateways to use H.323 gatekeepers:

Step 1.   Enable the H.323 VoIP gateway to register with a gatekeeper.

```
Router(config)#gateway
```

Sometimes, it helps to enable the gateway process at the end of your gateway configuration to avoid automatic gateway registration at the gatekeeper. For example, this is useful if you have multiple gatekeepers and want to make sure you are unicasting to a specific gatekeeper or using a specific H.323 ID. This allows all interface commands to be entered before the gateway attempts registration with the gatekeeper.

Step 2.   Enter interface configuration mode for the interface you intend to use for communication with the H.323 gatekeeper.

```
Router(config)#interface loopback 0
```

Step 3.   Give the interface an IP address.

```
Router(config-if)#ip-address 192.168.1.3 255.255.255.0
```

Step 4.   Configure the interface as an H.323 gateway interface.

```
Router(config-if)#h323-gateway voip interface
```

Step 5.   Define the IP address on the gateway to be used for H.323 communication.

```
Router(config-if)#h323-gateway voip bind srcaddr 192.168.1.3
```

Step 6.   Define the name and location of the gatekeeper.

```
Router(config-if)#h323-gateway voip id Houston ipaddr 192.168.1.15 1719
priority 1
```

This command is used to specify the IP address of the gatekeeper and the zone the gateway should register with, in this case Houston. Without the **voip id** parameter, the gateway will use multicast for gatekeeper discovery. When using multicast, the gateway will register with the first available zone on the gatekeeper. The gatekeeper ID is the zone the gateway should register with.

Step 7.   Specify the H.323 gateway name to identify it to its associated gatekeeper.

```
Router(config-if)#h323-gateway voip h323-id Houston
```

This is an optional command used to identify a gateway to its associated gatekeeper. In this case, the gateway will register with the name Houston at the gatekeeper.

Step 8.   Specify the technology prefix the gateway registers with the gatekeeper.

```
Router(config-if)#h323-gateway voip tech-prefix 1#
```

The gateway will inform the gatekeeper it wants to register with a technology prefix of 1#. Each technology prefix can contain as many as 11 characters.

Although not strictly necessary, a pound sign (#) is frequently used as the last digit in a technology prefix.

Table 6-3 provides a table of gateway interface configuration commands and explains their purpose.

Table 6-3 *Gateway Interface Configuration Commands*

Command	Purpose
Router(config-if)#**h323-gateway voip interface**	Identifies an interface as a VoIP gateway interface.
Router(config-if)#**h323-gateway voip id** *gatekeeper-id* {**ipaddr** *ip-address* [*port*] | **multicast**} [**priority** *priority*]	(Optional) Defines the name and location of the gatekeeper for this gateway. The following are the keywords and arguments: • *gatekeeper-id*: H.323 identification of the gatekeeper, which should match a zone configured on a gatekeeper. If no match is found, the gatekeeper registers the gateway with the first configured local zone. • **ipaddr** *ip-address*: IP address used to identify the gatekeeper. • *port*: UDP port number used for communicating with a gatekeeper. • **multicast**: Used by the gateway to locate a gatekeeper. • **priority** *priority*: This is the priority of this gatekeeper. The acceptable range is 1–127, and the default is 127.
Router(config-if)#**h323-gateway voip h323-id** *interface-id*	(Optional) Defines the H.323 name of the gateway that identifies this gateway to its associated gatekeeper. Usually, this ID is the name of the gateway, with the gatekeeper domain name appended to the end: name@domainname.
Router(config-if)#**h323-gateway voip tech-prefix** *prefix*	(Optional) Defines the numbers used as the technology prefix that the gateway uses to register with a gatekeeper. This command can contain up to 11 characters. Although it is not strictly necessary, a pound symbol (#) is frequently used as the last digit in a prefix. Valid characters are 0–9, #, and *.

Dial-Peer Configuration

The VoIP dial peer determines how to direct calls that originate from a local voice port into a VoIP cloud to the RAS session target. The session target indicates the address of the remote gateway where the call is terminated.

In the scenario presented in Figure 6-19 and Example 6-8, all calls designated for 2... will be routed from Houston to the gatekeeper.

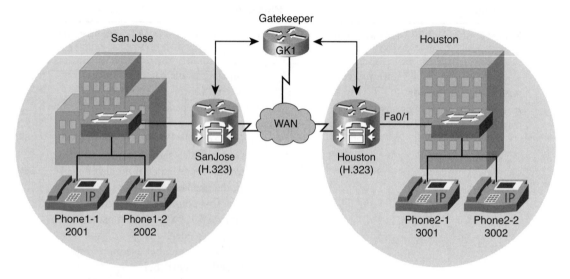

Figure 6-19   *Dial-Peer Configuration Topology*

Example 6-8   *Configuring a Dial Peer for Gatekeeper Operation*

```
Houston(config)#gateway
Houston(config)#dial-peer voice 1 voip
Houston(config-dial-peer)#destination pattern 2...
Houston(config-dial-peer)#tech-prefix 1#
Houston(config-dial-peer)#session target ras
```

You can use the following steps to create a dial peer to be used with a gatekeeper:

Step 1.   Enter dial-peer configuration mode.

```
Router(config)#dial-peer voice 1 voip
```

Step 2.   Specify the E.164 address associated with this dial peer.

```
Router(config-dial-peer)#destination pattern 2...
```

Step 3.   (Optional) Define the numbers used as the technology prefix that the gateway uses to register with the gatekeeper.

```
Router(config-dial-peer)#tech-prefix 1#
```

> **Note**   In this example, no prepending of a technology prefix is necessary because of the default technology configuration on the gatekeeper.

Step 4.   Specify that the RAS protocol is being used to determine the IP address of the session target (meaning a gatekeeper translates the E.164 address to an IP address).

```
Router(config-dial-peer)#session target ras
```

> **Note**   When dealing with services numbers, such as 911, make sure to include the **no e.164 register** command.

Example 6-9 shows the use of the **no e.164 register** command when configuring a dial peer for 911 operation.

Example 6-9   *911 Dial-Peer Configuration*

```
Router(config)#dial-peer voice 911 pots
Router(config-dial-peer)#destination pattern 911
Router(config-dial-peer)#prefix 911
Router(config-dial-peer)#no e.164 register
Router(config-dial-peer)#session target ras
```

Verifying Gatekeeper Functionality

Cisco IOS supports several commands for verifying and troubleshooting H.323 gateway and gatekeeper configuration, such as the following:

- **show gatekeeper gw-type-prefix:** Displays the technology prefix of a gateway
- **show gatekeeper status:** Displays the overall gatekeeper status, including zone status
- **show gatekeeper zone prefix:** Displays the zone prefixes known to a gatekeeper
- **show gatekeeper calls:** Displays current calls known to a gatekeeper
- **show gatekeeper endpoints:** Displays endpoints currently registered with a gatekeeper
- **show gatekeeper zone status:** Displays the status of zones registered with a gatekeeper
- **debug h225 {asn1 | events}:** Displays H.225 activity in real time
- **debug h245 {asn1 | events}:** Displays H.245 activity in real time
- **debug ras:** Displays RAS messages, in real time, to and from a gatekeeper

The following examples illustrate the output of a few of these commands. First, you can use the **show gatekeeper gw-type-prefix** command to display configured prefixes, as illustrated in Example 6-10.

Example 6-10   show gatekeeper gw-type-prefix *Command*

```
Router#show gatekeeper gw-type-prefix
GATEWAY TYPE PREFIX TABLE
========================================================
Prefix: 2#*
Zone HQ master gateway list:  10.1.250.102:1720 BR
```

The **show gatekeeper status** command, as shown in Example 6-11, displays the status of the gatekeeper.

Example 6-11   show gatekeeper status *Command*

```
Router#show gatekeeper status
     Gatekeeper State: UP
     Load Balancing:    DISABLED
     Flow Control:      DISABLED
     Zone Name:         HQ
     Zone Name:         BR
     Accounting:        DISABLED
     Endpoint Throttling:        DISABLED
     Security:          DISABLED
     Maximum Remote Bandwidth:            unlimited
     Current Remote Bandwidth:            0 kbps
     Current Remote Bandwidth (w/ Alt GKs): 0 kbps
```

Additionally, you can use the **show gatekeeper zone prefix** command to display configured zone prefixes, as demonstrated in Example 6-12.

Example 6-12   show gatekeeper zone prefix *Command*

```
Router#show gatekeeper zone prefix
       ZONE PREFIX TABLE
       =================
GK-NAME               E164-PREFIX
-------               -----------
HQ                    1...
BR                    2...
```

You can use the **show gatekeeper endpoints** command to display registered endpoints of the gatekeeper, as shown in Example 6-13.

Example 6-13 show gatekeeper endpoints *Command*

```
Router#show gatekeeper endpoints
                    GATEKEEPER ENDPOINT REGISTRATION
                    ==================================

CallSignalAddr   Port  RASSignalAddr    Port  Zone Name       Type      Flags
---------------  ----  ---------------  ----- ---------       ----      -----
10.1.250.101     1720  10.1.250.101     58963 HQ              H323-GW
    H323-ID: GW-A1
    E164-ID: 1101
    E164-ID: 1102
    Voice Capacity Max.=  Avail.=  Current.= 0
10.1.250.102     1720  10.1.250.102     58306 BR              VOIP-GW
    H323-ID: GW-A2
    Voice Capacity Max.=  Avail.=  Current.= 0
Total number of active registrations = 2
```

Providing Call Admission Control with an H.323 Gatekeeper

In this section, you learn how to implement gatekeeper-based CAC. You will also learn how CAC works and how it is responsible for managing admission control and bandwidth for both voice and video calls.

Gatekeeper Zone Bandwidth Operation

Consider the Cisco Unified IP Communications system shown in Figure 6-20. Because the IP network is based on a PSTN, no dedicated circuits are established to set up an IP communications call. Instead, the IP packets containing the voice samples are routed across the IP network together with other types of data packets. QoS is used to differentiate the voice packets from the data packets, but bandwidth resources, especially on IP WAN links, are not infinite. Therefore, network administrators dedicate a certain amount of "priority" bandwidth to voice traffic on each IP WAN link. However, after the provisioned bandwidth has been fully utilized, the Cisco Unified IP Communications system must reject subsequent calls to avoid oversubscription of the priority queue on the IP WAN link, which would cause quality degradation for all voice calls.

This function is known as CAC and is essential to guarantee good voice quality in a multisite deployment. The gatekeeper maintains a record of all active calls so it can manage bandwidth in a zone.

You can use CAC to help maintain a desired level of voice quality over a WAN link. For example, you can use CAC to regulate the voice quality on a T1 line that connects your main campus to a remote site.

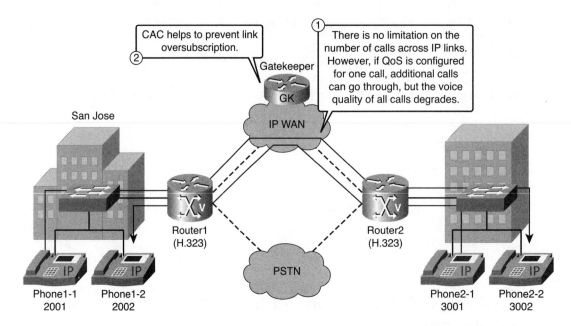

Figure 6-20   *Call Admission Control Sample Topology*

CAC regulates voice quality by limiting the number of calls that can be active on a particular link at the same time. CAC does not guarantee a particular level of audio quality on the link, but it does allow you to regulate the amount of bandwidth consumed by active calls on the link.

The Cisco IOS gatekeeper is the device in the IP communications network that is responsible for CAC between these devices:

■   Cisco Unified Communications Manager

■   Cisco Unified Communications Manager Express

■   H.323 gateways

The gatekeeper requires a static policy-based configuration of the available resources. The gatekeeper cannot assign variable resources like the Resource Reservation Protocol (RSVP) is able to do.

Zone Bandwidth Calculation

Zone bandwidth in a gatekeeper network can be calculated with this simple formula:

(Number of Calls) * (Codec Payload Bandwidth) * 2 = Zone Bandwidth

With this formula, the needed bandwidth in a gatekeeper network can be easily defined.

For example, following is a calculation for three simultaneous G.711 calls in a gatekeeper network:

3 * 64 kbps * 2 = 384 kbps

An important point for every bandwidth calculation is the number of devices for which you want to calculate the bandwidth. Gatekeepers and Cisco Unified Communications Manager servers have different bandwidth values for the same codecs. In a Cisco Unified Communications Manager environment, a G.711 call is assumed to use 80 kbps, and a G.729 call is assumed to use 24 kbps. However, in a gatekeeper environment, a G.711 call consumes 128 kbps, and a G.729 call consumes 16 kbps. If a call is signaled from a Cisco Unified Communications Manager server to a gatekeeper, Cisco Unified Communications Manager internally assumes that 80 kbps of bandwidth is required for a G.711 call, but will signal in its ARQ message to its gatekeeper a request for a G.711 call with 128 kbps of bandwidth required. Similarly, when using G.729, Cisco Unified Communications Manager will use 24 kbps for internal CAC calculations, but request 16 kbps from a gatekeeper.

Example 6-14 shows a gatekeeper with an active G.711 call requested by Cisco Unified Communications Manager. Note the 128 kbps in the BW column.

Example 6-14 *Viewing Active Gatekeeper Calls*

```
GK#show gatekeeper calls
Total number of active calls = 1.

                                    GATEKEEPER CALL INFO
                                    ====================
LocalCallID                         Age(secs)        BW
2-14476                             59               128(Kbps)
 Endpt(s): Alias                    E.164Addr
   src EP: CHI-CUCME                13125553001
                CallSignalAddr  Port   RASSignalAddr   Port
                192.168.3.254   1720   192.168.3.254   52668
 Endpt(s): Alias                    E.164Addr
   dst EP: ipipgw                   49895556666
                CallSignalAddr  Port   RASSignalAddr   Port
                192.168.1.3     1720   192.168.1.3     52060
```

The gatekeeper is the central device in the network. The bandwidth is configured for the network on the gatekeeper. The available bandwidth will be checked by the gatekeeper for every call, as illustrated in Figure 6-21.

The **bandwidth** command allows the gatekeeper to manage the bandwidth limitations within a zone, across zones, and at a per-session level. By default, the maximum aggregate bandwidth is unlimited.

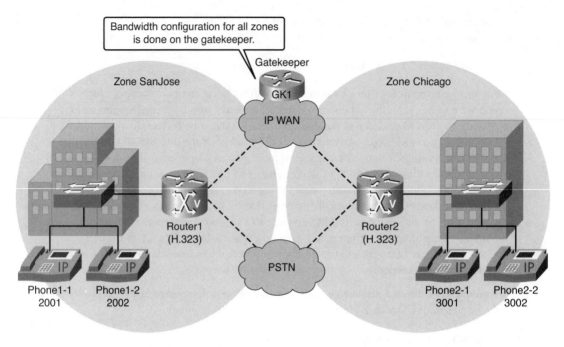

Figure 6-21   *Zone Bandwidth Sample Topology*

Example 6-15 configures the default maximum bandwidth for traffic between one zone and another zone to 128 kbps, the default maximum bandwidth for all zones to 5 Mbps, the default maximum bandwidth for a single session within any zone up to 384 kbps, and the default maximum bandwidth for a single session with zone "Denver" of up to 256 kbps.

Example 6-15   *Zone Bandwidth Command Example*

```
GK1(config)#gatekeeper
GK1(config-gk)#bandwidth interzone default 128
GK1(config-gk)#bandwidth total default 5000
GK1(config-gk)#bandwidth session default 384
GK1(config-gk)#bandwidth session zone denver 256
```

bandwidth Command

The full command syntax for the **bandwidth** command is as follows:

```
Router(config-gk)#bandwidth {interzone | total | session | remote | check-
   destination} {default |   zone zone-name} bandwidth-size
```

Table 6-4 describes the parameters of the **bandwidth** command.

Table 6-4 bandwidth *Command Parameters*

Parameter	Description
interzone	Total amount of bandwidth for H.323 traffic from a zone to any other zone.
total	Total amount of bandwidth for H.323 traffic allowed in a zone.
session	Maximum bandwidth allowed for a session in a zone.
remote	Total bandwidth for H.323 traffic between this gatekeeper and any other gatekeeper.
check-destination	Enables the gatekeeper to verify available bandwidth resources at a destination endpoint.
default	Default value for all zones.
zone *zone-name*	Specifies a particular zone.
bandwidth-size	Maximum bandwidth, in kbps. For **interzone**, **total**, and **remote**, the range is 1–10,000,000. For **session**, the range is 1–5000.

The following are Cisco-provided usage guidelines for the **bandwidth** command:

■ To specify maximum bandwidth for traffic between one zone and any other zone, use the **default** keyword with the **interzone** keyword.

■ To specify maximum bandwidth for traffic within one zone or for traffic between that zone and another zone (interzone or intrazone), use the **default** keyword with the **total** keyword.

■ To specify maximum bandwidth for a single session within a specific zone, use the **zone** keyword with the **session** keyword.

■ To specify maximum bandwidth for a single session within any zone, use the **default** keyword with the **session** keyword.

Zone Bandwidth Configuration Example

Figure 6-22 and Example 6-16 show a sample of a configuration for a gatekeeper.

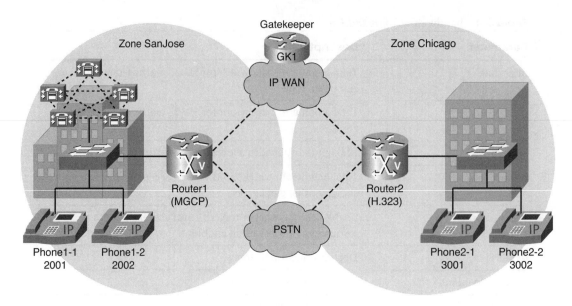

Figure 6-22   *Zone Bandwidth Configuration Topology*

Example 6-16   *Zone Bandwidth Configuration Example*

```
GK1(config)#gatekeeper
GK1(config-gk)#zone local SanJose cisco.com 192.168.1.15
GK1(config-gk)#zone local Chicago cisco.com
GK1(config-gk)#zone prefix SanJose 2... gw-priority 10 ICT_CM_1
GK1(config-gk)#zone prefix SanJose 2... gw-priority  9 ICT_CM_2
GK1(config-gk)#zone prefix Chicago 3... gw-priority 10 CME
GK1(config-gk)#gw-type-prefix 1#* default-technology
GK1(config-gk)#bandwidth interzone zone SanJose 384
GK1(config-gk)#bandwidth interzone zone Chicago 256
GK1(config-gk)#no shutdown
```

There are two local zones: SanJose and Chicago. Notice that the **bandwidth interzone** commands are highlighted. In the **bandwidth** command, the **interzone** option specifies the bandwidth from one zone to another zone. The first bandwidth command allocates 384 kbps of bandwidth for H.323 traffic between the SanJose zone and any other zone. The second **bandwidth** command allocates 256 kbps of bandwidth for H.323 traffic between the Chicago zone and any other zone.

Verifying Zone Bandwidth Operation

Example 6-17 shows the output of the **show gatekeeper zone status** command. In the Bandwidth Information output, you can see the maximum interzone bandwidth for all calls in the SanJose zone. In this scenario, a bandwidth of 384 kbps is configured.

Example 6-17 *Verifying Zone Bandwidth Operation*

```
Router#show gatekeeper zone status
                    GATEKEEPER ZONES

                    =================
GK name      Domain Name   RAS Address     PORT  FLAGS
-------      -----------   -----------     ----- -----


SanJose      cisco.com     192.168.1.15    1719  LS
  BANDWIDTH INFORMATION (kbps) :
    Maximum total bandwidth : unlimited
    Current total bandwidth : 0
    Maximum interzone bandwidth : 384
    Current interzone bandwidth : 0
    Maximum session bandwidth : unlimited
  SUBNET ATTRIBUTES :
    All Other Subnets : (Enabled)
```

Introducing the Cisco Unified Border Element Gateway

The Cisco Unified Border Element (Cisco UBE) is similar to a traditional voice gateway, the main difference being the replacement of physical voice trunks with an IP connection. This section describes the concepts and features of a Cisco UBE in enterprise environments.

Cisco Unified Border Element Overview

The Cisco UBE is an intelligent unified communications network border element. A Cisco UBE, formerly known as the Cisco Multiservice IP-to-IP Gateway, terminates and reoriginates both signaling (H.323 and SIP) and media streams (Real-time Transport Protocol [RTP] and RTP Control Protocol [RTCP]) while performing border interconnection services between IP networks. Cisco UBE, in addition to other Cisco IOS Software features, includes session border controller (SBC) functions that help enable end-to-end IP-based transport of voice, video, and data between independent unified communications networks.

Originally, SBCs were used by service providers (SP) to enable full billing capabilities within VoIP networks. But the functionality to interconnect VoIP networks is becoming more and more important for enterprise VoIP networks as well, because VoIP is becoming the new standard for any telephony solution.

Cisco UBE functionally is implemented on Cisco IOS gateways using a special Cisco IOS feature set. Using this feature set, a Cisco UBE can route a call from one Voice over IP (VoIP) dial peer to another VoIP dial peer.

VoIP dial peers can also be handled by either the Session Initiation Protocol (SIP) or H.323. As a result, the capability to interconnect VoIP dial peers also includes the capability to interconnect VoIP networks using different signaling protocols or VoIP networks using the same signaling protocols but facing interoperability issues.

Protocol interworking includes these combinations:

■   H.323-to-SIP interworking

■   H.323-to-H.323 interworking

■   SIP-to-SIP interworking

Figure 6-23 illustrates the capability of Cisco UBE to interconnect VoIP networks, including VoIP networks that use different signaling protocols. VoIP interworking is achieved by connecting an inbound VoIP dial peer with an outbound VoIP dial peer. A standard Cisco IOS gateway without the Cisco UBE functionality will not allow VoIP-to-VoIP connections.

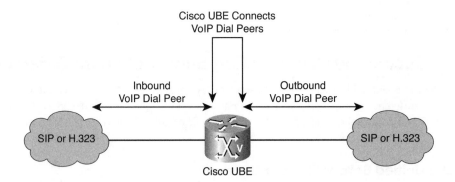

Figure 6-23   *Cisco UBE Functionality*

The Cisco UBE provides a network-to-network interface point for the following:

■   Signaling interworking (H.323, SIP)

■   Media interworking (dual-tone multifrequency [DTMF], fax, modem, and codec transcoding)

■   Address and port translations (privacy and topology hiding)

■   Billing and Call Detail Record (CDR) normalization

■   Quality-of-service (QoS) and bandwidth management (QoS marking using differentiated services code point [DSCP] or IP precedence, bandwidth enforcement using Resource Reservation Protocol [RSVP], and codec filtering)

A Cisco UBE interoperates with several network elements, including voice gateways, IP phones, and call control servers in many application environments, from advanced enterprise voice and/or video services with Cisco Unified Communications Manager or Cisco

Unified Communications Manager Express, as well as simpler toll-bypass and VoIP transport applications.

The Cisco UBE provides organizations with all the border controller functions integrated into the network layer to interconnect unified communications voice and video enterprise-to-service-provider architectures. The Cisco UBE is used by enterprise and small- and medium-sized organizations to interconnect SIP public switched telephone network (PSTN) access with SIP and H.323 enterprise unified communications networks.

Cisco UBE Gateways in Enterprise Environments

Cisco UBE in enterprise deployments serve two main purposes:

- **External connections:** A Cisco UBE can be used as a demarcation point within a unified communications network and provides interconnectivity with external networks. This includes H.323 voice and video connections and SIP VoIP connections.

- **Internal connections:** When used within a VoIP network, a Cisco UBE can be used to increase the flexibility and interoperability between different devices.

The following are some key features offered by Cisco UBE:

- **Protocol interworking:** The Cisco UBE supports interworking of signaling protocols, including H.323-to-H.323, H.323-to-SIP, and SIP-to-SIP.

- **Address hiding:** A Cisco UBE can hide or replace the endpoint IP addresses used for a media connection.

- **Security:** A Cisco UBE can be placed in a demilitarized zone (DMZ) and provide outside connectivity to external networks.

- **Video integration:** In addition to VoIP services, a Cisco UBE also supports H.323 video connections.

- **Call admission control (CAC):** A Cisco UBE can use Cisco IOS–based CAC mechanisms, including RSVP.

Table 6-5 lists key features and capabilities of the Cisco UBE

Figure 6-24 shows the various deployment options for a Cisco UBE. Depending on the deployment scenario, multiple Cisco UBEs might be required. Whether the gateways are being deployed within a single VoIP network or used to interconnect to external VoIP networks, the same concepts apply.

Table 6-5   *Key Features of the Cisco UBE Gateway*

Feature	Details
Protocols	H.323 and SIP
Network hiding	IP network privacy and topology hiding IP network security boundary Intelligent IP address translation for call media and signaling Back-to-back user agent, replacing all SIP-embedded IP addressing
CAC	RSVP Maximum number of calls per trunk CAC based on IP circuits CAC based on total calls, CPU usage, or memory usage thresholds
Protocol and signal interworking	H.323-to-H.323 (including Cisco Unified Communications Manager) H.323-to-SIP (including Cisco Unified Communications Manager) SIP-to-SIP (including Cisco Unified Communications Manager)
Media support	RTP and RTCP
Media modes	Media flow-through Media flow-around
Video codecs	H.261, H.263, and H.264
Transport mode	TCP UDP TCP-to-UDP interworking
DTMF	H.245 Alphanumeric H.245 Signal RFC 2833 SIP Notify Keypad Markup Language (KPML) Interworking capabilities: • H.323-to-SIP • RFC 2833-to-G.711 in-band DTMF
Fax support	T.38 fax relay Fax pass-through Cisco Fax Relay

Table 6-5 *Key Features of the Cisco UBE Gateway*

Feature	Details
Modem support	Modem pass-through Cisco modem relay
Supplementary services	Call hold, call transfer, and call forward for H.323 networks using H.450 and transparent passing of Empty Capability Set (ECS) SIP-to-SIP supplementary services (holds and transfers) support using a SIP REFER message H.323-to-SIP supplementary services for Cisco Unified Communications Manager with media termination point (MTP) on the H.323 trunk
NAT Traversal	NAT traversal support for SIP phones deployed behind non–Application Line Gateway (ALG) data routers Stateful NAT traversal
QoS	IP precedence and DSCP marking
Voice-quality statistics	Packet loss, jitter, and round-trip time
Number translation	Number translation rules for VoIP numbers Electronic Numbering (ENUM) support for E.164 number mapping into Domain Name System (DNS)
Codecs	G711 mu-law and a-law G723ar53, G723ar63, G723r53, and G723r63 G726r16, G726r24, and G726r32 G728 G729, G729A, G729B, and G729AB Internet Low Bitrate Codec (iLBC)
Transcoding	Transcoding between any two families of codecs from the following list: • G711 a-law and mu-law • G.729, G.729A, G.729B, and G.729AB • G.723 (5.3 and 6.3 kbps) • iLBC
Security	IP Security (IPsec) Secure RTP (SRTP) Transport Layer Security (TLS)
Authentication, authorization, and accounting (AAA)	AAA with RADIUS

Table 6-5   *Key Features of the Cisco UBE Gateway*

Feature	Details
Voice media applications	Tool Command Language (Tcl) script support for application customization Voice Extensible Markup Language (VoiceXML 2.0) script support for application customization
Billing	Standard CDRs for accurate billing available through: • AAA records • Syslog Simple Network Management Protocol (SNMP)

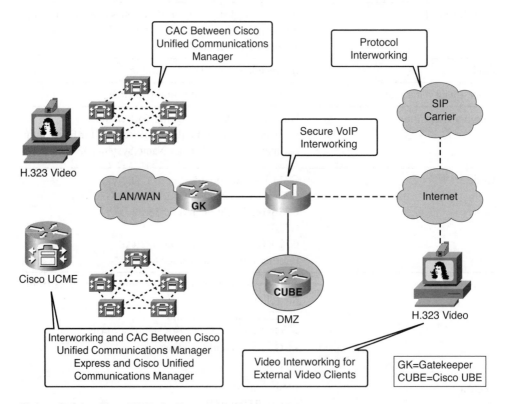

Figure 6-24   *Cisco UBEs in Enterprise Environments*

Protocol Interworking on Cisco UBE Gateways

Cisco UBE can interwork signaling protocols, similar to a proxy. This feature can be used for two scenarios:

- **Interworking between the same signaling protocol:** A Cisco UBE that is interworking between the same signaling protocol (for example, H.323-to-H.323) can be used to solve interoperability issues between two devices having different capabilities. Because Cisco UBE builds two call legs to each peer, it can interwork between those two call legs. For example, Cisco Unified Communications Manager Express uses H.450, a subset of H.323, for call transfers and call forwarding. When connected directly to a Cisco Unified Communications Manager, which does not support H.450, call forwarding and transfers might lead to hair-pinned calls and suboptimal WAN usage. A Cisco UBE at the Cisco Unified Communications Manager site can be used to solve these issues.

- **Interworking between different signaling protocols:** Cisco UBE can interconnect dial peers that use different signaling protocols, such as a SIP and an H.323 dial peer. This allows for greater flexibility when deploying an IP communications network.

Signaling Method Refresher

Table 6-6 provides a review of the signaling methods that are supported by H.323 and SIP.

H.323 version 1 supports only *Slow Start* call setup, in which the H.245 parameters are exchanged after the call has been answered.

H.323 version 2 introduced the *Fast Start* option, used by default on Cisco gateways, which expedites the call setup by embedding H.245 parameters in H.225 Call Setup and Proceeding or Alerting messages.

Early Media is an H.323v2 capability that allows the endpoints to establish RTP media flows before the call is answered. This option requires that Fast Start is used, but Fast Start does not necessarily entail Early Media cut-through, because it is negotiated separately.

Delayed Offer is a SIP signaling method that exchanges Session Description Protocol (SDP) information about the media types, codecs, and RTP numbers late in the exchange, namely in the 200 OK and ACK messages.

Early Offer, which is used by default on Cisco gateways, expedites the call setup by attaching the SDP information to earlier messages: Invite, and 200 OK, 183 Session Progress, or 180 Ringing. The relevant difference is that the Invite message carries the SDP information rather than the 200 OK message in Delayed Offer.

Early Media in SIP is the conceptual equivalent of Early Media in H.323 and allows an earlier cut-through of RTP flows. It requires Early Offer but is not enforced by it, because it is negotiated separately.

Table 6-6   *Signaling Method Refresher*

Method	Protocol	Characteristics
Slow Start	H.323v1	H.245 parameters exchanged after H.225 Connect
Fast Start (Cisco default)	H.323v2	H.245 parameters exchanged earlier, in H.225 Call Setup and H.225 Call Proceeding/Alerting
Early Media	H.323	Early Media cut-through after H.245 exchanged
Delayed Offer	SIP	SDP proposals sent late: From terminating gateway: • 200 OK From originating gateway: • ACK
Early Offer (Cisco default)	SIP	SDP proposals sent early: From originating gateway: • Invite From terminating gateway: • 200 OK • 183 Session Progress • 180 Ringing
Early Media	SIP	Early media cut-through after: • 183 session progress • 180 ringing

Cisco Unified Border Element Protocol Interworking

As illustrated in Figure 6-25, when you use interworking signaling protocols, a Cisco UBE supports these combinations:

- **H.323-to-H.323:** All combinations of Fast Start and Slow Start on both call legs

- **H.323-to-SIP:** H.323 Fast Start-to-SIP Early Offer and H.323 Slow Start-to-SIP Delayed Offer

- **SIP-to-H.323:** SIP Early Offer-to-H.323 Fast Start, SIP Early Offer-to-H.323 Slow Start, and SIP Delayed Offer-to-H.323 Slow Start

- **SIP-to-SIP:** All combinations of Early Offer and Delayed Offer on both call legs

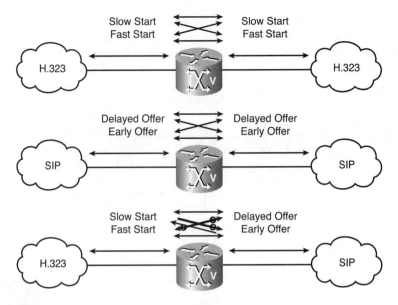

Figure 6-25   *Cisco UBE Interworking*

Media Flows on Cisco UBE Gateways

Because Cisco UBE is a signaling proxy, it also processes all signaling messages regarding the setup of media channels. This enables a Cisco UBE to affect the flow of media traffic. Two options exist: media flow-through and media flow-around.

When using media flow-through, Cisco UBE replaces the source IP address used for media connections with its own IP address. This operation can be utilized in different ways:

■ It solves IP interworking issues because Cisco UBE replaces potential duplicate IP addresses with a single, easy-to-control IP address.

■ It hides the original endpoint IP address from the remote endpoints.

This makes Cisco UBE with media flow-through ideal for interworking with external VoIP networks and enforcing a tighter security policy.

When using Cisco UBE internally, media flow-through might not be necessary or even desirable. One of the main drawbacks when using media flow-through is the higher load on a Cisco UBE router, which decreases the number of supported concurrent flows. In addition, media flow-through might result in suboptimal traffic flows because direct endpoint-to-endpoint communication is prohibited. Thus Cisco UBE can also be configured for media flow-around. When using media flow-around, Cisco UBE leaves the IP addresses used for the media connections untouched. Call signaling will still be processed by Cisco UBE, but after the call is set up, Cisco UBE is no longer involved with the traffic flow.

Figure 6-26 shows a Cisco UBE router configured for media flow-through. The signaling between the two Cisco Unified Communications Manager clusters is processed by Cisco UBE, and the source IP addresses of the endpoints are replaced by the Cisco UBE IP address.

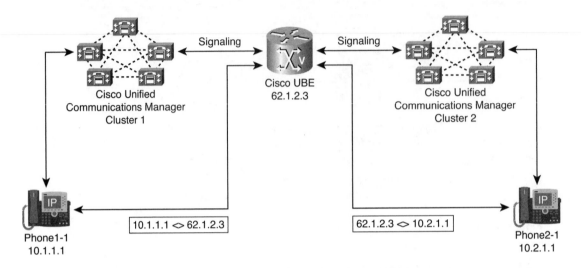

Figure 6-26   *Media Flow-Through Topology*

Figure 6-27 shows a Cisco UBE router configured for media flow-around. No duplicate IP address ranges exist, and IP address hiding is not required—so media flow-through is not required. Cisco UBE still processes all signaling traffic, but the endpoints have direct media channels. You might use media flow-around when you are not concerned with hiding your network addresses.

Codec Filtering on Cisco UBEs

VoIP networks usually support a large variety of codecs, and mechanisms exist to perform codec negotiations between devices. Regardless of which mechanisms are used, preferences determine which codecs will be selected over others.

Because a Cisco UBE router is essentially a Cisco IOS gateway with the capability to interconnect VoIP dial peers, the same codec selection mechanisms are available as on any other Cisco IOS gateway. A dial peer can be configured to allow a specific codec or to use a codec voice class to specify multiple codecs with a preference order. This enables Cisco UBE to perform codec filtering, because a dial peer will set up a call leg only if the desired codec criteria are satisfied. This adds to the Cisco UBE role of a demarcation point within a VoIP network.

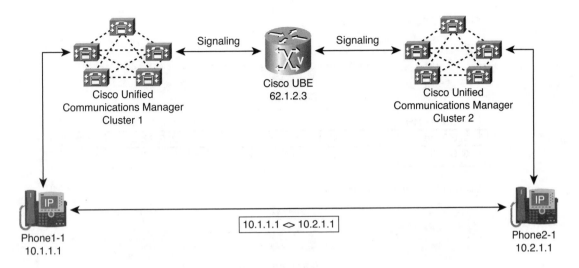

Figure 6-27 *Media Flow-Around Topology*

If codec filtering is not required, Cisco UBE also supports transparent codec negotiations. This enables negotiations between endpoints with Cisco UBE leaving the codec information untouched.

Whether performing codec filtering or operating in transparent mode, Cisco UBE is required to support the codec used between endpoints. The following codecs are supported:

■ **Audio codecs:** G.711u, G.711a, G.723, G.726, G.729r8, G.728, and AMR-NB

■ **Video codecs (H.323 only):** H.261, H.263, and H.264

Figure 6-28 shows how codec negotiation is performed on a Cisco UBE router. Two VoIP clouds need to be interconnected. In this scenario, both VoIP 1 and VoIP 2 networks have G.711 a-law as the preferred codec.

In the first example, the Cisco UBE router is configured to use the G.729a codec. This can be done by using the appropriate **codec** command on both VoIP dial peers. When a call is set up, Cisco UBE will accept only G.729a calls, thus influencing the codec negotiation.

In the second example, the Cisco UBE is configured for a transparent codec and will leave the codec information contained within the call signaling untouched. Because both VoIP 1 and VoIP 2 have G.711 a-law as their first choice, the resulting call will be a G.711 a-law call.

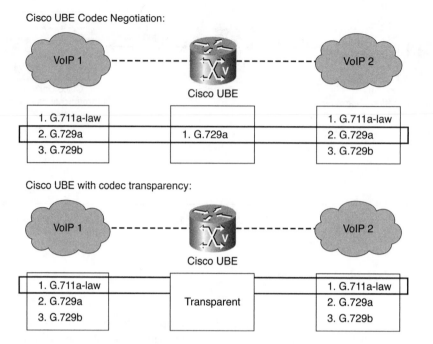

Cisco UBE Codec Negotiation:

Cisco UBE with codec transparency:

Figure 6-28 *Codec Filtering on Cisco UBEs*

RSVP-Based CAC on Cisco UBEs

Because a Cisco UBE router is a Cisco IOS gateway, it also supports RSVP-based CAC. Two Cisco Unified Communications Manager clusters can interconnect using Cisco UBE, thus enabling intercluster RSVP-based CAC. RSVP supports both voice and video calls.

RSVP requires at least two RSVP peers, so two Cisco UBE Gateways are required to enable RSVP-based CAC. When deploying Cisco UBE and RSVP-based CAC, ensure that the flows that should utilize RSVP are configured for media flow-through. Media flow-around is not supported with RSVP-based CAC.

RSVP-Based CAC

Figure 6-29 illustrates the placement of two Cisco UBEs to provide RSVP-based CAC. The calls are admitted to cross the WAN only when a reservation can be successfully made for a call.

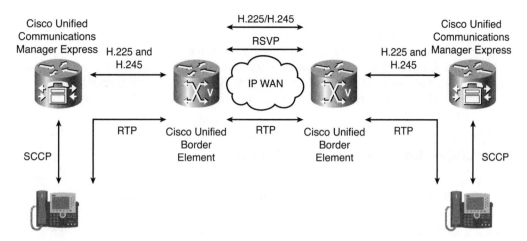

Figure 6-29 *RSVP-Based CAC*

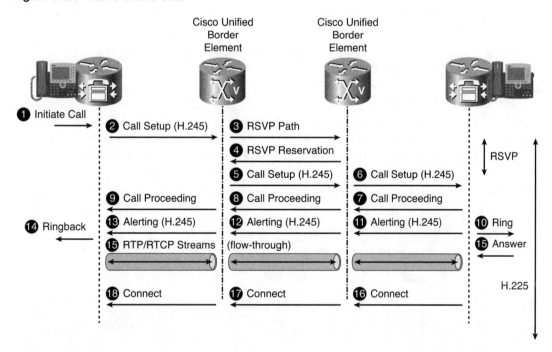

Figure 6-30 *RSVP-Based CAC*

RSVP-Based CAC Call Flow

Figure 6-30 depicts the signaling flow with two Cisco UBEs that provide RSVP-based CAC and use H.323 Fast Start on all call legs. The relevant step in this scenario takes place after the Call Setup message is received by a Cisco UBE. Before it forwards the Call Setup message to the other Cisco UBE, it checks the required bandwidth. The reservation process involves two messages: the RSVP Path message that is processed by each router in the path from the originating Cisco UBE to the terminating Cisco UBE, and the RSVP

Reservation message that flows in the reverse direction. The Path message carries the request with associated parameters, and the Reservation message is used to commit the reservation on all hops. The originating Cisco UBE sends the Call Setup message after a successful Reservation message is received. For RSVP-based CAC, media flow-through must be used to ensure that the media packets actually follow the reserved path. In this example, Early Media is negotiated that allows the gateways to establish the media flow before the call is answered.

Cisco Unified Border Element Call Flows

Call signaling depends on network topology and features that are implemented on the Cisco UBE. This section describes call flows for these Cisco UBE scenarios:

- Cisco Unified Communications Manager Express > Cisco Unified Border Element > SIP carrier

- Cisco Unified Communications Manager Express > Cisco Unified Border Element with RSVP > Cisco Unified Communications Manager Express

- Cisco Unified Communications Manager Express > gatekeeper > Cisco Unified Border Element > SIP carrier

SIP Carrier Interworking

Figure 6-31 shows a simple Cisco UBE deployment where the Cisco UBE is used to translate the H.323 call leg with the Cisco Unified Communications Manager Express to a SIP call leg point to a SIP carrier. Because this is a connection to an external VoIP network, media flow-through is required to hide internal IP addresses.

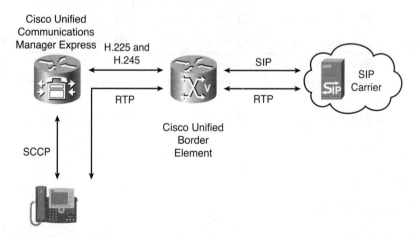

Figure 6-31   *SIP Carrier Interworking*

SIP Carrier Interworking Call Flow

Figure 6-32 illustrates the call signaling flow when Cisco UBE provides interworking service between H.323 Slow Start and SIP Delayed Offer.

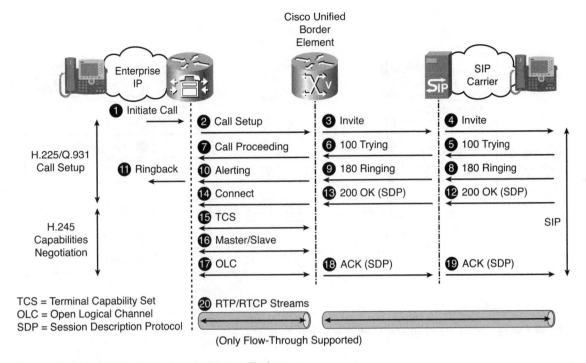

Figure 6-32   *SIP Carrier Interworking Call Flow*

Figure 6-33 illustrates the call signaling flow when Cisco UBE provides interworking service between H.323 Fast Start and SIP Early Offer.

SIP Carrier Interworking with Gatekeeper-Based CAC Call Setup

Figure 6-34 shows the signaling flow with two gatekeepers and one Cisco UBE, providing gatekeeper-based CAC in combination with SIP carrier interworking. The call flow from the Cisco Unified Communications Manager Express to Cisco UBE follows the regular H.225 RAS procedure, in which ARQs are sent by both gateways to their respective gatekeepers. Location Request (LRQ) and Location Confirmation (LCF) are exchanged between the gatekeepers. The Cisco UBE then connects the inbound H.323 call leg to the outbound SIP call leg. This example illustrates H.323 Slow Start-to-SIP Delayed Offer interworking on Cisco UBE. Interworking between different protocols (H.323 and SIP) supports media flow-through only.

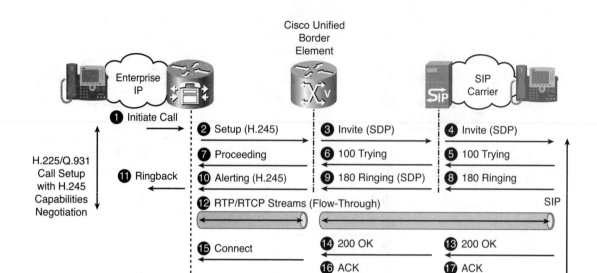

Figure 6-33   *SIP Carrier Interworking Call Flow (Continued)*

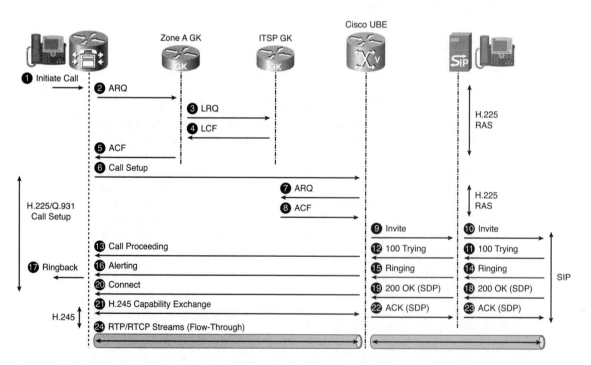

Figure 6-34   *SIP Carrier Interworking with Gatekeeper-Based CAC Call Setup*

Configuring Cisco Unified Border Elements

A Cisco UBE can be implemented in VoIP networks to enhance VoIP network interoperability. This section describes how to implement Cisco UBE routers to support protocol interworking between H.323 and SIP networks.

Protocol Interworking Command

To enable protocol interworking, use the **allow-connections** *from-type* **to** *to-type* command in voice service configuration mode. The *from-type* and *to-type* options specify the signaling protocols, as detailed in Table 6-7.

Table 6-7   allow-connections *Syntax Description*

Parameter	Description
from-type	Originating endpoint type. The following choices are valid: **h323:** H.323 **sip:** SIP
to	Indicates that the argument that follows is the connection target.
to-type	Terminating endpoint type. The following choices are valid: **h323:** H.323 **sip:** SIP

When interworking H.323 and SIP, the configuration is unidirectional; thus, if bidirectional interworking is required, you need to configure the mirroring statement as well. For example, if bidirectional H.323 to SIP interworking is required, you need to configure **allow-connections h323 to sip** as well as **allow-connections sip to h323**.

Figure 6-35 and Example 6-18 illustrate a sample protocol interworking configuration.

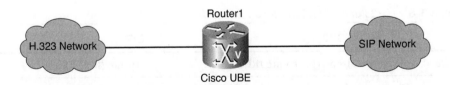

Figure 6-35   *Protocol Interworking Topology Example*

Example 6-18   *Protocol Interworking Configuration*

```
Router1(config)#voice service voip
Router1(config-voice-service)#allow-connections h323 to h323
Router1(config-voice-service)#allow-connections sip to sip
Router1(config-voice-service)#allow-connections h323 to sip
Router1(config-voice-service)#allow-connections sip to h323
```

Configuring H.323-to-SIP DTMF Relay Interworking

DTMF interworking is a subset of H.323-to-SIP interworking and supports these DTMF relay combinations:

- H.245 alpha/signal and SIP RTP-NTE (RFC 2833), as a function of basic DTMF interworking. This method converts an out-of-band DTMF relay method to an in-band relay. Its potential issue is that the DTMF digits are transported both in-band and out-of-band on the H.323 call leg.

Note   NTE is short for named telephony event.

- H.245 alpha/signal and SIP Notify, as a function of basic DTMF interworking. This method converts an out-of-band DTMF relay method to another out-of-band DTMF relay.

- G.711 inband DTMF to RTP-NTE, as a function of supplementary DTMF interworking. This method converts an in-band DTMF relay method to another in-band DTMF relay.

```
Router(config-dial-peer)#dtmf-relay [cisco-rtp] [h245-alphanumeric] [h245-signal]
  [rtp-nte [digit-drop]] [sip-notify]
```

The **digit-drop** keyword in the **dtmf-relay rtp-nte digit-drop** command prevents sending both in-band and out-of band tones to the H.323 leg. It is configured for the dial peer that provides the SIP call leg for the first DTMF relay method (H.245 alpha/signal and SIP RTP-NTE). It is useful only if either **dtmf-relay h245-alphanumeric** or **dtmf-relay h245-signal** is configured on the H.323 call leg.

Table 6-8 provides a review of in-band and out-of-band DTMF relay methods that are supported in H.323 and SIP.

Table 6-8   *H.323 and SIP DTMF Relay Methods*

	H.323	SIP
In-band	cisco-rtp, rtp-nte (RFC 2833)	rtp-nte (RFC 2833)
Out-of-band	h245-alphanumeric, h245-signal	sip-notify

Configuring Media Flow and Transparent Codec

The Cisco UBE media flow and codec transparency can be configured using various configuration elements.

media Command

To configure media flow-through or media flow-around, use the **media {flow-around |
flow-through}** command. This can be done in dial-peer configuration mode, globally
under the voice service voip configuration mode, or in a voice class that can then be referenced by multiple dial peers. The default is **media flow-through.**

Media flow-through is the only supported method for H.323-to-SIP interworking.

codec transparent Command

To configure transparent codec pass-through, use the **codec transparent** command. This
can be done in dial-peer configuration mode or via a codec class.

Media Flow-Around and Transparent Codec Example

Figure 6-36 illustrates a sample Cisco UBE configuration for media flow-around and
codec transparency. The configuration consists of H.323-to-H.323 signaling permission
and the respective VoIP dial peers. The dial peers are configured for media flow-around
and codec transparency. These settings can be configured in the voice class and codec
class and referenced by the dial peers.

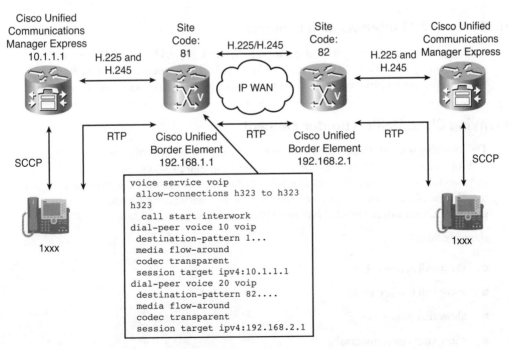

Figure 6-36   *Media Flow-Around and Transparent Codec Example*

Configuring H.323-to-H.323 Fast-Start-to-Slow-Start Interworking

The **h323** command issued in voice service voip configuration mode enters the h323 configuration mode.

```
Router(conf-voi-serv)#h323
```

H.323 Fast Start-to-Slow Start interworking is enabled using the **call start** command in h323 configuration mode.

```
Router(conf-serv-h323)#call start {fast | slow | interwork}
```

The **call start** command has three options:

- **fast:** This selection forces the H.323 gateway to use Fast Start (H.323v2) procedures for the dial peers using H.323. This is the default setting.

- **slow:** This option makes the H.323 gateway use Slow Start (H.323v1) procedures for the dial peers using H.323.

- **interwork:** This keyword allows Cisco UBE interoperability between Fast Start and Slow Start procedures. This option effectively disables the any-to-H.323 gateway operations on the Cisco UBE, because the gateway will not originate any H.323 calls (Fast Start and Slow Start are not enabled).

H.323-to-H.323 Interworking Example

Figure 6-37 illustrates a sample configuration for Cisco UBE H.323-to-H.323 interworking. The configuration consists of the H.323-to-H.323 signaling permission, Fast Start-to-Slow Start activation, and VoIP dial peers responsible for both call legs of the Cisco UBE.

Verifying Cisco Unified Border Element

The following lists summarize the commands that can be used to verify and debug Cisco UBE operations. All commands, except the **debug voip ipipgw** command, are typical commands that are known from traditional H.323 or SIP environments. To successfully troubleshoot Cisco UBE functionality in H.323-to-SIP interworking scenarios, both groups of commands are needed (SIP and H.323).

show commands:

- **show call active voice**
- **show call history voice**
- **show dial-peer voice**
- **show voip rtp connections**

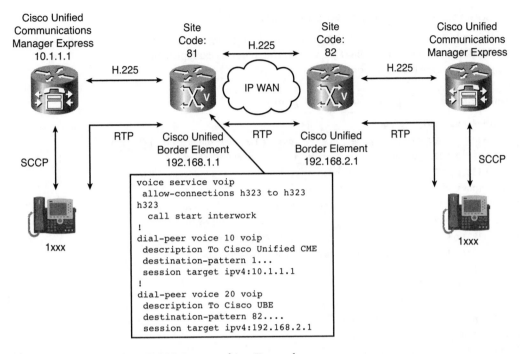

Figure 6-37   *H.323-to-H.323 Interworking Example*

debug commands:

- **debug voip ipipgw**

- **debug cch323 all**

- **debug ccsip messages**

- **debug h225 asn1**

- **debug h225 events**

- **debug h245 asn1**

- **debug h245 events**

- **debug voip ccapi inout**

A couple of the more commonly used commands are **debug voip ipipgw** and **show call active voice brief**.

Debugging Cisco Unified Border Element Operations

Example 6-19 shows sample output from the **debug voip ipipgw** command. It includes the description of the media flow (flow-through in this example), and lists negotiated parameters, such as RTP port numbers.

Example 6-19   *Debugging Cisco UBE Operations*

```
Router#debug voip ipipgw
.../H323/cch323_set_pref_codec_list: First preferred codec(bytes)=16(20)
.../H323/cch323_get_peer_info: Flow Mode set to FLOW_THROUGH
.../H323/cch323_build_local_encoded_fastStartOLCs: srcAddress = 0xA010665,
h245_lport = 0, flow mode = 1,
.../H323/cch323_generic_open_logical_channel: current codec = 16:20:20
.../H323/cch323_receive_fastStart_cap_response: Send cap ind to peer leg
.../H323/cch323_build_olc_for_ccapi: audioFastStartArray=0x49045794
.../H323/cch323_build_olc_for_ccapi: Channel Information:
Logical Channel Number (fwd): 1
Logical Channel Number (rev): 1
Channel address (fwd/rev): 10.1.250.102
RTP Channel (fwd/rev): 16764
RTCP Channel (fwd/rev): 16765
QoS Capability (fwd/rev): 0
Symmetric Audio Codec: 16
Symmetric Audio Codec Bytes: 20
Flow Mode: 0
Silence Suppression: 1
```

Viewing Cisco Unified Border Element Calls

The **show call active voice brief** command, as demonstrated in Example 6-20, can be used to validate that an active call has been established using the H.323-to-SIP interworking procedure. If so, there should be one SIP and one H.323 call leg. Additionally, the output displays other information, such as call duration and RTP parameters.

Example 6-20   *Viewing Cisco UBE Calls*

```
Router#show call active voice brief
...
Telephony call-legs: 0
SIP call-legs: 1
H323 call-legs: 1
Call agent controlled call-legs: 0
SCCP call-legs: 0
Multicast call-legs: 0
Total call-legs: 2
137C : 163 346116800ms.1 +1580 pid:40002 Answer 1010 active
```

```
dur 00:00:22 tx:1124/22480 rx:112/2050
IP 10.1.2.28:25850 SRTP: off rtt:0ms pl:0/0ms lost:0/0/0 delay:0/0/0ms
g729r8 TextRelay: off
media inactive detected:n media contrl rcvd:n/a timestamp:n/a
long duration call detected:n long duration call duration:n/a timestamp:n/a
...
```

Summary

The main topics covered in this chapter are the following:

- The Cisco IOS gateway was introduced, and its features were discussed.

- Gatekeeper configuration was explained, along with examples, which allowed H.323 devices to register with the gatekeeper and then use the gatekeeper for address resolution and call routing.

- The gatekeeper can act as a call admission control (CAC) mechanism, and the configuration of this CAC functionality was described.

- The Cisco Unified Border Element (Cisco UBE) was introduced, along with a discussion of its functions and features. Examples were provided as to how a Cisco UBE could be used in modern enterprise environments.

- Finally, this chapter demonstrated how to configure a Cisco UBE router to perform protocol interworking.

Chapter Review Questions

The answers to these review questions are in the appendix.

1. RAS is a subset of the _____ signaling protocol.

   a. H.323

   b. SIP

   c. H.225

   d. H.245

2. Which of the following RAS messages can be sent using either unicast or multicast?

   a. RRQ

   b. ARQ

   c. GRQ

   d. RIP

3. Given the following configuration, what IP address will GK1 use to send and receive RAS messages?

```
GK1(config)#interface serial 0/0/0
GK1(config-if)#ip address 192.168.0.2 255.255.255.0
GK1(config-if)#exit
GK1(config)#interface serial 0/0/1
GK1(config-if)#ip address 172.16.0.2 255.255.255.0
GK1(config-if)#exit
GK1(config)#gatekeeper
GK1(config-gk)#zone local SanJose cisco.com 172.16.0.2
GK1(config-gk)#zone remote Austin cisco.com 192.168.0.1
GK1(config-gk)#zone prefix SanJose 2...
GK1(config-gk)#zone prefix Austin 3...
```

   a. 192.168.0.2

   b. 172.16.0.2

   c. 192.168.0.1

   d. RAS messages will be load balanced between 192.168.0.2 and 172.16.0.2.

4. How much bandwidth does an H.323 gatekeeper assume will be required by a G.729 call?

   a. 8 kbps

   b. 16 kbps

   c. 24 kbps

   d. 64 kbps

5. What parameter of the **bandwidth** command, used in gatekeeper configuration mode, specifies the maximum amount of bandwidth that can be allocated in a zone?

   a. interzone

   b. total

   c. session

   d. remote

6. Cisco UBE features include _____, _____, codec filtering, and video interworking. (Choose two.)

   a. Phone registration

   b. Address hiding

   c. Protocol interworking

   d. Multiple gatekeeper registration

7. Protocol interworking interconnects VoIP networks, using the same or different _____ protocols.

   a. Signaling

   b. Compression

   c. Codec

   d. Transport

8. Choose the correct command to enable H.323-to-H.323 interworking.

   a. **allow-connections h323 to sip**

   b. **allow-connections sip to h323**

   c. **allow-connections sip to sip**

   d. **allow-connections h323 to h323**

9. Use the _____ command to configure codec pass-through.

   a. **transparent codec**

   b. **codec transparent**

   c. **codec auto**

   d. **codec preference**

10. When deploying Cisco UBE and RSVP-based CAC, ensure the flows that should utilize RSVP are configured for media _____.

    a. Flow-around

    b. Bypass

    c. Flow-through

    d. Parity

Chapter 7

Introducing Quality of Service

After reading this chapter, you should be able to perform the following tasks:

■ Explain the functions, goals, and implementation models of QoS, and what specific issues and requirements exist in a converged Cisco Unified Communications network.

■ Describe the characteristics and QoS mechanisms of the DiffServ model and contrast it to other models.

Converged networks must be engineered properly to guarantee satisfactory VoIP service. This chapter describes quality of service (QoS) requirements and conceptual models such as best effort, Integrated Services (IntServ), and Differentiated Services (DiffServ).

Fundamentals of QoS

IP networks must provide a number of services to adequately support voice transmission using VoIP. These services include security, predictability, measurability, and some level of delivery guarantee. Network administrators and architects achieve this service level by managing delay, delay variation (jitter), bandwidth provisioning, and packet loss parameters with QoS techniques. This section introduces the concept of a converged network, identifies four problems that could lead to poor quality of service, and describes solutions to those problems. It also explains and evaluates the three generic models of implementing QoS.

QoS Issues

Before networks converged, network engineering was focused on connectivity, as illustrated in Figure 7-1. The rates at which data came onto the network resulted in bursty data flows. Data packets tried to grab as much bandwidth as they could at any given time. Access was on a first-come, first-served basis. The data rate available to any one user varied depending on the number of users accessing the network at any given time.

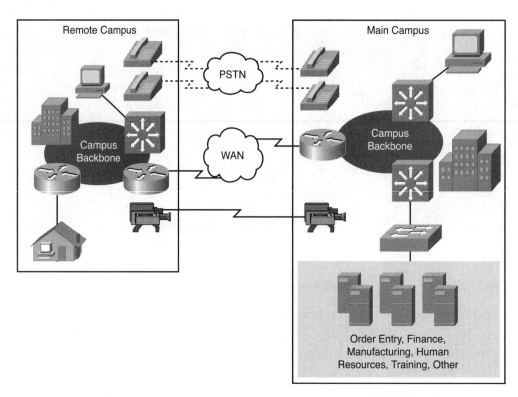

Figure 7-1 *Networks Before Convergence*

The protocols that have been developed have adapted to the bursty nature of data networks, and brief outages are survivable. For example, when you retrieve email, a delay of a few seconds is generally not noticeable. A delay of minutes is annoying but not serious.

Traditional networks also had requirements for applications such as latency-sensitive data, drop-sensitive data, and video. Because each application had different traffic characteristics and requirements, network designers deployed nonintegrated networks. These nonintegrated networks were designed to carry a specific type of traffic: data network, SNA network, voice network, and video network.

After Convergence

Figure 7-2 illustrates a converged network in which voice, video, and data traffic use the same network facilities.

Although packets carrying voice traffic are typically small, they cannot tolerate delay and delay variation as they traverse the network. Voices will break up, and words will become incomprehensible.

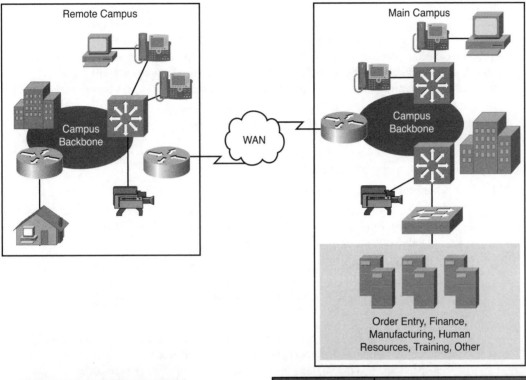

Traffic Characteristics
Constant small-packet voice flow competes with bursty data flow.
Critical traffic must get priority.
Voice and video are time-sensitive.
Brief outages not acceptable.

Technology	Problem Example
Telephony	"I cannot understand you; your voice is breaking up."
Teleconferencing	"The picture is very jerky. Voice is not synchronized."
Call Center	"Please hold while my screen refreshes."

Figure 7-2 *Converged Network*

On the other hand, packets carrying file transfer data are typically large and can survive delays and drops. It is possible to retransmit part of a dropped data file, but it is not feasible to retransmit a part of a voice conversation.

The constant, small-packet voice flow competes with bursty data flows. Unless some mechanism mediates the overall flow, voice quality will be severely compromised at times of network congestion. The critical voice traffic must get priority. Voice and video traffic is very time sensitive. It cannot be delayed, and it cannot be dropped, or the resulting quality of voice and video will suffer.

Finally, converged networks must not fail. While a file transfer or email packet can wait until the network recovers, voice and video packets cannot wait. Even a brief network outage on a converged network can seriously disrupt business operations. With inadequate preparation of the network, voice transmission is choppy or unintelligible. Gaps in speech are particularly troublesome when pieces of speech are interspersed with silence. In voice-mail systems, this silence is a problem. For example, when 68614 is dialed, and the gaps in speech are actually gaps in the tone, 68614 becomes 6688661144, because the gaps in speech are perceived as pauses in the touch tones.

Quality Issues in Converged Networks

The four major problems facing converged enterprise networks include the following:

- **Bandwidth capacity:** Large graphics files, multimedia uses, and increasing use of voice and video cause bandwidth capacity problems over data networks.

- **End-to-end delay (both fixed and variable):** Delay is the time that it takes for a packet to reach the receiving endpoint after being transmitted from the sending endpoint. This period of time is called "end-to-end delay," and consists of two components:

    - **Fixed network delay:** Two types of fixed delays are serialization and propagation delays. Serialization is the process of placing bits on a circuit. The higher the circuit speed, the less time it takes to place the bits on a circuit. Therefore, the higher the speed of the link, the less serialization delay that is incurred. Propagation delay is the time that it takes for frames to transit the physical media.

    - **Variable network delay:** Queuing delay is a type of variable delay. Specifically, the amount of time a packet spends in the output buffer (that is, the output queue) of an interface can vary based on network congestion. Therefore, this queuing delay is considered to be a variable delay.

- **Variation of delay (also called jitter):** Jitter is the delta, or difference, in the total end-to-end delay values of two voice packets in the voice flow.

- **Packet loss:** Loss of packets is usually caused by congestion in a WAN, resulting in speech dropouts or a stutter effect if the playout side tries to accommodate by repeating previous packets.

The following sections describe each problem in greater detail.

Bandwidth Capacity

Figure 7-3 illustrates an empty network with four hops between a server and a client. Each hop is using different media with a different bandwidth. The maximum available bandwidth is equal to the bandwidth of the weakest (slowest) link.

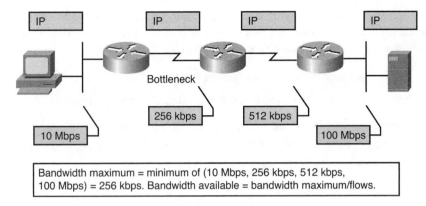

Bandwidth maximum = minimum of (10 Mbps, 256 kbps, 512 kbps, 100 Mbps) = 256 kbps. Bandwidth available = bandwidth maximum/flows.

Figure 7-3   *Lack of Bandwidth*

The calculation of the available bandwidth, however, is much more complex in cases where multiple flows traverse the network. The calculation of the available bandwidth in the illustration is an approximation.

The best way to increase bandwidth is to increase the link capacity to accommodate all applications and users, with some extra bandwidth to spare. Although this solution sounds simple, increasing bandwidth is expensive and takes time to implement. Fortunately, various QoS mechanisms, as depicted in Figure 7-4, can be used to effectively increase available bandwidth for priority applications.

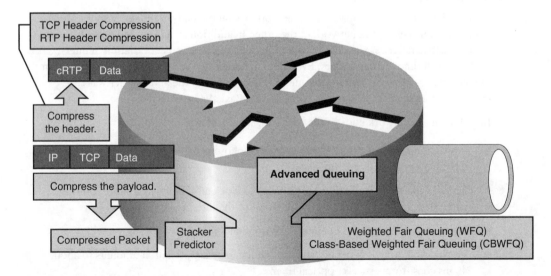

Figure 7-4   *Ways to Increase or Manage Available Bandwidth*

By classifying traffic into QoS classes and prioritizing traffic according to importance, voice and business-critical traffic can get sufficient bandwidth to support their application requirements; voice should get prioritized forwarding; and the least-important traffic should get whatever unallocated bandwidth is remaining. A variety of mechanisms such as these are available in Cisco IOS to provide bandwidth guarantees:

- Priority queuing (PQ) or custom queuing (CQ)

- Modified deficit round robin (MDRR) (on Cisco 12000 Series Routers)

- Distributed type of service (ToS)-based and QoS group-based weighted fair queuing (WFQ) (on Cisco 7x00 Series Routers)

- Class-based weighted fair queuing (CBWFQ)

- Low latency queuing (LLQ)

Optimizing link usage by compressing the payload of frames (virtually) increases the link bandwidth. Compression, on the other hand, might increase delay because of the complexity of compression algorithms. Using hardware compression can accelerate packet payload compressions. Stacker and Predictor are two compression algorithms that are available in Cisco IOS.

Another link-efficiency mechanism is header compression. Header compression is especially effective in networks in which most packets carry small amounts of data (that is, where payload-to-header ratio is small). Typical examples of header compression are TCP header compression and Real-time Transport Protocol (RTP) header compression.

End-to-End Delay and Jitter

Figure 7-5 illustrates the impact that a network has on the end-to-end delay of packets going from one end of the network to the other. In addition to end-to-end delay (that is, the cumulative delay), if the delay between packets varies (that is, a variation in inter-packet arrival times), *jitter* occurs. Even though packet drops do not necessarily occur in the presence of jitter, excessive jitter might result in gaps in the audio. Jitter was discussed in more detail in Chapter 2, "Configuring Basic Voice over IP."

Each hop in the network adds to the overall delay as follows:

- Propagation delay is caused by the speed of photons or electrons traveling in the media (fiber optics or copper media).

- Serialization delay is the time that it takes to clock all the bits in a packet onto the wire. This is a fixed value that is a function of the interface speed.

- There are processing and queuing delays within a router.

- Propagation delay is generally ignored but it can be significant. It amounts to about 40 ms coast-to-coast, over optical fiber.

Example: Effects of Delay

A customer has a router in New York and a router in San Francisco, each connected by a 128-kbps WAN link. The customer sends a 66-byte voice frame. To transmit the frame

(528 bits), it will take 4.125 ms to clock out (serialization delay). However, the last bit will not arrive until 40 ms after it clocks out (propagation delay). The total delay equals 44.125 ms.

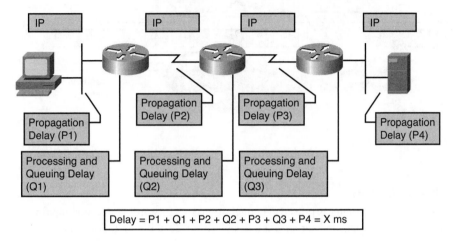

Figure 7-5 *End-to-End Delay*

This calculation will be different if the circuit is changed to a T1. To transmit the frame (528 bits), it will take 0.344 ms to clock out (serialization delay). However, the last bit will not arrive until 40 ms after transmission (propagation delay) for a total delay of 40.344 ms.

Types of Delay

In general, there are four types of delay, as follows, and as shown in Figure 7-6:

- **Processing delay:** The time it takes for a router to take the packet from an input interface and put the packet into the output queue of the output interface. The processing delay depends on factors such as:

    - CPU speed

    - CPU utilization

    - IP switching mode

    - Router architecture

    - Configured features on both input and output interfaces

- **Queuing delay:** The time a packet resides in the output queue of a router. Queuing delay depends on the number of and sizes of packets already in the queue, the bandwidth of the interface, and the queuing mechanism.

- **Serialization delay:** The time it takes to place a frame on the physical medium for transport.

- **Propagation delay:** The time it takes to transmit a packet, which usually depends on the type of media interface.

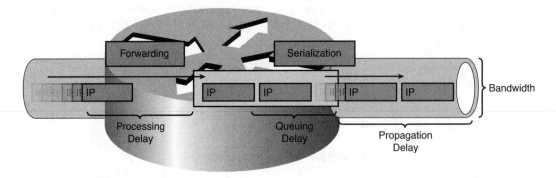

Figure 7-6   *Types of Delay*

Reducing Delay

Assuming that a router is powerful enough to make a forwarding decision rapidly, most processing, queuing, and serialization delay is influenced by the following factors:

- Average length of the queue
- Average length of packets in the queue
- Link bandwidth

The following approaches, which are illustrated in Figure 7-7, allow you to accelerate packet dispatching of delay-sensitive flows:

- **Increasing link capacity:** Sufficient bandwidth causes queues to shrink so that packets do not wait long before transmittal. More bandwidth reduces serialization time.

- **Prioritizing delay-sensitive packets:** This is a more cost-effective approach. PQ, CQ, strict-priority, or alternate-priority queuing within the MDRR (on Cisco 12000 Series Routers), and LLQ each have preemptive queuing capabilities.

- **Compressing the payload:** Payload compression reduces the size of packets, thereby virtually increasing link bandwidth. Because compressed packets are smaller, they take less time to transmit. Compression uses complex algorithms that take time and can add to delay. This approach is not used to provide low-delay propagation of packets.

- **Compressing the packet header:** Header compression is not as CPU intensive as payload compression, and you can use it with other mechanisms to reduce delay. Header compression is especially useful for voice packets that have a bad payload-to-header ratio, which you can improve by reducing the header size of the packet (RTP header compression).

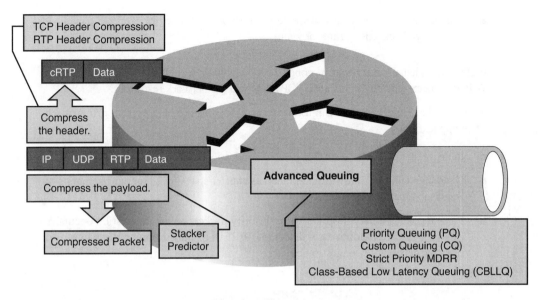

Figure 7-7 *Approaches to Reducing Delay*

Packet Loss

The usual packet loss occurs when routers run out of buffer space for a particular interface output queue. Figure 7-8 illustrates a full interface output queue, which causes newly arriving packets to be dropped. The term that is used for such drops is simply *output drop* or *tail drop* (that is, packets are dropped at the tail of the queue).

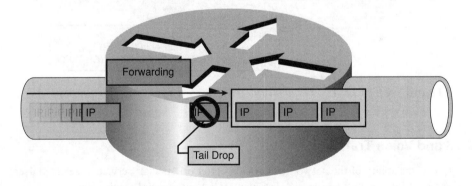

Figure 7-8 *Tail Drop*

Routers might also drop packets for these other, less common reasons:

■ **Input queue drop:** The main CPU is congested and cannot process packets (that is, the input queue is full).

■ **Ignore:** The router ran out of buffer space.

■ **Overrun:** The CPU is congested and cannot assign a free buffer to the new packet.

■ **Frame errors:** There is a hardware-detected error in a frame (for example, a cyclic redundancy check [CRC], runt, or giant).

Packet loss is usually the result of congestion on an interface. Most applications that use TCP experience slowdown, because TCP adjusts to the network resources.

As depicted in Figure 7-9, you can follow these procedures to help prevent drops of sensitive applications:

■ Increase link capacity to ease or prevent congestion.

■ Guarantee enough bandwidth, and increase buffer space to accommodate bursts of fragile applications.

■ Prevent congestion by dropping lower-priority packets before congestion occurs. You can use weighted random early detection (WRED) to start dropping these lower-priority packets before congestion occurs.

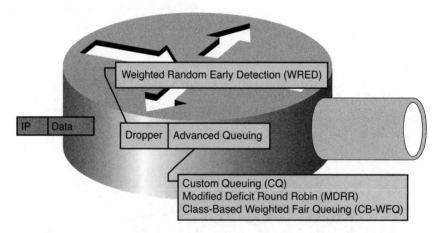

Figure 7-9   *Packet Loss Prevention*

QoS and Voice Traffic

QoS is the ability of the network to provide better or "special" service to selected users and applications, to the potential detriment of other users and applications.

The goal of QoS is to provide better and more predictable network service by providing dedicated bandwidth, controlled jitter and latency, and improved loss characteristics. QoS achieves these goals by providing tools for managing network congestion, shaping network traffic, using expensive wide-area links more efficiently, and setting traffic policies across the network. QoS offers intelligent network services that, when correctly applied, help to provide consistent, predictable performance.

QoS Policy

A QoS policy is a networkwide definition of the specific levels of QoS assigned to different classes of network traffic. In a converged network, having a QoS policy is as important as having a security policy. A written and public QoS policy allows users to understand and negotiate for QoS in the network.

Table 7-1 illustrates a sample QoS policy for an organization.

Table 7-1   *QoS Policy Example*

What	QoS	Security	When
Voice	< 150 ms one-way delay	Secure RTP (SRTP) over WAN	M–F
Enterprise Resource Planning (ERP)	Guarantee of 256 kbps of available bandwidth	Encrypted	24×7×365
Manufacturing traffic	Guarantee of 128 kbps of available bandwidth	Clear test	M–F
HTTP/HTTPS	Best effort	HTTP proxy	M–F, 6 a.m. to 10 p.m.

QoS for Unified Communications Networks

Follow these three basic steps to implement QoS on a network:

Step 1.   Identify traffic and its requirements. Study the network to determine the types of traffic running on the network and then determine the QoS requirements for the different types of traffic.

Step 2.   Group the traffic into classes with similar QoS requirements. For example, four classes of traffic can be defined: voice, high priority, low priority, and browser.

Step 3.   Define QoS policies that will meet the QoS requirements for each traffic class.

Example: Three Steps to Implementing QoS on a Network

In a typical network, voice always requires absolute minimal delay. Some data that is associated with key applications requires very low delay (for example, transaction-based data that is used in airline reservations or online banking applications). Other types of data can tolerate a greater amount of delay (for example, file transfers and email). Nonbusiness network surfing can also be delayed or even prohibited.

A one-to-one mapping between traffic classes and QoS policies is not necessary. For example, three QoS policies could be implemented to meet the requirements of the four traffic classes that are defined in the example:

- **NoDelay:** Assign to voice traffic

- **BestService:** Assign to high-priority traffic

- **Whenever:** Assign to both the low-priority and browser traffic

Step 1: Identify Traffic and Its Requirements

The first step in implementing QoS is identifying the traffic on the network and determining QoS requirements for the traffic. A network audit is recommended, because many enterprises have a false idea of what applications are running in their networks. If QoS mechanisms are deployed based on an unrealistic baseline, unexpected results might occur.

The next step is determining the QoS problems of users. Measure the traffic on the network during congested periods. Conduct CPU utilization assessment on each of their network devices during busy periods to determine where problems might be occurring.

Next, determine the business model and goals, and obtain a list of business requirements, in order to define the number of classes, so that you can determine the business requirements for each traffic class.

Finally, define the service levels that are required by different traffic classes in terms of response time and availability.

Step 2: Group Traffic into Classes

After you have identified and measured the majority of network traffic, you can use the business requirements to define traffic classes.

Because of its stringent QoS requirements, voice traffic almost always exists in a class by itself. Cisco has developed specific QoS mechanisms, such as LLQ, that ensure voice always receives priority treatment over all other traffic. After you define the applications with the most critical requirements, you can define the remaining traffic classes using the business requirements.

As illustrated in Figure 7-10, each application is not placed into its own class. Rather, applications with similar QoS requirements are grouped together into a common class.

Example: Traffic Classification   A typical enterprise might define five traffic classes as follows:

- **Voice:** Absolute priority for VoIP traffic

- **Mission-critical:** Small set of locally defined critical business applications

- **Transactional:** Database access, transaction services, interactive traffic, preferred data services

- **Best effort:** Internet, email

- **Scavenger (less than best effort):** KaZaa and other peer-to-peer applications

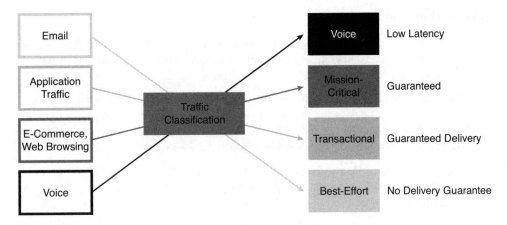

Figure 7-10   *Grouping Traffic into Classes*

Step 3: Define QoS Policies for Each Traffic Class

Finally, define a QoS policy for each traffic class, which involves these activities:

■   Set a minimum bandwidth guarantee

■   Set a maximum bandwidth limit

■   Assign priorities to each class

■   Use QoS technologies, such as advanced queuing, to manage congestion

Example: Defining QoS Policies   Using the traffic classes that were previously defined, you can determine QoS policies as follows:

■   **Voice:** Available bandwidth: 1 Mbps. Use QoS marking to mark voice packets with a DSC P value of EF; use LLQ to always give voice priority.

■   **Mission-critical:** Minimum bandwidth: 1 Mbps. Use QoS marking to mark critical data packets with a Differentiated Services Code Point (DSCP) value of AF31; use CBWFQ to guarantee specific bandwidth amounts for critical class traffic flows.

■   **Best effort:** Maximum bandwidth: 500 kbps. Use QoS marking to mark these data packets with a DSCP value of Default; use CBWFQ to specify a bandwidth amount for best-effort traffic flows that are below mission-critical and voice.

■   **Scavenger:** Maximum bandwidth: 100 kbps. Use QoS marking to mark less-than-best-effort (scavenger) data packets with a DSCP value of CS1; use WRED to drop these packets first when the network experiences congestion.

QoS Requirements

Voice traffic has extremely stringent QoS requirements. Voice traffic usually generates a smooth demand on bandwidth and has minimal impact on other traffic as long as the voice traffic is managed.

While voice packets are typically small (60 to 120 bytes), they cannot tolerate delay or drops. The result of delays and drops is poor, and often unacceptable, voice quality. Because drops cannot be tolerated, User Datagram Protocol (UDP) is used to package voice packets, because TCP retransmit capabilities have no value.

One-way delay for voice packets should be no more than 150 ms, according to the G.114 industry-standard recommendation. Also, voice packets should experience no more than 1 percent of packet loss.

A typical voice call will require 17 to 106 kbps of guaranteed priority bandwidth plus an additional 150 bps per call for voice control traffic. Multiplying these bandwidth requirements times the maximum number of calls expected during the busiest time period provides an indication of the overall bandwidth that is required for voice traffic.

Videoconferencing

Videoconferencing applications also have stringent QoS requirements, similar to voice. But videoconferencing traffic is often bursty and greedy in nature and, as a result, can impact other traffic. Therefore, it is important to understand the videoconferencing requirements for a network and to provision carefully for it.

The minimum bandwidth for a videoconferencing stream would require the actual bandwidth of a stream (dependent upon the videoconferencing codec being used) plus some overhead. For example, a 384-kbps video stream actually requires a total of 460 kbps of priority bandwidth (that is, 20 percent of extra bandwidth to accommodate for overhead).

Data

The QoS requirements for data traffic vary greatly. Different applications might make very different demands on the network (for example, a human resources application versus an automated teller machine application). Even different versions of the same application might have varying network traffic characteristics.

While data traffic can demonstrate either smooth or bursty characteristics, depending upon the application, data traffic differs from voice and video in terms of delay and drop sensitivity. Almost all data applications can tolerate some delay and generally can tolerate higher drop rates than voice and video.

Because data traffic can tolerate drops, the retransmit capabilities of TCP become important and, as a result, many data applications use TCP.

In enterprise networks, business-critical applications are usually easy to identify. Most applications can be identified based on TCP or UDP port numbers. Some applications use dynamic port numbers that, to some extent, make classifications more difficult.

Cisco IOS supports Network-Based Application Recognition (NBAR), which you can use to recognize dynamic port applications.

It is recommended that data traffic be classified into no more than four to five classes. There will still be additional classes for voice and video.

Methods for Implementing QoS Policy

Cisco offers multiple configuration approaches to QoS, including the following:

- **CLI:** Initially, the only way to implement QoS in a network was by using the command-line interface (CLI) to individually configure QoS policies within each interface. This was a time-consuming, tiresome, and error-prone task that involved cutting and pasting configurations from one interface to another.

- **MQC:** Cisco introduced the Modular QoS CLI (MQC) to simplify QoS configuration by making configurations modular. Using MQC, you can configure QoS in a building-block approach, using a single module repeatedly to apply a policy to multiple interfaces.

- **Cisco AutoQoS:** Cisco AutoQoS is a macro that enables you to enter one or two simple Cisco AutoQoS commands to enable all the appropriate features for the recommended QoS setting for an application on a specific interface. There are two versions of Cisco AutoQoS: Cisco AutoQoS VoIP (which can run on a Cisco IOS router or Cisco Catalyst switch) and AutoQoS for the Enterprise (which can run on a Cisco IOS router).

Implementing QoS Traditionally Using CLI

CLI was the first method to implement QoS in a network. It was a painstaking task, involving copying one interface configuration, and then pasting it into other interface configurations. The CLI method required much time and patience.

The original CLI method was nonmodular. Specifically, there was no way to separate the classification of traffic from the actual definition of policy. You had to do both on every interface. Example 7-1 illustrates an example of the complex configuration tasks involved in using the CLI approach.

Example 7-1 *CLI QoS Configuration Example*

```
interface Multilink1
  ip address 10.1.61.1 255.255.255.0
  ip tcp header-compression iphc-format
  load-interval 30
  custom-queue-list 1
  ppp multilink
  ppp multilink fragment-delay 10
  ppp multilink interleave
```

```
   multilink-group 1
   ip rtp header-compression iphc-format
!
```

Implementing QoS with MQC

MQC is a CLI structure that allows you to create traffic policies and then attach those policies to interfaces. A traffic policy contains one or more traffic classes and one or more QoS features. A traffic class is used to classify traffic. The QoS features in the traffic policy determine how to treat the classified traffic.

MQC offers significant advantages over the legacy CLI method for implementing QoS. By using MQC, you can significantly reduce the time and effort that it takes to configure QoS on a complex network. Rather than configuring "raw" CLI commands interface by interface, you develop a uniform set of traffic classes and QoS policies that can be applied on interfaces. Example 7-2 provides an example of an MQC configuration.

Example 7-2   *MQC QoS Configuration Example*

```
class-map VoIP-RTP
  match access-group 100
class-map VoIP-Control
  match access-group 101
policy-map QoS-Policy
  class VoIP-RTP
    priority 100
  class VoIP-Control
    bandwidth 8
  class class-default
    fair-queue
interface serial 0/0
  service-policy output QoS-Policy
access-list 100 permit ip any any precedence 5
access-list 100 permit ip any any dscp ef
access-list 101 permit tcp any host 10.1.10.20 range 2000 2002
access-list 101 permit tcp any host 10.1.10.20 range 11000 11999
```

Because the use of the MQC allows the separation of traffic classification from the definition of QoS policy, MQC enables easier initial QoS implementation and maintenance as new traffic classes emerge and QoS policies for the network evolve.

Implementing QoS with Cisco AutoQoS

The two versions of Cisco AutoQoS are

- **Cisco AutoQoS VoIP:** In its initial release, Cisco AutoQoS VoIP provided best-practice QoS configuration for VoIP on both Cisco switches and routers. This was accomplished by entering one global or interface command. Depending on the platform, the Cisco AutoQoS macro would then generate commands into the recommended VoIP QoS configurations, along with class maps and policy maps, and apply those to a router interface or switch port. Cisco AutoQoS is available on both LAN and WAN Cisco Catalyst switches and Cisco IOS routers.

- **Cisco AutoQoS for the Enterprise:** Cisco AutoQoS Enterprise relies on NBAR to gather statistics and detect as many as ten traffic types, resulting in the provisioning of class maps and policy maps for these traffic types. This feature deploys best-practice QoS policies for voice, video, and data traffic. Again, note that AutoQoS Enterprise is only supported on Cisco IOS routers, and not on Cisco Catalyst switches.

Cisco AutoQoS for the Enterprise, combined with the **auto qos voip** command, allows a novice network administrator to administer complex, detailed QoS policies throughout the enterprise network. Recall that Cisco AutoQoS for the Enterprise works only for Cisco IOS router platforms. The VoIP feature for Cisco Catalyst switches does not change.

There are some major differences between Cisco AutoQoS VoIP and Cisco AutoQoS for the Enterprise. Cisco AutoQoS VoIP does not detect traffic types. Cisco AutoQoS VoIP creates QoS policy only to provide priority of voice traffic. Cisco AutoQoS for the Enterprise, on the other hand, uses a discovery mechanism or traffic data collection process that uses NBAR. The Cisco AutoQoS VoIP macros use NBAR statistics to create QoS policies.

Comparing QoS Implementation Methods

Cisco recommends the use of MQC and Cisco AutoQoS VoIP when deploying voice over the LAN, and Cisco AutoQoS for the Enterprise on router WAN interfaces.

While MQC is much easier to use than CLI, Cisco AutoQoS VoIP and Cisco AutoQoS for the Enterprise can simplify the configuration of QoS. As a result, you can accomplish the fastest implementation with Cisco AutoQoS.

MQC offers excellent modularity and the ability to fine-tune complex networks. Cisco AutoQoS offers the fastest way to implement QoS, but has limited fine-tuning capabilities. When a Cisco AutoQoS configuration has been generated, you must use the CLI to fine-tune a Cisco AutoQoS configuration, if necessary.

Table 7-2 contrasts the CLI, MQC, AutoQoS VoIP, and AutoQoS for the Enterprise approaches to quality of service configuration.

Table 7-2 *Contrasting the Characteristics of QoS Implementation Approaches*

	CLI	MQC	AutoQoS VoIP	AutoQoS for the Enterprise
Ease of use	Poor	Easier	Simple	Simple
Ability to fine-tune	OK	Very good	Very good	Very good
Time to deploy	Longest	Average	Shortest	Shortest
Modularity	Poor	Excellent	Excellent	Excellent

QoS Models

The following three models exist for implementing QoS in a network:

- **Best effort:** With the best-effort model, QoS is not applied to packets. If it is not important when or how packets arrive, the best-effort model is appropriate.

- **IntServ:** Integrated Services can provide high QoS to IP packets. Essentially, applications signal to the network that they will require special QoS for a period of time and that bandwidth is reserved. With IntServ, packet delivery is guaranteed. However, the use of IntServ can severely limit the scalability of a network.

- **DiffServ:** Differentiated Services provides the greatest scalability and flexibility in implementing QoS in a network. Network devices recognize traffic classes and provide different levels of QoS to those different traffic classes.

Best-Effort Model

The Internet was designed for best-effort, no-guarantee delivery of packets. This behavior is still predominant on the Internet today. If QoS policies are not implemented, traffic is forwarded using the best-effort model. All network packets are treated exactly the same. For example, an emergency voice message is treated exactly like a digital photograph that is attached to an email. Without the implementation of QoS, the network cannot tell the difference between packets and, as a result, cannot treat packets preferentially.

When you drop a letter in standard postal mail, you are using a best-effort model. Your letter will be treated exactly the same as every other letter. It will get there when it gets there. With the best-effort model, the letter might actually never arrive. Unless you have a separate notification arrangement with the letter recipient, you might never know if the letter does not arrive.

IntServ Model

Some applications, such as high-resolution video, require consistent, dedicated bandwidth to provide sufficient quality for viewers. IntServ was introduced to guarantee predictable network behavior for these applications. Because IntServ reserves bandwidth throughout a network, no other traffic can use the reserved bandwidth. Bandwidth that is unused, but is reserved, is wasted. IntServ is similar to a concept known as *hard QoS*. With hard QoS, traffic characteristics such as bandwidth, delay, and packet-loss rates are guaranteed end-to-end. This guarantee ensures both predictable and guaranteed service levels for mission-critical applications. There will be no impact on traffic when guarantees are made, regardless of additional network traffic. Hard QoS is accomplished by negotiating specific QoS requirements upon establishment of a connection and by using call admission control (CAC) to ensure that no new traffic violates the guarantee.

Using IntServ is like having a private courier airplane or truck that is dedicated to the delivery of your traffic. This model ensures quality and delivery, can be expensive, and is not usually scalable.

IntServ is a multiple-service model that can accommodate multiple QoS requirements. IntServ inherits the connection-oriented approach from telephony network design. Every individual communication must explicitly specify its traffic descriptor and requested resources to the network. The edge router performs admission control to ensure that available resources are sufficient in the network. The IntServ standard assumes that routers along a path set and maintain the state for each individual communication.

The role of Resource Reservation Protocol (RSVP) is to provide resource admission control for VoIP networks. If resources are available, RSVP accepts a reservation and installs a traffic classifier in the QoS forwarding path. The traffic classifier tells the QoS forwarding path how to classify packets from a particular flow and what forwarding treatment to provide.

DiffServ Model

DiffServ was designed to overcome the limitations of both the best-effort and IntServ models. DiffServ can provide an *almost guaranteed* QoS, while still being cost-effective and scalable.

DiffServ is similar to a concept known as *soft QoS*. With soft QoS, QoS mechanisms are used without prior signaling. In addition, QoS characteristics (bandwidth and delay, for example) are managed on a hop-by-hop basis by policies that are established independently at each intermediate device in a network. The soft QoS approach is not considered an end-to-end QoS strategy, because end-to-end guarantees cannot be enforced. However, soft QoS is a more scalable approach to implementing QoS than hard QoS, because many (hundreds or potentially thousands) of applications can be mapped into a small set of classes upon which similar sets of QoS behaviors are implemented. Although QoS mechanisms in this approach are enforced and applied on a hop-by-hop basis, uniformly applying global meaning to each traffic class provides both flexibility and scalability.

With DiffServ, network traffic is divided into classes that are based on business requirements. Each of the classes can then be assigned a different level of service. As packets traverse a network, each of the network devices identifies the packet class and services the packet according to that class. You can choose from many levels of service with DiffServ. For example, voice traffic from IP phones is usually given preferential treatment

586 Implementing Cisco Unified Communications Voice over IP and QoS (CVoice) Foundation Learning Guide

over all other application traffic. Email is generally given best-effort service. Nonbusiness traffic can either be given very poor service or blocked entirely.

DiffServ works like a package delivery service. You request (and pay for) a level of service when you send your package. Throughout the package network, the level of service is recognized, and your package is given either preferential or normal service, depending on what you requested.

QoS Model Evaluation

DiffServ has these key benefits:

- It is highly scalable.
- It provides many different levels of quality.

DiffServ also has these drawbacks:

- No absolute guarantee of service quality can be made.
- It requires a set of complex mechanisms to work in concert throughout the network.

The main benefits of IntServ and RSVP are as follows:

- RSVP signals QoS requests per individual flow. The network can then provide guarantees to these individual flows. The problem with this is that IntServ does not scale to large networks because of the large number of concurrent RSVP flows.
- RSVP informs network devices of flow parameters (IP addresses and port numbers). Some applications use dynamic port numbers, which can be difficult for network devices to recognize. NBAR is a mechanism that has been introduced to supplement RSVP for applications that use dynamic port numbers but do not use RSVP.
- IntServ supports admission control, which allows a network to reject (or downgrade) new RSVP sessions if one of the interfaces in the path has reached the limit (that is, all reservable bandwidth is booked).

The main drawbacks of IntServ and RSVP are as follows:

- There is continuous signaling because of the stateful RSVP operation.
- RSVP is not scalable to large networks where per-flow guarantees would have to be made to thousands of concurrent RSVP flows.

The best-effort model has these significant benefits:

- The best-effort model has nearly unlimited scalability. The only way to reach scalability limits is to reach bandwidth limits, in which case all traffic becomes equally delayed.

■ You do not need to employ special QoS mechanisms to use the best-effort model. It is the easiest and quickest model to deploy.

The best-effort model also has these drawbacks:

■ Nothing is guaranteed. Packets will arrive whenever they can, in any order possible, if they arrive at all.

■ Packets are not given preferential treatment. Critical data is treated the same as email.

Table 7-3 summarizes the benefits and drawbacks of the DiffServ, IntServ, and best-effort QoS models.

Table 7-3 *QoS Model Evaluation*

Model	Drawbacks	Benefits
DiffServ	No absolute service guarantee Complex mechanisms	Highly scalable Many levels of quality possible
IntServ	Continuous signaling because of stateful architecture Flow-based approach not scalable to large implementations, such as ISP networks or the Internet	Explicit resource admission control (end-to-end) Per-request policy admission control Signaling of dynamic port numbers (for example, H.323)
Best effort	No service guarantee No service differentiation	Highly scalable No special mechanisms required

Characteristics of QoS Models

DiffServ is a multiple-service model for implementing QoS in the network. With DiffServ, the network tries to deliver a particular kind of service that is based on the QoS specified by each packet. This specification can occur in different ways, such as using the DSCP in IP packets or source and destination addresses. The network uses the QoS specification of each packet to classify, shape, and police traffic and to perform intelligent queuing. This section focuses on the DiffServ model and explains the mechanisms that are used to implement DiffServ.

DiffServ Model

As illustrated in Figure 7-11, discussions about the DiffServ model use three basic terms to describe DiffServ operations:

- **Behavior aggregate (BA):** A BA is a collection of packets with the same DSCP value crossing a link in a particular direction. Packets from multiple applications and sources can belong to the same BA. In Cisco IOS, classification of packets into BAs can be done by using Modular QoS CLI (MQC) class maps.

- **DSCP:** A DSCP marking is a value in an IP header that is used to select a QoS treatment for a packet.

- **Per-hop behavior (PHB):** A PHB is an externally observable forwarding behavior (or QoS treatment) applied at a DiffServ-compliant node to a DiffServ BA. The term PHB refers to the packet scheduling, queuing, policing, or shaping behavior of a node on any given packet belonging to a BA. The DiffServ model itself does not specify how PHBs must be implemented. A variety of techniques can be used to affect the desired traffic conditioning and PHB. In Cisco IOS, you can configure PHBs by using MQC policy maps.

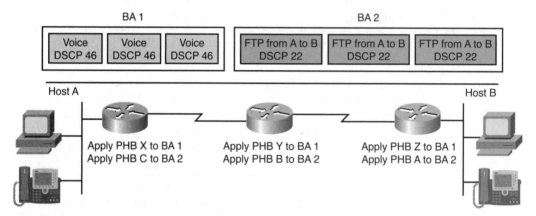

Figure 7-11   *DiffServ Terminology*

As shown in Figure 7-12, the DiffServ architecture is based on a simple model in which traffic entering a network is classified and possibly conditioned at the boundaries of a network. A traffic class is then identified with a DSCP or bit marking in the IP header. A primary advantage of DiffServ is scalability.

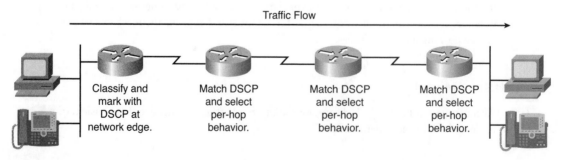

Figure 7-12   *DiffServ Model*

DSCP values are used to mark packets to indicate a desired PHB. Within the core of a network, packets are forwarded according to the PHB that is associated with the DSCP.

One of the primary principles of DiffServ is that packets should be marked as close to the edge of the network as possible. It is often a difficult and time-consuming task to determine the traffic class for a data packet, so the data should be classified as few times as possible. By marking the traffic at the network edge, core network devices and other devices along the forwarding path will be able to quickly determine the proper QoS treatment to apply to a given traffic flow.

DSCP supersedes IP Precedence, a 3-bit field in the type of service (ToS) byte of the IP header that was originally used to classify and prioritize types of traffic. However, DSCP maintains interoperability with devices that use IP Precedence.

DSCP Encoding

DiffServ uses the Differentiated Services (DS) field in the IP header to mark packets according to their classification into BAs. The DS field occupies the same 8 bits of the IP header that were previously used for the ToS byte, as depicted in Figure 7-13.

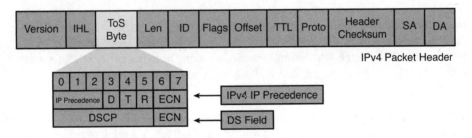

Figure 7-13 *DSCP Encoding*

The following three Internet Engineering Task Force (IETF) standards describe the purpose of the 8 bits of the DS field:

- RFC 791 includes specification of the ToS field, where the 3 low-order bits are used for IP Precedence. The next 3 bits are used for delay, throughput, reliability, and cost.

- RFC 1812 modifies the meaning of the ToS field by removing the meaning from the 5 high-order bits (those bits should all be 0). This gained widespread use and became known as the original IP Precedence.

- RFC 2474 replaces the ToS field with the DS field, where the 6 low-order bits are used for the DSCP. The remaining 2 bits are used for Explicit Congestion Notification (ECN). RFC 3260 ("New Terminology and Clarifications for DiffServ") updates RFC 2474 and provides terminology clarifications.

Each DSCP value identifies a BA. Each BA is assigned a PHB. Each PHB is implemented using the appropriate QoS mechanisms.

IP version 6 (IPv6) also provides support for QoS marking via a field in the IPv6 header. Similar to the ToS (or DS) field in the IPv4 header, the Traffic Class field (8 bits) is available for use by originating nodes and forwarding routers to identify and distinguish between different classes or priorities of IPv6 packets. The Traffic Class field can be used to set specific precedence or DSCP values, which are used the same way that they are used in IPv4.

DiffServ PHBs

The IETF standards define the following PHBs:

- **Default PHB:** Used for best-effort service (bits 0–2 of DSCP = 000)

- **Expedited Forwarding (EF) PHB:** Used for low-delay service (bits 0–2 of DSCP = 101)

- **Assured Forwarding (AF) PHB:** Used for guaranteed bandwidth service (bits 0–2 of DSCP = 001, 010, 011, or 100)

- **Class Selector PHB:** Used for backward compatibility with non-DiffServ-compliant devices (RFC 1812-compliant devices [bits 3–5 of DSCP = 000])

> **Note**   Bit position numbering can be confusing, because the numbering starts at 0. For example, when a reference is made to a Class Selector PHB having bits 3–5 set to 000, the bits being referred are the 4th, 5th, and 6th bits, counting from the left. Similarly, a reference to bits 0–2 refers to the 1st, 2nd, and 3rd bits, counting from the left.

Figure 7-14 illustrates the first 3 bits used by the Default, EF, and AF PHBs. It also points out that bit positions 3–5 (that is, the 4th, 5th, and 6th bits, counting from the left) are set to 0 for Class Selector PHBs.

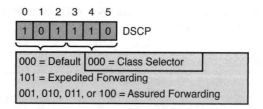

Figure 7-14   *Per-Hop Behaviors*

Expedited Forwarding PHB

Figure 7-15 shows the binary digits making up a DSCP value of 46, which is also known as a PHB of EF. The EF PHB has the following characteristics:

- The EF PHB ensures a minimum departure rate. The EF PHB provides the lowest possible delay to delay-sensitive applications.

- The EF PHB guarantees bandwidth. However, the EF PHB prevents starvation of the application if there are multiple applications using EF PHB.

- The EF PHB polices bandwidth when congestion occurs. The EF PHB prevents starvation of other applications or classes that are not using this PHB.

- Packets requiring EF should be marked with DSCP binary value 101110 (46 or 0x2E).

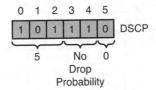

Figure 7-15 *Expedited Forwarding (EF) PHB*

Non-DiffServ-compliant devices will regard the EF DSCP value of 101110 as IP Precedence 5 (101), by examining the 3 leftmost bits.

This precedence is the highest user-definable IP Precedence and is typically used for delay-sensitive traffic (such as VoIP). Again, the 3 low-order bits of the EF DSCP value are 101, which matches IP Precedence 5 and allows backward compatibility.

Assured Forwarding PHB

Figure 7-16 shows the binary structure of an Assured Forwarding (AF) PHB. Twelve DSCP values correspond to the 12 AF PHBs. The AF PHBs have the following characteristics:

- An AF PHB guarantees a certain amount of bandwidth to an AF class.

- An AF PHB allows access to extra bandwidth, if available.

- Packets requiring an AF PHB should be marked with a DSCP binary value *aaadd*0, where *aaa* is the number of the class, and *dd* is the drop probability.

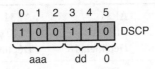

Figure 7-16 *Assured Forwarding (AF) PHBs*

As shown in Figure 7-17, there are four standard defined AF classes. Each class should be treated independently and should have allocated bandwidth that is based on the QoS policy. Each AF class is assigned an IP Precedence and has three drop probabilities: low, medium, and high. The AF drop probabilities are determined by the 4th and 5th bits (counting from the left).

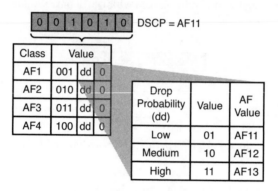

Figure 7-17   *Assured Forwarding (AF) Drop Probabilities*

AF*xy* represents an AF PHB, where *x* corresponds to the IP Precedence value (only IP Precedences 1 to 4 are used for AF classes), and *y* corresponds to the drop preference value (1, 2, or 3).

Interestingly, the AF PHB values do not necessarily follow the "bigger-is-better" logic used with IP Precedence markings, in which a packet with a higher IP Precedence received preferential treatment over a packet with a lower IP Precedence.

Table 7-4 lists the binary and decimal values for the four AF PHBs in three drop probability combinations. Interestingly, the drop probability values of 1, 2, and 3 are independent of the IP Precedence equivalent value of an AF PHB. For example, just as a DSCP PHB value of AF13 has a higher drop probability than AF11, a value of AF42 has a higher drop probability than AF11.

Table 7-4   *AF PHB Values*

Drop Probability	Class AF1	Class AF2	Class AF3	Class AF4
Low drop probability	AF11 001010 Decimal: 10	AF21 010010 Decimal: 18	AF31 011010 Decimal: 26	AF41 100010 Decimal: 34
Medium drop probability	AF12 001100 Decimal: 12	AF22 010100 Decimal: 20	AF32 011100 Decimal: 28	AF42 100100 Decimal: 36
High drop probability	AF13 001110 Decimal: 14	AF23 010110 Decimal: 22	AF33 11110 Decimal: 30	AF43 100110 Decimal: 38

DiffServ Class Selector

The meaning of the 8 bits in the DS field of the IP packet has changed over time to meet the expanding requirements of IP networks. The most common traditional use is provided by the 3 low-order (that is, leftmost) IP Precedence bits.

As shown in Figure 7-18, the Class Selector PHB provides bit-for-bit backward compatibility for DSCP with IP Precedence. The next 3 bits of the DSCP (bit positions 3–5), set to 0, identify a Class Selector PHB. The Class Selector PHB is defined as the probability of timely forwarding and is compliant with RFC 1812, which simply prioritizes packets according to the IP Precedence value. Packets with higher IP Precedence should generally be forwarded in less time than packets with lower IP Precedence.

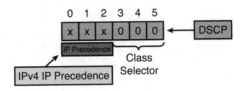

Figure 7-18   *Class Selector PHBs*

DiffServ QoS Mechanisms

The main categories of tools that are used to implement QoS in a network include the following:

- **Classification and marking:** The identifying and splitting of traffic into different classes and the marking of traffic according to behavior and business policies.

- **Congestion management:** The prioritization, protection, and isolation of traffic, based on markings.

- **Congestion avoidance:** Discards specific packets, based on markings, to avoid network congestion.

- **Policing and shaping:** Traffic conditioning mechanisms that police traffic by dropping misbehaving traffic to maintain network integrity. These mechanisms also shape traffic to control bursts by queuing excess traffic.

- **Link efficiency:** One type of link-efficiency technology is packet header compression, which improves the bandwidth efficiency of a link. Another technology is Link Fragmentation and Interleaving (LFI), which can decrease the "jitter" of voice transmission by reducing voice packet delay.

Classification

Classification, as depicted in Figure 7-19, is the identifying and splitting of traffic into different classes.

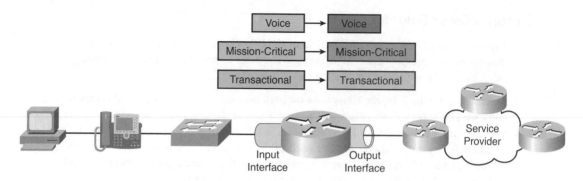

Figure 7-19   *Class-Selector PHBs*

In a QoS-enabled network, all traffic is classified at the input interface of every QoS-aware device. Packet classification can be based on many factors, such as

- DSCP

- IP Precedence

- Source address

- Destination address

The concept of trust is the key for deploying QoS. When an end device (such as a workstation or a Cisco Unified IP Phone) marks a packet with a Class of Service (CoS) or DSCP marking, a switch or router has the option of accepting or ignoring those values. If the switch or router chooses to accept the values, the switch or router trusts the end device. If the switch or router trusts the end device, it does not need to do any reclassification of packets coming from that interface. If the switch or router does not trust the interface, it must perform a reclassification to determine the appropriate QoS value for the packets coming from that interface. Switches and routers are generally set to not trust end devices and must specifically be configured to trust packets coming in an interface. Classification tools include Network-Based Application Recognition (NBAR), Policy-Based Routing (PBR), and classification and marking using MQC.

Marking

Marking, also known as coloring, involves marking each packet as a member of a network class so that devices throughout the rest of the network can quickly recognize the packet class. Marking is performed as close to the network edge as possible and is often done using MQC.

QoS mechanisms set bits in the DSCP or IP Precedence fields of each IP packet according to the class that the packet is in. Other fields can also be marked to aid in the identification of a packet class.

Other QoS mechanisms use these bits to determine how to treat packets when they arrive. If the packets are marked as high-priority voice packets, the packets will generally never be dropped by congestion avoidance mechanisms and might be given immediate preference by congestion management queuing mechanisms. On the other hand, if the packets are marked as low-priority file transfer packets, they will be dropped when congestion occurs and will generally be moved to the back end of the congestion management queues.

Congestion Management

Congestion management mechanisms (queuing algorithms), as illustrated in Figure 7-20, use the marking on each packet to determine in which queue to place packets. Different queues are given different treatment by a queuing algorithm that is based on the class of packets in the queue. Generally, queues with high-priority packets receive preferential treatment.

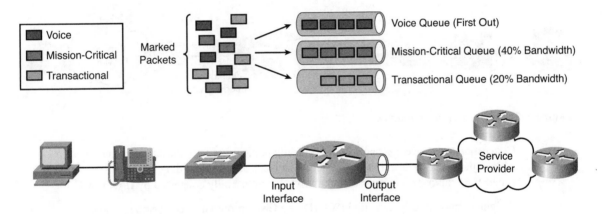

Figure 7-20 *Congestion Management*

Congestion management is implemented on all output interfaces in a QoS-enabled network by using queuing mechanisms to manage the outflow of traffic. Each queuing algorithm was designed to solve a specific network traffic problem and has a particular effect on network performance.

Cisco IOS features for congestion management (that is, queuing) includes these queuing methods:

- FIFO, priority queuing (PQ), custom queuing (CQ)

- Weighted fair queuing (WFQ)

- Class-based weighted fair queuing (CBWFQ)

- Low latency queuing (LLQ)

LLQ is currently the preferred queuing method. LLQ is a hybrid (PQ and CBWFQ) queuing method that was developed to specifically meet the requirements of real-time traffic, such as voice.

Congestion Avoidance

Congestion avoidance mechanisms, as shown in Figure 7-21, monitor network traffic loads in an effort to anticipate and avoid congestion at common network bottlenecks. Congestion avoidance is achieved through preemptive packet dropping.

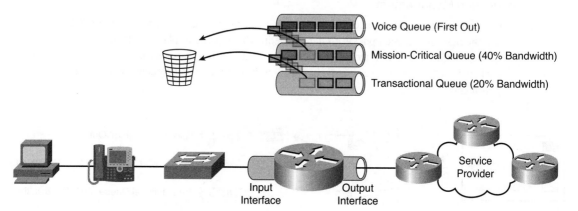

Figure 7-21   *Congestion Avoidance*

Congestion avoidance mechanisms are typically implemented on output interfaces where a high-speed link feeds into a lower-speed link (such as a LAN feeding into a slower-speed WAN link). This ensures that the WAN is not instantly congested by LAN traffic.

Weighted random early detection (WRED) is a Cisco-proprietary congestion avoidance technique. WRED increases the probability that congestion (that is, an output interface queue completely filling to capacity) is avoided by dropping low-priority packets rather than dropping high-priority packets.

WRED is not recommended for voice queues, because WRED influences TCP-based flows. However, voice traffic is UDP based.

Bonus Video   To view a video of the author discussing WRED theory, navigate to the CVOICE page on the 1ExamAMonth.com website. The video on WRED theory is titled *The 3 Most Challenging QoS Topics – Part 2*. Additional video tutorials from this website will be recommended later in the book.

Policing

Policing, as illustrated in Figure 7-22, is used to condition traffic before transmitting traffic to a network or receiving traffic from a network.

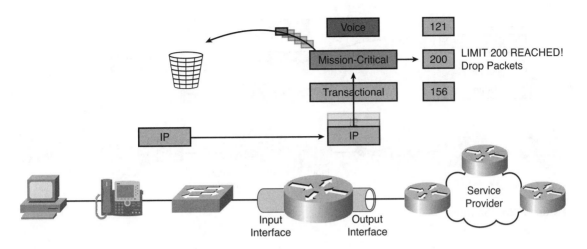

Figure 7-22   *Policing*

Policing is the ability to control bursts and traffic to ensure that certain types of traffic get certain amounts of bandwidth.

Policing drops or marks packets when predefined limits are reached. Policing mechanisms can be set to first drop traffic classes that have lower QoS priority markings.

Policing mechanisms can be used on either input or output interfaces. These mechanisms are typically used to control the flow into a network device from a high-speed link by dropping excess lower-priority packets. A good example would be the use of policing by a service provider to throttle a high-speed inflow from a customer that was in excess of their service agreement. In a TCP environment, this policing would cause the sender to slow its packet transmission.

Policing mechanisms include Class-Based Policing and Committed Access Rate (CAR).

Shaping

Shaping, as depicted in Figure 7-23, helps smooth out speed mismatches in a network and limits transmission rates.

Shaping mechanisms are used on output interfaces. These mechanisms are typically used to limit the flow from a high-speed link to a lower-speed link, ensuring the lower-speed link does not become overrun with traffic. Shaping could also be used to manage the flow of traffic at a point in the network where multiple flows are aggregated. Service providers use shaping to manage the flow of traffic to and from customers to ensure that the flows conform to service agreements between the customer and provider.

Cisco QoS software solutions include two traffic shaping tools to manage traffic and congestion on the network: Generic Traffic Shaping (GTS) and Frame Relay Traffic Shaping (FRTS).

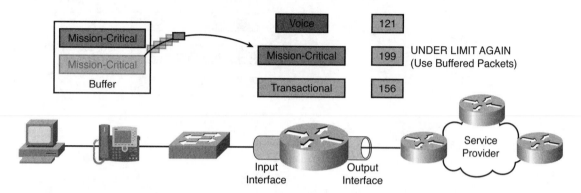

Figure 7-23   *Shaping*

> **Bonus Video**   To view a video of the author discussing the theory behind policing and shaping, navigate to the CVOICE page on the 1ExamAMonth.com website. The video on policing and shaping theory is titled *The 3 Most Challenging QoS Topics – Part 1*. Additional video tutorials from this website will be recommended later in the book.

Compression

Compression is one of the Cisco IOS link-efficiency mechanisms that work in conjunction with queuing and traffic shaping to manage existing bandwidth more efficiently and predictably.

Two types of compression are available:

- Payload compression of Layer 2 frames. One of two algorithms, Stacker or Predictor, can be configured for this type of compression.

- Compressed Real-time Transport Protocol (cRTP), as shown in Figure 7-24, maps the three headers, IP, UDP, and RTP, with a combined 40 bytes, to 2 or 4 bytes, depending on whether a CRC is transmitted. This compression can dramatically improve the performance of a link.

Compression should be used only on slow WAN links, because its drawback is the consumption of computational resources on a hop-by-hop basis.

Link Fragmentation and Interleaving

Interactive traffic, such as VoIP, is susceptible to increased latency and jitter when the network processes large packets, such as FTP packets, traversing a WAN link. This susceptibility increases as the traffic is queued on slower links.

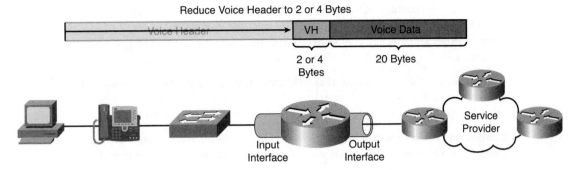

Figure 7-24 *RTP Header Compression*

LFI can reduce delay and jitter on slower-speed links by breaking up large datagrams and interleaving low-delay traffic packets with the resulting smaller packets, as demonstrated in Figure 7-25.

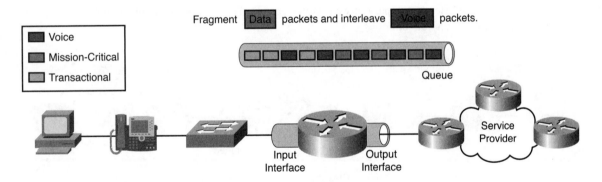

Figure 7-25 *Link Fragmentation and Interleaving*

LFI is used on slow WAN links to ensure minimal delay for voice and video traffic.

> **Bonus Video**   To view a video of the author discussing LFI theory and demonstrating the benefit of an LFI configuration, navigate to the CVOICE page on the 1ExamAMonth.com website. The video on LFI is titled *The 3 Most Challenging QoS Topics – Part 3.* Additional video tutorials from this website will be recommended later in the book.

Applying QoS to Input and Output Interfaces

In a QoS-enabled network, classification is performed on every input interface. Marking should be performed as close to the network edge as possible, in the originating network device, if possible. Devices further from the edge of the network, such as routers and switches, can be configured to trust or ignore the marking set by the edge devices. A Cisco Unified IP Phone, for example, will not trust the markings of an attached PC, while switches are typically configured to trust the markings of attached Cisco Unified IP Phones.

It only makes sense to use congestion management, congestion avoidance, and traffic shaping mechanisms on output interfaces. These mechanisms help maintain smooth operation of links by controlling how much and which type of traffic is allowed on a link.

Congestion avoidance is typically employed on an output interface where there is a chance that a high-speed link feeds into a slower link (such as a LAN feeding into a WAN).

Policing and shaping are typically employed on output interfaces to control the flow of traffic from a high-speed link to lower-speed links. Policing is also employed on input interfaces to control the flow into a network device from a high-speed link, by dropping excess low-priority packets.

Both compression and LFI could be used on slower-speed WAN links between sites to improve bandwidth efficiency.

Figure 7-26 offers a summary of what QoS mechanisms are supported in the inbound and/or outbound direction.

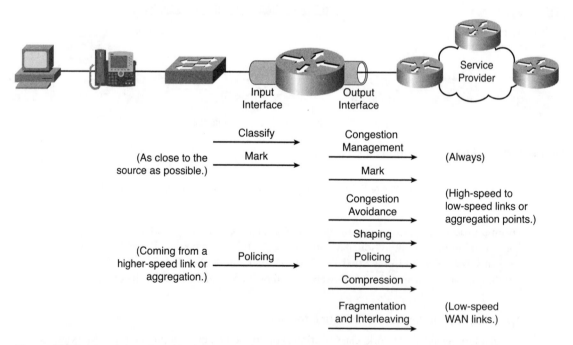

Figure 7-26   *Applying QoS Mechanisms Inbound and Outbound*

Cisco QoS Baseline Model

Although several sources of information can be used as guidelines for determining a QoS policy, none of them can determine exactly what is proper for a specific network. Each network presents its own unique challenges and administrative policies.

The Cisco baseline classification model provides one of the possible classification approaches. It consists of 11 traffic classes that are typically found in enterprise networks. The 11 traffic classes are described in Table 7-5 and provide enough granularity for a majority of organizations. The model can grow or shrink based on enterprise requirements. It should balance the need to differentiate between traffic categories with the goal of easy manageability.

Table 7-5 *Cisco QoS Baseline*

Traffic Class	Description
Routing	Network control traffic, such as routing protocols
Voice	Interactive voice-bearer traffic
Video Conferencing	Interactive video data traffic
Streaming Video	Streaming media traffic
Mission-Critical Data	Applications with critical importance to enterprise
Call Signaling	Call signaling and control traffic
Transactional Data	Database applications, transactional in nature
Network Management	Network management traffic
Bulk Data	Bulk data transfers, web traffic, general data
Scavenger	Casual entertainment, rogue traffic, less than best effort
Best Effort	Default class, all noncritical traffic

Cisco Baseline Marking

Table 7-6 lists the recommended markings for the 11 traffic categories that are defined by the Cisco baseline model.

QoS must be implemented consistently across the entire network. It is not so important whether Call Signaling is marked as DSCP 34 or 26, but rather that DSCP 34 and 26 are treated in a manner that is necessary to accomplish the QoS policy. It is also important that data marked DSCP 34 be treated consistently across a network. If data travels over even a small portion of a network where different policies are applied (or no policies are applied), the entire QoS policy is nullified. Whether the data is crossing slow WAN links or Gigabit Ethernet, being switched by a Layer 2 switch or routed in a Layer 3 router, the policies should be consistently implemented to satisfy the policy requirements.

Table 7-6 *Cisco QoS Baseline Markings*

Application	L3 Classification			L2
	IPP	**PHB**	**DSCP**	**CoS**
Routing	6	CS6	48	6
Voice	5	EF	46	5
Video Conferencing	4	AF41	34	4
Streaming Video	4	CS4	32	4
Mission-Critical Data	3	AF31	26	3
Call Signaling	3	CS3	24	3
Transactional Data	2	AF21	18	2
Network Management	2	CS2	16	2
Bulk Data	1	AF11	10	1
Scavenger	1	CS1	8	1
Best Effort	0	0	0	0

Originally, Cisco marked call signaling traffic as AF 31. The Cisco QoS baseline changed the marking recommendation for call signaling traffic to DSCP CS3, because Class Selector code points, as defined in RFC 2474, are not subject to markdown or aggressive dropping during times of congestion.

Cisco Baseline Mechanisms

Table 7-7 lists the QoS mechanisms recommended for each of the 11 traffic classes of the Cisco baseline model.

Table 7-7 *Cisco QoS Baseline Mechanisms*

Application	Recommendations
Routing	Rate-based queuing + RED
Voice	CAC + priority queuing
Video Conferencing	CAC + rate-based queuing + WRED
Streaming Video	CAC + rate-based queuing + WRED
Mission-Critical Data	Rate-based queuing + WRED
Call Signaling	Rate-based queuing + RED

Table 7-7   *Cisco QoS Baseline Mechanisms*

Application	Recommendations
Transactional Data	Rate-based queuing + WRED
Network Management	Rate-based queuing + RED
Bulk Data	Rate-based queuing + WRED
Scavenger	No bandwidth guarantee + RED
Best Effort	Bandwidth guarantee (rate-based queuing + RED)

Call admission control (CAC) ensures that only a defined number of simultaneous calls are admitted into the VoIP network.

Priority queuing (LLQ) and rate-based queuing (CBWFQ) are discussed in detail in the next chapter.

Random early detection (RED) and weighted RED (WRED) selectively drop packets when buffers are filling up. This random drop is used to avoid congestion and is most effective for TCP flows, which reduce their transmit window size.

Expansion and Reduction of the Class Model

Figure 7-27 shows other common classification models, based on three, five, or eight traffic classes, respectively. The expansion and reduction of the model causes some of the classes to be split or aggregated into more granular or more generic traffic categories. The selection of the most suitable model depends on enterprise needs.

Summary

The main topics covered in this chapter are the following:

- The need for and the purpose of quality of service (QoS) was discussed.

- Three QoS implementation models were introduced: best effort, Integrated Services, and Differentiated Services.

- QoS DSCP markings were discussed, including the four classes of per-hop behaviors (PHB): Default, Class Selector, Assured Forwarding, and Expedited Forwarding.

- An overview of various QoS mechanisms were presented. These mechanisms are elaborated upon in Chapter 8, "Configuring QoS Mechanisms."

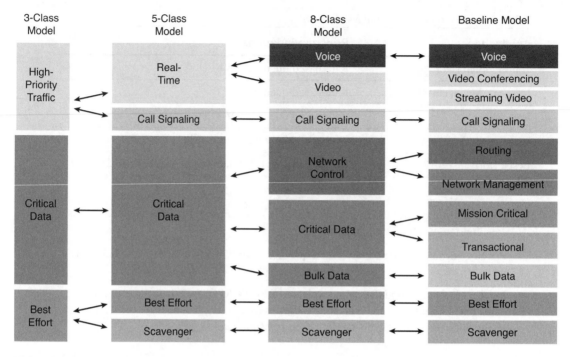

Figure 7-27   *Expansion/Reduction of Class Model*

Chapter Review Questions

The answers to these review questions are in the appendix.

1.   Which term describes the time that it takes to actually transmit a packet on a link ("put bits on the wire")?

   a.   Encoding delay

   b.   Processing delay

   c.   Serialization delay

   d.   Transmission delay

2.   How much one-way delay can a voice packet tolerate, according to the G.114 recommendation?

   a.   15 ms

   b.   150 ms

   c.   300 ms

   d.   200 ms

3. A variation in delay is called _____.

   a. LFI

   b. cRTP

   c. Tail drop

   d. Jitter

4. Which of the following is an advantage provided by MQC, as compared to the CLI approach to QoS configuration?

   a. GUI-based

   b. Ability to apply one policy to multiple interfaces

   c. Automatic generation of CLI commands from MQC macros

   d. Supports queuing mechanisms

5. Which QoS implementation method offers the shortest implementation time for simple networks?

   a. CLI

   b. MQC

   c. AutoQoS

   d. AutoTuner

6. Which class of DSCP PHBs offers bit-for-bit backward compatibility with IP Precedence markings?

   a. EF

   b. AF

   c. Default

   d. CS

7. What is the most important advantage of DiffServ over other QoS models?

   a. High scalability

   b. Offers FIFO treatment of traffic

   c. Guaranteed service

   d. Deterministic delays

8. Services are provided to which entities in the DiffServ model?

    a. Frames

    b. Packets

    c. Applications

    d. Classes of traffic

9. Which PHB is indicated by the DSCP value of 46 (101110)?

    a. Default PHB

    b. Selector PHB

    c. AF PHB

    d. EF PHB

10. Which AF class and which drop probability is indicated by the DSCP value of 100100?

    a. AF1 and medium

    b. AF4 and medium

    c. AF1 and high

    d. AF4 and high

Chapter 8

Configuring QoS Mechanisms

After reading this chapter, you should be able to perform the following tasks:

- Explain the operation and configuration of the QoS classification and marking mechanisms, including the concept of trust boundaries, and describe how LFI and cRTP provide link efficiency on WAN links and how they are configured.

- Explain how to configure policing, shaping, and LLQ, their operations and configuration, using MQC.

- Describe how Cisco AutoQoS works and what it achieves in a Cisco Unified Communications network.

This chapter covers the configuration of various QoS mechanisms to facilitate the creation of effective QoS administrative policies, with a special focus on voice transport. It provides design and usage rules for various advanced QoS features and for the integration of QoS with underlying Layer 2 QoS mechanisms.

Classification, Marking, and Link-Efficiency QoS Mechanisms

The Modular Quality of Service (QoS) Command-Line Interface (CLI), or MQC, provides a modular approach to the configuration of QoS mechanisms. MQC allows network administrators to introduce new QoS mechanisms and reuse available classification options.

MQC offers a scalable method to provide different levels of treatment to specific classes of traffic. Before any QoS applications or mechanisms can be applied, traffic must be identified and sorted into different classes. QoS is applied to these different traffic classes. Network devices use classification to identify traffic as belonging to a specific class. After network traffic is sorted, marking can be used to color (that is, tag) individual packets so that other network devices can apply QoS features uniformly to those packets as they travel through a network.

VoIP traffic is susceptible to latency when large packets, such as bulk FTP packets, traverse WAN links. Packet delay is especially significant when large packets are queued on slower links (that is, less than or equal to 768 kbps). To solve delay problems on slow bandwidth links, a method for fragmenting larger frames and then queuing smaller frames between fragments of the larger frames is required. To meet this requirement, Cisco IOS supports Multilink PPP (MLP), Link Fragmentation and Interleaving (LFI), and Frame Relay Fragmentation Implementation Agreement (FRF.12). In addition, complementary tools, such as header and payload compression techniques, can be deployed to reduce the size of frames sent over WAN links.

This section outlines how to implement QoS policies using MQC, and introduces the concepts of classification and marking. It explains the different markers that are available at the data link and network layers, and identifies where classification and marking should be used in a network. The section also describes different approaches for improving the efficiency of WAN links.

Modular QoS CLI

The MQC was introduced to allow any supported classification to be used with any QoS mechanism.

The separation of classification from the QoS mechanism allows new Cisco IOS versions to introduce new QoS mechanisms and reuse all available classification options. On the other hand, old QoS mechanisms can benefit from new classification options.

Another important benefit of the MQC is the reusability of the configuration. MQC allows the same QoS policy to be applied to multiple interfaces, as illustrated in Figure 8-1.

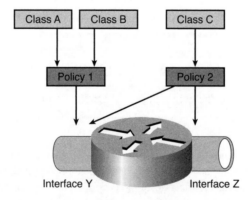

Figure 8-1   *Modular QoS CLI*

Example: Advantages of Using MQC

Configuring Committed Access Rate (CAR), which is an example of a policing mechanism, requires entire configurations to be repeated between interfaces and time-consuming configuration modifications. MQC allows class-based policing.

MQC Components

Follow these steps, which are depicted in Figure 8-2, to implement QoS by using MQC:

Step 1.   Configure classification by using the **class-map** command.

Step 2.   Configure traffic policy by associating the traffic class with one or more QoS features using the **policy-map** command.

Step 3.   Attach the traffic policy to inbound or outbound traffic on interfaces, subinterfaces, or virtual circuits using the **service-policy** command.

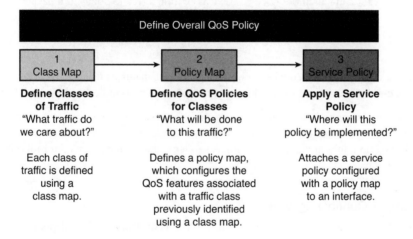

Figure 8-2   *MQC Components*

Class maps are used to create classification templates that are later used in policy maps in which QoS mechanisms are bound to classes.

You can create a class map by using the **class-map** global configuration command. Class maps are identified by case-sensitive names. Each class map contains one or more conditions that determine if a packet belongs to the class.

There are two ways of processing conditions when a class map has more than one condition:

■   **Match all:** This is the default match strategy. All conditions have to be met to bind a packet to the class.

■   **Match any:** At least one condition has to be met to bind a packet to the class.

The **policy-map** command is used to create a traffic policy. The purpose of a traffic policy is to configure the QoS features that should be associated with the traffic that has been classified in a user-specified traffic class or classes. A traffic policy contains three elements: a case-sensitive name, a traffic class (specified with the **class** command), and QoS policies.

The name of a traffic policy is specified in the policy-map CLI (for example, issuing the **policy-map class1** command would create a traffic policy named *class1*). After issuing the **policy-map** command, you are placed into policy-map configuration mode. You can then enter the name of a traffic class, and enter the QoS features to apply to the traffic that matches this class.

MQC does not necessarily require that you associate only one traffic class to a single traffic policy. When packets match more than one match criterion, multiple traffic classes can be associated with a single traffic policy.

Note   A packet can match only one traffic class within a traffic policy. If a packet matches more than one traffic class in the traffic policy, the first traffic class that is defined in the policy will be used.

The last configuration step when configuring QoS mechanisms using MQC is to use the **service-policy** command to attach a policy map to the inbound or outbound packets.

Using the **service-policy** command, you can assign a single policy map to multiple interfaces or assign as many as two policy maps to a single interface (a maximum of one in each direction, inbound and outbound). A service policy can be applied for inbound or outbound packets.

Example: Configuring MQC

Consider this example of configuring MQC on a network with voice telephony:

Step 1.   Classify traffic as voice, high-priority, low-priority, and browser in class maps.

Step 2.   Build a single policy map that defines three different traffic policies (different bandwidth and delay requirements for each traffic class): NoDelay, BestService, and Whenever. Assign the already-defined classes of traffic to the policies. Voice is assigned to NoDelay. High-priority traffic is assigned to BestService. Both low-priority and browser traffic is assigned to Whenever.

Step 3.   Assign the policy map to selected router and switch interfaces.

Configuring Classification

Classification is the process of identifying traffic and categorizing that traffic into different classes. Packet classification uses a traffic descriptor to categorize a packet within a specific group in order to define that packet. Typically used traffic descriptors include

CoS, incoming interface, IP Precedence, DSCP, source or destination IP address, application, and Multiprotocol Label Switching (MPLS) experimental (EXP) bits. After a packet has been defined (that is, classified), the packet is then accessible for QoS handling on the network.

Using packet classification, you can partition network traffic into multiple priority levels or classes of service. When traffic descriptors are used to classify traffic, the source agrees to adhere to the contracted terms, and the network promises a specific QoS level. Different QoS mechanisms, such as traffic policing, traffic shaping, and queuing techniques, use the traffic descriptor of the packet (that is, the classification of the packet) to ensure adherence to that agreement.

Classification should take place at the network edge, typically in a wiring closet, in IP phones, or at network endpoints. It is recommended that classification occur as close to the source of the traffic as possible.

MQC Classification Options

Classification using MQC is accomplished by specifying a traffic match criteria within a configured class map for each service class. In order for QoS mechanisms to use the class map, the class map must be referenced through the use of a policy map, which is subsequently applied to an inbound or outbound interface as a service policy.

MQC classification with class maps is extremely flexible, and you can classify packets by using these classification tools:

- **Access control lists (ACL):** ACLs for any protocol can be used within class-map configuration mode. MQC can be used for other protocols, not just IP.

- **IP Precedence:** IP packets can be classified by specifying IP Precedence values.

- **DSCP:** IP packets can be classified by specifying IP Differentiated Services Code Point (DSCP) values.

- **MPLS experimental bits:** Packets can be matched based on the value in the EXP bits of the MPLS header of labeled packets.

- **QoS group:** A QoS group parameter can be used to classify packets in situations where up to 100 classes are needed or the QoS group parameter is used as an intermediate marker. For example, the QoS group parameter can be used in an MPLS-to-QoS group translation on input and a QoS group-to-DSCP translation on output. QoS group markings are local to a single router.

- **Protocol:** Classification is possible by identifying Layer 3 or Layer 4 protocols. Advanced classification is also available by using the Network-Based Application Recognition (NBAR) tool, which identifies dynamic protocols by inspecting higher-layer information.

- **Class map hierarchy:** Another class map can be used to implement template-based configurations.

- **Frame Relay DE bit:** Packets can be matched based on the value of the underlying Frame Relay Discard Eligible (DE) bit.

- **CoS:** Packets can be matched based on the information that is contained in the three Class of Service (CoS) bits (when using 802.1Q encapsulation) or Priority bits (when using Inter-Switch Link [ISL] encapsulation).

- **Input interface:** Packets can be classified based on the interface from which they enter the Cisco IOS device.

- **MAC address:** Packets can be matched based on their source or destination MAC address.

- **User Datagram Protocol (UDP) port range:** Real-time Transport Protocol (RTP) packets can be matched based on a range of UDP port numbers.

- **All packets:** MQC can also be used to implement a QoS mechanism for all traffic in which case classification will put all packets into one class.

- **Field:** You can use the **match field** command to configure the match criteria for a class map based on the fields that are defined in Protocol Header Description Files (PHDF). Before configuring this match criterion, you must load a PHDF onto the router.

- **Frame Relay data-link connection identifier (DLCI):** You can use the **match fr-dlci** command to specify the Frame Relay DLCI number as a match criterion in a class map. This match criterion can be used in main interfaces and point-to-multipoint subinterfaces in Frame Relay networks. It can also be used in hierarchical policy maps.

- **MPLS EXP bit value in the topmost label header:** You can use the **match mpls experimental topmost** command to match the MPLS EXP value in the topmost label. You can use this match criterion on the input and output interfaces. It will match only on MPLS packets.

- **Packet length:** You can use the **match packet length** command to specify the Layer 3 packet length in the IP header as a match criterion in a class map.

- **Port type:** You can use the **match port-type** command to match traffic based on the port type for a class map.

Class Map Matching Options

Figure 8-3 illustrates the process of determining if a packet belongs to a class (match) or not (no match).

The process goes through the list of conditions and returns the following:

- A match results if one of the conditions is met and the match-any strategy is used.

- A match results if all conditions are met and the match-all strategy is used.

- No match results if none of the conditions are met.

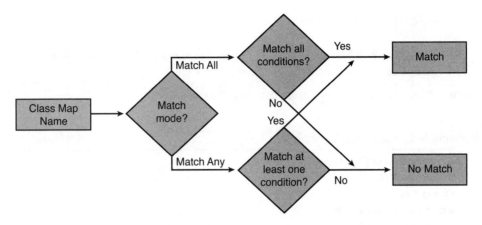

Figure 8-3 *Class Map Matching Options*

Configuring Classification with MQC

You can use the **class-map** global configuration command to create a class map and enter the class-map configuration mode. A class map is identified by a case-sensitive name. All subsequent references to the class map must use the same name.

```
Router(config)#class-map [match-any | match-all] class-map-name
```

You can use the **match** command to specify the classification criteria when in class-map configuration mode. You can use multiple **match** commands within a class map. At least one **match** command should be used within the class-map configuration mode. The default is **match none**.

```
Router(config-cmap)#match condition
```

You can also nest class maps in MQC configurations by using the **match class-map** command within the class-map configuration mode. By nesting class maps, the creation of generic classification templates and more sophisticated classifications are possible.

```
Router(config-cmap)#match class-map class-map
```

These additional options give extra power to class maps:

■ Any condition can be negated by inserting the keyword **not**.

■ The **any** keyword can be used to match all packets.

ACLs are one of the most powerful classification tools. Class maps can use any type of ACL (not only IP ACLs). The **match access-group** command is used to attach an ACL to a class map.

Example 8-1 shows these two class maps:

- Class map Well-known-services uses an ACL to match all the packets with a TCP source or destination port number lower than 1024.

- Class map All-services actually matches all packets.

Example 8-1   *Class-Map Example #1*

```
Router#show running-config
...OUTPUT OMITTED...
class-map Well-known-services
   match access-group 100
class-map All-services
   match any
access-list 100 permit tcp any any lt 1024
...OUTPUT OMITTED...
```

Configuring Classification Using Input Interface and RTP Ports

The **match input-interface** command classifies packets based on an input interface.

```
Router(config-cmap)#match input-interface interface-id
```

The **match ip rtp** command can be used to match RTP packets within a specific UDP port range.

```
Router(config-cmap)#match ip rtp starting-port-number port-range
```

Consider Example 8-2. In the first class map, called FastEthernets, the **match input-interface** will match any packet that arrives on either the FastEthernet 1/0 or FastEthernet 1/1 interface. In the second class map, called RTP, UDP packets in the port range starting with port 16384 and extending 16383 ports beyond the starting port (that is, port numbers 16384–32767) will be matched.

Example 8-2   *Class-Map Example #2*

```
Router#show running-config
...OUTPUT OMITTED...
class-map match-any FastEthernets
   match input-interface FastEthernet 1/0
   match input-interface FastEthernet 1/1
class-map RTP
   match ip rtp 16384 16383
...OUTPUT OMITTED...
```

Configuring Classification Using Marking

According to the DiffServ model, the per-hop behavior (PHB) applied to transit traffic is identified based on the markers that are set at the network edge. The most common markers are CoS, IP Precedence, and DSCP. The following **match** commands allow the matching of any specified value if multiple numbers are specified in a row:

```
Router(config-cmap)#match cos cos-value [cos-value cos-value cos-value]

Router(config-cmap)#match ip precedence ip-prec-value [ip-prec [ip-prec ]]

Router(config-cmap)#match [ip] dscp ip-dscp-value [ip-dscp-value ...]
```

Example 8-3 includes three class maps. Each matching is based on a different type of marker.

Example 8-3 *Class-Map Example #3*

```
Router#show running-config
...OUTPUT OMITTED...
class-map Low-priority
    match cos 0 1 2 3
!
class-map VoIP
    match ip precedence 5
!
class-map Voice
    match ip dscp ef cs5
...OUTPUT OMITTED...
```

Class-Based Marking Overview

Marking is related to classification. Marking allows network devices to classify a packet or frame based on a specific traffic descriptor. Typically used traffic descriptors include CoS, DSCP, IP Precedence, and MPLS EXP bits. The Frame Relay Discard Eligible (DE) bit and ATM Cell Loss Priority (CLP) have become less common, because service providers and enterprises have been replacing Frame Relay and ATM infrastructure with other transmission technologies. Marking can be used to set information in the Layer 2 or Layer 3 packet headers.

Marking a packet or frame with its classification allows network devices to easily distinguish the marked packet or frame as belonging to a specific class. After the packets or frames are identified as belonging to a specific class, QoS mechanisms can be uniformly applied to ensure compliance with administrative QoS policies.

Marking packets or frames sets information in the Layer 2 and Layer 3 headers of a packet so that the packet or frame can be identified and distinguished from other packets or frames.

MQC provides packet-marking capabilities using Class-based marking. MQC is the most flexible Cisco IOS marking tool, extending the marking functionality of Committed Access Rate (CAR) and policy routing.

Class-based marking can be implemented on input or output interfaces as part of a defined input or output service policy. On input, class-based marking can be combined with class-based policing, and on output, with class-based weighted fair queuing (CB-WFQ).

Configuring Class-Based Marking

Marking is configured using the **set** command in policy-map-class configuration mode. When configuring class-based marking, these three configuration steps are required:

Step 1.   **Create a class map.** The following command creates a class map and matches a condition within class-map configuration mode:

```
Router(config)#class-map [match-any | match-all] class-map-name
Router(config-cmap)#match condition
```

Step 2.   **Create a policy map.** The follow commands illustrate how to create a policy map, enter policy-map-class configuration mode, and mark packets in a traffic class using CoS, IP Precedence, DSCP, or MPLS EXP bits. The CoS option is available for interfaces with ISL/802.1Q encapsulation.

```
Router(config)#policy-map policy-map-name
Router(config-pmap)#class class-map-name
Router(config-pmap-c)#set cos cos-value
Router(config-pmap-c)#set ip precedence ip-precedence-value
Router(config-pmap-c)#set [ip] dscp ip-dscp-value
Router(config-pmap-c)#set mpls experimental mpls-experimental-value
```

Step 3.   **Attach the policy map to an interface using the** service-policy **command.** The following command associates the policy map to an input or output interface:

```
Router(config-if)#service-policy {input | output} policy-map-name
```

Class-Based Marking Configuration Example

Example 8-4 provides a sample configuration for marking RTP traffic with a DSCP value of 46 to ensure the EF PHB. This setting enables timely forwarding of VoIP media in a network with a DiffServ model. The marking is applied to UDP flows in the defined range, arriving on the Fast Ethernet 0/0 interface in the incoming direction.

Example 8-4   *Class-Based Marking Configuration*

```
Router#show running-config
...OUTPUT OMITTED...
class-map RTP_subnet_10_1_1
```

```
    match access-group 100
!
policy-map Set-EF-PHB
    class RTP_subnet_10_1_1
        set dscp ef
!
access-list 100 permit udp 10.1.1.0 0.0.0.255 range 8766 35000 any range 8766 35000
!
interface FastEthernet 0/0
    service-policy input Set-EF-PHB
...OUTPUT OMITTED...
```

Trust Boundaries

The concept of trust is important and integral to deploying QoS. After the end devices have set CoS or ToS values, the switch has the option of trusting them. If the switch trusts the values, it does not need to reclassify; if the switch does not trust the values, it must perform reclassification for the appropriate QoS.

The notion of trusting or not trusting forms the basis for the trust boundary. Ideally, classification should be done as close to the source as possible. If the end device is capable of performing this function, the trust boundary for the network is at the end device. If the device is not capable of performing this function, or the access layer switch (for example, a wiring closet switch) does not trust the classification that is done by the end device, the trust boundary might shift.

How this shift happens depends on the capabilities of the switch in the access layer. If the switch can reclassify the packets, the trust boundary is in the access layer. If the switch cannot reclassify the packets, the task falls to other devices in the network, going toward the backbone. In this case, one good rule is to perform reclassification at the distribution layer, which means that the trust boundary shifts to the distribution layer. It is likely that there is a high-end switch in the distribution layer with features to support the reclassification function. If possible, try to avoid performing the reclassification function in the core of the network.

In Figure 8-4, having a trust boundary at position 1 or 2 is optimal. However, an access layer switch might not be QoS-capable. In such a case, having a trust boundary at position 3 is acceptable.

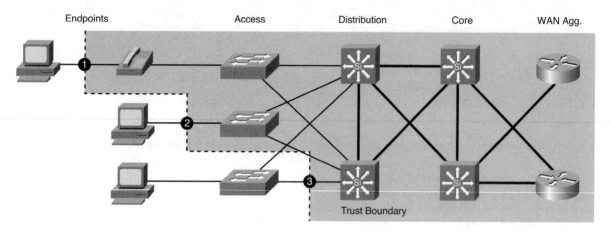

Figure 8-4   *Trust Boundary Options*

Trust Boundary Marking

Classification should take place at the network edge, typically in the access layer or within video endpoints or IP phones themselves.

Figure 8-5 shows an example of IP telephony packet marking. Packets can be marked using Layer 2 CoS settings, IP Precedence, or DSCP. Cisco IP Phones can mark voice packets as high priority using CoS and DSCP. By default, an IP phone sends RTP frames tagged with the CoS set to a value of 5 and the DSCP set to Expedited Forwarding (46).

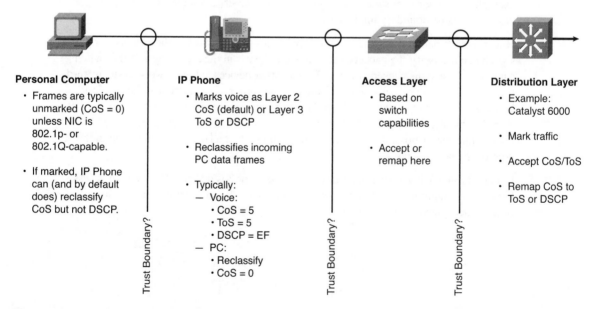

Figure 8-5   *Trust Boundary Examples*

In a Cisco IP telephony environment, PCs are placed in a native VLAN, meaning that their Ethernet frames are untagged. By default, DSCP values or packets originating from PCs are set to 0. Even if the PC sends tagged frames with a specific CoS value, Cisco IP Phones, by default, set the CoS values to 0 before sending the frames to the switch.

Configuring Trust Boundary

The **mls qos trust** command defines the type of trust that a Catalyst switch has for traffic arriving on a specific interface. By default, there is no trust.

```
Switch(config-if)#mls qos trust [cos [pass-through dscp] | dscp]
```

```
Switch(config-if)#mls qos trust device cisco-phone
```

If Layer 2 CoS is trusted (**mls qos trust cos**), the CoS marking of the incoming packets is used to select the ingress and egress queues. Two situations can arise:

■   If the **pass-through dscp** option is not configured, the DSCP value in the incoming packet is overwritten, using the CoS-to-DSCP mapping table.

■   The **pass-through dscp** option causes the original DSCP to be retained in the packet and be transmitted when the packet leaves the switch.

If DSCP is trusted, the DSCP field is retained and not overwritten by the CoS-to-DSCP mapping table. Instead, the CoS is modified according to the DSCP-to-CoS mapping table. For non-IP packets, CoS is set to 0 and the DSCP-to-CoS map is not applied.

The **mls qos trust device cisco-phone** command enables the CDP trusted boundary feature, which detects if a Cisco IP Phone is connected to the port. If one is not connected, the command disables the trusted setting on the switch port to prevent misuse of the priority queue.

Trust Boundary Configuration Example

Figure 8-6 and Example 8-5 illustrate a typical connection of a Cisco IP Phone to a switch port. Traffic that is sent from the telephone to the switch is marked with a tag that uses the 802.1Q header. The header contains the VLAN information and the CoS 3-bit field, which determines the priority of the packet. Usually, a switch is configured to trust the marking of the voice traffic, which is achieved by the **mls qos trust device cisco-phone** and the **mls qos trust cos** interface configuration commands. The upstream port (Fast Ethernet 0/16) is configured to trust the DSCP marking of traffic arriving from the distribution layer, which is typical for DiffServ deployment.

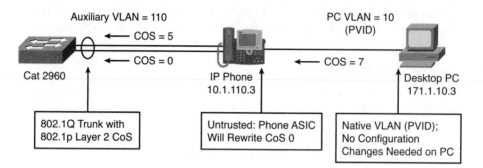

Figure 8-6   *Trust Boundary Configuration Example Topology*

Example 8-5   *Trust Boundary Configuration*

```
Router#show running-config
...OUTPUT OMITTED...
mls qos
interface FastEthernet 0/1
    description To Phone1
    switchport mode access
    mls qos trust cos
    mls qos trust device cisco-phone
    switchport voice vlan 110
    switchport access vlan 10
interface FastEthernet 0/16
    description To Distribution Switch
    switchport mode trunk
...OUTPUT OMITTED...
```

Mapping CoS to Network Layer QoS

IP headers are preserved end-to-end when IP packets are transported across a network. Data link layer headers are not preserved. This means that the IP layer is the most logical place to mark packets for end-to-end QoS. However, there are edge devices that can mark frames only at the data link layer, and there are many other network devices that operate only at the data link layer. To provide true end-to-end QoS, the ability to map QoS marking between the data link layer and the network layer, as illustrated in Figure 8-7, is essential.

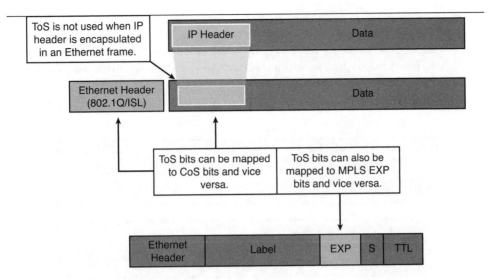

Figure 8-7   *Mapping Layer 2 CoS to Layer 3 QoS*

Default LAN Switch Configuration

By default, QoS is disabled on Cisco switches. When QoS is disabled, there is no concept of trusted or untrusted ports because the packets are not modified. The CoS, DSCP, and IP Precedence values in the packet are not changed.

When QoS is enabled on a switch, the default port trust state on all ports is untrusted. As a result, the switch resets the CoS and DSCP marking for all incoming packets to 0. This behavior can be changed

Mapping CoS and IP Precedence to DSCP

When QoS is enabled and a switch port is trusted, most Cisco Catalyst switches provide these classification options for IP traffic:

■ Trust the DSCP value in the incoming packet by configuring the port to trust DSCP. For ports that are on the boundary between two QoS administrative domains, you can modify the DSCP to another value by using the configurable DSCP-to-DSCP mutation map.

■ Trust the IP Precedence value in the incoming packet by configuring the port to trust IP Precedence, and generate a DSCP value for the packet by using the configurable IP Precedence-to-DSCP map.

■ Trust the CoS value (if present) in the incoming packet, and generate a DSCP value for the packet by using the CoS-to-DSCP map. If the CoS value is not present, use the default port CoS value.

■ Perform the classification based on a configured IP standard or an extended ACL, which examines various fields in the IP header. If no ACL is configured, the packet is assigned 0 as the DSCP and CoS value, which means best-effort traffic. Otherwise, the policy map action specifies a DSCP or CoS value to assign to the incoming frame.

Figure 8-8 shows the default CoS-to-DSCP and IP Precedence-to-DSCP mapping tables.

Default CoS-to-DSCP Map

CoS Value	0	1	2	3	4	5	6	7
DSCP Value	0	8	16	24	32	40	48	56

Default IP Precedence-to-DSCP Map

IP Precedence Value	0	1	2	3	4	5	6	7
DSCP Value	0	8	16	24	32	40	48	56

Figure 8-8 *Mapping CoS and IP Precedence to DSCP*

CoS-to-DSCP Mapping Example

Figure 8-9 provides an example of a CoS value that is mapped to the DSCP value in a Cisco Catalyst switch.

The trust boundary has been established on the switch port to trust the CoS setting from the Cisco IP Phone. By default, the phone marks voice traffic with DSCP EF value 46 and CoS value 5.

Because the switch port is configured to trust the CoS setting, the switch uses the CoS-to-DSCP map to find the appropriate DSCP for the packets. In this case, the map has default settings and the switch sets the DSCP value to 40. On the switch output, in the Layer 3 header, the DSCP will be set to 40. Note that this behavior is not optimal for voice RTP packets, which should typically have a DSCP value of 46. Therefore, a common practice is to reconfigure a switch to map a CoS value of 5 to a DSCP value of 46.

DSCP-to-CoS Mapping Example

Figure 8-10 shows the previous packet as it arrives to its destination after traversing the network. In this example, the ingress port of the egress switch is configured to trust DSCP. Therefore, the Layer 3 header will have a DSCP value of 40, which was set on the ingress switch. When the IP packet traverses the egress switch, its outgoing CoS value is set using the DSCP-to-CoS map. In this example, the map uses default values, and the switch sets CoS 5.

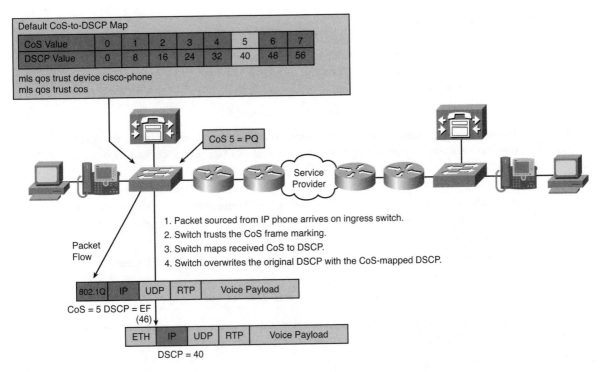

Figure 8-9 *CoS-to-DSCP Mapping*

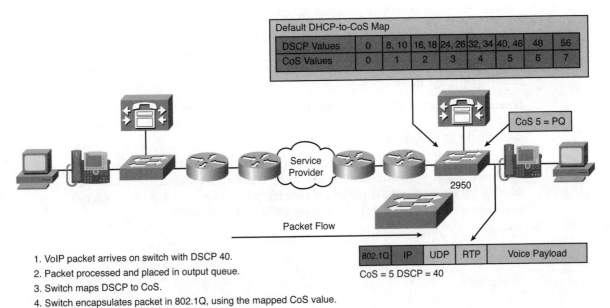

Figure 8-10 *DSCP-to-CoS Mapping Example*

Configuring Mapping

The **mls qos cos** interface configuration command defines the default CoS value on a port. It assigns a CoS and DSCP value to all incoming packets that are untagged (if the incoming packet does not have a CoS value). The **override** keyword is used to assign a default CoS and DSCP value to all incoming packets, even when the frame CoS is set.

```
Switch(config-if)#mls qos cos {default-cos | override}
```

The **mls qos map** global configuration command defines the Cisco Catalyst switch mapping between various packet markers. The command includes several options, two of which include

- **CoS-to-DSCP map:** This map defines eight DSCP values that correspond to CoS values 0 to 7. Mapping is performed only on ports that trust incoming CoS.

  ```
  Switch(config)#mls qos map cos-dscp dscp1...dscp8
  ```
- **DSCP-to-CoS map:** This setting maps *dscp-list* (as many as 13 DSCP values) to the defined CoS value (range from 0 to 7).

  ```
  Switch(config)#mls qos map dscp-cos dscp-list to cos
  ```

Other options of the **mls qos map** command, not discussed in this section, are the DSCP-to-DSCP mutation map, the IP Precedence-to-DSCP map, and the policed-DSCP map.

Mapping Example

Consider the mapping example presented in Figure 8-11.

The Catalyst switch has QoS enabled, which causes it to reset CoS and DSCP values of all incoming packets, unless configured otherwise. The **mls cos map cos-dscp** command defines the mapping between incoming CoS values and outgoing DSCP values, for ports that are configured to trust CoS.

Interface Fast Ethernet 0/1 is a trunk port that is configured to trust CoS, so all incoming 802.1Q packets will be subjected to the CoS-to-DSCP map before the packets are sent out from the outgoing port.

Interface Fast Ethernet 0/2 is configured to trust CoS, so the tagged packets sourced from the IP phone will be subjected to the CoS-to-DSCP map. Untagged packets sourced from the PC attached to the IP phone will have the default CoS set to 1 (with the **mls qos cos 1** command), and therefore their outgoing DSCP will be set to 10.

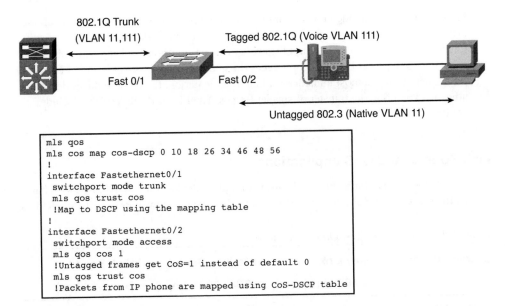

```
mls qos
mls cos map cos-dscp 0 10 18 26 34 46 48 56
!
interface Fastethernet0/1
 switchport mode trunk
 mls qos trust cos
 !Map to DSCP using the mapping table
!
interface Fastethernet0/2
 switchport mode access
 mls qos cos 1
 !Untagged frames get CoS=1 instead of default 0
 mls qos trust cos
 !Packets from IP phone are mapped using CoS-DSCP table
```

Figure 8-11 *Mapping Example Topology*

Link-Efficiency Mechanisms Overview

While many quality of service (QoS) mechanisms exist for optimizing throughput and reducing delay in network traffic, QoS mechanisms do not create bandwidth. QoS mechanisms optimize the use of existing resources and enable the differentiation of traffic according to a policy. Link-efficiency QoS mechanisms such as payload compression, header compression, and LFI are deployed on WAN links to optimize the use of WAN links.

Compression methods are based on eliminating redundancy. Using header compression mechanisms, most header information can be sent only at the beginning of the session, stored in a dictionary, and then referenced in later packets by a short dictionary index. Cisco IOS header compression methods include TCP header compression, Real-time Transport Protocol (RTP) header compression, class-based TCP header compression, and class-based RTP header compression. Header compression is the most effective method for VoIP traffic.

Payload compression is primarily performed on Layer 2 frames and therefore compresses the entire Layer 3 packet. The Layer 2 payload compression methods include Stacker, Predictor, and Microsoft Point-to-Point Compression (MPPC). Payload compression should not be used for VoIP.

LFI is a Layer 2 technique in which large frames are broken into smaller, equal-sized fragments, and transmitted over the link in an interleaved fashion with more latency-sensitive traffic flows (such as VoIP). Using LFI, smaller frames are prioritized and a mixture of fragments is sent over the link. LFI reduces the queuing delay of small frames, because the frames are sent almost immediately. Link fragmentation, therefore, reduces delay and jitter by expediting the transfer of smaller frames. The LFI methods available include MLP and FRF.12.

Link Speeds and QoS Implications

Table 8-1 explains which QoS mechanisms should be deployed on WAN interfaces, based on their link speed. Special consideration must be given to slow links (less than 768 kbps).

Table 8-1   *Link Speeds and QoS Implications*

Characteristics	Slow Link (< 768 kbps)	Medium Speed (768–2048 kbps)	High Speed (> 2048 kbps)
Support for interactive video	Not recommended	Yes	Yes
LFI	Mandatory	Not required	Not recommended
cRTP	Recommended	Optional	Not recommended
Recommended class model	3–5 classes	3–5 classes	5–11 classes

These mechanisms should not be used to transport video conferences, because they must have LFI, and they should have header compression. Medium-speed interfaces can have LFI and cRTP configured, but these mechanisms are not required. Fast links should not have any link-efficiency mechanisms deployed on them. The class models should not exceed five classes on slow and medium-speed links and can be extended to as many as 11 classes on high-speed links (more than 2048 kbps).

Serialization Issues

When considering delay between two hops in a network, queuing delay in a router must be considered, because it might be comparable to, or even exceed, the serialization and propagation delay on a link. In an empty network, an interactive or voice session experiences low or no queuing delay, because the session does not compete with other applications on an interface's output queue. Also, the small delay does not vary enough to produce considerable jitter on the receiving side.

In a congested network, however, interactive data and voice applications compete in the router queue with other applications. Queuing mechanisms can prioritize voice traffic in the software queue, but the hardware queue (TxQ) always uses a FIFO scheduling mechanism. After packets of different applications leave the software queue, the packets will mix with other packets in the hardware TxQ, even if their software queue processing was expedited. Therefore, a voice packet might be immediately sent to the hardware TxQ, where two large FTP packets might still be waiting for transmission. The voice packet must wait until the FTP packets are transmitted, thus producing an unacceptable delay in the voice path. Because links are used variably, the delay varies with time and might produce unacceptable jitter in jitter-sensitive applications, such as voice, as shown in Figure 8-12.

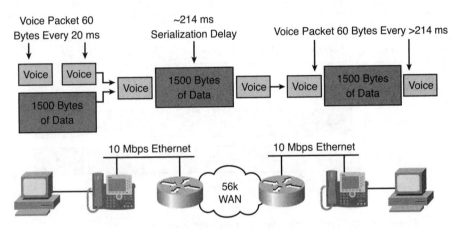

Figure 8-12 *Impact of Slow Serial Links on VoIP*

Serialization Delay

Serialization delay is the fixed delay that is required to clock a voice or data packet onto the network interface. Serialization delay is directly related to the link speed and the size of the packet, as shown in this formula:

Serialization Delay (in seconds) = [(Packet Size in Bytes) * 8] / (Link Speed in bps)

Table 8-2 shows serialization delay as a function of the link speed and packet size. For example, the serialization delay for a 1500-byte packet over a 56-kbps link will be 214 ms, while the serialization delay drops to 15 ms over a 768-kbps link for the same 1500-byte packet.

Link Fragmentation and Interleaving

LFI is a Layer 2 technique, in which all Layer 2 frames are broken into small, equal-sized fragments and transmitted over a link in an interleaved fashion, as shown in Figure 8-13. LFI reduces delay and jitter by expediting the transfer of smaller frames through a hardware TxQ. LFI should be used on slow links (that is, links with a bandwidth less than 768 kbps).

Table 8-2   *Serialization Delay*

Link (kbps)	1 Byte	64 Bytes	128 Bytes	256 Bytes	512 Bytes	1024 Bytes	1500 Bytes
56	143 us	9 ms	18 ms	36 ms	72 ms	144 ms	214 ms
64	125 us	8 ms	16 ms	32 ms	64 ms	128 ms	187 ms
128	62 us	4 ms	8 ms	16 ms	32 ms	64 ms	93 ms
256	31 us	2 ms	4 ms	8 ms	16 ms	32 ms	46 ms
512	15.5 us	1 ms	2 ms	4 ms	8 ms	16 ms	23 ms
768	10 us	640 us	1.28 ms	2.56 ms	5.1 ms	10.2 ms	15 ms

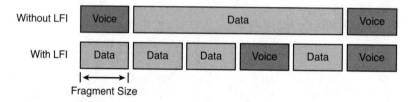

Figure 8-13   *Link Fragmentation and Interleaving*

These two LFI mechanisms are most commonly implemented in Cisco IOS:

- **MLP LFI:** By far the most common and widely used form of LFI

- **FRF.12 Frame Relay LFI:** Used with Frame Relay data connections

Fragments that are transmitted over slow WAN links are self-contained frames, consisting of Layer 2, 3, and 4 headers and payload. The Layer 2+ headers must be considered when calculating a recommended fragment size.

Fragment Size Recommendation

Acceptable one-way delay in a VoIP network is 150 ms. Considering the fact that the network consists of multiple hops and links, the recommended serialization delay on a single link should not exceed 20 ms. This per-link delay translates, for a given link speed, to a maximum frame size. Because the endpoints transmit data in packets up to the maximum transmission unit (MTU) size, the fragmentation must be performed on a per-link basis.

Table 8-3 illustrates fragment sizes for various link speeds that result in acceptable serialization delays.

Table 8-3   *Recommended Fragment Sizes*

Link (kbps)	10 ms (Bytes)	20 ms (Bytes)	30 ms (Bytes)	40 ms (Bytes)	50 ms (Bytes)	100 ms (Bytes)	200 ms (Bytes)
56	70	140	210	280	350	700	1400
64	80	160	240	320	400	800	1600
128	160	320	480	640	800	1600	3200
256	320	640	960	1280	1600	3200	6400
512	640	1280	1920	2560	3200	6400	12,800
768	1000	2000	3000	4000	5000	10,000	20,000

An appropriate fragment size, for a given delay and a given link speed, can be calculated with this formula:

Fragment Size (in bytes) = [(Link Speed in bps) / 8 bits] * Serialization Delay (in sec)

Configuring MLP with Interleaving

Follow these steps to configure MLP with interleaving:

Step 1.   Enable MLP on a PPP interface.

Step 2.   On the multilink interface, enable interleaving within MLP.

Step 3.   In the multilink interface configuration, specify the maximum fragment size by specifying the maximum desired serialization delay in milliseconds.

Interestingly, Multilink PPP (MLP) does not require multiple links. In fact, MLP can be set up over a single router interface. The reason is that a virtual multilink interface is created, which creates a *multilink bundle*. Then, one or more individual interfaces can be made members of this bundle.

To begin the configuration of MLP, create a virtual multilink interface with the **interface multilink** *bundle-number* command.

```
Router(config)#interface multilink bundle-number
```

The **ppp multilink** command enables MLP on a PPP interface.

```
Router(config-if)#ppp multilink
```

The **ppp multilink interleave** command enables interleaving of fragments within the multilink connection.

```
Router(config-if)#ppp multilink interleave
```

The **ppp multilink fragment delay** *delay* command specifies the maximum desired fragment delay for the interleaved multilink connection. The maximum fragment size is calculated from the interface bandwidth and the specified maximum delay. The default is set at 30 ms. To support voice packets, a maximum fragment size of 10 to 20 ms should be used.

```
Router(config-if)#ppp multilink fragment delay delay
```

MLP with Interleaving Example

Figure 8-14 shows a configuration of MLP with interleaving on a multilink group interface.

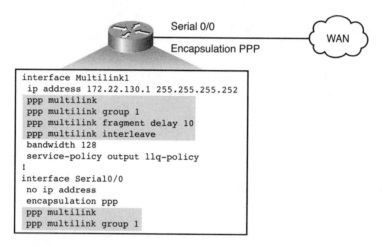

Figure 8-14   *MLP with Interleaving Example*

A multilink group interface is a collection of interfaces that is bundled together in the Multilink PPP configuration. With a multilink group interface, you can bundle interfaces into logical multilink groups. The **interface multilink** command creates a multilink bundle. A serial interface requires two commands to be assigned to a multilink bundle: the **ppp multilink** command, which enables Multilink PPP, and the **ppp multilink group** command, which specifies the multilink bundle to which the serial interface should belong.

A maximum desired delay of 10 ms is configured to ensure timely forwarding of VoIP traffic.

The **show interfaces multilink** command output includes MLP LFI statistical information and indicates whether MLP interleaving is enabled on an interface. Multilink should be in the open state along with Link Control Protocol (LCP) and IP Control Protocol (IPCP). Example 8-6 provides sample output from the **show interfaces multilink** command.

Example 8-6   show interface multilink *Sample Output*

```
Router#show interfaces multilink 1
Multilink1 is up, line protocol is up
Hardware is multilink group interface
...OUTPUT OMITTED...
Encapsulation PPP, loopback not set
Keepalive set (10 sec)
DTR is pulsed for 2 seconds on reset
LCP Open, multilink Open
Open: IPCP
Input queue: 0/75/0/0 (size/max/drops/flushes); Total output drops: 0
Queueing strategy: weighted fair
Output queue: 0/1000/64/0/2441 (size/max total/threshold/drops/interleaves)
Conversations 0/7/16 (active/max active/max total)
Reserved Conversations 0/0 (allocated/max allocated)
5 minute input rate 0 bits/sec, 0 packets/sec
5 minute output rate 7000 bits/sec, 6 packets/sec
```

The statistics for the output queue include a counter for interleaved frames, which provides a fair estimate of the mechanism's effectiveness.

Configuring FRF.12 Frame Relay Fragmentation

FRF.12 fragmentation allows long data frames to be fragmented into smaller pieces and interleaved with real-time frames. In this way, real-time voice and nonreal-time data frames can be carried together on lower-speed Frame Relay links without causing excessive delay and jitter to the real-time traffic such as VoIP.

Because Frame Relay is a Layer 2 protocol, it has no way to tell which frame contains voice (VoIP) or data. Therefore, Frame Relay will fragment all packets larger than the fragment size into smaller frames, including VoIP packets. In a VoIP over Frame Relay network, it is important to configure the fragment size on the data-link connection identifier (DLCI) so that VoIP frames will not get fragmented. For example, a G.711 VoIP packet without cRTP is 200 bytes long. For this DLCI, do not set the fragment size to less than 200 bytes.

Cisco IOS supports the end-to-end FRF.12 method, with the following characteristics:

■   Packets contain the FRF.12 fragmentation header.

■   Fragmentation occurs at the permanent virtual circuit (PVC) level.

■   LMI packets are not fragmented.

FRF.12 is configured on a per-PVC basis. Cisco's FRF.12 implementation requires that traffic shaping is configured (either Frame Relay Traffic Shaping [FRTS] or Generic Traffic Shaping [GTS]) for FRF.12 to be effective. If traffic shaping is not configured, FRF.12 is inactive, even when configured.

Configuring FRF.12 Fragmentation

FRF.12 fragmentation is configured within a Frame Relay map class. The **frame-relay fragment** *size* command sets the maximum fragment size in bytes. On an interface, the **frame-relay class** command applies the map class to the interface or subinterface. To associate a map class with a DLCI, use the **class** command in Frame Relay DLCI configuration mode.

```
Router(config)#map-class frame-relay map-class-name
Router(config-map-class)#frame-relay fragment fragment-size
Router(config-if)#frame-relay class name
```

or

```
Router(config-subif)#frame-relay class name
```

or

```
Router(config-fr-dlci)#class name
```

FRF.12 Configuration Example

Figure 8-15 shows a configuration example where FRF.12 fragmentation is applied to a Frame Relay circuit configured on the Serial 0/0.1 subinterface.

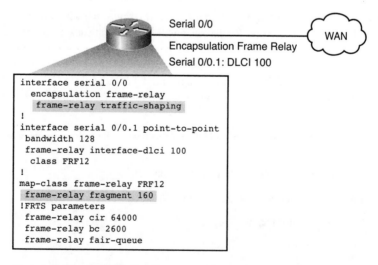

Figure 8-15 *FRF.12 Configuration Example*

The maximum fragment size is set to 160 bytes. The required fragment size is computed using the previously presented formula:

Fragment Size (in bytes) = [(Link Speed in bps) / 8 bits] * Serialization Delay (in sec)

In the case of the desired delay of 10 ms and link speed of 128,000 bps, the required fragment size is 160 bytes. It ensures that VoIP packets, using any audio codec, are not fragmented.

FRTS is enabled on the interface and FRTS parameters are configured within a Frame Relay map class.

The **show frame-relay fragment** command displays information about the FRF.12 Frame Relay fragmentation process. The fragment type will always display end-to-end because this is the only type that is currently supported on Cisco IOS. In addition to fragment type, the fragment size in bytes and associated DLCI are displayed. Example 8-7 shows sample output from the **show frame-relay fragment** command.

Example 8-7   show frame-relay fragment *Sample Output*

```
Router>show frame-relay fragment
interface dlci frag-type frag-size in-frag out-frag dropped-frag
Serial0/0.1 100 end-to-end 80 1298 1563 0
The show frame-relay pvc command output includes settings that are related to the
FRF.12 fragmentation process. This output shows the fragment size (80 bytes in
this example) used on the Frame Relay PVC. The fragment type is end-to-end.
router> show frame-relay pvc 100
PVC Statistics for interface Serial0/0 (Frame Relay DTE)
DLCI = 100, DLCI USAGE = LOCAL, PVC STATUS = INACTIVE, INTERFACE = Serial0/0.1
   ...OUTPUT...
   Output queue size 0/max total 600/drops 0
   fragment type end-to-end fragment size 80
   cir 64000 bc 2600 be 0 limit 325 interval 40
   mincir 32000 byte increment 320 BECN response no IF_CONG no
   frags 1563 bytes 121914 frags delayed 0 bytes delayed 0
```

Class-Based RTP Header Compression

Two standards-based methods are commonly used to compress headers:

■ **RTP header compression:** Also written as *cRTP*, RTP header compression is used to compress the packet IP, UDP, and RTP headers, thus lowering the delay for transporting real-time data, such as voice and video, over slower links. This method is recommended on slow WAN links carrying VoIP packets.

■ **TCP header compression:** Also known as *Van Jacobson Header Compression*, TCP header compression is used to compress the packet IP and TCP headers over slow links. It is most effective for small TCP packets, typical for interactive traffic, where the header-to-payload ratio is high.

When header compression is enabled, the compression occurs by default in the fast-switched path or the Cisco Express Forwarding–switched path, depending on which switching method is enabled on the interface. Class-based header compression enables RTP or TCP header compression on a per-class basis. Decompression is not based on the class map. The receiving end decompresses all packets that come compressed from the other side. Header compression is performed on a link-by-link basis. Header compression is performed on a hop-by-hop basis, because routers need full Layer 3 header information to be able to route packets to the next hop.

RTP Header Compression Example

Figure 8-16 shows the packet size before and after RTP header compression for VoIP packets using G.729. The IP, UDP, and RTP headers are reduced to 2 bytes, resulting in 8 bytes of overall headers. The VoIP overhead is reduced from 70 to 29 percent. Because of the packet size reduction, the serialization delay decreases from 8 ms to 3.5 ms. The bandwidth that is used to transport a single voice call (using the G.729 codec) drops from 26.4 kbps (66 bytes per frame * 50 frames per second [fps] * 8 bits per byte) to 11.2 kbps (28 bytes per frame * 50 fps * 8 bits per byte). Therefore, a 64-kbps link can support up to two G.729 voice calls without cRTP, but up to five G.729 voice calls with cRTP.

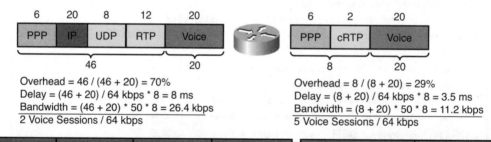

Overhead = 46 / (46 + 20) = 70%
Delay = (46 + 20) / 64 kbps * 8 = 8 ms
Bandwidth = (46 + 20) * 50 * 8 = 26.4 kbps
2 Voice Sessions / 64 kbps

Overhead = 8 / (8 + 20) = 29%
Delay = (8 + 20) / 64 kbps * 8 = 3.5 ms
Bandwidth = (8 + 20) * 50 * 8 = 11.2 kbps
5 Voice Sessions / 64 kbps

Codec	Voice Bandwidth	PPP Layer 2+ Bandwidth	Layer 2+ Overhead	PPP Layer 2+ Bandwidth with cRTP	Layer 2+ with cRTP Overhead
G.711	64 kbps	82.4 kbps	22%	67.2 kbps	5%
G.729	8 kbps	26.4 kbps	70%	11.2 kbps	29%

Figure 8-16 *RTP Header Compression Example*

When G.711-based VoIP is deployed, the overhead that is created by the Layer 2 (PPP), IP, UDP, and RTP headers consumes 18.4 kbps of bandwidth, just as in G.729. This overhead equals 22 percent of the overall throughput requirement. The overhead can be reduced by using cRTP, thus consuming 3.2 kbps of bandwidth, representing 5 percent of the total call bandwidth.

Configuring Class-Based Header Compression

Configure class-based TCP and RTP header compression within a policy map using the **compression header ip** command. The command can be applied at any level in the policy map hierarchy configured with MQC.

```
Router(config-pmap-c)#compression header ip [rtp | tcp ]
```

If you do not specify either RTP or TCP header compression, both RTP and TCP header compressions will be configured.

> **Note**   Header compression is autonegotiated only on PPP links. On Frame Relay or High-Level Data Link Control (HDLC) links, both ends of the links must match.

Class-Based RTP Header Compression Configuration Example

In Figure 8-17, the **compression header ip** command has been configured to use RTP header compression for a traffic class called *voip*. The voip traffic class is part of a policy map called *cust1*. This cust1 policy map is applied to the Serial 0/0 interface in the outbound direction.

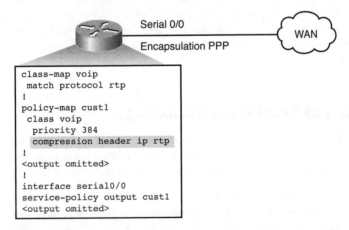

Figure 8-17   *Class-Based RTP Header Compression Configuration Example*

This policy provides a maximum bandwidth guarantee of 384 kbps for the voip traffic class and will perform RTP header compression on the voip traffic class leaving the Serial 0/0 interface.

Consider Example 8-8. The **show policy-map interface** command output displays the type of header compression configured (RTP, in this example), the interface to which the policy map called cust1 is attached (Serial 0/0), the number of packets that are sent, the number of packets that are compressed, the number of bytes saved, and the number of bytes sent.

Example 8-8   show policy-map interface *Sample Output*

```
Router#show policy-map interface serial0/0
Service-policy output:cust1
Class-map: voip (match-all)
1005 packets, 64320 bytes
30 second offered rate 16000 bps, drop rate 0 bps
...OUTPUT...
compress:
header ip rtp
UDP/RTP Compression:
Sent:1000 total, 999 compressed,
41957 bytes saved, 17983 bytes sent
3.33 efficiency improvement factor
99% hit ratio, five min miss rate 0 misses/sec, 0 max rate 5000 bps
```

Other statistical information that is provided in the output includes the efficiency improvement factor, which indicates the percentage of increased bandwidth efficiency as a result of header compression. For example, an efficiency improvement factor of 3.33 means 330 percent efficiency improvement. The hit ratio is the percentage of packets that are found in the context database. In most instances, this percentage should be high. The five-minute miss rate is the number of traffic flows in the last five minutes that were not found in the context database. The rate is the actual traffic rate after the packets are compressed.

Queuing and Traffic Conditioning

Queuing algorithms are one of the primary ways to manage congestion in a network. Network devices manage an overflow of arriving traffic by using a queuing algorithm to sort traffic and determine a method of prioritizing the traffic onto an output link.

Traffic policing controls the maximum rate of traffic that is sent or received on an interface. Traffic policing is used on interfaces at the network edge to limit traffic into or out of the network.

Traffic shaping controls outgoing traffic on an interface to match the transmission rate to the speed of the remote end, and ensures that the traffic conforms to administrative quality of service (QoS) policies.

Class-based weighted fair queuing (CB-WFQ) extends the standard weighted fair queuing (WFQ) functionality, providing support for user-defined traffic classes. A queue is reserved for each class, and traffic belonging to a class is directed to the queue for that class.

Low latency queuing (LLQ) brings strict priority queuing to CB-WFQ. Strict priority queuing allows delay-sensitive traffic such as voice to be dequeued and sent first (before packets in other queues are dequeued), giving delay-sensitive data preferential treatment over other traffic. This section describes the queuing architectural components, including traffic-policing, traffic-shaping, CB-WFQ, and LLQ.

Congestion and Its Solutions

Congestion can occur anywhere within a network where there are points of speed mismatches (for example, a Gigabit Ethernet link feeding a Fast Ethernet link), aggregation (for example, multiple Gigabit Ethernet links feeding an upstream Gigabit Ethernet link), or confluence (the flowing together of two or more traffic streams).

Queuing algorithms are used to manage congestion. Many algorithms have been designed to serve different needs. A well-designed queuing algorithm will provide some bandwidth and delay guarantees to priority traffic. Speed mismatches, as depicted in Figure 8-18, are the most typical cause of congestion in a network.

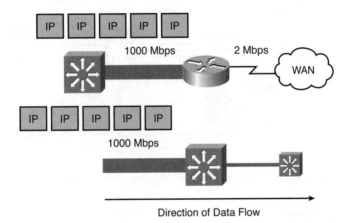

Figure 8-18 *Congestion and Queuing: Speed Mismatch*

Speed mismatches are most common when traffic moves from a high-speed LAN environment (1000 Mbps or higher) to lower-speed WAN links (1 or 2 Mbps). Speed mismatches are also common in LAN-to-LAN environments when, for example, a 1000-Mbps link feeds into a 100-Mbps link.

Congestion and Queuing: Aggregation

The second common type of congestion occurs at aggregation points, as shown in Figure 8-19.

In a WAN environment, aggregation congestion is typical on routers that are attached to WANs when multiple remote sites feed back into a central services site.

In a LAN environment, congestion resulting from aggregation often occurs at the distribution layer of networks, where the different access layer devices feed traffic to the distribution-level switches.

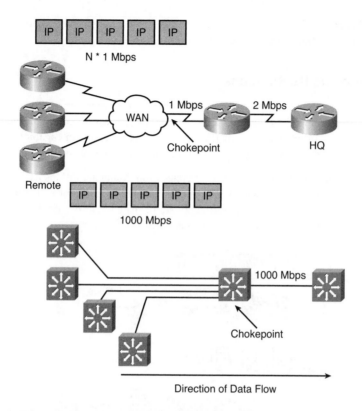

Figure 8-19   *Congestion and Queuing: Aggregation*

Queuing Components

Queuing on routers is necessary to accommodate bursts when the arrival rate of packets is greater than the departure rate, usually because of one of the following two reasons:

■   The input interface is faster than the output interface.

■   The output interface is receiving packets coming in from multiple other interfaces.

The queuing structure is split into two parts, as follows:

■   **Hardware queue:** Uses FIFO strategy, which is necessary for the interface drivers to transmit packets one-by-one. The hardware queue is sometimes referred to as the transmit queue (TxQ). Packets in the hardware queue cannot be reordered.

■   **Software queue:** Schedules packets into the hardware queue based on the QoS requirements. Software queuing is implemented when the interface is congested. The software queuing system is bypassed whenever there is room in the hardware queue. The software queue is, therefore, used only when data must wait to be placed into the hardware queue.

The software queue is much larger than the hardware queue, which has a capacity of only a few packets (typically two to three). The software queue can hold tens of packets and allows their reordering prior to transmission.

Figure 8-20 illustrates the following actions that have to be taken before a packet can be transmitted:

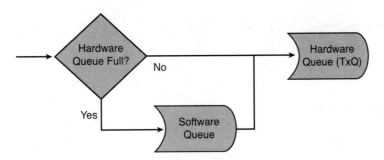

Figure 8-20 *Queuing Components*

■ Most queuing mechanisms include classification of packets.

■ After a packet is classified, a router has to determine whether it can put the packet into the queue or drop the packet. Most queuing mechanisms will drop a packet only if the corresponding queue is full (that is, tail drop). Some mechanisms use a more intelligent dropping scheme, such as weighted random early detection (WRED).

■ If the packet is allowed to be queued, it will be put into the FIFO queue for that particular class.

■ Packets are then taken from the individual per-class queues and put into an interface's hardware queue.

Software Interfaces

Software-only interfaces, such as subinterfaces or tunnels, have no concept of departure rate, because there is no hardware interface that is directly tied to them. No congestion can occur, and they cannot perform queuing. Therefore, it is impossible to configure a queuing service policy directly to a software interface.

Hierarchical MQC provides a solution by emulating congestion and dividing the forwarding resources among the subinterfaces, or traffic classes that are received over specific subinterfaces, as shown in Figure 8-21. The congestion is emulated by configuring a shaper that throttles the traffic rate to a configured value. Class-based queuing is used to map the subinterfaces or traffic classes to individual software queues with bandwidth guarantees.

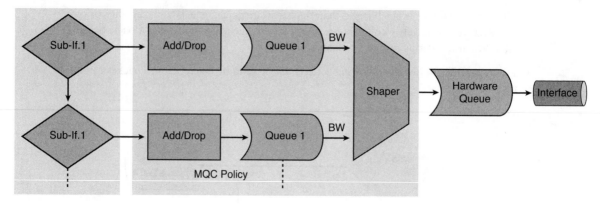

Figure 8-21   *Software Interfaces*

Policing and Shaping

Both traffic shaping and policing mechanisms are traffic conditioning mechanisms used in a network to control traffic rates. Both mechanisms use classification so that they can differentiate traffic. They both measure the rate of traffic and compare that rate to the configured traffic shaping or traffic policing policy.

As illustrated in Figure 8-22, the difference between traffic shaping and policing can be described in terms of their implementation. Traffic shaping buffers excessive traffic so that the traffic stays within a desired rate. With traffic shaping, traffic bursts are smoothed out by queuing the excess traffic to produce a steadier flow of data. Reducing traffic bursts helps reduce congestion in the network.

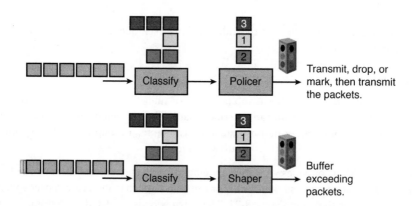

Figure 8-22   *Policing and Shaping Overview*

Traffic shaping is typically used for the following:

■   To prevent and manage congestion in WAN or MAN networks, where asymmetric bandwidths are used along the traffic path. If shaping is not used, buffering can occur at the slow (usually the remote) end, which can lead to queuing, causing delays, and overflow, causing drops.

■   To prevent dropping of noncompliant traffic by the service provider. This allows the customer to keep local control of traffic regulation, but the customer must not exceed the committed rate.

Traffic policing drops excess traffic in order to control traffic flow within specified rate limits. Traffic policing does not introduce any delay to traffic that conforms to traffic policies. Traffic policing can cause more TCP retransmissions, because traffic in excess of specified limits is dropped.

Traffic policing is typically used to satisfy one of these requirements:

■   Limiting the access rate on an interface when a high-speed physical infrastructure is used in transport. Rate limiting is often used by service providers to offer customers subrate access.

■   Engineering bandwidth so that traffic rates of certain applications or classes of traffic follow a specified traffic rate policy.

■   Re-marking excess traffic with a lower priority at Layer 2 and Layer 3, or both, before sending the excess traffic out. Class-based policing can be configured to mark packets at both Layer 2 and Layer 3.

Traffic policing mechanisms such as Class-based policing or Committed Access Rate (CAR) also have marking capabilities in addition to rate-limiting capabilities. Instead of dropping the excess traffic, traffic policing can alternatively mark and then send the excess traffic. This allows the excess traffic to be re-marked with a lower priority before the excess traffic is sent out. Traffic shapers, on the other hand, do not re-mark traffic; these only delay excess traffic bursts to conform to a specified rate.

Policing and Shaping Comparison

Shaping queues excess traffic by holding packets inside a shaping queue. Use traffic shaping to shape the outbound traffic flow when the outbound traffic rate is higher than a configured shape rate. Traffic shaping smoothes traffic by storing traffic above the configured rate in a shaping queue. Therefore, shaping increases buffer utilization on a router and causes unpredictable packet delays. Traffic shaping can also interact with a Frame Relay network, adapting to indications of Layer 2 congestion in a WAN. For example, if the Backward Explicit Congestion Notification (BECN) bit is received, the router can lower the rate limit to help reduce congestion in a Frame Relay network.

You can apply policing to either the inbound or outbound direction, while you can apply shaping only in the outbound direction. Policing drops nonconforming traffic instead of queuing the traffic, as shaping does. Policing also supports marking traffic. Traffic policing is more efficient in terms of memory utilization than traffic shaping, because no additional queuing of packets is needed.

As depicted in Figure 8-23, both traffic policing and traffic shaping ensure that traffic does not exceed a bandwidth limit, but each mechanism has different impacts on the traffic:

- Policing drops packets, generally causing more retransmissions of connection-oriented protocols such as TCP. TCP reacts to packet loss by not only retransmitting the packet, but also reducing the transmission window size, which defines the number of octets that can be sent unacknowledged. The reduction of the window size effectively lowers the data throughput of a TCP session.

- Shaping adds variable delay to traffic, possibly causing jitter.

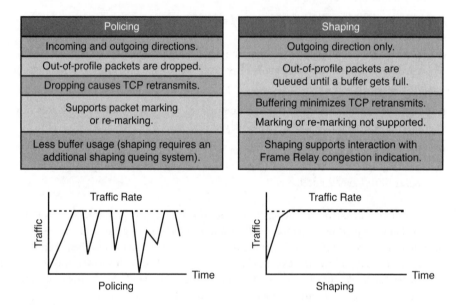

Figure 8-23   *Policing and Shaping Comparison*

Measuring Traffic Rates

The token bucket is a mathematical model that is used by routers and switches to regulate traffic flow. Figure 8-24 illustrates the operation of a single token bucket.

The token bucket model has the following two basic components:

- **Tokens:** Each token represents permission to send a fixed number of bits into the network. Tokens are put into a token bucket at a certain rate by Cisco IOS.

- **Token bucket:** A token bucket has the capacity to hold a specified number of tokens. Each incoming packet, if forwarded, takes tokens from the bucket, representing the packet size. If the bucket fills to capacity, newly arriving tokens are discarded. Discarded tokens are not available to future packets. If there are not enough tokens in the token bucket to send the packet, the traffic conditioning mechanisms might take these actions:

- Wait for enough tokens to accumulate in the bucket (traffic shaping)

- Discard the packet (traffic policing)

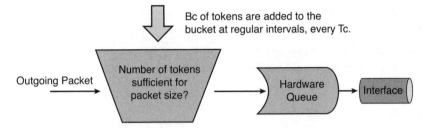

Bucket Size = Bc + Be (Bytes)
Each forwarded packet consumes tokens (equal to packet size).
On average, Bc of data is transmitted every Tc.
Occasionally, Bc + Be of data can be transmitted if unused
tokens have been accumulated in previous intervals.

Bc = Committed burst (amount of data guaranteed to be delivered in one time interval).
Be = Exceed burst (additional amount of data attempted to be delivered if no congestion).

Figure 8-24 *Single Token Bucket Operations*

Using a single token bucket model, the measured traffic rate can conform to or exceed the specified traffic rate. The measured traffic rate is conforming if there are enough tokens in the single token bucket to transmit the traffic. The measured traffic rate is exceeding if there are not enough tokens in the single token bucket to transmit the traffic.

The committed burst (Bc) is the amount of data that is guaranteed to be delivered by the network within one committed rate measurement interval (Tc). It corresponds to a committed information rate (CIR) using the formula CIR = Bc / Tc. Data is always sent in bursts, and not evenly with the CIR speed because the frames are put on the wire using the clock rate of the physical circuit. Thus, the committed burst specifies how many octets can be sent out in one interval.

The excess burst (Be) is the amount of data that the network agrees to deliver to the destination if there is no congestion in the network. The Bc and Be values are part of the contract that an enterprise or user signs with a service provider.

Example: Token Bucket as a Coin Bank

You can think of a token bucket as a coin bank. You can insert a coin into the bank every day (the token bucket). At any given time, you can only spend what you have saved in the bank. On the average, if your saving rate is $1 per day, your long-term average spending rate will be $1 per day if you constantly spend what you saved. However, if you do not spend any money on a given day, you can build up your savings in the bank to the maximum that the bank can hold. For example, if the size of the bank is limited to $5, and if you save and do not spend for five straight days, the bank will contain $5. When the bank fills to its capacity, you will not be able to put any more money into it. Then, at any time, you can spend up to $5 (bursting above the long-term average rate of $1 per day).

The conforming rate (or the Bc) (using the coin bank example) means that if you have $2 in the bank and you try to spend $1, that is considered conforming because you are not spending more than you have saved.

Exceeding rate (or the Be) (using the coin bank example) means that if you have $2 in the bank, and you try to spend $3, it is considered exceeding, because you are spending more than you have saved.

Single Token Bucket

Figure 8-25 shows a single token bucket traffic policing implementation. Starting with a current capacity of 700 bytes' worth of tokens accumulated in the token bucket, when a 500-byte packet arrives at the interface, its size is compared to the token bucket capacity (in bytes).

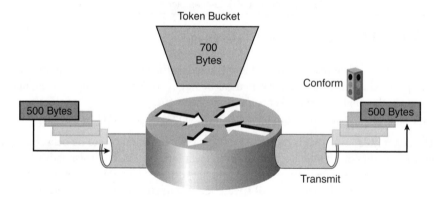

Figure 8-25   *Single Token Bucket in Operation*

The 500-byte packet conforms to the rate limit (500 bytes < 700 bytes), and the packet is forwarded. 500 bytes' worth of tokens is taken out of the token bucket, leaving 200 bytes' worth of tokens for the next packet.

When the next 300-byte packet arrives immediately after the first packet, as shown in Figure 8-26, and no new tokens have been added to the bucket (tokens are added periodically), the packet exceeds the rate limit.

The current packet size (300 bytes) is greater than the current capacity of the token bucket (200 bytes), and the exceed action is performed. The exceed action can be to drop or mark the packet during traffic policing.

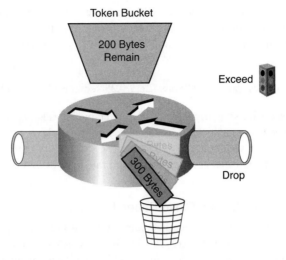

Figure 8-26 *Single Token Bucket in Operation (Continued)*

Class-Based Policing

As shown in Figure 8-27, token bucket operations rely on parameters such as CIR, Bc, and Tc. Bc is known as the normal burst rate.

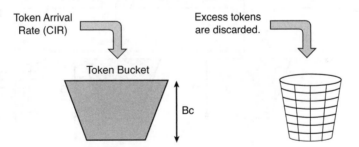

Figure 8-27 *Single Token Bucket Class-Based Policing*

The mathematical relationship between CIR, Bc, and Tc is as follows:

CIR (bps) = Bc (bits) / Tc (sec)

With traffic policing, new tokens are added into the token bucket based on the inter-packet arrival rate and the CIR. Every time that a packet is policed, new tokens are added back into the token bucket. The number of tokens added back into the token bucket is calculated as follows:

(Current Packet Arrival Time − Previous Packet Arrival Time) * CIR

An amount (Bc) of tokens is forwarded without constraint in every time interval (Tc). For example, if 8000 bits' (Bc) worth of tokens is placed in the bucket every 250 ms (Tc), the router can steadily transmit 8000 bits every 250 ms if traffic constantly arrives at the router.

CIR (normal burst rate) = 8000 bits (Bc) / 0.25 seconds (Tc) = 32 kbps

Without any excess bursting capability, if the token bucket fills to capacity (Bc of tokens), the token bucket will overflow and newly arriving tokens will be discarded. Using the example, in which the CIR is 32 kbps (Bc = 8000 bits and Tc = 0.25 seconds), the maximum traffic rate can never exceed a hard rate limit of 32 kbps.

Single-Rate, Dual Token Bucket Class-Based Policing

You can configure class-based policing to support excess bursting capability. With excess bursting, after the first token bucket is filled to Bc, extra (excess) tokens can be accumulated in a second token bucket. Excess burst (Be) is the maximum amount of excess traffic over and above Bc that can be sent during the time interval after a period of inactivity. With a single-rate metering mechanism, the second token bucket with a maximum size of Be fills at the same rate (CIR) as the first token bucket. If the second token bucket fills up to capacity, no more tokens can be accumulated and the excess tokens are discarded. Figure 8-28 illustrates the operation of a single-rate, dual token bucket.

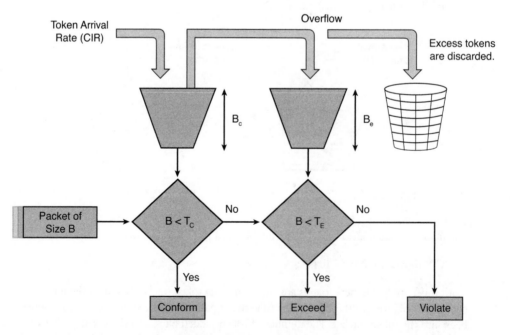

Figure 8-28   *Single-Rate, Dual Token Bucket Operation*

When using a dual token bucket model, the measured traffic rate can be as follows:

■   **Conforming:** There are enough tokens in the first token bucket with a maximum size of Bc.

■   **Exceeding:** There are not enough tokens in the first token bucket, but there are enough tokens in the second token bucket, with a maximum size of Be.

■   **Violating:** There are not enough tokens in the first or second token bucket.

With dual token bucket traffic policing, the typical actions that are performed are sending all conforming traffic, re-marking (to a lower priority), sending all exceeding traffic, and dropping all violating traffic. The main benefit of using a dual token bucket method is the ability to distinguish between traffic that exceeds the Bc but not the Be. This enables a different policy to be applied to packets in the Be category. Referring to the coin bank example, think of the CIR as the savings rate ($1 per day). Bc is how much you can save into the bank per day ($1). Tc is the interval at which you put money into the coin bank (one day). Be ($5) allows you to burst over the average spending rate of $1 per day if you are not spending $1 per day.

Using a dual token bucket model allows traffic exceeding the normal burst rate (CIR) to be metered as exceeding, and traffic that exceeds the excess burst rate to be metered as violating traffic. Different actions can then be applied to the conforming, exceeding, and violating traffic.

Dual-Rate, Dual Bucket Class-Based Policing

With dual-rate metering, as depicted in Figure 8-29, the traffic rate can be enforced according to two separate rates: CIR and peak information rate (PIR). Before this feature was available, you could meter traffic using a single rate that was based on the CIR with single or dual buckets. Dual-rate metering supports a higher level of bandwidth management and supports a sustained excess rate that is based on the PIR.

With dual-rate metering, the PIR token bucket fills at a rate that is based on the packet arrival rate. The CIR token bucket fills at a rate that is based on the packet arrival rate and the configured CIR.

When a packet arrives, the PIR token bucket is first checked to see if there are enough tokens in the PIR token bucket to send the packet. The violating condition occurs if there are not enough tokens in the PIR token bucket to transmit the packet. If there are enough tokens in the PIR token bucket to send the packet, then the CIR token bucket is checked. The exceeding condition occurs if there are enough tokens in the PIR token bucket to transmit the packet but not enough tokens in the CIR token bucket to transmit the packet. The conforming condition occurs if there are enough tokens in the CIR bucket to transmit the packet.

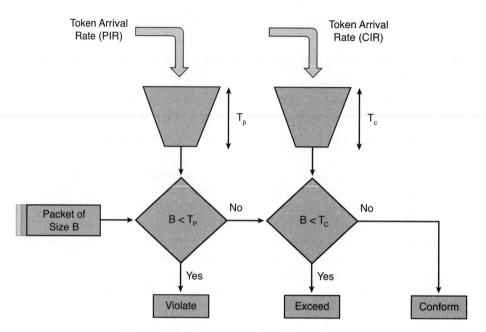

Figure 8-29   *Dual-Rate, Dual Bucket Class-Based Policing*

Dual-rate metering is often configured on interfaces at the edge of a network to police the rate of traffic entering or leaving the network. In the most common configurations, traffic that conforms is sent and traffic that exceeds is sent with a decreased priority or is dropped. You can change these configuration options to suit your network needs.

This token bucket algorithm provides users with three different actions for each packet:

- A conform action

- An exceed action

- An optional violate action

Traffic entering the interface with dual-rate policing configured is placed into one of these categories. Within these three categories, users can decide packet treatments. For example, a user can configure a policing policy as follows:

- Conforming packets are transmitted. Packets that exceed might be transmitted with a decreased priority; packets that violate are dropped.

- The violating condition occurs if there are not enough tokens in the PIR bucket to transmit the packet.

- The exceeding condition occurs if there are enough tokens in the PIR bucket to transmit the packet but not enough tokens in the CIR bucket to transmit the packet. In this case, the packet can be transmitted and the PIR bucket is updated to Tp – B remaining tokens, where Tp is the size of the PIR bucket and B is the size of the packet to be transmitted.

- The conforming condition occurs if there are enough tokens in the CIR bucket to transmit the packet. In this case, the packets are transmitted and both buckets (Tc and Tp) are decremented to Tp – B and to Tc – B, respectively, where Tc is the size of the CIR bucket, Tp is the size of the PIR bucket, and B is the size of the packet to be transmitted.

Configuring Class-Based Policing

The class-based policing feature performs these functions:

- Limits the input or output transmission rate of a traffic class that is based on user-defined criteria

- Marks packets by setting different Layer 2 or Layer 3 markers, or both

Class-based policing can be implemented by using a single or double token bucket method as the metering mechanism. When the **violate** action option is not specified in the **police** MQC command, the single token bucket algorithm is engaged. When the **violate** action option is specified in the **police** MQC command, the dual token bucket algorithm is engaged.

A dual token bucket algorithm allows traffic to do the following:

- Conform to the rate limit when the traffic is within the average bit rate

- Exceed the rate limit when the traffic exceeds the average bit rate, but does not exceed the allowed excess burst

- Violate the rate limit when the traffic exceeds both the average rate and the excess bursts

Depending on whether the current packet conforms with, exceeds, or violates the rate limit, one or more of these actions can be taken: transmit, drop, or set a marker and transmit.

Multiaction policing is a mechanism that can apply more than one action to a packet—for example, setting the Differentiated Services Code Point (DSCP) as well as the Cell Loss Priority (CLP) bit on the exceeding packets.

Configuring Class-Based Policing

The MQC-based **police** command defines policing parameters for either a single- or dual-rate policer. The **cir** parameter defines the policed CIR; Bc and Be define the token bucket sizes in bytes; and the *action* defines an action for conforming, exceeding, or, optionally, violating traffic.

```
Router(config-pmap-c)#police {cir cir} [bc conform-burst] {pir pir} [be peak-
   burst] [conform-action action] [exceed-action action] [violate-action action]
```

If Bc (in bytes) is not specified, it will default to CIR / 32, or 1500 bytes, whichever is higher. When using the formula CIR / 32 to calculate the default Bc (in bytes), Cisco IOS uses a Tc of 0.25 second, where:

Bc (in bytes) = (CIR * Tc) / 8

Bc (in bytes) = (CIR * 0.25 seconds) / 8 = CIR / 32

If Be (in bytes) is not specified, it will default to Bc. In a single token bucket case, Cisco IOS ignores the Be value. This means that excess bursting is disabled.

The Be rate can be specified when a violate action is configured. Therefore, using a dual token bucket allows Be to be explicitly configured instead of using the default value of Be = Bc. Be specifies the size of the second (excess) token bucket.

Definition of the **pir** parameter enables dual-rate policing, which uses two separate rates: CIR and PIR. The Bc and Be keywords and their associated arguments (*conform-burst* and *peak-burst*, respectively) are optional. If Bc is not specified, Bc (in bytes) will default to CIR / 32, or 1500 bytes, whichever is higher. If Be is not specified, Be (in bytes) will default to PIR / 32, or 1500 bytes, whichever is higher.

Class-Based Policing Example: Single Rate, Single Token Bucket

Figure 8-30 shows a class-based policing configuration example with two configured traffic classes that are based on upstream MAC addresses.

Traffic from the particular web server, which is classified by its MAC address, is policed to a fixed bandwidth with no excess burst capability using a single token bucket. Conforming traffic is sent as-is and exceeding traffic is dropped. In this case, the www.123.com web server is policed to a rate of 512 kbps, and the www.456.com web server is policed to a rate of 256 kbps. Because the violate action is not specified, this will use a single token bucket scheme and no excess bursting is allowed.

In this example, the Bc is not specified, and therefore it will default to 512,000 / 32 (16,000 bytes) and 256,000 / 32 (8000 bytes), respectively.

The default Bc setting can be examined by showing the policy map. The Be is not displayed, because no excess bursting is allowed using a single token bucket with class-based policing.

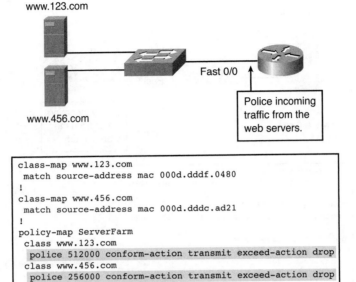

```
class-map www.123.com
 match source-address mac 000d.dddf.0480
!
class-map www.456.com
 match source-address mac 000d.dddc.ad21
!
policy-map ServerFarm
 class www.123.com
  police 512000 conform-action transmit exceed-action drop
 class www.456.com
  police 256000 conform-action transmit exceed-action drop
!
interface FastEthernet 0/0
 service-policy input ServerFarm
```

Figure 8-30 *Class-Based Policing Example: Single Rate, Single Token Bucket*

Class-Based Policing Example: Single Rate, Dual Token Bucket

The class-based policing configuration example in Figure 8-31 shows two configured traffic classes that are based on upstream MAC addresses.

Traffic from the particular web server, which is classified by its MAC address, is policed to a fixed bandwidth with excess burst capability using a dual token bucket, by configuring a violate action. Conforming traffic will be sent as-is, exceeding traffic will be marked to IP Precedence 3 and transmitted, and all violating traffic will be dropped.

In this example, because the violate action is specified, a dual token bucket scheme with excess bursting will be used. The committed burst size (Bc) is not specified, and therefore it will default to the 512,000 / 32 (16,000 bytes) and 256,000 / 32 (8000 bytes), respectively. The excess burst size (Be) is also not specified, and therefore it will default to Bc.

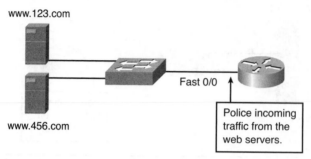

```
class-map www.123.com
 match source-address mac 000d.dddf.0480
!
class-map www.456.com
 match source-address mac 000d.dddc.ad21
!
policy-map ServerFarm
 class www.123.com
  police 512000 conform-action set-prec-transmit 4 exceed-action
  set-prec-transmit 3 violate-action drop
 class www.456.com
  police 256000 conform-action set-prec-transmit 4 exceed-action
  set-prec-transmit 3 violate-action drop
!
interface FastEthernet 0/0
 service-policy input ServerFarm
```

Figure 8-31   *Class-Based Policing Example: Single Rate, Dual Token Bucket*

Class-Based Shaping

Class-based shaping applies for outbound traffic only. Class-based shaping can be configured in the following two ways:

- **Shaping to the configured average rate:** Shaping to the average rate forwards up to a Bc of traffic at every Tc interval, with additional bursting capability when enough tokens are accumulated in the bucket. Bc of tokens are added to the token bucket at every Tc time interval. After the token bucket is emptied, additional bursting cannot occur until tokens are allowed to accumulate, which can occur only during periods of silence or when the transmit rate is lower than the average rate. After a period of low traffic activity, up to Bc + excess burst (Be) of traffic can be sent. This is the most common method of configuring class-based shaping.

- **Shaping to the peak rate:** Shaping to the peak rate forwards up to Bc + Be of traffic at every Tc time interval. Bc + Be of tokens are added to the token bucket at every Tc time interval. Shaping to the peak rate sends traffic at the peak rate, which is defined as the average rate multiplied by (1 + Be / Bc). Sending packets at the peak rate might result in dropping in the WAN cloud during network congestion. Shaping to the peak rate is recommended only when the network has additional available bandwidth beyond the CIR and applications can tolerate occasional packet drops.

Configuring Class-Based Shaping

The **shape average** and **shape peak** commands configure average and peak shaping, respectively. The Bc and Be value in bits can be explicitly configured, or Cisco IOS can automatically calculate their optimal value. It is not recommended that you configure the Bc and Be in order to let the Cisco IOS algorithm determine the best Bc and Be value to use. Class-based shaping uses a single token bucket with a maximum token bucket size of Bc + Be.

```
Router(config-pmap-c)#shape {average | peak} average-bit-rate [Bc] [Be]
```

The **shape percent** *percent* command is often used in conjunction with the **bandwidth** and **priority** commands. The **bandwidth** and **priority** commands can be used to calculate the total amount of bandwidth available on an entity (for example, a physical interface). When the **bandwidth** and **priority** commands calculate the total amount of bandwidth available on an entity, the total bandwidth is the bandwidth on the physical interface.

```
Router(config-pmap-c)#shape {average | peak} percent percent [sustained-burst-in-
   msec ms] [be excess-burst-in-msec ms] [bc committed-burst-in-msec ms]
```

Class-Based Shaping Example

Figure 8-32 shows an example configuration for standalone class-based shaping (no CB-WFQ). Citrix traffic is classified into the Shape class.

The Shape class is then shaped to different rates on two interfaces:

- On the Serial 0/0 interface, traffic is shaped to the average rate. The Bc and Be values are not configured, allowing Cisco IOS to automatically calculate their optimal values. The Citrix traffic is shaped to the average rate of 16,000 bps. The resulting automatically determined Be and Bc values will both be 8000 bits with a Tc of 500 ms.

- On the Serial 0/1 interface, the Citrix traffic is shaped to the peak rate. Because the Be and Bc are not specified, Cisco IOS automatically calculates the optimal value for Tc, Bc, and Be. The shape statement is **shape peak 16000**. The resulting automatically determined Be and Bc values will each be 8000 bits with a Tc of 500 ms. Therefore, the peak rate will be as follows:

peak rate = average rate * (1 + Be / Bc) = 16000 * (1 + 8000 / 8000) = 16000 * 2 = 32000 bps

Hierarchical Class-Based Shaping with CB-WFQ Example

The example in Figure 8-33 uses hierarchical policy maps and configures CB-WFQ inside the class-based shaping. The parent policy is the *shape-all* policy. This parent policy references a child policy named *child-cbwfq*. The parent policy map *shape-all* specifies an average shape rate of 384 kbps for all the traffic (matched by *class-default*) and assigns the service policy that is called *child-cbwfq* as the child policy.

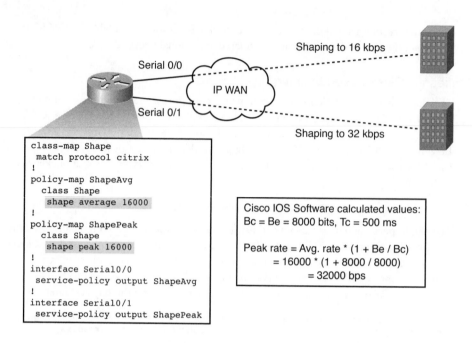

Figure 8-32   *Class-Based Shaping Example*

— Moves the bottleneck to the local interface
  • To manage congestion and prevent uncontrolled drop in WAN

— Divides the aggregate bandwidth among classes
  • Can be used to map packets from software interfaces

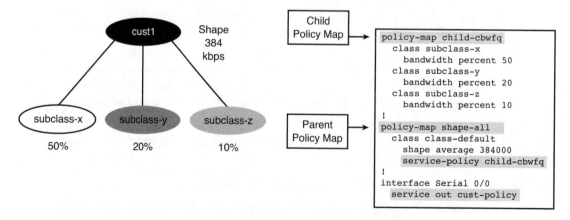

Figure 8-33   *Hierarchical Class-Based Shaping with CB-WFQ Example*

The shaped traffic is further classified into three distinct traffic subclasses, with bandwidth guarantees of 50, 20, and 10 percent of the shaped bandwidth, respectively.

The traffic that is transmitted over the Serial 0/0 interface is rate-limited to a total of 384 kbps. Subclass-x has a minimal guarantee of 192 kbps (384 * 0.5), subclass-y has a guarantee of 76.8 kbps (384 * 0.2), and subclass-z has a guarantee of 38.4 kbps (384 * 0.1).

Hierarchical Class-based shaping with CB-WFQ is used to throttle the transmission rate and thus manage congestion locally instead of relying on the network to deliver or drop the packets to the destination. The class-based bandwidth guarantees within the parent shaper ensure a certain forwarding rate for each class.

Hierarchical class-based shaping with CB-WFQ can be used to manage congestion on software-based interfaces, such as subinterfaces or tunnels, because they do not have a hardware queue that is directly associated with them.

Low Latency Queuing

CB-WFQ defines multiple traffic classes that are based on match criteria. Packets satisfying the match criteria for a class constitute the traffic for that class. A queue is reserved for each class, and traffic belonging to a class is directed to that class queue. A class is characterized by bandwidth, weight, and maximum packet limit. The bandwidth that is assigned to a class is the minimum bandwidth that is delivered to the class during congestion.

CB-WFQ supports multiple class maps to classify traffic into its corresponding FIFO queues. Tail drop is the default dropping scheme. WRED can be used in combination with CB-WFQ to prevent congestion of a class.

For CB-WFQ, the weight for a packet belonging to a specific class is derived from the bandwidth that you assigned to the class when you configured it. Therefore, the bandwidth that is assigned to the packets of a class determines the order in which packets are sent. A class gets more than its reserved bandwidth if there is no congestion. The unused bandwidth is shared among the classes proportionally to their guarantees.

In CB-WFQ, all packets are serviced fairly based on weight. No class of packets can be granted strict priority. This scheme poses problems for voice traffic, which is largely intolerant of delay, especially variation in delay. For voice traffic, variations in delay introduce irregularities of transmission that are heard as jitter in the conversation.

The LLQ feature brings strict priority queuing to CB-WFQ. Strict priority queuing allows delay-sensitive data such as voice to be dequeued and sent first (before packets in other queues are dequeued), giving delay-sensitive data preferential treatment over other traffic.

LLQ Architecture

When CB-WFQ is configured as the queuing system, it creates a number of queues, into which it classifies traffic classes. These queues are then scheduled with a weighted scheduler, which can guarantee bandwidth to each class. Figure 8-34 illustrates the architecture of LLQ.

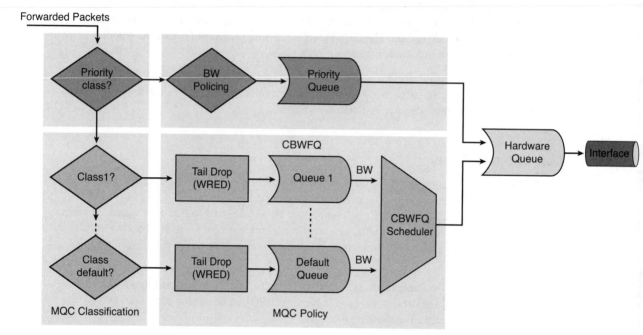

Figure 8-34   *LLQ*

If LLQ is used within the CB-WFQ system, it creates an additional priority queue in the WFQ system, which is serviced by a strict priority scheduler. Any class of traffic can therefore be attached to a service policy, which uses priority scheduling, and hence can be prioritized over other classes.

Classes to which the **priority** command is applied are considered priority classes. Within a policy map, you can assign priority status to one or more classes. When multiple classes within a single policy map are configured as priority classes, all traffic from these classes is queued to the same, single, strict priority queue.

LLQ Benefits

The LLQ priority scheduler implements the Expedited Forwarding per-hop behavior (EF PHB) of the DiffServ model by guaranteeing both low-latency propagation of packets and bandwidth to high-priority classes. Low latency is achieved by expediting traffic using a priority scheduler.

Bandwidth is also guaranteed by the nature of priority scheduling, but is policed to a user-configurable value. The strict priority scheme allows delay-sensitive data such as voice to be dequeued and sent first (that is, before packets in other queues are dequeued).

Policing of priority queues also prevents the priority scheduler from monopolizing the CB-WFQ scheduler and starving nonpriority classes, as legacy PQ does. By configuring the maximum amount of bandwidth that is allocated for packets belonging to a class, you can avoid starving nonpriority traffic.

The nonpriority class queues within the LLQ (or CB-WFQ) structure implement the Assured Forwarding (AF) PHB of the DiffServ model by guaranteeing a defined service level to each class. The differential drop is controlled by WRED, which can be configured individually for each class, and specifies the drop characteristics of the traffic in the class.

Configuring LLQ

The two main commands that are required to configure an LLQ system are the **priority** and **bandwidth** commands.

The **priority** command is used to identify a class as a strict priority class and allocate bandwidth to that class. The bandwidth can be specified either in kilobits per second or percentage of the configured or default interface bandwidth. Traffic exceeding the specified bandwidth is dropped if congestion exists. The *burst* option defines the amount of data that can be sent at once. The default burst size is based on 200-ms interval and LLQ bandwidth.

```
Router(config-pmap-c)#priority bandwidth [burst]
Router(config-pmap-c)#priority percent percentage [burst]
```

The **bandwidth** command is used to allocate bandwidth to nonpriority classes. It applies to the CB-WFQ portion of the LLQ system, not to the priority queue. The bandwidth can be specified in kilobits per second or in percent of the configured or default interface bandwidth. The **remaining** keyword allows the allocation of a percentage of remaining (nonallocated) bandwidth.

LLQ Configuration Example

Consider Example 8-9. This LLQ configuration forwards the voip class as strict priority traffic and allocates it 10 percent of the interface bandwidth (configured using the **bandwidth** command or default).

Example 8-9 *LLQ Configuration Example*

```
Router#show running-config
...OUTPUT OMITTED...
class-map voip
   match ip precedence 5
!
class-map mission-critical
```

```
    match ip precedence 3 4
!
class-map transactional
    match ip precedence 1 2
!
policy-map Policy1
    class voip
        priority percent 10
    class mission-critical
        bandwidth percent 30
        random-detect
    class transactional
        bandwidth percent 20
        random-detect
    class class-default
        fair-queue
        random-detect
...OUTPUT OMITTED...
```

The *mission-critical* class is allocated 30 percent of the interface bandwidth. It uses WRED to randomly drop packets when the queue is filling up, to prevent congestion.

The *transactional* class gets 20 percent of the interface bandwidth and also uses WRED. The *class-default* class matches all other packets that are not classified into the previous classes, is scheduled using the WFQ algorithm, and also uses WRED.

Monitoring LLQ

The **show policy-map interface** command displays the packet statistics of all classes that are configured for all service policies on the specified interface. Example 8-10 provides sample output from the **show policy-map interface** command.

Example 8-10   show policy-map interface *Command Output for LLQ*

```
Router#show policy-map interface fastethernet 0/0
 FastEthernet 0/0
  Service-policy output: LLQ
   Class-map: LLQ (match-any)
       0 packets, 0 bytes
       5 minute offered rate 0 bps, drop rate 0 bps
       Match: any
       Weighted Fair Queueing
         Strict Priority
         Output Queue: Conversation 264
         Bandwidth 1000 (kbps) Burst 25000 (Bytes)
```

```
    (pkts matched/bytes matched) 0/0
    (total drops/bytes drops) 0/0
Class-map: class-default (match-any)
  0 packets, 0 bytes
  5 minute offered rate 0 bps, drop rate 0 bps
  Match: any
```

Table 8-4 describes some of the key fields shown in the output.

Table 8-4   *Monitoring LLQ*

Parameter	Description
Class-map	Class of traffic being displayed. Output is displayed for each configured class in the policy.
offered rate	Rate, in kbps, of packets coming into the class.
drop rate	Rate, in kbps, at which packets are dropped from the class. The drop rate is calculated by subtracting the number of successfully transmitted packets from the offered rate.
Match	Match criteria that are specified for the class of traffic.
pkts matched/bytes matched	Number of packets (also shown in bytes) matching this class that were placed in the queue.
total drops/bytes drops	Number of packets/bytes that are discarded for this class.

Calculating Bandwidth for LLQ

The bandwidth allocation is specified using two commands within the LLQ structure: the **priority** and **bandwidth** commands. While the **bandwidth** command does not include a policing mechanism, the **priority** command defines the bandwidth guarantee and policing rate. The policing rate is enforced only during congestion. The bandwidth must include the Layer 2 and Layer 3 overhead of the packets that are forwarded within a class.

Figure 8-35 illustrates how to compute the bandwidth required for an LLQ queue that should ensure timely forwarding of ten G.729 calls with 20-ms packetization over a MLP link.

The frame size is 73 bytes: 20 bytes (payload) + 40 bytes (IP/UDP/RTP) + 13 bytes (MLP). The bandwidth of a single call is 29.2 kbps. The aggregate of ten calls totals to 292 kbps and can be rounded up to 300 kbps.

Bandwidth Reservation Should Include Overhead:
- Bandwidth used for guarantees and policing with LLQ.
- For proper operation, it should include Layer 3 and Layer 2 overhead; otherwise, it guarantees less than expected.
- Example: Setting up priority queue to support 10 x G.729 calls (20-ms packetization) on MLPPP link.

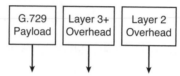

LLQ Priority Bandwidth = 10 x (20 bytes + 40 bytes + 13 bytes) x 50 p/s x 8 bits/byte
 = 10 x 29.2 kbps = 292 kbps
LLQ Priority Bandwidth rounded up to 300 kbps

```
router(config-pmap-c)# priority 300
```

Figure 8-35   *Calculating Bandwidth for LLQ*

Figure 8-36 illustrates how to compute the bandwidth required for an LLQ queue that should ensure timely forwarding of ten G.711 calls with 20-ms packetization over a Frame Relay link configured for Frame Relay Fragmentation Implementation Agreement FRF.12 LFI.

Codec	Packetization Period	Voice Payload	Packets per Second
G.711	20 ms	160 bytes	50
G.711	30 ms	240 bytes	33
G.729	20 ms	20 bytes	50
G.729	30 ms	30 bytes	33

Layer 2 Headers [Bytes]	
802.3 Ethernet	18
802.1Q Ethernet	18+4
PPP	6-9
Multilink PPP with Interleaving	13
Frame Relay	6
Frame Relay with FRF.12	8

Example: 10 G.711 calls, 20-ms packetization, FRF.12:

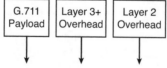

LLQ Priority Bandwidth = 10 x (160 bytes + 40 bytes + 8 bytes) x 50 p/s x 8 bits/byte
 = 10 x 83.2 kbps = 832 kbps
LLQ Priority Bandwidth rounded up to 840 kbps

```
router(config-pmap-c)# priority 840
```

Figure 8-36   *Calculating Bandwidth for LLQ (Continued)*

The frame size is 208 bytes: 160 bytes (payload) + 40 bytes (IP/UDP/RTP) + 8 bytes (FRF.12). The bandwidth of a single call is 83.2 kbps. The aggregate of ten calls totals to 832 kbps and can be rounded up to 840 kbps.

Introduction to Cisco AutoQoS

Cisco AutoQoS represents two technologies, Cisco AutoQoS VoIP and Cisco AutoQoS for the Enterprise. These technologies simplify network administration challenges, reducing QoS complexity, deployment time, and cost in enterprise networks.

Cisco AutoQoS VoIP incorporates value-added intelligence in Cisco IOS and Cisco Catalyst software to provision and manage large-scale QoS deployments. It provides QoS provisioning for individual routers and switches, simplifying deployment and reducing human error. Cisco AutoQoS VoIP offers straightforward capabilities to automate VoIP deployments for customers who want to deploy IP telephony but who lack the expertise and staffing to plan and deploy IP QoS and IP services.

Cisco AutoQoS for the Enterprise is a process in which two intelligent mechanisms are deployed to detect voice, video, and data traffic in Cisco networks. The mechanisms generate best-practice QoS policies and apply those policies to WAN interfaces.

This section explores the capabilities, requirements, and configuration of Cisco AutoQoS VoIP and Cisco AutoQoS for the Enterprise.

Cisco AutoQoS VoIP

Cisco AutoQoS VoIP provides the ability to deploy QoS features for converged IP telephony and data networks fast and efficiently, by simplifying and automating the MQC policy. Cisco AutoQoS VoIP generates traffic classes and policy map CLI templates. When Cisco AutoQoS VoIP is configured on an interface or permanent virtual circuit (PVC), the traffic receives the required QoS treatment automatically. There is no need for in-depth knowledge of the underlying technologies, service policies, and link-efficiency mechanisms. Cisco AutoQoS VoIP implements best practice for VoIP transport. Figure 8-37 illustrates typical locations within a network that might benefit from Cisco AutoQoS VoIP.

Cisco AutoQoS VoIP can be beneficial in these scenarios:

■ Small- to medium-sized businesses that must deploy IP telephony quickly but lack the experience and staffing to plan and deploy IP QoS services

■ Large enterprises that need to deploy Cisco telephony solutions on a large scale while reducing the costs, complexity, and time frame for deployment, and ensuring that the appropriate QoS for voice applications is being set in a consistent fashion

- International enterprises or service providers requiring QoS for VoIP in different regions of the world where little expertise exists and where provisioning QoS remotely and across different time zones is difficult

- Service providers requiring a template-driven approach for delivering managed services and QoS for voice traffic to many customer premises devices

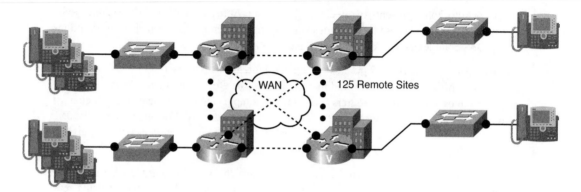

Figure 8-37   *Locations for Cisco AutoQoS VoIP*

Cisco AutoQoS VoIP Functions

Cisco AutoQoS VoIP simplifies and shortens the QoS deployment cycle in five major aspects:

- **Application classification:** Cisco AutoQoS VoIP leverages intelligent classification on routers using Cisco Network-Based Application Recognition (NBAR) to provide deep and stateful packet inspection. Cisco AutoQoS VoIP uses Cisco Discovery Protocol (CDP) for voice packets to ensure that the device attached to the LAN is really an IP phone.

- **Policy generation:** Cisco AutoQoS VoIP evaluates the network environment and generates an initial policy. Cisco AutoQoS VoIP automatically determines WAN settings for fragmentation, compression, and encapsulation, eliminating the need to understand QoS theory.

- **Configuration:** With one command, Cisco AutoQoS VoIP configures the port to prioritize voice traffic without affecting other network traffic, while still offering the flexibility to adjust QoS settings for unique network requirements. Cisco AutoQoS VoIP–generated router and switch configurations are customizable using the standard Cisco IOS CLI.

- **Monitoring and reporting:** Cisco AutoQoS VoIP provides visibility into the classes of service that are deployed via system logging and Simple Network Management Protocol (SNMP) traps, with notification of abnormal events (that is, VoIP packet drops).

- **Consistency:** When deploying QoS configurations using Cisco AutoQoS VoIP, configurations that are generated are consistent among router and switch platforms. This level of consistency ensures seamless QoS operation and interoperability within the network.

Cisco AutoQoS VoIP Router Platforms

Support for Cisco AutoQoS VoIP includes the Cisco 1800, 2800, 2900, 3800, 3900, and 7200 Series Routers.

The Cisco AutoQoS VoIP feature is supported on the following interfaces and PVCs:

- Serial interfaces with PPP or High-Level Data Link Control (HDLC)

- Frame Relay DLCIs (point-to-point subinterfaces only, because Cisco AutoQoS VoIP does not support Frame Relay multipoint interfaces)

- ATM PVCs

  - Cisco AutoQoS VoIP is supported on low-speed ATM PVCs on point-to-point subinterfaces only (link bandwidth less than 768 kbps)

  - Cisco AutoQoS VoIP is fully supported on high-speed ATM PVCs (link bandwidth greater than 768 kbps)

Cisco AutoQoS VoIP Switch Platforms

Support for Cisco AutoQoS VoIP includes all current Cisco Catalyst switches. You can implement the voice QoS requirements without extensive knowledge of the trust boundary theory, CoS-to-DSCP mappings, and weighted round robin (WRR) and priority queuing (PQ) implementation on a given switch platform. Once the automatic policy is applied, it can be modified to match the needs of a specific environment.

To configure the QoS settings and the trusted boundary feature on the Cisco IP Phone, CDP version 2 or later must be enabled on the port. If the trusted boundary feature is enabled, a syslog warning message displays if CDP is not enabled or is running version 1.

CDP needs to be enabled only for the **ciscoipphone** QoS configuration. CDP does not affect the other components of the AutoQoS VoIP features. When the **ciscoipphone** keyword with the port-specific AutoQoS VoIP feature is used, a warning displays if the port does not have CDP enabled.

When executing the port-specific AutoQoS VoIP command with the **ciscoipphone** keyword without the **trust** option, the trust-device feature is enabled. The trust-device feature is dependent on CDP.

Configuring Cisco AutoQoS VoIP

Before configuring Cisco AutoQoS VoIP, you must meet these prerequisites:

- Cisco Express Forwarding (CEF) must be enabled on the interface or subinterface. Cisco AutoQoS VoIP uses NBAR to identify various applications and traffic types, and CEF is a prerequisite for NBAR.

- No QoS policies (that is, service policies) can be attached to the interface. Specifically, Cisco AutoQoS VoIP cannot be configured if a QoS policy is applied to an interface in the same direction (that is, inbound or outbound) as an existing policy.

- Cisco AutoQoS VoIP classifies links as either low-speed or high-speed depending upon the link bandwidth. The default bandwidth of a serial interface, if the **bandwidth** command is not configured, is 1.544 Mbps. Therefore, correct bandwidth must be specified on the interface or subinterface where Cisco AutoQoS VoIP is enabled.

- If the interface or subinterface has a link speed of 768 kbps or lower, an IP address should be configured on the interface or subinterface using the **ip address** command. By default, Cisco AutoQoS VoIP will enable Multilink PPP (MLP) and copy the configured IP address to the multilink bundle interface.

In addition to the Cisco AutoQoS VoIP prerequisites, the following are recommendations and requirements when configuring Cisco AutoQoS VoIP:

- The Cisco AutoQoS VoIP feature is supported only on PVCs and these interfaces:
  - ATM PVCs
  - Serial interfaces with PPP or HDLC
  - Frame Relay DLCIs (point-to-point subinterfaces only) (Cisco AutoQoS VoIP does not support Frame Relay multipoint interfaces.)

- The configuration template that is generated by configuring Cisco AutoQoS VoIP on an interface or PVC can be tuned manually, via a CLI configuration, if desired.

- The **no auto qos voip** command removes Cisco AutoQoS VoIP.

- Cisco AutoQoS VoIP SNMP traps are only delivered when an SNMP server is used in conjunction with Cisco AutoQoS VoIP.

- If the device is reloaded with the saved configuration after configuring Cisco AutoQoS VoIP and saving the configuration to NVRAM, some warning messages might be generated by Remote Monitoring (RMON) threshold commands. These warning messages can be ignored. (To avoid further warning messages, save the configuration to NVRAM again without making any changes to the QoS configuration.)

Configuring Cisco AutoQoS VoIP: Routers

To configure the Cisco AutoQoS VoIP feature on an interface, use the **auto qos voip** command in interface configuration mode or Frame Relay DLCI configuration mode. To remove the Cisco AutoQoS VoIP feature from an interface, use the **no** form of the **auto qos voip** command. The **trust** keyword indicates that the DSCP markings of a packet are trusted for classification of the voice traffic. If the optional **trust** keyword is not specified, voice traffic is classified using NBAR, and the packets are marked with the appropriate DSCP value. The **fr-atm** keyword enables Cisco AutoQoS VoIP on Frame Relay-to-ATM interworking links.

```
Router(config-if)#auto qos voip [trust] [fr-atm]
```

or

```
Router(config-fr-dlci)#auto qos voip [trust] [fr-atm]
```

The bandwidth of the serial interface is used to determine the link speed at the time the feature is configured. Cisco AutoQoS VoIP does not respond to changes made to bandwidth after the feature is configured. If the bandwidth is later changed, the Cisco AutoQoS VoIP feature will not update its policy. To force the Cisco AutoQoS VoIP feature to use an updated bandwidth, use the **no auto qos voip** command to remove the Cisco AutoQoS VoIP feature, and then reconfigure the feature.

Configuring Cisco AutoQoS VoIP: Switches

When the Cisco AutoQoS VoIP feature is initially enabled on a switch, QoS is globally enabled with the **mls qos** global configuration command.

When the **auto qos voip trust** interface configuration command is entered, the ingress classification on the interface is set to trust the CoS QoS label that is received in a frame, and the egress queues on the interface are reconfigured. QoS labels in ingress frames are trusted.

```
Switch(config-if)#auto qos voip {cisco-phone | trust}
```

When the **auto qos voip cisco-phone** interface configuration command is entered, the trusted boundary feature is enabled. The trusted boundary feature uses CDP to detect the presence or absence of a Cisco IP Phone. When a Cisco IP Phone is detected, the ingress classification on the interface is set to trust the QoS label that is received in the packet.

When a Cisco IP Phone is absent, the ingress classification is set to not trust the QoS label in the packet. The egress queues on the interface are also reconfigured. This command extends the trust boundary if an IP phone is detected.

Monitoring Cisco AutoQoS VoIP

Cisco AutoQoS VoIP activates different QoS mechanisms on routers and switches, and the configuration varies slightly. However, you can use similar commands for verifying what Cisco AutoQoS VoIP does to your router or switch configuration.

Monitoring Cisco AutoQoS VoIP: Routers

When the **auto qos voip** command is used to configure the Cisco AutoQoS VoIP feature, configurations are generated for each interface or PVC. These configurations are then used to create the interface configurations, policy maps, class maps, and ACLs.

```
Router>show auto qos [interface interface-id]
```

The **show auto qos interface** command can be used with Frame Relay DLCIs and ATM PVCs.

When the **interface** keyword is used along with the corresponding interface type argument, the **show auto qos interface** [*interface-id*] command displays the configurations that are created by the Cisco AutoQoS VoIP feature on the specified interface.

When the **interface** keyword is used but an interface type is not specified, the **show auto qos interface** command displays the configurations that are created by the Cisco AutoQoS VoIP feature on all the interfaces or PVCs on which the Cisco AutoQoS VoIP feature is enabled.

Example 8-11 offers sample output from a **show auto qos interface** command.

Example 8-11 show auto qos interface *Command Output*

```
Router>show auto qos interface Serial0/1/1
!
interface Serial0/1/1
   service-policy output AutoQoS-Policy-UnTrust
```

The **show auto qos** command provides more information than the **show auto qos interface** command, which shows only the service policy that is applied to an interface. The **show auto qos** command can be used to verify the contents of the interface configurations, policy maps, class maps, and access control lists (ACL).

Example 8-12 presents output from the **show auto qos interface** command in a scenario in which the Cisco AutoQoS VoIP feature was configured at a low-speed Frame Relay subinterface.

Example 8-12 show auto qos interface *Command Output on a Frame Relay Subinterface*

```
Router#show auto qos interface s6/1.1

Serial6/1.1: DLCI 100 -
```

```
!
 interface Serial6/1
  frame-relay traffic-shaping
!
 interface Serial6/1.1 point-to-point
  frame-relay interface-dlci 100
    class AutoQoS-VoIP-FR-Serial6/1-100
  frame-relay ip rtp header-compression
!
map-class frame-relay AutoQoS-VoIP-FR-Serial6/1-100
 frame-relay cir 512000
 frame-relay bc 5120
 frame-relay be 0
 frame-relay mincir 512000
 service-policy output AutoQoS-Policy-UnTrust
 frame-relay fragment 640
```

Monitoring Cisco AutoQoS VoIP: Switches

To display the initial Cisco AutoQoS VoIP configuration, use the **show auto qos**
[**interface** [*interface-id*]] privileged EXEC command. To display any user changes to that
configuration, use the **show running-config** privileged EXEC command. You can compare the **show auto qos** and the **show running-config** command output to identify the
user-defined QoS settings.

```
Switch#show auto qos [interface interface-id]
```

Example 8-13 shows sample output from the **show auto qos** command on a Cisco
Catalyst switch.

Example 8-13   show auto qos *Command Output on a Cisco Catalyst Switch*

```
Switch#show auto qos
Initial configuration applied by AutoQoS:
wrr-queue bandwidth 20 1 80 0
no wrr-queue cos-map
wrr-queue cos 1 0 1 2 4
wrr-queue cos 3 3 6 7
wrr-queue cos 4 5
mls qos map cos-dscp 0 8 16 26 32 46 48 56
!
interface FastEthernet 0/3
mls qos trust device cisco-phone
mls qos trust cos
```

Automation with Cisco AutoQoS VoIP

Cisco AutoQoS VoIP performs these functions in a WAN:

■ Automatic classification of Real-time Transport Protocol (RTP) payload and VoIP control packets (H.323, H.225 Unicast, Skinny Client Control Protocol [SCCP], Session Initiation Protocol [SIP], and Media Gateway Control Protocol [MGCP]) using NBAR and ACLs. The **trust** option enables classification using DSCP values.

■ Marking, when the **trust** option is not used.

■ Builds service policies for VoIP traffic that are based on Cisco MQC.

■ Provisions low latency queuing (LLQ) for VoIP bearer and bandwidth guarantees for control traffic.

■ Enables Frame Relay Traffic Shaping that adheres to Cisco best practices, where required.

■ Enables link-efficiency mechanisms such as Link Fragmentation and Interleaving (LFI) and compressed Real-time Transport Protocol (cRTP) on slow links.

■ Provides SNMP and syslog alerts for VoIP packet drops.

Cisco AutoQoS VoIP performs these functions in a LAN:

■ Enforces the trust boundary on switch access ports, and uplinks and downlinks.

■ Enables Cisco Catalyst strict PQ (also known as *expedited queuing*) with WRR scheduling for voice and data traffic, where appropriate.

■ Configures queue admission criteria (maps CoS values in incoming packets to the appropriate queues).

■ Modifies queue sizes and weights where required.

Table 8-5 summarizes the features which can be applied by Cisco AutoQoS VoIP.

Cisco AutoQoS for the Enterprise

The Cisco AutoQoS for the Enterprise feature automates the deployment of QoS policies in a general business environment. The policies that are deployed by Cisco AutoQoS for the Enterprise are not solely focused on VoIP convergence, but also on convergence of voice, video, and data applications. Cisco AutoQoS for the Enterprise is generally deployed in midsize companies and branch offices of larger companies. It is used to provide best-practice QoS policy generation for voice as well as to provide for classification of as many as ten traffic classes.

Existing QoS policies can be present during the first configuration phase of Cisco AutoQoS for the Enterprise, that is, during the *autodiscovery* (data collection) phase. However, any existing QoS policies must be removed before the Cisco AutoQoS–generated policies are applied during the second configuration phase of this feature.

Table 8-5 *Automation with Cisco AutoQoS VoIP*

DiffServ Function	Cisco IOS QoS Feature	Applicability	Description
Classification	NBAR, DSCP, ACL	Trust option: only DSCP-based	Classification of VoIP; when trust option used, classification based on DSCP only
Marking	Class-based marking	Only when untrusted	Set Layer 2 and Layer 3 attributes when trust option not set
Congestion management	Percentage-based LLQ	Always	Provide EF treatment to voice and best-effort treatment to data
Shaping	FRTS	Frame Relay	Shape to CIR to smooth traffic to configured rate
Compression	RTP header compression	Slow links (<768 kbps)	Increases throughput; enabled only on slow links
LFI	MLP with interleaving or FRF.12	Slow PPP and Frame Relay links	Reduces voice jitter; enabled only on slow links

Cisco AutoQoS for the Enterprise classifies the traffic using a ten-class model, which is too wide for many environments, especially with low-speed interfaces. In such cases, manual tuning should be performed to merge the classes into fewer traffic classifications.

Figure 8-38 identifies typical network locations that could benefit from Cisco AutoQoS for the Enterprise.

Cisco AutoQoS for the Enterprise is performed in the following two phases:

- **Autodiscovery:** The autodiscovery process detects applications and protocol types. The autodiscovery phase gives the discovery period enough time to gather traffic statistics before applying Cisco AutoQoS. The time for gathering traffic statistics before applying Cisco AutoQoS depends upon the actual highs and lows of traffic patterns of a network.

- **Provisioning:** Cisco AutoQoS policy is the provisioning stage, in which the appropriate MQC configuration is applied to the router. It includes the recommended QoS policy that is generated and installed by the AutoQoS macros, based on the data that is gathered by the autodiscovery process.

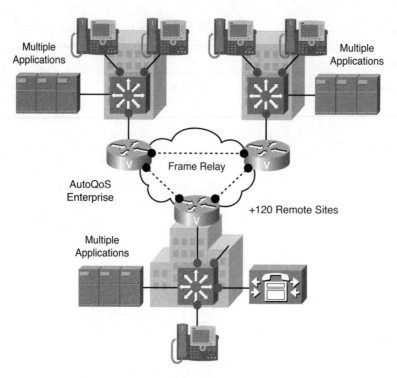

Figure 8-38   *Cisco AutoQoS for the Enterprise Typical Implementation Locations*

Figure 8-39 shows the ten traffic classes that can be classified by Cisco AutoQoS for the Enterprise. They might have to be aggregated into fewer classes during the manual tuning of the automatic Cisco AutoQoS configuration.

Configuring Cisco AutoQoS for the Enterprise

The **auto discovery qos [trust]** command starts the discovery phase on a router interface, subinterface, or Frame Relay DLCI. The discovery stage must be completed before a recommended Cisco AutoQoS policy can be applied to the router interface. When the discovery is complete, the results can be viewed using the **show auto discovery qos [interface]** command. The router will not accept the **auto qos** command until statistics have been gathered.

```
Router(config-if)#auto discovery qos [trust]
```

or

```
Router(config-fr-dlci)#auto discovery qos [trust]
```

Traffic Class	DSCP
IP Routing	CS6
Interactive Voice	EF
Interactive Video	AF41
Streaming Video	CS4
Telephony Signaling	CS3
Transactional/Interactive	AF21
Network Management	CS2
Bulk Data	AF11
Scavenger	CS1
Best Effort	0

Figure 8-39 *Cisco AutoQoS for the Enterprise Traffic Classes*

The **trust** keyword is used to make the router rely on the markings in ingress packets. Cisco AutoQoS for the Enterprise has the same prerequisites as Cisco AutoQoS VoIP, such as the following:

- Cisco AutoQoS uses NBAR to identify various applications and traffic types, and CEF is a prerequisite for NBAR.

- Although an existing QoS policy is allowed during the discovery stage, it must be removed before Cisco AutoQoS commits its policy.

- Cisco AutoQoS classifies links as either low-speed or high-speed, depending upon the link bandwidth. The correct bandwidth configuration is necessary to apply the correct policy. When the bandwidth is changed during the discovery phase, the autodiscovery must be stopped (using the **no auto discovery qos** command) and restarted (using the **auto discovery qos** command) to take the new setting into account.

The discovery period should cover the complete business cycle of an enterprise and typically ranges between 2 and 7 days.

The **auto qos** command commits the automatically generated QoS policy to the router. This command is accepted after the discovery statistics have been gathered. No QoS service policy should previously exist on the interface.

```
Router(config-if)#auto qos
```

or

```
Router(config-fr-dlci)#auto qos
```

On slow Frame Relay links (less than 768 kbps), the Cisco AutoQoS policy provisions the Frame Relay Fragmentation Implementation Agreement (FRF.12). The fragmentation breaks connectivity over the link, unless it is also configured on the other side of the PVC.

Monitoring Cisco AutoQoS for the Enterprise: Phase 1

The **auto discovery qos** command displays the results of the discovery phase. Example 8-14 shows an example of NBAR recognizing traffic classes that have been detected on a WAN interface. The information includes the length of the discovery period and the detected traffic classes, with their throughput rates.

Example 8-14   show auto discovery qos *Command Output*

```
Router#show auto discovery qos
 AutoQoS Discovery enabled for applications
 Discovery up time: 2 days, 55 minutes
 AutoQoS Class information:
  Class VoIP:
  Recommended Minimum Bandwidth: 517 Kbps/50% (PeakRate)
    Detected applications and data:
    Application/ AverageRate PeakRate Total
    Protocol (kbps/%) (kbps/%) (bytes)
    rtp audio 76/7 517/50 703104
  Class Interactive Video:
  Recommended Minimum Bandwidth: 24 Kbps/2% (AverageRate)
    Detected applications and data:
    Application/ AverageRate PeakRate Total
    Protocol (kbps/%) (kbps/%) (bytes)
    rtp video 24/2 5337/52 704574
...OUTPUT OMITTED...
```

Monitoring Cisco AutoQoS for the Enterprise: Phase 2

The **show auto qos** [**interface** *interface-id*] command displays the initial policy that is committed by Cisco AutoQoS for the Enterprise. The **interface** keyword allows a more selective display of interface-specific configuration.

Example 8-15 shows a sample QoS policy configuration that is generated by Cisco AutoQoS templates, based on NBAR statistics gathered during the data discovery phase. The configuration is built in a modular way, based on MQC building blocks (class maps, policy maps, and service policy). The committed rules can be tuned. Tuning is often performed to reduce the number of traffic classes from ten to a lower number.

Example 8-15   show auto qos *Command Output for AutoQoS for the Enterprise*

```
Router#show auto qos interface Serial2/1.1
class-map match-any AutoQoS-Voice-Se2/1.1
  match protocol rtp audio
class-map match-any AutoQoS-Inter-Video-Se2/1.1
  match protocol rtp video
class-map match-any AutoQoS-Signaling-Se2/1.1
  match protocol sip
  match protocol rtcp
...OUTPUT OMITTED...
policy-map AutoQoS-Policy-Se2/1.1
 class AutoQoS-Voice-Se2/1.1
  priority percent 33
  set dscp ef
 class AutoQoS-Inter-Video-Se2/1.1
  bandwidth remaining percent 1
  set dscp af41
...OUTPUT OMITTED...
```

Summary

The main topics covered in this chapter are the following:

- The three-step MQC process was used to configure classification and marking.

- Theory and configuration examples for multiple QoS mechanisms were covered. Examples of these mechanisms include LFI, cRTP, policing, shaping, and LLQ.

- Configuration for both AutoQoS VoIP and AutoQoS for the Enterprise was examined.

Bonus Video   To reinforce the QoS configuration tasks presented in this chapter, you can view a series of 12 QoS video labs on the author's website. Navigate to the CVOICE page on the **1ExamAMonth.com** website to access these bonus videos.

Chapter Review Questions

The answers to these review questions are in the appendix.

1. Which command would you use to attach a QoS policy to an interface?

   a. policy-set-interface

   b. policy-map

    c. policy-interface

    d. service-policy

2. Which command will display both the CoS-to-DSCP and DSCP-to-CoS mappings on a Catalyst switch?

    a. show mls maps

    b. show mls qos maps

    c. show mls maps both

    d. show qos mls maps both

3. Which two factors influence the serialization delay? (Choose two.)

    a. Link speed

    b. Speed of light in the media

    c. Router CPU processing power

    d. Packet size

4. Which configuration element is used to provision FRF.12 fragmentation?

    a. Class map

    b. Policy map

    c. Service policy

    d. Map class

    e. Map policy

5. Which of these is the default dropping scheme for CB-WFQ?

    a. RED

    b. WRED

    c. Tail drop

    d. Class-based policing

6. In which way does LLQ extend CB-WFQ?

    a. Strict priority scheduling

    b. Alternate priority scheduling

    c. Non-policed queues for low-latency traffic

    d. Special voice-like traffic classification and dispatch

7. What are the two configuration options when configuring class-based shaping? (Choose two.)

   a. Shape average

   b. Shape peak

   c. Single or dual token bucket

   d. Single or multiaction traffic shaping

   e. Single- or dual-rate traffic shaping

8. What is "trusted" when the **auto qos voip** command is configured with the **trust** parameter on routers?

   a. Source address

   b. MAC address of sender

   c. DES keyword

   d. DSCP

9. Which of these terms is displayed by the **show auto qos interface serial0/0** command on a router?

   a. ACL configuration that is applied to the Serial 0/0 interface

   b. Class maps configuration

   c. Policy maps configuration

   d. Service policy configuration on the Serial 0/0 interface

10. Which statement is true of Cisco AutoQoS on a Cisco Catalyst switch?

   a. Neither Cisco AutoQoS VoIP nor Cisco AutoQoS for the Enterprise is supported.

   b. Cisco AutoQoS VoIP is supported, but Cisco AutoQoS for the Enterprise is not supported.

   c. Cisco AutoQoS VoIP is not supported, but Cisco AutoQoS for the Enterprise is supported.

   d. Both Cisco AutoQoS VoIP and Cisco AutoQoS for the Enterprise are supported.

Appendix A

Answers to Chapter Review Questions

Chapter 1

1. B and D
2. A and D
3. D
4. A and D
5. D
6. D
7. D
8. C
9. C
10. A and D

Chapter 2

1. B
2. C
3. A and C
4. D
5. A, C, D, and E
6. A

7. C
8. D and E
9. B
10. B

Chapter 3

1. B
2. A, B, C, and E
3. D
4. A and E
5. B
6. A and D
7. C
8. C
9. A and B
10. B

Chapter 4

1. B
2. D
3. C
4. B
5. A, C, and D
6. B, C, and D
7. B
8. A
9. B
10. A

Chapter 5

1. C
2. A
3. D
4. A
5. D
6. A
7. C
8. D
9. B
10. B

Chapter 6

1. C
2. C
3. B
4. B
5. B

6. B and C
7. A
8. D
9. B
10. C

Chapter 7

1. C
2. B
3. D
4. B
5. C
6. D
7. A
8. D
9. D
10. B

Chapter 8

1. D
2. B
3. A and D
4. D
5. C
6. A
7. A and B
8. D
9. D
10. B

Index

H

R

S

ciscopress.com: Your Cisco Certification and Networking Learning Resource

Subscribe to the monthly Cisco Press newsletter to be the first to learn about new releases and special promotions.

Visit **ciscopress.com/newsletters.**

While you are visiting, check out the offerings available at your finger tips.

–Free Podcasts from experts:
- • OnNetworking
- • OnCertification
- • OnSecurity

View them at **ciscopress.com/podcasts**.

–Read the latest author **articles** and **sample chapters** at ciscopress.com/articles.

–Bookmark the Certification Reference Guide available through our partner site at **informit.com/certguide**.

Connect with Cisco Press authors and editors via Facebook and Twitter, visit **informit.com/socialconnect**.

FREE Online Edition

Your purchase of **Implementing Cisco Unified Communications Voice over IP and QoS (CVOICE)** includes access to a free online edition for 45 days through the Safari Books Online subscription service. Nearly every Cisco Press book is available online through Safari Books Online, along with more than 5,000 other technical books and videos from publishers such as Addison-Wesley Professional, Cisco Press, Exam Cram, IBM Press, O'Reilly, Prentice Hall, Que, and Sams.

SAFARI BOOKS ONLINE allows you to search for a specific answer, cut and paste code, download chapters, and stay current with emerging technologies.

Activate your FREE Online Edition at www.informit.com/safarifree

> **STEP 1:** Enter the coupon code: AXZFQGA.

> **STEP 2:** New Safari users, complete the brief registration form.
> Safari subscribers, just log in.

If you have difficulty registering on Safari or accessing the online edition, please e-mail customer-service@safaribooksonline.com